# AMERICANA

## Readings in Popular Culture

Revised Edition

Edited by Leslie Wilson

PRESS AMERICANA

Hollywood Los Angeles
2010

Press Americana
The Press of Americana: The Institute for the Study of American Popular Culture
7095 Hollywood Boulevard, 1240, Hollywood, California 90028-8903
http://www.americanpopularculture.com



Library of Congress Cataloging-in-Publication Data

Americana : readings in popular culture / edited by Leslie Wilson. -- Rev. ed.
p. cm.
Summary: "Americana : readings in popular culture, revised edition, is a collection of essays examining American culture from 1900 to present. Dozens of scholars investigate five aspects of our society offering insights into 'What we hear,' 'What we watch,' 'What we read,' 'Where we go,' and 'The American identity'"--Provided by publisher.
Includes bibliographical references.
ISBN 978-0-9789041-8-0
1. Popular culture--United States. 2. United States--Civilization. 3. National characteristics, American. 4. United States--History. 5. Mass media--Political aspects--United States. 6. United States--Politics and government. 7. United States--Social conditions. I. Wilson, Leslie, 1967-
E169.1.A471913 2010
973--dc22

2010009900

# AMERICANA

## Readings in Popular Culture

Revised Edition

# Table of Contents

# Preface

As Executive Director of Americana: The Institute for the Study of American Popular Culture (1900-present) and Editor-in-Chief of the Institute's publications, *Magazine Americana* and *Americana: The Journal of American Popular Culture*, I have been reminded that we have accumulated a harvest of excellent essays examining our American culture and history, essays ripe for the picking. Thus we decided it was high time we collected some of the best of what we had published in a general reader. We also decided to include essays that would premiere in the collection as well.

You will find that some of the work is written in journalistic style with the references included within the text itself following our tradition of magazine publishing while other essays are formal research papers including parenthetical references and a works cited page following the tradition within the journal publishing world.

We hope you enjoy what we have assembled for you. Please visit us on the web at http://www.americanpopularculture.com. There you will find even more articles in American Studies.

Leslie Wilson

# Introduction

Americans have long held as true that the study of American history is not only a worthy endeavor it is a critical one. Only after knowing and understanding our past can we insure positive change for the future.

Many of us believe that there exists no better record of the history of America and Americans than in our popular culture. There we will find the hopes, needs, dreams, and desires of the people.

Through the careful analysis of our American popular culture (and in this text, we focus on 1900-present), we can more clearly understand where we have been and who we have been and thus consciously consider where we want to go, who we want to be, how we want to live, and what public policies we want to endorse as twenty-first century Americans. This process will also help us formulate our identities and find our political, sociological, intellectual, and spiritual direction. For those who read this book who are not Americans, we hope that these essays open doors to a better understanding of American issues and challenges.

As you can see and no doubt already know, the impact of popular culture on our lives is substantial, and we have divided this book into five sections that underscore this point.

**What We Hear** examines the impact of music in our society. The writers discuss topics as diverse as Tin Pan Alley, Jewish musical theater, Dizzy Gillespie's jazz, and the lyrics of Bruce Springsteen, Steve Earle, John Mellencamp, and Jimmy Buffett.

**What We Watch** features essays on film, television, and video games. Here, the writers consider the Shakespearean *10 Things I Hate about You*, the political allusions in *Star Wars*, Clint Eastwood's Academy Award winning *Unforgiven*, popular military-style video games, *American Idol*, cable news, and children's cartoons.

**What We Read** features essays on magazines, bestsellers, newspapers, Internet articles, comic books, and cereal boxes. Here, you will flip through the pages of *The Catcher in the Rye*, Stephen King, and Harry Potter. You will also find yourself scouring newspapers studying George W. Bush and the myth of the cowboy, reading post-World War II men's magazines, and enjoying an old comic book called *Space Museum*.

**Where We Go** features essays on public spaces. You will travel on a train with hobos then visit Silver Springs, the Bonneville Salt Flats, the county fair, Bike Week in Daytona Beach, and the rodeo. In the end, you will stop for a steaming cup of joe at a coffeehouse.

Lastly, the essays in **The American Identity** document the struggles in the American experiment. In other words, the authors ask what it means to be an American and examine the difficulties in a project of this kind. The issues they address include religion, the Vietnam War, nostalgia, Latina body image in *Real Women Have Curves*, and African-American identity politics in *Hustle and Flow*.

This section also includes a **Casebook** of three readings that examine health issues in American culture. The authors investigate the language of disease, the image of the IV drug user in the context of AIDS, and Asian-American scapegoating due to SARS.

And now we invite you to read on…

# What We Hear

*As popular Tin Pan Alley music emerged at the turn of the twentieth century, critics debated the value of the "syncopated pastiche." In "An 'Invasion of Vulgarity,'" Matthew Mooney documents the debate between the defenders of the new music and the traditionalists.*

## An "Invasion of Vulgarity": American Popular Music and Modernity in Print Media Discourse, 1900-1925

Matthew Mooney

> Ragtime is the musical expression of an attitude toward life only too familiar to us all, an attitude shallow, restless, avid of excitement, incapable of sustained attention, skimming the surface of everything, finding nowhere satisfaction, realization, or repose. It is a meaningless stirabout, a commotion without purpose, an epilepsy stimulating controlled musical action. It is a musical counterpart of the sterile cleverness we find in so much of our contemporary conversation, as well as in our theater and our books. No candid observer could deny the prominence in our American life of this restlessness of which ragtime is one expression.
>
> -Daniel Gregory Mason, March 1918, *New Music Review*

Throughout the summer and early fall of 1912 readers of *Musical America*, a monthly magazine devoted to classical music and of special interest to opera aficionados, were treated to a heated debate between columnist Arthur Farwell and a series of correspondents who criticized his stand on ragtime, the reigning popular music of the era. Farwell, while expressing no great love for the syncopated pastiche pouring forth from Tin Pan Alley, argued that ragtime was created by and for the masses and served, therefore, a legitimate function in bringing pleasure to the working class millions.[1] "Popular music," argued Farwell, "is not forced upon the people; it is created out of their own spirit…what right has the man of culture to pass judgment upon the goodness or badness of ragtime, of popular music as a whole – in short, to make out a case against the popular song?" (24). Disagreeing, his critics pronounced ragtime unequivocally "bad"; for them, popular music was a consequence of America's ever more disparate distribution of resources. Money-grubbing capitalists, they argued, forced popular music down the throats of an ignorant and exhausted proletariat. Rudolph Bismarck Von Liebich, replying to Farwell's assertion that popular music represented the needs and desires of its consumers, wrote:

> With the advent of the machine age, when the giant tools of production (machines, factories, railroads) are owned by the few for their private gain and the worker is compelled to beg for work, which may at any time be denied him, he has no heart for song. Music as a spontaneous means of self-expression is no longer for him. He accepts songs like his clothes, made for one reason only – profit; and songs and clothes alike are shoddy, to his dire and tragic impoverishment. (26)

George Hamlin, primarily concerned with the aesthetic qualities of ragtime and its caustic effects on consumers, charged:

> Trash is always trash no matter in what form it exists. It is always worthless and often noxious unless disposed of. Mr. Farwell overlooks the fact that there is music of a depraved nature that is malevolently conceived and has a wide and powerful influence; that this music is at present rife in every part of the United States. (36)

While Farwell's defense of ragtime's modest virtues makes for interesting reading, early twentieth century polemics against popular music, such as those quoted above, are far more intriguing because they indict it as both a source of social disintegration and as a symptom of the dehumanizing industrial order relentlessly transforming America into a spiritually empty, impersonal realm where nothing was safe from the commodifying effects of the market. The contentious debate carried out in the pages of *Musical America* was echoed incessantly throughout the American popular press (though rarely in the explicitly Marxian formulation espoused by Von Liebich) of the era. An analysis of the discourses created in reaction to the popular music of the early twentieth century allows us to grasp more clearly how certain Americans resisted what they perceived to be the final dissolution of a pre-capitalist, nineteenth century, paternalistic mentality.

As the modernizing forces of industrial capitalism and bureaucratic rationality molded early twentieth century America into the world's foremost manufacturer of consumer goods, many Americans paradoxically perceived this transformation as engendering social chaos rather than order and stability. In the eyes of America's traditionalist middle-class, the nation was socially and culturally descending into a primitive morass of irrationality, a tribal barbarism guided not by the cherished achievements of the European Enlightenment but by the lowest common denominator of the mass market. They were appalled by the seething, heterogeneous mob of urban working class America, swollen to appalling dimensions by decades of immigration from Eastern and Southern Europe, which they believed threatened to swamp the remaining citadels of bourgeois culture in a torrent of ignorant sentimentality designed to satiate only the most vulgar, unrefined corporeal impulses. As one commentator baldly stated, "One thing is certain: the voice of the people is not the voice of culture and art" (Smith 183). Yet, there was no denying that the voice, or choices, of the masses in a dollar-directed nexus increasingly determined the tenor of American culture. Indeed, the nineteenth century dictum attributed to master huckster P.T. Barnum, "Give the people what they want," found its fruition in early twentieth century consumerism. This culture of the popular, both arising from and directed at the masses, was widely recognized as a sphere central to the struggle to define and direct the evolution of American society. Of course, not only did few Americans agree on what it was the people wanted, but many disdained Barnum-style populism altogether and advocated, instead, that they knew best what it was Americans needed (whether the masses themselves knew it or not). Film historian Charles Musser identifies these traditionalist advocates of a restrained moral conservatism with the "semi-official, elevated Protestant culture and its stamp of social responsibility and respectability" (9). Their fight to defend a culture of learned gentility against the tyranny of the marketplace and the teeming masses who drove it (and were driven by) are plainly evident in the contentious discourses surrounding the era's most popular musical genres: ragtime and early jazz, both of which represented America in its most modern guise: urban, restless, pleasure-seeking, pragmatic, and avowedly materialist.

The emergent "culture industry" that manufactured and distributed popular music came to fruition in the mid to late 1890's and increasingly challenged traditionalist values thereafter. Tin Pan Alley's entertainment entrepreneurs fashioned commercial amusements not in correspondence with the venerated models of "high" European classicism, but for an ever-expanding working-class audience demanding immediate and uncomplicated pleasures. This gradual turn away from entertainments justified by their ostensibly "uplifting" didacticism and towards modern amusements, such as ragtime and early jazz, did not occur in the absence of opposition, of course. Traditionalists vociferously resisted this trend in, among other places, the pages of the early twentieth century press. The resulting confrontation between modern and traditionalist discourses was described by a period sociologist as a battle between "warring sides of human nature – appetite and will, impulse and reason, inclination and idea" (Musser 9). The character of discourses generated in response to popular music depended primarily upon an author's impression of the emerging, mass-marketed American culture: modernity as indicative of profound cultural degradation or modernity as the triumph of the people's will over an exclusionary, elitist tradition.

Although jazz is musically distinct from ragtime, traditionalist discourses opposing the spread of popular music made little or no distinction between them.[2] For most, "jazz" was simply a new label applied, around the end of the First World War, to the ragtime menace they had been combating for a generation. Therefore, an analysis of opposition to early popular music should not commence in 1917, with the abrupt explosion of jazz into the national consciousness, but should instead view opposition to ragtime and early jazz as constituting an unbroken discursive continuum stretching back into the final few years of the nineteenth century (1896 is often acknowledged as the beginning of the ragtime era). Therefore, utilizing the turn-of-the-century as a starting point and continuing into the mid-1920's, this paper will examine both affirmative responses (popular music as triumph) to ragtime and early jazz as well as oppositional discourses (popular music as cultural degradation) that sought to arrest and reverse the burgeoning popularity of these early mass-marketed musics. Oppositional discourses will constitute the primary subject of analysis, however, because the unqualified acceptance of ragtime and early jazz in contemporary Americacontrasts so starkly with the fervent disapproval that greeted their initial appearance. This sharp discontinuity between past and present perceptions provides a unique opportunity to examine fears about modernity, the maturation of industrial capitalism, and the growing hegemony of the market in the first three decades of the twentieth century.

Both ragtime and early jazz have long-since been incorporated into national memory as benign, wholly inoffensive artifacts worthy of cultural veneration and early twentieth century predictions that they might become "the much vaunted music of the future" appear quaintly prescient (Sherlock 639). While today relatively few Americans are intimately familiar with these genres, no one feels, upon hearing a snippet of ragtime, as though their aesthetic sensibilities have been assaulted. "Alexander's Ragtime Band" fails to generate fears of moral degeneracy, and American teenagers are quite unlikely to draw any parallels whatsoever between the music of Irving Berlin and Eminem. In contrast, fervent denunciations of popular music as a harbinger of cultural decline were common in the early twentieth century popular press. Ragtime, for instance, was often described as a "virulent poison" or "malarious epidemic" to which the nation's youth were especially susceptible ("Musical Impurity" 16). Detractors condemned ragtime and early jazz with an intensity reminiscent in tone and content to that which greeted rock 'n' roll in the 1950's and rap in the 80's and 90's. Indeed, early twentieth century popular music never denoted "innocence" for contemporaries. Both enthusiasts and detractors agreed that ragtime and early jazz were culturally potent, powerfully affecting consumers. Traditionalist opponents contended "ragtime was an insult to public taste; that popular music was a degradation to the cultured mind; that it provided entertainment for the MASSES [sic] only, and that its very sound was obnoxious to the refined and cultivated instincts of the better class of Americans" (Meyer 3), while popular music's modernist champions countered that, "If any musician does not feel in his heart the rhythmic complexities of 'The Robert E. Lee,' [an enormously successful ragtime number about a steamboat named after the iconic Confederate general] I should not trust him to feel in his heart the rhythmic complexities of Brahms" ("Ragtime Wrangling" 69).

The insistent, syncopated rhythm pulsating through the music seemed to compel men and women into joyously promiscuous interaction on dance floors throughout America, a development that critics feared would contribute to the moral degradation of (white) Americans. Traditionalists denounced popular music not only because the working class masses preferred it to the high culture cultivated by America's "better classes," but also because it became increasingly clear that their own sons and daughters were very often attracted to these highly rhythmic, racialized musics that, according to the May 1900 edition of *The Musical Courier*, exploited the "lowest, basest passions" ("Rag-Time Rage" 20). As one exasperated observer reported, "Our girls will spend hundreds of dollars taking grace lessons and as soon as a ragtime piece of music starts up, they will grasp a strange man in any outlandish position that will often put the lowest creature to shame" (Peiss 103).

Opponents objected not only to popular music's savage, primal rhythm but also to its often-uncouth lyrics. While even ragtime enthusiasts conceded that ragtime lyrics might often be meaningless, critics charged Tin Pan Alley wordsmiths with cranking out messages that were unequivocally toxic. They objected to "young men and ladies of the best standing" delighting in popular songs that referenced "a nauseating twaddle about 'hot town,' 'warm babies,' and 'blear-eyed coons' armed with 'blood-letting razors'" along with a whole host of other objectionable images ("Musical Impurity" 16). How do we account for the intensely negative reaction of so many to a music that would not only eventually be proudly embraced as distinctively American, but harmless as well? Ultimately, opposition to early twentieth century popular music was rooted in the unsettling effects that mass market commerce, with which popular music was intimately linked, produced in traditional social hierarchies and power relations. Oppositional discourses represented a quixotic attempt by America's old bourgeoisie to maintain their positions of influence and authority in a modernizing, dollar-directed world that increasingly regarded them as both irrelevant and antiquated.

Such an argument does not, however, imply that race was absent from discourses surrounding ragtime and early jazz. Indeed, the growing popularity of ragtime and early jazz parallels the institutionalization of legalized segregation and the growing stream of African-Americans migrating from the rural South into Northern urban centers like Chicago. Most Americans assumed without question that ragtime and jazz were primarily of African-American origin. In the early days of the ragtime craze, a 1903 article reported, "There can be little doubt that 'Rag-time' is a genuine creation of Negro blood," and this perception was rarely challenged in mainstream periodicals ("Musical Possibilities" 11). For white critics, however, the "blackness" of popular music was simply another avenue through which to disparage it. Locating the origins of jazz in Africa itself, the *Ladies Home Journal* claimed, "Jazz originally was the accompaniment of the voodoo dancer, stimulating the half-crazed barbarians to the vilest deeds. The weird chant, accompanied by the syncopated rhythm of the voodoo invokers, has been employed by other barbaric people to stimulate brutality and sensuality" (Faulkner 16). The ever-growing popularity of this music alarmed those who feared the growing influence of cultural forms associated with African-Americans. By 1913, the prevalence of popular music in American consciousness seemed so widespread as to prompt this letter to the editor of the *Musical Courier*:

> SIR – Can it be said that America is falling prey to the collective soul of the Negro through the influence of what is popularly known as "rag time" music? Some sociological writers of prominence believe so; all psychologists are of the opinion. One thing is infallibly certain: if there is any tendency toward such a national disaster, it should be definitely pointed out and extreme measures taken to inhibit the influence and avert the increasing danger – if it has not already gone too far. (Kenilworth 22)

Interestingly, bourgeois critics did not condemn all "black" music. African-American "folk" music (spirituals and plantation chants) was often approved of and accorded a guarded acceptance alongside the cherished masterworks of Beethoven, Mozart, and Brahms (among others). It is likely that many white critics deemed African-American folk music "safe" because it represented a time when Blacks "knew their place" at the bottom of the social hierarchy under slavery; they likewise approved of the oft-religious themes. As a critic patiently explained, Americans, in their enthusiasm for "manufactured" popular music, failed to appreciate "the wealth and beauty of the true Negro songs" from the antebellum era. Indeed, she went on to argue that

> Side by side with the too highly civilized white race the Negro must in time have eliminated from him all his God-given best instincts and so fail utterly. For are they not already ashamed of their old African music? They should be taught that slavery, with its occasional abuses, was simply a valuable training in their evolution from savagery, and not look upon their bondage and their slave music with shame. (Murphy 1730)

The middle class African-American response to such racial discourse was complex. African-Americans were integral to the formation and expansion of both ragtime and early jazz, yet their relationship to American popular music was ambivalent and contested. While white critics readily assigned an African origin to the popular music they so despised, black writers sought to complicate such assumptions. "I do not see why this music should be put upon the shoulders of the Negro solely," argued the editor of the *Negro Music Journal*, "for it does not portray his nature, nor is its rhythm distinctly characteristic of our race" ("Our Musical Condition" 138).

Popular music in all its permutations was often subject to sweeping condemnations by these arbiters of Black middle-class propriety. As Kevin Gaines argues, "Virtually all but the most unchurched and bohemian black elites were unable to distinguish the aesthetically ambitious ragtime piano compositions of, for example, Scott Joplin, from humiliating coon songs and minstrel characters" (76). Instead, critics struggled to maintain a strict separation between classical music, with its connotations of learning and respectability, and popular forms associated, unfairly or not, with demeaning racial stereotypes.

Racism as entertainment was nothing new, of course. The blackface minstrel show, which bequeathed its rhythms and representations to ragtime and the vaudeville music hall, delighted white audiences for much of the nineteenth-century. Since the antebellum era, minstrelsy had demeaned blacks and effectively equated bourgeois morality with whiteness

(Gaines 67). Beginning in the 1890's, however, the power of mass-marketed popular music to spread and further reinforce racist stereotypes was of increasing concern to uplift-minded African-Americans. The *Negro Music Journal* explicitly referenced the rapidly expanding music industry when it maintained the races bore equal culpability for the popularity of ragtime: "The whole country is responsible, both black and white. Neither side can be excused for the part it has played in creating, publishing, and distributing this low and degrading class of music. Publishing houses in all parts of the country have, with few exceptions, published this music more or less" ("Our Musical Condition" 138).

In response to the power of the music publishing and vaudeville industries, many middle-class African Americans believed that achievement in "legitimate" cultural endeavors, like opera, which demanded "high-class performance and artistic execution" rather than the "droll song and dance" associated with popular music and minstrelsy held the promise of disrupting vicious racial stereotypes.

As the *Colored American Magazine* argued, in favor of cultivating an appreciation of opera, "At these gatherings the refined and cultured of our race assemble, and from them the Caucasian learns that all of the Negro race are not ragtime characters, but that a great number of us possess a discriminating and cultivated taste for the fine arts" ("Drury" 507).

Ultimately, the black bourgeoisie's rejection of popular music was rooted in an effort to de-emphasize perceived racial differences and achieve a semblance of social equality by carefully identifying their cultural aspirations with those cultivated by the white middle-class. It sought to demonstrate African-Americans' essential sameness with those who despised their growing aspirations. Unlike a later generation that would embrace jazz within a wider celebration of their uniquely African-American heritage, the early twentieth-century black bourgeoisie, in pursuit of an uplift ideology emphasizing class over race, disavowed popular music and instead overwhelmingly sought to distinguish themselves in cultural endeavors deemed legitimate by "the better sort" of whites. African-American discourse in middle-class periodicals echoed white assumptions that classical music embodied universal values that edified, enriched, and purified its adherents while ragtime and jazz were, in contrast, repugnant productions imposed upon ignorant consumers by a venal horde of unscrupulous music publishers. They consistently argued that a livable, civilized future lay in venerating tradition rather than in embracing the latest novelty manufactured to amuse the masses. For both Black and White traditionalists, the past denoted a realm safe from the vacuous mob and the market that privileged its unenlightened choices.

Traditionalists stridently rejected the argument justifying the worth of ragtime and early jazz based on their widespread and ever growing appeal in the mass marketplace. Furthermore, critics refused to accept the notion that even if popular music truly arose from, and in response to, the people themselves, that this qualified it as a legitimate cultural production. Traditionalists strove to refute modernist arguments such as the following:

> "The people" have created their popular music precisely to their need and their taste. As to its having a deteriorating effect on them, vulgarities and all, such a claim is absurd in view of the fact that it is not the music which makes the people, but the people who make the music to suit them. ("Ethics" 225)

Traditionalists countered,

> Because there is a large demand for yellow newspapers, burlesque shows, saloons, gambling houses, and other dens of the underworld, could we with justice say that

> these things are created by and for the public, and are, therefore, creative and good? ("Dangers" 8)

In short, according to traditionalist discourse, it did not matter if popular music arose spontaneously from the people themselves because the masses were ignorant and immoral. Like children let loose in a candy store, they clamored to stuff themselves with that which made them ill. When modernists argued that "you may take it as certain that if millions of people persist in liking something that has not been recognized by the schools, there is vitality in that thing," the obvious retort was that mass popularity denoted nothing but the power of money-hungry sensationalists to exploit the venality of the masses ("Ragtime Wrangling" 69). According to such discourse, popular music was but one of a host of media that prostituted itself in pursuit of the widest audience possible. Inevitably, this appealing to the lowest common denominator of the masses supplied

> The editor with his dozen reports of murder and sexual laxity flashing from the front page of his morning paper; the novelist and dramatist with their liberal laxative of filth and crass sugaring of sentiment; the minister with his vulgarity and hypnotism; the music master with his ragtime - all these bow the knee to Baal. These men, however, insist that they are expressing the true American feeling by giving the people what they want. ("Will Ragtime" 407)

Such was the fruit of pandering to the masses. Not only did the market valorize the charlatan, the demagogue, and the acquisitive materialist but, more alarmingly, it simultaneously degraded legitimate cultural forms, such as Western classical music, as it nourished the vulgarity of the masses.

Traditionalist discourse argued that popular music contributed directly to the decay and neglect of the music the old bourgeoisie held most dear – the symphonic masterpieces of European classical composers. As early as 1900, the *Musical Courier* reported that "rag-time – a ragweed of a music – has grown up everywhere in the Union and its vicious influences are highly detrimental to the cause of good music" ("Rag-time Rage" 20). Almost thirty years later, critics were still vainly declaiming against popular music, asserting that jazz was a "rhythm without music and without soul…undoubtedly it stifles the true musical instinct, turning many of our talented young people from the persistent, continuing study and execution of good music" ("Damrosch" 26). This strand of traditionalist discourse argued that popular music positively hindered a "musically uncultured person in gaining an appreciation of higher music…ragtime has dulled their taste for pure music just as intoxicants dull a drunkard's taste for pure water and so fascinates them that they cannot even listen to higher music, much less enjoy it" ("Dangers" 8). According to traditionalists, a veneration of "higher music" was essential to developing one's moral, spiritual, and intellectual nature. Of course, the elevated character of classical music could not be grasped without the proper training; to grasp it required assiduous and respectful study. "By music," clarified one music teacher, "I mean that which demands much time and thought; the music of artistic cultivation, of humble ambitions, prayerfully and earnestly followed; of obedience to teachers; of self denial" ("Music Versus" 42). A devotee had not only to be carefully trained to properly appreciate classical music but he or she must also be shielded from the infectious degradation of popular entertainment forms.[3] As an 1899 *Etude* editorial entitled, "The Invasion of Vulgarity In Music," argued:

> This cheap trashy stuff [ragtime] cannot elevate even the most degraded minds, nor could it possibly urge any one on to greater effort in the acquisition of culture in any phase…If you are endeavoring to cause an elementary musical mind to appreciate Beethoven, you must not let him escape you and visit a vaudeville show, even for a single night, or you will find yourself the next day set back weeks in your work. (Weld 52)

While the cultivation of an elevated character capable of appreciating "higher music" required cloistered, diligent study, indulgence in popular music required no great intelligence or aesthetic effort on the part of the listener.

Music teachers and other traditionalists invested in the maintenance and promotion of classical music decried the increasing influence of popular music over America's youth. As the German composer Dr. Karl Muck proclaimed in 1916, "What you call here ragtime is poison. It poisons the very source of your musical growth, for it poisons the taste of the young" (qtd. in "Ragtime Wrangling" 68). Teachers echoed Dr. Muck's trepidations. Their very livelihoods seemingly threatened, instructors despaired that popular music and mass entertainment in general discouraged the serious, long term, and expensive dedication required for achievement in classical music. Many young Americans abandoned such spiritually strenuous aspirations. In a 1922 article entitled, "Music Versus Materialism," a music teacher decried the effects of the "amusement-mill of our suburban community life" which left young music students profoundly ignorant, superficial, conformist, and dismissive of anything (like music) not immediately and obviously practical to material ambitions. According to this author, the attitude of America's young music student now amounted to a petulant complaint, "What good is all this high-class music, anyhow, except just to harrow up your feelings? Let's play something lively and cut out the sob stuff!" Again, the decline of classical tradition and civilized life in America more broadly, was attributed to shallow pragmatism and an overweening preoccupation with material success:

> [T]he scion of the new democracy…not only does he frankly prefer rag-time to Beethoven, he is no longer ashamed of the fact. And he has taken a new stand – he absolutely refuses to practice. He is going to be an electrical engineer, anyhow, so what's the use of bothering with five finger exercises and all that sort of foolishness?

Ultimately, traditionalists argued, ragtime and jazz were detrimental to the future greatness of American classical music because the public's insatiable appetite for popular music allowed no appreciation for the geniuses who, undoubtedly, labored unrecognized in their midst. "It is my firm belief," argued a respondent in the *Musical America* debate of 1912, "that many an undiscovered Beethoven, Wagner and Liszt has trashy music to thank for his obscurity. Musical nature may become truly perverted, just as a highly imaginative reader may injure his brain by constant perusal of 'cheap, trashy' fiction" (Hamlin 36).

The traditionalist idea that ragtime and jazz "perverted" an individual's musical nature was rooted not only in a despair for the future of classical music but also in the perception that popular music seemed to possess a unique power over the physical bodies of its consumers. In this respect, traditionalist and modernist discourses were in substantial agreement. No one disputed the notion that ragtime and jazz were aimed at the body, rather than the intellect (as was claimed for classical music). They differed fundamentally, however, on whether popular music's corporeal power was destructive or liberatory. For instance, while the *Ladies Home Journal* argued that "those moaning saxophones and the rest of the instruments with their broken, jerky rhythm make a purely sensual appeal…they call out to the low and rowdy instinct" (McMahon 34), the *Ragtime Review* countered, "The fact remains that ragtime is the most popular music in the world today – the kind that makes your feet shuffle and the mouth pucker – that makes you forget your troubles and worries and feel at peace with the entire universe" ("What Is Ragtime?" 8). Both agreed that the irresistibly syncopated rhythms of popular music, bypassing one's mental faculties and moral sensibilities, left listeners "powerless" to resist the appeals it made to the body. Although the earliest published accounts of ragtime often focused on professional entertainers, recounting "a distinct rhythm and mode, so to speak, throughout the Negro melodies… [which] lend themselves to the dance which usually accompanies the popular song when sung on the stage," writers soon began to describe the dramatic (and often unsettling) effects of popular music on its listeners ("Music Halls" 536). In 1903, a music professor intending to dispassionately observe ragtime music at a masquerade ball instead found himself caught up in the energy:

> Suddenly I discovered that my legs were in a condition of great excitement. They twitched as though charged with electricity and betrayed a considerable and rather dangerous desire to jerk me from my seat. The rhythm of the music, which had seemed so unnatural at first, was beginning to exert its influence over me.

He concluded, "The continuous reappearance and succession of accentuations on the wrong parts of the bar and the unnatural syncopations impart somewhat of a rhythmic compulsion to the body which is nothing short of irresistible" ("Musical Possibilities" 11). While the discourses emanating from social commentators concurred with the professor that popular music possessed the distinct ability to operate directly upon the body, opinion was sharply split regarding the consequences of this power. Modernists associated the enjoyment of popular music with a healthy ability to express emotion and experience pleasure. American composer Howard Brockaway opined, "It is fairly well established that only an oyster can resist the appeal of syncopated rhythm" ("Delving" 97). While traditionalist discourse agreed that popular music had the power to manifest itself directly on the body it argued, unsurprisingly, that this was a wholly destructive rather than a liberating influence. Giving oneself over to the power of syncopated rhythm resulted in the abdication of moral restraint and, consequently, the destruction of all civilized decorum.

Beginning in the early 1910's, traditionalist discourse identifying popular music with the abandonment of moral restraint in favor of a primitive hedonism began to appear more frequently. The impetus for much of this discourse was undoubtedly the dance craze that swept America around this time. *Musical America* approvingly reprinted the reaction of a Polish conductor visiting America in 1912, "Day and night you Americans tingle tangle and jingle jangle ragtime band stuff with [dances like the] grizzly bear, tom cat and turkey trot. This is not music; this is madness. Awful. Terrible!" ("Ragtime Is Madness" 43). Ragtime and jazz were responsible, according to traditionalist discourse, for compelling Americans into modern dances that were "as much a violation of the seventh commandment as adultery" ("Pulpit" 894). Traditionalists regularly claimed Americans, having had enough of these immoral dances and the popular music that propelled them, were on the verge of a moralistic crusade to purge the nation of these vices. In 1913, for instance, the *Literary Digest* reported, "Police, church, and school authorities everywhere are stirred to conference and action over the demoralization that is plainly evident though the incoming of these indecent dances which are sweeping over the country like an epidemic"("Carnality" 102). To their dismay, however, the appeal of popular music and the new dances only continued to grow, especially with the jazz phenomenon that gripped America near the end of World War One. By 1921, the *Ladies Home Journal* argued, in an article hopefully entitled, "Back To Prewar Morals" (conveniently forgetting that, in the opinion of many, America's prewar morality had been little better than a cesspool), "In so far as jazz dancing relaxes morality and undermines the institution of the family, it is an element of tremendously evil potential" (13). Whether its target was ragtime or jazz, however, traditionalist discourse consistently recognized the corporeal appeal of popular music. The elevated, spiritual tone of classical music simply could not compete with popular music for the hearts and minds (and feet) of the masses.

Although traditionalist discourses condemned ragtime and jazz for their relentless assault upon the American body, critics also argued that the damage inflicted by popular music went far beyond the dance madness denounced from the bench as "a series of snakelike gyrations and weird contortions of seemingly agonized bodies and limbs" ("Judge Rails" 15). Some critics preached that ragtime and jazz ultimately produced mental degeneration or hysteria in their listeners. Popular music not only made Americans lose control of their bodies and their better judgment on the dance floor, but it actually rendered them mentally unstable. The earliest denunciations of popular music had characterized it as a "dangerous epidemic," and by the twentieth century's second decade it was increasingly associated with the degeneration of mental health. Critics tied the appeal of popular music and its relentless, hypnotic beat to the increasingly frenetic rhythm of modern American life. A 1911 article in the *New York Times* approvingly quoted a visiting German music professor's opinion that ragtime would "eventually stagnate the brain cells and wreck the nervous system" ("Music in America" 10), while in a 1913 article entitled "Ragtime: The New Tarantism" (the original tarantism being a wild dancing mania, prevalent in thirteenth-century western Europe and supposedly incited by the bite of a tarantula), Francis Toye opined, "I believe that it [ragtime] is a direct encouragement to hysteria…in a society where the social needs and restraints of modern civilized life unite with subtle hereditary nervous defects to make hysteria as common as it is" (Toye 654-655).

Critics often fused a smattering of psychoanalytic hearsay with a facile authority borrowed from the scientific realm to "prove" that popular music was mentally degenerative. As the *Ladies Home Journal* asserted, "That it [jazz] has a demoralizing effect upon the human brain has been demonstrated by many scientists." This article went on to claim that a number of scientists, working with the insane, had discovered that "the effect of jazz on the normal brain produces an atrophied condition on the brain cells." Ultimately, it concluded, jazz music inhibited a patient's ability to distinguish between "good and evil, between right and wrong" (Faulkner 16). The orchestra leader at the Napa State Hospital wrote an article for *The Metronome* to warn, "I can say from my own knowledge that about fifty percent of our young boys and girls from the age of 16 to 25 that land in insane asylums these days are jazz crazy" (Guilliams 59). While many commentators stopped short of charging popular music with directly causing mental illness or hysteria, they asserted, alternatively, that popular music contributed to an emotional malaise increasingly infecting Americans. After informing readers that he did not approve of jazz because it was "doing a vast amount of harm to young minds and bodies not yet developed to resist evil temptations" the author of an editorial in the January 1925 edition of *Etude* went on to approvingly quote an "expert" in these matters, the "eminent" Dr. M.P. Schlapp. "We are headed for a smash in this country if we keep on the way we are going," reported Dr. Schlapp. "Our emotional instability is the product of immigration, automobiles, jazz and the movies" (qtd. in "Is Jazz the Pilot" 7). Attempts to associate popular music with a generalized sense of psychological fragility reflecting the tenor of modern American life were increasingly common throughout this period.

Beginning in the second decade of the century, both modernists and traditionalists began to identify popular music as broadly evocative of the economic and cultural transformations remolding America. The most obvious example of this trend, of course, identifies the 1920's as the "Jazz Age." Despite the inability of this label to accurately characterize the complexities of an entire historical era (in the sense that all such labels are inadequate), Americans of the early twentieth century often did just this, utilizing images and attitudes associated with popular music to define the times in which they lived. The associations authors chose to take from popular music and apply to the nation more generally, of course, depended upon their stance toward industrial modernity and the marketplace. For those who embraced America's consumerist promise of unlimited abundance and liberatory technology, the frenetic liveliness of ragtime and early jazz provided an apt metaphor. Despite its earlier appropriation of "plantation" and "darkie" images, ragtime was not often associated with the quiet repose of rural retirement or contemplation. Instead, it was "the perfect expression of the American city, with its restless bustle and motion, its multitude of unrelated details, and its underlying rhythmic progress toward a vague Somewhere" ("Great American" 317). As *The Ragtime Review* claimed in December of 1914:

> [Ragtime] is the music of the hustler, of the feverishly active speculator; of the "skyscraper" and the "grain elevator." Nor can here be any doubt about its vigor – vigor which is, perhaps, empty sometimes and meaningless, but, in the hands of competent interpreters, brimming over with life. ("Why Ragtime" 3)

The energy of popular music was associated with the creative forces rapidly binding the continent together, increasing the speed with which goods and information could be transferred across the nation and delivered swiftly to the benefit of consumers, fulfilling their rapidly multiplying desires. In a lyrical description of popular music's evocation of a pragmatic, modern America, Grace Hodsdon Boutelle wrote that the rhythm of ragtime existed

> in every factory and mill, on the elevated and in the subway. It sings in the wireless and flies in the aeroplane. It blossoms in the fertilized desert and flows in the toil-created waterways. It streams, visible and splendid as flying banners, along the skyline in New York Harbor. Here is architectural syncopation, if you like, an accent withheld here, anticipated there, nothing happening exactly according to the traditional rhythm of architecture, yet this very freedom demonstrates its loyalty to the basic law of building – that law which demands that skyscraper or government shall definitely meet the needs and coherently express the purpose of its builders. (qtd. in "Ragtime Wrangling" 69)

With the conclusion of the First World War, jazz displaced, or mutated out of, ragtime but the images utilized in popular discourse remained essentially unchanged. "Jazz," wrote the *Etude,* "has come to stay. It is an expression of the times, of the breathless, energetic, superactive times in which we are living and it is useless to fight against it" ("Where Is Jazz"

595). For champions of modernity, popular music represented the fierce creative energy of an industrializing, urban America, the ceaseless enterprise of its people, and the mountain of desirable consumer goods it showered upon them.

Like modernists, traditionalists increasingly appropriated images associated with popular music in order to broadly characterize the tenor of American life and society. The connotations employed by traditionalists, obviously, were quite different. Traditionalists recognized the profound changes reshaping America, but they chose, in contrast tomodernist discourses, to use popular music to emphasize the indecision, indeterminacy, and fragmentation of modern life. As Americans became ever more responsive to the dictates of the market, traditionalist discourses reflected a perception that the cultural authority of the old middle class was slipping away, along with the standards of conduct they espoused. The "cheap, trashy" music so popular with the masses was supposedly indicative of a malaise infecting all of American life. Careful scrutiny of ragtime music, for example, allegedly revealed that "every one of the songs is insidiously perverting; they are indicative of relaxitive morality, of disparagement of the marital tie...of the entire moral code" ("Remarks" 22). After the end of World War One, many authors were convinced that the nation had lost its traditional moral restraints and much of this discourse, in fact, referenced the war as an explanation for the "jazz spirit" apparently affecting the nation. Discussing the rage for jazz which gripped the nation with the end of World War One, the *Ladies Home Journal* explained in 1921, "There is always a revolutionary period of the breaking down of old conventions and customs which follows after every great war; and this rebellion against existing conditions is to be noticed in all life today. Unrest, the desire to break the shackles of old ideas and forms are abroad" (Faulkner 16). The *Journal*, unsurprisingly, foresaw only disaster in Americans' desire to "break the shackles of old ideas," but, by identifying these urges with a transitional period following the tribulations of war, it was able to claim that jazz signified only a temporary period of readjustment; America would see a "Return to Pre-War Morals" soon enough. Jazz, however, did not immediately disappear, and three years later the *Etude* still found it necessary to declaim, "Jazz is one of the inevitable expressions of what might be called the jazzy morale of mood of America...when America regains its soul, jazz will go, not before – that is to say, it will be relegated to the dark and scarlet haunts whence it came and wither unwept it will return, after America's soul is reborn" ("Where is Jazz" 595).

Mass-produced popular music, of course, never disappeared from American life, and the genres that eventually displaced ragtime and jazz, such as rock 'n' roll and rap, would have been just as upsetting, if not more so, to the traditionalists who denounced Tin Pan Alley's ubiquitous creations.[4] Hopes that America's "jazz spirit" was only a peculiar manifestation of the post-war era were bound to be disappointed because the transformations so often signified by popular music had begun long before and were tied to the growth of industrial capitalism in America, rather than to a temporary upset of social relations caused by a year and a half of America's participation in The Great War. The garish materialism denounced by traditionalists could not be reversed by their fervent denunciations of cultural decay, and the popular music they so detested grew in popularity along with the burgeoning consumer culture of the 1920's. These changes could be resisted but not overturned by appeals for Americans to return to an orderly, pre-capitalist past sanctified and largely created in traditionalist discourse. For traditionalists, popular music symbolized the lamentable and growing hegemony of the market and its ability to commodify all that it touched. A 1921 article in *Ladies Home Journal* encapsulated many of their fears about modern capitalism's omnipresence in one short passage that evoked popular music, mass amusements, the displacement of traditional religion, the vulgar materialism of the masses, the frenetic rhythm and mental confusion of modern life, and the visceral power of advertising images to permeate modern consciousness. Describing a stroll through Manhattan in search of immoral jazz dens, John R. McMahon wrote, with Beat-like intensity, "We walked up Broadway encompassed with a fierce jazz of light, barbaric in color, savage in gyrating motion, stupefying the optic nerves and conveying to the brain confused messages of underwear, chewing gum, and automobile parts. It seemed an appropriate vestibule to the temple of the modern dance" ("Back To Pre-War Morals" 13).

## Notes

1. The literal and metaphoric center of the modern popular song industry, beginning in the early 1890's and continuing through the middle of the twentieth-century, was an area originally located on New York City's West 28th Street known as Tin Pan Alley.
2. According to one observer in 1920, however, "the jazz" was simply ragtime speeded up and "raised to the Nth power" ("Jazz and Ragtime" 200).
3. Interestingly, one of the most successful, popular composers in American history disdained acquiring any formal musical training whatsoever. According to author E.M. Wickes, Irving Berlin once said that "he feared to study music, as he had an idea that the knowledge of music-construction and its laws would have a tendency to kill his originality and spontaneity" ("The Birth" 893). Berlin reportedly composed all of his songs in F-sharp, constructing million-selling melodies using only the black keys on the piano.
4. The conviction that popular music was literally everywhere constituted a prevalent theme in traditionalist discourse. In the article touching off the popular music debate in *Musical America,* for instance, a music teacher by the name of Minna Kaufmann argued, "In these songs, which are heard everywhere, one gets a very good idea of the state of mind and feeling of the public...The language used in the verses is always the 'catchy' kind. You can't avoid quoting some of the songs, because the verses are made up of everyday expressions twisted into other and often unsavory meanings. These songs are especially bad for children, yet it is impossible to keep them in ignorance of them, for the bands, the phonographs and street singers proclaim that this is the kind of music the public wants and pays for" ("The Case" 13).

## Works Cited

"Back to Prewar Morals." *Ladies Home Journal* November 1921: 13+.
"The Birth of Our Popular Songs." *Literary Digest* 7 October 1916: 893.
"Carnality in Song, Dance, and Dress." *Literary Digest* 19 July 1913: 101-102.
"The Case against the Popular Song." *Musical America* 8 June 1912: 13.
"Damrosch Assails Jazz." *New York Times* 17 April 1928: 26.
"Dangers That Lie in Ragtime." *Musical America* 21 September 1912: 8.
"Delving into the Genealogy of Jazz." *Current Opinion* August 1919: 97-99.
"The Drury Opera Company in Verdi's 'Aida.'" *Colored American Magazine* August 1903: 595-599.
"Ethics of Ragtime." *Literary Digest* 10 August 1912: 225.
Farwell, Arthur. "The Ethics of 'Ragtime.'" *Musical America* 22 June 1912: 24.
Faulkner, Anne Shaw. "Does Jazz Put the Sin in Syncopation?" *Ladies Home Journal* August 1921: 16+.
Gaines, Kevin. *Uplifting the Race: Black Leadership, Politics, and Culture in the Twentieth Century.* Chapel Hill: U of North Carolina P, 1996.
Guilliams, A.E. "Detrimental Effects of Jazz on Our Younger Generation." *The Metronome* February 1923: 59.

"The Great American Composer – Will He Speak in the Accent of Broadway?" *Current Opinion* November 1917: 316-317.

Hamlin, George. "Popular Songs Bad." *Musical America* 13 July 1912: 36.

"Is Jazz the Pilot of Disaster?" *Etude* January 1925: 6-7.

"Jazz and Ragtime Are the Preludes to a Great American Music." *Current Opinion* August 1920: 199-200.

"Judge Rails at Jazz and Dance Madness." *New York Times* 14 April 1926: 15.

Kenilworth, Walter Winston. "Remarks on Ragtime." *Musical Courier* 28 May 1913: 22-23.

Mason, Daniel Gregory. "Concerning Ragtime." *The New Music Review* March 1918: 112-116.

McMahon, John R. "Unspeakable Jazz Must Go." *Ladies Home Journal* December 1921: 34+.

Meyer, Peter Frank. "The Potency of Ragtime." *Ragtime Review* April 1916: 3.

Murphy, Jeanette Robinson. "The True Negro Music and its Decline." *The Independent* July 1903: 1723-1730.

"Music Halls and Popular Songs." *Cosmopolitan* July 1897: 531-540.

"Music in America." *New York Times* 9 October 1911: 10.

"Music Versus Materialism." *Musical Quarterly* January 1922: 39-42.

"Musical Impurity." *Etude* January 1900: 16.

"The Musical Possibilities of Rag-Time." *The Metronome* March 1903: 11.

Musser, Charles and Carol Nelson. *High-Class Moving Pictures: Lyman H. Howe and the Forgotten Era of Traveling Exhibition, 1880-1920.* Princeton: Princeton UP, 1991.

"Our Musical Condition." *Negro Music Journal* March 1903: 137-139.

Peiss, Kathy. *Cheap Amusements: Working Women and Leisure in Turn-of-the-Century.* New York. Philadelphia: Temple UP, 1985.

"The Pulpit and the New Dances." *Literary Digest* 19 April 1913: 894.

"Ragtime Is Madness Says Sirota." *Musical America* 23 March 1912: 43.

"The Rag-Time Rage." *The Musical Courier* 23 May 1900: 20.

"Ragtime Wrangling." *Literary Digest* 8 January 1916: 68-70.

"Remarks On Ragtime." *The Musical Courier* 28 May 1913: 22-23.

Sherlock, Charles Reginald. "From Breakdown To Rag-Time." *Cosmopolitan* October 1901: 630-639.

Smith, Wilson G. "The Vagrant Philosopher." *Negro Music Journal* May 1903: 181-183.

Toye, Frances. "The New Tarantism." *English Review* March 1913: 654-655.

Von Liebich, Rudolph. "The Benighted Lover of Ragtime as a Musical 'Man with the Hoe.'" *Musical America* 31 August 1912: 26.

Weld, Arthur. "The Invasion of Vulgarity in Music." *Etude* February 1899: 52.

"What Is Ragtime?" *The Ragtime Review* January 1915: 8.

"Where Is Jazz Leading America?" *Etude* September 1924: 595-596.

"Why Ragtime Is the True Music of 'Hustlers.'" *Ragtime Review* December 1914: 3-4.

"Will Ragtime Save the Soul of the Native American Composer?" *Current Opinion* December 1915: 406-407.

*In "How Deep Is the Ocean? How High Is the Sky?" Jill Gold Wright examines the lyrics of the most popular songs in American musical theater history. "Intrinsic in the theme of question-asking," she explains, "is my argument that the Jewish composers and lyricists who pioneered the American musical stage did so from a place of marginalization." This marginalization, Wright theorizes, stems from the immigrant Jews finding that they had "entered a lion's den of intolerance and discrimination upon their arrival in America. They often did not have the power or the confidence to use statements or commands." Wright also argues that the tradition of religious inquiry further influenced the development of this lyrical form.*

# "How Deep Is the Ocean? How High Is the Sky?": The Question Song and the Jewish Lyricist in American Musical Theater

## Jill Gold Wright

There is an old Jewish joke which goes something like this: a young boy wanders into the kitchen to ask his grandmother a question. "Grandma, why do Jewish people always answer a question with another question?" The grandmother looks at him and says, "Why? Who wants to know?"

Leo Rosten's *The Joys of Yiddish* is a lighthearted lexicon of Yiddish words that have made their way into English usage and are most well known to Americans. He tells a variation of the same story:

> Mr. O'Neill and Mr. Pinsky were chatting. O'Neill said, "Did you hear about the fight between Cooley and McGraw?"
>
> "How could I miss it?" said Pinsky. "Wasn't it in front of my eyes?"
>
> "I didn't know you were there."
>
> "What then? I was maybe in the White House?"
>
> "Whose fault was it: Cooley's?"
>
> "Who else?"
>
> O'Neill sighed, "Pinsky, why do Jews answer every question with another question?"
>
> Pinsky pondered. "Why not?"

Rosten's anecdote confirms how common question-asking is in the Jewish-American dialect; after the introduction of Yiddish into AmericanEnglish, people came to recognize this syntactical pattern as a distinctlyJewish trait. Even more interesting is Rosten's placing the joke in thesection of his book that attempts to define the difference between a "goy" and a "Jew." Rosten clearly sees question-asking as a conspicuous way of distinguishing between Jews and Gentiles.

But besides noting that the pattern of question-asking is typical to Jewish speech, not much more has been made of this phenomenon. Never has this linguistic pattern been linked to or placed in a discussion of American musical theater, a field dominated by Jews. In the first half of the twentieth century, Broadway was pioneered largely by Jewish composers and lyricists, and it was Jewish writers, most specifically, who created this definition of America on the American stage for musical theater audiences.

The theater attracted Jewish writers. It may seem paradoxical, but it took a Russian-born cantor's son, Irving Berlin, to write "God Bless America" and the musical of quintessential Americana, *Annie Get Your Gun.* It was Jerome Kern and Oscar Hammerstein II, both Jews, who wrote the American masterpiece *Show Boat.* George and Ira Gershwin composed *Porgy and Bess*, often considered America's first and best opera. Richard Rodgers and Oscar Hammerstein II created and defined aspects of the American landscape in *Oklahoma!* and explored American values in *South Pacific.* And, in the latter half of the twentieth century, Jerry Bock and Sheldon Harnick wrote the prototypical "Jewish" musical, *Fiddler on the Roof.*

The composers and lyricists I focus on here were either born in Eastern Europe, came from immigrant families newly arrived in America, or were native to a society where Jews were outcasts. It is not a coincidence, then, that these "non-Americans" were the ones who clearly saw the American landscape and who considered America a worthwhile topic to sing about on stage.

To study these writers as a group, it is necessary to illuminate some of the commonalities shared by the Jewish composers and lyricists. This paper will discuss a specific trait that all these Jewish lyricists had in common: their linguistic heritage of Yiddish and how that legacy formed the lyrics that pioneered the American musical stage.

Irving Berlin, Ira Gershwin, Oscar Hammerstein II, and Sheldon Harnick all spoke and wrote in English throughout their careers. But what is more important is that they came from Jewish backgrounds in which Yiddish had an enormous influence. There is a very distinctive element in their collective work, one that has unquestionable ties to their Jewish culture and which is all but absent in the work of their Gentile counterparts. It is the simple syntactical form of asking a question, instead of making a direct statement. Especially in the new world of America, audiences began to understand this syntax as a specifically "Jewish" way of using language.

In the beginning of the twentieth century on the Lower East Side, Yiddish became a primary marker of the Jews' newfound freedom. According to Sol Gittleman in *From Shtetl to Suburbia: The Family in Jewish Literary Imagination*, "After centuries of restriction and censorship, the Jew could walk…with his eyes off the ground. He could also read, write and speak freely, and the Jews took full advantage of this opportunity to create one of the great immigrant cultures of America, in an immigrant language, Yiddish." Newly-arrived American Jews infused Yiddish into every aspect of their community; indeed, it was one of the forces that bound the community together. Uriel Weinreich states, "For almost a thousand years it has been the language of the largest and most creative branch of the Jewish people." Yiddish was not only the language of conversation, but of all of life's intricacies. Weinrich says, "While serving as the vernacular of millions of Jews, it came to express their fears and hopes. In folk songs and informal prayer, it has been enriched by high emotional overtones; as the language of instruction in the Law, it has become capable of great intellectual subtlety."

Among the Jewish immigrants living on the Lower East Side, Yiddish literacy was extremely high, and texts written in Yiddish were readily available. As Sol Steinmetz reminds us in *Yiddish and English: The Story of Yiddish in America*, "In New York City, the center of the Yiddish-speaking population, over 150 different Yiddish newspapers, magazines, and other periodicals made their appearance between 1885 and 1914." Further, these publications were not intended merely for the educated or upper classes. Gittleman states, "Literally every adult Jew read a Yiddish newspaper. In the peak years of the 1920s, the circulation of the Yiddish daily press in New York City alone was nearly seven hundred thousand, and conservative estimates suggested that each paper was read by three adults, accounting for a readership of over two million people."

It is important to understand that the Yiddish texts did not preach exclusion. The publications were not intended as a tool for the Jewish community to isolate itself but as an in-road to assimilation. Numerous publications "became famous for the beauty of their work and the particularly modern American view of life they held out. The Yiddish newspapers and magazines were, as a rule, openly in favor of assimilation to the American way of life and had no scruples about freely admitting into Yiddish all types of Anglicisms," Steinmetz states. This linguistic exchange was mutual; Yiddish became affected by American English, and the reciprocal occurred. We know that numerous Yiddish words became part of the English vernacular, but it is not only Yiddish vocabulary that changed the American landscape. The Yiddish heritage of the Jewish lyricists affected the songs they wrote and changed American musical theater as well.

Beyond that, Yiddish folk music influenced the American Jews. Of course, the immigrants brought with them the songs of their childhoods, and they continued to sing them in the new world. One example is the prototype of the Yiddish cradle song: "It may be that the chapter of anonymous Yiddish lullabies ended with the close of the nineteenth century." According to Ruth Rubin in *Voices of a People: The Story of Yiddish Folksong*, Yiddish cradle songs, however, continued to be written by Jewish poets and composers during the twentieth century, both in Eastern Europe and America and wherever Yiddish-speaking Jews settled." The following lyrics of a Yiddish lullaby are representative of an entire musical genre which began in Eastern Europe and flourished in America. Its form is especially significant; nearly the whole song is a series of questions:

> My child, who will comb and caress you?
> My child, who will clean your cradle?
> Without a mother, there is no comfort!
> My child, who will clothe and adorn you?
> My child, who will take you to cheder?
> My child, who will make a man out of you?
> My child, who will bless you under the canopy?

But the question form is not limited to the cradle song. The following lyrics come from a protest song, also written in Yiddish. This song, written by David Edelshtat in the late nineteenth century, uses the question to incite a strong reaction in his listeners:

> How long, oh, how long will you slaves yet remain
> And bear the shameful chain?
> How long will you glorious wealth create
> For him, who robs you of your bread?
> How long will you stand with your backs bended low
> Humbled, homeless, and wan?

One reason the question-song was so natural to Jewish lyricists is that the rhetoric of question asking is absolutely pivotal in Jewish theology andideology. From the earliest centuries of Judaism, human inquiry and analysis have reigned supreme, even in questioning the sacred texts. The Talmud specifically states, "As the hammer [striking a rock] causes numerous sparks to flash forth, so a scriptural verse engenders many interpretations."

Modern rabbis describe this essentiality of Judaism in less archaic terms, but the central message is the same. Rabbi Adin Steinsaltz writes:

> The questioning, searching and skeptical man is not excluded from the circle of believers; he becomes, rather, the spokesman of the central work of the Jewish religion, the prime source for halakhah [traditional Jewish law] and daily conduct. This very process creates the unique blend of profound faith and questioning skepticism that has characterized the Jewish people throughout the ages.

The lyricists I discuss here were quite comfortable with question-asking as a core part of their discourse. Beyond the nuances of their everyday conversation, they were taught in both their formal Jewish instruction and in their casual contact with Jewish adults that they could reach the most profound truths through questions. By doubting all assumptions, and analyzing the world they lived in, they could create a new set of truths for themselves.

There is no question that the lyricists I discuss were familiar with and influenced by the nuances of Yiddish. For Irving Berlin and Ira Gershwin, Yiddish was the language of their first neighborhoods and certainly of the home. Even for Oscar Hammerstein II and Sheldon Harnick, who did not grow up in the tenements of New York, Yiddish would have been deeply ingrained in their psyches and in their ears, simply from their families and social circles' knowledge and usage of it.

Each of these lyricists uses the pattern of question-asking. But it is important first to understand the pattern in general terms to provide a context for the specific examples. Though all of these examples illustrate the question form, the Jewish lyricists employ variations of the same pattern.

In some examples, Jewish lyricists write a series of questions but provide no answer. The song's content is communicated via a list of questions, left in a hypothetical mode, implying that an answer is either unknown, unnecessary or would be redundant. Hammerstein uses this pattern in Tuptim's song "My Lord and Master" from *The King and I*:

> He is pleased with me, my Lord and Master,
> Declares he's pleased with me; what does he mean?
> What does he know of me, this Lord and Master?
> When he has looked at me, what has he seen?

Hammerstein also follows this pattern later in *The Sound of Music* when describing the protagonist, Maria:

> How do you solve a problem like Maria?
> How do you catch a cloud and pin it down?
> How do you find a word that means "Maria?"
> A flibberty-jibbit, a will-o'-the wisp, a clown!...
> But how do you make her stay, and listen to all you say?
> How do you keep a wave upon the sand?
> Oh, how do you solve a problem like Maria?
> How do you hold a moonbeam in your hand?

In these examples, Hammerstein leaves his questions unanswered either because there is no answer, or because the character singing lacks the power to obtain it. Tuptim, the slave, will never know what the King thinks of her or means when he speaks about her because he leaves her in ignorance. The nuns, who exasperatedly sing about Maria, cannot answer these questions. They find that this rhetoric is the only way they can explain the free-spirited nonconformity of their new novice. This is the exact point. Hammerstein uses this very Judaic pattern to pose questions for examination, leaving the audience to understand that at times, questions do not have answers.

In other examples, the Jewish lyricists create a list of questions, and then answer them with a small but definitive word, phrase or sentence. This is a particularly effective technique; that final "answer" packs a large punch, providing closure to the song. Therefore, the character does find some answer to the question, brief though it may be. Hammerstein relies often on this pattern. One example, which emerges from his collaboration with Jerome Kern, is the famous question-song, "Why Was I Born?" Notice how each stanza's long list of questions is answered by a simple half-line response:

> What is the good of being by myself?
> Why was I born? Why am I living?
> What do I get? What am I giving?
> Why do I want a thing I daren't hope for?
> What can I hope for? I wish I knew.
> Why do I try to draw you near me?
> Why do I cry? You never hear me.
> I'm a poor fool, but what can I do?
> Why was I born? To love you.

Hammerstein later creates this pattern again in his collaboration with Richard Rodgers. In *The King and I*, this technique works perfectly in the mouth of the King, whose question-song replaces the traditional form of the soliloquy. Singing alone on stage, the King intellectually explores his options, wondering aloud how best to govern his ancient country in a modern age:

> Shall I join with other nations in alliance?
> If allies are weak, am I not best alone?
> If allies are strong with power to protect me,
> Might they not protect me out of all I own?
> Is there danger to be trusting one another?
> One would seldom wants to do what other wishes.
> But unless someday somebody trust somebody,
> They'll be nothing left on earth, excepting fishes!
> Is a puzzlement!

Other than to recognize that they stem from Yiddish syntax, it is difficult to pinpoint why these language patterns exist in the Jewish vernacular, but there is no question that they do. The pattern of asking questions appears time and again as a standard lyrical form for Jewish songwriters, too many times to be ignored or disregarded as "unscientific." Further, it is telling to consider the differences between Jewish and non-Jewish lyricists. Let us do a brief comparison of the Jewish lyricists' work to the songs of their most prominent non-Jewish colleagues, Cole Porter and George M. Cohan.

Cole Porter was acutely aware of being a Gentile in a theatrical world that seemed to be dominated by Jews. He came onto the theatrical scene later than Berlin, Kern, and Gershwin and felt he needed the key to success. There is an often-quoted conversation Porter had with his friend and colleague, Richard Rodgers. Porter told Rodgers that he had found the secret to writing successful theater music. "What is it?" asked Rodgers. "Simplicity itself," said Porter. "I'll write Jewish tunes."

However, even though Porter successfully emulates Jewish music by using minor chords and keys, thus creating many of his beautiful ballads, his pattern of writing lyrics is distinctly non-Jewish. Where Jewish lyricists use questions to communicate, Gentile writers use direct statements to create meaning in song. Porter's lyrics are poetic, extremely clever and often ironic, but are written in the exact opposite of the Jewish writers' patterns. Consider Porter's witty lyric from his 1948 musical *Kiss Me, Kate*:

From Milwaukee, Mr. Fritz
Often dines me at the Ritz.
Mr. Fritz invented Schlitz, and Schlitz must pay.
But I'm always true to you, darling, in my fashion;
Yes, I'm always true to you, darling, in my way.

Porter relies on the form of the statement to push forward a song, even when it is the simple construction of a subject followed by a being-verb. The examples "I'm always true to you," "I'm in love again," "It was just one of those things" and "You're the top" make clear how some of Porter's most popular songs use a straightforward statement, much more an answer than a question. In sum, Porter writes, "That's why the lady is a tramp," where a Jewish writer might question, "Why is this lady called a tramp?"

George M. Cohan is another early Gentile songwriter who favors the statement over the question, also using the subject/being-verb construction. This directed syntax appears in his most famous songs: "I'm a Yankee Doodle Dandy" and "You're a Grand Old Flag." But Cohan even extends past the statement to communicate his message; in one of the greatest musical tributes to *Broadway* (1904), Cohan's lyrics are not just straightforward sentences, but commands:

Give my regards to Broadway,
Remember me to Herald Square.
Tell all the folks at Forty-Second Street
That I will soon be there!

This format of command-writing also appears in Cohan's World War One hit, "Over There" (1917), illustrating that Cohan still employs the command form nearly fifteen years later:

Johnny, get your gun, get your gun, get your gun.
Take it on the run, on the run, on the run …
So prepare, say a prayer, spread the word to beware!

If we compare Cohan's lyrics to some written by Oscar Hammerstein II, we see that instead of demanding that the character follow a list of commands in the song, the Hammerstein character uses the Judaic form of asking a list of questions to communicate his desires:

Shall we dance?
On a bright cloud of music, shall we fly?
Shall we dance?
Shall we then say "Goodnight," and mean "Goodbye?"
Or perchance, when the last little star has left the sky,
Shall we still be together with our arms around each other,
And shall you be my new romance?
On the clear understanding that this kind of thing can happen,
Shall we dance, shall we dance, shall we dance?

If readers know this scene in *The King and I*, they remembers that the action, not the lyric, answers this series of questions, since Anna and the King actually polka around the hall as they sing this song. The scene would seem absurd if the lyrics were written in a statement form, since they would stupidly state the obvious. "We shall dance /On a bright cloud of music, we shall fly" would not form the magical scene that Hammerstein otherwise creates.

In other songs, Porter combines the two characteristics of the "Gentile" song in his "Let's Do It (Let's Fall in Love)" (1928). Notice how the lyrics include a series of statements and then climax in a series of commands:

Birds do it, bees do it,
Even educated fleas do it.
Let's do it; let's fall in love.
In Spain the best upper-sets do it,
Lithuanians, and let's do it,
Let's do it; let's fall in love.

In the first few decades of the twentieth century, the distinction between the Jewish lyricist writing question-songs and the Gentile writing statement-songs was clear. It must be admitted, however, that this was not a longtime trend. These innovators knew each other and studied each other's compositions to learn what became successful and popular. Soon enough, they began to imitate each other's patterns, and the distinction became blurred.

Evidence of this change again lies in careful study of Cole Porter. From the time Porter began publishing music with the song "Bridget" in 1910, and for twenty years following, all but three songs hepublished were statement-songs. However, in his later years, after watching the question-song flourish on Broadway, Porter regularly tried the form himself. In the second half of his career, Porter averaged at least one question-song per show, including: "What Shall I Do?" (1938), "Do I Love You?" and "Well, Did You Evah?" (1939), "Who Would Have Dreamed?" (1940), "Could It Be You?" (1941), "Should I Tell You I Love You?" (1946), "Why Can't You Behave?" and "Where Is the Life that Late I Led?" (1948).

Although some of Porter's question-songs became quite popular, his composition of them was not entirely natural. Porter's lyrics in his very late song, "I Love Paris" (1953) illuminate his discomfort in shifting from the statement form to the question-song. Porter begins the song in his standard form of writing direct sentences:

I love Paris in the Springtime,
I love Paris in the Fall.
I love Paris in the Winter, when it drizzles,

> I love Paris in the Summer, when it sizzles.

He then moves to the question pattern; however, when Porter writes in this form, it seems forced and does not further the audience's understanding of the song. In fact, his question lyrics become repetitious and cumbersome, slowing down too much the pace of the song:

> I love Paris.
> Why, oh, why do I love Paris?
> Because my love is near.

To an even greater detriment, Porter's lyric of "Why, oh, why?" seems to be a direct appropriation of E.Y. (Yip) Harburg's lyric in *The Wizard of Oz*. Harburg, a Jewish lyricist collaborating with Harold Arlen, wrote this phrase in 1939, fourteen years earlier, in "Somewhere Over the Rainbow:" "Birds fly over the rainbow / Why, oh, why can't I?" There is no question that Porter's "I Love Paris" has a hauntingly beautiful and memorable tune. But under deeper scrutiny, Porter's lyrical attempt to imitate his Jewish colleagues, indeed to write "good Jewish music," seems just that: an imitation. Porter wrote no more question songs after this attempt in 1953.

It must be said that the Jewish lyricists also transitioned into writing statement-songs. Even though Irving Berlin wrote question-songs throughout his entire career, some of his most famous lyrics segue to use the basic subject/verb syntax of the statement song; consider his "This Is the Army, Mr. Jones" (1942), and *Annie Get Your Gun's* "I Got the Sun in the Morning" and "There's No Business Like Show Business" (1946). Some of Ira Gershwin's statement songs became his biggest hits: "I Can't Get Started" (1935), "Let's Call the Whole Thing Off" (1937), and the final song he and George wrote together, "Love Is Here to Stay" (1938). Finally, the Rodgers and Hammerstein partnership created a list of very famous statement songs, including: "I Cain't Say No" (1943), "You'll Never Walk Alone" (1945), "I'm Gonna Wash That Man Right Outa My Hair" (1949), and "Climb Ev'ry Mountain" (1959).

Despite this ultimate blending of forms, the pattern had been set. Stemming directly from their Yiddish heritage, the Jewish songwriters introduced the question-song to Broadway, and its success turned the question-song into a standard.

Proof of this lies in an analysis of the most famous "Jewish" musical ever written, *Fiddler on the Roof*. Besides being written by a Jewish composer and lyricist, Jerry Bock and Sheldon Harnick, *Fiddler* has a distinctly Jewish plot. Based on the stories of Yiddish author Sholom Aleichem, the story follows the residents of the Jewish shetl of Anatevka, who live in constant fear of pogroms. Unlike the other musicals discussed here, *Fiddler* is a Jewish story that purposely "sounds" Jewish; the characters are consciously given a Jewish dialect. Having demonstrated that Jewish lyricists tend to use the question form, it is interesting to view this libretto as a litmus test. The result does not come as any surprise: from the very opening words of the show, the Jewish question pattern we have come to know emerges. Harnick relies on the pattern of asking questions because it is an authentically Jewish mode.

The effect here is different than Hammerstein's prototypical question-song. Hammerstein uses the question to embed in his characters feelings of subservience, self-doubt or fear, and the actual act of questioning communicates these emotions to the audience. But Harnick writes question-songs for his characters because this is the way they would speak! When I interviewed Sheldon Harnick himself about how he came to use this linguistic pattern, he told me about his "own memories of going to a small synagogue in

Chicago" which was "upstairs from a secretarial agency." He thought back on "the men who were there…how they were, how they talked." He concluded that the "rhythm of their speech… worked its way into the lyrics."

The lyrics of *Fiddler on the Roof* are centered on the form of the question throughout the show. The opening line of the prologue immediately establishes this pattern: "A fiddler on the roof…sounds crazy, no?," and from there, Fiddler's opening song, "Tradition," maintains the pattern of asking questions:

> Who day and night must scramble for a living,
> feed a wife and children, say his daily prayers?
> And who has the right, as master of the house,
> to have the final word at home?

As in all strong opening numbers, this song introduces the themes, characters and attitudes of the entire show. As the next verses continue to introduce the papas, mamas, sons and daughters of Anatevka, significantly, they do so in series of questions.

As the musical develops, the major life-cycle events that occur in the family are also sung about in questions. At the eldest daughter Tzeitel's wedding, the epic song "Sunrise, Sunset" begins this way:

> Is this the little girl I carried?
> Is this the little boy at play?
> I don't remember growing older.
> When did they?
> When did she get to be a beauty?
> When did he grow to be so tall?
> Wasn't it yesterday when
> They were small?

As the song continues, the parents ask, "What words of wisdom can I give them? / How can I help to ease their way?," and the younger siblings wonder, "Is there a canopy in store for me?"

Later, in what could be the most heart-wrenching scene in the show, one of Tevye's daughters decides to leave her family to marry a rebel who is imprisoned in Siberia. When the couple approaches her father about their plans, he responds by falling again into his typically Jewish pattern, the question:

> So what do you want from me?
> Go on, be wed.
> And tear out my beard and uncover my head.
> Tradition! They're not even asking permission from the papa.
> What's happening to the tradition?
> One little time I pulled out a thread.
> And where has it led? Where has it led?

When the daughter leaves Anatevka to follow her destiny in Siberia, the farewell lyrics she sings to her father have a distinctly Jewish sound:

> How can I hope to make you understand why I do what I do?
> Why I must travel to a distant land, far from the home I love?...
> Who could imagine I'd be wandering so far from the home I love?
> Yet, there with my love, I'm home.

Intrinsic in the theme of question-asking is my argument that the Jewish composers and lyricists who pioneered the American musical stage did so from a place of marginalization. As immigrants or sons of immigrants, they had huge obstacles to overcome in understanding American ways. They were outsiders and were often pushed to the sidelines. Perhaps because of their status as unknowledgeable newcomers, or because the Jews were discriminated against in the new land as they were in the old, they sometimes adopted the language of weakness. Along with finding a land of opportunity and success, the immigrant Jews found that they entered a lion's den of intolerance and discrimination upon their arrival in America. They often did not have the power or the confidence to use statements or commands. My earlier example of Tuptim shows how question-asking can reveal a powerlessness and a deep anxiety about being seen as wrong. In circumstances like these, asking a question is safer than making a definitive statement, and safety was a concern for the Jew.

Therefore, the question-song brings the listener into a world far beyond the scope of the play. It not only invites the listener into the song, but it brings him into the experience of the American Jew as well. Because these poignant question-songs are written by a specific group, they insist that the audience listen to the subtext of the lyrics. The songs seem to plead, "Listen to what our experiences have been! Provide your own answers for it! What are your answers for my experiences of racism, isolation and marginalization?"

Jewish lyricist Yip Harburg once commented, "A song is the pulse of a nation's heart, a fever chart of its health. Are we at peace? Are we in trouble? Do we feel beautiful? Are we violent? Listen to our songs." Jewish-American composers and lyricists grew into adulthood knowing their roots as well as feeling the sting of discrimination in their own lives. Stemming from their shared experience, they each grew to translate into their creative work the positive and negative experiences they faced in the new world. Their nuanced Yiddish mother tongue, their painful brushes with anti-Semitism, and their rich Jewish heritage all combined to dictate the major themes of their musicals and, ultimately, led to creating a renaissance on the American musical theater stage.

*Constructed as racist and oppressive by Cold War propagandists, the United States government sent jazz musicians overseas as "jambassadors" in an effort to improve our image. In "Jazz Strategy," Scott Gac documents the journeys of one such musician, Dizzy Gillespie.*

# Jazz Strategy: Dizzy, Foreign Policy, and Government in 1956

Scott Gac

***1955:*** *Legendary Radio Corporation of America chairman David Sarnoff calls a conference in Midtown Manhattan. He presents a ten-ounce turntable, which seems ordinary except for its portability and the fact that the United States government has already tossed several of these record players out of military planes. Sarnoff's introduction is serious. There is no dispute over sound theory. Packaged with various pro-American recordings, some members of the federal government believe that lightweight phonographs can help win the Cold War. The self-powered players are the latest device to further American empire (James).*

Sarnoff, the visionary who helped launch television in 1939 – "Now we add sight to sound," he said – was, in 1956, more a stargazer than a prophet when adding flight to sound (qtd. in Casey and Werner 88). The conference on the skydiving phonograph, though, pointed to a much larger postwar theme: the emphasis on sound in foreign policy. Long before the American military serenaded Manuel Noriega with ear-splitting rock tunes, the government spent millions blanketing foreign nations with more soothing sounds of America through radio programs, live performances, and library recordings.

The sudden jump in funding for government sponsored cultural programs showcased a new commitment made after World War II. From 1947 through 1951, an average of $37 million was set aside for cultural endeavors, with a 1951 high of $57 million and a 1948 low of $14 million. The average from 1952 through 1956 was $109 million. These figures, while calculated separately as budget items, represent part of a broader foreign policy that included military and diplomatic resources. The increased funds available for government sponsored cultural events reveal a great concern with how other nations viewed the United States. "In recent years," wrote Franz Joseph in *As Others See Us*, "the social scientists have given much attention to the 'images' that each nation has of other nations" (vi).[1]

***1955:*** *"Coke, Boogie-Woogie, and Gum Not So Bad" states the* New York Times *(Raymond). An official visit to the United States by a Polish observer appears to work. Jerzy Putrament publishes a popular article in Poland saying that the widespread denunciation of American goods is misguided. He thinks that many commercial items in America have no connection to a capitalist conspiracy (as he had been taught) and everything to do with their pleasurable effects. The Pole proposes that Coca-Cola be used in his nation's campaign against alcoholism. "It Isn't the Gum" – a tongue-in-cheek, op-ed piece printed a few days later hopes that gum users in New York and in Moscow will build on Putrament's enlightenment and stop leaving their non-conspiratorial chewing gum around the subways.*

Inviting foreign nationals to witness the evils of capitalism first hand was part of changing the international view of America. Following the collapse of the anti-fascist alliance and the onset of the Cold War, the Soviet Union restarted its criticism of America, which had been suspended during the two countries' war coalition. In 1945 and 1946, *L'Humanité*, the official organ of the French Communist Party, which was faithful to the

Soviet stance, portrayed the promise of Hollywood with extensive coverage of the visits of Rita Hayworth and other American icons. Abruptly, in 1947, the United States appeared in the paper's pages as a failing imperial power on the precipice of social and economic upheaval. All things American were derided and, according to Cora Sol Goldstein, "American cinema and the American film industry were a particular target, and Hollywood was accused of introducing American ideology and values through entertainment" (19-20).[2]

The relentless Soviet criticisms of the capitalist country were, by and large, dismissed as propaganda and Putremant's revelation, while entertaining, did not signify any great victory. It was taken for granted that communist and capitalist countries fundamentally disagreed on basic social issues. The one censure that stuck, though, was the charge of racism. The Soviet Union and her allies pointed to segregation and the violence that accompanied it as evidence of an unenlightened America.

Of course, with pictures of tortured black bodies and Josephine Baker decrying a new slavery in the South, communist media accessed a seemingly endless stream of material to present to their readers. Clearly, this was not the American way of life that the United States government wanted foreigners to see. Yet, there it was, not only in communist sponsored publications, but in the popular presses in India, Mexico, Greece, Haiti, and Great Britain; the United States was being characterized worldwide through racial conflict. To counter this image, the American government sponsored a host of cultural activities (radio programs, libraries, concerts, and plays) that presented American achievement rather than American failure (Goldstein 21).

***Remembering 1956:*** *"Adam Powell surprised me," Dizzy Gillespie later recalled, "I went to Washington once, in 1956, playing with a small group at the Showboat, and received a call from him saying come down to the House Office Building the next day because he had something to tell me. I arrived there and all these reporters were standing around, and then Adam made a statement: 'I'm going to propose to President Eisenhower that he send this man, who's a great contributor to our music, on a State Department sponsored cultural mission to Africa, the Near East, Middle East, and Asia'" (Gillespie and Fraser 413).*

The United States government was relatively new to artist support, yet the international cultural invasion of the 1950s by American artists was largely inconceivable without federal assistance. Prior to the Cold War, World's Fairs, Expositions, and shows for American servicemen were about the only foreign venues for which state assistance for the arts was available (Kammen 793-803). On the domestic front, attitudes toward government cultural funding had changed drastically during the Depression. The first sustained venture in state support for the arts took place under the auspices of the Works Progress Administration (WPA). Starting in 1932 and ending in 1943, the WPA supported many cultural undertakings in an effort to employ artists as social relief for a nation suffering an epic economic crisis.

The end of the unemployment dilemma, helped largely by the war effort, ensured an end to the WPA. When government funding for the arts reemerged in the post-war era, its object was far less altruistic. Cultural productions developed into one of the nation's preferred methods to vaunt overseas. The result? Federal funding for the arts became a focal point for the debate over an appropriate postwar American image for foreign consumption.[3]

"What then is the American, this new man?" asked St. John de Crevecoeur in the eighteenth century. This question demanded an answer, again, as the United States looked to become a global leader in the mid-twentieth century. Congressman Adam Clayton Powell, Jr., representative from New York City's Harlem, had an answer: Dizzy Gillespie.

By 1956, John Birks "Dizzy" Gillespie had long since risen from his impoverished South Carolina childhood and was recognized as one of the leaders of the recent musical revolution that spawned a new form of jazz called bebop. Gillespie may already have been an international superstar, yet the proposal for the trumpeter to front a jazz tour on the behalf of the United States government was daring. With the South in disarray over segregation, the suggestion that a black man represent the nation seemingly would not pass. For years, Powell made little headway when pleading with the Eisenhower Administration for his own worldwide speaking tour in defense of American racial progress. In 1956, he temporarily transferred his own goal to music and Gillespie. The Congressman's idea was not without some precedent – African American baritone William Warfield had performed in Cairo in 1955 thanks to support from the federal government. A jazz musician, however, was an entirely different proposition (Hamilton 290-294).

Music, part of the country's Cold War propaganda from the start, had an interesting beginning as an American symbol. When the Department of State looked for performers from New Orleans, its symphony was chosen time and again. If, in the supposed birthplace of jazz, musicians such as the enormously popular Louis Armstrong were ignored, securing sufficient support for a Gillespie tour was certainly going to be troublesome. Classical music and classically trained musicians were the initial cultural cold warriors of choice, ensuring that the majority of the performers (with exceptions such as Warfield) on those early government sponsored tours were white men.

By the mid-1950s, it was clear, though, that American classical musicians were fighting a losing battle – having great orchestras succeeded only in placing American culture upon a crowded mantle. Asserting American superiority in art music (classical music), competing against a hallowed European institution, was not really impressing many foreigners. At best, the country's art musicians would be applauded for their skill, but, in this arena, the American orchestra was viewed suspiciously by Europeans nurturing prejudice about American cultural inferiority. Americans performing within, or even excelling within, what was clearly a European-dominated tradition was not great promotional material. Classical music would help portray the United States as civilized by a Western standard; it could not offer up something widely understood as American to the world.[4]

Jackson Lears wrote that "the essence of hegemony is not manipulation but legitimation" (50); the story of American music at mid-century documents the nation's quest for validation in light of its new status as a global leader. The federal government was slow to comprehend that jazz, particularly swing, was widely understood as an American icon. There was no disputing this fact. Made fashionable by American troops and by privately financed performances, foreigners turned toward American popular music and jazz *en masse* after Word War II. Jazz had been the sound of the Depression, and its fans tracked band roster changes as sports enthusiasts tracked the players on their favorite teams. During the war, swing music evoked visions of "'home' values," becoming a symbol "of a war to defend the American way" (Erenberg 234-5). At home and abroad, jazz became increasingly synonymous with American values – particularly freedom.[5]

Foreigners were thus annoyed after the war when, time and again, they requested jazz performers from the United States and, instead, found themselves listening to groups like the New York Philharmonic (Wagnleitner iv). When the State Department finally recognized the broad appeal of jazz as an inherently American art form – deciding in 1955 to emphasize "real Americana" – the face and the sound of government sponsored music tours changed ("Remote Lands"). Classical musicians were no longer the exclusive representatives of America and a host of other musical styles gained access to federal sponsorship. (Alden;

Sheed).

The evening of May 9, 1956, displayed the nation's newfound musical diversity that was exported overseas. That night there were five government funded concerts, three of which presented the usual classical fare – the Los Angeles Philharmonic in Bangkok, pianist Eugene Isthmian in Japan, and Robert Shaw's Chorale in Cologne – while the other two presented the new amalgamation – Native American Tom Two Arrows in Burma and Dizzy Gillespie's band in Belgrade ("ANTA").

***February 1956:*** "DIZZY TO ROCK INDIA" — *a short article with an exciting headline ran in* the New York Times *in February 1956 announcing that "Dizzy Gillespie and his band will make a ten-week tour of India, the Near East and the Balkans beginning in April." The tour will be the first foreign visit of jazz music sponsored by the American National Theatre and Academy (a group which recommends "artistically qualified" entertainers to the State Department for federally funded international tours). Gillespie's troupe will consist of about twenty performers.*[6]

The Department of State thought better of pushing Dizzy Gillespie and his band out of the back of a plane, but, like the skydiving phonograph, the Gillespie tour started with a big crash. Just before the troupe was to fly to Bombay, tensions between India and the United States resulted in concert cancellations ("Dizzy to Rock"). Officially, Jawaharlal Nehru refused to sacrifice his policy of nonalignment. But the Indian leader was particularly upset by the continued U.S. military aid to Pakistan, so he spoiled the State Department's plans for Gillespie (Shipton 281; Gillespie and Fraser 417). If, as Penny Von Eschen writes, the State Department tours "tried to make critics of U.S. policy identify with America or the idea of America independently of American policies," Nehru saw through the cultural game that the Americans were playing — rightly linking American foreign policy to the Gillespie show ("Satchmo" 172). Before the tour even started, Gillespie got a good feel for what he later called the "political implications" of his trip (Gillespie and Fraser 417).

The bandleader remembered that American papers criticized Nehru as "ungrateful" (417). After all, he turned away a free concert. Meanwhile, the State Department quickly rescheduled the group to start in Abadan, Iran, a city close to the Iraqi border (Shipton 281). The India incident was the first of several skirmishes that set the tone for the musicians. As the jazz group traveled to places harboring valuable natural and military resources, several of the host countries expressed displeasure with the make-up of Gillespie's troupe.

The trumpeter's big band had been sporadically employed during the late 1940s and the early 1950s, so its personnel was constantly changing. There was nothing unusual in the fact that Gillespie had to choose several musicians before his 1956 State Department tour. But Gillespie's band, typically staffed by black men, was now a remarkable, to use its leader's terminology, "'American assortment' of blacks, whites, males, females, Jews and Gentiles" (Gillespie and Fraser 414). While there is scant evidence, there is little doubt that the State Department greatly influenced the band's new look (Shipton 280). The addition of white musicians, altoist Phil Woods and trombonist Rod Levitt, and also women, singer Dotty Saulter and trombonist/arranger Melba Liston, were most noticeable. That Gillespie recalled the assembly over twenty years later revealed just how unusual it was for his group (Gillespie and Fraser 414-16).

The 1956 version of the Gillespie band, like any group of mixed racial composition, would have stirred disapproval in America, especially in the South. But a greater controversy erupted abroad over the women in the group and the religious affiliation of one of the musicians. During a layover in the Cairo airport, American racial strife was the last thing on the minds of Gillespie and Rod Levitt. After the band was served a free drink, Levitt remembered, "they turned all the lights out and started showing a movie" (qtd. in Gillespie and Fraser 416-17). The film was a virulent anti-Israeli propaganda film. Gillespie, who laughed at almost anything, turned to his Jewish trombonist and joked, "How do you like it?" (417).

Levitt's troubles did not stop there. For several hours, it looked as if Pakistani officials were not going to allow him to leave their country because he wrote "Jewish" on his visa. The band, set to leave for Syria, impatiently awaited resolution. The State Department defused the situation by refiling Levitt's visa, listing him as a Christian; the Gillespie band left Karachi together (Gillespie and Fraser 414-16).

Far more radical for Muslim nations, though, was the independence of the two women in the group. Melba Liston remembered a stream of questions regarding gender dynamics in the United States: "I had lots of women come to me in the Middle East tours to find out how life was over here for women and how in the world I could be running around there traveling and single" (qtd. in Gillespie and Fraser 415-16). The relative freedom that the two women presented on and off stage was a primary focus of their audience. No doubt their accomplishments affected their female listeners who were confused and awed at the situation and wanted to learn more. There existed a clear disjunction between the interests of foreign listeners and the interests of the foreign press, which reported on race in America when covering the musical act.

***April 1956:*** *"Professor Joins the Gillespie Band," reports the* New York Times. *Dr. Marshall Stearns, a professor at Hunter College who teaches a jazz course at the New School, takes over the role of music educator on the Gillespie tour.*

Three years after the inaugural jazz concerts, Leonard Bernstein, on tour in the Soviet Union, introduced Igor Stravinsky's *Le Sacre du Printemps* as a work central to the musical revolution of the early twentieth century. For years, Soviet leaders slandered Stravinsky's work as academic and bourgeois, so Bernstein's talks, which preceded an actual performance of the work by the New York Philharmonic, were not welcome. By the time the New York Philharmonic reached Leningrad, the *New York Times* said "the request that he [Bernstein] say nothing about Stravinsky was transmitted through Americans from Russian sources" ("Bernstein Drops"). This was not the first time that the famous musician was quieted during this trip. A week earlier in Moscow, Bernstein's copious program notes for his own Symphony No. 2 – based on W. H. Auden's Age of Anxiety, a commentary "on the search for happiness in Western society" – were omitted from the program ("Bernstein Work").

Despite regular censure in Russia, Bernstein continually lectured about music during the New York Philharmonic's summer concerts abroad (Frankel). In his role as a music teacher, the conductor continued in a long tradition of art music analysis. In 1956, Dizzy Gillespie could not benefit from centuries of jazz scholarship because there was no such thing. But the trumpeter was one of a handful of jazz innovators in the relatively short history of the musical style. This fact did not salvage the role of jazz lecturer for Gillespie in the eyes of the State Department ("Professor"). Early on in the tour, the State Department made certain that Gillespie would teach jazz through performance, not oration (Gillespie and Fraser 418; "Gillespie's Band").

One very clear purpose of the Gillespie band was to present a program illuminative of jazz's development. It is quite remarkable, then, that Dizzy Gillespie, recognized as a musical modernizer for his contribution to bebop in the 1940s, was replaced by a professor of English ("Professor"; "Gillespie's Band"). Not only was he humorous, entertaining, and eloquent, Gillespie had lived through most of jazz history. Seemingly, the famed trumpeter was a better choice than a New York professor whose status was clinched by an impressive collection of jazz paraphernalia and a jazz history course that he started teaching in 1951 at the New School ("Institute of Jazz Studies"). No doubt Oxford University Press, the publisher behind Stearns's 1956 book The Story of Jazz, was thrilled by the selection of their author to such a visible post. Less than a month into the tour, Stearns was telling the audience all about jazz before Gillespie and company came on stage and played the history to them.

Stearns's appointment, especially in light of Bernstein's role with the Philharmonic, replaced an empowered minority with a white man. Reading Stearns's selection purely in terms of race, though, distracts from the very important issue surrounding jazz and federally funded concerts. At the time of Gillespie's government tour, jazz was beginning to shed its image as the "unwanted stepchild of the arts" (Korsky 112). Schools and classes for jazz sprung up at a surprising rate both in the United States and in Europe. More importantly, the bebop revolution had ensured that jazz, already a popular art form, developed into an intellectual one as well.

Swing, the predominant sound of jazz in the 1930s and a most popular style in its heyday, was music created for immediate consumption through commercial channels and was directly dependent upon audience approval. Bebop overturned this relationship and built its reputation on a divide between artist and fan. Gillespie, along with Charlie Parker, Thelonius Monk, and others, fashioned a confusing array of innovations and played them to often puzzled listeners (Deveaux 3-8, 20-27, 273-294; Gillespie and Fraser 190). Swing had benefited from the likes of white performers like Woody Herman and Glen Miller, but bebop, much like ragtime, was fundamentally a black musical innovation (Deveaux 20-27; Tucker xii, 3-27; Gerard 314-15). Removed from the dance halls of Harlem where the big bands wailed, jazz became the more reclusive art of a small ensemble within the poorly lit clubs of New York's Fifty-Second Street. Bebop marginalized the role of jazz in American culture by making it avant-garde and ultimately secured a future for jazz through the institutionalization that accompanied jazz's status as an object for serious study.[7]

The creation of centers like the Institute for Jazz Studies (founded by Marshall Stearns in 1952 and taken over by Rutgers University in 1966) and the Lenox School of Jazz brought Czech composer Anton Dvorak's 1893 statement that "Negro melodies…must be the real foundation of any serious and original school of composition to be developed in the United States" closer to reality ("Institute"; qtd. in Murray 22). Businessman Norman Granz captured the development by promoting the aptly titled series Jazz at the Philharmonic. Dr. Stearns was chosen to lecture during Gillespie's tour to add, according to a 1956 *New York Times* piece, "a highbrow touch" ("Gillespie's Band"). When the government began its Cold War jazz crusade, jazz was chosen not only for its American pedigree and its seeming denial of American racial conflict but also because it was fast becoming recognized as a scholarly form (Von Eschen, "Satchmo" 164; Gerard xi-xx).

***June 1956:*** *United States Ambassador to Turkey, Donald Heath, senses that something is wrong, but as embassy security summons him to the stage area, he isn't sure what. Heath approaches the famed trumpeter and asks: "Mr. Gillespie, there's supposed to be a jam session. What's happening? Why don't you want to play?" Gillespie should be on stage performing with his band and local Ankaran musicians. Instead, he is seething backstage. When he entered the embassy earlier, Gillespie noticed a large crowd, mainly children, trying to get into the show. As the Turkish band took the stage, the trumpeter clambered up the reviewing* *stand which allowed him to reach over the railing and to sign autographs. From this vantage point, he witnessed a young boy scale the fence of the embassy, only to be immediately hurled back by security. Now, Gillespie explains to Heath, he will not play until the children are allowed to see the concert. "You see those people out there?" Gillespie responds to the ambassador. "We're trying to gain their friendship, not these people, big shots here with the tickets" (Gillespie and Fraser 422).*

"GILLESPIE REFUSES TO PLAY FOR THE ELITE" reports one paper the day after Gillespie's standoff in the embassy (Gillespie and Fraser 422). That day, a musician's idealism proved stronger than policy; Ambassador Heath ordered the guards to let the children in. Gillespie's antics did not cloak his basic purpose. Time and again, he placed the concerns of the "common people" – those who were priced out of his shows – on par or above those who could pay to attend his concerts. In Dacca, Gillespie repeated the demands he made in Turkey. In Damascus, he paused the show precisely at sundown so that the audience could break their Ramadan fast with him backstage. With characteristic political tact, Gillespie presented a resolute, yet affable face to U.S. officials to ensure that his concerts reached the foreigners who he thought should witness American music. Gillespie explained five years after his 1956 tour that his private shows abroad were about money; the government-sponsored shows were about the people (*An Electrifying*).

The gulf dividing jazz performers and the Department of State did not subside in future years. Officials of the American government catered to the leaders of other countries, and it was only the musicians themselves who espoused a more widespread cultural experience. Seven years later after Gillespie's inaugural tour, the State Department still had not altered their policies, and Duke Ellington was frustrated by the elite composition of his audiences during his government-sponsored tour of the oil-rich Middle East (Von Eschen, "Satchmo" 171). The jazz tours were part of a diplomatic package, used as propaganda, incentive, and reward, to convince foreign leaders of American solidarity. Many of the sponsored musicians saw matters differently.

***July 1956:*** *From the* New York Times*: "If Congress goes along with the Senate Appropriations Committee, foreigners may come to think of Americans as a nation of chorus-singing athletes. Alarmed by the impression of the United States conveyed by officially sponsored tours of performers such as Louis Armstrong and Dizzy Gillespie...the committee urges Government-aided travel for choral groups and miscellaneous sports projects" ("Biceps and Choirs").*

Five months before the article "Biceps and Choirs" appeared in the *Times*, Autherine Lucy was admitted as the first African American student to the University of Alabama while the black community in Montgomery was in the midst of a now famous bus boycott. Studying the debate over the early jazz tours makes the present-day reader squeamish. I wonder if the unnamed author who contributed "Biceps and Choirs" understood the implications of the Congressional debate. Looking at the context in which the deliberations took place, it is hard to imagine that the reporter was oblivious. Gillespie and Armstong were not the only jazz musicians to receive federal funds for international concerts. Benny Goodman, for example, traveled as well, yet the famed trumpeters's names were the ones emphasized by opponents of government jazz programs. The discussion over funding jazz made clear that jazz itself was not the issue; the argument revolved around the race of the performers. So while Gillespie enjoyed the privilege of representing the supposed success of diversity in the United States to foreign nationals in 1956, certain members of Congress worked to remove his African American face from the program.

Senator Barry Goldwater wrote to Assistant Secretary of State, Robert Hill:

> This particular item has reference to the recent tour of a negro band leader, Dizzy Gillespie, which apparently involved an expenditure by the Federal Government of the outrageous sum of $100,839…Without any intention of criticizing you, I am wondering just what there is about a program of this type which would more properly fulfill the Government objectives in the area of cultural assistance to foreign countries as opposed to the excellent presentation offered by a group of young boys who have joined together for the purpose of contributing to the musical life of our country, and who have indicated a willingness to share these accomplishments with peoples abroad. (032 Tucson Kids Band, Letter to Robert C. Hill, 19 April 1957)

Goldwater could not believe that "a negro band leader" (who, by implication, did not contribute to the "musical life of our country") was chosen over a local group from his home state of Arizona, the Tucson Kids Band. The $100,000 face of America that Goldwater wanted foreigners to see was youthful, from his district, and white.

Government sponsored cultural programs aimed to offset reports of the exact kind of race-based thinking embedded in Goldwater's response to the Gillespie tour. Reports covering concerts of black musicians who had been sent abroad prior to Gillespie's inaugural jazz tour demonstrated the concerted effort of State Department officials to track the perception of race in America. A statement from the American Embassy in Cairo regarding the 1955 Egyptian tour of *Porgy & Bess* stated that "the impact achieved outside of the theater by the personalities of the cast can easily be rated as excellent. USIS arranged three major receptions for the cast in Cairo: one primarily for Egyptian theater and radio leaders…; another for the press; and a third for cultural, social, and civic leaders" (qtd. in 511.003/1-3155, Report From American Embassy Cairo, To State Dept /USIA, 31 Jan. 1955). These receptions evoked a "highly enthusiastic acclaim" (qtd. in 511.003/1-3155, Report From American Embassy Cairo, To State Dept /USIA, 31 Jan. 1955). Translations of local newspaper accounts included in the file show the kind of influence the State Department expected:

> 1) "The members of the group showed unwillingness to discuss racial discrimination in the United States. They however pointed out that such discrimination is being gradually eliminated in the United States." (qtd. in 511.003/1-3155, *Al Guil Al Guedid*, 17 January 1955). 2) "The American negro opera now called 'Porgy and Bess,' has interpreted this living community into music that now portrays the suffering, poverty, hardship and discrimination that is the lot of the negroes in America…Negroes attach great importance and significance to the recent rulings of the American Supreme Court giving the equal right to education to both whites and negroes." (qtd. in 511.003/1-3155, "Negro Screams on the Stage of the Opera House," *Al Ahram*, 5 January 1955).

The gradual elimination of racism, or at least an idea that racial discrimination was waning, was the message that the State Department wished to convey through cultural tours that included black Americans. Dizzy Gillespie and his band operated in this environment during their 1956 tour.

Federal support for black musicians did not start (or stop) with jazz performances (511.003/1-3155). But, in 1956, the international demand for and popularity of jazz performers made them the focal point of the federal funding dispute.

Gillespie was acutely aware of the racial performance that he led in the Middle East. In true minstrel show tradition, the United States government "blacked up" when sending Gillespie abroad. When the State Department asked to brief Gillespie before the tour, he refused: "They laid it all right in front of me, and I sort've liked the idea of representing America, but I wasn't going over to apologize for the racist policies of America." Gillespie explained to his wife, "I've got three hundred years of briefing. I know what they've done to us, and I'm not gonna make any excuses. If they ask me questions, I'm gonna answer them as honestly as I can" (Gillespie and Fraser 414).

The government's refusal to allow eminent black intellectuals such as W.E.B. DuBois and Paul Robeson the right to travel, assigned musicians like Gillespie and Louis Armstrong the "official" international spokespeople for black Americans (Von Eschen, *Race* 167). Jazz, though, had brought different privileges to the two generations of trumpeters. For Armstrong and an older generation of jazz musicians, performing often represented a way out of a life in manual labor, while, for Gillespie and his cohorts, becoming a performer was akin to becoming a doctor – it was a respectable profession (DeVeaux 46-50; Tucker 28-46). In the 1950s, Armstrong proved a far more vocal critic of events than Gillespie. The elder jazz statesman gained notoriety in government circles for canceling a state sponsored tour of the Soviet Union due to his disgust over 1957 events in Little Rock.

Earlier, in 1956, Gillespie lead the way with a more muted tone, one that, despite the antagonistic stance he struck prior to the tour, appeared to gel with State Department objectives. On the racial implications of his band, he wrote:

> They [foreign audiences] could see it wasn't as intense because we had white boys and I was the leader of the band. That was strange to them because they'd heard about blacks being lynched and burned, and here I come with half whites and blacks and a girl playing in the band. And everybody seemed to be getting along fine. So I didn't try to hide anything. I said, "Yeah,...We have our problems but we're still working on it. I'm the leader of this band, and those white guys are working for me. That's a helluva thing." (Gillespie and Fraser 421)

Gillespie certainly knew that the United States had problems. The bandleader, along with Ella Fitzgerald and others, was picked up backstage at a Texas concert for gambling before his international tour – an arrest clearly motivated by racism (Shipton 266). But his success, measured in dollars and by the white musicians in his band, indicated to Gillespie that things were, indeed, improving. Nonetheless, the irony in Gillespie's message to President Eisenhower at the close of his 1956 tour jumps at the modern reader: "I urge you to do all in your power to continue exploiting this valuable form of American expression of which we are so proud" ("Diz Set"). Gillespie meant "exploit" in a most positive way. But by the early 1960s, many black nationalists thought that Gillespie and his fellow "U.S. jambassadors" sounded too much like Uncle Tom and too little like Nat Turner (Von Eschen, *Race* 178).

It is a familiar debate. But just as Frederick Douglass changed his mind about minstrelsy in the 1840s and 1850s – first, calling blackface performers "the filthy scum of white society" and, later, stating that minstrel songs "awaken the sympathies for the slave, in which anti-slavery principles take root, grow and flourish" – the role of the jazz musicians and the State Department needs to be reevaluated in a new light (qtd. in Lott 4, 15; Douglass 40). Were the State Department jazz tours emblematic of a larger push in national government for a gradual easing of racial tensions in the nation, or merely an interesting footnote to the Cold War? Situating black musicians as actors for foreign policy had domestic ramifications. Not only did the United States government publicly acknowledge the contribution of black culture to American history and contemporary society, the use of jazz contributed to a then raging debate over nation, race, and representation.

***1957:*** *An article defends the musical politics that the United States is promoting through state sponsorship of jazz. It is believed to be so influential that communist governments might soon be "more friendly to the United States." Donald B. Cook of the State Department stands up for the Gillespie tours – by this time there had been two – stating that "the $141,000 invested by the Government in tours by Dizzy Gillespie's jazz band…had helped to offset reports of radical prejudice in the United States" by showcasing a preeminent black American ("U.S. Finds").*

Gillespie was hardly a pawn of United States foreign policy. He pointed out an important fact about his situation: "We didn't have to lay out any money to support it and didn't have to worry about jobs because all the jobs were preset" (Gillespie and Fraser 414). A government tour was the kind of institutional support that only a few fortunate musicians would ever receive – Gillespie could not lose playing for the State Department. He was paid a prorated weekly salary of $2,150 (which exceeded that of the President of the United States) whether one or 100,000 tickets sold (032 Tuscon Kids Band, *Congressional Record*). Ultimately, the $16,458 worth of ticket sales did not come close to covering the price tag for the tour, which was over $100,000.

Yet the government hardly bought itself a Cold War operative. The back and forth between Gillespie and his State Department handlers makes it difficult to read his tour as pure propaganda. If anything, the tour mirrored the divisiveness regarding race and class back in the States.

Clearly, the State Department did not sponsor jazz musicians to make money but rather to make a point. Jazz was a "sonic weapon" for the United States government (Belair). Cheaper than researching a new military machine, jazz was sent on the near impossible mission to battle the perception of the United States as a racist society. In the midst of black protests and Southern response, State Department officials stood by their support of jazz and continued the program at a time when the federal government is often understood to have been aloof on racial issues ("U.S. Defends").

We need more scholarship that researches the intertwined role of politics and culture in the 1950s. A host of issues revolving around foreign policy, the cultural status of an art form, the individual musicians, foreign listeners, race, gender, and religion surrounded the joint venture of Gillespie and the American government international policy. To say that jazz was manipulated in the American quest for global resources is trite. Of course, American performers were sent to regions harboring crucial economic and military resources. But what happened there, as Reinhold Wagnleitner demonstrated in Austria, is a more complex story. Insofar as the United States was definable as a culture in the postwar era, it was defined by jazz, which was achieving new heights in the cultural hierarchy. And this, especially for foreigners, meant that American cultural life greatly depended on African Americans – a remarkable idea that was hotly contested, more at home than abroad.

Gillespie wired President Eisenhower after his tour: "Our trip through the Middle-East proved conclusively that our interracial group was powerfully effective against red propaganda" ("Dizzy Urges"; Von Eschen, *Race* 178). Christian Herter, acting Secretary of State, agreed, telling critics in 1957 that the government would continue to pay top dollar to showcase the very best of American culture abroad ("U.S. Defends"). "The language of diplomacy," wrote one foreign music critic, "ought to be translated into a score for bop trumpet" ("Indians Dizzy"). Gillespie started the negotiations on March 23, 1956, the day of the first foreign concert of jazz sponsored by the American government.

## Notes

1. For a table on government funding for cultural programs, see Table 1 in Wagnleitner, 57.
2. See also, Wagnleitner, ix-xv, 1-7.
3. Michael Kammen considers government funding during the 1950s to be insignificant stating that the U.S. has no cultural policy until the establishment of the NEA in 1965, but notes "an awakening sense of popular pride in American cultural activities" in Cold War America (801). This view misses the link between government funding and the "discovery" of American cultural producers.
4. Wagnleitner superbly illuminates this contest: during the war, the National Socialists used Beethoven's *Fifth Symphony* to demonstrate German genius; later the BBC employed it for their propaganda broadcasts in Germany; American orchestras played it to display their cultural maturity; lastly, communist politicians utilized it to claim the mantle as the legitimate heirs of the European humanistic tradition. See especially 194.
5. By 1949, the *New York Herald Tribune* had declared that jazz was one of the "most exportable commodities – second, perhaps, only to dollars" (qtd. in Wagnleitner 202.)
6. Gillespie's name was selected as a result of a combination of forces that opened the way for his inaugural jazz tour. Changing ideas about the significance and stature of jazz at home and abroad played a big role. There was also, of course, the authorized process set by the Department of State. This decision-making process for state backed foreign tours is rather arbitrary. One connection to the right political figure – especially someone with pull in the Department of State – and the sanctioned procedure quickly turned into a show. Nonetheless, the official procedure employed the following steps. An artist was first recommended to the board members of the American National Theatre and Academy (ANTA), initiating the process that would allow for monetary support from a special Presidential fund. At the time, the ANTA board was made up of prestigious members of the artistic community representing all fields of American culture. Their responsibility was to determine whether or not the proposed musicians are "artistically qualified." After the ANTA panel approved the group, a special committee of delegates from various government agencies including the State Department, named the Operations Coordinating Board, deliberated further. At this juncture, the judgment of the Department of State's appropriate field post was heavily relied upon. For example, if a tour was slated for England, the London field office was queried about foreign relations' advantages and revenue potential. (511.003/2-1556, Department of State, Telegram to Mission in Tripoli, Consulates in Algiers, Casablanca, Tangier and Tunis, 15 February 1956; 032 Tucson Kids Band, Robert C. Hill, Letter to Barry Goldwater, 18 April 1957.)

If approved the performers received funds from the President's Special International Program for Cultural Presentation, administered by ANTA. Despite the formalities, there was never any question that the State Department controlled the process. In Gillespie's case, the State Department sends a one-line telegram to the American National Theatre and Academy stating, "Dizzy Gillespie project approved" (032 Gillespie, Douglas N. Batson, Telegram to Mr. Robert C. Schnitzel, 25 January 1956). The amount requested for the Presidential fund for cultural programs in 1956 was $6 million, a decent sum when compared to the cost of the entire USIA for the same year, which totaled $87,336,630. (110.11-HE/9-1859, David M. Keiser, Letter to Christian R. Herter, 18 September 1959; "$12,650,000"; Rubin 51.)

The Department of State set the boundaries for cultural programs. The most crucial of which was how many and what type of groups could travel to certain regions of the world. In 1958, State Department officials allotted five openings for cultural groups to be sent to Europe and decided that only one could be a symphony orchestra. The program and the selection process had several flaws that were acknowledged at the time. The first was that performers with established international reputations were highly favored. There was no substitute for an artist's prior experiences outside of the United States in order to evaluate revenue potential abroad. A far more severe consequence of these measures was that it ultimately relied upon a judgment concerning who and what was deemed "artistically qualified" (032 Tucson Kids Band, Robert C. Hill, Letter to Barry Goldwater, 18 April 1957). From the onset of the program until 1955, a jazz performance was never certified. Then, rather suddenly, jazz became the focus of government funding efforts. How and why this happens goes a long way towards uncovering the drastic changes in who and what was to represent Cold War America.

7. This position modifies Wagnleitner who writes of jazz concerts representing the opposite of "'serious' music from the United States" (221).

## Works Cited


032 Gillespie, Dizzy/1-2556; General Records of the Department of State, Record Group 59; National Archives at College Park.

032 Tucson Kids Band/4-1957; General Records of the Department of State, Record Group 59; National Archives at College Park.

110.11-HE/9-1859; General Records of the Department of State, Record Group 59; National Archives at College Park.

"$12,650,000 Asked For Atomic Ship: Eisenhower Requests Funds to Design, Start Work on Global Cruise Vessel." *New York Times* 27 May 1955: 1.

511.003/1-3155; General Records of the Department of State, Record Group 59; National Archives at College Park.

511.003/2-1556; General Records of the Department of State, Record Group 59; National Archives at College Park.

Alden, Robert. "Hands of U.S. Tied in Asia 'Cold War': Best Weapons, Such as Jazz and Movies, Not Exploited Information Aides Say." *New York Times* 11 June 1956: 11.

*An Electrifying Evening with the Dizzy Gillespie Quintet: Recorded Live in Concert.* 314 557 544-2 Verve Master Edition. New York: Polygamy Records, Inc., 1999.

"ANTA Concerts Listed In 5 Countries Tonight." *New York Times* 9 May 1956: 36.

Belair, Felix, Jr. "United States Has Secret Sonic Weapon – Jazz: Europe Falls Captive as Crowds Riot to Hear Dixieland." *New York Times* 6 November 1956: 1+.

"Bernstein Drops Talk With Music: Leads 2 Stravinsky Works Without Explanation to Leningrad Audience." *New York Times* 1 September 1959: 21.

"Bernstein Work Heard in Moscow: 'Age of Anxiety' is Offered by New York Philharmonic – Program Notes Omitted." *New York Times* 24 August 1959: 16.

"Biceps and Choirs: Senate Group Backs Them to Promote U.S. Abroad." *New York Times* 18 July 1956: 54.

Casey, Marcy and Tom Werner. "Father of Broadcasting – David Signoff." *Time* 7 December 1998: 88-90.

Devious, Scott. *The Birth of Bebop: A Social and Musical History.* Berkeley: U of California P, 1997.

Douglass, Frederick. *The Anti-Slavery Movement. A Lecture by Frederick Douglass before the Rochester Ladies' Anti-Slavery Society.* Rochester: Press of Lee, Mann & Co., 1855.

"Diz Set for Tour of South America." *Pittsburgh Courier* 21 July 1956: 23.

"Dizzy to Rock India: Gillespie and Jazz Group Tour East and Balkans." *New York Times* 2 February 1956: 19.

"Dizzy Urges Ike to Back Jazz Tours." *Pittsburgh Courier* 4 August 1956: 21.

Greenberg, Lewis. "Things to Come: Swing Bands, Bebop, and the Rise of a Postwar Jazz Scene." *Recasting America: Culture and Politics in the Age of Cold War.* Ed. Larry May. Chicago: U of Chicago P, 1989.

Frankel, Max. "Critic in Moscow Scores Bernstein." *New York Times* 28 August 1959: 26.

Gerard, Charley. *Jazz in Black and White; Race, Culture, and Identity in the Jazz Community.* Westport: Pager, 1998.

Gillespie, Dizzy and Al Fraser. *To Be or Not to Bop: Memoirs of Dizzy Gillespie.* New York: Ad Capo Press, 1979.

"Gillespie's Band a Hit in Beirut." *New York Times* 29 April 1956: 124.

Goldstein, Cora Sol. "Ideological Constraints and the American Response to Soviet Propaganda in Europe: The Case of Race." Paper for the Conference of Europeanists, Chicago, March 2004.

Hamilton, Charles V. *Adam Clayton Powell, Jr.: The Political Biography of an American Dilemma.* New York: Athenaeum Press, 1991.

"Indians Dizzy Over Gillespie's Jazz." *Pittsburgh Courier* 2 June 1956: 18.

"Institute of Jazz Studies: History." *Institute for Jazz Studies.* 1997. Rutgers University. 29 June 2005. http://newarkwww.rutgers.edu/IJS/Plain/jazz2n.html.

"It Isn't the Gum." *New York Times* 25 November 1955: 26.

James, Michael. "A 50c Phonograph Is the Newest U.S. Weapon: Can Be Air-Dropped with Messages for Red-Ruled People." *New York Times* 11 November 1955: 1+.

Joseph, Franz M., ed. *As Others See Us: The United States through Foreign Eyes.* Princeton: Princeton UP, 1959.

Kammen, Michael. "Culture and the State in America." *Journal of American History* 83.3 (December 1996): 791-814.

Corky, Frank. *Black Nationalism and the Revolution in Music.* New York: Pathfinder Press, 1970.

Leers, Jackson. "A Matter of Taste: Corporate Cultural Hegemony in a Mass-Consumption Society." *Recasting America: Culture and Politics in the Age of Cold War.* Ed. Larry May. Chicago: U of Chicago P, 1989.

Lott, Eric. *Love & Theft: Blackface Minstrelsy and the American Working Class.* New York: Oxford UP, 1995.

McRae, Barry. *Dizzy Gillespie: His Life & Times.* New York: Universe Books, 1988.

Murray, Albert. "Ellington Hits 100." *The Nation* 22 February 1999: 22-26.

"Professor Joins Gillespie Band." *New York Times* 17 April 1956: 28.

Raymond, Jack. "Coke, Boogie-Boogie and Gum Not So Bad, Says Pole after Visit." *New York Times* 24 November 1955: 1.

"Remote Lands to Hear Old Democracy Boogie." *New York Times* 18 November 1955: 16.

Rubin, Ronald I. *The Objectives of the U.S. Information Agency: Controversies and Analysis.* New York: Frederick A. Pager, 1966.

Shed, Wilfred. "Les Jazz Fans Hot – and Cool – of Europe." *New York Times* 18 November 1956: 248.

Shipton, Alyn. *Grooving' High: The Life of Dizzy Gillespie.* New York: Oxford UP, 1999.

Stearns, Marshall W. *The Story of Jazz.* New York: Oxford UP, 1956.

Tucker, Mark. *Ellington: The Early Years.* Urbana: U of Illinois P, 1991.

"U.S. Defends Trips by Entertainers." *New York Times* 5 May 1957: 55.

"U.S. Finds Unrest in Soviet Sphere: Information Chief Believes Reds May Face Shake-up – Gillespie Tour Hailed." *New York Times* 11 April 1957: 11.

Von Eschen, Penny. *Race Against Empire: Black Americans and Anti-colonialism, 1937-1957.* Ithaca: Cornell UP, 1997.

----. "'Asthma Blows Up the World': Jazz, Race, and Empire During the Cold War." *"Here, There And Everywhere:" The Foreign Politics of American Popular Culture.* Eds. Reinhold Wagnleitner and Elaine Tyler May. Hanover: UP of New England, 2000.

Wagnleitner, Reinhold. *Coca-Colonization and the Cold War: The Cultural Mission of the United States in Austria after the Second World War.* Trans. Diana M. Wolf. Chapel Hill: U of North Carolina P, 1994.

*In this essay, Alexander Pitofsky argues that far from merely celebrating the working class, Bruce Springsteen, especially on* Darkness on the Edge of Town, *offers a more nuanced reading of their experience, both optimistic and anguished.*

# *Darkness on the Edge of Town*: Bruce Springsteen's Representations of Working-Class Distress

Alexander Pitofsky

In the 1990s, Bruce Springsteen occasionally performed "In Freehold," an unreleased song in which he reflects on his youth in a small town. Some of the lyrics are nostalgic, emphasizing that Freehold, New Jersey was the place where Springsteen "had [his] first kiss at the YMCA canteen on a Friday night" and played in his first rock-and-roll band. Elsewhere, he accuses the town of harassing anyone who happened to be "different, black, or brown" and not showing much compassion when one of his sisters "got pregnant" late in her teens. Springsteen's rapid shifts from lighthearted autobiography to poetic revenge are at odds with his usual songwriting practices, but his complicated view of his small-town origins should seem familiar to anyone who has listened to *Darkness on the Edge of Town* (1978). Throughout that album, Springsteen portrays the lives of working-class Americans as an endless struggle. Some of his characters convince themselves to persevere, believing that better times may arrive in the future. Others chase after excitement in the present through love, sex, and fast cars. The album also contains a few traumatized characters who seem unable to find any sense of purpose.

This essay discusses *Darkness*'s representations of working-class distress and suggests that the album casts doubt on the notion that Springsteen's music "celebrates" working people. (This reading, which came to light around the time *Darkness* was released, is still commonplace in critical and journalistic discourse about Springsteen. In *A Race of Singers: Whitman's Working-Class Hero from Guthrie to Springsteen* [2000], for example, Bryan K. Garman asserts that Springsteen's career has been, among other things, a realization of Walt Whitman's wish to inspire future poets "who would celebrate the working class and fulfill the promise of American democracy." Similarly, the *Pittsburgh Post-Gazette* announced in 2004 that "Rock superstar Bruce Springsteen, whose songs celebrate the working man, will join Joe Grushecky and the Houserockers and other local musicians Dec. 2 at Heinz Hall in a benefit concert...") Springsteen's empathy for blue-collar Americans is unmistakable, but it does not follow that his principal aim is to praise them. *Darkness* does not offer purely positive remarks about "the working man." Springsteen's small towns are complex, and his characters embody many kinds of anguish and optimism.

Critics have often observed that Springsteen's approach to songwriting changed during the time in which he recorded *Darkness*. Robert Hilburn interprets the album's relatively simple arrangements as a rejection of the Phil Spector-style grandeur of *Born to Run* (1975): "Where *Born to Run* was mixed at symphonic fullness, the sound on *Darkness* was moodier. Songs like 'Promised Land' still featured the dense mix of keyboards, guitars, and drums, but the solos are short, the players who blew so lustily on *Born to Run* are kept in check. . . . *Darkness* is not a recitation of the great party sounds. That would have to wait until Bruce's mood changed." Other commentators attribute the album's somber tone to Springsteen's frustrations during his two years of litigation with his former manager Mike

Appel. In Dave Marsh's August 1978 *Rolling Stone* cover story on the *Darkness* tour, Springsteen worried that his audience was hearing dejection and hopelessness in his new songs:

> It's the title, [Marsh suggests]. "I know, I know," [Springsteen] says impatiently. "But I put it in the first few seconds of 'Badlands,' the first song on the album, those lines about 'I believe in the love and the hope and the faith.' It's there on all four corners of the album." By which he means the first and last songs on each side: "Badlands" and "Racing in the Street," "The Promised Land" and the title song. He is clearly distressed. He meant *Darkness* to be "relentless," not grim.

Another interpretation holds that the explosive drums, guitars, and vocals featured in songs like "Adam Raised a Cain" and "Candy's Room" demonstrate that Springsteen was writing under the influence of Patti Smith, The Clash, Elvis Costello, and other punk and new wave musicians of the time. Several critics have also pointed out that *Darkness* marks the time when Springsteen stopped writing about adolescents in abandoned beach houses and dusty arcades. Hilburn, for instance, writes that the album's characters are "men well into adulthood caught up in the now-joyless rituals of adolescence. Preeminent among these songs was the stirring 'Racing in the Street' . . . The title and chorus played on Martha and the Vandellas' 'Dancing in the Streets,' but there was little happiness for the aging drivers on the dragstrip, or for their forgotten wives and girlfriends. What's left after youth and its passions have gone?"

All of these observations are worth considering, but they overlook *Darkness*'s central theme: the struggles of blue-collar Americans who live in small towns. If you doubt that the album is a meditation on working-class distress, read Springsteen's essay introducing the album in *Songs* (1998). In the opening sentence, he recalls that "[a]fter *Born to Run* I wanted to write about life in the close confines of the small towns I grew up in." Then he elaborates on the subject matter he had in mind:

> I was searching for a tone somewhere between *Born to Run*'s spiritual hopefulness and '70s cynicism. I wanted my new characters to feel weathered, older, but not beaten. The sense of daily struggle in each song greatly increased. The possibility of transcendence or any sort of personal redemption felt a lot harder to come by. . . . I intentionally steered away from any hint of escapism and set my characters down in the middle of a community under siege.

A community under siege – that phrase captures the spirit of *Darkness on the Edge of Town*. The album's characters are trapped, surrounded by various forms of pressure that never seem to let up. And while they all feel the anxieties of small-town life, they respond to those anxieties in a number of different ways.

The response that probably comes to mind first for most Springsteen fans is the mixture of determination and hope expressed in "Badlands." The words this character uses – *lights out, trouble, head-on collision, caught in a crossfire, fear, waste* – suggest that he feels as though his surroundings were a combat zone. He seems convinced that his troubles are inescapable, yet he delivers a high-spirited chorus that pulls together stoicism, optimism, and slang: "Badlands, you gotta live it every day / Let the broken hearts stand / As the price you gotta pay / We'll keep pushin' 'til it's understood / And these badlands start treating us good." Later in the song, the character's protests give way to a secular prayer: "I believe in the love that you gave me / I believe in the faith that can save me / I believe in the hope and I pray / That someday it may raise me above these badlands." Where does he find this love, faith, and hope? The question is left unanswered. Springsteen simply implies that there is something heroic about this character – he has what it takes to keep moving forward. The same could be said of the character whose story we hear in "The Promised Land." He admits that he feels powerless and worries that he may be wasting time "chasing some mirage," but near the end of the song, in what A. O. Scott describes as "a climactic vision of purifying destruction," he imagines that the future will take the form of a tornado with the power to blow away his disappointments.

Springsteen's examination of perseverance becomes more complicated in "Racing in the Street." Early in the song, Springsteen's racer, like the drivers in "Don't Worry Baby" and "Little Deuce Coupe," boasts about his success on the dragstrip:

> We take all the action we can meet, and we cover all the northeast stat
> When the strip shuts down, we run 'em in the street, from the fire roads to the interstate
> Some guys they just give up living, and start dying little by little, piece by piece
> Some guys come home from work and wash up, and go racing in the street.

The Beach Boys' characters keep the focus on their cars: "I got the fastest set of wheels in town . . . comin' off the line when the light turns green / She blows 'em outta the water like you never seen." Springsteen's racer, by contrast, emphasizes his own ability not to be overwhelmed by his everyday struggles. His life sounds exciting – and too effortless for the world of *Darkness* – until the third verse. As Hilburn observes, the racer understands that the satisfaction he finds in competition does nothing to comfort his girlfriend, whose unexplained despair causes her to stare "into the night, with the eyes of one who hates for just being born." Suddenly, Springsteen inverts the relationship featured in "Don't Worry Baby": in this song, the racer seems confident and his girlfriend needs to hear some reassuring words. Will she hear them? Again, the question is leftunanswered. The racer speaks mysteriously about riding to the sea and washing away sins, but his closing lines focus on new possibilities, not necessarily on reconciliation or relief.

For another group of *Darkness*'s characters, love and sex provide temporary distractions. The young man in "Candy's Room" says a few ominous words about "strangers from the city" and the "sadness hidden in [Candy's] face," but throughout most of the song his erotic daydreams force everything else out of his mind:

> We kiss, my heart's pumpin' to my brain
> The blood rushes in my veins . . .
> We go driving, driving deep into the night,
> I go driving deep into the light in Candy's eyes.
> She says, Baby if you wanna be wild, you got a lot to learn
> Close your eyes – let them melt, let them fire, let them burn . . .

The character in "Prove It All Night" seems more easygoing than his counterpart in "Candy's Room," but even he feels the pressures that torment every character on the album. His curiously old-fashioned references to pretty dresses and long white bows are apparently meant to console his girlfriend, but phrases such as *you deserve much more than this*, *pay the price*, and *what it's like to steal, to cheat, to lie* continually darken the song's atmosphere.

"Something in the Night" offers a portrait of resentment, isolation, and defeat. "You're born with nothing," the character wails, "and better off that way / Soon as you've got something they send someone to try and take it away / You can ride this road 'til dawn, without another human being in sight / Just kids wasted on something in the night." "Streets of Fire" may be Springsteen's bleakest narrative. First of all, the doom-filled organ and slashing guitar make the song the closest thing to heavy metal Springsteen has ever recorded. "Streets of Fire" also stands out because its main character is incoherent. Why doesn't he care anymore when the night's quiet? What does he mean when he says he's dying and can't go back? His reference to being "strung out on the wire" suggests that he may be an addict, but he isn't even able to make that clear. In one respect, however, this character is representative of the album in general – he finds it impossible to explain what has been troubling him. Springsteen's characters speak at length about their problems, but their remarks about the sources of their problems are brief and laced with abstractions. One character wants to tear *this old town* apart. Another wants to spit in the face of *these badlands*. A third, forced to settle for a pronoun, says that *it's* never over; *it's* as relentless as the rain. (Marsh suggests that the absence of clearly defined antagonists on the album may be connected to Springsteen's admiration of the 1940 film adaptation of *The Grapes of Wrath*: "For Springsteen, the most striking part of [the film] is the early scene when the Dust Bowl farmer is trying to find out who has evicted him from his land and is confronted with . . . images of faceless corporations. Similarly, a vague, disembodied 'they' creeps into songs like 'Something in the Night,' 'Prove It All Night,' and 'Streets of Fire' to deny people their most full-blooded possibilities."

"Adam Raised a Cain" and "Factory" begin Springsteen's emotionally charged sequence of "father songs," which would later include "Independence Day," "My Father's House," and "Walk Like a Man." They might also help to account for *Darkness*'s preoccupation with the fears and disappointments of working men. Springsteen's earliest exposure to working-class distress was probably his childhood observation of his father, who struggled to find steady employment and eventually gave up on Freehold, moving the family (with the exception of Bruce, who refused to leave his friends and the Jersey Shore music scene) to California in 1969. The elder Springsteen's anxieties, then, could be the underlying model for these songs, framed by the experiences of a variety of characters. Another interesting feature of *Darkness*'s father songs is that they are not, strictly speaking, about fathers. It would be more accurate to call them narratives about young men's observations of their fathers. In "Adam Raised a Cain," the son snarls that his father, like the father in the Animals' "We Gotta Get Out of this Place," has been cheated out of the best years of his life: "Daddy worked his whole life for nothing but the pain / Now he walks these empty rooms looking for something to blame." We do not see the father in these lines; we see the son as he catalogues the ways in which his father has suffered. "Factory" also portrays a father's daily routine as an alarming spectacle. The narrator watches his father leave home in the morning and walk through the factory gates. At the end of a shift, he thinks he can see death in the eyes of the workers. The son does not comment directly on his father's way of life, but the words he chooses to evoke it – *fear, pain, someone's gonna get hurt tonight* – suggest that he despises "the working life" and has no intention of following his father's path.

The title song closes the album with a strong dose of mystery and ambiguity. The main character seems solitary, determined, and resilient, but aside from those traits the audience learns very little about him. How did he lose his money and his wife? What does he mean when he says he'll be "on that hill"? Why, in these soul-searching verses, does he spend so much time commenting on other people's experiences? (*They're* still racing out at the Trestles. *They* cut their secrets loose or let themselves be dragged down. *Some folks* are born into a good life. *Other folks* get it anyway, anyhow.) What is "the darkness on the edge of town"? Is it a place? A state of mind? What are the things he wants, and why can they only be found in the darkness? This song, it seems to me, is one of the most daring moves in Springsteen's career, a conclusion in which nothing is concluded. The title songs of most of his albums – "The River," "Tunnel of Love," "The Ghost of Tom Joad" – are detailed introductions to some of the themes he wants to examine. In this title song, Springsteen suggests that words cannot express this character's anguish. Part of what he feels has to reach the audience through the sound of Springsteen's voice, his guitar, and his band.

The core of *Darkness* is a paradox: the album's characters are united by the fact that they all feel the pressures of day-to-day life in small towns, but they are divided by their responses to those pressures. Thus, to conclude that Springsteen "celebrates" working people in these songs is to miss the point. *Darkness* does not generalize about the kinds of people Springsteen knew when he lived in Freehold; it insists that their experiences and temperaments are as diverse as those of people in any other community. Springsteen's commitment to complexity and ambiguity may help to explain why listeners often find his representations of small-town Americans even more compelling than those of talented blue-collar songwriters such as John Mellencamp and Steve Earle. The resentment of the farmer in "Rain on the Scarecrow" and the critique of Reaganomics offered by the disillusioned Texan in "Good Ol' Boy (Gettin' Tough)" are staged with clarity and passion, but they seem two-dimensional, smaller than life, when compared to the confessions of Springsteen's characters.

Springsteen's music has had had a cinematic quality ever since he included "Lost in the Flood," "Incident on 57th Street," and other story-songs on his first two albums, but on *Darkness* Springsteen's informal but broad-ranging study of film begins to pay off in a new way. How do John Ford's characters feel about their surroundings in the old West? How do Martin Scorsese's characters feel about turning to crime on dangerous city streets? These questions cannot be answered in a sentence or two. Directors like Ford and Scorsese choose narrow areas of experience and then demonstrate how much drama and mystery those strictly limited spaces can contain. Springsteen began to experiment with that method of storytelling in the 1970s and has continued to use it throughout his career. How would you describe the relationship between the character in "Brilliant Disguise" and his wife? Is it dominated by love? Suspicion? Confusion? Shame? What does the character in "The Rising" have to say about his violent death? Is he wounded by his separation from his family? Proud that he did his job under extraordinary pressure with courage and skill? Shaken by the moments of crisis that made him a victim and a hero at the same time? Any effort to sum up a "message" conveyed by these songs would be futile. Like *Darkness on the Edge of Town*, they demonstrate that Springsteen's aim is to represent experience in convincing ways, not to sing his characters' praises.

*Through an analysis of the lyrics written and sung by John Mellencamp and Jimmy Buffett, Precious McKenzie-Stearns come to the following conclusion: "Though Mellencamp and Buffett share roughly the same generation, a current of optimism and hope threads itself through Jimmy Buffett's lyrics. Mellencamp's lyrics are not as hopeful; he challenges American political and economic policies and refuses to paint a shining portrait of a country that, in his perception, marginalizes the poor."*

# "Those Old Crazy Dreams": The Threads of Discontent in the Lyrics of John Mellencamp and Jimmy Buffett

## Precious McKenzie-Stearns

George Lipsitz in his book *Time Passages: Collective Memory and American Popular Culture* acknowledges the importance of marginalized and fragmented histories that popular musicians invoke in the collective public psyche. Indeed, the production and reception of popular music has impact because of the large size of the audience. Furthermore, for Lipsitz, popular musicians, "At their worst, perform the dirty work of the economy and the state. At their best, they retain memories of the past and contain hopes for the future that rebuke the injustices and inequities of the present."

John Mellencamp and Jimmy Buffett are two such songwriters. Both artists' sales over the past thirty years illustrate the strong, personal connection they have established with Americans. Well-loved songs such as Mellencamp's *Jack and Diane* and Buffett's *Margaritaville* are testimonies to middle class America's desire for love, nostalgia, personal agency, and happiness. In other songs, Mellencamp and Buffett explore more complex political and social issues as related to everyday American life. Their political platforms and responses to issues and life in the late twentieth century take divergent paths; however, both artists use their lyrics to represent disenchantment, frustration, and escape from an America that no longer offers the American dream. Over the last three decades, both artists have become cultural eidolons; Buffett is the quintessential wander luster whereas Mellencamp is, as Wilbur Zelinsky phrased it in *Nation into State: The Shifting Symbolic Foundation of American Nationalism,* Mr. Midwest. Jimmy Buffett and John Mellencamp are modern America's underdogs; they are working men's heroes who are trapped, confused, and abused by institutions, jobs, and relationships. The villains are, more often than not, abstractions – systems and ways of living that have been created and enforced by bureaucracy and proliferated as the status quo.

Born in Mississippi in 1946, Jimmy Buffett states that ninety percent of his songs are autobiographical ("Jimmy Buffett Biography"). John Mellencamp, born in 1951 in Indiana, maintains that his songs are not "necessarily autobiographical," and he publicly resists the label of "spokesman for America" ("John Mellencamp Biography"). Autobiographical or not, their songs reflect the growing unease and unhappiness with the American condition. Though the two men were born after World War II, the reoccurring theme in their music is the poetic exploration of marginalization and disenfranchisement. Analyzing their lyrics from the 1970s through 2003 explores not only the state of the nation, but also reveals the tattered psychological state of American men. Twentieth century history makes it easy for us to understand such disenchantment. After the heroic defeat of Nazism and Fascism, sparks of hope quickly began to fade. The 1950s saw the rise of McCarthyism and the Korean War; the 1960s: Watergate, the Vietnam War, the Bay of Pigs Invasion, the assassinations of John F. Kennedy and Martin Luther King, Jr.; the 1970s and 1980s: the Cold War, the rise of nuclear weapons, the Invasion of Panama, Three Mile Island, AIDS, urban rioting, and terrorist bombings in the Middle East. The decade of the 1990s saw war and terrorism at home and abroad with the Persian Gulf War, the Bosnian War, Rwandan genocide, the Oklahoma City bombing, and ended with the shootings at Columbine High School in 1999.

Mellencamp and Buffet are critics of the nation and, rather than glorify the past or present, instead challenge or run from the white, male, upper class experience. In *Rhythm and Resistance: Explorations in the Political Uses of Popular Music*, Ray Pratt finds that "Springsteen has found the traditional promises and vision of America to be unfulfilled for large sectors of the population." Mellencamp and Buffett, like Springsteen, lament the condition of modern America. The past, as well as current events, for these two songwriters is not a simple list of military, economic, or political confrontations, rather history is comprised of the emotional and psychological effects on individuals, lovers, and families. Political strife and unrest manifests in Mellencamp's lyrics as despair, anger, andcynicism whereas Buffett's lyrics acknowledge despondency and then offer escapism as the route to find happiness. As Mel Van Elteren points out in his article "Populist Rock in Postmodern Society: John Cougar Mellencamp in Perspective," Mellencamp writes of the common American man, often times as a plurality and by doing so, he becomes the spokesman for the American working class and poor, especially of the impoverished Midwestern farmers. Buffet's escapist lyrics trace the disenfranchisement of (usually) one man, with which listeners seem to readily identify. Mellencamp and Buffet's music is successful because their music challenges the dominant white, male, upper class discourse of the politicians (and businessmen) in power. More specifically, their lyrics challenge dominant political discourse because their songs borrow, as Lipsitz reminds us, "from the ideas, actions, and experience of the past, all of which contain potential for informing a radical critique of the present."

Mellencamp released the album *Uh-Huh* in 1983. His song "Pink Houses" rapidly gained recognition and popularity, and with this song Mellencamp became America's newest troubadour. Ironically, however, "Pink Houses" is not a love song about America; rather the lyrics criticize the American economic system. Mellencamp chronicles the life of a black man with an "interstate runnin' through his front yard," a young, already disillusioned man who was told "boy, you're gonna be president" and quickly realizes that "just like everything else those old crazy dreams / just kinda came and went." The black man and the nameless young man are victims of the powerful men who "go to work in some high rise / and vacation down at the Gulf of Mexico." Ultimately, "the simple man baby pays for the thrills, the bills / the pills that kill." "Pink Houses" identified the socio-political divide operating in the 1980s; the lyrics identified the working class by citing examples of nameless, yet seemingly "common" *everyman* kinds of men. The song also identified holders of economic power, though not necessarily by name or political affiliation; however, the implications are clear. The Reagan era trickle down economics policy brought unease and disenchantment to millions of working class Americans, many of whom felt they carried the financial tax burden while large corporations prospered.

Ten years before "Pink Houses" debuted, Jimmy Buffett released "He Went to Paris" on *A White Sport Coat and a Pink Crustacean* (1973). The song begins with a nameless man who leaves his homeland in order to find "answers to questions that bothered him so." The man settles in Paris, is lulled by the climate and cuisine, and ends up spending a decade there. Then the man moves to England, marries, and has a son. Twenty years "slip away." After the war, most likely World War II, the man who is left both a widower and childless, is devastated: "All he could do was just cry." On the run from the problems of modernity, the man flees to the "islands," and there he writes, drinks, and forgets about current events. Contrary to Mellencamp's cynicism about the fate of *everyman* in the early 1980s, Buffett's nameless *everyman*, offers this advice regarding life: "Some of it's magic, some of it's tragic / But I had a good life all the way."

1977, two years after Springsteen released his *Born to Run* album, Buffett released *Changes in Latitudes, Changes in Attitudes*, another escapist melody. The narrator, or perhaps Buffett himself, reminisces about his travels, and his "running" and "cunning." He focuses on his past glories and good times rather than the negative events of the era. However, resilience seems to be the key to survival in the 1970s. Buffett sings: "If it suddenly ended tomorrow / I could somehow adjust to the fall / Good times and riches and son of a bitches / I've seen more than I can recall." In this song, Buffett's narrator differs from Mellencamp's as Buffett's narrator has the privilege of experiencing wealth and exotic destinations. Buffett's narrator seems more resigned to the bureaucratic power superstructure of America. Laughter, travel, and "boat drinks" numb the pain of powerlessness and voicelessness associated with life in the twentieth century.

Mellencamp's song "Rain on the Scarecrow" (1985) on *Scarecrow* describes the desolation and loss of identity a man experiences as his family's farm faces foreclosure. The man's identity is deeply connected to the soil on which his family lived and worked. The land and the labor required bestow dignity on the man because this "land fed a nation / this land made me proud." A traditional way of American life, family farming, was rapidly vanishing. In the 1980s, corporate owned farms began to spread across the Midwest and because of this, American farm families were displaced and disenfranchised. Mellencamp sings, the American Dream is "just memories for you now." Nevertheless, Mellencamp's everyman stays rooted in American soil. On *Scarecrow*, the soil grows the man. Buffett's everyman, on the other hand, traverses the globe in search of pleasure in order to forget the turmoil in America.

Mellencamp's song "The Face of the Nation," also on *Scarecrow*, describes elderly citizens, women, and children "stumblin' their way through the dark" city. The chorus bemoans the changing 'face' of America, the face the singer does not recognize "no more." In this song, American citizens are disillusioned because of loneliness, starvation and "broken dreams;" however, the narrator perseveres and "put[s] things right." The singer will not abandon America but will instead struggle and fight for his survival and for his rights.

Six years before *Scarecrow*'s release, Jimmy Buffet released *Volcano* (1979). In the title song, the narrator, stranded on a volcanic island, feels the trembling earth below his feet. Read metaphorically, Buffett may be reflecting on political unrest or disagreement and its affects on civilians. The singer contemplates possible destination (or exile) choices. Interestingly enough, the singer refuses to "land" in America or any nation touched by imperialistic American capitalism. His "don't want to land" list includes New York City, Mexico, Three Mile Island, Nashville, San Juan, the Yukon Territory or "on no Ayatollah." Where will such an expatriate bury his head in the late twentieth century? Ultimately, he doesn't know. He just knows that he must "get away from it all." As is clear by the number of shark fins donned by his Parrothead fans during his live concerts, such escapist tendencies in Jimmy Buffett's lyrics endear him to his audience. Young and old raucously sing along to his songs wearing Hawaiian shirts, fins, coconuts, straw hats, and consuming boat drinks. Clichés aside, such an ideological paradigm represents not only isolationism but also personal disillusionment regarding the state of the nation and the world. His songs happily dream of isolated, primitive islands in which modern man can lose himself and find a more satisfying way of being. Ironically though, such islands may not exist especially since Buffett's songs have inspired the American tourist colonization of the Caribbean and the Florida Keys.

Appearing in many of Buffett's lyrics is the globetrotter's dream of home. When the narrator rhapsodizes about finding a home, or a retreat, he says he searches for "a magic kind of medicine / that no doctor could prescribe" ("One Particular Harbour"). More often than not, paradise includes "Caribbean sunshine," oceans, and primitiveness. Buffett's songs are indeed a musical form of travel writing. Like many travel writers, especially nineteenth century travel writers, through the writer's discourse, foreign people acquire an innocence and purity that cannot be found in the Western world of corruption, greed, and politics. The exotic island locale transforms itself into paradise on earth regardless of the actual politics and social conditions operating on the foreign island. The writer, or traveler, ignores the real conditions of the place and instead envisions paradise. Buffett's songs are a welcome respite from the anonymous, mechanized hustle and bustle of late twentieth century living; however in the post-colonial world, it seems highly unlikely that he will be able to find a place untainted by American imperialism.

Mellencamp's "Country Gentleman" (1989) from *Big Daddy* echoes contemporary American populist doubt. This song draws attention to the failure of American politics to help the poor and working class. Once again, the wealthy politician "ain't a-gonna help no poor man / he's just gonna help his rich friends." Whereas Buffett's narrators have the economic means by which to escape the turmoil and disenchantment at home, Mellencamp's do not and are constantly bombarded with images of the politician "glad handin' folks and chattin' to the nation." Mellencamp's everyman "feels like he is being used." Yet, escapism is impossible because of economic obstacles. Denied the economic privilege required for travel or expatriation, Mellencamp's Americans are marginalized because of their lack of economic power and must watch their beloved nation's domestic and foreign policies deteriorate. In "Love and Happiness," Mellencamp's America is sadly "droppin' our bombs" and killing people in the Middle East "in the name of peace." America, by 1991, has become a "battlefield" "with wounds that fester and bleed / but never heal."

Three years later, 1994, brings about Jimmy Buffett's escape to Africa in "Six String Music" on *Fruitcake*. At such a late date in the century, it seems as if Africa is the last untouched place on Earth; he travels to Africa because he is searching for a place with no "TV" and no "crap." He reminisces about a night spent "straddling the equator" with "Those shy black hidden faces." He revels in the simple life, a life filled with simple music, simple people, and simple pleasures. "Six String Music" begs to travel back in time, before the problems of civilization and technology. Not so very different from Joseph Conrad's protagonist in *Heart of Darkness*, Buffett's narrator is enchanted with the exotic, primitive appearing African tribal customs. Even on the cusp of the twentieth-first century, African Zanzibar in *Six String Music* seems untouched and unconquered by Europeans and Americans. The narrator does not see starvation, oppression or political unrest in modern Africa; in short, the post-colonial world's discontent largely escapes the narrator. The song's pastoral simpleness enchants listeners and romanticizes Africa. His songs proliferate the dreams of paradise found only at the far side of the world, such dreams cannot be found in his own American backyard.

By 2002, however, Buffett's naïve escapism has matured. "Far Side of the World" is groundbreaking in that this is the first time Buffett seems cognizant of the unrest in the post-colonial world. In the song's opening stanza, the singer acknowledges a religion, Muslim, historically marginalized by Americans and Europeans. Still, exoticism persists. In this "most unlikely place" he observes, "bamboo shacks and shops / behind a jitney packed like sardines / with bananas piled on top." The singer admits that he "ran away from politics / it's too bizarre at home." Assuming his home is America, this is a revelatory statement from an artist who has spent the last twenty-five years running from American socio-political problems. Buffett finally explicitly acknowledges he has been searching for "that one particular harbour" because his rose colored vision of America, like Mellencamp's, has been destroyed. The American dream of safety, prosperity, and freedom crumbled with the imperialistic wars of the mid to late twentieth century. All that remains is nostalgia, shame, anger, and regret.

Nevertheless, like the Crusaders from the Middle Ages, the narrator in "Far Side of the World" wakes up and finds his "threshold of adventure" is Spain. The singer adopts a metaphorical persona of a colonizer. Similar to the early adventurers, as he travels "up and down a Spanish highway / some things remain the same." The highway might be found on any ancient Spanish territory, or in Spain itself, but the patterns of traveling, "othering," and conquering changes little from century to century. From the Spanish civilized (or perhaps conquered) location, the singer embarks "for the far side of the world." Spanish, presumably Catholic civilization, is abandoned in the quest for new knowledge, new territory and newer, more exotic experiences. He runs across "oceans, mountains, saloons" and settles for a time, in the desert. Master-of-all-he-surveys, he sits "atop this dune." Then the singer traces the path of French colonialism: "From Paris to Tunisia / Casablanca to Dakar / I was riding long before I flew / Through the wind and sand and stars."

Whether intentionally or not, Buffett tells the brief history of European colonialism in just one song. He describes Spanish and French endeavors and hints that this procession of exploration and conquest has happened since the beginning of time and will continue. More specifically, he explores the conscious and subconscious experience of exploration and conquest. As he sings of native religious incantations "while the embers from the log fire / flicker, fly and twirl / then drift off toward the cosmos / from the far side of the world," he also sings, in the preceding stanza, of Western sleeping bags and battle flags situated in the "far side of the world."

Divergent from the usual horror stories of Western exploration, Buffett's colonizer and colonized associate but do not dominate or oppress the other. *Far Side of the World* asks for balance and respect in the post-colonial world. On Christmas, Masai "circle" his tent and (presumably) joyfully: "I teach them how to play guitar / They show me how to dance / We have rum from the Caribbean / And burgundy from France." Relics from separate world civilizations meet; legends and customs from past colonial projects mingle and merge but unlike the bloodshed caused by past colonial projects, Buffett's global community is joyous, hopeful and cooperative. The New Year, as a literal and metaphorical construction for beginning life anew, is ushered in with cross cultural dancing and music. In the fragmented and fractured post-colonial world, Buffett optimistically writes "time to sing time to dance / living out my second chance." "Far Side of the World" is not only Buffett's second chance to experience peace and happiness (and always adventure), but also the modern world's second chance to heal the wounds of the past, accept cultural differences, and revel in diversity. Nonetheless, peace in Buffett's new world is never secure. The cobras will remain, but as a representative of America, he must decide and commit totaking "chances on the far side of the world." *Far Side of the World* suggests the possibility for adventure and peace if Westerners embrace cultural diversity and the challenges global peace demands. It seems as if Buffett's days of isolationism are over as he moves between the West and the far sides of the world.

Buffett's optimism for the future is a striking contrast to Mellencamp's cynical observations during this period. In 1997, Mellencamp released *The Best That I Could Do 1978-1988.* This album is a compilation album; it features "Pink Houses," "Small Town," "Paper in Fire," and "Jack and Diane." Perhaps, reflecting on the condition of American domestic and foreign policies, Mellencamp felt it was once again time to sing for the marginalized and give credence to American disillusionment by re-releasing classic working class tributes. Mellencamp wrote new material for the 2003 album *Trouble No More.* However, his cynicism remains, as does his outspokenness for justice and equality in America. Specifically, his acoustic song "To Washington" briefly chronicles the scandals of the Clinton presidency and then describes the Bush/Gore election fiasco: "So America voted on a president / No one kept count / On how the election went / From Florida to Washington / Goddamn, said one side / And the other said the same / Both looked pretty guilty / But no one took the blame." He proceeds to question Bush's "fresh ideas" and explicitly criticizes Bush's foreign policy: "He sent out the National Guard / to police the world / From Baghdad to Washington." As the song progresses, the singer's disgust increases. The song concludes: "What is the thought process / To take a human life / What would be the reason / To think that is right / From heaven to Washington / From Jesus Christ to Washington."

For Mellencamp, separation between church and state seems impossible during this administration. Even with Jesus Christ on America's side, Mellencamp's Americans are still marginalized and discounted.

Analyzed collectively, what are the songs of John Mellencamp and Jimmy Buffett doing? Both artists combine a curious blend of Romanticism and Modernism. In their more Romantic songs, they explore musical and cultural tradition, utilize "natural" sounds, and sing ofcommunity. Nevertheless, as Keir Keightley reminds us in "Reconsidering Rock," other songs feature more Modernist tendencies in that they write of elitism, progress and are unafraid to experiment with technology, style and sound. As these two artists move in and away from the mainstream, they explore and reconstruct themes such as identity, gender, classism, racism and politics. These men are not simply pop stars. Both artists are builders and transmitters of American culture. While Raymond Williams asserts that "culture is ordinary," John Street in "Rock, Pop, and Politics" clarifies that "ordinariness is not, however, mundane. Culture is part of, and derived from, the circumstances of people's lives. It does not just reflect daily existence, though, it both orders it and looks to better ways of living." Millions of "ordinary" Americans identify with, take consolation in, laugh along with, and hope for better ways of living in Mellencamp and Buffett's lyrics.

From his earliest songs, Mellencamp created an American everyman, a common, simple person the American working class could identify with. He invents, performs, and shapes an American working class identity. Mellencamp, not unlike fiction writer Kurt Vonnegut, exposes disenchantment and frustration as he witnesses the destruction of the American Dream. His songs, for the common man, not only represent but also empower ordinary Americans. More specifically, as Ray Pratt maintains, "To speak of empowerment and popular music is to focus on the possibilities provided by musical forms for investment of psychic energies and how, for example, 'rock and roll organizes one's ability, need and possibility for investing affectively in the world.'" In vastly different ways, Mellencamp and Buffett beg their listeners to invest affectively if not in the world, then at least in themselves. Though Mellencamp and Buffett share roughly the same generation, a current of optimism and hope threads itself through Jimmy Buffett's lyrics. Mellencamp's lyrics are not as hopeful. Yet, he challenges American political and economic polices and refuses to paint a shining portrait of a country that, in his perception, marginalizes the poor. Buffett's chipper optimism is a result of socio-economic power, which allows an escape from American domestic problems.

Whether imaginatively or literally, by sailing (or flying) to an island, Buffett escapes political and economic conflicts and marginalization. His "particular harbours" are timeless, peaceful and isolated. Indeed, isolationism seems to be the prescription for sanity and survival in the twentieth century. By striving for a perpetual vacation in paradise, he eludes the forces of history. Disillusioned listeners escape their angst through his songs. In his quest for the perfect world, Buffett's tongue in cheek humor and upbeat musings resonate with many modern Americans. His exoticism transcends time and reaches into the vast collective of Western Enlightenment philosophies. Buffett's escapist poetry searches for a simpler way of life in a world without complicated problems; he searches for a world of love, good times, and boat drinks whereas John Mellencamp resists and instead tries to recover and repair an American paradise.

*In this essay, David Carithers argues that Steve Earle's lyrics are situated in a history of American pragmatism, which can be traced through such thinkers as Walt Whitman, Ralph Waldo Emerson, and John Dewey. This pragmatism seeks not just to express ideas in writing but also to enact positive, transformational change in our lives. In other words, Earle, like so many other American philosophers before him, "finds a usable past in American history to galvanize his present efforts to create a more just and equitable – though contingent and revisable – future."*

# Steve Earle and the Possibilities of Pragmatism

David Carithers

## "Everything Good Is on the Highway:" The Pragmatist Tradition and Steve Earle

In December of 2003, NPR's Steve Inskeep commented that "the songwriter Steve Earle is playing a role that brings some people great respect and causes others to look like fools. He's an artist who speaks out about politics" (Earle, "Interview" 2). Since the attacks of 9/11 in New York and Washington D.C., Earle has turned his attention to democracy and patriotism while retaining his interest in the stories of marginal individuals. In this essay, I consider Steve Earle's art as pragmatic poetry in the Emersonian tradition, the purpose of which is to provoke listeners to action. The link between Emersonian pragmatism and Steve Earle can be found on the highway.

Long before Jack Kerouac affixed the highway in the American imagination as the ultimate experience where movement through the vast land and encounters with its diverse people were tantamount to creation of the new, the open road held a mythical place in the American mind in general and was a particularly powerful metaphor for pragmatism. "Everything good is on the highway," quipped Emerson in "Experience," and John Dewey added that one "finds truth in the highway, in the untaught endeavor, the unexpected idea" (Emerson 481; Dewey *75*). If the Emersonian self is, as Cornel West maintains, "a rather contingent, arbitrary, and instrumental affair, a mobile, performative, and protean entity perennially in process, always on an adventurous pilgrimage" (26), then the highway, either literally or metaphorically, is its natural home.

One might dismiss the metaphor of the highway as a mindless philosophy valuing movement for movement's sake only, but the American pragmatists viewed movement and flux as more than just random motion. Activity itself was a method of invention, especially if it involved provocation of the active mind. West writes that "for Emerson, the goal of activity is not simply domination, but also provocation; the telos of movement and flux is not solely mastery but also stimulation" (26). Stimulation of the mind was William James's goal as well, another American pragmatist who borrowed his meliorative pragmatism from Emerson. As West notes, "James's pragmatic theory of truth affirms the basic Emersonian notion that powers are to be augmented by means of provocation for the purpose of the moral development of personalities" (65).

It was in John Dewey, though, "the greatest of the American pragmatists" according to West, that American pragmatism reached its full potential, "After him, to be a pragmatist is to be a social critic, literary critic, or a poet – in short, a participant in cultural criticism and cultural creation" (71). Dewey helped us "see the complex and mediated ways in which philosophical problems are linked to societal crises" (West 71). He democratized pragmatism by maintaining that personal experiences are legitimate points of inquiry, and artists such as Steve Earle and Bruce Springsteen have certainly used them as such. A close listen to a Steve Earle song such as "Billy Austin" (on *The Hard Way*), in which the audience is asked to take the place of the executioner ("Could you pull that switch yourself, sir?"), at least provides the opportunity for a novel personal experience from which the listener may launch a new mode of inquiry. In "Does Reality Possess Practical Character?" Dewey explains why the practical and personal are valuable modes of inquiry:

> If we suppose the traditions of philosophic discussion wiped out and philosophy starting afresh from the most active tendencies of to-day, – those striving in social life, in science, in literature, and art, – one can hardly imagine any philosophic view springing up and gaining credence, which did not give large place, in its scheme of things, to the practical and the personal, and to them without employing disparaging terms, such as phenomenal, merely subjective, and so on. (80)

We might ask what qualifies an artist to be an active participant in cultural criticism. In the interview mentioned above, Steve Inskeep asks Earle, "What makes you qualified to talk politics, the war in Afghanistan, health care, any of the other things you've talked about?" Earle quickly replies,"I'm a citizen in a democracy. That makes me qualified and all of us" ("Interview" 2). The focus on democracy in his art has intensified since 9/11. In track eight on the second CD of *Just an American Boy* (appropriately titled "Democracy"), Earle addresses a direct message to the listener: "No matter what anybody tells you, it is *never ever* unpatriotic or un-American to question any…thing in a *democracy*." Steve Earle enacts an Emersonian brand of pragmatism in his provocative stories meant to rouse the mind to action, and a Whitmanesque poetics in his vision of a better democracy. Earle creates stories out of questionable or problematic circumstances, presenting these scenes to any curious mind that dares approach and apprise them.

This provocation-by-narration can be considered a theory of rhetorical invention in which a listener is exposed to a situation that challenges part of his or her belief system. The personal becomes the rhetorical as soon as it is shared with others. Emerson favored this mode of invention, which is based on the twin ideas that we learn and create mostly in social ways and that invention involves figurative movement to new places, reminiscent of Aristotle's *topoi.* Emerson wrote: "When I converse with a profound mind, or if at any time being alone I have good thoughts, I do not at once arrive at satisfactions, as when, being thirsty, I drink water, or go the fire, being cold: no! but I am at first apprised of my vicinity to a new and excellent region of life" (485). Dewey, somewhat characteristically, takes this Emersonian idea of provocation and makes it the basis of his education modeled on the pragmatic method developed by C.S. Peirce in which the action of thought is excited by an irritation or doubt that ceases only when belief is attained. Dewey explains further in the following quote:

> The natural man is impatient with doubt and suspense: he impatiently hurries to be shut of it. A disciplined mind takes delight in the problematic, and cherishes it until a way out is found that approves itself upon examination. The questionable becomes an active questioning, a search; desire for emotion of certitude gives peace to quest for the objects by which the obscure and unsettled may be developed into the stable and clear. (qtd. in West 97)

The Brazilian educator Paulo Freire argued in favor of a "'problem-posing' education" that focuses on "the posing of the problems of human beings in their relations with the world" (60). I argue that Steve Earle does just this in his work. By presenting narratives from the point of view of the outcasts of our society – especially the accused or the condemned – Earle plants a doubt in the receptive listener's mind, a doubt that may become "an active questioning" of the listener's beliefs. In the following section, I discuss some of Earle's pre-9/11 songs to describe how he enacts the pragmatic poet's aim to provoke the active mind. The final section will focus on Earle's overtly political work since 9/11.

## Confronting the Other Here and "Over Yonder": Steve Earle, the Pragmatic Poet

Steve Earle's primary area of activism has involved his opposition to the death penalty, but he did not write a song on the subject until Tim Robbins asked him to do so for *Dead Man Walking*, the film based on Sister Helen Prejean's book by the same name. The result was "Ellis Unit One" (on *Sidetracks*), which is based on Earle's father's experience working in a Texas prison and is told from the perspective of a prison guard who has witnessed many executions during his career. Earle has also written songs told from the perspective of the condemned, such as "Billy Austin," a brooding narrative on the album *The Hard Way* that challenges preconceived notions about the death penalty. Accompanied only by a quiet acoustic guitar, Earle delivers the stanzas of "Billy Austin" slowly, methodically, inviting the listener to savor each word and digest each line fully. The B-minor chord, considered by some to be the darkest of the minor keys, accentuates every fourth line and grounds the song in a somber mood.

The opening stanza reveals the protagonist's relative youth and his racial ethnicity that will figure prominently in one of the challenges the reader must face later in the song concerning racism in the penal system. "My name is Billy Austin / I'm twenty-nine years old.

/ I was born in Oklahoma / Quarter Cherokee I'm told." Deracination, with its side effects violence and loneliness, dominates the second stanza: "I don't remember Oklahoma / Been so long since I left home / Seems like I've always been in prison / Like I've always been alone."

In the middle stanzas, the narrator describes the night of the murder and wonders what made him "cross that line." Listeners also witness the coldness of the court-appointed lawyer, who would not look him in the eye even after Billy was sentenced to death. The story then invites the reader to reconsider the demographic of the inmates on death row and poses the possibility that some of them may be innocent.

Now my waitin's over
As the final hour drags by
I won't stand here and tell you
That I don't deserve to die

But there's ninety-seven men here
Mostly black, brown, and we're all poor
Most of us are guilty
Who are you to say for sure?

It is in the final stanzas that Earle's rhetorical aim becomes clear; the narrative takes a turn here that may challenge some listeners' conceptions about capital punishment. Imagining ourselves as the condemned prisoner invites the kind of empathy that humanizes. Nobles and others like him, but when Earle asks his audience if they could actually execute the condemned one, he brings up the issue of civic responsibility in a democracy. "My theory is that in a democracy, if the government kills someone, then I'm killing someone," Earle says. "And I object to the damage that does to my spirit, period" ("Interview" 2). In "Billy Austin," Earle first takes the audience to a melancholy place (or mood) by appealing to universal human emotions connected with loneliness, pain, and death, themes reinforced by the rhythmic drone of the dark minor chord. Having secured the audience's attention with this appeal to *pathos*, considered the most effective appeal since ancient times, Earle then uses the logical appeal by suggesting that the listener – as a citizen of the state – is complicit in the act of execution. Through these rhetorical techniques, Earle questions the moral right and superiority of the state (and the citizen represented by that state) to kill a human. For many listeners, being made accomplice to murder is a problematic situation. The final stanzas address the listener directly:

So when the preacher comes to get me
And they shave off all my hair
Could you take that long walk with me
Knowing hell is waitin' there?

Could you pull that switch yourself sir
With a sure and steady hand?
And then go home and tell yourself, sir,
That you're better than I am?

The listener has several rhetorical options here, one of which may involve a change in his or her beliefs. Challenged by the moral question, the listener makes his or her choices, one of which, of course, is to ignore the question altogether. The attention given the reader in this form of direct address is reminiscent of Walt Whitman, who addressed his audience so directly and hauntingly at times, such as in "Crossing Brooklyn Ferry": "And you that shall cross from shore to shore years hence are more to me, / and more in my meditations, than you might suppose" (35).

"Billy Austin" is a convincing fiction, but another song in the Earle anti-death penalty canon is written from the perspective of a real condemned man, Jonathan Wayne Nobles, an inmate in Texas whom Earle befriended and whose execution Earle witnessed. Many of the words in the song are Nobles's. "Over Yonder (Jonathan's Song)" is about "giving Jon a voice," explains Earle in the NPR interview, and does not address an explicit challenge to the listener's beliefs on capital punishment. But the story certainly has its rhetorical motivations, mainly its challenge to listeners to think about the humanity of the people on death row. Just as Ernest Gaines leads us through an emotional experience in his novel *A Lesson Before Dying*, culminating in our reading of the executed Jefferson's posthumous diary that documents the condemned boy's last hours, Steve Earle draws the listener into the mind of Jonathan Nobles before he takes his final walk. The result is not only an aesthetic experience, but also a rhetorical situation because it has the potential to lead listeners to action.

Like "Billy Austin," "Over Yonder (Jonathan's Song)" on *Transcendental Blues* features sparse instrumental accompaniment, mostly limited to Earle finger-picking an acoustic guitar and a slow, deliberative delivery of the lines. These effects allow the song slowly to draw the reader into the personal experience of a condemned man. In the first stanza, the speaker describes where he is physically and mentally, hours before his execution and mercifully close to the end of his painful existence: "The warden said he'd mail my letter. / The chaplain's waiting by the door. / Tonight we'll cross that yard together. / Then they can't hurt me anymore." In this short narrative, the accused longs for the afterlife "over yonder," where he believes he will be "free." He only hopes his death in some way helps the people who hate him: "The world will spin around without me. / The sun will come up in the east, / Shinin' down on all of them that hate me. / I just hope my going brings them peace."

In *Poetry and Pragmatism*, Richard Poirier writes that Emersonian pragmatists "promise to help effect transformations not just in writing, but in the actual forms of individual and communal life." Their rhetoric "is mostly in a socially optative mood" (112). Steve Earle's rhetoric, too, is mostly aimed at social improvement. When he asks his listeners to reconsider the guilty ones, the dregs of our society, he is reminding usto be humane to one another. In the Preface to *Leaves of Grass*, way helps the people who hate him: "The world will spin around without me. / The sun will come up in the east, / Shinin' down on all of them that hate me. / I just hope my going brings them peace."

In *Poetry and Pragmatism*, Richard Poirier writes that Emersonian pragmatists "promise to help effect transformations not just in writing, but in the actual forms of individual and communal life." Their rhetoric "is mostly in a socially optative mood" (112). Steve Earle's rhetoric, too, is mostly aimed at social improvement. When he asks his listeners to reconsider the guilty ones, the dregs of our society, he is reminding us to be humane to one another. In the Preface to *Leaves of Grass*, Whitman advised his readers to "stand up for the stupid and crazy" (15) and one way that Earle does this is by penning songs about condemned people. If Cornel West is correct in his assertion that "the aim of Emersonian pragmatism is to subjectify and humanize unique individuals" (27), then Earle's narratives are Emersonian to the core. It should not be surprising, then, to find that after 9/11 Earle focused his imaginative powers of provocation on one of the most prominent recent outcasts in American history: John Walker Lindh.

## Explaining America to Itself: Steve Earle's Poetic Pragmatism after 9/11

Two distinct ways of thinking about 9/11 offer different modes of thought and action. On one hand is the romantic-pragmatic outlook, which views 9/11 as a new experience to test old beliefs, a provocation for self-reflection on both the individual and the national levels. Our biggest failure after 9/11 would be an inability or unwillingness to engage in such a debate. But there is an opposite view, we might call it the militaristic or official governmental position, which holds the United States wholly blameless for 9/11, which it views as an act of war motivated by pure evil, the only response to which is to wage war. While I in no way condone the despicable terrorist acts of 9/11, I *do* believe that 9/11 calls for intense self-inquiry of the kind promoted by pragmatism. Borrowing the language of Kenneth Burke's dramatic pentad, I submit that these parties profoundly disagree over the nature of the "scene" of post-9/11 America. For many pragmatists, 9/11 provided a new scene for investigation of the connections between beliefs and actions. The event provides the impetus for thoughtful inquiry that may lead to new theories and practices. The militaristic philosophy also emphasizes the way the scene calls for certain acts after 9/11, but the scene in this case is defined as a state of war in which the terms "good" and "evil" and "us" and "them" are off-limits to criticism.

Narrowing our focus from the overall scene of 9/11 to one specific incident, the actions of "the American Taliban" John Walker Lindh, we find some of the same disagreements arising between these opposing worldviews over the nature of the scene and the motivations for acting within it. If we consider the scene to be a state of war against terrorism in which a person is either on the side of the United States or on the side of the terrorists, then Lindh is a traitor to his country. But if the scene opened by 9/11 is one of renewed inquiry into America as an *idea* (and ourselves as Americans), then Lindh's story becomes a narrative of persuasion that asks listeners to re-think assumptions about treason, guilt, and freedom. The difference is a matter of different terministic screens that direct the attention in different ways. Steve Earle's interpretation of Lindh's story takes this second, pragmatic approach.

John Walker Lindh was nineteen years old when he was found in November 2001 among Taliban forces in a holding facility in Afghanistan where an uprising had caused the death of CIA agent Johnny Michael Spann. Apparently, the teenager decided not only to convert to Islam, but to leave his California home and study Arabic in Yemen, a country considered to be a crucible for Islamic extremism. He then joined the Taliban in Afghanistan as a soldier. The response from conservative commentators and writers can be summed up well in the words of one of my students at the time who said that Lindh "should be summarily executed." The website of *The New York Post* headlined its dispatch on the Lindh story "Twisted Ballad Honors Tali-Rat" and claimed "American Taliban fighter John Walker Lindh is glorified and called Jesus-like in a country-rock song…by maverick singer-songwriter Steve Earle" (Sujo). This opinion is in keeping with what I've called the militaristic philosophy that defines the scene after 9/11 as an unambiguous moral battlefield pitting the forces of good and evil. Lindh, in this view, is a traitor pure and simple because he was found fighting with the enemy, even though the Taliban was supported and funded by the U.S. when Lindh joined and right up to the time of the events of 9/11. Burke explains in *A Grammar of Motives* that stressing "the term, agent, encourages one to be content with a very vague treatment of scene, with no mention of the political and economic factors that form a major aspect of national scenes" (17). Describing Lindh simply as a traitor that deserves to be hanged is a way of deflecting "attention from scenic matters by situating the motives of an act in the agent" (17).

But a more romantic-pragmatic approach to the story of John Walker Lindh, which is the approach taken by Steve Earle in his song"John Walker's Blues" on *Jerusalem*, illuminates new ideas in which Burke's ratios are at work. When the post 9/11 scene is viewed as a new experience to test our old beliefs and not as a clearly defined battlefield, then the scene-act ratio offers more insight into the situation than the agent-purpose ratio. By shifting the focus away from Lindh as a traitor (agent-purpose) and toward the scene that moved him to act (scene-act), then we unmask unfair assumptions about Lindh and his purposes. My aim here is to, in Burke's words, "deflect attention from the criticism of personal motives by deriving an act or attitude not from traits of the agent but from the nature of the situation" (*Grammar* 17).

In "John Walker's Blues," the scene is a materially-oriented world dominated by the global market and the proliferation of American icons and goods worldwide, or what Benjamin Barber calls "McWorld" in his book *Jihad vs. McWorld: How Globalism and Tribalism are Reshaping the World.* It is this vacuous scene that has driven Lindh to search for meaning through radical Islam. He is captured but not defeated and, faced with a hostile audience, attempts to explain his purpose in fighting with the Taliban. When using Burke's pentad to explore human motivations, we often find that one term is clearly dominant as the first cause of action and the other elements follow. In this case, the dominant term is the scene of a spiritually bankrupt culture, the darkness out of which the speaker seeks the light. Like many of his other thoughtful songs, "John Walker's Blues" is written in the dark key of B-minor, but with its quick chord changes and marching rhythm accompanied by distorted electric guitar, the song evinces a tense and edgy mood indicative of the subject matter. The opening stanzas suggest the scene:

> I'm just an American boy, raised on MTV.
> And I've seen all those kids in the soda pop ads
> But none of 'em looked like me.
> So I started lookin' around for a light out of the dim.
> And the first thing I heard that made sense was the word
> Of Mohammed, peace be upon him

In Earle's interpretation, and borrowing again from Burke's dramatic theory of rhetoric, it was Lindh's search for a life worth living within the context of globalization (scene) that led him to Islam as the means (agency) to achieve this end. In this case, "the scene contains the act," to use a Burke-ian phrase. For the speaker in this song, the act of fighting with the Taliban is honorable and although Lindh is defeated, he defends his right to act on his beliefs: "If my daddy could see me now – chains around my feet. / He don't understand that sometimes a man / Has got to fight for what he believes." The next stanza includes the lines in which, as Earle explained in an interview (Zengerle), were meant to show that Islam shows respect for Christianity by viewing Jesus as a prophet: "And I believe God is great, all praise due to him. / And if I should die, I'll rise up to the sky / Just like Jesus, peace be upon him." Here is a rhetorical move apparently intended, like Springsteen's "World's Apart" on *The Rising*, to mediate between what are considered – especially after 9/11 – the extremes of Christianity and Islam. "John Walker's Blues" shares something else with "World's Apart": lyrics in Arabic. While the Arabic is a mostly unintelligible background chant in "Worlds Apart," it is placed in the most prominent place in "John Walker's Blues": the chorus. Taken from a verse in the Koran meaning in part, "I am a witness," the chorus sounds like part battle-cry and part dirge, its brooding tone accentuated by the E-minor chord at the end of each line: "A shadu la ilaha illa Allah. / There is no God but God."

The final stanzas of the song focus on Lindh's act, which in this context is described as heroic and more meaningful than the typical life of an American teenager: "We came to fight the Jihad and our hearts were pure and strong. / As death filled the air, we all offered up prayers / And prepared for our martyrdom." The final lines reveal the speaker's faith in his God, even while he is being dragged back, "with my head in a sack, / to the land of the infidel." The chorus is then repeated as the song fades and ends.

In "John Walker's Blues," Steve Earle reminds us that there is a real person with human dignity underneath the label of scapegoat. "It's not about an agreement with what John Walker Lindh did," Earle explains. "It's just about not forgetting, when everyone else was lining up to lynch him, that he was a human being. And I've done that pretty consistently throughout my career" ("Interview" 3). Now more than ever, after 9/11, it is important to remember the humanity of those who are quickly labeled as traitors or enemies of the United States. This acknowledgment of the other, which Earle indeed has achieved in his art consistently throughout his career, is an important part of education. In her argument for "cosmopolitanism," Martha Nussbaum explains that students must "learn to recognize humanity wherever they encounter it, undeterred by traits that are strange to them, and be eager to understand humanity in all its strange guises" (9). Earle's narrative about John Walker Lindh, his "vivid imagining of the different," in Nussbaum's terms, is a pragmatic act of education. This is difficult work, as it is always much easier to rest assured in one's old conclusions than to dump a whole cartload of beliefs when experience proves them wrong. It is difficult work because, as Rowan Williams explains, "it means putting on hold our most immediate feelings – or at least making them objects of reflection; it means trying to put apart the longing to re-establish the sense of being in control and the longing to find a security that is shared" (270).

Cornel West explains that Emersonian pragmatism "is less a philosophical tradition putting forward solutions to perennial problems in the Western philosophical conversation initiated by Plato, and more a continuous cultural commentary or set of interpretations that attempt to explain America to itself at a particular historical moment" (5). The particular historical moment in American history opened by 9/11 inspired Steve Earle to explain America to itself through his songs. Just as he does in his anti-death penalty songs, Earle presents in "John Walker Blues" a narrative to be experienced by the listener as a moment of inquiry. Such aesthetic experiences can be understood, from a Deweyan perspective, as grounds for human reasoning. Art highlights the context of specific experiences, holding them up for our inspection and our edification, as Thomas Alexander explains:

> Objects, things, actions, events – all have their being by being situated within a context. The qualitative unity of the context may be subliminal, or, as in the experience of art, heightened into conscious experience. The transformative nature of situations, part of their reconstructive temporality, involves the constant use of imagination, conceived here as the ability to employ and play with alternative

interpretive schemata. (136)

Earle has always had a fondness for alternative interpretive schemata, especially those that represent the viewpoint of the outcast. Earle writes about "despicable people," in his own words, to remind us that these people are still human. Lindh was objectified into a traitor by some Americans, and Earle made him human again in "John Walker Blues." Earle would, I am sure, agree with Anne Slifkin, as she writes, "It is easier to scapegoat one person who has aligned himself with our new enemy than to take a critical look at cold war and post-cold war U.S. foreign policy initiatives and decisions" (423). In "John Walker's Blues," Earle asks listeners to put aside the view of Lindh as traitor and think about his motivations as a human being looking for meaning in a spiritually vacuous culture. Lindh is an anomaly for most Americans: one of "us" who volunteered to become one of "them." In keeping with the pragmatic tradition in which I place him, Earle mediates between these extremes through this powerful narrative of persuasion.

Steve Earle, agitator and activist, attempts to provoke his audience to action by describing the experiences of real and fictional "unfamiliar" characters through the careful choice of terministic screens. Earle's songs remind us of the humanity in the unrecognizable "other" whose experience we may think we understand until moved to reflect on it. Through his choice of terministic screens for describing people like John Walker Lindh, Jonathan Nobles, or the fictional Billy Austin, Earle provokes the audience members to test their previous conclusions concerning these people and their experiences.

With his hope for a better America, his concern with democracy, and his activist tendencies, Steve Earle is a romantic pragmatist for the twenty-first century. What Cornel West said of William James's pragmatic theory of truth (as always "in the making") holds true for Steve Earle's art: they both affirm "the basic Emersonian notion that powers are to be augmented by means of provocation for the purpose of the moral development of human personalities" (65). Steve Earle's pragmatism shares the vision of John Dewey's pragmatism as "a political form of cultural criticism and locates politics in the everyday experiences of ordinary people" (West 213). And like James's moral heroism, Earle's rhetoric "intends to energize people to become exceptional doers under adverse circumstances, to galvanize zestful fighters against excruciating odds" (West 59). Invoking the best of America's past through figures such as Malcolm X, Martin Luther King, Jr., and Woody Guthrie, all of whom he calls on in "Christmas in Washington" (*El Corazón*) to figuratively "come back to us now," Earle finds a usable past in American history to galvanize his present efforts to create a more just and equitable – though contingent and revisable – future.

## Works Cited


Alexander, Thomas. *John Dewey's Theory of Art, Experience, and Nature: The Horizons of Feeling.* Albany: State U of New York P, 1987.

Barber, Benjamin. *Jihad vs. McWorld: How Globalism and Tribalism are Reshaping the World.* New York: Random House, 1995.

Burke, Kenneth. *A Grammar of Motives.* New York: Prentice-Hall, 1945.

----. "Terministic Screens." *Language as Symbolic Action: Essays on Life, Literature, and Method.* Los Angeles and London: U of California P, 1966. 44-62.

Dewey, John. "Does Reality Possess Practical Character?" *Essays, Philosophical and Psychological.* New York: Longmans, Green, and Co., 1908. 53-80.

Earle, Steve. *El Corazòn.* E-Squared, 1997.

----. *Jerusalem.* E-Squared / Artemis, 2002.

----. *Just an American Boy: The Audio Documentary.* E-Squared / Artemis, 2003.

----. *The Hard Way.* MCA, 1990.

----. *Sidetracks.* E-Squared / Artemis, 2002.

----. "Interview with Steve Inskeep." *All Things Considered.* National Public Radio. 7 Dec. 2003.

Emerson, Ralph Waldo. *Essays and Lectures.* New York: Library of America, 1983.

Freire, Paulo. *Pedagogy of the Oppressed. New Revised Twentieth-Anniversary Edition.* New York: Continuum, 1997.

Nussbaum, Martha. *For Love of Country?* Boston: Beacon Press, 1996.

Poirier, Richard. *Poetry and Pragmatism.* Cambridge: Harvard UP, 1992.

Slifkin, Anne. "John Walker Lindh." *Dissent from the Homeland: Essays after September 11. South Atlantic Quarterly* 101 (2002): 417-424.

Springsteen, Bruce. *The Rising.* Columbia, 2002.

Sujo, Aly. "Twisted Ballad Honors Tali Rat." *New York Post* 21 July 2002: 3.

West, Cornell. *The American Evasion of Philosophy: A Genealogy of Pragmatism.* Madison: The U of Wisconsin P, 1989.

Whitman, Walt. "Crossing Brooklyn Ferry." *Complete Poetry and Collected Prose.* New York: The Library of America, 1982. 35-40.

----. "Preface to Leaves of Grass, 1855." *Complete Poetry and Collected Prose.* New York: The Library of America, 1982. 5-26.

Williams, Rowan. "End of War." *Dissent from the Homeland: Essays after September 11. South Atlantic Quarterly* 101 (2002): 267-284.

Zengerle, Jason. "Sympathy for a Rebel." *New York Times Magazine* 25 August 2002: 17.

# What We Watch

*Based on Shakespeare's* The Taming of the Shrew, 10 Things I Hate about You *premiered in 1999 and won Julia Stiles the MTV Award for Breakthrough Female Performance as the sassy Katarina (or Kat) Stratford. In this article, Melissa Croteau argues that the screenwriters and director actually improved on the problematic* Shrew.

## Kat and Bianca Avenged: Or, Things to Love about *10 Things I Hate about You*

Melissa Croteau

In our contemporary cultural climate, which thankfully recognizes the battered and abused woman as a victim and the perpetrator of that violence as a criminal, Shakespeare's *The Taming of the Shrew* is undoubtedly a difficult play to stage in any type of venue or medium. Like other of his plays of questionable ideology, particularly *The Merchant of Venice* and *Othello*, *Shrew* has been attacked by critics, playgoers, and readers alike, accused of sending a morally untenable message to masses of people who may be swayed or placated by its portrayal of sado-masochistic gender relations.

Critics like Barbara Hodgdon argue that *The Taming of the Shrew* normalizes and reifies domestic abuse and master-servant dynamics in male-female relationships. Diana E. Henderson writes that this play "highlights the culture's traffic in women," and a *Los Angeles Times* theater critic penned an editorial about *Shrew* entitled, "The Beast of a Play that Can't Be Tamed," insisting that "until someone can make better sense of the Bard's battle-of-the-sexes comedy, it's time to declare a moratorium on the oft-staged *Shrew*."

Despite the pervasive misgivings about this play, it has seen prolific production in the twentieth century, spawning numerous film and television versions since its silent picture debut in Biograph's brief 1908 *Shrew*, directed by famed filmmaker D.W. Griffith. At least eighteen screen versions of *The Taming of the Shrew* have been made in North America and Europe. In her fine article "Katherine Bound," scholar Hodgdon examines several twentieth century productions of Shrew on stage and on celluloid and concludes that "*Shrew* continues to enfold women within representation to make and remake cultural myths with which to negotiate her use" and that these representations "perfectly exhibit how the containing illusions of popular patriarchies are engendered and sustained." In other words, all *Shrews* are inevitably (and always already) works of ideological containment.

In her study of the illustrious and notorious film and television production history of this play, Diane E. Henderson notes that *Shrew* seems to experience popularity particularly during those decades in which women are being encouraged to return to or take pleasure in domestic space and duties and eras in which American culture is backlashing against feminism. Henderson also claims that "*Shrew* occurs at moments of new viewing technologies and is promptly reproduced in the new media before most if not all other Shakespeare plays," remarking that the "agents of culture seem anxious to make sure *The Taming of the Shrew* is preserved."

It would seem that *Shrew* has indeed been used as an instrument of ideological containment for women throughout the last century. However, there is one notable and recent exception to this rule. As the century drew to a close, one film genre resurfaced on the mass market in a new and powerful way: the teen movie. This genre exploded after the 1995 and 1996 box office hits *Clueless*, *Scream*, and *Romeo + Juliet* proved to filmmakers and studios that teen films could be extremely lucrative because of their low production costs and large audience with plenty of free time and discretionary cash. Like the new technologies that have sought to produce new *Shrews* at their inceptions, this new genre quickly generated its *Shrew* for the times in 1999's *10 Things I Hate about You.*

The teen film genre has been much maligned by critics all over the country for the past several years; indeed, Shakespeare scholars often disdain such free adaptations of his work and claim that this sort of American pop culture version of a Shakespeare classic is nothing but a reflection of the "dumbing-down" of high culture to pander to and profit from the degenerate taste of the voracious and vapid teen audience.

But much of the critical work done on Zeffirelli's *Romeo and Juliet* (1968) and Baz Luhrmann's William Shakespeare's *Romeo + Juliet* (1996) has argued to the contrary: that mass market films made of Shakespeare's work can be crafted for the teen audience and still be effective, intelligent, and illuminating adaptations. First time film director Gil Junger, a twenty-two year veteran of television direction, made *10 Things I Hate About You* from a script written by two young novice scriptwriters, Karen McCullah Lutz and Kirsten Smith. Together, they offered a revision of *The Taming of the Shrew* which finally put women on top, leaving Kat and Bianca united in the end, not divided, and stronger than ever.

While nearly all of the film and video *Shrews* have focused on how the male characters in the play position themselves and relate to one another through the purchasing and possession of the female characters, *10 Things* is truly a film about the Stratford sisters, Katarina and Bianca, students at Padua High School. Unlike the *Shrew* text, most of this film's dialogue belongs to the sisters, and theirs is the only home we are allowed to explore via the camera. It is the sisters' struggle to grow up, to deal with family and personal demons, and to understand one another that dominates this comedy.

Of course, refocusing the attention on the activity and agency of the female characters does require a thorough rewriting of the play. Actress Fiona Shaw, who played Kate on stage for over a year, notes the irony embedded in a play which claims to be about a "shrew" yet does not allow this egregiously open-mouthed woman to speak: "I think Shakespeare is making a point of it. This man comes to tame Kate and speaks through the whole play…for almost five acts we never hear her speak…So we have to interpret her silence."

In fact, when Kate finally does find her voice, she speaks the infamous, lengthy subservient monologue in which she lectures her sister Bianca and the newlywed widow that their husband is their "lord," their "king," and their "governor" and instructs them to "serve, love, and obey" their husbands in all situations. This searing diatribe Kate delivers at the close of the play is certainly one of the most difficult Shakespearean passages to negotiate on a stage or screen today. It would be extremely politically incorrect to play it straight, and no North American audience could tolerate it well. Hodgdon insists that the only way audience members can endure Kate's final speech is "by gliding over the signs of the father…(accepting them as 'natural') or choosing to assume Kate is merely performing and does not believe what she says (or both)." She further suggests that by doing so readers or viewers "can produce a scene similar to a happy rape, the fully authorized scene of female sexuality – authorized precisely because it is mastered and controlled."

Screenwriters Lutz and Smith have created a text that ends Kate's silence in *The Taming of the Shrew* and gives her a voice, loud and strong. Their screenplay also praises the intelligence and insight of the mind behind that voice. Highlighting this point, toward the beginning of the film, Kat defiantly declares to Ms. Perky, her guidance counselor, "Expressing my opinion is not a terrorist action." Perhaps this is the pivotal difference between early modern gender politics and those of the 1990s. Moreover, the screenwriters have also transformed Kate's final patriarchal paean to wifely domesticity into a public reading of a Shakespearean sonnet she has written to her would-be boyfriend, Patrick, who has betrayed her trust. In the sonnet, she explains the many things she "hates" about him in order to communicate her affection for and disappointment in his treatment of her. Like her counterpart in *Shrew*, Kat is expressing her care for her partner; however, this Kat does not lose her edge. The servile flattery is lost; she is not accepting a "happy rape." Instead, Kat is asking for a renewal of a "marriage of true minds."

As I have mentioned, the film is about two sisters, Katarina and Bianca Stratford, a high school senior and sophomore respectively, who are complete opposites. Kat is a willful, intellectual, sharp-tongued young woman who is universally feared as a "mewling rampallian wretch." She reads Sylvia Plath and Simone de Beauvoir, listens to "angry girl" indie rock, and wants to attend prestigious Sarah Lawrence College. Bianca is a popular, pretty girl who constantly seeks the approval of others and debates the relative value of her fashion accessories, at one point declaring that she has discovered the difference between like and love because she "likes" her Skechers (sneakers) but she "loves" her Prada backpack.

One of the most entertaining and innovative features of this film is its portrayal of the sisters' father, played by comedian Larry Miller. He is an obstetrician who spends every day "up to his elbows in placenta" and is paranoid that if he allows his daughters to date they will become a teen pregnancy statistic. He continually lectures them about the horrors of teenagers giving birth and insists that they stay close to home. At one point in the film, he forces Bianca to wear a weighted vest which is shaped like the torso of a pregnant woman, called "the belly," to keep her from getting into trouble with the opposite sex at a party. For all his paranoia, he is a loving father who cares about what his daughters want. The screenplay goes further to explain the situation by revealing that the Stratford mother abandoned the family three years before the opening of the film, and the father feels overwhelmed with the roles of both mother and father.

Kat has clearly taken on some of the motherly functions in the house, including the role of protector in Bianca's life. Kat insists she does not desire to date the "unwashed miscreants" that deck the halls of her high school, but she is also hiding a secret. She has had a negative sexual encounter with Joey Donner, the school narcissist, and she is trying to save Bianca from a similar fate by encouraging her father to retain the no-dating rules for both sisters. When Bianca begs Daddy for permission to go out like "normal" girls, he placates her by giving her a condition: if Kat dates, she can date. He clearly relies on Kat not to do what she has sworn disgusts her and believes he is safe in this ruling.

The contemporary high school setting of this adaptation of *The Taming of the Shrew* greatly lessens the consequences of the male-female relationships in the play. Like the *Shrew* plot, this film begins with a newcomer to Padua High, Cameron, spotting Bianca across a crowded quad and declaring Lucentio's words, "I burn, I pine, I perish," to which his guide Michael replies dryly, "Of course you do." This anti-Petrarchan sentiment echoes that in *Shrew* as well as plays like *Romeo and Juliet* and sonnets such as "My mistress' eyes are nothing like the sun." Cameron then claims to be a French tutor in order to get to know Bianca, as Lucentio disguises himself as a tutor for his Bianca.

Petruchio's transformation is more complicated. Patrick Verona is a wild high school senior whose reputation as an insane renegade, like Kat's, allows him to escape the economy of high school hierarchies. It is common knowledge that he sold his liver on the black market to buy a new pair of speakers, spent a year in San Quentin, and ate a live duck. But the truly shrewish traits of Petruchio are found in the character of Joey, the self-obsessed underwear model who three years before had deflowered Kat and who now has made a bet with his friends that he can do the same to Bianca.

As in *Shrew*, money changes hands concerning the possession of a female. In this case, Cameron and Michael, in an Iago-like move, inveigle Joey into paying Patrick to date Kat so that Bianca can date, as per the new rule set by their father. Of course, Patrick succeeds in winning the heart of the wily Kat after several amusing mishaps, including her vomiting on his shoes after drinking too much at a party and him performing "Can't Take My Eyes Off of You" for her in the high school stadium, sacrificing himself on the altar of dignity. Their public humiliation is mutual.

In fact, the most important cross-gender relationship in *10 Things I Hate About You* is the one between Kat and her father. Like Kate in *Shrew*, Kat believes that her father wants her to be more like Bianca and feels that he loves Bianca more; however, unlike Kate, Kat has a father who not only listens to her, but also learns from her.

In *Shrew*, when Kate's father Baptista informs Petruchio that he may wed her only if he obtain the "special thing…her love; for that is all in all," he quickly forgets his pledge to honor her will and expressly acts against her wishes in marrying her to Petruchio.

In *10 Things*, Kat's overprotective father has been thinking about Kat's accusation that he does not trust his daughters to make their own decisions because he lost his wife and feels out of control himself. By the conclusion of the film, father Stratford has put forth money on behalf of Katarina: he has paid her deposit for Sarah Lawrence College. He has relinquished his desire to keep her close to home and decides to trust her judgment and support her education on the east coast.

Bianca's fate is more interesting. Bianca seems to be the same simpering, manipulative fool at the start of *10 Things* as she does throughout *Shrew*; however, this Bianca is a cat of a different color. This Bianca may be sophomoric, but she is not stupid.

She realizes, all on her own, that Joey is a pompous windbag and finds him ultimately repugnant, despite his popularity. Instead, she chooses the kind, smitten Cameron, who confronts her with the frustrated question, "Have you always been this selfish?" After a shamed pause, she answers quietly, "Yes." This Bianca allows herself to be chastened by her suitor and then attempts to mend her ways, having obviously learned some valuable lessons.

When Kat finally tells Bianca about her damaging sexual experience with Joey, Bianca confronts Kat with her own duplicity, asking Kat why she had never told of this before and insisting that this was not a valid reason for Kat to help their father keep Bianca hostage.

Bianca understands that this has been a house of damaging secrets and denial. Of the three remaining members of her broken family, she is the only one who accepts that her mother is gone for good and attempts to recapture some normalcy in a house of extremes. The symbolism in the film is subtle, but potent. Bianca wears her mother's pearls, emblem of maternal domesticity, which enrages Kat, who declares that they should not be worn at all and look terrible on Bianca. Clearly, Kat holds on to the expectation that her mother is coming home. Their father tries to hold on to his daughters so as not to lose them as he did his wife. Only Bianca knows that life must move on.

In one of the final scenes of the film, Bianca, like her counterpart in *Shrew*, proves more shrewish than her sister: she punches Joey Donner twice in the nose (once for making Cameron bleed, once for what he did to her sister) and kicks him in the groin, saying "and that's for me!" The next day, when Kat admits to her father that Bianca "beat the hell" out of Joey, she expects her father's censure: "What's the matter? Upset that I rubbed off on her?" Their father responds honestly, "No. Impressed." It turns out that Kat has succeeded in protecting her sister after all, by teaching her to be strong and to be herself. In the end, the audience sees the end of domestic containment, which had been maintained by both the father and by Kat, creates a closer, more unified family.

Thus, rather than the "dumbing-down of high culture to pander to and profit from the degenerate taste of the voracious and vapid teen audience," screenwriters Lutz and Smith and director Junger have created a skillful revision of the problematic *Shrew*, endowing Kat and Bianca with strength, intelligence, agency, and, perhaps most importantly, a voice. The two sisters have indeed been transformed into role models for women in the twenty-first century.

*In a 1983 speech, then President Ronald Reagan called for a Strategic Defense Initiative (SDI), otherwise known as Star Wars. This space-based program would strike down missiles aimed at the United States and was widely denounced as unrealistic, expensive, even foolish. Randy Fallows believes that George Lucas's* Star Wars, Episode I, The Phantom Menace *continues that critique.*

# *Star Wars Episode I:* The "Reagan" Menace?

Randy Fallows

As difficult as it is to feel sorry for someone with lots of money, artistic success, and millions of adoring fans, I feel sorry for George Lucas. Years ago, he made *Star Wars*, a film that shows the power of humanity over machinery when a young man armed only with a tiny space ship and a distilled version of Taoist philosophy overcomes a moon-sized weapon capable of annihilating a planet. But instead of making audiences aware of the foolishness of relying on technology to solve our problems, "Star Wars" became the nickname for the ultimate mechanical panacea, the Strategic Defense Initiative. To add insult to injury, President Reagan, who first proposed SDI, borrowed other terminology from the series to cash in on the collective resonance it inspired. The Soviet Union became known as "the evil empire," a huge bureaucratic machine that had to be kept in check by those homespun freedom loving individuals, the Jedi Knights of NATO. Much more recently, *The Phantom Menace* inspired an equally surprising response when some argued that it was full of offensive racial stereotypes. What must have made this response particularly upsetting to Lucas is that a closer viewing of his latest installment reveals that if anyone should have been offended, it should have been conservatives not liberals, for the political subtext of the film disparages both SDI and the man who introduced it to us.

However, this is not to say the film is all that good, even for liberals like myself. The plot is constructed with the hardcore *Star Wars* fan in mind, and as such it simply gives more of the same with few new insights or surprises. The film is the first of a three-part prequel to the original *Star Wars* trilogy which was released between 1977-1983, taking place an even longer time ago in that far, far away galaxy. Queen Amidala of the Naboo is taken hostage on her planet by the Trade Federation, a nasty group of capitalists who complain that their taxes are too high. Obi Wan Kenobe, a Jedi apprentice on the verge of graduating to full knighthood, arrives with his mentor, Qui-Gon Jinn, to try to resolve the conflict. They fail in this regard, but do manage to help the queen escape to Tatooine, a desert planet full of slave traders. There they meet young Anakin Skywalker who will later grow up to become the infamous Darth Vader of the original series. At this point, however, he's just a precocious kid who helps them repair their ship, so they can travel to the capitol planet to lodge an official complaint with the Imperial Senate. There they meet their representative, Senator Palpatine, who unbeknownst to them is actually Darth Sidious, the evil-dark-side-of-the-force-master who's behind all the trouble in the first place. He claims to want to help them, but only on the condition that they will support his bid to become first chancellor. That accomplished, he betrays their trust and secretly orders the Trade Federation to "utterly destroy" their opposition. Fortunately, however, before they can carry out this order, the good guys return and defeat the Trade Federation with the help of the Gungans, a less advanced fishy race, and, of course, The Force. Palpatine returns to "celebrate" the victory, letting young Annakin Skywalker know that he will be keeping an eye on him, thus moving the film to conclude like the first installment, with both a celebration and an ominous warning of things to come.

The film has all the familiar ingredients of the *Star Wars* formula: the cool Jedi knights doing amazing things with their light sabers, the extraordinary lad escaping from imposed limitations, a number of cute characters to please the younger viewers (and toy shop owners), and, most importantly, several extraordinary special effects. Yet while it recreates the mythological feel of the original series, it lacks the originality, humor, and character development. Had it appeared first, I doubt the series would have generated even half the interest that it has. So in general I have no quibbles with the overall critical assessment of the film, but I think that it is strange that with all the scrutiny it received concerning its lack of quality and its questionable stereotypes that no attention has been directed at its more progressive subtext, a subtext which attempts to disassociate *Star Wars* from SDI, and to attack the conservatives who made this connection in the first place.

As mentioned earlier, even in the original trilogy there are many places where promises of technological imperviousness get broken down, so in retrospect it is odd that SDI should be nicknamed "Star Wars." Nonetheless, the original series showed that it was very, very difficult to penetrate the enemy's defenses, a process which required a lot of help from The Force. However, in *The Phantom Menace* everyone's "strategic defenses" break down. First to go are the Trade Federation's when the Jedis, armed only with light sabers, manage to escape from the heavily guarded flagship. Shortly after, the Jedis lose their own ship's shields when they try to escape from the occupied planet. In the final battle sequence, the Gungans lose their shields, and the Trade Federation allows a child to stumble through and destroy theirs. In fact, the Achilles' heel of the Trade Federation is that they rely too much on technology, allowing their mechanical creations to fight their battles for them. Remember that all of these "people," even the Gungans, are light years ahead of us technologically, which should lead us to ponder the question that if none of them can construct an impervious shield, then how can we be expected to?

Of course, most scientists already acknowledge how unlikely it is that SDI could ever work. So why is it that taxpayers have allowed the Pentagon to spend over four billion dollars to develop it – and the permutations thereafter? Certainly, in part it is because of its association with *Star Wars*; both are fantasies, but they are fantasies that people want to believe in. The very words "Star Wars" conjure up hope that we can survive our own planet-wrecking weapons, hope that the technology used by freedom loving people can negate the weapons used by "evil empires." Arguments that appeal to the emotions, to collective pathos almost always trump those that appeal to the intellect (especially in post-September 11th America). Perhaps that's why Lucas shows so many instances of failing shields, to make it absolutely clear that there are no mechanical panaceas, neither in the *Star Wars*' galaxy nor in our own.

The film's strongest critical subtext, however, is not focused on SDI but on the man who first proposed it, President Ronald Reagan. There are several connections between the former president and Senator Palpatine (a.k.a. Darth Sideous, the future evil emperor). Many mistakenly labeled Reagan as a bad actor, when in fact the opposite was true. Though he cut programs for the poor, for students, for the environment, he always projected a kindly grandfather façade, appearing as a nice man who seemed to care for our collective welfare. Senator Palpatine also has these two sides to him, especially in his relation to Queen Amidala. On the one hand, he acts like a concerned father, smiling, warm, caring, but at the same time he is the hidden cause behind her concern, for it is he who secretly pulls the Trade Federation's strings, giving the order for them to take over her planet.

This is why I do not think that it is a coincidence that the relationship between Palpatine and the Trade Federation closely resembles Reagan's relationship with Iran. While Palpatine outwardly condemns the Federation, especially in how they take the Naboo hostage, he secretly collaborates with his supposed enemy, using them to advance his own power by accusing the current chancellor of being too weak, too tied up in bureaucratic procedures to take action. In the same way, President Reagan gained substantial support by criticizing how his predecessor, Jimmy Carter, handled the crisis with Iran, calling his political rival to task for being too weak, especially in the way he responded to the hostage issue. At the same time, Reagan, like Palpatine, would soon secretly collaborate with his outward enemy, by selling weapons to the Iranians in order to use the profits to advance his own political agenda without the knowledge or approval of the Senate.

In fact, the whole conservative agenda that Reagan set in place is reflected in Palpatine's political stance. First, he gets the Trade Federation riled up over having to pay high taxes, an issue that has been the cornerstone of almost every Republican campaign. To make this connection even more blatant, the head of the Trade Federation is named Nute Gunray, which sounds very similar to Newt Gingrich, the House Speaker who rose to power on anti-tax campaigns. The related conservative concern is their belief that the government is too big, resulting in an unnecessary bureaucracy where nothing gets done. When Palpatine makes statements like "our best choice would be to push for the election of a new supreme chancellor – one who can take control of the bureaucrats, enforce the laws, and give us justice," he sounds like Reagan in his 1980 campaign. Of course, despite all of Reagan's complaints about taxes and government spending, he ended up guilty of both, increasing taxes and spending more than all his predecessors combined, mostly on a massive military build up. With tour memory of storm troopers, battleships, and planet-wrecking stations from the original *Star Wars*, we know that Palpatine will soon do the same.

Finally, it's important to note that despite all the recent criticism of racial stereotypes, there is still a very strong endorsement for multiculturalism in the film. Palpatine is almost always surrounded by white males, he belongs to a race of Naboo who consider themselves superior to the other races on his planet, and he feels no compunction about giving the order to wipe out the "insignificant" Gungans. This contrasts with the actions of Queen Amidala. Although she also is a Naboo, she learns to regret her race's dismissal of the Gungans and begs their forgiveness for how they had been treated in the past. Furthermore, in contrast to Palpatine's entourage, the Jedi council, the undisputed good guys, are made up of the most imaginative assortment of creatures Lucas has yet put together. Throughout the film, he shows us the galactic races are stronger together than apart.

Perhaps one reason this subtext was too submerged for most people to see was that Lucas tried too hard to make the film fit the traditional *Star Wars* formula that served him in the past; the glitter of the overly cute, contrived characters and plot blinded people to the film's subtle political commentary. Perhaps if Lucas had studied the *Tao Te Ching* more carefully rather than just extracting nice sounding phrases to describe The Force, he would have come across one of the many maxims, which tell us success can be as hollow as failure. While the film's financial success must certainly be pleasing, it must bother him that it did very little to remove *Star Wars* from the political camp that continues to misappropriate it.

*In 1993,* Unforgiven, *a film released the year before, made a substantial impact on the award show circuit. Clint Eastwood, for example, won best director honors at the Golden Globes, the Director's Guild, and the Academy Awards. The film was also a box office success clearing $100 million, the benchmark of a hit in Hollywood terms. Critics were abuzz claiming that Eastwood had deconstructed the western. According to Clay Motley, however,* Unforgiven *ultimately reaffirms the western ethos.*

# "It's a Hell of a Thing to Kill a Man": Western Manhood in Clint Eastwood's *Unforgiven*

## Clay Motley

Upon my first viewing of Clint Eastwood's 1992 western *Unforgiven*, I was drawn to its aging, reluctant protagonist, William Munny (Clint Eastwood), because he seemed so different from traditional western and action heroes. Tired and remorseful, years removed from a bloody career as an outlaw, Munny appeared to be the opposite of the youthful and exuberant "hero" of traditional gunslinger movies who reveled in violence. I envisioned the film as a complex subversion of devices traditionally associated with the Western, such as the glorification of violence, the salvation of a helpless heroine, and stock heroes and villains. I was not alone in this belief: Sara Anson Vaux asserts that the film calls "into question any legendmaking that would glamorize or valorize violence" (445), and Michael Kimmel notes that as the film concludes with Munny killing his antagonists and thereby "reclaim[ing] his manhood," "we realize that it is a manhood that no one in his right mind would want" (325). This belief that *Unforgiven* approaches the familiar touchstones of the Western genre in an unfamiliar and somewhat subversive way was undoubtedly shared by many of the voters who vaulted it to the Academy Award for Best Picture.

After considering the film carefully, I have come to realize that *Unforgiven*, while retaining the complexity I suspected it of having, has none of the subversive elements. In fact, the elements of the film often noted as critiquing traditional notions of western manhood – such as Eastwood's portrayal of the aging killer-turned-unimpressive "pig farmer" William Munny – actually are the mechanics enabling the attainment of a manhood predicated on critic Richard Slotkin's redemptive violence and manly aggression. The bulk of the film appears to subvert our conception of western manhood only to allow for the vindication of Munny's manhood during the climactic ending. The audience is shown that when manhood is challenged, it is that very challenge which allows it to emerge triumphant, a fact particularly comforting for a contemporary male audience.

## "Real Life" and Domestication

The primary reason *Unforgiven* is often considered subversive to traditional forms of western manhood is that it portrays a fairly mundane picture of the usually mythologized West. It is not rare for reviewers to comment on the film's exceedingly "realistic" portrayal of its subject matter. Typically, when we describe something as "realistic," we are attributing to it the quotidian qualities and relative uneventfulness of our daily lives: it is something we can relate to in our average experiences rather than something fantastic. *Unforgiven e*arns the appellation "realistic" through its unglamorous view of western life when compared to most movies of the genre. For example, the once-wild gunfighters, Will Munny and Ned Logan (Morgan Freeman), have married and become farmers. The typical frontier town, in this case Big Whisky, Wyoming, doesn't allow guns anymore; current gunfighters, like English Bob (Richard Harris), are so scarce that they have hack writers following them around to distort the mundane truths of their lives into mythic fodder for an eastern reading audience. The next generation of gunfighter, represented by The Schofield Kid (Jaimz Woolvett), is a braggart who balks when violence becomes actualized. And when cowboys are gunned down, like the man Munny is hired to kill, it is while defenseless on the toilet rather than during a duel on Main Street.

We are witnessing in *Unforgiven,* then, a version of the West that conforms much more closely to our own subdued, unheroic modern lives than most Westerns do. It is a West that has lost its wildness and is modernized to the point of reconcilability. On the surface, these changes seem to challenge the mythic manhood of the western hero who typically proves his manhood violently in a glamorous and exotic setting. To this point, Jane Tompkins asserts that the feminized "feelings of triviality, secondariness, [and] meaningless activity" are "everything that readers of westerns are trying to get away from" (14). Some critics assume *Unforgiven* subverts traditional western manhood because so many of the markers of that manhood are missing or undermined. In actuality, the film invites us to identify with a world where heroic manhood has vanished – to see it as "realistic" and much like our own – so the audience's identification with the realized manhood of William Munny at the end of the story is all the stronger. The audience is not to view William Munny's progression from pig farmer to Western hero as something isolated and fantastic, but rather we are invited to see Munny's attainment of manhood in a "realistic" world as what is possible for all men when their manhood is challenged.

## Little Bill

This theme, the challenge to manhood, is presented in the first seconds of the film when the prostitute Delilah (Anna Levine) giggles at a cowboy's "teensy little pecker" and has her face cut up for it. Mirroring the Biblical Delilah's theft of Samson's power, the prostitute Delilah damages the cowboy's manhood by suggesting his virility is comical and inadequate. The cowboy lashes out at Delilah with his knife to redeem his injured manhood, establishing the pattern in which manhood is achieved through violence. Significantly, however, the cowboy is ultimately stopped and punished by the sheriff of Big Whisky, Little Bill Daggett (Gene Hackman). Little Bill, though unequivocally manly himself, is paradoxically the primary domesticating agent in the film. He is always stopping the development of manhood in others and is ultimately Munny's nemesis in his own quest for manly redemption.

Little Bill, in his role as sheriff, does not allow guns in the town of Big Whisky, and when people do come to town to for violent purposes, like English Bob and William Munny, they are quickly subdued and sent away from the town's peaceful confines. When the cowboy who disfigures Delilah is restrained, Little Bill refuses the prostitutes' calls for his whipping by asking, "Haven't you seen enough blood for one night?" Little Bill does use, on occasion, violence to control violent characters, but it is clear he prefers placid domestic life as he builds his new house, so he "can sit of an evening, drink [his] coffee, and watch the sun set." Therefore, an ideal Big Whisky for Little Bill would be a domesticated, civilized town: one with no violence, no guns, no outlaws, and one in which everyone stays at home watching the sun set (or at least allowing him to do so).

While it may seem paradoxical that Little Bill is both manly and the film's primary inhibitor of manhood, Bill's function is clear when we consider that Munny must eventually defeat a man to be a man. As Jane Tompkins notes, "Men prove their courage to themselves and to the world by facing their own annihilation" (31). Munny cannot achieve his manhood by besting Little Bill's scared and inept deputies. Instead, Munny must defeat his manly counterpart to fully regain his manhood. Little Bill dominates all other candidates for manhood in the story: Delilah's attacker, English Bob, and Ned Logan; he even gives William Munny a profound beating upon their first meeting. In other words, for the protagonist to fulfill his goal of reclaiming his manhood, he must not only thwart the source of domestication in the story, but he must also stand up to and surpass the only other viable man present: Little Bill represents both.

## The Kid and Ned

William Munny's partners, The Schofield Kid and Ned Logan, also serve important roles in the redemption of his manhood, but unlike Little Bill, it is their failure to achieve manhood that is significant. Lee Clark Mitchell observes that in Westerns "the failed man offers a foil against which the true man…can be measured" (167). The Schofield Kid taunts Munny and his seeming lack of manhood when he sees Munny on his pig farm, declaring, "You don't look like no rootin' tootin'…cold blooded assassin." And when Munny is convalescing after his beating at the hands of Little Bill, The Kid declares, "I told you I'm a damn killer. I done it before. I'm more of a killer than he [Munny] is anyhow." However, we soon learn that The Kid's boasts of previously killing five men are false when he breaks down after shooting his first person, an unarmed man on a toilet. The Kid's change in attitude is complete when afterwards he gives his gun to Munny, declaring, "You go on and keep it. I'm never going to use it again. I don't kill nobody no more. I ain't like you, Will." What we are supposed to understand that The Kid is not, is a man. With The Kid's relinquished gun, so much a symbol of manly virility and violence in westerns, Munny will, mere moments later, kill Little Bill and fulfill his own manly redemption. The Schofield Kid's disillusionment with violence is often noted as an important moment in the film's subversion of traditional western manhood; in actuality, his lying, verbosity, bragging, ineptness, and ultimate refusal to partake in violence, only highlights Munny's bedrock manhood.

Ned Logan's failed attempt at manhood stands even more starkly in relief to Munny's successful bid. Ned closely resembles Munny in that they were partners in their wild, violent youths; like Munny, Ned married and became a farmer, and, with Munny, Ned embarks on the mission to kill the cowboys and collect the prostitutes' gold. However, when Ned is presented the chance to finish off one of the men he has rode all the way from Kansas to kill, he balks. Significantly, Munny picks up Ned's rifle and kills the cowboy without any qualms while Ned can only stare at the ground. Thus, the failed men in the film reveal that manhood is very difficult to attain, and thus precious.

## Munny

Of course, the most important character in *Unforgiven's* portrayal of western manhood is William Munny himself. For much of the film, Munny is depicted as a hollow shell of the typical western hero. We see him, clearly aged, ineptly wallowing in the mud trying to separate pigs; later, he repeatedly misses when trying to shoot a can off a stump, humorously resorting to using a shotgun. Even though his wife died years before, he is still under her domestic influence, as he declares to his children, "Your ma showed me the errors of my ways." And most tellingly, Munny repeatedly has trouble mounting his horse, frequently being tossed to the ground after feebly attempting to mount. As John Cawelti notes, the western hero "is a man with a horse and the horse is his direct tie to the freedom of the wilderness, for it embodies his ability to move freely across it and to dominate and control its spirit" (57). Thus, Munny's clumsiness with his horse, and indeed with most actions we see him attempting, reveals a person clearly contradicting traditional modes of western manhood.

Most critics of the film take Munny's difficulty with such manly markers as firearms and horses to be unequivocal evidence of the film's subversion of manly ideals. However, Munny's difficulties only set the stage for his future redemption. As Mitchell explains:

> The frequency with which the body is celebrated, then physically punished, only to convalesce suggests something of the paradox involved in making true men out of biological men, taking their male bodies and distorting them beyond any apparent power of self-control, so that in the course of recuperating, an achieved masculinity that is at once physical and based on performance can be revealed. (155)

Thus, for manhood in westerns to be achieved, the male body must be challenged, beaten, convalesce, and recuperate to earn the mantle of manhood. It is the ability to persevere and triumph over hardship that is the mark of a man in the western.

And so it is with William Munny. The trials and tribulations that distinguish him as unmanly only set up the necessary hurdles he must conquer to be a true man. He can't ride a horse; he can't shoot straight; he is beaten nearly to death by Little Bill in Greeley's tavern. At this point, the discrepancy between Munny and ideal Western manhood is at its height, as the Schofield Kid is too happy to point out when remarking to Ned, "He ain't nuthin' but a broken down old pig farmer." Not only has Munny been badly beaten without even throwing a punch, but he has been bested by the sole masculine force in the story to that point, Little Bill. After the beating, Munny hovers near death as he convalesces in the tomb-like darkness of a shed for three days. At the height of this struggle with death, he even envisions his dead wife, with "her face. . .all covered in worms." Munny, however, emerges from this deathbed, reborn, into the bright morning air, with a fresh blanket of snow on the ground, now ready to assume his manhood. Soon, Munny does reclaim that mythic manhood as he kills five men nearly simultaneously at Greeley's – including Little Bill – but it is his long convalescence starting from the first time we see him as a pig farmer – and played out most dramatically after his beating by Little Bill – that makes his manly redemption possible.

## The Ending

The climactic shootout in Greeley's tavern is the full renaissance of western manhood in Munny and in the movie. Munny kills Little Bill, the one true man in town and its primary domesticator, along with four of his deputies. Notably, he does so in the same place where Delilah first laughed at the cowboy's manhood, in the very place where the movie's original threat to manhood was unleashed. Similarly, the final shootout is the only scene in the movie that conforms to what we recognize as typically western action: men shooting armed men in a public setting, such as a saloon. Although the movie may have shown us nearly two hours of manhood failing, we are left with the image of Munny's singular, triumphant figure riding out of Big Whisky on his horse, declaring to the people cowering in the darkness, "Any son of a bitch that takes a shot at me, not only am I going to kill him, but I'm going to kill his wife, and all his friends, and burn his damn house down!" This is the image of manhood *Unforgiven* ultimately leaves us with; Munny's previous tribulations only serve as a pedestal for him to mount to reach the crowning moment of his realized masculinity.

Importantly, during the shootout at Greeley's, Eastwood as director employs first-person camera angles that put the viewer in the perspective of Munny. We see the world through Munny's eyes as he rides into town past the sign proclaiming no guns in Big Whisky; we see the empty whiskey bottle being tossed to the ground, and we see a barrel of a rifle push the saloon doors open as Munny enters the scene of the killing. These camera angles, used only during the final scene, suggest that we, the viewers, are to identify with Munny during his reclamation of his manhood. The audience, at least the male members of it, is invited to believe that the reclamation of this manhood is not just Munny's, but all of ours.

This reading of the film is supported by Munny's actions after the shootout at Greeley's. We are told through a postscript that Munny settled back into his domestic life, but this time in the burgeoning town of San Francisco – the symbol of the urbanizing West – as he becomes a business man. This plot turn mirrors how we, the audience, will return to our domestic (sub)urban lives after the movie ends. But the film has left us with the reassurance that manhood is essential, and though a domesticated veneer may cover it, it can be summoned if needed.

This lesson that, even in the mundane routine of modern life, a virile manhood is waiting to be reclaimed seems particularly appealing to a contemporary male audience. As Mitchell points out, "We should recall that the emergence of the Western coincides with the advent of America's second feminist movement, and that the genre's recurrent rise and fall coincides more generally with interest aroused by feminist issues, moments when men have invariably had difficulty knowing how manhood should be achieved" (152). *Unforgiven's* popularity in the 1990s coincided with widespread male discomfort at a Clintonian American in which many men felt marginalized. Press accounts trumpeted tales of the "angry white male," who was lashing out due to a perceived loss of power. Affirmative Action, gays in the military, increased attention to sexual harassment suits, and women further pushing new social boundaries, all pointed towards a defensive feeling pervasive in a group of American men who usually are the audience for westerns. As Kimmel reminds us, "The breadwinner role left men feeling like cogs in the corporate machine, and conspicuous consumption in sprawling suburban shopping malls was hardly a compensation" (265).

Thus, *Unforgiven's* mix of the mundane and the manly, the "realistic" and the fantastic, stepped into this cultural moment, assuring its male audience that when manhood is cornered, threatened, it is only an opportunity, a stage, for it to emerge triumphant.

## Works Cited

Cawelti, John. *The Six-Gun Mystique*. Bowling Green, OH: Popular Press, 1970.
Kimmel, Michael. *Manhood in America: A Cultural History*. NY: The Free Press, 1996.
Mitchell, Lee Clark. *Westerns: Making the Man in Fiction and Film*. Chicago: U of Chicago P, 1996.
Tompkins, Jane. *West of Everything: The Inner Life of Westerns*. NY: Oxford UP, 1992.
*Unforgiven*. Screenplay by David Webb Peoples. Dir. Clint Eastwood. Warner Brothers, 1992.
*Vaux, Sara Anson*. "*Unforgiven*: The Sentence of Death and Radical Forgiveness." *Christianity and Literature* 47 (1998): 443-460.

*For the last several years, video games have figured prominently on the fiscal landscape grossing literally billions. The military, ever eager to tap into the youth market, has seen this popularity and tried its hand in the market. In "Playing War," Brian Cowlishaw investigates this phenomenon.*

# Playing War:
# Real Virtual Combat in Current Video Games

## Brian Cowlishaw

While video games have been around for some time now, they have emerged, in recent years, as a major player on the profit scene. Indeed, for the past few years, the video game market has made more money than the motion picture business. Perhaps that's why filmmakers often release video game versions of their films months before theatrical release – in order to heat up the marketplace for their film.

The latest trend in video games, such as the *Medal of Honor* series, the *Battlefield* series, and *America's Army*, is to be especially "realistic." Such games proudly transport the gamer into immersive, gut wrenching virtual battlefields. They persuade the gamer that, in an echo of WWII-era journalism, "You Are There" – on the beaches of Normandy, in the jungles of Vietnam, in modern military hotspots.

Upon examination, this now-common claim raises other key questions. First, and perhaps most obviously: To what degree is this claim to realism justified? In other words, are the games truly as historically accurate as their makers and players claim? Answering that question raises a series of more significant and telling questions: What do these games signify? Being war games, why are they so popular now? Who benefits from this popularity, and how?

The games that most stridently and persuasively claim to be realistic, and therefore those games on which I will focus, are first-person shooters (FPSs), which purport to recreate full-scale, real-world battles. For the uninitiated, the phrase "first-person" in "first-person shooters" refers to the player's point of view: onscreen appears a pair of forearms and hands aiming a weapon forward "into" the screen. The hands are "you." That gun is "your" gun. Players use controls (keyboard, mouse, and/or game controller) to virtually look up, down, and around onscreen, and the result looks and feels like brandishing a weapon. The word "shooter" in "first-person shooter" refers to what the player does: move around a "map" (virtual battlefield) and deploy an arsenal of weapons against virtual enemies.

*Unreal Tournament* provides clear examples of standard FPS conventions. One key convention is that weapons, ammunition, armor, and first-aid kits regularly and frequently "spawn," that is, suddenly appear out of nowhere. Simply running over them onscreen confers their benefits immediately; there is almost no time wasted simulating using the first-aid kits, or reloading the weapons. Second, all FPS players die a lot, even when they're winning. The goal is to rack up the most "frags," or kills, so how often they die is really irrelevant. Dead players immediately respawn at a semi-random spot on the map, then get right back to killing. Finally, FPSs revel in offering ungenteel, gore-intensive gameplay. Players can be slimed, shot, sniped, razored, exploded, or chainsawed to death onscreen. Bodies hit just right, with the right weapon, fly apart into bloody chunks of flesh.

Realistic war games are recent specialized offshoots of the broader FPS genre. The first FPS was *Wolfenstein*; *Medal of Honor*, published a decade later, probably the first realistic war game. This genealogical relationship – realistic war games' direct descent from FPSs – becomes apparent with close scrutiny. This genealogical relationship also means that while realistic war games are generally more realistic than other FPSs, they still retain significant unrealistic qualities.

One key unrealistic quality of putatively realistic war games might be called "self-assessment." Players have onscreen at all times thorough, accessible-at-a-glance information regarding their condition. They can see the status of their armor, their physical health expressed as a precise percentage, and their ammunition stores for every single weapon. Obviously, this level of self-knowledge is unavailable in real life. We may have a fairly keen sense of how healthy or unhealthy we feel, and if we have just had a blood or other test we may even be able to express this feeling with some precision. But this precision never approaches that in a FPS: we could never say, "I'm 81% healthy, and my clothes are providing 34% protection." Thus, for a simulation of war truly to be realistic, such information would have to remain vague or difficult to obtain. Yet there it is, right onscreen constantly in all of the new war games – just as in unashamedly unrealistic other FPSs.

Surprisingly, another FPS convention preserved by the realistic war games is respawning. For example, in the *Medal of Honor* games, when players die they are magically transported back to the beginning of the scenario, with all their original weapons and health restored, to try again. This makes sense not only from a games-history perspective, but also from an entertainment perspective: it's no fun if dying onscreen means the game is over. Players want to get right back up and fight some more. Obviously, though, real life does not work this way. Death tends to be final – but not in war video games.

Not only is death in this way banished from the games, but significantly, so is bodily dismemberment. Game makers systematically exclude it, much in the way Paul Fussell shows it was excluded from images and accounts of World War II. He observes that in such accounts, with very few exceptions, "the bodies of the dead, if inert, are intact. Bloody, sometimes, and sprawled in awkward positions, but except for the absence of life, plausible and acceptable simulacra of the people they once were. . . . American bodies (decently clothed) are occasionally in evidence, but they are notably intact." The famous photographic collection *Life Goes to War*, for example, shows only three dismembered bodies – specifically, heads. It is significant that they are not American but Asian heads. They are displayed as trophies of our soldiers' prowess. Always showing American bodies intact directly counters real-world factsand probabilities: as Fussell points out, it was "as likely for the man next to you to be shot through the eye, ear, testicles, or brain as (the way the cinema does it) through the shoulder. A shell is as likely to blow his whole face off as to lodge a fragment in some mentionable and unvital tissue." In fact, it was also quite common for a soldier to be wounded or killed not by a bullet or shell but by a flying body part – a foot, a skull, a ribcage.

Obviously, game makers could include such graphic details if they wanted to: *Unreal Tournament* displays gore galore. The technology for depicting dismemberment convincingly onscreen is quite capable nowadays, so clearly war game makers choose not to do it. They do in war video games what wartime journalists such as Ernie Pyle did in writing: purposely, systematically remove gory details so as to make the war more palatable – as opposed to more truly realistic. One of Pyle's best-known stories involves the return of the body of one Captain Henry T. Waskow "of Belton, Texas," to his grieving company. One of the men reportedly sat by the body for a long time, holding the captain's hand and looking into his face; then he "reached over and gently straightened the points of the captain's shirt collar, and then he sort of arranged the tattered edges of the uniform around the wound." As Fussell points out, Pyle's geographical and behavioral precision calls attention to the essential information that he glosses over:

> 1. What killed Captain Waskow? Bullet, shell fragments, a mine, or what?
> 2. Where was his wound? How large was it? He implies that it was in the traditional noble place, the chest. Was it? Was it a little hole, or was it a great red missing place? Was it perhaps in the crotch, or in the testicles, or in the belly? Were his entrails extruded, or in any way visible?
> 3. How much blood was there? Was the captain's uniform bloody? Did the faithful soldier wash off his hands after toying with those "tattered edges"? Were the captain's eyes open? Did his face look happy? Surprised? Satisfied? Angry?

Like wartime press reports, war video games carefully elide this most basic fact of wartime: bodily damage.

The most plainly unrealistic element of the war games is the existence of the games themselves. That is, players always remain inescapably aware of two very important facts. First, the war is never finally real. Players are not, in fact, dashing around a battlefield but rather sitting in a comfortable chair. They grip a controller, or keyboard and mouse, not a Garand rifle. There is no actual danger of being killed, or physically harmed beyond getting stiff and fat from playing video games too long. No matter how immersive or even realistic the game, one can never forget that it is "just a game." Second, players may play the game, but in an important sense the game plays them. There is always a "proper" outcome, a pre-scripted story one must complete correctly, especially when the game pits the player against the computer rather than against other flesh-and-blood players. There is always a specific task to carry out, such as to storm Normandy Beach and rout the Germans from their bunkers; the ideal for game programmers is to make such tasks challenging but possible. Players' job, then, is to find the correct solution to a puzzle someone else constructed; they are in a significant sense acted upon rather than acting. In life, of course, we can choose badly or well, but we can choose. This rat-in-a-maze aspect, together with the game's inescapable "game-ness," reminds players every moment that games fundamentally differ from real life; playing a game is inherently unrealistic.

Nevertheless, talk abounds regarding how realistic the current war video games are. *Official Xbox Magazine*'s comments on *Full Spectrum Warrior* are typical of the glee with which players and critics greet the newly "realistic" war games. The magazine effuses, "Now when you send your troops into a slaughter in *Full Spectrum Warrior*, you'll have to look in their eyes and hear their screams." Apparently this is a good thing. *OXM* also raves, "with [its] 5:1

[sound] it really feels like you are in the middle of a combat zone (turn it up loud enough and your neighbors might think so as well)." One fan anticipating *Battlefield: Vietnam*'s release on EBGames.com writes, "this will alow a more real taste of the war [sic]." Another, purporting to speak for all of us, claims, "U know how u always wanted to know what the Vietnam War was like [sic]. I think this game will show you."

There is some justification for these claims to realism. Sound is one area in which the new war games truly do reproduce wartime accurately. Sound effects are as accurate and inclusive as visual representations are sanitized and edited. The realistic war games – for example, *America's Army*, the *Battlefield* series, and the *Medal of Honor* series – reproduce all of the rumbling machinery, gunfire, artillery, explosions, footsteps, splats, ricochets, shouted orders, swearing, and wounded cries one would hear in a real war. And current computer/television sound technology – now standardized at seven points in the room – reproduces all these sounds with perfect clarity at 100+ decibels.

In addition to sound, the war games also reproduce historical circumstances with comparative accuracy. The games do allow players to virtually fight in battles that really did occur – famous ones such as the Normandy invasion, Pearl Harbor, and the Tet Offensive. In-game soldiers use weapons that look and perform more or less like real weapons that real soldiers used. In-game soldiers dress, look, and speak like real soldiers did. The games may not be completely historically faithful in these elements, but they certainly are more so than other, older FPSs. The genealogical relationship makes the newer war games seem more realistic than they are.

Compare any realistic war game, for example, with *Unreal Tournament.* In *UT*, the voices and character models ("skins") are a self-consciously over-the-top assortment of idealized macho warriors and ridiculous comic figures. In addition to the macho grunts, my copy features the downloaded voices of Fat Bastard (from the Austin Powers movies), Eric Cartman (from *South Park*), and Homer Simpson (from *The Simpsons*). Players can choose *UT* deathmatchers' appearances: onscreen fighters can be assigned any skin from a giant, scary lizardman, to a stereotypical macho male (or female), to Captain America, to Dr. Frankenfurter (from *The Rocky Horror Picture Show*). Any voice can be assigned to any skin: one might arrange a Dr. Frankenfurter with Cartman's voice, or a skull-faced villain who talks like Homer Simpson. These zany characters' weapons similarly aim for entertaining gameplay rather than factual accuracy. *UT* features rocket launchers, handheld frag cannons, plasma rifles, and sludge guns. The battles in which these crazy weapons are used take place on obviously artificial, nonreferential staging grounds. That is, the in-game battle sites are not intended to reproduce historical locations. They clearly exist solely so that players can virtually blast the hell out of each other in visually interesting, strategically challenging settings – and the more fantastic, the better. References to real-world locales tend to be ironic, humorous: "Hey look, here's a map like a football field!" "Here's one set on a cruise ship!" I certainly hope real deathmatches never take place in such locales. Classic FPSs, as opposed to realistic war games, are judged by how intense a deathmatch they can produce, not by how accurately they reproduce "the real Normandy."

Overall "presentation," too, proves comparatively realistic in the new war games. "Presentation" refers to the way a game is laid out for the player in terms of menu choices, art, and sound; we might call it "atmosphere." In *Medal of Honor: Frontline*, for example, menu choices take the form of file folders stamped with the (now-defunct) Office of Strategic Services logo. All in-game fonts look typewritten by period typewriters. "Your" portrait in the menu file appears attached by low-tech paper clip. Selecting a menu option produces a gunshot or file-rustling sound. In the *America's Army* game, menu headings use terminology lifted from the real-world America's Army: "Personnel Jacket," "Training Missions," "Deployment," and so on. This kind of attention to making the presentation realistic enhances the overall impression that the game accurately recreates history. Compared to the three-ring FPS circus that is their origin, the new realistic war games appear positively photographic in their historical fidelity. Even gamers, disposed by nature to find all flaws, perceive them as faithful to what the games purport to recreate.

So far, I have discussed two fairly black-and-white categories, "realistic" and "unrealistic," so that I can make descriptions clearly. But the truth is, the issue is much more complicated than that binary choice. It's more accurate to say that the games blur the boundaries between real and virtual, or mix elements of the one in among the other, so thoroughly that players finally cannot tell where reality ends and virtual reality begins.

One telling example appears in the required marksman-training mission that begins *America's Army*. The player must hit a specified number of targets within a time limit. After passing the test, the player receives hearty applause from the drill sergeant: "Congratulations, soldier! You have just qualified as a marksman in the United States Army!" I must admit: the first time I passed this test, I became moderately alarmed – he did mean I virtually qualified, right? So many other kinds of transactions take place online nowadays; why not real-life recruitment and qualification?

The idea that by playing a realistic war game for a few minutes I may have inadvertently enlisted is not as outlandish as it may seem out of context. Consider the fact that the real-world *America's Army* was created, programmed, and distributed for free online specifically for the purpose of recruitment. Anyone can download it for free, right now, at americasarmy.com. The real army counts on people, mostly young men ripe for recruitment, to download the game, enjoy it, think to themselves, "Hey, you know, I should do this for real," and then go enlist.

Apparently, the strategy is working very effectively. In late March 2004, the *CBS Evening News* reported on a huge *America's Army* gaming tournament. Hundreds of thousands of dollars in prize money and computer equipment were at stake. Several recruiters sat in the competition room. Hundreds of players walked directly from their round of competition over to sign up with recruiters. CBS reported that since the game was released in 2002, recruitment has spiked; the video game is the most effective recruitment tool since the Uncle Sam "I Want You" posters during World War II.

This video game recruitment strategy meshes very neatly with the Army's recent advertising campaign. The Army shows images of underage kids essentially playing games – flying a remote – controlled plane in one, and actually playing a video game in another. Then the same people (presumably) are shown as young adults doing pretty much the same activities in the Army: the model plane flyer pilots a decoy drone plane, and the video gamer efficiently directs real tanks and troops around a battlefield. The clear message is: "You should join the real Army because we will pay you to play pretty much the same games you play for fun right now. You were born for this."

*Full Spectrum Warrior* blurs reality and gaming perhaps even more thoroughly. Like *America's Army*, this game was produced by the real U.S. Army. In fact, it's not entirely clear that the end result was the choice of the game's original developer, William Stahl. In an interview with *Official Xbox Magazine*, Stahl describes how the game got made: "Three years ago, I was pitching a…game for the PC. Representatives of the Army were looking for a developer to create a training simulation on a videogame console. They got ahold of those early documents and thought the concept was right in line with what they wanted to achieve. …This game was developed in conjunction with the Army. They were essentially our publisher, and as such, they had the final say on what they wanted in the game, how it looked, etc." This statement raises worrisome questions:

1. How did the Army get "ahold" of those early documents"?
2. How much choice of publisher did Stahl and company actually have?

In any case, the Army ultimately made two versions, one of which is being used right now by real American soldiers for training, and a very similar version being sold in stores. Real soldiers and couch bound warriors alike learn battle tactics by playing a video game. Thus, the real and the virtual become indistinguishable. The U.S. Army recruits real soldiers by appealing to them through video games and suggests that video gamers' virtual prowess and enjoyment translate directly into real-world Army suitability and success.

In one important sense, the first-person-shooter genre itself contributes to this fusion of the real and the virtual. In recent years, in-game instructions have become standard parts of all FPSs and most video games in general; James Paul Gee explains in detail, in his book *What Video Games Have to Teach Us about Learning and Literacy*, how they help the player learn to "read" and understand the game, to figure out what to do in the game world. So, for example, in *America's Army*, the sergeant character gives the player basic directions to get started. He gives commands like, "Press <G> to fix jammed weapon," "Press <T> to bring up sights," and "Press <B> to reload." In doing so, he merges the player's onscreen and real-life identities. The sergeant is onscreen, talking to the player's onscreen representation, but he's giving directions that only the real-world person can carry out. The onscreen representation doesn't have a G, T, or B button to push – it's the real-world person doing that. Similarly, in *Medal of Honor: Frontline* the player is to "press Select to get hints from HQ," and "press Start to review mission objectives." In-game, players are spoken to as their real-world self and their onscreen self simultaneously and without differentiation, which means those identities merge.

With the real and the virtual mingling so thoroughly in war video games, perhaps it's only natural that both players and game makers reproduce and perpetuate this fusion in the way they talk. It's not some kind of schizophrenia or delusion, it's the ordinary, proper response to the postmodern facts. For example, imagining someone playing *Full Spectrum Warrior* with guns blazing rather than cautiously and strategically, William Stahl predicts, "His men will die. Mothers will lose their son, wives will lose their husbands, and children will lose their fathers." *OXM* also warns, "Don't press [the Action] button [in this game] until you've assessed the situation and made the right plan or it'll be the last button you press." Er, they do mean in-game…right? Thus, it's not so outlandish for the magazine to call *Full Spectrum Warrior* "The Game That Captured Saddam." *OXM* explains, "This game was made to train the US Army infantry…they're the ones who dug Saddam out of his hole. So technically this game caught Saddam." Nor is it as insane as it might first appear when one gamer writes in anticipation of playing *Battlefield: Vietnam*, "The Vietnam War was said to be a draw, but when this game comes out everyone will see that the U.S.A. is the best army in the world." His comment suggests that an alleged misperception of history – namely, that the U.S. did not decisively win that war – will be corrected by people's playing the game. He's epistemologically assuming, and rhetorically suggesting, that not only do video games refer to and simulate real-world battles, but because this is so, they also provide players an accurate recreative picture of history. In this understanding, war games not only borrow from history, they also teach it.

Many veterans' and historical organizations have bestowed awards on games such as the *Medal of Honor* series for their educational value. *Medal of Honor: Frontline*'s official sales copy at EBGames.com boasts, "Authentic WWII content with the assistance of the Smithsonian's . . . expert Russ Lee and renowned technical consultant Capt. Dale Dye," and, "The MOH team continues to work closely with the Congressional Medal of Honor Society to ensure the ideals and integrity of this prestigious commendation." Not incidentally, that game awards the Congressional Medal of Honor for especially meritorious military action – in-game. If players complete a given mission quickly enough and safely enough, they win a virtual medal. *MOH: Frontline* also unlocks documentary movie clips and historical speech excerpts as rewards for good performance in the game, and it mixes game elements, such as the game's logo and menus, and historical elements, such as documentary film clips and an exhortative speech by Dwight D. Eisenhower, without any differentiation of importance or validity. They all "feel real." Current war video games have blended and blurred the real and the virtual.

Because that is so, the games' romanticizing of war becomes all the more seductive and powerful. Any truly realistic recreation of war would cast some doubt on the idea that war is cool and enjoyable, and that, as in sports, all one has to do is "step up" and become an instant hero. But the titles alone hint at how current war video games support this old myth: *Call of Duty*, *Full Spectrum Warrior*, *Medal of Honor*. Players can almost taste the medals, just reading the game box. In-game, it immediately becomes clear that the war effort would never get off the ground without the player's personal, constant heroics. What the U. S. Army claims in its current advertising slogan is absolutely true: the player really is "An Army of One." Never mind the Army's famous unwieldy, illogical bureaucracy made famous in works such as *Catch-22* and *M*A*S*H*. Never mind the fact that boot camp is famously designed to tear down the individual to replace that entity with a small cog in a giant machine. Contrary to common-sense facts, the war game player is always "An Army of One." *Medal of Honor: Frontline*'s first mission provides a brilliant example of this. During this mission, "you" are ordered onscreen to storm the beach at Normandy under heavy machine-gun and rifle fire, provide covering fire for three soldiers widely separated along the beach, run lengthwise down the beach to an engineer then cover his run all the way back, cross a minefield, storm a machine-gun nest and take it over, mow down a wave of advancing German soldiers with that machine-gun, and finally snipe two far-off machine-gunners while still under fire. And that's just the first mission! What must the odds be that any individual would a) be present at D-Day; b) be asked to personally complete every single necessary task at that battle; and c) survive to complete them all successfully, thus winning that battle singlehandedly? The whole game continues like that: the player is assigned all the work at all the key European battles, eventually bringing about V-E Day completely solo.

This fact begins to answer the important question, "Why would someone want to realistically recreate the experience of war? Isn't it just common sense to avoid being there?" One game magazine editor raises exactly this question when he writes, "With the new wave of games pushing the envelope of realism it begs the question: how real do we want it? Do we want games that'll simulate war to such a degree that it's possible to suffer from post-game-atic syndrome?" Judging by the state of the games now, the answer for both gamers and game makers is a resounding "No." For all their attention to accurately recreating sounds, weapons, locales, and uniforms, and for all their visual drama and flair, the new "realistic" war video games do not, in fact, reproduce the real conditions of war. They still play too much like other FPSs, and significantly, like goreless FPSs. Although players see soldiers being blown into the air by mines, riddled with machine-gun fire, and sniped from all directions, they never see blood or a flying body part, ever.

Thus, I would argue, what the new war games are is not realistic, but cinematic. They don't reproduce the real world experience of war; they do reproduce the theatrical experience of war. Games use all of the same techniques as movies for framing shots, editing, pacing, and narration. Playing one of the new war video games is very much like starring in a war movie. For example, the *MOH: Frontline* opening mission is a rather accurate, if condensed, version of the first thirty minutes of *Saving Private Ryan*, even down to individual camera shots: bullets whizzing along underwater past slowly sinking soldiers, and the company's seeking cover under a low hill while the engineer blows away the barbed wire barrier. *Medal of Honor: Rising Sun* similarly steals heavily from the much less well-made movie Pearl Harbor. H. L. Mencken once described art as "life with all the boring parts taken out." War has been described as 99 percent boredom punctuated by short bursts of abject terror. No one in their right mind would want to reproduce that, and, in recent war video games, no one does. Instead, the games are, in essence, interactive movies about war with all the boring parts taken out. But the boring parts were already pretty much taken out by the movies, so in the games, all that's left is action, action, action – the player winning a war single handedly. The war games make players heroes, in a bloodless, risk-free environment where they can show off their "mad skillz."

As it turns out, then, logical answers do exist for the question, "Why in the world would anyone want to recreate the experience of war?" First, the games don't do quite that; rather, they recreate movies about the experience of war. The additional remove is key. Playing the games provides an entertaining, cinematic experience, rather than the horrible one a true recreation would give. Even if the imagery is not pleasing, it certainly is immersive. And as Miroslaw Filiciak points out, we value the experience of immersion in itself. We intentionally overlook unconvincing elements of the experience so as to become more fully immersed: "We desire the experience of immersion, so we use our intelligence to reinforce rather than to question the reality of the experience." In short, it doesn't really matter that the war games aren't fully realistic; gamers enjoy them for what they are, interactive movies that temporarily immerse us in the games' battles. The second answer to the question, "Why would anyone want to recreate the experience of war?" is to play the hero, in a cinematically intense experience in which we can play an active part rather than just settling passively down into our couches and watching as movies force us to do. And third, we get to see ourselves onscreen playing the hero. Filiciak observes: "Contemporary people have a fascination with electronic media, something we cannot define, something that escapes our rationalizations.... We make the screen a fetish; we desire it, not only do we want to watch the screen but also to 'be seen' on it...being on the screen ennobles. All the time we have the feeling (more or less true) thatothers are watching us. The existence of an audience is an absolute necessity." We can see "ourselves" onscreen in any video game, but in online war games such as *America's Army* and *Battlefield: Vietnam*, we can also be seen by other players. We can show off our skills, and brag about our victories, to others who have just witnessed them. We can enact the electronic equivalent of dancing in the end zone.

The reasons for making the new war video games are even more obvious than those for playing them. Foremost, there's the money. As I mentioned at the beginning of this article, Americans now spend more money on video games than on movies. Games are huge business, and they're steadily getting huger. One key game maker, the real-world U.S. Army – and by extension, the other service branches and the federal government as a whole – reaps huge benefits from the games' popularity. Not only does the current hawkish regime gain flesh-and-blood recruits for the armed services, it also gains general credibility and support as the games work their propagandist magic. By hiding ugly realities and producing cinematic cotton candy, the games make real war seem exciting, heroic, even fun. And so hawkish political candidates seem not bellicose, but reasonable. Rapidly escalating defense costs look not wasteful, but common-sensical. Thus our two-front war rolls on and on and on.

*Alarmed by the cultural messages surrounding the images of Asians and African-Americans on the popular television show* American Idol, *David J. Leonard and Carmen R. Lugo-Lugo examine these messages and show us what they say about the current state of racism in America.*

# Welfare Queens, Model Minority, and Racialized Bodies: Lessons from the Third Season of *American Idol*

David J. Leonard and Carmen R. Lugo-Lugo

In hindsight, the televised auditions for the third season of *American Idol* foretold the makings of a show that would be replete with lessons about twenty-first century race relations in the U.S. (including special illustrations of the new racism as described by Eduardo Bonilla-Silva). These lessons began with the audition of William Hung, a young Asian American college student with absolutely no musical talent who converted this lack of skills into an immense amount of popularity. Hung's audition – and its aftermath – compelled us (a white, American man and a Puerto Rican woman) to watch the show more seriously, in order to garner greater understanding of the racial text within *American Idol.* This interest became a point of academic or pedagogical inquiry (and obsession), as other events unfolded in the show, including the vote that put three black women (collectively known as "the three divas") in the bottom three of the competition. Despite widespread belief that these three women represented the show's best talent, voters gave them the least number of votes, resulting in the dismissal of one of them: Jennifer Hudson. This moment, along with the William Hung phenomenon, Fantasia Barrino's election as the third *American Idol*, and the significant protest/discussion that ensued after each event, revealed the power of this show as a contemporary racial text and its function as a cultural space where ideologies disguised as entertainment are constantly recreated.

The racial (and racist) overtones of the third season of *American Idol* culminated, on May 26, 2004, after a much-dragged-out results show, when Ryan Seacrest announced to millions of American viewers that Fantasia Barrino had been voted the new *American Idol*, the third Idol in a period of two years. Barrino, a nineteen-year-old, black, single mother from High Point, North Carolina, defeated sixteen-year-old Diana DeGarmo, a white teenager from Snellvile, Alabama. On that date, Fantasia Barrino became the first African American woman to hold thetitle of *American Idol*, and Diana DeGarmo became the first "all-American girl" runner up. Moreover, since then, the producers of *American Idol*, Fox network, and those paying attention have witnessed one of the biggest controversies surrounding the show.

This paper explores the pervasive manifestations of and provides tools to analyze white supremacy in U.S. popular culture, by way of the Fox powerhouse show. We will pay special attention to three aspects of white supremacy: colorblindness, meritocracy, and the demonization and fetishization of racialized bodies. Though these are not the only traits of white supremacy in our post-Civil Rights era, we decided to focus on these three particular aspects of contemporary expressions of white supremacy ideologies, for, in our view, they are the most pervasive elements (especially as they are manifested in contemporary expressions of popular culture). In order to talk about these expressions of white supremacy, we will focus on the way two particular events associated with specific contestants unfolded: William Hung's audition and its aftermath and Fantasia Barrino winning the competition. Concentrating on how these two events (and the contestants associated with them) were treated, portrayed, marketed, and talked about in the third season of the show, we can begin to see the workings of demonization, fetishization, colorblindness, and meritocracy, pillars of contemporary expressions of white supremacy (see Bonilla-Silva, *Racism without Racists* and *White Supremacy and Racism*). We go beyond flat discussions of representations or images in a purely textual analysis to interrogate the ways in which dominant discourses, ideologies, and struggles infect and play through the production and consumption of *American Idol* (see Omi and Winant). We examine the sharp and distinct ways in which the bodies of these contestants were unable to transcend their own racial signifiers, putting into questions the predominant arguments of colorblindness and a merit-based society. We reveal how neither Hung, nor Fantasia Barrino, despite their celebrity and celebration, were able to outrun the racial inscriptions onto their respective bodies: as a model minority/nerd in the case of Hung and single black mother in the case of Barrino. Despite numerous claims of colorblindness and hyped celebrations of meritocracy, we argue that fan reaction to, and the representations and positioning of both William Hung and Fantasia Barrino were over-determined by the racialized status of their bodies.

Specifically, we contend that *American Idol* represents a contested space of racialized meaning; a place where advocates of meritocracy, colorblindness, and the efficacy of the American Dream resist examples of racism while simultaneously participating in new manifestations of post-civil rights racism (see Bonilla-Silva, *Racism without Racists* and *White Supremacy and Racism*). Thus, the show becomes a place where the racialized bodies over-determine the celebrations and condemnations of contestants, whereupon their bodies are read through dominant tropes and discursive fields, whether they be those of Asian model minorities or single black mothers. Our discussions of the participation of William Hung and Fantasia Barrino on *American Idol* attempt to give "notice to the unnoticed and to interrogate the taken-for-granted" (Whannel 11). As part of a society drowned in talks of colorblindness and meritocracy, *American Idol* represents a contested space of racial meaning that reinforces hegemonic ideas of race, at the same time that it manages to reinscribe Asian masculinity as passive, black femininity as aggressive, *and* racism as obsolete in the twenty-first century. Our discussions never stray far from power, in terms of the ways white supremacist discourses (in the form of fetishization, colorblindness, and meritocracy) reify white privilege at the expense of its impact on communities of color (see Johnson and Rothenberg). As Robert Ferguson reminds us, issues of representation are, undoubtedly, questions of power. In his words: the "ways in which relations of power and subordination are signified with particular reference to media representations of 'race' need to be set alongside questions about individual or other forms of identity" (5).

Moreover, we demonstrate that the contest does not merely take place around the next American idol or even the predominant vision of twenty-first century race relations within the United States, but over the more concrete meanings of blackness, whiteness, and Asianness. *American Idol* does not merely provide a competitive reality show to which contestants battle for the approval of fans and judges, but a cultural terrain in which individuals and (racist) ideologies compete to define the meaning of race within contemporary America. Thus, as any other cultural text, *American Idol* offers interpretations, representations, and explanations of race, meritocracy, colorblind ideologies, post-civil rights America, whiteness, and the nature of American race relations. Disguised as a mere television show, *American Idol* is a space that engages in and deploys dominant American discourses, ideologies, and racial dynamics. As Douglas Kellner suggests, "the artifacts of media culture are thus not innocent entertainment, but are thoroughly ideological artifacts bound up with political rhetoric, struggles, agendas, and policies" (93). We are not talking about the banality of popular culture or about examining shows exclusively based on entertainment, but about an ideological project that provides explanations to race, gender, sexuality and a host of other hegemonic ideologies (see Omi and Winant, Giroux, Giroux & Giroux).

Before we go on, we would like to say that while never wavering from our positionality as academics or avid watchers of the show, we are not writing this paper because we secretly love and watch the show (though we do both) nor are we treating it as a simple academic exercise. Rather, our discussion of contemporary expressions of white supremacy alongside a discussion of the struggles over the meaning of racism and race provide a pedagogical moment to "make knowledge meaningful in order to make it critical and transformative," while simultaneously "intervening into contexts and power…in order to enable people to act more strategically in ways that may change their context for the better" (see Giroux & Giroux 101; Grossberg 143; see also McLaren, hooks, and Kellner). Given the popularity of *American Idol* and the significant racialized discourse that infects and surrounds popular culture in general, it is crucial to interrogate the ways in which racial meaning is (re)conceived, (re)deployed, challenged, (re)worked and ultimately reified.

## Meritocracy, Colorblindness, and *American Idol*: The Case of William Hung

In one of the initial episodes during season three (the auditions), in which contestants vie for the opportunity to move to Hollywood to compete for the crown of *American Idol*, William Hung, an Asian American college student from UC Berkeley, launched his "career" with a ghastly rendition of Ricky Martin's "She Bangs." Off key, out of tune, and screaming each note, Hung made us either laugh or feel sorry for him. Neither Randy Jackson nor Simon Cowell, two of the show's three judges, could contain their laughter. Amazingly, his dancing was even more precarious than his singing.

While Cowell and Jackson offered several insults guised as professional critique, Hung stood with a look of joy, telling the judges that he did his best, only hoping that he touched the hearts of million of watchers. As William Hung was one of many obviously tone-deaf *American Idol* contestants, we assumed that his three minutes of fame had ended at the conclusion of that episode. However, after this initial appearance, websites dedicated to Hung sprang up. At one point, typing his name on google.com produced nearly one million hits with dozens of fan sites, discussion groups, and petitions of support. Specifically, Hung was often praised for his love of music, for his selflessness, and for his desire to make people happy. For example, after appearing on the show, Hung became a folk hero at UC Berkeley; his peers could not get enough of him. "I'm in love with William Hung," noted Student Action SenatorLauren Hubbert, adding: "It's fantastic…that's the kind of determination you don't see everyday and I think a lot of people appreciate that" (qtd. in Lin). On multiple fan websites, similar remunerations appeared with fans describing him as having "great spirit," a "wonderful attitude," and being "sweet," "humble," "genuine." Others went so far as to link his work ethic and humility to his academic success in that his lack of talent reflected his focus on school rather than music, making him that much more appealing. One writer even noted how he could not do many interviews because he was too busy studying. The focus on his intellectual abilities, and his humility, as something of an anti-celebrity happy to "make people laugh and smile," embodies the discursive articulations of Hung as model minority. Even his critics invoke model minority discourse, noting that his fame reflected his brilliance and intelligence, which served him well as he found ways to convert his talentless body into a hot commodity.

The outpouring of love and adoration evident on the Internet prompted a return appearance on Idol, a performance at a UC Berkeley volleyball match, and visits to *Good Morning America*, *The Today Show*, *Ellen*, and *Jay Leno*. As contestants continued to battle for the ultimate crown of American Idol, and the all-important record contract, Koch Records had already put Hung under contract. His album, which included covers of "I Believe I Can Fly," "Hotel California," "Rocket Man," "Y.M.C.A," and, of course, "She Bangs," was released on April 6, 2005, debuting in the top thirty, amassing sales of over 30,000 albums.

While his fans raved about his genuine outlook, gumption, and "scrappy underdog" mentality, all playing on signifiers of body, his popularity cannot be understood outside of a discussion on race and gender. Many commentators have specifically cited his acceptance as evidence of the insignificance of his Asianness. Alan Grumblatt, general manager and executive VP called William Hung "the perfect artist for our culturally diverse society. He is the new Elvis" (qtd. in Guillermo). Sharon Mitzota agreed, reclaiming Hung as an alternative vision of Asian masculinity.

> Hung has struck a chord with so many, not just because he fits into a familiar stereotype, but because he showed fortitude, and yes, grace, in the face of rejection. It was his humility, not his race that made him stand out from the parade of crybabies and divas churning through the *American Idol* machine. Despite his awkward appearance, voice and dance moves, Hung dared to put his dream to the test. He may have been delusional, or simply naive, but he *tried*. And then, when he failed, he took it "like a man."…We laugh at Hung because he's inept, accented, and awkward, and we admire him because he's brave, self-confident, and a little bull-headed (all masculine traits). In combining the feminized Asian American with the self-reliance and fortitude of a "man," Hung embodies a new kind of male ideal.

While recognizing the potential for stereotypes and "racist love," Oliver Wang, like Mitzota, questioned the single-minded focus on racism: "He enters the media spotlight and lets it all hang out. His earnestness, call it naiveté if you insist, can be painful to watch, but it is also what Hung contributes. Far from the one-dimensional cartoon his critics paint him as, Hung comes off instead as vulnerable, confused, optimistic, and joyful, all at once." He goes on to say: "'It's good to be Hung,' because to be Hung means admitting to your limitations, knowing that some will laugh at you, but boldly striding onto the stage anyway. It's as complex and inspiring a portrait of humanity as one could hope for, and truly, when was the last time we've seen that in any American idol, Asian or otherwise?" Each, to varying degrees, argues that Hung, like other racialized "artists" (Jay-Z, J-Lo, and MJ all come to mind), transcends the limitations of his racial identity.

As popular culture commentators and music executives celebrated his popularity as evidence of racial transcendence and the fulfillment of the "American Dream," others found less to celebrate linking his popularity to a history of racism, American minstrelsy, and Orientalism. David Ng and Emil Guillermo both offered scathing diatribes against Hung's fifteen minutes of fame, each focusing on the racist context of Hung's fanatical reception. Jimi Izrael even called him an "American Sambo" noting there is nothing worthy of celebration in Hung's stardom: "Hung fits into a stereotype, and his audition seemingly gave some permission to revive it. The goofy, buck-toothed dancing Chinaman hasn't persevered like some other Sambos, but Hung's rise to popularity proves that it ages well." Ng specifically linked Hung's popularity to longstanding constructions of Asian sexuality, "For Asian Americans, Hung represents everything we don't want to be seen as (foreign, nerdish, a joke), and thus his oddball fame reinforces our own happily assimilated identities." In his estimation, representations of Hung and the fanfare that resulted from his performance reflected a hegemonic willingness to embrace and celebrate an Asian American male who fulfilled dominant expectations regarding Asian American masculinity. Whereas Hung fulfilled longstanding western discourses that imagine Asian masculinity as that of the "feminine," of "weakness," of "submissive" woman, his celebrity was over-determined by the meaning and significance of his body, especially in juxtaposition to both the imagined white and black bodies of contemporary American popular culture (Eng 1, 18).

Despite the hegemony of discourses of colorblindness and meritocracy, both of which have been inscribed in the course of the William Hung spectacle, the representation and positioning of Hung has not erased race (ism) from the scene. Although the comparison offered by Ng lacks complete synchronicity with the history of African American minstrelsy, his focus on body, on the ways in which popular culture markets bodies of color by dehumanizing and mocking them and by turning them into profit and pleasure, is crucial in comprehending the continuity of new racism. Mainly, just as blackness or the site of a black male body over-determines audience reception or public engagement, so too did William Hung's Asianness.

America's love affair with William Hung reflects a historic taste for the savage, buffoon, and otherwise laughable other. With African Americans, this historically took the form of the coon, often a white actor in black face whose stupidity always matched his gullibility and difficulty with the English language. Similar to the Jim Crow stereotype, the Zip Coon, or the Red Man, John Chinaman represented the hegemonic image of Chinese immigrants an inassimilable racialized other, who despite every effort could never overcome an insurmountable cultural difference. As noted by Robert Lee, Asian Americans have long been demonized through popular culture, as the pollutant, the collie, the deviant, the yellow peril, the model minority, and the gook," all of which have rendered Asian Americans as "alien body and a threat to the American national family" (8). While each of these representations is historically specific and unique in their visual orientation, they collectively mark Asians as an inassimilable "other." Specifically, the presence of Asian minstrelsy or Yellow face through the history of popular culture marks "the Oriental as indelibly alien. Constructed as a race of aliens, Orientals represent a present danger of pollution" (Lee 2).

Throughout U.S. history, the physical and cultural signifiers of Asians (including Orientalism) have required surveillance and control from the state and dominant institutions. Despite the widespread celebration of William Hung by commentators and fans alike, Hung follows in this tradition, embodying virtually all of these images, demonstrating the absurdity of colorblind rhetoric.

William Hung certainly fulfills the longstanding images and stereotypes of Asians as an infantilized, incompetent, and feminized (impotent) male, who will never assimilate. In both celebration and condemnation, online discourses and fans alike fixated on his body, on his voice, on his inability to dance, as a nerdy Asian male. In other words, both the demonization and fanfare focused on the beauty or disgust resulting from the performative "power" of his Asian body. The commodity of William Hung cannot be understood outside white supremacist ideologies that have perpetually castrated the Asian male. Nor can he be understood outside images of Asians as heavily accented and having bad teeth, bad hair, and bad clothes. On eBay, shoppers can buy t-shirts of a cartoonish Hung, buckteeth and all, with "She Bangs" inscribed below it. Beyond embodying a clownish representation, the absurdity of Hung rests with a nerdy Asian man "banging" anything. William Hung, thus, fulfills white fantasies of Asian men as non-threatening, asexual, and backwards, serving as the basis of our laughter/love (see Lee and Lott). America does not love William Hung purely because of his attitude or his dreadful singing, but because the history of popular culture is a story of love, contempt, and yearning for the exotic and the buffoonish "other," whether he is Tonto, Amos, Andy, Stepin Fetchit, or William Hung.

The minstrelsy effect in William Hung's popularity is never more evident than with his music video for "She Bangs." Mimicking Martin's own video, Hung is surrounded by scantily clad women whose breasts overwhelm the screen. However, unlike in the majority of music videos, including that of Martin, Hung shows little interest in the women, keeping his distance. In fact, in a documentary chronicling its production, Hung's mother puts her foot down on several occasions, forbidding any contact between her son and these women. She even instructs the director to provide her son with a raincoat for a particular scene in which he is supposed to get wet with a group of women. Thus, he wears a raincoat in the scene, while several women dance in erotic ways. The sight of a singing William Hung wearing a raincoat as the wetness sexualizes the women is striking. The video undoubtedly plays into the idea of the model minority who not only tries hard in spite of limitations, but also repels cultural pollutants (see Abelmann and Lie, Lee, and Takagi). His popularity or lovability is very much connected to this infantilization, feminization, and desexualization, all of which are wrapped up within white supremacist ideologies and the history of racist representations of Asians within western popular culture (see Lee).

More importantly, both those who celebrate (the era of colorblindness) and those who condemn (the persistence of American racism) the William Hung phenomenon ignore his positioning within a larger discourse of popular culture and race, in which blackness has come to signify the artistic, moral, and political stench of the entertainment world, where bodies on the basketball court or through hip hop have come to signify and embody all that is wrong with popular entertainment. Whether it be scantily-clad, hip-hop divas or the physically intimidating and tattooed arms of any number of black athletes, American popular cultural discourses are increasingly demonizing bodies of color as pollutants, as source of denigration, and as invading and diseased cultural bodies. Frustrations with artists who ignore fans, who over-indulge in excessive materialism, or who promote misogyny often come through denunciations of blackness. The celebration of Hung as pure, as motivated by heart, and as a breath of fresh air not only bespeaks to societal frustration with millionaire entertainers of color, but Hung also functions as a model minority. While writing about a different context in the Los Angeles riots, Nancy Abelmann and John Lie encapsulate the interconnectedness between model minority, racism, and the condemnation of blackness:

> The American dream presents a problematic ideal of individual life and community. More crucially for our purpose, however, the constellation of attitudes and institutions that constitutes the American dream has found a powerful articulation in the contrast between the model minority and the urban underclass: Korean Americans embody the American dream, while African Americans betray its promise. The ideological constitution and construction of the "black-Korean conflict" should alert us not only to the importance of the broader political economy but also to the necessity of rethinking dominant American ideologies. (179-180)

We can say that ultimately, although America's love affair with William Hung is a love of (laughter at) his accent, buckteeth, and his asexual interaction with women – his imagined Asian masculinity, more broadly, reflects a fascination for the incompetent, yet happy, racialized other. His popularity embodies an anti-blackness (i.e. bling-bling, arrogance, and hypersexuality) as it reflects his position as a model minority within popular culture. He, unlike the black entertainer, does it for the love of singing, of making people happy. So as others celebrate William Hung, citing his Asian American fans as proof against racism, let us remember history, minstrelsy, and the manner in which racialized constructs of blackness, Asianness, and whiteness all emanate from popular culture, an ever-evolving cultural force. One of the central features of new racism, especially as it relates to American popular culture, is the simultaneity of commodification and demonization, of rhetoric of celebration and denunciation, which is most certainly evident with the positioning and reaction to the emergence of William Hung. Yet, to truly understand this process, we must remain focused on bodies, on the ways in which racialized meaning is inscribed onto "bodies of color," and the ways in which the signified meanings contribute to a hegemonic common sense. With William Hung, both celebration of his stardom, of his work ethic, and his ability to capitalize on his talents, and denunciations that focused on his unmasculine, nerdy, and asexual physical presence reveal the powerful ways in which his racialized body predicted the possibility of his fifteen minutes of fame and, of course, its conclusion.

## New Racism in *American Idol 3*: The Controversy over Fantasia Barrino's Election

The controversy over *American Idol 3* intensified after the final results, when Fantasia Barrino was proclaimed the new Idol. Mainly, those opposing Barrino's election became highly vocal about their (op)position. One avenue these folks used to express their views was the community forum in the official *American Idol* website. These postings are important because they recreate historical notions (and ideologies) of race relations even as these same chatters embraced the legitimacy of their own and society's colorblindness, a central tenet of the new racism in the U.S. Moreover, an analysis of this lone website elucidates the profound way in which race impacts and is situated within American popular culture, revealing how this fan site does not merely serve as a site of debate over the strengths and merits of individual contestants, but a space in which ideologies over the meaning of race and race relations are disseminated and sometimes challenged. In this case, and similar to the case of William Hung, Fantasia Barrino's black and female body served to rehearse contemporary notions of racism. We will use a few examples to illustrate this point.

Though varied and numerous, the messages posted revolved around one underlying theme: Fantasia's race and gender. Given the pervasiveness of meritocracy and colorblindness, we would expect the discourses within the community forum to embody these prevalent ideologies exclusively. However, we found that, along with manifestations of a new kind of racism, old rhetorical tools were also employed, when/if folks felt (or their whiteness felt) perhaps threatened (see Gilroy and Collins). As we will show, the postings in the *American Idol* community forum deployed both old and new racial(ized) discourses. We found that the majority of the discussions fell within three overlapping frames: Fantasia's attitude (mainly, chatters complained about her perceived arrogance); Fantasia's mannerisms (she was frequently described as animal-like); and Fantasia's status as a single mother (the welfare mother stereotype was consistently deployed by chatters to argue against her being voted that year's American Idol). These three topics camouflaged (rather precariously) objections to Fantasia's race. Moreover, these topics revealed the powerful imagery invoked by the black female body, especially when it validates dominant discourses of single black mothers.

Interestingly, many of the postings loyally followed the new racism script, by sprinkling the discussion with versions of the "I'm not a racist but…" statement. (For an in-depth description of this element of the new racism, see the works of Bonilla-Silva). For instance, here is a reaction from one of the chatters to Barrino's crowning as the new American Idol. In his/her words:

> Well I can honestly say that I hope Fox goes off the air because that Fantasia Barinno won and I hope she just shut's [sic] Fox down all together. She has the worst singing voice I have ever heard I would have been happier if Osama Benladen [sic] won this stupid competition. This is the worst season of American
>
> Idol I have ever seen and I also know that it will be another Clay and Ruben scenario. Diana will do a hell of a lot better than Fantasia. The only reason that Fantasia won is because (and I'm not a racist I swear) she had all the black people voting for her!!!!!!!! DIANA IS THE REAL AMERICAN IDOL!!

The "I'm not a racist I swear" statement corroborates Bonilla-Silva's research on racism after the civil rights era. The statement is used to validate an otherwise scathingly racist statement, but since, in this case, the person swears not to be racist, then the statement is supposed to be unbiased and, of course, true. Also, by alluding to American Idol's second season, the person establishes a history in which his/her racist ideologies have developed. That is to say, "another Ruben and Clay scenario" is supposed to imply that runner up Clay (who is white) has been more successful than winner Ruben (who is black) because Clay is the real *American Idol*, even though Ruben won. Looking at the historical treatment of the female black body in this country, it should be no surprise that this person prefers (socially constructed terrorist) Osama Bin Laden to a black American woman (see Collins and hooks, *Black Looks* and *Outlaw Culture*). Though different from the constructions of Hung's male Asian body discussed above, constructions of Barrino's female black body also follow the racialized and racist social script. In this case, different from the "friendly" and un-intimidating male Asian body, the female black body is ridden with threats to white supremacy. Thus, the same racism that turned William Hung into a caricature of Asianness alsoturned Fantasia Barrino into a dangerous and representative body of blackness in the U.S. Of course, in the case of Barrino, she is a representative of a bigger threat: the black community. In this respect, the viewer invokes the "blacks stick together" age-old ideology as a justification as to why Diana was not voted in as the new idol. According to this mentality, blacks will vote their own in, regardless of whether the person is "qualified" or not, as opposed to whites, who will presumably base their unbiased votes exclusively on merit. This logic, of course, ties into contemporary discussions of Affirmative Action programs, which are regarded by many whites as anti-merit (i.e anti-white) efforts to advance blacks and leave whites behind. Thus, according to this aspect of the new racism, whites are associated with true and impartial practices (based, undoubtedly, on meritocratic ideals), something that blacks are not able to do, because they lack impartiality and "stick together" instead.

Meritocracy was consistently invoked by way of race. For instance, this person offered that Barrino's election as the new American Idol could only happen if the show was rigged:

> [All in caps] This contest is sooooo setup I dont [sic] even know why I watch it anymore. Other than the first season, all of the sucky singers are winning. Is it because the producers feel so bad they cant [sic] sing they let them win or do the winners just pay off the producers to let them win either way it is setup. Plus I also think they are being raced to[o] since only African Americans can win and nobody else.

There are a few interesting aspects to this chatter's post, all of them involving race, racism, and meritocracy. For instance the "sucky singers" this person is alluding to are black singers (who won seasons two and three). Kelly Clarkson, the winner from the first season (whom the person seems to approve in the statement "other than the first season"), is white. What's interesting here is that the posting does not say anything directly negative about blacks themselves. In fact, the person uses the politically correct term "African Americans" to describe these contestants. The implication that blacks are cheaters (they "pay off the producers") or the pathetic subject of pity ("the producers feel so bad they can't sing they let them win") plays directly into historical stereotypes in the U.S. of blacks as untrustworthy and child-like being.

Though still playing into racialized discourse, other "fans" were a bit more measured in their statements and tried to divert the attention from Fantasia as a black singer to Fantasia as a black person/woman. For instance, here is what one fan had to say about Fantasia's personal life:

> My biggest problem with Fantasia, however, does have to do with her being a single mother. I don't have a problem with the fact that she is a single mother or that dropped out of high school. That's not my beef. My problem is that she is neglecting her responsibility as a single mother to her daughter.

We wonder if this person feels the same way about soldiers fighting in Iraq (including single moms), or parents who decide to go back to college or to graduate school, or about single white mothers who have to work all day to make ends meet. In the end, this kind of statement is very similar to statements made by white people as to why they are "uncomfortable" with interracial marriage: "the kids are the ones who suffer" (see Bonilla-

Silva, *Racism without Racists* and *White Supremacy and Racism*). Thus, diverting the attention away from Fantasia's merits as a singer, this chatter is objecting to having an American Idol who is not taking care of her child, and thus questioning Barrino's very right to be part of the competition, and thus her right of becoming the American Idol. Race, in this instance, was, of course, the underlying text, as we are all too familiar with discourses about (neglectful and/or irresponsible) single black mothers.

As it is to be expected, Fantasia's "personality" was also part of the discussion and produced one of the biggest exchanges in the community forum. An integral part of race relations in the U.S. involves recreating perceptions of racialized groups and systematically deploying them to explain the behavior of members of those groups. Here is one example of a posting in which Fantasia is described in a way historically used to describe blacks in the U.S.:

> I dislike her personality! She seems arrogant and rude. Her attitude really turned me off to her. Dianna is gracious and classy! I dislike her voice…she often seems as though she is screaming. In my opinion, she does not have the voice of an American Idol.

Again, given the history of perceptions of African Americans in this country, we could have predicted that a self-assured black woman would be accused of behaving with arrogance and being rude, two descriptors often used to describe blacks in the U.S. What is also interesting about this posting is the direct comparison made by the person between Fantasia's "arrogance" and "rudeness" (two words usually used in reference to black bodies) and Diana Degarmo's "graciousness" and "classiness" (two highly coded words, used often to describe white women). We have further insight into the mind of this person when she follows her previous statements with the following comments on Fantasia's status as a single mother:

> I don't believe that an unwed teen mom should be the role model for teens. She made bad choices [in] life and should not be rewarded for them…I thought using her child was in very bad taste. I also found it very disturbing and selfish that she would leave her young daughter for months to persue [sic] her dreams, a child needs her mother.

Similar to the person claiming that Fantasia was neglecting her child by participating in the competition, this person also indicates that Fantasia's place was not in the competition, but with her child. However, this person takes it a step further and questions Fantasia's status as a role model for teenagers. Also, in an interesting rejection of meritocratic ideals, s/he sees Fantasia's election as "reward" for her "bad behavior" (i.e., having a child in her teens, and without a husband), not as a reward for her hard work and talent (which would be the response that meritocracy dictates). A similar sentiment was expressed in the following posting:

> Congratulations America! You have voted in a high school dropout and unwed mother for your childrens [sic] American Idol role model! I hope all your children follow in her footsteps and give grandma lot's [sic] of little BoBo's [sic] to support. Oh, I'm sorry, I mean taxpayers! Way to go America!

Another person suggested that maybe *American Idol* executives should have tighter screening processes. The person created a laundry list of what s/he does not like about Fantasia to suggest that maybe those are things that need to be "screened" for future installments of the show:

> I can't stand her voice. Her rudeness at the beginning of the competition. The "in your face" look she gets after she sings. Being a single teen mother! High school dropout. The flouncing she does on stage. I can go on. I just think the idol qualifications need to be stricter.

After reviewing the "laundry list" provided by this person, we realize there really is little the producers could do about things like "voice," "perceived rudeness," and "flouncing on stage." We wonder if by suggesting that qualifications need to be stricter the person is really arguing that blacks (with an attitude) need to be weeded out early in the competition. The "flouncing" on the stage critique was made by many, every single comment containing particular racial connotations and racist overtones. For instance, here is what one person had to say about Fantasia's performing style:

> I just feel that Fantasia likes to jump around like a wild animal on stage and when she can't hit a high note, she shouts "yeah, yeah, yeah"… Fantasia acts as if she was just let out of a cage. She needs speech classes and needs to carry herself a little better. More people may respect her.

The comparison between Fantasia (a black woman) and animals (i.e. "she jumps around like a wild animal," and "Fantasia acts as if she was just let out of a cage") is alarming, though highly disingenuous if we again think of historical notions of the black body as not fully human (see Collins, Marriot, hooks, *Black Looks and Outlaw Culture*). These arguments serve to illustrate how, in times of the new racism, explicit connections are not necessary, for the rhetoric has become sophisticated enough to allow for tacit (re)constructions of racialized bodies. The person need not say "because Fantasia is black, she jumps around like a wild animal," for at this point, the "she jumps around like a wild animal" implies her blackness. As with many of the postings, the final sentence of the statement is key, for the person is suggesting that if Fantasia stops "acting like an animal," maybe more people would respect her. We are left to assume that those people gaining respect for a less animal-like Fantasia would be white people, who would "respect her more" if she stopped acting "black," including talking "black."

Sometimes the coded statements were not so coded. Here is an example of a Diana fan who also concludes that the competition was rigged:

> [Diana] was robbed everyone knows it. If I were Diana I would ask for a recount of the votes. The producers messed with her earpiece so she wouldn't win this hole [sic] show was planned out from the start. Diana deserves to be the winner not a[n] ugly unwed dropout girl.

An "ugly dropout girl" says it all. In this case, the association of blackness with ugliness, presupposes beauty with whiteness. Moreover, this juxtaposition of beauty and ugliness suggests that beautiful (white) should always win and ugliness should always lose. Thus, this "argument" does not specify what makes Diana more deserving to win the competition other than her whiteness. Following the logic of the argument, Diana deserves to win, not because she has more merits, but because she is not an ugly, unwed mother. Insofar as blackness is coded as ugliness and unbecoming behavior, whiteness then is coded as deserving and beautiful.

Of course, some postings were outright blatant, as if they had come out of a 50's KKK rally or a contemporary white nationalist website. In these kinds of postings, we find not even the slightest attempt to use the more subtle, new racism language. For instance, here is what a person replied to a Fantasia fan, who (without identifying racially) was arguing that Fantasia won the competition fair and square, because of her talent and her hard work (i.e. because of merit): "Take your bootlip family and head back to Africa and be with the monkey's [sic]." The assumption that all Fantasia fans were black (because again, "blacks stick together"), suggests that not only the rhetoric of new racism allows room for old-fashioned blatantly racist rhetoric, but also that a seemingly innocuous talent show can reproduce embedded notions of race wars and racial competition.

## *American Idol*, Blindness, Merit, and Race Relations in the U.S.: Final Thoughts

*American Idol* demonstrates that even though discourses surrounding the myth of merit are alive and well, in many instances these discourses mask a new kind of racism (as discussed by Bonilla-Silva) in which ideals of merit are intertwined with a not-so-colorblind colorblind ideology. The workings of these ideologies are evident in the public's reaction to the third season of *American Idol*, and they become even more significant when we realize that, as a cultural artifact, *American Idol* is a reflection of the larger society. Fantasia's election as the third American Idol may lead some to argue that meritocracy is alive and well in the U.S. After all, critics, the judges, and an overwhelming number of those watching the show considered her the best singer of the season. Thus, her election as the *American Idol* may indicate that the right qualifications, along with hard work, do pay off. Simon Cowell's constant effort to rebuff accusations of racism with persistent references to her victory, always noting that in the end the most talented (qualified) person secured the crown of American Idol, reflects the discourse of reaction and the manner in which meritocracy and race seek to trump accusations of racism. However, as we discussed above, there were key aspects leading to Barrino's election that directly contradict meritocracy, such as the craze over William Hung and the treatment of the "three divas."

In the absence of Klan rallies and Jim Crow signs, racism is often difficult to both define and locate within contemporary discussions (see Gilroy and Omi and Winant). Responding to hegemonic discourses dismissing contemporary manifestations of racism, scholars have recently written about a "new racism" that is defined less by overt forms of racial discrimination, with an increased level of visibility and representation of people of color, but by a series of codes and colorblind tropes all of which maintain white supremacist discourses and societal organization (see Collins and Bonilla-Silva, *Racism without Racists*). The deployment of colorblind language and emphasis of "not seeing any color" does not reflect American reality in that "racial considerations shade almost everything in America" (Bonilla-Silva, *Racism without Racists* 1). This point is clear in the way Barrino is described by most of the chatters as African American (an ethnicity, not a color), although the message was clear: she was less deserving of the crown because she was black. Even though *American Idol* saw no racial slur (at least not before Barrino's election), the contested meaning of race or racism sits at the center of its textual renderings and societal importance. In each instance, fans, commentators and participants demonstrate the ways in which *American Idol* functions as a space of ideological struggle over the importance and meaning of racism, colorblindness, meritocracy, and the universal availability of the American Dream, as well as the dynamic meaning of blackness (black femininity), Asianness (Asian masculinity), and whiteness. *American Idol* is not merely a weekly talent show that allows fans to vote for the ultimate American Idol, but a means and mechanism to express, legitimize, or challenge hegemonic notions of race.

As if to prove internet critics wrong, in July 2004, Fantasia's single "I Believe" reached number one on the Billboard Hot 100 singles and tracks chart, something that neither season two's winner Ruben Studdard nor Season three's runner up Diana Degarmo have accomplished thus far. Regardless of how many compact discs Fantasia is selling, however, we can say that while participating on *American Idol*, she "pushed some buttons," not necessarily because of her talent, but because of her status as a single black woman. Thus, even though we live in a different era from the one in which Jim Crow laws ruled race relations in the U.S., at times we find ourselves subject to similar discourses of that era, supplemented with new (more subtle) racist techniques (colorblindness, meritocracy, etc.). That is to say, the old ideas of blacks' racial inferiority or sub-human status, or those about un-masculine Asian (male) bodies, for instance, have not completely left the U.S.'s collective unconscious. In fact, they are still very much present in the images and messages we get from popular culture. As a racial project, a cultural artifact, a contested space of debate, a discursive field embodying the deployment of colorblind rhetoric in the face of accusations of white supremacy, *American Idol* represents a powerful text of inquiry. From season one, with the popularity of Kelly Clarkson (white) over Tamara Gray (black), to the persistent visibility of Clay Aiken (white) over Ruben Studdard (black) the winner of season two, to the third season with William Hung (Asian), "the thee divas" (who were black) and Barrino's victory marred in white supremacist rhetoric, *American Idol* does embody a post-civil rights racial discourse. Offering a text to which we could explore the interplay between race, meritocracy, colorblind rhetoric and televisual representation through both popular, liberal, and white supremacist medias, our analysis demonstrates the powerful ways in which constructions of race infects contemporary popular culture. Documenting the persistence of racial meaning within *American Idol*, as well as the powerful discursive field that surrounds its reception, with accusations and denials of racism, our effort sheds light on the nature of contemporary racial discourses, while providing analytical tools and demonstrating the importance of engaging in a pedagogy of popular culture toward anti-racist media literacy based on critical multiculturalism.

Finally, we should place this analysis within the larger context of race relations in popular culture. In his new book, *Scripting the Black Masculine Body: Identity, Discourse, and Racial Politics in Popular Media*, Ronald Jackson maps out the longstanding practices of controlling, demonizing, and policing black male bodies as part of an American white supremacist project.

> The reservoir of negative inscriptions of the Black body is very extensive. No one book can claim to catalogue all the examples of racially inscribed bodies. From early black corporeal inscriptions established during slavery and minstrelsy to more contemporary inscriptions within cinema, television, and music, at least one aspect is common to all – black bodies have been thingafied, socially rejected, and treated as foreign to the American ethos. (44)

He most certainly could be writing about Asians, Latinos, or Native Americans, as white supremacy has been and continues to be about profiting from, surveilling, owning, consuming, determining, defining, and ultimately controlling othered bodies. Building on the work of Robyn Wiegman, Kobena Mercer, Frantz Fanon and others, Jackson argues that white supremacy not only infects representations and those associated discursive fields of meaning, but the way in which we view these bodies as well. As he tells us, a white gaze "is a spectacular event, a tool for examining sites of obsessive desire that admit the visibility of difference, but remained troubled by it" (10). The celebration and condemnation of both Hung and Barrino not only reveal the power of race despite claims of meritocracy and the ways in which their racialized bodies over-determined their representation and positioning, but the ways in "which corporeal zones such as that of skin color and hair texture automatically evoke the feelings, thoughts, perhaps, anxieties," functioning within this new racist moment (Jackson 10). In the end, it is important to keep in mind that the text presented by Fox's *American Idol* is a (re)creation of the text we can find in the larger society, and the forces that produce discourses of buckteeth and accented Asian men as funny "creatures" are the same that produce discourses of irresponsible, unwed black mothers as a burden to society. Thus, in early twenty-first century American popular culture, we can find vestiges of early twentieth century ideologiesmerged with a new understanding of race, that is to say, a new and enduring racism.

## Works Cited

Abelmann, Nancy, and John Lie. *Blue Dreams: Korean Americans and the Los Angeles Riots.* Cambridge: Harvard UP, 1995.

Bonilla-Silva, Eduardo. *Racism without Racists: Color-Blind Racism and the Persistence of Racial Inequality in America.* New York: Rowan and Littlefield, 2003.

----. *White Supremacy and Racism in the Post-Civil Rights Era.* Boulder: LynneRienner Publishing, 2001.

Collins, Patricia Hill. *Black Sexual Politics: African Americans, Gender and the New Racism.* New York: Routledge, 2004.

Eng, David. *Racial Castration: Managing Masculinity in Asian America.* Durham: Duke UP, 2001.

Ferguson, Robert. *Representing 'Race': Ideology, Identity and the Media.* New York: Oxford UP, 1998.

Gilroy, Paul. *Against Race: Imagining Political Culture beyond the Color Line.* Boston: Harvard UP, 2001.

Giroux, Henry, and Susan Searls Giroux. *Take Back Higher Education: Race, Youth, and the Crisis of Democracy in the Post-Civil Rights Era.* New York: Palgrave-Macmillan, 2004

Giroux, Henry. *The Abandoned Generation: Democracy Beyond the Culture of Fear.* New York: Palgrave-Macmillan, 2003.

Grossberg, Lawrence. "Toward a Genealogy of the State of Cultural Studies." *Disciplinarity and Dissent in Cultural Studies.* Eds. Cary Belson and Dilip Parameshawar Gaonkar. New York: Routledge, 1996.

Guillermo, Emil. "William Hung: Racism or Magic?" *Sfgate.com.* 6 April 2004. http://www.sfgate.com/cgibin/article.cgi?file=/gate/archive/2004/04/06/eguillermo.DTL

hooks, bell. *Killing Rage: Ending Racism.* New York: Outlet Publishers, 1996.

----. *Outlaw Culture: Resisting Representation.* New York: Routledge, 1994.

----. *Black Looks: Race and Representation.* Boston: South End Press, 1992.

Izrael, Jimi. "What It Iz: William Hung, American Sambo." *Africana.com.* 17 March 2004. http://www.africana.com/columns/izrael/ls20040317hung.asp

Jackson, Ronald. *Scripting the Black Masculine Body: Identity, Discourse, and Racial Politics in Popular Media.* New York: State of New York UP, 2006.

Johnson, Allan G. *Privilege, Power and Difference.* New York: McGraw-Hill Publishers, 2001.

Kellner, Douglas. *Media Culture: Cultural Studies, Identity, and Politics between the Modern and the Postmodern.* New York: Routledge, 1995.

Lee, Robert. *Orientals: Asian Americans in Popular Culture.* Philadelphia: Temple UP.

Lin, Rong-Gong. "Elect William Hung!" *Daily California* 20 February 2004: 1A.

Lott, Eric. *Love & Theft: Blackface Minstrelsy and the American Working Class.* New York: Oxford UP. 1993.

McLaren, Peter. "Multiculturalism and the Post-Modern Critique: Toward a Pedagogy of Resistance and Transformation." *Between Borders: Pedagogy and the Politics of Cultural Studies.* Eds. Henry Giroux and Peter McLaren. New York: Routledge, 1994. 192-222.

Mitzota, Sharon. "Can the Subaltern Sing? Or Who's Ashamed of William Hung?" Popmatters.com. 4 May 2004. http://www.popmatters.com/tv/features/040504-williamhung-mizota.shtml

Ng, David. "Hung Out to Dry." *Village Voice* 6 April 2004: http://radio.villagevoice.com/issues/0414/ng.php

Omi, Michael and Howard Winant. *Racial Formation in the United States: From the 1960s to the 1990s.* New York: Routledge, 1994.

Rothenberg, Paula. *White: Essential Readings on the Other Side of Racism.* New York: Worth Publishers, 2002.

Takagi, Dana. *The Retreat from Race: Asian American Admissions and Racial Politics.* New Brunswick, NJ: Rutgers UP, 1992.

Wang, Oliver. "Full Circle: No False Idol." *San Francisco Bay Guardian* 21 April 2004: http://www.sfbg.com/38/30/x_full_circle.html

Whannel, Gary. *Media Sports Stars: Masculinities and Moralities.* New York: Routledge, 2002.

*Far from pure, objective news, cable news channels, Jonathan Morris argues, impose a sensational melodramatic narrative structure onto their stories in an effort to increase ratings.*

# Car Crashes and Soap Operas: Melodramatic Narrative on Cable News

## Jonathan S. Morris

In Late April, 2001, a young California woman, scheduled to arrive home from an internship in Washington, DC, vanished. This disappearance was not particularly unique in the context of a missing persons case. Across the nation, hundreds of young women vanish every year with each individual case bringing little national attention. The parents of the missing intern were understandably distraught and contacted the police to file a missing persons report. Because they were an affluent family, they hired a private investigator, which is common under such circumstances. Then, less common to be sure, the parents of the missing intern hired a public relations firm (Nolan).

The intern, Chandra Levy, was allegedly involved in an intimate affair with a married congressional Representative, Gary Condit (D-CA). The parents of Ms. Levy, through their public relations firm, strategically leaked information regarding their daughter's relationship with the Congressman in order to keep the story in the news and increase the chances of finding her. This strategy contributed toward creating a news story that unfolded in the media over the course of several weeks, especially on the cable news stations, which devoted countless hours to covering and discussing the circumstances surrounding the Levy disappearance.

The Levy case was, to say the least, dramatic. There was a dynamic cast of characters, mystery, suspense, allegations of sexual impropriety, political intrigue, and a gut-wrenching tragic sense surrounding the entire ordeal. Cable news stations, particularly Fox News, CNN, and MSNBC, featured this story with theatrical flair as the major news event of the summer. These stations did not simply cover the drama of the Levy story, they accentuated and perpetuated it, thus creating a melodramatic narrative. This approach obviously worked from a ratings perspective, as the audience share for each channel increased dramatically from the same time one year earlier.

This essay argues that, in the modern media era, the cable news stations pursue melodramatic narrative as a strategy for attracting a larger share of the audience. I also discuss the specific elements of melodrama in cable news stories and discuss possible consequences. My argument follows from the 1981 work of David L. Paletz and Robert M. Entman who note that news stories lacking compelling drama will "have drama grafted on" (16). Likewise, in his 1988 discussion of general news coverage in America, Lance Bennett states, "The trend toward ever more dramatic and entertaining news may mean that a new form of mass communication is emerging. This evolving communication form may still go by the term 'news,' but it would be a serious mistake to assume that the traditional meanings of that term still apply" (37).

As Bennett predicted, cable news has become increasingly theatrical. With striking frequency, cable news producers and reporters turn political and social events into melodramatic stories with multiple plot lines, conflict, tragedy, a dynamic cast, and even the possibility of redemption. Tabloid style titles and themes are now assigned to the stories: "The Search for Chandra," "The Search for Natalie" (referring to the Natalie Holloway disappearance in Aruba), and "Democracy in Crisis" (referring to the 2000 Presidential election and Florida recount). In addition to creating melodrama, cable news stations have also employed the use of audio and visual effects to grab the attention of passive television watchers. One journalist noted, "The [cable news] networks now generally use a 'whooshing' sound to precede an on-screen headline. There is far more frequent use of the words 'Breaking News' or 'News Alert,' even for events that in the past would not have called for urgent treatment. The technique is used largely to catch and keep channel surfers" (Rutenberg, "War or No").

Even when stories are inherently dramatic, such as the aftermath of September 11th, the war in Iraq, or the recent disappearance of twelve coal miners in West Virginia, cable news sources have become impressively adept at perpetuating and even accentuating the drama. Before the 2003 Iraq war, for example, the stations devoted energy toward soliciting viewers ahead of time using the impending drama as an enticing factor. Journalist Jim Rutenburg observes that "each channel is trying to distinguish itself and outdo its rivals. And because cable news success often seems to rest as much on the presentation of the programs as the journalism itself, executives are looking for different production twists to enhance their war, and prewar, coverage. As a result, the reports are taking on a hypercharged tone as the cable networks try to persuade viewers ahead of time that they are the ones to watch should war break out" ("War or No").

Another journalist argued, "These days, it's hard to tell when you're watching *Inside Politics* (CNN) and when you've tuned in to *Melrose Place*. Both feature unhealthy quantities of lust, lies, betrayal and adultery, though the latter has more believable scripts" (Chapman). This is certainly overstating the case, but it does illustrate the growing belief that cable news coverage is now heavily focused on accentuating the dramatic. The goal is to highlight intriguing plot lines that viewers are compelled to follow, much like fictional programming, but with the flare of reality.

This is not, of course, to say that cable news channels crave carnage or conflict in the pursuit of highlighting the dramatic. Clearly, the journalists covering recent disasters such as Hurricane Katrina were upset by the devastation, hardship, and loss of life – as were all Americans. But cable news producers have also learned from past events and understand that ratings increase when dramatic events unfold. When nothing dramatic is transpiring, ratings slip. Thus, when drama is not present, it is created. We can see an example of this phenomenon in the media firestorm surrounding the "runaway bride" in 2005.

## Car Crashes and Soap Operas

In the pursuit of melodramatic narrative, cable news often creates a news product that is unsettling for viewers, often featuring crime and personal anguish. Although this coverage can be troubling and sometimes disturbing, it appears as though the public cannot look away – much like staring at a car crash. Also, many Americans are acquiring the habit of consulting the twenty-four hour cable news stations for frequent updates on how the aftermath of the "car crash" is transpiring – much like viewers might tune in daily to a soap opera.

In the summer of 2001, survey data from the Pew Research Center indicated that the public did not show much interest in coverage of the disappearance of Chandra Levy. The survey report, titled "Missing Intern Stirs Media Frenzy, Lukewarm Public Interest," argued that less than half the public was closely following the news on the search for the former intern (16 percent very closely, 33 percent fairly closely), a number much lower than many major stories of the past and present. Indeed, the report even indicated that the Levy story was not even the biggest story of the summer. Andrew Kohut, Director of the Pew Research Center made the argument that "the vast majority of the public is put off by coverage of these stories once it becomes so extensive as to be inescapable for viewers…One can only question the wisdom of alienating a large percentage of a public that now has the ability to screen out the news it does not want."

One puzzling question arises from Kohut's accusations: Why, then, do cable news stations' ratings skyrocket when dramatic or melodramatic political events are accentuated in the media? In July 2001, cable news networks saw their ratings go up significantly from the preceding year (CNN grew 44 percent, MSNBC was up 19 percent, and Fox News increased by 136 percent). Interestingly enough, the cable news channel that saw its ratings increase the most, Fox News, came under scrutiny for covering the Levy case with the most intensity (Kurtz and Rutenberg, "Cable's Instinct").

If the public is so fed up with cable's style of coverage, as Kohut argues, why does its use continue to rise? Although the public may not admit they like melodramatic news, they are drawn in by continual updates and storyline twists which create compelling, addictive entertainment.

## Elements of Drama on Cable News

Drama on cable news takes several forms. First, the stories are personalized. The human element is the driving force behind melodrama. The introduction of identifiable characters is necessary for the viewers of a melodrama to relate on a human level. Political events often do revolve around one or a few individuals, and coverage of such events are given a great deal of overall media attention. In recent years, however, it has been recognized that the media go out of their way to focus coverage on individual actors instead of policy and process. Often, journalists will forgo covering the important issues to focus on the dynamics of personalities (see Fallows, Lichter and Amundson, and Rozell). While this trend is certainly evident in all media, it is particularly present on cable news. Because cable news is interested in *hooking* the audience into actively following long-running stories, they work to develop the characters involved. In this sense, cable news providers will not only spend a great deal of time covering stories that involve significant individual characters, they will also work to personalize stories in which individual actors are not so identifiable. Most cable news viewers are very familiar with photos and video footage of Natalie performing with her high school marching band, as well as Joran van der Sloot's drinking and gambling habits. In political news coverage, budget battles and debate over the more mundane public policy issues often are covered on cable not from a policy or process perspective, but rather as a conflict between competing personalities, George Bush vs. Ted Kennedy, for example.

A second element of melodrama in the news is the use of the scandalous and sensational. Viewers are not typically drawn to the ordinary or mundane. Instead, compelling melodrama relies on the unexpected and extraordinary. Incorporating such elements into news coverage draws the viewer in and compels him or her to follow the story as it unfolds. The tendency to gravitate toward the scandalous and sensational is present in all of today's news (see Fallows; Mann and Ornstein; Sabato; and Sabato, Stencel, and Lichter). Cable news stations, however, have found that intense and prolonged focus on scandalous events typically leads to increased ratings. Therefore, the scandalous and sensational events are more intensely covered on cable than in traditional news. As Rutenberg noted during the Condit affair, "In the dual world of Condit-saturated television, there is, on one side, Dan Rather of CBS barely reporting the Levy case, on principle. On the other are the cable new networks, which seem to be talking about almost nothing else all day, even though the police say that Mr. Condit is not a suspect" ("Cable's Instinct"). The nature of scandals and sensational events provide the perfect material for melodramatic narrative as we have seen in the Duke lacrosse rape case. Cable providers have also capitalized on the opportunity to make non-stop coverage of political scandals a major aspect of their political news coverage as well. Such news as Patrick Kennedy's driving accident while under the influence of prescription medicine dominates the cable cycle.

The third element of melodrama in the news is conflict. Conflict is the most basic and necessary component of a dramatic story. Drama cannot exist without conflict between groups and/or individuals. Of course, it is not difficult to find conflict in many of today's newsworthy events. In fact, it is often the conflict itself that makes the event newsworthy. To heighten conflict, anchors such as Greta Van Susteren will bring on panelists who are sure to disagree and argue with each other during the show.

Negativity stems from conflict in the cable news environment and is the fourth aspect of its melodramatic coverage. To maintain a desired level of melodramatic conflict in their news coverage, the journalists will often approach a story with a very negative, even cynical, tone. Partly, this negative approach is the result of the past cable journalists being left out of the inner circle of high-powered reporters and decision-makers, which consists primarily of political elites and traditional journalists (see Davis and Owen). In recent years, however, the cable news personalities have gained a great deal of power and legitimacy and thus have forced their way into ranks similar to that of traditional journalists. The negativity, however, remains primarily due to the fact that it perpetuates melodramatic stories and – especially on talk shows – provides an endless supply of discussion and debate. In recent weeks, for example, reporters have been disdainful and dismissive of the woman who brought the rape charges against the Duke lacrosse players. At the outset of the scandal, however, the disdain was pointed at the Duke lacrosse players and Duke University in general.

Melodrama cannot be maintained in a straight news environment. Subjective analysis and opinion, therefore, is the fifth component of melodramatic news coverage on cable. Journalists must go beyond any attempt at objective news coverage to maintain the dramatic storyline in a news story. Allowing more subjectivity into news coverage provides more freedom to discuss an issue or event from several possible angles. This approach makes it easier for journalists to implant new dramatic angles in a story that may be losing some of its dramatic steam.

The sixth element of the cable news media's dramatic coverage is the game-schematic approach. This perspective has been articulated in the past as a critique of mainstream political campaign coverage. Thomas E. Patterson argues that modern political journalists have fallen into a "game schematic" approach to covering political campaigns (57). Covering the news in the context of a game is more dramatic than covering the particulars of public policy proposals and initiatives (see Hovind). Patterson states, "The game schema dominates the journalist's outlook in part because it conforms to the conventions of the news process…The plotlike nature of the game makes it doubly attractive. The campaign 'is a naturally structured, long-lasting dramatic sequence with changing scenes.' The game provides the running story in which today's developments relate to yesterday's, and probably tomorrow's events" (61).

The tendency of traditional journalists to focus on stories about politics as a game has accelerated on cable. The more an event can be framed in the context of a sporting event, or a "horserace," the easier it is to attract viewers and keep them coming back to "check the scores." The nature of cable's continuous coverage fits very well with game schema. Cable news provides for countless updates, debate, and discussion regarding current situations of the players in various political "games," such as elections, policy initiatives, and political scandals. There is a wide range of perspectives regarding who is ahead, who is behind, and what strategies should be employed to win these political games.

Discussion of strategy, while present in all media, resonates with more frequency on cable. Not only is the frequency of strategic discussion high, but the intensity is extreme as well. Consider the following comment made by Chris Matthews on *Hardball* during the Clinton/Lewinsky scandal as an example:

> Let's talk about the president. It seems to me that everybody agrees that he's – your brother's a basketball player, and we're watching in – the NBA playoffs now. You have that shot clock and you have that game clock, and everybody plays the clock. It looks to me like Clinton has been playing down that clock. Every time he gets the ball, I'm gonna use up the whole 24 seconds. I – and it – and eventually, this year is passing quickly.

In the above example, the political world is likened to a sporting event, where the "clock" is running out and the defense is attempting to "stall." In this sense, cable news not only borrows tricks from the entertainment world to create melodrama, but from the sports world as well.

## Conclusion

Melodrama intrigues viewers. However, one of the dangers in melodramatic news lies in the specific elements of melodrama: manufactured scandal, conflict, strategy, characters, negativity, and excess subjectivity. The various elements of drama, while entertaining and often compelling, may have considerable implications for the public. Research indicates dramatic portrayals of government and politics, for example, can contribute to a contemptuous public (see Morris). In other words, the practice of attracting an audience with melodramatic news coverage could disrupt the effective function of institutions necessary in a democratic society. Secondly, journalism itself has lost some credibility. The emphasis on affect and the blurring of fact with fiction transforms objective reporting into subjective storytelling creating a cable news cycle in which the public hunts for the truth like the needle in the proverbial haystack.

## Works Cited


Bennett, Lance W. *News: The Politics of Illusion*, Second Edition. New York: Longman, 1988.

Chapman, Steve. "Could 2000 be the Real Year of the Woman?" *Chicago Tribune* 7 January 1999: A19.

Davis, Richard and Diana Owen. *The New Media and American Politics.* New York: Oxford UP, 1998.

Fallows, James. *Breaking the News: How the Media Undermine American Democracy.* New York: Pantheon Books, 1996.

Hovind, Mark B. "The Melodramatic Imperative: Television's Model for Presidential Election Coverage." *The Electronic Election: Perspectives on the 1996 Campaign Communication.* Eds. Lynda Lee Kaid and Dianne G. Bystrom. Mahwah, New Jersey: Lawrence Erlbaum Associates, 1999.

Kohut, Andrew. "America is Getting Sick and Tired of Scandal News." *The San Diego Union-Tribute* 25 July 2001: B7.

Kurtz, Howard. "The Slow Start of Something Big; From Marvin Kalb, a Reminder of Cautious Scandal Coverage." *The Washington Post* 30 July 2001: C1.

Lichter, Robert S. and Daniel Amundson. "Less News is Worse News: Television Coverage of Congress, 1972-1992." *Congress, the Press, and the Public.* Eds. Thomas Mann and Norman Ornstein. Washington, DC: American Enterprise Institute and Brookings Institute and Brookings Institute, 1994.

Mann, Thomas and Norman Ornstein. *Congress, the Press, and the Public.* Eds. Washington, DC: American Enterprise Institute and Brookings Institute, 1994.

Morris, Jonathan S. "The Effects of Dramatized Political News on Public Opinion." *The American Review of Politics* 25 (2004): 321-343.

Nolan, Martin F. "An Unsavory Recipe Feeds Condit Story." *The Boston Globe* 19 July 2001: A17.

Paletz, David L., and Robert M. Entman. *Media Power in Politics.* New York: Free Press, 1981.

Patterson, Thomas E. *Out of Order.* New York: Knoft, 1993.

Pew Research Center Report. "Missing Intern Stirs Media Frenzy, Lukewarm Public Interest." Report Published by The Pew Research Center for the People and the Press. 18 July 2001. http://www.people-press.org

Rozell, Mark. "Press Coverage of Congress, 1946-1992." *Congress, the Press, and the Public.* Eds. Thomas Mann and Norman Ornstein. Washington, DC: American Enterprise Institute and the Brookings Institution, 1994.

----. *Contempt of Congress: Postwar Press Coverage on Capitol Hill.* Westport, CT: Praeger, 1996.

Rutenberg, Jim. "War or No, News on Cable Already Provides the Drama." *The New York Times* 14 January 2003: C1.

----. "Cable's Instinct for the Racy and Repetitive." *The New York Times* 30 July 2001: C1.

Sabato, Larry J. *Feeding Frenzy: How Attack Journalism has Transformed American Politics.* New York: Free Press, 1991.
Sabato, Larry J., Mark Stencel, and Robert S. Lichter. *Peepshow: Media and Politics in an Age of Scandal.* Lanham, MD: Rowman and Littlefield, 2000.

*Impressed with the children's animated show* Maya and Miguel, *Debra Smith shows us the ways in which it exceeds the standards of the Children's Television Act.*

# Cartoon Culture: How *Maya and Miguel* Excel beyond the 1990 Children's Television Act

Debra Smith

*Dora the Explorer* and *Bob the Builder*, you're model students, but *Kim Possible* and *Penny Proua* report to the back of the classroom please. The former are cartoons that educate as well as entertain while the latter two fall short of the 1990 Children's Television Act requirement that broadcasters make educational and informational television available for children. Also belonging in the first group – *Maya and Miguel*, the first animated show featuring a Latino family. The creation of this show reflects the shift in demographics in the United States as minority groups continue to grow. Hispanics account for 35 million or close to 14 percent of the population of America according to the 2000 census. The population of Hispanic groups in North America is growing rapidly as the census reported a 25 percent growth among combined Hispanic groups, which now constitute the largest ethnoracial minority group in North America ("Census 2000 Briefs"). The producers of *Maya and Miguel* acknowledge that, in creating a show that centered upon a Latino family, they were responding to the fact that Hispanic households are expected to grow from 5.5 million to 8.2 million by 2010 (*Ready to Learn*).

In this article, I will examine the effectiveness of the cartoon not only in responding to the two basic tenets of the Children's Television Act of 1990 but also in placing a special emphasis on Latino and African culture to promote positive identity development for that population of children.

Since the 1974 Federal Communications Commission (FCC) published guidelines, an increased effort has been made to produce educational television for children up to age eighteen. The 1990s Children's Television Act (CTA) set out to regulate children's television by requiring broadcasters to meet educational needs of children which were defined as cognitive/intellectual or social/emotional need. Cognitive/intellectual television includes thinking, reasoning, remembering, imagining, or learning words as examples while social/emotional television engages the child in learning about self, feelings, actions, consequences, others' feelings and perspectives, social skills, and caring.

You may remember singing along to schoolhouse rock with a congressional bill or melodically interrogating the "function" of a "conjunction." And not many of us have never heard of *Sesame Street*, the revolutionary 1969 show. Always progressive, since the 1990s it is even more so. Watched by over 6 million preschoolers weekly in the U.S. and nationally,

*Sesame Street* not only teaches it now serves the dual purpose of exposing children to ideas about culture, inclusion, tolerance, and potential. Countries such as Egypt, South Africa, Israel, and Bangladesh each has special and unique characters on the show. Egypt's version of *Sesame Street*, *Alam Simsim*, for example, introduces Khokha a female muppet who teaches girls that they have limitless potential; South Africa's *Takalani Sesame* uses Kami to help children overcome prejudice about having HIV/AIDS; meanwhile, Israel's *Sippuray Sumsum* encourages mutual respect for the cultures of Jewish and Arab Israeli children. And, in Bangladesh, *Sismpur* reflects the diversity of Bangladeshi children (Germain). Likewise, *Maya and Miguel* follows these shows in presenting television that teaches children values, language, identity, and respect for cultural difference. The cartoon, which debuted in the fall of 2004 and is funded by a grant from the United States Department of Education, is geared toward a young school-age audience (age 6-11) and is the first bilingual cartoon for this age group.

The first episode of *Maya and Miguel* rapidly established itself as the premier show on PBS Kids Go. *Maya and Miguel*'s popularity is further evident in that the show's website has received over 160 million page views, over 180,000 emails from kids and parents, and almost 400,000 average daily users in close to merely two years of existence ("It's a Very Merry"). Based on an original concept by Scholastic Media president Deborah Forte, the series portrays culture and language learning as fun for every child though it especially emphasizes the Latino population. The goals of the series are to promote the value of a culturally diverse society and to support English language learners through the presentation of language in a natural context with a special emphasis on vocabulary ("It's a Very Merry"). *Maya and* Miguel casts its net wide as a learning tool, using not only the show itself but also its website and other media like DVDs and its toys to reinforce the themes and lessons of the show.

Despite the surge in population, there is a scarcity of current Latino culture information though some reference type publications have emerged. Children especially are impacted by the invisibility of certain cultures reflected by electronic media. And, as Giroux and Simon advise that we reveal the relationship between pedagogy and popular culture, educators acknowledge that popular culture forms like television are instrumental in how students look at themselves, in how they relate to pedagogy and their learning experience (15).

Elizabeth Ellsworth states that "educational media incorporate popular cultural forms for the teaching of concepts, processes, and the modeling of behavior" (Giroux and Simon 48). *Maya and Miguel* confirms Ellsworth's claim, as each episode is crafted to show acceptable modes of behavior and views toward diverse cultures. The twins' endorsement of diversity is demonstrated by their cultural participation. For example, in one episode, African traditions are particularly highlighted when Maya neglects to secure tickets for the premiere day of a popular movie. Her brother and friends Theo and Maggie, learn of her oversight just as Maya's father Santiago is set to drop them off at the theater. Mr. Santos then suggests that the children accompany him on his cultural excursion instead. Disappointed, they reluctantly agree to go to the museum, presumably one of cultural history. The museum becomes the setting through which the show demonstrates its allegiance to valuing cultural difference. At the museum, Maggie, a Chinese-American girl insists: "What are we going to do, stare at dioramas of West Africa a gazillion years ago?" Theo, who is African-American responds: "West Africa? My mom's ancestors came from there. Those warrior kings could be interesting." Maggie appears uninterested. Undeterred, Theo enters a section of the museum, flanked by two African warriors. There, he becomes spellbound by the epic of Sundiata, a 700-year-old West African epic playing on one of the museum monitors. The story recalls a weak boy, Sundiata, who grew to become a great warrior. During the story,

Sundiata is successful in ridding his community of a brutal warrior and uniting his countrymen, despite not being able to stand on his feet for many years due to illness. Introducing African values and other tenets of African culture to children at an early age helps dispel many notions about Africa as a "dark continent," non-contributory to any aspect of society. Later, Maggie embarks on her own cultural journey to discover ancient Chinese history and culture that teaches her more about her own ancestry.

Ellsworth reminds us that "the incorporation of popular cultural forms into educational films and videos has a long history" (48). Indeed, thirty-five-year-old *Sesame Street* is testament to this fact (Fisch). Ellsworth continues by saying that "dramatizing" knowledge assists with comprehension and retention (53). In fact, sometimes children are learning when more marginalized curriculum is present. For instance, children may identify with a character who has a less prominent role in the plot of the show. One such veiled curriculum in *Maya and Miguel* is the daily vocabulary lesson that satisfies the CTA's cognitive/intellectual component. Each episode introduces viewers to Spanish vocabulary words that are repeated throughout the thirty-minute show by the characters, as well as by *Maya and Miguel*'s pet parrot "Paco." In his "normal" behavior, Paco repeats words, which assists in child viewers' practice of Spanish and English vocabulary and committing the new words to memory. I'll elaborate on Paco later.

In addition to a language lesson, *Maya and Miguel* offers child viewers a look into Latino culture including food and holidays. The premise for many of the show's episodes, according to the PBS website, is to present family as the "preserver of traditions, beliefs, customs and cultures." An example is one episode in which Maya is set to make a presentation about Mexico for a school project. Her abuela (grandmother) Elena entrusts Maya with a coveted calavera. The calavera, a skull made from sugar, is a fixture during the annual Dia de los Muertos commemoration. Children are introduced to an ancient festival that in pre-Hispanic Mexico, celebrated children and the dead. The Mexican celebration of *Dia de los Muertos* is different in that it is a holy day set aside to remember and pray for the souls of deceased family members. The celebration is commemorated by the construction of altars bearing photographs of the dead, Calaveras, candy, and special food in acknowledgment of the dead.

Additionally, Maya and Miguel, share a close relationship with their Mexican cousin "Tito." In the "Tito's Mexican Vacation" episode of the show, their cousin, missing his homeland, becomes bored with his normal activities which include playing soccer and mimicking his older cousin Miguel. Determining that Tito is homesick, Maya and Miguel re-create Mexico for Tito. They study Mexico to determine what food and memorabilia will comfort him. The result was to include the audience in learning about Mexico as Tito reminisced about his friends and family, Mexican beaches, piñatas, the warm climate, and his diet staple – tortillas. The episode also situates Tito in a position of fond remembrance of his homeland, which he loves as much as his new home in America.

Univision news anchor Jorge Ramos calls *Maya and Miguel*, aired in more than thirty countries, a show in which Latino children can relate to the protagonists. Ramos' own bi-lingual son joins other children in determining that their dual language capability makes them "distinguishable" (*Maya, Miguel*); while Michelle Valdovino from Cultural Access Group says Latino children "tell us that language is a key factor in the definition, the recipe of who [they are], even if they are not using it [Spanish] as much" (qtd. in Clemens). In a survey commissioned by Nickelodeon and conducted by Cultural Access Group, a marketing research company, close to 70 percent of young Latinos said they felt it important for them to see themselves on television (Clemens). Maya and Miguel demonstrate that language is a key component of identity. Their bird, Paco, a fixture on every episode, repeats key words that the children use interchangeably in Spanish and English.

Typically, when Maya and Miguel go to school, their culture follows them. For a school assignment, Maya reads *Don Quixote de la Mancha*, a novel that is universally acknowledged as a great Spanish work. Maya is "inspired by the themes of truth, honor, and courage found in the novel" (*Maya and Miguel* website). So, she goes on a Don Quixote-style quest when a beloved flavor is taken off the menu at her local ice-cream parlor. The episode's theme of "helpful knights" is advanced by references to Sancho Panza who represents the honorable and insightful common man.

Studies (see Calvert and Kotler; Fisch, Truglio, and Cole among others) validate the notion that educational television is beneficial for children. The FCC's report on the value of educational television states, "Children can benefit substantially from viewing educational television. In one such study, children who watch *Barney* showed greater counting skills, knowledge of colors and shapes, vocabulary, and social skills, than children who did not watch the program" (FCC 1996). The report continues by saying that children from lower-income families are particularly receptive to the benefits of educational television. The real median income for the period between 2002 and 2003 for non-Hispanic white households was about $48,000 compared to $30,000 for black households and $34,241 for Hispanic households according to U.S. Census (Census 2000 Briefs). Fisch points to the fact that "children from low- and moderate-income families who frequently watch *Sesame Street* and other educational programs from ages two to four performed better on vocabulary, school readiness, pre-reading, and math tests than non-viewers as much as three years later" (11). To further illuminate the teaching value of television, according to the Children's Television Workshop ("CTW") "preschoolers from low-income families who watch *Sesame Street* demonstrated more advanced literacy and numeric skills than their counterparts who did not watch the program" (FCC 1996).

In the 1970s, networks began a concerted effort to enlist educational consultants during the weekend morning television slot geared toward children. A primary goal during that time was to reduce the amount of advertising directed toward this vulnerable viewing audience. *Maya and Miguel* arrives on the strength of a 1990s re-commitment to educational television following the 1980s removal of FCC enforcement. The FCC's 1996 report clearly outlined the obligations of broadcasters with regard to children's television to include, among other objectives, the following:

> Broadcasters must introduce "core" programming that would fulfill children's educational television obligations. Broadcasters must abide by the FCC's "core" programming definition. This means the program must air for 30 minutes each week between the hours of 7:00 am and 10:00 pm. Broadcasters must list core programming as a children's program and keep this information in their public file.

While PBS is certainly not a surprise venue for the display of educational television, *Maya and Miguel* emerges during a time when higher education recognizes, perhaps in hindsight, that the cultural and racial changes in the census will be reflected on its campuses. For example, San Diego State University's Department of Africana Studies now offers a certificate program with the focus on how to effectively teach African-American students. Meanwhile scholars at the University of Arizona and Florida State University consider questions like "what is important for teaching Latino students?" and "how do we incorporate Latino parents' perspectives into teacher preparation?" The foundation for this foray must begin with teaching early-age children about diversity and pride in their culture and capabilities. *Maya and Miguel* convey messages about culture by enhancing images of Latino and African culture to provide an affirmative sense of identity for children. For instance, when Miguel enters a comic book writing contest, his story much like the premise of the show, reflects Aztec mythology. The connection between *Maya and Miguel*'s emphasis on Latino and other cultures along with Miguel's Aztec comic topic speaks to the universality and interrelatedness of culture and the importance of ethnic identity confirmation. In this particular episode, each of the primary characters in *Maya and Miguel* suggest an ending for Miguel's comic story that acknowledges their own race and ethnicity. The result is what the show's producers call a "cooperative ending" that connects all of the children (*Maya and Miguel* website).

*Maya and* Miguel's ties to contemporary and historic literature and culture are further reflected in the episode in which one African-American teacher takes maternity leave and is replaced by another African-American. In the show titled "The Taming of Mr. Shue," the substitute teacher is judged by the children's expectation of how he should behave. In Shakespeare's *The Taming of the Shrew*, the characters in the play hold specific social and behavioral roles. Social status is influenced by wealth, age, gender, education, etc. and is reinforced by the society as a whole. In comparison, when Maya, Miguel, and friends recognize their prejudgment of Mr. Shue, they do damage control by determining that, although he is different from their permanent teacher Mrs. Langley, Mr. Shue should be given a "chance" to prove himself based upon his own personality and merit.

The variety of ethnic backgrounds in *Maya and Miguel* reflects the model that the 1970s and later versions of School House Rock utilized in that the cast is diverse. Joining the title characters, their cousin Tito and Theo who, as aforementioned, is Afro-American, is Chrissy who is Afro-Dominican, Maggie who is Chinese-American and Andy who is Euro-American. In addition, the show conforms to one of Fisch's features of an effective educational show in that it reinforces "concepts by repeating them over the course of an episode or segment" (13). Paco, the children's parrot, reinforces the Spanish language lesson by repeating the words *Maya and Miguel* use. The colorful, energetic bird is an eye-catcher for child viewers as he flies wildly behind the children supplementing their social and cultural messages. Fisch asserts that child learning is encouraged by "using engaging or action-filled visuals rather than static visuals or 'talking heads'" (13).

Similarly, in every episode, Maya exclaims "eso es" ("that's it!") when she comes up with an idea. Her hair bow also glows wildly when she repeats this Spanish phrase. Meanwhile, Miguel responds with "yo te conozco, Maya" (I know you, Maya) to express his wariness toward a forthcoming scheme that will likely require his assistance.

While the show certainly makes a signficant impact on children's prosocial behavior, the challenges Maya and Miguel met in responding to the Children's Television Act of 1990 included the revision of the show's original theme song, which hinged upon gender stereotyping. The lyrics of the song called Miguel a boy who "leads with his head," while Maya, his sister, "follows her heart." While the show's content did not depict Maya as less astute than Miguel, the theme song was adjusted in the middle of the second season. The lyrics were changed to "they make a great team as they each do their part." Clearly, the show's producers and consultants took a second look at the point of entry to the show that would stereotype the girl as being emotional and spontaneous in contrast to the boy's pensive, serious, intelligent nature. Another potentially problematic angle to the show is its conclusion. When the "story" part of *Maya and Miguel* ends, and the appropriate lesson and vocabulary words are learned, Maya returns, (we hear her voice) apart from the show, yet before the final credits run, to "introduce" some of her "friends." Maya says "here's what some of our friends are doing" prior to showcasing talent, service projects, etc. from children in their hometowns. Maya, who is not real, becomes a "friend" to viewers and the children she introduces who are primarily Latino and black children filmed while they are dancing, doing crafts, helping their families or introducing an ethnic food. Maya – away from the show and introducing real people as her "friends" – is moderately problematic because it gives children the impression that Maya is real outside the setting of the show and has "friends" outside of the characters on the show. On the other hand, the case can be made that it is reinforcement that, outside the show, real-life children not unlike the viewers, are demonstrating cognitive/intellectual or social/emotional mastery.

Still another challenge is reliance upon partial funding from the U.S. Department of Education, which has awarded $23.4 million the Ready To Learn program of which *Maya and Miguel* is a beneficiary. When the Senate reviews its budget, it could potentially be swayed by the fact that many networks and cable stations are already carrying the torch for educational television. As of yet, however, funding cuts are not a threat, but censorship may be. In 2005, the *Posters from Buster* series that runs on PBS had an episode censored because it showed Buster, the lead character in the show, visiting children in Vermont who had same-sex parents. In a letter to PBS and the show's producers, Education Secretary Margaret Spellings not only demanded that the episode not air, but reiterated that the Ready to Learn funding was "to use the television medium to help prepare preschool age children for school. The television programs that must fulfill this mission are to be specifically designed for this purpose, with the highest attention to production quality and validity of research-based educational objectives, content and materials" (qtd. in de Moraes). As a recipient of this funding as well, *Maya and Miguel* writers and producers must be aware of this mandate.

While a few have argued that some of the behavior on the show reflects stereotypes, for the most part, *Maya and Miguel* excels in offering a guide for children's television producers by celebrating diverse cultures and identities and, further, by having them validated due to their very existence on our most ubiquitous popular culture form – the television show.

## Works Cited


Calvert Sandra L. and Jennifer A. Kotler. "Lessons from children's television: The Impact of the Children's Television Act on children's learning." *Journal of Applied Developmental Psychology* 24.3 (2003): 275-335.

"Census 2000 Briefs." U.S. Census Bureau. http://www.census.gov/population/www/cen2000/briefs.html

Children's Television Act of 1990. http://www.fcc.gov/cgb/consumerfacts/childtv.pdf

Clemens, Luis. "Next-Gen Hispanics Reshape the Market." *Multimedia News* 13 February 2006. http://www.multichannel.com/article/CA6306528.html

de Moraes, Lisa. "PBS's 'Buster' Gets an Education." *Washington Post* 27 January 2005: http://www.washingtonpost.com/wpdyn/articles/A40188-2005Jan26.html

Ellsworth, Elizabeth. "Educational Media, Ideology, and the Presentation of Knowledge through Popular Culture Forms." *Popular Culture, Schooling & Everyday Life.* Ed. Henry Giroux and Roger I. Simon. Westport, CT: Bergin and Garvey Publishers, 1989. 47-66.

Federal Communications Commission. (1974). Children's Television Programs: Report and Policy Statement. Federal Register, 39, 39396-39409. Washington, DC.

Federal Communications Commission (1996). Policies and Rules Concerning Children's Television Programming. Revision of Programming Policies for Television Broadcast Stations. FCC 96-335. Washington DC.

Fisch, Shalom M. "Children's learning from television: It's Not Just Violence." *Televizion* 18 (2005): 10-14.

Fisch, Shalom M., Rosemarie T. Truglio, and Charlotte F. Cole. "The Impact of Sesame Street on Preschool Children: A Review and Synthesis of 30 Years' Research." *Media Psychology* 1.2 (1999): 164-190.

Germain, David. "The World According to Sesame Street." *Charlotte Observer* 29 January 2006: 7E.

Giroux, Henry A. and Roger I. Simon. *Popular Culture, Schooling & Everyday Life.* Westport, CT: Bergin and Garvey Publishers, 1989.

"It's a Very Merry Maya & Miguel Christmas!" *Scholastic.com.* 30 November 2005. http://www.scholastic.com/aboutscholastic/news/press_11302005_CG.htm

Lieberman, David. "Media tune in to ethnic audiences." *USA Today* 7 April 2006: 1B.

*Maya and Miguel* (television show). PBS.

*Maya and Miguel* (website). PBS Kids. http://pbskids.org/mayaandmiguel/flash.html

*Maya, Miguel and the Future of Latinos.* Univision. October 2005.

*Ready to Learn Seminar.* "Life of a child today/A child's life: Learning, Literacy and the Role of Media." Baltimore, MD. 3 February 2005. Accessed from pbs.org.

*In this essay, Ann Kordas argues, "The exceedingly negative portrayal of females, especially adolescent girls, in men's pulp magazines in the 1940s and 1950s was undoubtedly influenced by the new challenges confronting men in the postwar world. No longer the sole economic support of their families, perhaps even unable to find a job, many American men fretted over their diminishing power and authority."*

# "Women Don't Rape – But They Do Kill": The Crisis of Masculinity in Post World War II Men's Magazines

Ann Kordas

Since the latter half of the nineteenth century, magazines have played an important role in formulating images of masculinity in American society. Many early magazines created an ideal image of American masculinity based on strength, courage, and mastery over the environment. Dime novels, inexpensive short "novels" which first became popular in the 1860s among both boys and adult men, portrayed cowboys, outlaws, detectives, military scouts, Indian fighters, and hunters as male icons through whom lesser men could vicariously experience the thrills of "true" masculinity (Smith 90, 92, 95, 99, 103-104, 109). In the 1870s, the *National Police Gazette*, a magazine that targeted a primarily working-class male audience, featured both stories about sports and crime and, to appeal to male sexual desires, pictures of female burlesque performers. In the late nineteenth and early twentieth centuries, other magazines, such as *Physical Culture* (1908), a magazine for "bodybuilders" and exercise enthusiasts, attracted working-class male readers by focusing "on tough, male physicality and…lurid stories of sexual sensationalism" (Osgerby 22). *Physical Culture*, it should be noted, also attracted numerous female readers with its articles on love and its pictures of handsome, unclothed men (Hooven 20).

As late as the 1930s, magazines aimed at both male and female blue-collar readers, such as *True Story* and *True Confessions*, continued to consist largely of tales of adventure and thrilling accounts of bloody crimes, sports victories, and masculine derring-do (Pendergast 223, 224). During World War II, however, significant changes in the format and content of blue-collar magazines began to take place. New pulp magazines aimed at an exclusively male audience emerged, and the *True* magazine series began to eliminate features intended to appeal to female readers (Pendergast 222). After World War II, further changes occurred. Although men's pulp magazines continued to include heroic stories of masculine exploits, they also began to contain a significant number of articles, photos, and advertisements that emphasized male vulnerability and inadequacy and stressed the perils faced by American men in the postwar world. Indeed, the content of many men's magazines from this period seems almost deliberately calculated to strike fear in the hearts of male readers.

In *Men in the Middle: Searching for Masculinity in the 1950s*, historian James Gilbert characterizes the years following World War II as a time of "male panic," one of several such periods in American history when men, confronted by "changes in work or family relationships," feared losing their political, economic, and cultural dominance in American society (3). In the late 1940s, many American men found their traditional authority in the workplace and the home threatened by an array of forces. Postwar unemployment jeopardized men's role as family provider at precisely the same time that more women than ever before in American history were becoming part of the paid workforce. Many of the men who did find employment worked for corporations (if they were middle class) or factories (if they were working class) in positions in which they were unable to exercise authority or make important decisions on their own (Atwan 45-46; Kimmel 239-42). In the words of sociologist David Riesman, American men had become "other directed" as they strove to please others and blend into the corporate work environment (qtd. in Kimmel 241).

In addition to these changes in men's work experience in the postwar period, many middle- and working-class families moved from crowded cities to new suburban housing developments. In the short time between 1947 and 1950, 70,000 new homes were built in Nassau County, Long Island, alone (Baxandall and Ewen 165). As a result of this mass exodus, men, Gilbert and others argue, found themselves trapped in the "feminizing and debasing" atmosphere of suburbia, caring for children and assisting their wives with household chores (Gilbert, *Men* 4; Kimmel 245-46). Adolescents, newly enriched by part-time employment during the war and accustomed to absent fathers and lack of supervision by working mothers, also posed a threat to the authority of adult men (Palladino 82, 93). Although it is impossible to determine precisely how much fear these changes in American society actually aroused, men's pulp magazines from the time clearly convey the impression that American men lived in a state of peril, facing danger on all sides.

Advertisements in post World War II men's magazines, for example, were designed to create (or prey upon) fears and insecurities by calling into question male strength, health, attractiveness to women, and ability to support a family. Many of the ads exploit fears regarding the traditional physical components of manliness – better than average height, thick heads of hair, and strong bodies (Luciano 13). For example, an advertisement for Sloan's Liniment in the November 1946 issue of *Inside Detective* asks readers, "Muscles Ache? Feel Like You've Been 'Through a Wringer'?" The ad features a picture of a man scowling in pain as he rubs the product on his shoulder, a shoulder clearly not as strong as it should be (Sloan's Liniment). An ad for the Charles Atlas muscle-building program appearing in the same issue of *Inside Detective* offers to reveal the answer to "How Joe's Body Brought Him Fame Instead of Shame," doubtlessly awakening fears lurking within many men that, like Joe, they were also "spindle-shanked, scrawny weakling[s]" with "shameful" bodies (Charles Atlas).

Accompanying advertisements proclaiming the average man's physical shortcomings were ads suggesting that such inadequacies would cause a man both to lose the respect of his peers and to be slighted by women. For example, an ad in the November 1949 issue of *Sir!* trumpets the benefits of elevator shoes through the use of "before" and "after" pictures. In the "before" picture (a line drawing), a diminutive man laments, "For years I was called Shorty. I was unpopular…was laughed at by the men in the office…by girls everywhere." In the "after" picture, "Shorty," now transformed by the shoes, is shown dancing with a beautiful blonde who previously had towered over him. He exults, "Now the men have changed towards me. And I am popular with the girls, too. No longer embarrassed, I command attention…everywhere" (Elevator Shoes). Not only is "Shorty" no longer ashamed of his height – he is in "command."

Other advertisements preyed upon men's fears that they might prove unable to earn a living and support a family. Such fears were undoubtedly common among men of all classes in the years immediately following the end of World War II, when unemployment plagued the American economy. Men who could not find work could not provide for their families and thus failed in the most fundamental of all male roles, that of breadwinner (Kimmel 245). Advertisements in men's magazines played upon the anxieties of both white- and blue-collar workers. An ad for International Correspondence Schools in the November 1946 edition of *Inside Detective*, for example, impertinently asks men, "How's Your Post-War Progress?" The ad is accompanied by a picture of a man wearing a suit and carrying a briefcase, symbols of the middle-class businessman or middle-manager. The image of the man is partially obscured by the title question; his face is completely hidden by the word "Your" (International Correspondence Schools). The implication is obvious: The failure of men to earn a living could destroy their sense of self and rob them of their identity; men who lacked a well-paying job literally lost face. Another correspondence school advertisement, this one for the Institute of Applied Science, queries, "Want a Regular Monthly Salary?" (Institute of Applied Science). The presumption, of course, was that the magazine's readers had trouble finding steady employment.

Besides the advertisements warning men of their financial and physical inadequacies, articles in postwar men's pulp magazines also raised the fear of outside threats to the power, authority, and dominance of American men. For example, an article in the January 1953 issue of *Sir!* tells the story of American soldiers who had been captured while fighting in Korea and had been sent to the Soviet Union, where they were interrogated, beaten, and used as slave labor (Watson 8, 9). The article is accompanied by a photograph of slumped male bodies, American soldiers, the caption states, who had been murdered by North Korean troops. The Americans' boots, the caption further informs the reader, had been stolen from them by the North Koreans shortly before they were killed (Watson 8). This image surely struck a cord with male readers who knew, as a result of years of watching Hollywood westerns, that the desire of all true American men was to die with their boots on.

Many of the articles appearing in Cold War men's magazines, however, focused not on the communist menace but on the dangers posed by women. These articles seem to be a response to new social and economic realities in postwar society. As historians Maureen Honey and Elaine Tyler May respectively argue, following the end of World War II, many women who held jobs in wartime industries (jobs previously held by men) were reluctant to return to the home and to their role as homemaker. The majority of women employed in war industries, Honey reveals, wished to remain part of the labor force. Surveys taken at the end of the war indicated that at least 75% of such women wanted to work at the same jobs after the war was over (23). Indeed, even married women wished to continue working outside the home after the war. According to May, 69% of married female workers hoped to retain their wartime jobs even after their husbands returned home (75-76). By 1945, 25% of married women were employed outside the home, and the percentage of wives who worked for wages grew even larger in the postwar period (Osgerby 51; Hartmann 92). The growing financial power of women and the potential independence that this gave them distressed many American men. The fear of women usurping men's place in the workforce may have inspired fears that women would challenge male dominance in other areas as well (May 89; Gilbert, *Men* 67).

Such fears became a recurring theme in the pages of both general-interest and men's pulp magazines. In 1949, a writer for *Reader's Digest* complained that women were becoming "aggressive" and "unfeminine" (Gilbert, *Men* 70). In men's magazines, such fears often rose to the level of hysteria as articles repeatedly warned men that they might one day find not only their position in the workplace but also their physical safety, perhaps even their very lives, threatened by women. In postwar men's magazines such as *Sir!*, *Mr.*, *Famous Police*, *True Detective*, *Inside Detective*, and *Women in Crime*, females of all ages were routinely depicted as robbers, rapists, and murderers. Indeed, one magazine, *Women in Crime*, devoted itself, as its title indicates, exclusively to the topic. In the April 1957 issue of the magazine, one article relates the story of a woman who had falsely accused a man of murder because he had refused to leave his wife to be with her ("Trial By Fury"). The same issue features a photograph of Opal Collins, a woman who had dispatched with her mother-in-law, sisters-in-law (ages fourteen and eleven), and "crippled, war-veteran husband" with a few well-aimed rifle blasts ("Sentenced to Die").

Although postwar men's pulp magazines portrayed women in general as dangerous, lesbians were depicted as posing a special threat to American men. Homosexuality in general frightened Americans in the postwar period just as it had since the beginning of the twentieth century. In the decades following World War II, however, homosexuality was especially feared and loathed. Gay men, who were generally perceived as weak and effeminate, were believed to pose a threat to American security, presumably because gay men employed by the federal government could easily be blackmailed by communist agents into revealing important national secrets (D'Emilio and Freedman 293). Furthermore, in a period in which men feared social and economic "emasculation," homosexual men may have represented to many heterosexual men a foreshadowing of the "fate" that supposedly awaited them if they lost the competition with women for dominance over American society.

Although both before and after World War II male homosexuality occupied the American imagination to a greater extent than did lesbianism, in the postwar world, lesbians came under greater scrutiny than in previous decades. The greater interest in lesbians may, perhaps, be attributed to their greater visibility in wartime and postwar society. As lesbians left home to join the military or to work in defense industries located in other parts of the country, they encountered many other women with sexual desires like their own, perhaps for the first time in their lives (D'Emilio and Freedman 289-90; Faderman 120-21). Such women frequented public places of amusement just as heterosexual couples did, and gay bars sprang up around the country to accommodate them (Hartmann 180; D'Emilio and Freedman 290-91; Faderman 127). The visibility of lesbians in the postwar world was further enhanced by Alfred Kinsey's publication of *Sexual Behavior in the Human Female* in 1953. In the book, Kinsey revealed that approximately one-quarter of American women reported having felt sexually attracted to another woman at least once in their lives. Kinsey also stated that as many as 12% of American women might be lesbians (Hartmann 180).

In the postwar world, lesbians may have seemed not only more ubiquitous but also more frightening than they previously had. The American psychiatric community in the years following World War II considered homosexuality a sickness and stressed the supposed unhappiness and "antisocial" tendencies of lesbians (Faderman 130-32). In addition, for men who worried that their wives no longer needed to depend on them for financial support, the thought that women might no longer need men for sexual fulfillment either must have occasioned great distress. The fear that women, including married women, might reject male lovers in favor of female ones was often exploited in the pages of men's pulp magazines. For example, in "The Unspeakable Vice," a man tries to pick up a beautiful, seemingly-unaccompanied blonde in what is obviously a gay bar (occupied by "pairs" of women wearing "mannish-cut clothes and haircuts") in Greenwich Village. His advances, however, provoke the anger of a "mannish-looking woman" who goes "berserk" and attacks him, "ripp[ing] his cheek with fingernails as sharp as tigerclaws." Such a vicious response, the author, L. MacKay Phelps, chides, should not have been completely unexpected, given the violent nature of lesbians. He then proceeds to warn readers of the possibility that innocent men might find themselves accidentally "married to lesbians" (Phelps, "Unspeakable" 12). Indeed, Phelps cautions, this is entirely possible given the "alarming" number of lesbians in the American population, many of whom were to be found at "girls' colleges" whose campuses veritably "swarm with lesbians" ("Unspeakable" 44). Unfortunately, he laments, "many men" have found themselves in this predicament, and a man who marries a lesbian is "foredoomed to a wretched experience" ("Unspeakable" 12, 44) .

Other authors also agonized over the supposed dangers posed by lesbians masquerading as heterosexual women. In "Sappho and the Modern Showgirl," George Gale relates the story of another hapless man who finds himself unwittingly married to a lesbian. "George M.," a successful businessman, marries a beautiful dancer only to learn later that she is "a devotee of Sapphism, an abnormal lover of her own sex who was frigid toward all men." Like Phelps, Gale also warns that such an "experience is not uncommon among American husbands" (23).

Besides the dangers posed by adult women, both homosexual and heterosexual, to male safety and self-esteem, adolescent girls also, or so men's magazines implied, represented a threat to male authority and well-being. Such claims probably did not seem implausible to men in postwar America. In the years following World War II, American adults found themselves confronted by the growth of a youth culture that valued the opinions of peers over the directives issued by adults. Increasingly, adolescents turned to friends for advice and guidance instead of to their parents, a situation that undoubtedly caused consternation among many fathers. To make matters worse, rejection of parental authority was accompanied by access to automobiles, which placed teens beyond adult scrutiny (Gilbert, *Cycle* 12). Furthermore, historian Kelly Schrum reveals, the new prosperity of American adolescents in the postwar period gave them considerable economic power (136). Indeed, during the late 1940s and the 1950s, many advertisers identified the adolescent girl as the family's chief consumer, an expert who advised her parents on what new items to purchase and insisted that they replace beloved but outdated possessions, such as "Daddy['s]…smoking chair" (qtd. in Palladino 104).

Although advertisers rejoiced in the increased independence and economic power of American adolescents, fears of adolescent autonomy consumed postwar society, and, as James Gilbert reveals in *A Cycle of Outrage: America's Reaction to the Juvenile Delinquent in the 1950s*, Americans became obsessed with the subject of juvenile delinquency. In postwar America, adults agonized over the seemingly dramatic leap in the rates of juvenile delinquency from the first decade of the twentieth century to the late 1940s (Gilbert, *Cycle* 55, 66-67). Such fears, especially those of violent female delinquents, were not necessarily grounded in fact. Although the Senate delinquency subcommittee, claimed that juvenile delinquency after World War II had increased significantly (45%) from the prewar period, it is unclear that American teens in the 1940s and 1950s were actually committing more crimes (Gilbert, *Cycle* 67). As Gilbert points out, new concerns regarding adolescents may simply have made youthful crime more visible and thus more likely to have been reported (*Cycle* 69, 70-71). The seeming increase in delinquency in the postwar period, Gilbert further argues, might also have been the result of an increase in the number of status offenses (acts classified as criminal because of the offending party's age), such as "sex delinquency" and underage drinking, instead of an increase in the kinds of violent crime that adults most feared. Most female delinquents were arrested for status offenses not for committing acts of violence (*Cycle* 69).

The fact that teenage girls rarely committed violent crimes meant little, however, in a world in which both women and adolescents appeared as unruly elements threatening the established social order. Fear of female adolescents was especially pronounced in men's pulp magazines, which often dwelled upon acts of brutality carried out by teenage girls. In keeping with fears regarding the usurpation of male power by women, magazine articles frequently portrayed girl criminals as masculine in nature. Such girls were often depicted as wearing men's clothing or using "male" (i.e. profane) language. Other girl criminals were depicted as ignoring traditionally female household chores. Clearly, it was believed, girls who rejected conventionally feminine roles would reject other limitations on their behavior as well.

To better draw the line between properly feminine and improperly masculine girls, "good" girls who displayed appropriately feminine behavior were sometimes portrayed as the victims of mannish "bad" girls in men's magazines. For example, an April 1957 article, "No Place for Virgins," which appeared in *Women in Crime*, gives a graphic account of an attack on a group of female adolescents by a gang of teenage girls called the Hawks, who supposedly terrorized the Williamsburg section of Brooklyn. In the article, the victims are described as "walking peacefully homeward from a church meeting" when the Hawks "[sweep] down upon their quarry yelling like a Comanche war party, lusting for blood." The Hawks viciously attack their victims who, the reader is told, are unable to defend themselves with their "prayer books and dainty purses." So horrendous is the attack that even adult men are afraid to intervene (Sawyers 22).

In contrast to their "dainty" and pious victims, the Hawks are described as "a ruthless gang of teen-age terrorists; a mob of Amazons" who dress in boys' clothing (blue jeans, buttoned shirts, and leather jackets). Not only do these "deadly dungaree dolls" dress like boys, but they also carry the same deadly weapons as male gang members – knives and "garrison belts" (lengths of chain ending in razor-sharp belt buckles) (Sawyers 24). Especially troubling to both the article's author, Frank Sawyers, and to the police who rescue the gang's victims is the Hawks' use of profanity. When the Hawks attacked the young churchgoers, according to the author, "the air was blue with the obscenity of their curses" (22). The Hawks' response to the arrival of the police was to "hur[l] curses of almost inconceivable filth" at them (Sawyers 24). Indeed, the girls' use of profanity caused one policeman to describe them as worse than the mobsters and professional hit men of Murder, Inc., a Brooklyn-based organized crime syndicate. According to the police officer, "As vile as the Murder, Inc. [sic] mob was, their language was not anywhere near so foul and obscene as the filth these gang-girls spew out with almost every breath" (Sawyers 25).

Although violent acts committed against other girls were disturbing, violence on the part of female delinquents was portrayed as particularly troublesome when it was directed against males, especially fathers or father substitutes. In such accounts, the masculine tendencies of girl criminals, the girls' rejection of traditional feminine roles, the girls' dislike of the male sex, and/or the girls' anger at their fathers were typically emphasized. For example, in the April 1957 issue of *Women in_Crime*, a short story told the tale of a fourteen-year-old North Carolina girl who one Sunday morning calmly loaded a shotgun and patiently waited until the end of the day before "blast[ing] her father into eternity" as he sat watching television. The reason for her crime was that her father had "nagged her about not doing enough housework" ("Unavoidable Delay" 35). In a January 1951 article, "The Urge to Kill," several of the cases related involved the impulsive killing of men or boys by teenage girls. In each of the cases profiled, either the girl's dislike or her envy of the male sex was emphasized. For example, when discussing the motives of a fifteen-year-old girl named Helen, who shot a man in his own home for no apparent reason, the author explains this seemingly random crime by attributing it to the girl's hatred of her father. The author explicitly notes "that Helen hated her father, whom she hadn't seen in a long time. And she told the sheriff she wanted to kill him" (Ives 65). The same article also contained the story of thirteen-year-old Diane Allen from Joliet, Illinois, who "kept wishing she were a boy." Seemingly unable to control her frustration, Diane drowns Charles Jackson, her seven-year-old male playmate, whose masculinity she supposedly envied (Ives 65).

Of all the disturbing and dreadful acts of violence thought to be committed against men by adolescent girls, the most fear inspiring of all was surely rape. Such fears doubtlessly derived from, and were yet another expression of, men's fear of women's and girls' usurpation of male power and privilege. Although, for physiological reasons, the rape of men by women is extremely rare, the subject of male rape was intriguing enough to warrant an article in the January 1953 issue of *Sir!* magazine. The article, "Why Men Can't be Raped," authored by the lesbian-fearing L. MacKay Phelps, debunks one account of male abduction and rape. However, another account, in which the attackers are teenage girls, is presented as a true story of rape committed by young women. In this account, a young man is driving from Providence to Narragansett, Rhode Island, when he is flagged down by three teenage girls – an attractive blonde, a pretty brunette, and "a short, dumpy girl." They tell him they are hitchhiking to New York. The gallant young man agrees to give them a ride for at least part of their journey. However, once in the car, the girls begin to make "suggestive remarks" and, according to the boy, "discus[s] which one of them was going to make love to me." The girls pull out a knife and, warning him that they have stabbed men before, order him to pull off on a side road. The blonde holds the knife against the driver's throat while, again in the words of the young man, "the short girl had her way with me in the rear seat. I had to submit to save my skin. It was simply awful!" The two attractive girls then also rape him. The group then drives to a nearby town to buy some peroxide for the girls' hair. While the girls are making their purchases in the drug store, the police are summoned. They promptly arrest the girls on the charge of "lewd and lascivious behavior," indicating that they believe the young man's claims may be true (Phelps, "Why Men" 66).

Worthy of note is the general tone of the article. The piece does not contradict the apparent belief that swarms of young women were lying in wait to rape men. Instead, it merely reassures men that, if they should happen to find themselves in such a situation, the physical realties of male sexual response will make it virtually impossible for the women or girls to carry out their plan (Phelps "Why Men" 66-67). However, lest men feel too secure and thus lapse into complacency, the article warns that even though women are rarely successful at committing acts of rape, they are eminently capable of murder. "Women don't Rape – but they do kill" warns a caption beneath an accompanying photo. The picture shows a man's body sprawled across the passenger seat of a car as a pretty blonde behind the wheel smiles smugly at the corpse (Phelps, "Why Men" 14).

Perhaps the most graphic portrayal of female delinquents' encounters with men, however, is described in the aforementioned "No Place for Virgins!," the account of the depredations of the indescribably profane girl gang, the Hawks. When the police, who are described as the "most despised of all [the Hawks'] enemies," attempt to rescue the girls who have been assaulted, they find themselves under attack as well (Sawyers 24). When one police officer manages to grab one of the Hawks, the other gang members turn on him and begin to assault him, beating him over the head and slashing his face. The fearsome nature of the girl gang members is summarized in a statement by the victimized policeman that conveys the terror that even law enforcement officers supposedly felt at the sight of these girls gone astray: "Any cop who has been forced to deal with the like of these gang girls, who has seen their eyes narrowed to blazing points of murderous hatred, knows what he is up against – and would almost sooner step naked into a den of wild and starving beasts" (Sawyers 25).

The exceedingly negative portrayal of females, especially adolescent girls, in men's pulp magazines in the 1940s and 1950s was undoubtedly influenced by the new challenges confronting men in the postwar world. No longer the sole economic support of their families, perhaps even unable to find a job, many American men fretted over their diminishing power and authority. Such anxieties readily translated into fears regarding their physical strength, appearance, and ability to retain the role as family provider (and leader). Feelings of vulnerability led easily to fears of attack by both foreign and domestic "enemies." This sense of weakness and defenselessness, combined with men's resentment of the growing economic and social independence of women and adolescents, often translated into fears of women and teenagers themselves. Such fears made adolescent girls seem a particular source of worry. These fears, based on real changes in the postwar world, were reflected in the horrific depiction of women and female adolescents in the pages of men's pulp magazines of the late 1940s and 1950s.

## Works Cited


Atwan, Robert, Donald McQuade, and John W. Wright. *Edsels, Luckies, and Frigidaires: Advertising the American Way*. New York: Dell, 1979.

Baxandall, Rosalyn, and Elizabeth Ewen. *Picture Windows: How the Suburbs Happened.* New York: Basic, 2000.

Charles Atlas. Advertisement. *Inside Detective* November 1946: 42.

D'Emilio, John, and Estelle B. Freedman. *Intimate Matters: A History of Sexuality in America.* New York: Harper, 1988.

Elevator Shoes. Advertisement. *Sir!* November 1949: 73.

Faderman, Lillian. *Odd Girls and Twilight Lovers: A History of Lesbian Life in Twentieth-Century America.* New York: Penguin, 1991.

Gale, George. "Sappho and the Modern Showgirl." *Sir!* January 1953: 28+

Gilbert, James. *A Cycle of Outrage: America's Reaction to the Juvenile Delinquent in the 1950s.* New York: Oxford UP, 1986.

----. *Men in the Middle: Searching for Masculinity in the 1950s.* Chicago: U of Chicago P, 2005.

Hartmann, Susan M. *The Home Front and Beyond: American Women in the 1940s.* Boston: G.K. Hall, 1982.

Honey, Maureen. *Creating Rosie the Riveter: Class, Gender, and Propaganda during World War II.* Amherst: U of Massachusetts P, 1984.

Hooven, F. Valentine, III. *Beefcake: The Muscle Magazines of America 1950-1970.* New York: Taschen, 2002.

International Correspondence Schools. Advertisement. *Inside Detective* November 1946: 12.

Institute for Applied Science. Advertisement. *Inside Detective* November 1946: 12.

Ives, Frank. "The Urge to Kill." *Sir!* January 1951: 32+.

Luciano, Lynne. *Looking Good: Male Body Image in Modern America.* New York: Hill, 2001.

May, Elaine Tyler. *Homeward Bound: American Families in the Cold War Era.* New York: Basic, 1988.

Osgerby, Bill. *Playboys in Paradise: Masculinity, Youth and Leisure-Style in Modern America.* New York: Berg, 2001.

Palladino, Grace. *Teenagers: An American History.* New York: Basic, 1996.

Pendergast, Tom. *Creating the Modern Man: American Magazines and Consumer Culture, 1900-1950.* Columbia, MO: U of Missouri P, 2000.

Phelps, L. MacKay. "The Unspeakable Vice." *Mr.* September 1951: 28+.

----. "Why Men Can't Be Raped." *Sir!* January 1953: 14+.

Sawyers, Frank. "No Place for Virgins!" *Women in Crime* April 1957: 22+.

"Sentenced to Die!" *Women in Crime* April 1957: 6.

Schrum, Kelly. "'Teena Means Business': Teenage Girls' Culture and *Seventeen* Magazine, 1944-1950." *Delinquents and Debutantes: Twentieth-Century American Girls' Cultures.* Ed. Sherrie A. Inness. New York: New York UP, 1998.

Sloan's Liniment. Advertisement. *Inside Detective* November 1946: 4.

Smith, Henry Nash. *Virgin Land: The American West as Symbol and Myth.* 1950. Cambridge, MA: Harvard UP, 1978.

"Trial By Fury." *Women in Crime* April 1957: 58.

"Unavoidable Delay." *Women in Crime* April 1957: 34-35.

Watson, Hugh. "What Russia Does to GI Prisoners." *Sir!* January 1953: 6+.

*In this essay, Albert Wendland explores the 1950s comic* Space Museum *to reveal the contradictions that we can find even in "this most un-radical and unquestioning of comic book series."*

# *Space Museum*: Heroism, Conformity, and the Conflicts of an Age[1]

Albert Wendland

From 1959 to 1964, DC's science-fiction comic *Strange Adventures* ran in every third issue an almost ideal anthology-format for science-fiction stories. The premise was simple: each month a father and his fourteen-year-old son visited the Space Museum, "one of the wonders of the 25th century," which housed "mementos of the daring and heroism of the men who venture into space" (Fox, "Secret of the Space-Jewel" 2). On each visit, the father, Howard Parker, told his son, Tommy, the story behind a particular display that had been chosen by the boy. Since the reader heard the story too, this format was perfect for generating and framing a new plot for each installment, for arguing the heroism and worth of humanity, and for sharing the adolescent listener's "sense of wonder" with the reader, whose assumed similar background encouraged identification. Tommy was white, male, middle class (he raced futuristic "soap-box" cars and was a member of that century's version of the Boy Scouts), and thus the values and aspirations of his and the audience's assumed social group, as they existed for the era, could be communicated and reinforced through example – as Tommy is socialized, so is the reader. Furthermore, the editor of the series knew how to appeal to the sensibility of his market. He was Julius Schwartz, famed for being the main force behind the successful "Silver Age" resurgence of DC (or National) superheroes.[2] The writer of the series was his often-used and science-minded Gardner Fox, who also wrote *Adam Strange* and the popular *Justice League of America.* And the artist was Carmine Infantino, who drew *Adam Strange* and *The Flash*, the last being a seminal Silver Age work.

*Space Museum* was only a minor comic book installment (just one story appeared on the magazine's cover, when the series began), and it receives only brief if respectful mention in the studies of SF comics. Mike Benton says that the "concept was simple yet open-ended" (72) while Gerard Jones and Will Jacobs claim it was the "best realized" of the series that Schwartz introduced into the magazine (22); indeed, the art and not the content is usually the focus of commentary, since it represents one of the few times when Infantino was allowed by Schwartz to ink his own work.[3] But the series provides an interesting example of how popular culture can support the values of its era and yet show conflicts at the same time, can even suggest other values that are not those most obviously expected. Given the Cold War background of the period, the sense of democracy/capitalism versus communism, the supposed "missile gap" between the U.S. and the U.S.S.R., and a space race that began with the embarrassment of Sputnik in 1957, one would expect the series to be little more than a showcase – a museum – for the cultural imperialism of the era, for the Cold War brought out into space, and for futuristic soldiers of Earth's expansion (whether colonial or economic) who are white, male, and middle class – whose values are then passed on, in true patriarchal fashion, by the father to the son. And, to be sure, these assumptions are justified: the series *was* heavy with evil aliens and militant solutions – the first object Tommy points to in his first visit to the museum is a ray-gun "used to fight off single-handedly a hundred winged creatures of Saturn" ("World" 2).

But, as John Fiske has argued, popular culture can be "progressive" even while its popularity prevents it from being "radical" (133), that it can encourage its consumers to be active social "agents" and not just passive social "subjects" (180), that readers of popular culture are not over-determined by marketing dictates but that they often choose how much to be involved. This essay points out that contradictions can be seen in even this most un-radical and unquestioning of comic book series. They arise in three areas. First, a museum – just by being a museum – gives a vague official approval to any acts of cultural or militant imperialism that are housed there. But, though the Cold War was obviously influential, much of the activity celebrated in the series is defensive, aggression is often seen as futile, and most of the main characters are not soldiers but explorers, or agents of peace. Second, the heroes are both solitary and yet connected to a larger society, making them both extraordinary and ordinary at the same time; such a contradiction reflects major conflicts of the era, like the uneasy balance between conformity and individualism seen in suburbia and white-collar labor. Finally, the boy listener, Tommy, is more the main subject of the series than the museum itself, for his growing-up and education are emphasized (in some ways, they even become part of the museum), and his development both supports and yet counters late fifties stereotypes, especially the militarism of the times, the ideal of individualism, and the attitudes toward women. Exploring these topics shows that the series, though in no way radical, still offered tentative reconciliations for American middle-class conflicts, for exposing the dreams and frustrations of an age, and for thus "cooking" and not always just "serving" the underlying social conditions.

## Imperialism: "The Toy Soldier War"

As in much science fiction of that age, human expansion into space was a given, seldom examined for root causes like economic growth, population pressure, or cultural and political conflict with a rival nation supposedly expanding too. But selected artifacts of such expansion housed in a museum raise questions about the nature of the institution in the first place. Jane Thompkins, writing about the American West, has argued that museums store "safeguards of our own existence," that the objects preserve "a source of life from which we need to nourish ourselves when the resources that would normally supply us have run dry" (188). For example, she describes the Buffalo Bill Historical Center in Cody,

Wyoming, (a showplace for the art of taxidermy) as

> a kind of charnel house that houses images of living things that have passed away but whose life force still lingers around their remains and so passes itself on to us. We go and look at the objects in the glass cases and at paintings on the wall, as if by standing there we could absorb into ourselves some of the energy that flowed once through the bodies of the life things represented. A museum, rather than being, as we normally think of it, a place most distant from our savage selves, actually caters to the urge to absorb the life of another into one's own life. (188)

Such images of death on display and the vampire-like feeding from it exemplify the notion that even after dying life-forms cannot escape exploitation (and, given the history discussed by the passage, the tone is not overly exaggerated). For viewers to enjoy any museum means for them to buy into the values represented, to absorb the inherent "life" of past events no matter how one-sided or exploitive they might have been. In a similar way, Fiske has said that the price of admission to a traditional art gallery is to accept middle-class definitions of aesthetics (79). Both writers thus suggest that visiting a museum is not free of social and ideological concerns; even if alone, a visitor partakes of this social "gathering place," and just the choice to attend suggests some participation in whatever ideology is on display.

The Space Museum, since touted as a showcase of how the "name and fame of Earth" was spread "throughout the stars" ("World" 2), suggests such a latent cultural imperialism. When the first noted exhibit is a weapon that fought off aliens, a sense of racial survival results, of us against them, of heroes who are soldiers carrying "Earth's banners to the far-flung star-systems" ("Threat" 2). But, as it turns out, the object Tommy picks for the tale is not the weapon but an average pair of contact lenses, which were used as defensive and not offensive devices; the villain is not even an alien race but a supposedly "perfect" robot created by one – it absorbs the "mind-energy" of people and enslaves them. One Earthman ingeniously uses his own personal accidental protection to defeat the threat: he's not affected by the robot because of the contact lenses he wears. The story thus reverses historical expectations. The appeal is not to technological or military strength but to the hero's skillful deduction and Tommy's curiosity over why contact lenses are important enough to be in a museum. What is central here is the narrative context of the object – "story" itself, the unique and surprising tale behind each artifact. Indeed, the museum was not well-labeled; Tommy's father had to relate almost every tale – no placards gave it away. Such encouragement for cross-generational bonding and oral story-telling – if only for reasons of plot-production – seems quaintly attractive when today's technology, like the Internet and email, provides "participation" only when people are already divided by distance and machines. A past future holding a major social museum where stories are not so much housed as told, where objects (technology) have significance only in how they are narrated face-to-face, is, in retrospect, a naïve, idyllic, and yet still unachieved dream.

The emphasis on context can be seen in the list of objects chosen by the curious Tommy: a tree branch, a human strand of hair, a goblet of water, a document saying "son of two worlds," a stuffed magpie, a jewel that is said not to be a jewel, a silver (not gold) medal, a wrist-watch, a sewing needle. One is struck by the lack of imperialistic overtones and an emphasis on the organic or ironic instead. These objects are ordinary but made extraordinary by the story each tells; they seem hardly unique, but they must be special since housed in the museum. Indeed, their unlikelihood for uniqueness always leads Tommy to ask "why?" thus generating the story. Though many of the objects do tell of confrontational events (the stick was used as an energy weapon), even obviously militaristic symbols have a quirk of difference: an alien rifle shoots "crookedly," the model of a futuristic soldier is a *toy* soldier. Again, it is the quirk that produces the wonder. The items are not heirlooms or antiques; they are unique only in their context. They represent actions more than "thingness," agency instead of objecthood. Their "sustenance" – in Jane Thompkins' sense – exists more in the sharing between the teaching father and the receptive son, of the boy's self-application and imitation of the model behavior – and not through the accumulation of relics of conquest or possession (like the coins in a Scroogian money bin, to use another icon from the period). Furthermore, since the museum for the reading audience was *science fiction*, it contained a posed imaginary future and not a completed real past – in essence, there's nothing to "preserve" yet. Any life-force that might be sustaining is still in the inspiration and goal stage, not products of a past that now seem to exist only to be deconstructed and re-evaluated. The museum supplied models for behavior-to-come and not embarrassments of behavior-that-was, or examples famous now made historically infamous.

These differences can be seen in the appropriately entitled, "The Toy Soldier War." An alien race, the Jorgans, specializes in making toys, and their planet is threatened by alien invaders. The Jorgans have no defense system (they just make toys), and thus they are coerced into doing the invaders' bidding. A buyer from Earth persuades a craftsman to use the toys themselves as weapons. (That the Earthman comes up with the idea demonstrates the self-serving nature of the series – and maybe a contradicting suggestion that only an Earthman could ever think of using toys as weapons.) In lines that would sound terrifying today, the gentle and hardly militant toy-maker considers the idea: "Yes – I can make this space-dragon exhale atomic fire instead of sparks, and arm this battle-cruiser with tiny nuclear warheads!" And the Earthman adds, "These toy soldiers could carry real ray-guns!" (3). But there's a catch. The toys have a weakness, not revealed until the end of the story. They are purely self-defensive; they can't attack, they can only *re*act to hostile acts against them. The invaders, so ruthless they can't help blasting at the toys even when they are not threatened by them, are thus defeated because of their *own* "brutal, warlike nature" (5).

The story thus answers the charge of militarism. All the aliens had to do to escape was never shoot at the toys in the first place. The defense is not built on bigger bombs but on the fault – and it's highlighted as a fault – of aggressive ruthlessness in the enemy. Against the Cold War mood of the time, this story argues pacifism – certainly no radical idea but somewhat progressive given the era (with its still latent McCarthy jitters) and the medium of comic books (with its Comics Code and post-Wertham restrictions). After all, Heinlein's *Starship Troopers* had just come out (1959), Khrushchev was saying, "We will bury you," and the Cuban Missile Crisis was only a few years away. Instead of this example working as energy-feed for jaded observers, it provides a model of behavior that questions the assumptions of "shooting first," that does not praise "the everlasting glory of the infantry" (the last statement in the Heinlein book), and that can be modeled by a simple businessman in an interstellar free market whose ingenuity is more important than the ray-gun technology.

## Heroism: "Son of Two Worlds"

Since behind every object in the museum was a "story of heroism, daring, self-sacrifice" ("World" 2), the kind of hero exemplified deserves attention. Jones and Jacobs define the "unvarying" Schwartzian hero as a "positivist in a positivistic world, using reason and knowledge to master an ultimately knowable universe and thus restore our unquestioned status quo to proper order" (22). This emphasis on active ingenuity, a scientifically knowable world (material, rational, confidently manipulative), and how that world supports the dominant culture of the time, I have explored elsewhere.[4] In addition, we can see how ordinary objects were used ingeniously in new and extraordinary ways. But also addressed here will be three other related characteristics of these heroes: they were alone, they were ordinary, and they were different – that the last two ideas contradict each other demonstrates the conflicts of the age.

## The Solitary Hero

This contradiction, which in many ways is also the contradiction of popular culture (that it can be supportive of the status quo and yet question it at the same time), can be seen in the *aloneness* of the main characters. Their heroic deeds were often performed in solitude, yet not done for the glorification of an individual ego but as self-sacrifice for the survival of a larger group (usually, in sweeping comic book terms, a whole planet or the entire human race). The individualism was not "possessive"; social interaction was not made subordinate to a solitary human enterprise motivated by manipulation of others or a brooding self-enclosure.[5]

A net of solitude and self-sacrifice can be seen in "Secret of the Space Jewel," the second story in the series. The main character is a great space hero who once saved an alien world, yet the story is about the inhabitants who, years later, suddenly despise him: "They treat me with scorn and contempt! *Why*?" (1). This is not contemporary post-colonial reaction lifted to the stars; instead, a villain pretended to be the hero and made a bad impression with exploitation and greed. The man is isolated, made "lonely" by the composition of the panels, often framing the contemplative hero in empty space, but not by the dialogue or plot. He does not retreat into Romantic self-absorption or robber-baron manipulation. His primary concern is just to do his job: he's an ambassador from the interstellar "United Nations," and he needs to clear his reputation before he can begin work. To find the villain impersonating him, he simply has to act alone. He does catch the villain, is accepted again by the world that shunned him, and thus he is able to fulfill his still solitary role as a foreign representative supporting a collectivity. Aloneness did not imprison or torment him, or preclude him from working for others.

Similarly in "Revolt of the Spaceships!" the pilot hero has only one "friend," his spaceship, yet he is able to help in saving humanity. He built the ship himself and named it "Ike" (obviously appropriate for that era). He becomes a planetary surveyor, a job where he is alone, and he relieves tension by treating the spaceship like a pal: "The space-trails are lonely for a man who works by himself and 'Ike' became like a buddy" (4). But later in the story, all spaceships become possessed with an alien intelligence, which makes them – sentient now – rebel against Earthmen. The pilot convinces Ike to remain loyal by arguing their friendship: "We're more than pilot and ship! We're *buddies*!" (5). Ike sacrifices its "life," its self-awareness, to defeat the aliens and save the humans. The ship thus is awarded a medal of honor and is eventually housed in the Space Museum – giving it a home, a final resting spot for a loved and faithful object (and the motivation here counters the view of the museum as an energy bank for consuming visitors). Even though this "buddy" relationship is between a man and a machine, the personal devotion between them saves other people and thus extends into a loyalty to the race. Even Ike, the machine, says, "It is the *humans* who count in space" (6). This is not so much a sublimation of affection onto technology as a celebration of connection to a larger group, that even loners – and their machines – are part of a whole, and devotion to that "whole" by individuals is sanctified by the museum.

So these heroes are not rogues, rebels, or Byronic outsiders. They support the middle-class ideals of the time (devotion, hard work, materialism, loyalty), but they still walk a balance between independence and self-sacrifice. They thus appeal to *both* fifties habits of wanting to be different and yet wanting to be the same, of, for example, loving suburbia and yet fearing its conformity, of wanting advancement in corporate business but wary of losing oneself in the "team." Two great fears of the time were suburban and corporate sameness. The harrowing film *Invasion of the Body Snatchers* (1956), in which humans turn into pods and think utterly the same, was as much inspired by suburbia as fear of communistic uniformity; the maker of the film has said that the original idea was of aliens taking over suburbia – and no one would notice (Halberstam 140). Influential books like *The Lonely Crowd* (1950), *White Collar* (1951), *The Manin the Gray Flannel Suit* (1955), and *The Organizational Man* (1956) expressed the fears that corporate sameness would dry up individual initiative. But, at the same time, we forget that the early criticism of suburbia often had an elitist slant to it, and that many middle-class families were quite happy with their new homes, feeling empowered at the sense of independence (many having moved from urban apartments) and freedom to enjoy the open space of new backyards or the highways of the growing interstate system.[6] For all the corporate sameness of the era, this was also the time of such financial independents as Ray Kroc (McDonalds), Kemmons Wilson (Holiday Inn), and Ed Cole (the '55 Chevy, or "the poor man's Caddy") and such charismatic leaders as Martin Luther King and, in the early sixties, John F. Kennedy. So the interaction of solitude and suddenly-being-the-savior-of-civilization seen in these comic book stories can yet suggest a response to underlying historical tensions, the argument – or at least the dream – that one could be independent and depended on at the same time, can follow one's call and yet help others – that one could be a "hero."

## The Ordinary Hero

Many stories stressed that the heroes were ordinary. Even though the pilot mentioned above is portrayed as exceptional – he's smart enough to build his own spaceship – he's not a genius, and he's certainly not self-important. His defining characteristic is more his affection for his spaceship. The heroes are special because they solve extraordinary problems – like invasions from space and whole Earth dangers – but they are ordinary in that they have qualities that anyone can obtain, like insight, inventiveness, and bravery. They are average people rising to the occasion, fulfilling a responsibility placed on them and willing to act for others. Here too they are separate – acting alone – and yet part of a group, for their "ordinariness" makes them like everyone else, and thus not lonely.

A story in which the "ordinary" is openly stressed is "Threat of the Planet Wreckers!" where three unarmed asteroid miners, "ordinary men – neither soldiers nor heroes" (5), find themselves, by chance, to be the only people who can stop ruthless aliens who want to rule the Solar System.[7] Though feeling inadequate, they know they've "got to try" (5). Their plan is simple (each man one-at-a-time attacks the aliens so that the next man can learn more about their weapons). Tommy, the boy listener, comments, "Golly! Those men were ordinary people, but they saved us all! They never sought to be heroes, but they sure turned out to be!" (8). It's a lesson for humility – they simply accepted the responsibility of the moment. Since they were not mutations, "more than human," X-Men, Supermen, or the next evolutionary step, they prove that greatness is contained in the ordinary, that being average does not prevent one from achieving. This notion relates to the historical era. In David Halberstam's words, the family sitcoms of the fifties seemed to argue that "to be ordinary is to be better" (510). This idea only intensifies the tension between conformity and individualism, arguing that "being the same" is more a strength than a weakness. Indeed, given the Cold War attitudes, such an idea is not surprising: going along with traditional middle class norms provides a unified bloc against the threat of communist takeover. In some ways, the *Space Museum* stories argue this idea more pointedly than the sitcoms, since Ozzie Nelson was never threatened by galactic invaders or the end of the world. These stories don't act to "reduce" oneself to the ordinary (and thus produce an ambiguity that the ordinary is supposed to be "better"), but to use the strength *in* the ordinary to perform heroic world-saving tasks – to be lifted up instead of pulled down, to placate the ambiguity and tension by demonstrating the optimism that anyone with insight can be a hero.

## The Unique Hero

Yet several stories do stress uniqueness, that the hero *is* different from everyone else. These stories, however, emphasize more the hero *wanting* to be ordinary so as to fit in with others. At this point, it is important to remember the adolescent or pre-adolescent readers, for underlying the need to "fit in" is the adolescent sense of awkwardness, of being different and unaccepted, which is part of the stories' appeal for the young reader. The important thrust is identity, the need to find one's own self – very pertinent to the adolescent – and an identity within the greater collectivity: not just a growing "up" but a growing "into" the dominant culture. While the ordinary hero feels part of the group already, the character who seems different searches for acceptance, for reasons behind the personal uniqueness, for the secret of self and one's true name. The rest of society does not need to conform to him (the use of the male pronoun is intentional) as its people would if he were the next evolutionary step; instead he conforms to them. He's an outsider wanting in and not an overlord trying to lead the pack; the emphasis is not on Nietzschean *or* comic book supermen.

An excellent example of such desire to know where one fits occurs in "Son of Two Worlds!" in which the main character since childhood has wondered why he is different – he sees strong emotions in people as emitted colored rays, stress in materials as peculiar glows. His father tells him only: "I'll explain . . . when you're old enough to understand" (2). (And what youth would not identify with *that*?) But when he's six years old, his parents die before they can tell him the secret of his capabilities. As he grows, he keeps them to himself since, "Other boys merely laughed at him and he didn't want to be 'different'" (3) (more appeal to adolescents, especially "nerd" SF comic book readers). His only clue is that he remembers his parents mentioning a planet whose name he cannot find in any registry. So he devotes his life to finding that world: he attends Space Academy and studies hard – alone, of course – to become a space pilot. And eventually, in a kind of male Cinderella story, he finds he's the "lost prince" or rightful ruler of another world and that the tyrant reigning there had tried to kill his father (the tyrant's brother) who had escaped to Earth. Only members of the royal family can see the colors of emotion or stress. So he finds his lineage – and fulfills the adolescent dream of secretly being more than someone just laughed at by others. However, his growth in power is hardly emphasized. We never see him don the trappings of rule, and his one "political" event in the story is to lead the escape of prisoners he's been jailed with (and this event is described as more intellectual than political – he deduces how to counter the power of the electric force field imprisoning them by not grounding himself). More important to him is finding who he is, his family and his name. Furthermore, at the end of the story, his identity is defined as "son of two worlds…citizen of one, ruler of the other" (8). So an ordinary Earth citizen can also be a ruler of an entire planet – ordinary and extraordinary at the same time. Indeed, one can argue that in these stories finding identity alone makes one heroic. Since other installments argue that heroism is latent in ordinary people, then finding one's identity is also to find one's own true heroic self.

In short, this blending of ordinary and extraordinary, of solitude and connection to society, offers a tentative reconciliation for the problem of individuality in a conformist culture – the stories say you can have both. You can be "better" by being not just ordinary but extraordinary too. Saving civilization – and thus being connected to it – is also to find your unique self. You can be the next-door suburban neighbor and the prince of another planet at the same time.

## Identity: "Earth Victory – By a Hair"

As seen above, into this brew of social contradictions comes the adolescent, the child growing up and about to enter the adult world – knowing he's close to doing so, pondering the ramifications of the act. The adult American world of the late fifties-early sixties is a conformist block, a monolithic culture defined by class, race, lifestyle, television, and the culture of suburbia. It is not the pluralistic, fragmented, and de-centered culture(s) of today's postmodern world. Though juvenile delinquency, the Beats, and rock-and-roll complicated the stage of adolescence in the fifties, making it a lifestyle unto itself (a *Rebel without a Cause* interlude), growing up was still assumed to be manageable – as the problems of outer space technology and meetings with interstellar aliens could still be controlled if one was just careful and rational enough.[8] Physics, and becoming an adult, were knowable – if being questioned. All that an adolescent had to do was, so to speak, pass the entrance exam – recognize the requirements and necessary skills. Though the culture joined would still be contradictory (in matters of race, sex, work, and consumerism), the process of joining it was still the easiest way of finding a place and a self – even if that self was already defined and provided little choice for variety. (To the adolescent, the problem of no adult variety was still down the road, yet to be encountered, and although "dropping out" soon would become more attractive to youth, this was an alternative of denial and not a solution for someone wanting to join). Simply to arrive was to be defined.

So the emphasis on ordinary heroism and on a museum full of role-model *stories* more than objects comes together in the character of the adolescent listener, Tommy – in his development, his growing up, and especially in his finding who he was. Indeed, the real subject of the series was not so much the museum but Tommy himself – to the point at which a trophy to him is eventually placed in the museum where he joins an even more hallowed group than just the society of adulthood.

First of all, the stories provided Tommy with an education, a kind of core curriculum in basic skills. In "Second-Best Spaceman!"[9] he's encouraged to keep trying no matter how often he is defeated. Tommy is disappointed over placing second in a "jetbox derby" and receiving only a silver medal. So his father tells him the story behind a silver medal in the museum: a most decorated officer of the Star Patrol is also disappointed because all his medals were silver. Then a situation arises in which the officer prevents an invasion by using the silver in his medals, the exact substance needed (if they had been gold, the Earth would have been conquered). The lesson is spelled out by Tommy's father: "No matter how often you fail – victory can eventually be yours if you try hard enough to win!" (8). And from there on, Tommy says he will wear his second-best medal proudly. In "Secret of the Energy Weapon!" he learns the need to trust one's self, one's own innate capabilities (the story is about activating our full brain power). In "The Tree of 1000 Colors!" he comes to appreciate and mimic the rational skills of analytic reasoning the story's hero demonstrates. His father says to him, "Observation and deduction are important traits out among the stars, Tommy! I'm glad to see you've learned them at an early age!" (8).

But more emphasized than this general education – which makes him "ordinary," or, rather, socialized into a basic competency (rational, male, scientific) that contains, according to the stories' ideology, the capacity for heroism – is the achievement of his own identity. "The Gem Invasion of Earth!" explains how Tommy got his name. His father brings him to the museum on his fourteenth birthday to show him a special exhibit, a stuffed magpie that, when alive and a boy's pet, saved the Earth from destruction. This event occurred fourteen years ago, on the day Tommy was born. Because of it, his parents chose the name of the magpie – Tommy – for their son. In "The Mass-Energy Robbers of Space!" Tommy *becomes* the protagonist and the episode's hero. Only three "interplanetary boy scouts" from Mars, Venus, and Earth are free to repel an alien invasion, which they succeed in doing through an ingenuity that, as demonstrated, is not an exclusive prerequisite of adulthood. The story also emphasizes interplanetary – and thus international and interracial – cooperation. It was predictable that such a story starring Tommy would be included in the series. But it did not come without the preparation, the progression of lessons taught to him, and a successive unveiling of his own identity.

Then, in probably the best story of the series, "Earth Victory – By a Hair," we learn how Tommy's parents met, though not until the end of the story is that fact revealed. The social actions of establishing identity – the naming and heroism described above – are supported in this story by the biological act too. Though this act is not free of social influence and the gender-role stereotypes of the time, the story questions those very stereotypes and thus provides both an ordinary and extraordinary background for Tommy. The trophy is a blonde human hair, and when Tommy wants to know why it's in the museum, the father says, "I've waited a long time for you to ask about that" (2). The main character in the tale is called the Wrecker, a tough Major-General of the space-marines. He's assigned to meet an Admiral "Blondy" – who has a "good rep," according to the all-male and no-nonsense Wrecker, who has always wanted to meet "him." But finding that Blondy is a woman, he at first is not happy: "an admiral in skirts?!...This is ridiculous!...I don't approve" (3). But she's not fazed by his criticism, and she quickly proves her piloting skills. When the General tries to tell her how to destroy two attacking enemy craft, she says bluntly, "I'll fight my ship . . . without your advice!" (4). After handling those enemy ships easily, she says: "Any complaints, General?" He doffs his hat to her and replies, "None at all, Admiral!" (5). They then work together to defeat the aliens. One of her blonde hairs has to be used as a sight in an Earth weapon; the General and an "editor's note" explain that female blonde hairs were used in bombsights in WWII because they performed "better than any other material" – to which the Admiral comments, "We women do come in handy now and then, don't we, General?" (7).

Of course, after such romantic play (like the humorous formality of the repeated address to "General" and "Admiral"), they fall in love and are married. Tommy, at the end of the story, learns they're his parents and delivers a line that has to be the dream of all boys for that militant Cold War age: "I wonder if any other kid ever had a General for a father – and an Admiral for a mother?" (8). Identity is established: Tommy learns his heritage – *and* gains an immense respect for his parents. The most militant story in the series is also the most domestic – a blend of *Starship Troopers* and *Ozzie and Harriet* – and thus obviously hints at the contradictions of the time. When bomb shelters were built in backyards, "enemy" satellites could be seen passing overhead, and the suburban home was like a miniature fortress of American values – self-contained, stuffed with consumer goods, ready for the Bomb, attended by made-attractive-in-media stay-at-home housewives – the story playfully desensitizes Cold War fears and sexual inequality by making the military domestic and by giving a woman a position equal to that of the man, and a skill – piloting – that is even better than his. It's no drastic reversal of cultural expectations; the story is just lightly progressive, certainly not radical. And one might argue that it uses a standard fifties device – domesticity turned into a weapon against the Cold War enemy (as the romance comics used it in the early part of the decade[10]). But this is less "family as fortress" than "fortress as family." The surprise is not that the family can be a first line of defense, but that the first line of defense was a family, and a somewhat liberated one at that. For the age, Tommy's shock at his mother's role must have been equaled by the reader's.[11]

Ultimately, and predictably, Tommy himself becomes a part of the Space Museum, and at that point his entrance into the culture is complete. In "Prisoner of the Space Flowers!" a picture of Tommy at age three is unveiled as a trophy (after a required twelve-year consideration-for-acceptance period). On that day, his fifteenth birthday, his mother comes for the ceremony, and a story is told which Tommy never knew. Through an elaborate and outlandish ploy (the plots became more contrived as the series went on), Tommy, the child, helped save his parents which, in turn, saved the Earth. Indeed, it is a downright family story, with the mother demonstrating her incredible piloting skills, the father being ingenious, and Tommy, having watched his father so much, apparently working the spaceship himself – just the exploits of a "standard" American family out driving for the weekend (in a spaceship), who happen to prevent the destruction of their homeworld. As Tommy says at the end: "Boy oh boy! Did any fella ever have a birthday present as wonderful as this?" (8). His ordinary and extraordinary qualities, which socialize and distinguish him at the same time, are thus proven, and he is granted a home in the Space Museum itself. He is grounded in domesticity, the shared realm of ordinary competence, and in a distinctive social place, an institution that will last through history – like being rooted on Earth (or in a specific Earth culture) and yet climbing into space. Such "doubleness" or equal footing demonstrates the historical turning-point of the era itself, with its science-fictional (and scientific) emphasis on the present vision and coming reality of the space program, on the dream and assumed realization that humans were about to leave the "cradle" of Earth. Perhaps only during that era was the dream of spaceflight so "potential," so possible and so not yet buried under economic constraints and the disappointing lifeless environments soon-to-be-found on other planets. The age was in its own adolescent moment of expectation for the future as much as was Tommy.

## Conclusion

For all of these ways in which the series demonstrated a reconciliation of the major fifties contradiction between conformity and personal identity, such compromises were still only temporary, a buying of time before the identity crises of the late sixties, the "consciousness-raising" and political ferment with its you-can't-straddle-the-fence attitudes. It was strictly a mild resolution fit for the surface placidity of the era, well within its social assumptions and class structures, and hardly disturbing to them. (The only real "surprise" of the series is the mother being an Admiral and having a skill that is stronger than the father's.) Furthermore, as argued, the real unifying subject of the series was not the Space Museum, nor the heroism and bravery on display. It was Tommy. Not just how he learned life skills but how he learned to be himself, and how, through identification, the young boy reader was encouraged to do the same. With his unique parents and yet his conformist upbringing, by entering the social institution of a museum that houses individual achievements (a compromise of the contradiction itself), Tommy answers even more directly the "charnel house" label sometimes given to any museum. For he is very much alive when he joins it; he is still growing, still has a future, and is still poised on the adventure of adulthood. He is no dead relic of the past whose only value is a weak nutrition. He is a living agent, ready for action, and though he might never change his world (never be encouraged to do so, never question his class, race, or privilege, never find in himself the need for such), his learning – from the Museum, his father, *and* his mother – readies him for saving it from fictional threats (if the bigger – more outlandish and more external – the better). Who knows? If the readers fully identified with Tommy's "lessons," then such an upbringing might have contributed to the actual self-examination that would occur historically as they grew older: 1968 wasn't that far away.

## Notes

1. An earlier version of this article was presented at the International Conference for the Fantastic in the Arts, Fort Lauderdale, Florida, May 2001.
2. See Schwartz and Thomsen for a biography of this famous editor.
3. Jones and Jacobs also describe an average story, define the typical Schwartzian hero, and then discuss the uniqueness of the artwork in relation to the rest of Infantino's career. They describe how Infantino's own personal inking created a "loose and exuberant line that suggested rather than delineated, a line sometimes rough and scratchy, sometimes delicate and wistful, but never merely illustrative" – which Schwartz found too "impressionistic" for the major comics (22-23). Also, see Infantino and Spurlock (60-61, 92-93), for more on this artist's own inking style.
4. In "Touching the Night Sky: 'Progressing' the 50s in *Strange Adventures* and *Mystery In Space*," *Journal of the Fantastic in the Arts*, 13: 4 (2003), 389-402.
5. I paraphrase here language used by Eagleton (171).
6. Halberstam covers both sides of this contradiction (131-143, 521-536). The conformity of the era and its resulting tensions are discussed also in Carter (90-113) and Patterson (337-342).
7. But the situation is made a bit more poignant, the aliens given sympathetic motivation for what they are doing. They originally came from a planet that used to orbit the area where the asteroid belt exists now and that was destroyed after they left. They are homesick, they long for their planet back, and they gather up the asteroids to reform it and then insist that the rest of the solar system provide them with laborers who will rebuild their civilization, to make their homeworld "fair and fertile" (3). Their approach, of course, is megalomaniacal, but their sorrow and bitterness is made to be understandable. "Bad" aliens were sometimes handled with such sympathy in the series.
8. For more on prose science fiction's faith in rationality see Huntington (passim).
9. This same story is mentioned in Jones and Jacobs (22).
10. See White (131-133) for how romance comics supported Cold War attitudes.
11. Jones and Jacobs also have pointed out Schwartz's insistence on strong women characters in other comics he edited (37). But a later story in *Space Museum*, "The Evolutionary Ensign of Space!" is more ambiguous. In this one, Tommy's mother takes him to the Museum instead of his father, and she shows how she once defeated aliens with a sewing needle. That she's the best space-pilot is stressed – she can "turn a ship inside a bucket of paint" (4). But Tommy's reactions at the end of the story demonstrates stereotypes of the time. First, he's disappointed that she, unlike "Dad," did not stop

short toward the end of the story to give him the chance to deduce the solution. He frowns while saying, "[Dad] stops at a critical point and challenges me to figure out how the memento in the *Space Museum* was used! You didn't give me the chance" (8). The series never questioned the patriarchal educational bond. But then he's happy, smiling in the next moment, because he has "the prettiest mother in the universe!" (8) – and thus great piloting is hidden behind "looks."

## Works Cited

Benton, Mike. *Science Fiction Comics: The Illustrated History*. Dallas: Taylor Publishing, 1992.
Carter, Paul A. *Another Part of the Fifties*. New York: Columbia UP, 1983.
Eagleton, Thomas. *Literary Theory: An Introduction*. 2nd ed. Minneapolis, MN: U of Minnesota P, 1996.
Fiske, John. *Understanding Popular Culture*. 1989 rpt. London and New York: Routledge, 1996.
Fox, Gardner. "Earth Victory – By a Hair!" *Strange Adventures* 124 (January 1961): 1-8.
----. "The Evolutionary Ensign of Space!" *Strange Adventures* 148 (January 1963): 1-8.
----. "The Gem-Invasion of Earth!" *Strange Adventures* 115 (April 1960): 1-8.
----. "The Mass-Energy Robbers of Space!" *Strange Adventures* 145 (October 1962): 1-8.
----. "Prisoner of the Space-Flowers!" *Strange Adventures* 142 (July 1962): 1-8.
----. "Revolt of the Spaceships!" *Strange Adventures* 112 (January 1960): 1-8.
----. "Second-Best Spaceman!" *Strange Adventures* 136 (January 1962): 1-8.
----. "Secret of the Energy Weapon!" *Strange Adventures* 139 (April 1962): 1-8.
----. "Secret of the Space-Jewel!" *Strange Adventures* 106 (July 1959): 1-8.
----. "Son of Two Worlds!" *Strange Adventures* 127 (April1961): 1-8.
----. "Threat of the Planet Wreckers!" *Strange Adventures* 118 (July 1960): 1-8.
----. "The Toy Soldier War!" *Strange Adventures* 130 (July 1961): 1-8.
----. "The Tree of 1000 Colors!" *Strange Adventures* 151 (April 1963): 1-8.
----. "World of Doomed Spacemen!" *Strange Adventures* 104 (May 1959): 1-8.
Halberstam, David. *The Fifties*. New York: Ballantine, 1993.
Huntington, John. *Rationalizing Genius: Ideological Struggles in the Classic American Science Fiction Short Story*. New Brunswick: Rutgers UP, 1989.
Infantino, Carmine and J. David Spurlock. *The Amazing World of Carmine Infantino*. Lebanon, NJ: Vanguard Productions, 2000.
Jones, Gerard and Will Jacobs. *The Comic Book Heroes*. Rocklin, CA: Prima Publishing, 1997.
Patterson, James T. *Grand Expectations: The United States, 1945-1971*. Oxford: Oxford UP, 1996.
Schwartz, Julius and Brian M. Thomsen. *Man of Two Worlds: My Life in Science Fiction and Comics*. New York: HarperCollins, 2000.
Thompkins, Jane. *West of Everything*. New York: Oxford UP, 1993.
White, Bradford W. *Comic Book Nation: The Transformation of Youth Culture in America*. Baltimore: Johns Hopkins, 2001.

*J.D. Salinger's 1951 novel is, without question, one of the most read in American history – to call it a bestseller is truly to understate the matter. Generations of high school and college students have had it as assigned reading in their literature classes. Ironically perhaps, because Lawrence Bowden would argue, "You can't teach* The Catcher in the Rye."

# The Ducks in Central Park, Or Why You Can't Teach *The Catcher in the Rye*

## Lawrence Bowden

The "catcher in the rye" proceeds from a mistake, a mistake that we as readers and we as teachers are prone to make as well. I'm not talking about the *novel*; I'm referring to Holden's fantasy vocation of becoming a "catcher," the fantasy after which the novel takes its name. I can't help but wonder whether Salinger ever regrets his choice of title.... How many of us, at some time in our reading, have blundered into thinking that "to become a catcher in the rye is the story's culminating vision"? You recall the passage I'm referring to? – Where in response to his worries about becoming a "phony" Holden says to his sister Phoebe:

> I keep picturing all these little kids playing some game in this big field of rye and all. Thousands of little kids, and nobody's around – nobody big, I mean – except me. And I'm standing on the edge of some crazy cliff. What I have to do, I have to catch everybody if they start to go over the cliff – I mean if they're running and they don't look where they're going I have to come out from somewhere and catch them. That's all I'd do all day. I'd just be the catcher in the rye and all. I know it's crazy, but that's the only thing I'd really like to be. I know it's crazy.

That's probably the most frequently quoted passage from the novel and, as an image, was immortalized on the cover of *Time* magazine. But remember how Phoebe points out Holden's misappropriation of Robert Burns? She makes it clear that it's about *meeting*, not *catching*. Why, then, is it that students and professional readers alike so easily fail to see that the end of *The Catcher in the Rye* (the novel) is the end of the "catcher in the rye" (the fantasy)? The fact that the fantasy has become virtually the controlling image of the novel is problematic not simply because it eclipses Holden's most authentic realization at the very end of his story, but also because it can seduce us as teachers into becoming "catchers" in the classroom.

As events unfold on that Advent weekend in New York City, what comes to Holden arrives with the force of an epiphany as he watches Phoebe go around on the carrousel in Central Park. "All the kids," he observed, "kept trying to grab for the gold ring, and so was old Phoebe, and I was sort of afraid she'd fall off the goddam horse, *but I didn't say anything or do anything. The thing with kids is, if they want to grab for the gold ring, you have to let them do it, and not say anything. If they fall off*, they fall off" (emphasis mine). When the carrousel stops old Phoebe comes running over to Holden elated. Holden gives her more money for more tickets, gets an unexpected kiss, and sends her off for another try, successfully resisting the temptation to be the catcher in the rye. The power in this moment – not only for what he has realized but also for what he has resisted – is signaled by his feeling so "damn happy" all of a sudden that he was "damn near bawling." In letting Phoebe go, he realizes that there is really nothing that he can or should say or do to protect her from the risks of the ride. Holden has overcome his temptation to shape her experience of the carrousel with his own "greater awareness." He has also discovered, as Rilke said, that one happy smile going "around and around," with no end in mind, "dazzles and dissipates / over this blind and breathless game" we call life. If ever there were a religious epiphany! At that moment *The Catcher* ends and we are left with a brief, but important, postscript in which Holden meets anew, re-members, even the most objectionable encounters of his life.

So what has this to say about the way teachers approach *The Catcher in the Rye* with their students? Well, I would think that one thing it implies if it does not outright proclaim is that we must think carefully about our need to control the text, indeed, to "teach" *The Catcher in the Rye*. That is, if we begin with the assumption that our "greater awareness" of things as professional readers delights in things like plot, structure, character analysis, critical commentary and grants us power over the text (and by extension, then, power over our students) we have unwittingly fallen into a "catcher" role for ourselves however benign our intent.

Our role as teachers often places us in a position to assume that our responsibility is "to get students to see" what Salinger is doing and how he does it – to show them what we believe they can't see for themselves. Indeed, to catch them before they tumble over a precipice into the danger of allowing a text to become a story in which they themselves are implicated and involved. Our apprehensions may lead us to fear that precisely this kind of personal reading and involvement with *The Catcher in the Rye* leads to the making of a John Hinckley…to appropriate the story as explanation or justification for one's own paranoia or delusion. As experienced and seasoned readers familiar with the critical and interpretative literature that has overgrown the text like a field of rye, have we not an obligation to come between students and the precipice of wrong-headed reading? Is not our job to generate analytical and critical distance, to interpret metaphor, elucidate connections, and mediate meaning?

Certainly such assumptions keep CliffsNotes and a number of state mandated "standards of learning" instruments in business. CliffsNotes, in fact, has an expanded edition of *Salinger's The Catcher in the Rye*. Not only does it offer a chapter-by-chapter summary with commentary and a glossary of terms and idioms, but also it contains an expanded critical section that treats the major themes, symbols, and "The Coming of Age Genre." And just to be sure students "get it," there is a review section with Q & A, identification, essay questions, and even creative projects calculated to demonstrate "standards of learning" beyond all reasonable doubt. Just the sort of approach you might assume is tailor-made for a student like Holden…but you'd be wrong.

English was the one subject, you recall, that Holden didn't fail at Pencey Prep. It's pretty clear that he likes to read and its unarguably clear that he loves to write – remember Allie's baseball glove? When it came to the classroom however, he just didn't "do one damn thing the way you're supposed to…not one damn thing." He flunked Vinson's Oral Expression class because he wouldn't "unify and simplify." And contrary to instructions about the need to focus and stay on task, Holden preferred "digression." "I mean," says Holden, "lots of time you don't *know* what interests you most till you start talking about something that *doesn't* interest you most…. I like it when somebody gets excited about something. [But] this teacher…he could drive you crazy sometimes…I mean he'd keep telling you to *unify* and *simplify* all the time. Some things you just can't *do* that to. I mean you can't hardly ever simplify and unify something just because somebody *wants* you to." And doesn't he have a point?

We too like it when a student gets excited about *something* – and especially literature, reading, thinking, writing! But how does that happen? By ingesting CliffsNotes or our notes? Or, by recovering the wide-eyed, palpitating, heart-rending immediacy of the first time – the first time a particular turn of phrase, a familiar voice, or an intimate moment unexpectedly awakened a sense of knowing and of being known? It was that moment when no one stood between us and those words, words sounding in our soul an unanticipated welcome to our own life! To use the jargon, we could relate.

When asked, as a college student, how he would account for his connection with *The Catcher*, Chris Parker in "Why the Hell Not Smash All the Windows?" says,

> I think the language is a big part of it – absurd exaggeration and complete vagueness. "One of those little English jobs that can do around 200 miles an hour." "My parents would have about two hemorrhages apiece if I told them…." It's a way of being casual – the use of "or something," "and all," "the thing" in every other sentence. The whole idea about being completely unconcerned about anything – except absurd little things, idiosyncrasies. Like [Holden's] great interest in the ducks in Central Park, and his complete lack of interest in school. [What's that all about?!]

In his book *J.D. Salinger*, James Miller, former editor of *College English*, says, "what it's all about" is exactly what CliffsNotes and much of our concern in the classroom is not: "plot irrelevancies." Miller suggests that the reason synopses and so much critical interpretation are inadequate to *The Catcher* is that they are inadequate to the *experience* of the novel. What a skeleton of events or a character analysis reveals, ironically, is how relatively *un*important the events are. They show, by contrast, "how dependent [the book] is on incidental detail…for its most moving and profound meanings. Such detail and such crucially relevant irrelevancies are woven into the book's very texture." Just like real life. This kind of detailing creates not only character and atmosphere. It makes Holden authentic and real – even with all of his hypocrisy and his own kind of phoniness. These plot irrelevancies are Holden's digressions, the play of mind free of mediating constraints that dares to be interested and even excitable.

Let's take the ducks in Central Park…. In classroom terms you could almost identify them as a unifying theme or metaphor since Holden's interest in them appears at the very beginning of the story, a couple of times in the middle, and then again near the end. In fact, one might argue that it was that walk over to the park to "see what the hell the ducks were doing, see if they were around or not" that signals the denouement. Following that decision to "see what the hell the ducks were doing," Holden decides that he's got to sneak back home and see old Phoebe before heading west. It is only after Phoebe is on the scene that the knots in Holden's mind and heart begin to loosen. But, of course, the ducks are neither a "major theme" nor a "major symbol" in CliffsNotes because they are not a major theme or a major symbol in the interpretative literature – at least as far as I have read. So Holden's interest in them, no matter how often that interest surfaces, must indeed qualify as a plot irrelevancy. And it is…until a mind like that of Chris Parker's, whom I quoted earlier, notices and begins to wander about with Holden free from the rules of engagement. Then the ducks in Central Park, or their absence, get interesting. Here's how…

One of the things we know about *The Catcher in the Rye* is that the version we have is not Mr. Salinger's first. He'd been exploring the themes and characters of the novel in six other stories, the earliest of which appeared in the *Saturday Evening Post* in 1944. Two of those early stories, one from *Collier's* and one from *The New Yorker*, are substantially incorporated into the novel as we have it. But before *The Catcher* was published in 1951, Mr. Salinger submitted another 90-page version for publication in 1946. Just before going to press he withdrew it from publication and, obviously, went back to work. In those years between the 1946 version and 1951, Mr. Salinger discovered D.T. Suzuki and R.H. Blyth. Suzuki and Blyth more than anyone else are responsible for the burst of popular interest in Zen in America following the war. Protestations not withstanding, Mr. Salinger was studying Zen Buddhism right along with the Beat poets and writers of the post-war era. Knowing that, listen to this Zen mondo that R. H. Blyth translates for us in his 1976 book *Games Zen Masters Play*. It is interesting to consider in association with the ducks in Central Park:

> One day Hyakujo was out taking a walk with his master Baso when a flock of ducks flew overhead. "What are they" Baso asked. "They are wild ducks." "Where are they flying?" [the master continued] "They have already flown away, Master." At that point in the game, Baso suddenly grabbed Hyakujo's nose and twisted it until, overcome by pain, Hyakujo cried out. "You say they have flown away," said Baso, "but really they have been here from the very beginning."
>
> [Blyth comments:] Hyakujo's statement "they have flown away" is true enough on the ordinary level of common sense. They are no longer here but have gone someplace else. But at the moment of acute pain his normal thinking process was stopped and he saw directly what Baso was pointing to in his statement, "they have been here from the very beginning." The point of the statement is not a new kind of logic or belief but a new way of seeing…an "open secret" which has been right in front of our eyes from the very beginning.

The ducks, whether physically evident or not, *are* present to the mind that thinks about them.

Now I have no intention of suggesting that Holden's query about the ducks in Central Park is anything more than curiosity, but isn't it an odd kind of thing to ask a New York taxi driver? From the beginning, Holden wants to know, "Where did the ducks go?" When he blurts his question out in the taxi, the driver's response is hardly surprising, "What're ya tryna do, bud? Kid me?" It's our response as well…you can't tell me that Holden Caulfield is such an urban dunce that he knows nothing about birds and migration however often he brings it up. But what else are we to conclude? Either he knows or he doesn't and in any case the "answer" (if you will) is obvious, an "open secret" which has been right in front of his eyes from the very beginning. After dropping Phoebe's record, breaking it into about fifty pieces and "damn near crying" because it made him feel so terrible, he enters the park, wanders all around the lagoon looking for the ducks, nearly falls in, then finds a bench and sits shivering imagining that he will get pneumonia and die. It's not his own death that seems so troubling, but "thinking how old Phoebe would feel." In that moment of acute pain, his normal thinking process stops, his mind clears, and he sees as plainly as ever he will what he must do.

Now I think that one could go on to show how from this moment on Holden awakens to that "open secret" which has been right in front of his eyes from the very beginning. But rather than pursue that academic exercise, I want to shift our attention back to what the ducks in Central Park suggest to us about teaching (or not teaching) *The Catcher in the Rye*.

Holden's mind first drifts toward the ducks on page thirteen while he's telling old Spenser "how most people didn't appreciate how tough it is being a teacher." Then comes this bit of trenchant musing to himself: "I'm lucky, though. I mean I could shoot the bull to old Spencer and think about those ducks at the same time. It's funny. You don't have to think too hard when you talk to a teacher." Insulting? Maybe…but I don't think that's to the point. His point is that as teachers we're so programmed and predictable because we spend more energy on producing what passes for measurable achievement than we do cultivating imaginative minds. By "shooting the bull" Holden is "following the program," saying what he knows old Spenser, teachers, want to hear. Holden has "learned his teacher" so well that he conducts his conversation almost mechanically, leaving his mind free to wander. But in the process he realizes just how "poles apart" he and old Spenser really are, and how empty the conversation can't help but be. It's a painful realization, and not only for students like Holden. It is devastating for authors as well, authors who, in Mr. Salinger's view, are poles apart from their interpreters. His disdain for the intellectual arrogance of the northeastern establishment, Ivy League snobs, and professional readers like English professors and literary critics is well documented. Bruce Bawer reminds us in "Salinger's Arrested Development," "Referring to a controversy between Sinclair Lewis and the critic Bernard De Voto over the merits of Lewis's novel, *Arrowsmith*, Mr. Salinger [once] observed that De Voto was probably in the right but had 'no right to be right.' In a just world [he claimed] novelists like Lewis would be criticized not by 'small-time' opinionizers like De Voto but 'by men of their own size' – that is, by writers of fiction."

It is such a tempting affliction to know it all! Mr. Salinger himself succumbed to it, and despised himself for it. Shortly before *The Catcher* was published, he was invited to speak to a short story class at Sarah Lawrence. According to William Maxwell in the 1951 *Book of the Month Club News*, Salinger said, "I went, and I enjoyed the day, but I wouldn't want to do it again. I got very oracular and literary. I found myself labeling all the writers I respect. A writer, when he's asked to discuss his craft, ought to get up and call out in a loud voice just the *names* of the *writers* he loves." No need for labeling. No need for interpretation or justification or explanation. But we're so schooled for doing it! These labels and interpretations, Mr. Salinger seems to be suggesting, too easily eclipse or supplant the writing itself. The writing deserves, indeed, needs to be met directly, immediately – amateurishly.

In Zen, one strives for what the masters call "beginner's mind," a mind that sees directly into the true nature of oneself and one's world. Beginner's mind is a mind uncluttered by years of being taught – being told – what to think and feel, how to think or feel, and even when to think and feel. The games Zen players play are games to uncover our original mind, our beginner's mind – strategies designed, first, to pare away all of the clutter and opinion that actually filters, shapes, and colors our perception of everything. Overwhelmed by such clutter, overpowered by all we've been given to believe, we can scarcely be said to have what Emerson called an "original relationship" with the universe. What makes Holden so compelling is that we can see that he is just as overwhelmed by what he criticizes as Mr. Salinger was at Sarah Lawrence. He is believable because he is just as much a phony as we are, and is sickened by it. We approach life with a beginner's mind when we remove what comes between us and our experience of the world – or of literature. Beginner's mind is the mind of Mr. Salinger's "amateur reader," to whom he dedicates his last published book, to "anyone who just reads and runs."

It might be argued that "reading and running" is something Mr. Salinger knows a bit about. He had as rough a time negotiating high school as did Holden, finally graduating from Valley Forge Military Academy in 1936. He did some time at NYU and Ursinus College, without graduating, before sitting in on a short-story writing class taught by Whit Burnett in 1939 at Columbia. That experience changed his life. Burnett, then editor of *Story* magazine, recognized young Salinger's talent and published his first story in

1940. In 1964, Salinger was invited to write the Introduction for *Story Jubilee: 33 Years of Story*. Rather than the expected "Introduction," what he chose to do was to pen "A Salute to Whit Burnett," a tribute that didn't appear until 1975. It is the only piece of non-fiction that Mr. Salinger has published. It's important because of what we learn about good teaching – at least as far as one student is concerned – but also because it comes as close as anything to seeing the ducks on the pond.

The tribute begins by making it clear that Whit Burnett saw the classroom not as a staging area to display his own personal interests or to use for his own professional advancement, but as an arena to serve the interests of the "Short Story" itself. (Salinger, by the way, capitalizes "Short Story," as if to emphasize its integrity as a living form.) In Salinger's words, Burnett "conducted a short-story course, never mugwumped over one…. He plainly had no intention of using fiction as a leg up for himself." In other words, teaching was about *meeting* rather than *catching*. Burnett was able to get out of the way and create a moment for meeting – not between himself and his students, but between his students and the story. Here's what Salinger says:

> In class, one evening, Mr. Burnett felt himself in the mood to read Faulkner's "That Evening Sun Go Down" out loud, and he went right ahead and did it…most singularly and indescribably….Almost anybody picked at random from a crowded subway car would have given a more dramatic or "better" performance. But that was just the point. Mr. Burnett very deliberately forbore to perform. He abstained from reading beautifully. It was as if he had turned himself into a reading lamp…. By and large, he left you on your own to know how the characters were saying what they were saying. You got your Faulkner straight, without any middlemen between. Not before or since have I heard a reader make such instinctive and wholehearted concessions to a born printed-page writer's needs and, aye, rights…. Not once…did Burnett come between the author and his beloved silent reader. [He left Faulkner] intact, unfinagled with, suitably content.

Well, this is rich. The relationship "between the author and his beloved silent reader" as Salinger sees it is very nearly sacred. The author has a "right" to meet his beloved on her own terms, "intact and unfinagled with." The skilled teacher, then, should be less concerned about having command over the text and more concerned with forbearance and illumination. It's such a wonderful metaphor! How easily we confuse illumination with interpretation. We assume that to illuminate text means to give our students our own reading. But illumination is always invisible, it reveals without itself being seen.

The irony for us, then, is that what students need to know about *The Catcher* is already there in the reading – not in the analysis we make, however textually implicit or logically consistent we believe our insights to be. That's another literature. What students need to know is there in the unmediated magic that transpires between the author and his beloved silent reader. Our job is not to mugwump over *The Catcher in the Rye*, but to become their "reading lamp," to illumine a story our students already know and are searching for a way to tell in their own voice. It's about *meeting*, not *catching* – make no mistake about that.

*Could it be that we are fascinated with the horror genre because the monster lives within us? In "The Monster Never Dies," Heidi Strengell looks at Stephen King novels to examine the possibility that "good and evil can and do exist within a single person and, concomitantly, we are ultimately unable to evolve, to purge our baser selves from our psyche."*

# "The Monster Never Dies": An Analysis of the Gothic Double in Stephen King's Oeuvre

Heidi Strengell

In *Danse Macabre* (1981), his non-fiction study of the horror genre, Stephen King distinguishes three Gothic archetypes that embody the central issues with which the Gothic era was concerned. To be more precise, *Mary Shelley's Frankenstein or, the Modern Prometheus* (1818) deals with "the refusal to take personal responsibility for one's actions because of pride" (62); Bram Stoker's *Dracula* (1897) portrays perverse or, in medical terms, abnormal and repressed sexuality as well as double standards of sexuality; and, finally, Robert Louis Stevenson's *The Strange Case of Dr. Jekyll and Mr. Hyde* (1886) exploits the possibilities provided by the discovery of the human psyche during the Gothic period, that is, the question of the double. Taking this third archetype as the subject for this paper, I will show that one of the central issues in the Gothic era, namely the paradoxical existence of both good and evil in a single person, remains an important issue in the fiction of Stephen King. This perpetuation reveals our inability to evolve past our base instincts, to purge them completely from the human psyche. The appearance and reappearance of the Gothic double also shows us that popular fiction provides a useful repository for our deepest fear – specifically the fear that each of us is capable of great evil.

## The Gothic Double

I will begin by distinguishing *the Gothic double* from the terms related to it. Alongside Frankenstein's monster, the Wandering Jew, and the Byronic vampire, David Punter sets a fourth Gothic character, the *Doppelganger* which, in his view, signifies "the mask of innocence" and which is found in, for instance, *Dr. Jekyll and Mr. Hyde* (21). On another occasion, Punter refers to the novel as a record of a *split personality* (2), and since the terms are far from being identical, they need to be defined at the outset. The term *Doppelganger* is defined in *The New International Webster's Comprehensive Dictionary of the English Language* (1999) as "1 A person exactly like another; a double. 2 A wraith, especially of a person not yet dead" (378). Since the German equivalent, too, primarily assumes that the word refers to two separate entities, the term Doppelganger is rejected in this context, although it is widely used in literary criticism. The term *split personality* is not included in *The New International Webster's Comprehensive Dictionary of the English Language*, rightly so, because such a diagnosis is no longer considered scientifically valid. After Eugen Bleuler in the late nineteenth century coined the term *schizophrenia* to replace the old one, *dementia procox*, the lay public mistakenly understood it as an equivalent to the term *split personality*. The confusion of the terms meant that the lay term *split personality* became replaced in scientific usage by *dissociative identity disorder* (Kaplan, Sadock and Grebb 457). The latter includes various states and signifies a personality disorder in which the person is unaware of what his "other half" is doing. Whether Dr. Jekyll/Mr. Hyde can be diagnosed as a dissociative disorder patient or possibly a borderline personality may occupy a few psychiatrists, but the term Gothic double will do for my purposes.

Like *Doppelganger*, the word *double* calls upon ambiguous interpretations and needs therefore to be defined. My definition takes as a starting point the concept of personality. According to *The New International Webster's Comprehensive Dictionary of the English Language*, personality is: "1 That which constitutes a person; also, that which distinguishes and characterizes a person; personal existence" (942). As the unity of the personality was endangered by Freudian notions, similarly, many Gothic narratives were consumed "by a paranoid terror of involution or the unraveling of the multiformed ego" (Halberstam 55). *Dr. Jekyll and Mr. Hyde* fittingly displays this juxtaposition of the smooth surface of Dr. Jekyll and that of the "dwarfish" (18), "ape-like" (27) Mr. Hyde. While Dr. Jekyll is pleasant and sophisticated, Mr. Hyde, stunted, crumpled, and ugly, is designed to shock. Indeed, the "Gothic effect depends upon the production of a monstrous double" (Halberstam 54). Thus, for my purposes, the term *Gothic double* refers to the essential duality within a single character on the further presumption that the duality centers on the polarity of good and evil.

Like many of King's works, Stevenson's novella examines the conflict between the free will to do good or to do evil as well as the theme of hypocrisy. King believes the conflict between good and evil is the conflict between, in Freudian terms, the id and the superego and refers also to Stevenson's terms: the conflict between mortification and gratification. In addition, King views the struggle both in Christian and mythical terms. The latter suggests the split between the Apollonian (the man of intellect, morality, and nobility) and the Dionysian (the man of physical gratification) (Danse 75). Influenced by James Hogg's *Confessions of a Justified Sinner* (1824) and Edgar Allan Poe's "William Wilson" (1839), Stevenson wrote his novella in three days in 1886 (Punter 1; Danse 69). King expresses his admiration for *Dr. Jekyll and Mr. Hyde*, regarding it as a "masterpiece of concision" (Danse 69, 80-81).

*Dr. Jekyll and Mr. Hyde*, the story of a Victorian gentleman who leads a secret life of vice, uses multiple narrators to relate the story of a man doomed by the chemical reproduction of his double. "Man is not truly one but two," says Dr. Jekyll, tormented by a sense of "the thorough and primitive duality of man" (Stevenson 70). Through chemical experimentation, he discovers a potion, which dissociates the "polar twins" of the self, transforming his body into that of his other self (70). The other self, Mr. Hyde, allows Dr. Jekyll to satisfy his undignified desires untrammeled by moral scruples. Haunting the streets of London, this small and indescribably ugly character "springs headlong into the sea of liberty" which finally leads him to murder a respectable gentleman (75). Frightened, Dr. Jekyll determines never to use the potion again. However, the metamorphosis has become spontaneous, and, as King aptly notes, Dr. Jekyll "has created Hyde to escape the strictures of propriety, but has discovered that evil has its own strictures" (Danse 73). In the end, Dr. Jekyll has become Mr. Hyde's prisoner, and Jekyll/Hyde's life ends in suicide.

Many of the themes of *Dr. Jekyll and Mr. Hyde* appear in King's work. Like Dr. Jekyll, Reverend Lester Lowe of *Cycle of the Werewolf* bases his influence on moral superiority, and his high views of himself produce morbidity in his relations with his own appetites. Arnie Cunningham of *Christine* illustrates another angle of the werewolf myth even more clearly, that is, the werewolf as an innocent victim, predestinated to its destruction. While the Gage creature in King's *Pet Sematary* constructs part of its maker, the dialectic between monster and maker is resolved in, for instance, *Cycle of the Werewolf* as a conflict in a single body. Gage Creed's monstrosity in *Pet Semetary* depends upon the fragility of his father's humanity, whereas the repulsive nature of the werewolf can only be known through the failed respectability of Reverend Lester Lowe. King characterizes Lowe as genuinely evil, whereas Jekyll, although a hypocrite and a self-deceiver, only desires personal freedom and keeps certain pleasures repressed. Punter points out that while Hyde's behavior manifests an urban version of "going native," Jekyll struggles with various pressures (3). Similarly, Lester Lowe who embodies social virtue takes great pleasure in his bloody nocturnal adventures.

Thad Beaumont's alter ego in *The Dark Half* expresses the violent part of the protagonist's character, of which he himself is not constantly aware. Likewise, the degree to which Dr. Jekyll takes seriously his public responsibilities determines the "hidden-ness" of his desire for pleasure. Punter notes that since the public man must appear flawless, he must "hide" his private nature, to the extent of completely denying it (3). Defying all logic, Beaumont's "dark half," George Stark, has somehow come into existence, and Beaumont must literally face his dark half in a confrontation in which either Beaumont's Jekyll or Stark's Hyde has to die.

*The Drawing of the Three* introduces a dissociative patient, Odetta Holmes/Detta Walker, who through Roland the Gunslinger and Eddie Dean's intervention is able to merge her two personalities into the woman named Susannah Dean. Odetta developed a second personality as a young girl, when Jack Mort dropped a brick on her head. Her two personalities – the sophisticated and wealthy Odetta and the uneducated and vulgar Detta – lead separate lives, completely unaware of each other. Since both are aspects of her self, she cannot become a whole until those "polar twins" are united in Susannah Dean. When the compassion of Odetta and the strength of Detta merge into Susannah, she becomes a worthy gunslinger on Roland's team.

The dark halves of King's Gothic doubles express unrestrained sexuality. Reverend Lester Lowe "wolf-rapes" Stella Randolph, and the shy Arnie Cunningham transforms into a vulgar senior citizen in the form of the beast; the sexually insatiable Detta Walker uses both foul language and teases men, whereas George Stark commits a sexually charged murder of Miriam Cowley – not to mention the rape-murders of Frank Dodd and the child murders of Carl Bierstone/Charles Burnside. Gothic monsters underline the meaning of decadence and are thus concerned with the problem of degeneration. Punter maintains that they pose, from different angles, the same question appropriate to an age of imperial decline: how much can one lose – individually, socially, nationally – and still remain a man? (1). The question has remained a central issue in the modern Gothic and in King's fiction in particular.

*Dr. Jekyll and Mr. Hyde* was published at a time when the problem of prostitution was receiving considerable public attention in England. As in *Frankenstein* and *Dracula*, the protagonist's vice and decadence are once again sex-related, but also clearly sadistic – the serial killers, Frank Dodd (*Dead Zone*) and Charles Burnside (*Black House*), feature these sadistic traits in King. Stevenson had read W. T. Stead's series of articles on child prostitution and was aware that the demand for child prostitutes was being stimulated by the sadistic tastes of the Victorian gentlemen (Clemens 123). More importantly, the theme is evoked at the outset of the novella when Mr. Hyde tramples on a young girl. The violation of the girl's body is settled with a hundred pounds, which reinforces the prostitution motif. Also, the foggy night side of Mr. Hyde's London gives a glimpse of the Victorian gentlemen's subculture: "Once a woman spoke to him, offering, I think, a box of lights" (Stevenson 85) – clearly, she was offering something else. As in *Black House* where the Fisherman lusts for a young boy's buttocks, the hints of sexual exploitation also suggest male victims, as for instance, in the scene in which Mr. Utterson, "tossing to and fro" on his "great, dark bed," imagines Mr. Hyde blackmailing Dr. Jekyll. This dark "figure to whom power was given" would stand by Jekyll's bedside, "and even at that dead hour he must rise and do its bidding" (20). A disturbing novella, *Dr. Jekyll and Mr. Hyde* gave a detailed depiction of some upper-class gentlemen, but, as Valdine Clemens notes, criticized moralistic middle-class sexual repression (for instance, the prevalent homosexual abuse in public schools and prostitution) and patriarchal power (124, 132).

Arnie Cunninham of *Christine* perishes because of his desperate loneliness. An unattractive teenager who finds little solace at home or at school, Arnie falls in love with a 1958 Plymouth Fury. Possessed by the evil spirit of Christine's earlier owner, Roland LeBay, Arnie is alienated from his family, best friend Dennis, and even his high school sweetheart Leigh Cabot. Like *Dr. Jekyll and Mr. Hyde*, *Christine* focuses on "humanity's vulnerability to dehumanization" which coexists with the fear of internal evil: "the upsurge of the animal, the repressed unconscious, the monster from id," or, as Douglas E. Winter points out, "the monster from the fifties" (137, 139; *Danse* 75). The novel also discusses the conflict between the will to do evil and the will to deny evil; the car becomes a symbol of the duality of human nature, as telling as the two sides of Henry Jekyll's town house which bordered both a graceful Victorian street and a slumlike alley (Winter 139-140; *Danse* 75): "It was as if I had seen a snake that was almost ready to shed its old skin, that some of the old skin had already flaked away, revealing the glistening newness underneath" (*Christine* 57-58). As Christine magically returns to street condition, Arnie also begins to change, at first for the better, but then he matures beyond his years: "a teenage Jekyll rendered into a middle-aged Hyde" (Winter 140).

In brief, although Stevenson's classic finds no single counterpart in King, its motifs occur in several of King's works.

## The Werewolf

*Cycle of the Werewolf* and *The Talisman* introduce us to another Stephen King double: the werewolf. Perhaps nowhere else in King's fiction is the Gothic double more pronounced than in this figure.

Beginning as a calendar, displaying twelve colored drawings by Bernie Wrightson with brief accompanying text by King, *Cycle of the Werewolf* evolved into a twelve-chapter novella. Each successive segment takes place on a specific holiday of the year, from January to December, relating the story of the recurring appearance of a werewolf in isolated Tarker's Mills, Maine, and its destruction at the hands of a crippled boy. King defines the predestined nature of the disaster: "It is the Werewolf, and there is no more reason for its coming now than there would be for the arrival of cancer, or a psychotic with murder on his mind, or a killer tornado" (*Werewolf* 14). Although the werewolf arouses fear and suspicions, only in October do the residents take systematic action to defend themselves. Like "Salem's Lot, Castle Rock, or Derry, Tarker's Mills keeps its secrets, and, similarly, the residents of Tarker's Mills embody all of the diversifying virtue and ugliness found in everyday people" (Larson 104).

What is more, each of the werewolf's victims expands the constant sense of isolation, due to the flaws in their physiques and in their characters (Collings, *The Many Facets of Stephen King* 80). As an illustration, the February victim, Stella Randolph, is isolated by her skewed romanticism and by her corpulence (80). However, this Valentine's day the lonely old maid receives a visitor: "a dark shape – amorphous but clearly masculine" (*Werewolf* 21). King depicts Stella's encounter with the werewolf in Gothic terms, combining dreams, sex, and death (21-24). He uses the common French metaphor "orgasm is a little death" to reinforce the Gothic effect of the February section. Indeed, what takes the place of the Valentine figure is a "beast" with "shaggy fur in a silvery streak" (22) its breath "hot, but somehow not unpleasant" (23). Despite Berni Wrightson's illustration of a lustful redhead embracing a werewolf, King never graphically describes the wolf-rape and killing of the fat old maid, but veils it in quasi-romantic images that might have derived from John Keats's classic poem, "The Eve of St. Agnes" (Reino 136).

Like the wheelchair bound protagonist Marty Coslaw, the Reverend Lester Lowe did nothing to deserve his destiny. Until May, he remains as unaware of the werewolf's identity as anybody else in Tarker's Mills. On the night before Homecoming Sunday, he has, however, a most peculiar dream. In his dream, Lowe has been preaching with fire and force, but has to break off, because both he and his congregation are turning into werewolves. Lester Lowe's relief after the nightmare turns into knowledge when he opens the church doors next morning, finding the gutted body of Clyde Corliss.

King refers to the werewolf in biblical terms as "the Beast" and "the Great Satan," and in the Gothic manner the Beast can be anywhere or, even worse, anybody (*Werewolf* 45). Unlike a number of other monsters, werewolves, however, frequently arouse pity. Aptly, Collings states that the werewolf is more sinned against than sinning, and that the curse works in two ways: on the level of plot, it transforms an otherwise sensible man into a rapacious monster; on the level of theme and symbol, it divorces him from reality, isolating the person from society and from personal standards of morality (*Facets* 78).

Although Reverend Lester Lowe shares a fate similar to that of Arnie Cunningham of *Christine*, he does not evoke fear and pity to the same extent. In the same way as his hypocritical predecessor in *Dr. Jekyll and Mr. Hyde*, Lester Lowe makes excuses for his behavior without fighting against it. In November, having found out that hunters have been sent out after the werewolf, he deliberately takes the role of the beast and defends himself by comparing the hunters with irrational animals. Ignoring the threat of these adult men, Marty Coslaw's lined notepads, and his direct question – "*Why don't you kill yourself?*" (*Werewolf* 108, 111; italics original) – the Reverend Lester Lowe (that is, the werewolf) is forced to analyze his situation. With hubris like that of Victor Frankenstein, he turns to God: "*If I have been cursed from Outside, then God will bring me down in His time*" (*Werewolf* 111; italics original). In other words, against the advice of his own creator, Stephen King, Reverend Lester Lowe readily lays the guilt on "God the Father" (*Danse* 62) and refuses to take responsibility for his actions or to fight his werewolf instincts. Moreover, blinded by his own logical reasoning, Lester Lowe succumbs to even greater evil by deliberately contemplating the murder of Marty Coslaw – this time both premeditated and in full possession of his senses (*Werewolf* 111).

While many contemporary treatments tend to glamorize the virtues of evil, King's approach is more traditional (Larson 106-107). Larson regards Reverend Lowe as a man unable to free himself from the overwhelming influence of evil, and he is eventually only able to do so through the aid of an outside agency, through the sympathy and concern of Marty Coslaw (107). Despite his fear of the werewolf, Marty recognizes the human being beneath the beast. While aiming his pistol with silver bullets towards the attacking werewolf, he says: "Poor old Reverend Lowe. I'm gonna try to set you free" (*Werewolf* 125). In the same way, Mina Harker pities the vampire in *Dracula*: "The poor soul who has wrought all this misery is the saddest case of all" (367). Clearly, King's allusion to this sentiment reinforces the moral tradition that has lain at the heart of the horror genre and has been much absent in contemporary horror fiction (Larson 108).

Undoubtedly, King takes a traditional stand by letting evil perish in the end of the novella, thus, unlike Larson or Anthony Magistrale in *The Moral Voyages of Stephen King* (57-67), I argue that evil can often be conquered in King's fiction. Although Jack Torrance of *The Shining* succumbs to evil and takes the mallet to attack his family, Dick Hallorann is able to resist the same evil influence of the hotel – similarly, Lowe could have acted otherwise. In *The Talisman*, we encounter Wolf, a slow-witted werewolf from the Territories. When he senses that the full moon is rising and that his instincts might lead him to hurt Jack Sawyer who has become his "herd" and whom he is thus expected to defend against all imaginable threats, this righteous creature takes measures to prevent possible accidents and locks up the herd, that is Jack Sawyer, in a shed for three days: "He Would Not Injure His Herd" (321). Unlike the godly Lowe who attempts to silence his crippled eyewitness, the animal-like Wolf avoids killing people. Lowe considers his werewolf nature alien to his true self and allows this alien part to commit even grimmer crimes, which pushes him toward greater levels of moral corruption. Wolf, in contrast, lives by the laws of nature, takes into account the facts caused by his instincts, and respects himself. It is interesting to note, however, that while an evil impulse may be conquered the temptation toward evil is never entirely eliminated.

## The Writer/His Pseudonym

Another variation of the Gothic double in Stephen King's work is Thad Beaumont/George Stark or the writer/his pseudonym. In the author's note of *The Dark Half,* King expresses his gratitude to his pseudonym, Richard Bachman, maintaining that the "novel could not have been written without him." In an interview with Walden Books (November/December 1989) and quoted in Magistrale, King acknowledged prior to the publication of *The Dark Half* that Richard Bachman is the darker, more violent side of Stephen King, just as Stark is the dark half of Thad Beaumont (*The Second Decade* 66). Remarkably, then, the Gothic double resides within the Gothic double, that is, the reality of the novel reflects reality. Undoubtedly, both pseudonyms function as a dark alter ego for the artist, a chance to realize his most violent and pessimistic visions. Tony Magistrale notes that the details surrounding the union between Beaumont and Stark underscore King's intimate relationship with Bachman. Furthermore, even information relevant to those trusted persons who knew, protected, and finally revealed King's pseudonym corresponds to the fictional events that the reader discovers in *The Dark Half* (Decade 63-64).

Like Dr. Jekyll/Mr. Hyde, whose transformation is occasioned by scientific explanation, King attempts to establish credibility by the means of medicine. Having suffered from constant headaches, the eleven-year-old Thad Beaumont is operated on, and, instead of a supposed brain tumor, a fetal twin is discovered in his brain. In addition to being Thad's physical twin, George Stark has his origin in the writer's imagination. Considering George "a very bad man," Thad knows that he has "built George Stark from the ground up" (*The Dark Half* 155). The symbolic funeral of George Stark becomes a moral stand for Thad's part, because he has both indulged his dark fantasies in Stark's fiction and profited financially from his success (Magistrale, *Decade* 64). Wendy and William, Beaumont's identical twins, underscore the symbiotic relationship of Stark and Beaumont. While responding with similar affection to these different looking men, Wendy and William sense their identical nature. Sharing identical fingerprints and a capacity for mental telepathy, it becomes more obvious that George has a right to feel insulted (*The Dark Half* 331). Not even Thad is able to make a clear distinction between himself and George: "*Who are you when you write, Thad? Who are you then?*" (*The Dark Half* 129; italics original).

Since George constitutes an integral part of Thad's psyche, he does not genuinely attempt to get rid of George. Elisabeth compares the relationship with alcohol or drug addiction, stating that Thad revealed George's identity only through the force of circumstances: "If Frederick Clawson hadn't come along and forced my husband's hand, I think Thad would still be talking about getting rid of him in the same way" (*The Dark Half* 202). Indeed, this contradiction has resulted in alcohol addiction, a suicide attempt, and lifelike dreams. However, only as Stark threatens Beaumont's immediate circle, does he realize the intimacy of their relationship and its fatal consequences. Starting as a thriller, the final confrontation of the two brothers and its victory for Thad receives a mythological explanation.

Conducting human souls back and forth between the land of the living and the land of the dead, sparrows are able to distinguish the original brother from the dead one and to take the latter where he belongs. Nevertheless, Thad's victory may prove of short duration, and he is referred to in a less pleasant context later in King: in *Needful Things* (1991) we learn that Thad Beaumont has broken up with his wife and in *Bag of Bones* (1998) that he has committed suicide.

## The Serial Killer

The serial killer also represents the modern counterpart of Dr. Jekyll/Mr. Hyde. *The Dead Zone*, for example, concerns the removal of masks, both political and psychological. The Gothic duality is displayed even in the novel's central symbol, the wheel of fortune, which, apart from representing blind chance, reveals a second disc. Winter explains that at its heart is the Presidential Seal, a symbol of a different game of chance – politics – and its paradoxes (76). Focusing on the masquerade of politics, Greg Stillson, a Congressional candidate whose name is an intentional conjunction of "still" and "Nixon" (263), takes the Vietnamese masquerade-game of the "Laughing Tiger" a step further: "inside the beast-skin, a man, yes. But inside the man-skin, a beast" (*The Dead Zone* 297). *The Dead Zone* also connects the fates – and masks – of Johnny Smith whose resemblance to Everyman is signaled in the prosaic simplicity of his name and Frank Dodd, the strangler-rapist whose identity is withheld until one of "Faithful John's" psychic revelations.

As a consequence of a car crash, Johnny lies in a coma for four and a half years. Awakening in May 1975 at the age of twenty-seven, he discovers that the world has changed: the war in Vietnam has ended, a Vice-President and President have resigned, Johnny's girlfriend is married and has borne a child, Stillson has made his political move, and an unidentified rapist is killing young women in Castle Rock. Apart from regaining consciousness, Johnny has acquired occult powers of precognition and telepathy, which both cause his estrangement from his past life and force him to take a moral stand: whether or not to stop Stillson and Dodd. Although this Faithful John serves the purpose of good, his Jekyll-and-Hyde mask (*The Dead Zone* 14) haunts his girlfriend Sarah Bracknell (later Sarah Hazlett) throughout the novel.

While Johnny is comatose, the policeman Frank Dodd commits his brutal rape-stranglings. Joseph Reino maintains that the crimes seem to emerge from the blankness of the coma, as if they were merely the dark side of the otherwise sunny personality, and as if Frank was Johnny's evil "other" – this pair thus possessing something like Edgar Allan Poe's "bi-part soul" (67). Despite the grim verdict, King provides the character with a background that explains some of the hideous acts. While awaiting a young victim (Alma Frechette) to walk into his trap, Dodd's mind is momentarily obsessed with an embarrassing childhood memory: a lesson in sexual education given by his abusive mother. When Frank was innocently playing with his penis, his mother, a huge woman, caught him in the act and began to shake him back and forth. Here King emphasizes parental responsibility for aberrant personality development, arguing that Frank "was not the killer then, he was not slick then, he was a little boy blubbering with fear" (*The Dead Zone* 65). Albeit somewhat simplistically, King underscores the significance of the formative years.

When Alma Frechette appears, fate plays a decisive role in a genuinely Gothic manner, and, again, everybody must be suspected. Familiar with the killer, Alma does not suspect anything but wonders at his Little Red Riding Hood outfit (*The Dead Zone* 66). Before long, she is strangled at the moment of Dodd's ejaculation. "Surely no hometown boy could have done such a dreadful thing," states the pious narrator (*The Dead Zone* 68), and from then on almost two years pass without more killings.

Significantly, Johnny Smith's awakening from the coma coincides with the fourth murder. However, it takes deep self-exploration on the recovered Johnny's part before he accepts the sheriff George Bannerman's request to assist in the murder investigation. By acknowledging his psychic abilities and acting accordingly, Johnny humbles before fate. In King's world, nobody escapes his destiny, and, at any rate, a well-developed brain tumor would cause Johnny's death within a few months. However, by bearing responsibility for his next, Johnny prevents Greg Stillson's presidency and its likely consequence, a nuclear war, as well as Frank Dodd from continuing his murder series. After all, the investigation turns out to be of short duration, since the deputy Frank Dodd commits suicide the same evening the two men meet at the police department. Remarkably, the childish face hides the Gothic mark of the beast (*The Dead Zone* 233), evil actions having their root in childhood. After gathered enough evidence, Bannerman and Smith visit Dodd's house and find him dead: "*Knew, Johnny thought incoherently. Knew somehow when he saw me. Knew it was all over. Came home. Did this*" (*The Dead Zone* 253). In other words, the two men are connected, and their interrelations are further reinforced by the nature of their mothers: the sexual neurotic, Henrietta Dodd, who "knew from the beginning" (*The Dead Zone* 252) and Vera Smith who marks her son with her religious frenzies: "God has put his mark on my Johnny and I rejoice" (*The Dead Zone* 61).

The opening page of *Cujo* repeats the story of Frank Dodd, stating that "he was no werewolf, vampire, ghoul, or unnameable creature from the enchanted forest or from the snowy wastes; he was only a cop named Frank Dodd with mental and sexual problems" (*Cujo* 3). Like Buffalo Bill in *The Silence of the Lambs* (1991), Frank Dodd personifies a victimized human being who does not "suit in his skin." Although regarded as a respected resident of Castle Rock, Frank Dodd lacks identity and perhaps therefore need for disguise.

A number of serial killers suffer from impotence except during their violent acts and are not considered genuinely males, but are despised as freaks and monsters. Charles Burnside a.k.a. Carl Bierstone and the Fisherman of *Black House* has all but one of these characteristics: born evil and without conscience, he justifies cruelty as an end in itself.

*Black House* is a kind of sequel to *The Talisman*, both works being jointly authored by Peter Straub and Stephen King. A Victorian novel with allusions to Charles Dickens's *Bleak House*, Dickensian characters, and references to Edgar Allan Poe and Mark Twain, *Black House* reads as a tale of horror or a detective story with a blend of thriller and fantasy (Gaiman 2). The narrative reintroduces the then twelve-year-old Jack Sawyer of *The Talisman.* Now this retired, burned out ex-LAPD homicide detective lives in the small Wisconsin town of French Landing – interestingly, in scenery resembling Tom Sawyer's and Huckleberry Finn's foggy riverside. Children are being abducted from French Landing by a cannibal named "The Fisherman" who has disguised himself as an Alzheimer's patient in the local old people's home and is aided in his dastardly misdeeds by a talking crow called "Gorg." The Fisherman is a pawn in the hand of the Crimson King, evil monarch of End World, who attempts to abduct a wunderkind in order to annihilate the universe with his powers. Jack and a gang of philosophically inclined motor bikers called the Hegelian Scum take action to save the wunderkind, Ty Marshall, and arrest the Fisherman.

Parodying the thriller formula, the narrator takes us to the murder scene of Irma Freneau:

> We are not here to weep.... Humility is our best, most accurate first response. Without it, we would miss the point, the great mystery would escape us, and we would go on deaf and blind, ignorant as pigs. Let us not go on like pigs. We must honor the scene – the flies, the dog worrying the severed foot, the poor, pale body of Irma Freneau, the magnitude of what befell Irma Freneau – by acknowledging our littleness. In comparison, we are no more than vapors. (*Black House* 35-36)

The Fisherman himself is named after Albert Fish, a real-life child-killer and cannibal, whose crimes he imitates in the novel's fictional world. In his study of the interrelationship between the reader and the novel, Edward Bullough states that a work of fiction has succeeded when the reader participates in the communication process so completely as to be nearly convinced that the art is reality (758). In *Black House*, the authors gap the bridge between the reader and the text by equating the reader with the narrator (a first-person plural narration), by using the present tense, and even by letting the reader choose the story ending that best serves his purpose. Perhaps the otherwise too fantastic occurrences of the story become more realistic by these means, combined with King's usual artillery: lifelike characters and initially realistic settings.

The serial killer turns out to be a tall, skinny, and senile old man (*Black House* 22). Although a soul brother to the other men who reside at the Maxton Elder Care Facility with his "sly, secretive, rude, caustic, stubborn, foul-tongued, mean-spirited, and resentful" character (*Black House* 23), Charles Burnside hides his true self:

> Carl Bierstone is Burny's great secret, for he cannot allow anyone to know that this former incarnation, this earlier self, still lives inside his skin. Carl Bierstone's awful pleasures, his foul toys, are also Burny's and he must keep them hidden in the darkness, where only he can find them. (*Black House* 26)

The secrets with which Charles Burnside indulges himself turn him into a loner, forcing him to hide his misdeeds. As a tool in the hands of a greater evil, Burnside takes his pleasure feeding on children who are not worth sending to the End-World to the Crimson King, a creature who ultimately hides beneath the Fisherman mask.

Assisted by Gorg, the speaking crow, Charles Burnside addresses the End-World like a vassal or a stray dog fed with crumbs. While action is needed, the senior citizen undergoes a transformation. In Charles Burnside's place is Carl Bierstone and something inhuman (*Black House* 111). The inhuman inside Burny's head signifies Mr. Munshun, Crimson King's close disciple and servant, a vampire-like figure. Nearing the end of his usefulness, Burny is at Mr. Munshun's request forced to take Ty Marshall, a promising breaker to an appointed meeting place. The term breaker is used for those slaves of Crimson King who break the beams leading to the Tower, thus aiming at the total annihilation of the universe. Driven by contradictory urges, this odd serial killer is afraid of the consequences of his actions (*Black House* 541), but, despite a deadly wound, still lusts for Ty Marshall's "juicy buttocks." Like the witch of "Hansel and Gretel," he is reluctant to hand over his prey: "A good agent's entitled to ten percent" (*Black House* 550). Only seldom can a parallel be drawn between a serial killer and a wicked witch from a fairy tale, which perhaps bears further witness to King's genre blending.

## Conclusion

The Gothic double of *Dr. Jekyll and Mr. Hyde* shares some traits with characters in King's work. First, flawed humanity moves between the two poles of good and evil, causing contradiction and anguish to the subject. Second, the Gothic gnome, that is, the "dwarfish" and "ape-like" half of the personality is hidden at the cost of hypocrisy and oft hideous crimes. Therefore, a disguise is needed, which causes further tension and the fear of getting caught. Tension also intensifies from the constant threat of transformation.

Monsters of the nineteenth century scare us from a distance while at the same time, as Halberstam notes, "We wear modern monsters like skin, they are us, they are on us and in us" (163). King, too, states that "the monsters are no longer due on Maple Street, but may pop up in our own mirrors – at any time" (*Danse* 252). Presumably, both convictions are based on two facts; good and evil can and do exist within a single person and, concomitantly, we are ultimately unable to evolve, to purge our baser selves from our psyche. King puts it straightforwardly: "Werewolf, vampire, ghoul, unnameable creature from the wastes. The monster never dies" (*Cujo* 4).

## Works Cited


Briggs, Julia. *Night Visitors: The Rise and Fall of the English Ghost Story*. London: Faber & Faber, 1977.

Bullough, Edward, "'Psychical Distance' as a Factor in Art and an Aesthetic Principle." *Critical Theory since Plato*. Ed. Hazard Adams. New York: Harcourt Brace Jovanovich, 1971: 758.

Clemens, Valdine. *The Return of the Repressed: Gothic Horror from The Castle of Otranto to Alien*. New York: State U of New York, 1999.

Collings, Michael R. *The Many Facets of Stephen King*. Mercer Island, WA: Starmont House, 1985.

----. *Stephen King as Richard Bachman*. Mercer Island, WA: Starmont House, 1985.

Halberstam, Judith. *Skin Shows: Gothic Horror and the Technology of Monsters*. Durham: Duke UP, 2000 1995.

Kaplan, Harold I., Benjamin J. Sadock, Jack A. Grebb. *Kaplan and Sadock's Synopsis of Psychiatry: Behavioral Sciences, Clinical Psychiatry*. Baltimore: Williams & Wilkins, 1994.

King, Stephen. *Black House*. London: HarperCollins Publishers, 2001.

----. *Carrie*. New York: Pocket Books, 1999.

----. *Christine*. London: Hodder and Stoughton, 1983.

----. *Cujo*. New York: Signet, 1982.

----. *Cycle of the Werewolf*. New York: Signet, 1985.

----. *Danse Macabre*. New York: Berkley Books, 1983.

----. *The Dark Half*. New York: Signet, 1990.

----. *The Dead Zone*. New York: Signet, 1980.

----. *The Gunslinger: The Dark Tower I*. New York: Plume, 1988.

----. *On Writing*. New York: Scribner, 2000.

----. *Pet Sematary*. New York: Signet, 1984.

----. *The Talisman* (with Peter Straub). New York: Berkley, 1985.

Larson, Randall D. "*Cycle of the Werewolf* and the Moral Tradition of Horror." *Discovering Stephen King*. Ed. Darrell Schweitzer. Mercer Island, WA: Starmont House, Inc., 1985. 102-108.

Magistrale, Anthony, *The Moral Voyages of Stephen King*. Mercer Island, WA: Starmont Studies, 1989.

----. Stephen King: *The Second Decade, Danse Macabre to The Dark Half*. New York: Twayne Publishers, 1992.

*The New International Webster's Comprehensive Dictionary of the English Language*. Florida: Trident Press International, 1999, 1958.

Punter, David. *The Literature of Terror. A History of Gothic Fictions from 1765 to the Present Day. Volume 2. The Modern Gothic*. Harlow, Essex: Pearson Education Limited, 1996.

Reino, Joseph. *Stephen King: The First Decade, Carrie to Pet Semetary*. Boston: Twayne, 1988.

Stevenson, Robert Louis. *The Strange Case of Dr. Jekyll and Mr. Hyde*. London: Penguin Books, 1994.

Stoker, Bram. *Dracula*. London: Penguin, 1994.

Tropp, Michael. *Images of Fear: How Horror Stories Helped Shape Modern Culture (1818 -1918)*. Jefferson, NC: McFarland and Co., 1990.

Winter, Douglas E. *Stephen King: The Art of Darkness*. New York: Signet, 1986.

*In this essay, Karen Dodwell examines newspaper, magazine, and Internet articles in order to show us how both those who supported the war in Iraq and those who did not were able to use the myths of the cowboy effectively.*

# The Cowboy Myth, George W. Bush, and the War with Iraq

Karen Dodwell

In an address to the nation, on March 17, 2003, George W. Bush declared, "Saddam Hussein and his sons must leave Iraq within 48 hours. Their refusal to do so will result in military conflict, commenced at a time of our choosing." The ultimatum aroused a multitude of commentary in editorials and news articles that depicted George W. Bush as a cowboy sheriff who told outlaws to get out of town or face the consequences. On March 19, for instance, Reuters ran a story titled "High Noon for Cowboy Era" in which the lead sentence declared that, for Arabs, Bush's ultimatum was a throwback to the Wild West. The commentary prompted by the forty-eight hours ultimatum was not the first time Bush's actions had been referred to as cowboy-esque. After September 11, 2001, as editorial writers and public figures discussed terrorism more vigorously, they frequently described Bush in terms of a variety of cowboy images that went well beyond the cowhand who works cattle and drives them to market miles away. In the months leading up to the war with Iraq, commentators began to portray Bush as a sheriff in the Old West who would go it alone without a posse if need be in order to defeat what he saw as lawlessness and evil. Europeans, who would not join the posse to defeat the outlaw, were compared to timid saloonkeepers and shopkeepers, afraid to confront evil and afraid of the sheriff who might shoot up the town while getting his man. Eventually, the sheriff realized he had to ride out without a big posse. Tony Blair became Tonto to Bush's Lone Ranger and rode along to cover his boss's back.

As the image of the cowboy dominated debates over the war with Iraq, it became obvious that the term "cowboy" was lodged securely in the national and international consciousness as a means of delineating positions. I examined editorials and news articles published in newspapers and magazines both in print and on the Internet, beginning September 11, 2001, and continuing through April 2003 in order to explore the ubiquitous representations of George W. Bush as a cowboy. I read these editorials and news articles to answer one primary question: How and why has the myth of the cowboy been used in shaping public opinion about the war with Iraq? Answering the question was a challenge because I immediately confronted the slipperiness of the signifier "cowboy" and the generative quality of the story of the American cowboy, now widely called the cowboy myth. As I will discuss in more detail below, numerous writers have traced the evolution of the myth from the original era of the trail-riding cowboy in the late 1800s through contemporary images that are a mixture of the historical and the fictional. In understanding the news commentary, then, I was first caught up in the structuralist endeavor of investigating the myth as a pattern for understanding a certain type of persona. I then recognized that the cowboy myth appeared in so many editorials and news articles, building and growing from writer to writer, that it formed a multi-faceted story.

I also wondered why the cowboy myth was still being used in political rhetoric early in the twenty-first century. In 1955, Franz and Choate asked the following question in their work, *The American Cowboy: The Myth and the Reality*: "Why this everlasting preoccupation with the cowboy in a country that is supposed to be crassly treadmilling its way to an ever increasing urbanization and ulcerated pursuit of happiness through money?" The question seemed even more puzzling in the context of urbanization and consumerism that have proliferated beyond what most individuals in the mid-1950s could have imagined. Most editorialists and politicians who exploited the cowboy myth likely lived in urban areas and were far removed from the austerities of life on the cattle trail and the frontier. Obviously, the myth of the cowboy persists not because many people live like cowboys but because it defines something significant about the character of the U.S broadly and the character of George W. Bush specifically. What the cowboy myth means, however, is complicated because, as Frantz and Choate have explained, the cowboy represents both a desire for violence and recklessness and also the pursuit of heroism and integrity. Furthermore, as recent theorists have also explained, the line between the good and the bad cowboy is ambiguous because some people view the cowboy's will to act, even violently, as an honorable trait while others are repelled by the aggressive, eager-to-shoot image. Given the blurry line between the bad cowboy and the good cowboy, I was surprised that editorialists and politicians had adopted the cowboy myth in conveying their views of an international conflict.

I will argue that in spite of the slipperiness of the term cowboy, the complex evolution of the cowboy myth, the anachronistic aspects of the historical cowboy, and the blurry line between the good and bad cowboy, both those who supported and those who opposed the war with Iraq used the cowboy myth successfully to influence public opinion. Many columnists and public figures outside and within the U.S. used the cowboy myth to create a very negative image of George W. Bush as a blood-thirsty, trigger-happy loner. The love of the cowboy in the U.S., however, became a potent means of coalescing support for George W. Bush as a fast-acting, straight-shooting, brave president. The cowboy myth produced positive associations for segments of the U.S. public that held conservative views while the myth produced negative associations for segments of the public with more liberal views. As I will explain, this dichotomy aligned with a view of the frontier promoted by Frederick Jackson Turner and the opposing view promoted by New Western Historians and those who have called for the abandonment of the cowboy myth. My reading of editorials that analyze the presence of the myth in the discussions about the war with Iraq (the meta-commentary) leads me to believe that Bush's image as a cowboy president was more positive than negative in the U.S.; in Europe, however, a negative image of the cowboy reinforced a disgust with Bush's handling of the war with Iraq.

## Patterns of the Cowboy Myth

In his essay "The Structural Study of Myth," Claude Levi-Strauss clarifies how myths become timeless and operational: "On the one hand, a myth always refers to events alleged to have taken place long ago. But what gives the myth an operational value is that the specific pattern described is timeless; it explains the present and the past as well as the future." He also tells us to analyze myths by breaking down their patterns into constituent units. His detailed process is clearly beyond the scope of this essay; however, he provides a good starting point for briefly thinking about the timeless quality and the specific patterns of the cowboy myth that operate in defining contemporary political positions.

As many writers have explained, the patterns that define the cowboy myth have little to do with the historical cowboy of the open range in the American West. Paul H. Carlson's designation of the classical era of the cowboy is helpful in understanding the genesis of the term "cowboy" and its contemporary applications. Carlson considers 1865-1890 the classical period, a time when cowhands, with an average age of twenty-four, road the open range. As he explains, many early cowboys were overworked, illiterate, inexperienced laborers who wore ill-fitting clothes and developed outlaw reputations. At least a third were Hispanic or African American, and some scholars claim many were Indian and Chinese. By the late 1880s, however, with the demise of the open range, more settled cattlemen took over the wilder business of the cowboy. With the end of the classical cowboy came fictionalized versions, changing the cowboy image. Buffalo Bill Cody's Wild West Exhibition in 1883 marked the beginning of a new image of the cowboy as "young, white, and virile." Prentis Ingraham's novel, *Buck Taylor, King of the Cowboys*, Charlie Russel's paintings of cowboys, and Owen Wister's novel *The Virginian* also transformed the image of the cowboy from the illiterate, overworked cowhand to an idealized hero. Frantz and Choate claim the cowboy came to embody the qualities of a number of folk heroes: Daniel Boone, Indian fighter, buffalo hunter, gold washer, and mountain man. None of these images, however, persisted through time like that of the cowboy – which soon merged with that of the sheriff of the Old West, the gunslinger, and the frontiersman. "Reel cowboys" in movie and television productions have expanded the cowboy myth through characters such as Wyatt Earp and The Lone Ranger and through actors such as John Wayne, Gary Cooper, and Clint Eastwood. The rodeo cowboy, the urban cowboy, and the cowboy depicted in country western music have also expanded the cowboy myth by combining aspects of historical and fictional cowboys.

One important and timeless pattern in the construction of the historical and the mythical cowboy is the contrast between the heroic good cowboy and the rogue, bad-man cowboy. Frantz and Choate describe the idealized cowboy tradition: The good cowboy is brave and up for a challenge. He promotes justice and defends the honor of women; he is "the implacable foe of the Indian; and a man to whom honor and integrity come naturally." As I will illustrate, George W. Bush and many editorialist have adopted the myth of the idealized cowboy in promoting the war with Iraq, while Bush's opponents have adopted the tradition of the rogue cowboy in promoting their opposition to the war. The bad cowboy is associated with such notables as Wild Bill Hickock and Billy the Kid. As a reckless ruffian, the bad cowboy is a pistol-shooting, merciless, hard-living man who roamed the boom towns of the Old West.

Some scholars have critiqued the cowboy myth and called for abandoning it because the good and the bad cowboy become intermingled; they argue that the violent aspects of the bad cowboy are idealized as embodying the essence of the American character. Richard Slotkin, for one, in *Regeneration Through Violence* (1973) and *Gunfighter Nation* (1992), explains how the myth of the frontiersman and the cowboy have sanctioned local and national violence; he argues the U.S. needs to cast off the cowboy myth because of its advocacy of violence and because it idealizes "the white male adventurer as the hero of national history." Slotkin believes the U.S. needs a new myth that represents the changing demographics of the nation and that "does not reduce the parties of the American cultural conversation to simple sets of paired antagonists." Sharmon Russell also calls for the abandonment of the cowboy myth and even goes so far as to urge us to "kill the cowboy" in his book title. While primarily arguing in favor of new ways of preserving the ecology of the Western States, he also asserts, "We need new myths and new role models, one that includes heroines as well as heroes, urbanites as well as country folk, ecologists as well as individualists." Nevertheless, judging by the ubiquitous use of the cowboy myth in the commentary leading up to the war with Iraq, the cowboy myth has not been abandoned in favor of a new myth. Perhaps this results in part from the ongoing disagreements about the meaning of the West and the frontier in the development of the American experience.

In his 1893 essay, "The Significance of the American Frontier in American History," Frederick Jackson Turner announced that the American West and the frontier developed the freedom-loving democratic character of the United States. Turner claimed the American frontier was closed by 1890, and, up until that time, the westward movement was central in American history and in the American experience. He claimed, "This perennial rebirth, this fluidity of American life, this expansion westward with its new opportunities, its continuous touch with the simplicity of primitive society, furnish the forces dominating the American character." The frontiersman, according to Turner, defined what it meant to be an American as he moved west and left European influence behind. Most importantly, frontier life developed the individualism that promoted democracy, and it created a buoyant American character that thrived on freedom, strength, inquisitiveness, invention, and expansion.

John Mack Faragher contends that "Turner's essay is the single most influential piece of writing in the history of American history," and in *Rereading Frederick Jackson Turner*, he traces the emergence of other histories of the west, including Richard Slotkin's, that contest Turner's glorification of the American frontier. One "New Western Historian," Patricia Nelson Limerick, redefines the West as a site of "invasion, conquest, colonization, exploitation, development, [and] expansion of the world market." In her focus on the West, Limerick includes "women as well as men, Indians, Europeans, Latin Americans, Asians, Afro-Americans." She rejects Turner's idea of the closing of the frontier in 1890, and she contests the belief that westward expansion primarily meant progress and improvement. She, like many other New Western historians, points to the injuries to the environment and to individuals that resulted from the expansion into the West.

In the editorial clashes, Turner's glorification of the frontier conflicts head on with New Western condemnations of the violence and exploitation in the American West. The two conflicting versions of the West and the two conflicting images of the cowboy help explain why the cowboy myth has been used both to condemn the war with Iraq and to call the U.S. to war. The image of the cowboy gunfighter with a frontiersman mentality is offensive to those who resist the war with Iraq and who call for settling international conflict without violence and exploitation. At the same time, the image of the cowboy gunfighter is positive to those who support the war with Iraq and call on the U.S. to uphold the frontier ideal of bravery and integrity in the face of danger.

## The Bad Cowboy

Politicians and columnists outside the U.S. almost unanimously use the bad man tradition of the cowboy myth to generate negative associations about George W. Bush's policies after 9/11. For many columnists in non-European countries, the term "cowboy" was a means of condemning a bullying, ruthless U.S. military apparatus led by a cowboy-style leader. Praful Bidwai, for instance, writing in the *Daily Star* in Bangladesh about the U.S. policy on Afghanistan and Iraq in March of 2002, declared the cowboy style of U.S. militarism "unbecoming of a civilized state." Bidwai believed India should protest the cowboy-style militarism instead of groveling before it, and he used the term "cowboy" to represent not just Bush but the entire U. S. military operation. Fahd Diab, editorialist for *Al-Thawra* in Syria, claimed Bush wanted "America to have the final word in every conflict as if it were the era of the strong conservative President Reagan, who led the world by his cowboy stick." Regardless of the mixed metaphor, the word "cowboy" seemed to signify for Diab the presence of columnists in Europe also adopted the cowboy as bad man in clarifying their opposition to U.S. policy. In May of 2002 when George W. Bush traveled to Germany to build European support for a war on Iraq, Cameron Brown reported on NBC Nightly News that even the "German media are portraying Bush as a Rambo-like cowboy intent on going after Saddam Hussein with or without Europe's support." David E. Sanger analyzed the European reaction to Bush's political style and declared that Europeans did not like Bush's tendency to paint political issues as "black-and-white certainties." They didn't like Bush's religiosity, his "provocative manner, the jabbing of his finger at you." The Texas culture was unfamiliar to the Germans, Sanger claimed, and Bush reminded the Europeans of what they disliked about Reagan. CNN's Walter Rodgers summed up the perceptions of Bush by the Europeans, claiming Bush's cowboy image "doesn't play well" in Europe. He quoted Piers Morgan editor of London's Daily Mirror: "I think people look at him [Bush] and think John Wayne. We in Europe like John Wayne, we liked him in cowboy films. We don't like him running the world." Europeans, who are somewhat attuned to U.S. movies and culture, seemed to view the American cowboy through the lens of movies about Rambo and John Wayne and through images of Ronald Reagan and his cowboy persona. The result was an image of the cowboy with an assortment of cultural nuances, most of them removed from the cowboy who rides the range herding cattle; the cowboy image for Europeans seemed to center around a dominating man of action who always got his way.

Many columnists and reporters in the U.S. also used the bad man tradition in describing George W. Bush and seemed to relish extending and clarifying the negative connotations of the cowboy. After Bush spoke to the United Nations General Assembly in September 2002 to present his case on attacking Iraq, columnist William Saletan wrote in *Slate* that, prior to the speech, Saddam Hussein was widely considered a reckless troublemaker who required the attention of the international community. After the speech, according to Saletan, diplomats realized that now "another cowboy is riding into town, less crazy but with much bigger guns: the president of the United States." For Saletan, the cowboy was the individual who rode into a town ready to shoot, and this image of the cowboy with big guns was extended in other editorials: Bush became a tough talking Clint Eastwood type with such a huge ego that he could not back down once he gave his word. John Ed Pearce writing for the *Herald-Leader* in Kentucky asserted Bush did not carry through on his promises regarding Afghanistan and eliminating terrorists. He wrote that Bush, however, continued to be "riding high with his cowboy motif. He has a big white cowboy hat and a ranch. He talks tough like Clint Eastwood. He has the mightiest military machine, and it looks like he is going to use it. If he doesn't, the tyrants of Central and Southeast Asia will make fun of him. Can't have that." Les Payne, writing for Newsday.com, extended the image of the cowboy riding into town with big guns in his critique of President Bush whom he claimed acted like a Texas Ranger, "one of the cold-blooded, bloodthirsty Texas lawmen" who are eager to dispense justice. Payne called attention to Bush's tendency for beaded eyes and finger pointing, which he claimed impeded U.S. diplomacy. Bush would attack Iraq, Payne claimed, in order to show that he was not "all hat and no cattle." In summary, editorialists in the U.S. portrayed Bush, the cowboy riding into town, as a crazed, egoistic Texas Ranger, eager to shoot in the name of justice.

As the cowboy myth was widely used in the U.S. press as a weapon for ridiculing Bush and his policy on Iraq, Vice President Al Gore joined in the process, condemning Bush's policies on Iraq and making use of the bad man tradition of the cowboy to reinforce his point. Speaking before a crowd of five hundred people in California, Gore claimed Bush should focus on the war on terror first before engaging with Iraq and should garner international cooperation in any action against Iraq. After the speech, Gore told reporters that the Bush Administration had adopted a "do-it-alone, cowboy-type reaction to foreign affairs," and that "there's ample basis for taking off after Saddam, but before you ride out after Jesse James, you ought to put the posse together."

## The Good Cowboy

The posse aspect of the cowboy myth was off and running after Gore's comments, and the lone cowboy riding out without a posse is a particularly damaging image when one considers the cowboy also has been portrayed as an evil guy out for revenge and eager to shoot in the name of justice. With such an image in the public consciousness, the adoption of a cowboy persona by George W. Bush amazed me. After the injurious connotations associated with Bush's "cowboy diplomacy" abroad and in the U.S., Bush continued to play directly into the cowboy president image. Was this a calculated risk taken by Bush and his image consultants?

The lack of ambiguity in Bush's references to cowboy images, I believe, indicates that Bush purposely adopted the heroic, idealized version of the cowboy in defining his presidency. Even before September 11, Bush was cultivating a cowboy image of himself. In August of 2001, he provided photo opportunities to the press during his vacation at his Texas ranch. As several news articles commented, he road around dusty roads in his white Ford pickup with Rumsfield at his side "riding shotgun." After 9/11, Bush clarified his desire to kill or capture Osama bin Laden by stating, "There's an old poster out West that I recall that said 'wanted, dead or alive'." In making such a statement, Bush was obviously not shying away from the image of the cowboy sheriff who dispenses justice, and he continued to reinforce his cowboy persona. At a National Cattlemen's Beef Association meeting in February 2002, Bush told the crowd, "Either you're with us, or you're against us." After the Senate approved the War Powers Resolution in October of 2002, Bush thanked members of Congress and said, "The days of Iraq acting as an outlaw state are coming to an end." The statements to the cattlemen's association and to Congress were somewhat veiled allusions to thecowboy, but by late 2002, Bush clearly embraced the cowboy myth.

In November 2002 at the NATO summit in Prague Castle, where Bush was generating international support for a war with Iraq, he said, "Contrary to my image as a

Texan with two guns at my side, I'm more comfortable with a posse." The timing of this statement is particularly interesting since Al Gore made his statements about Bush's willingness to ride out without a posse in late September 2002. Just before the war with Iraq began, Bush solidified his cowboy image by declaring that Saddam and his sons had forty-eight hours to leave Iraq. As the *OTC Journal* emphasizes, "This statement did nothing to mitigate Bush's cowboy image on the International political scene as it sounded like Wyatt Earp telling the bad guy he had 48 hours to get out of Dodge." As the war with Iraq became imminent, the president, indeed, appeared ready to ride out to dispense justice without a posse.

## Tony Blair as Cowboy

Bush was not without one steadfast companion in the lead-up to war with Iraq, and because Tony Blair solidly aligned himself with Bush's stance on Iraq, he was identified as a cowboy also. Whether or not Blair's intent was as obvious as Bush's is not clear, and whether or not Blair was a good or a bad cowboy in the British press is also not obvious. It is clear, though, that the press relished using the image of the cowboy in illustrating Blair's support of Bush's position on Iraq. The British press, for instance, published photos of Blair with what was described as a "thumbs-in belt" position before a news conference on Iraq. The *Daily Telegraph* asked if Blair was "spending too much time down on the ranch with Dubya" and whether he was becoming a "faithful deputy, the meanest gunslinger in Durham County, strolling into the Sedgefield corral." The *Mirror*, a popular London tabloid, printed a photo of Blair with the headline "Unforgiven" (the title of a Clint Eastwood movie) and called Blair's involvement with Bush a "two-hour epic starring Tony Blair: a man with a mission: to follow America's cowboy trail to war." Blair's thumbs-in-the-belt stance was not lost on the international press. The BBC News reported that *The Gulf Today*, located in Dubai, analyzed Blair's posturing, claiming, "When Britons saw him with thumbs tucked into his belt cowboy-style ahead of his news conference on Iraq, his political stance on the Iraq issue crumbled….A body-language expert even suggested that Blair is subconsciously mimicking Bush." One political cartoon even showed Blair as Tonto, the companion to Bush as Lone Ranger. The portrayal of Blair as a cowboy in the British press adds an intriguing twist to the image of the cowboy as it was used in editorials; Bush became the Lone Ranger with Tony Blair as his loyal companion, and he also became a sheriff with a faithful deputy, also played by Tony Blair.

## Meta-Commentary on the Cowboy Myth

As editorial writers began to recognize the ubiquity of the cowboy myth in commentary on the war with Iraq, some began to analyze Bush's cowboy image and tried to sort out the references to the good and the bad cowboy. Two editorials, for instance, analyzed how Bush fit or should fit Gary Cooper's image of the cowboy in the movie *High Noon*. An article in *The All-American Post* published by the Vietnam Veterans and Airborne Press asserts that George W. Bush should "examine his cowboy image" and try to be more like Gary Cooper than Clint Eastwood in *Unforgiven* who issues cruel threats as he leaves town. The article claimed Bush resembled the Gary Cooper style cowboy after 9-11 in his deliberate approach and gained much political capital; however, in his dealings with Iraq, Bush emulated Eastwood in *Unforgiven*. Brant Ayers, publisher of the *Anniston Star*, claimed the Bush administration had "blurred the quiet cowboy as a self-defining allegory" by being more like "a bad-humored, 20-foot American cowboy [who] tells the whole saloon he's going to drill the 3-foot bad guy, who doesn't stand a chance." Ayers analyzed the Gary Cooper style cowboy and explained that Americans have looked up to the image of the quiet cowboy, personified by Gary Cooper as Sheriff Kane in *High Noon*, who only lost his quiet demeanor and fought when he was provoked by an outlaw.

As a result of my reading of other pieces of meta-commentary, I believe that the image of Bush as a heroic cowboy president had more currency in the U.S. than the images of him as an outlaw bad-man cowboy. Several elements appeared to reinforce the positive image of the cowboy president: the increasing popularity of Ronald Reagan who played into the image of the cowboy president during the dismantling of the Soviet Union; the American love of the cowboy – the impetus that generated so many westerns in the first place; and the ability to use the image of the cowboy to clearly distinguish a U.S. view of the war with Iraq from a European view. Many Americans relish the idea that they are different from the Europeans because of the experience of the American frontier and the cowboy who rode in it; consequently, many Americans promote Frederick Jackson Turner's version of the frontier as a means of defining differences between the U.S. and Europe.

Two prominent news analysts, William Schneider and William F. Buckley Jr., explored how Bush as cowboy was a favorable image because of the positive impression Reagan generated as a cowboy politician. As early as March of 2002, William Schneider, writing in the *National Journal*, explained how Bush's use of a cowboy image worked to his advantage in positioning himself in the attack on Afghanistan in the aftermath of 9/11. He pointed out that Ronald Reagan also used his cowboy image to affirm his positions by wearing big cowboy hats and using the phrase, "Go ahead. Make my day!" Schneider also explained how Reagan's tough talk about the "Evil Empire" shocked allies and correlated with Bush's own tough talk. Schneider summarized Bush's approach: "Talk tough and carry a big stick, but act with prudence. It's Reagan diplomacy with a Bush twist – just right for an Ivy League cowboy." Reagan, however, also generated ridicule in the international community with his tough stance and "big cowboy stick." William F. Buckley Jr. analyzed in the January 24, 2003, *National Review* what people in the international community found so offensive about Reagan. The diplomatic community, which Buckley claimed "lives and breathes off ambiguity," was taken aback by Reagan's talk about the Soviet Union being an "evil empire." According to Buckley, moving forward as a loner with a clear will to take action was antithetical to the international community. Buckley claimed that Bush, if he was like other cowboys, Winston Churchill and Ronald Reagan, would go forward with removing Saddam Hussein from power in Iraq. The cowboy image of Reagan and of Bush for those who endorse Buckley's line of thinking, was not that of the crazed gunman riding out alone, but instead of the man of courage who left ambiguity behind and clearly named the evil doer. Apparently, after the horrendous images of 9/11, the U.S. public was more open to image of the cowboy as a courageous straight-shooting leader than many editorialists realized when they used the word "cowboy" to generate extremely negative associations.

A number of commentators claimed many Americans maintain their love for the cowboy of the Old West repeatedly portrayed in movies and other forms of narrative. Wayne Lutz explored the statements made around the world that portrayed Bush negatively as a cowboy and claimed the statements contrasted with the feelings of most Americans. Lutz provided quotation after quotation referencing Bush as a cowboy and concluded that liberals, "superior Europeans, frightened Canadians, and Al Gore" consider the term cowboy disdainfully and enjoy feeling superior to Bush; but, said Lutz, the American people of the heartland admired the cowboy nature of George W. Bush and calling him a cowboy "stirs the cowboy in us all." In line with Turner's theory of the frontier, Lutz said America was built by individuals with a cowboy mentality, which meant straight shooting and honesty to most people. The public, Lutz claimed, liked Bush's moral clarity; they admired the fact that he risked an unpopular war, but a war he believed was just. In my opinion, Lutz revealed what should have been obvious in the editorial wars all along: many Americans believe in and love the cowboy. They see the cowboy as central to the identity of Americans and to themselves. We have only to think of the popularity of country western music, of western movies, and the cowboy image in general. When Tim McGraw sings, "I guess that's just the cowboy in me," he is not anticipating that his words will generate negative associations. Likewise when Ralph Lauren wears a beat up cowboy hat and denim jacket, he is counting on positive associations with the cowboy. So do marketers who use the cowboy image to sell perfume, trucks, and cigarettes.

The love of the cowboy in the U.S., however, did not translate well into other countries, and, in fact, some editorialists analyzed how irksome the love of the cowboy was to many Europeans. Kathleen Parker, writing for *Sun News*, believed the cowboy spirit in America, based on a love of freedom, troubled other countries. She claimed "most tax-paying Americans grew up watching cowboy shows" and loved what she defined as the "real" cowboy: "the genuine driver of cattle across lonely, death-around-every-corner prairies and torrential rivers [who] was the American heroic prototype – strong, brave, trustworthy, loyal, wise, resourceful, self-reliant and dutiful." In fact, according to Parker, the word "cowboy" has "become an epithet from the freedom-hating masses." Parker claimed, "Averring that Bush is a cowboy is like saying he's an honorable man whose word is his bond. Whoa, that hurts." She ended her article with this statement: "The world has become a global Dodge City. Lucky for us, a Wild West sheriff is in charge." For Parker, the love of the cowboy translated to the sheriff president who was willing to take charge of his town, the global community. The image of the cowboy acting on the international scene, not just creating law and order in the U.S., seemed to have an appeal for the U.S. public. Robert Kagan in *The Globalist* approved of the global role of the cowboy president and claimed the U.S. had become a self-appointed "international sheriff" who kept law and order and defeated the outlaws. Kagan viewed Europe as a saloonkeeper, who was not only afraid of the outlaw but also the violent sheriff. If some Americans love the cowboy, and correspondingly George W. Bush as lawmaker of the international community, then perhaps it is not surprising that the press and citizenry of other countries have come to disdain the image of the cowboy and of George W. Bush.

My scrutiny of editorials revealed a belief that Bush took on a largely self-appointed role, and Europeans (in particular the French and the Germans) disdained his will to action. Fernando Oaxaca writing for *Latinola's Forum* claimed there was a cultural gap between the "French, the Germans and their liberal media sympathizers," and those who understood cowboys. Vaqueros are the opposite of the wealthy and the elitists, says Oaxaca, and he believes his father, an "old school Mexican," would have admired Bush's plain speaking and risk taking. Likewise, Andrew Bernstein, a writer for the Ayn Rand Institute, claimed the American public admires the hardworking, courageous, and heroic cowboy. He said when "European critics use the 'cowboy' image as a symbol of reckless irresponsibility, they implicitly reveal the real virtues they are attacking." Europeans, Berstein said, disdained the "black and white certainties" and bluntness of the cowboy. They were "worse than the timid shopkeeper in an old Hollywood Western" because they were afraid to stand up to evil and were afraid of anyone else who was willing to do so.

Christopher Hitchens, a *Vanity Fair* writer and frequent analyst on televised news editorial programs, provided perhaps the most thorough analysis of the use of the cowboy myth and a provocative examination of the contrast between U.S. and European attitudes about it. After proclaiming how frequently Bush had been labeled a cowboy in the European press, Hitchens reviewed the meanings of the word "cowboy": the tough, fatalistic cattle driver, the uncouth Indian fighter on the frontier, and the lone horseman with a six shooter who held up stage coaches or fought for justice. Hitchens clarified that in England the word "cowboy" "described a fly-by-night business or a shady or gamey entrepreneur" and that cowboys were especially connected to Texas. Hitchens stated, "Boiled down, then, the use of the word 'cowboy' expresses a fixed attitude and an expectation on the part of non-Texans, about people from Texas." Regarding the European reaction to Bush's stance on Iraq, Hitchens stated, "What we are really seeing, in this and other tantrums, is not a Texan cowboy on the loose but the even less elevating spectacle of European elites having a cow." Hitchens' analysis made clear that how one defines "cowboy" was significant in shaping perspectives of George W. Bush and the war with Iraq.

## Conclusion

I believe the cowboy myth highlights a significant division in perspectives on U.S. foreign policy. Those who view the cowboy as heroic (more Americans than Europeans and, in general, those who adhere to Turner's version of the American frontier) tend to look at political problems in a sharply focused way and are willing to take big political risks in acting on their vision. Bush and conservative editorialists apparently adopted the cowboy myth in order to clarify their adherence to a no nonsense policy on Iraq. Like a sheriff of the Old West who clearly delineates the difference between good and evil, Bush as a straight-shooting cowboy declared the aims of the U.S. were good and those of Iraq under Saddam Hussein were evil. The president was justified, then, in leading the charge for good to win out over evil.

Not everyone, of course, admires the straight-shooting keeper of the law who sees good and evil clearly. Those who view the cowboy as a bad man (more Europeans than Americans and, in general, the New Western Historians) are more comfortable with dealing in ambiguities and complexities and prefer to continue talking and delaying action. They observe the social and political world in a more nuanced way and find the president's unproblematic will to take action very troublesome. They are more likely to look for ambiguities in political and cultural issues and to see less black and white certainties. They view Bush as too eager to take action, and they deconstruct the good versus evil binary he promoted in his 2003 State of the Union address in which he sets out his axis of evil.

What I find disquieting is that the cowboy myth has become not only a pattern in the mind but also a pattern on the printed page that generates action. In *Regeneration Through Violence*, Richard Slotkin emphasizes that myths generate not only thoughts but also action. He defines mythology as "a complex set of narratives that dramatizes the world vision and historical sense of a people or culture, reducing centuries of experience into a constellation of compelling metaphors." The human mind, as Slotkin explains, generates the myth, but myths "ultimately affect both man's perception of reality and his actions."

In the case of the lead up to the war with Iraq, comparisons of Bush to a heroic cowboy may have propelled the U.S. into a war in a faster and more determined way than might otherwise have been the case, and thus the use of the cowboy myth in defining contemporary political positions confers additional weight to Joseph Campbell's well-known phrase "the power of myth."

*In "Reading Cereal Boxes," Lesley V. Kadish explores "the ways exoticized histories and representations of otherness are deployed on organic cereal boxes to frame the healthy breakfast as an ancient ritual." She also analyzes "the ways ethnicities are constructed and commodified on organic brand cereals and the aesthetic construction of opposing histories through nostalgia for an idealized agrarian past."*

# Reading Cereal Boxes: Pre-packaging History and Indigenous Identities

Lesley V. Kadish

> In my hungry fatigue, and shopping for images, I went into the neon fruit supermarket.
>
> -Allen Ginsberg," A Supermarket in California," 1955

## Introduction

Welcome to H.E.B., one of Texas's largest grocery chains with over 300 stores throughout the state. Inside, we find the visual trappings that are typical of the large-scale supermarket industry: linoleum tiles, stadium ceilings, florescent lighting, and clearly gridded aisles. At selected H.E.B. stores, however, a new section called Nature's Harvest has been created to serve the needs of a different brand of shopper, a group I am calling the "thoughtful class." This class can be defined by disproportionate access to education, wealth, and transportation. They shop with moral and intellectual intention, putting their money where their mouths are. The section of H.E.B that caters to this type of consumer specializes in organic, "healthy foods" and is visually separate from the managed aesthetics (or lack thereof) governing the rest of the store; track lighting, lowered ceilings, angled aisles, and hardwood floors greet H.E.B.'s Nature's Harvest shoppers. An exotic oasis among the clamor of shopping carts, the natural food section provides the artificial comfort of a local co-operative in the jowls of corporate consumption. For the thoughtful class, shopping is a personal experience in the moral landscape of organics. Imagined cultural ideals of eating healthily while supporting cultural and biological diversity are encouraged within the constructed supermarket space and are reinforced through the commodification of historical and indigenous images. In this paper, I will explore the ways exoticized histories and representations of otherness are deployed on organic cereal boxes to frame the healthy breakfast as an ancient ritual. I will also analyze the ways ethnicities are constructed and commodified on organic brand cereals and the aesthetic construction of opposing histories through nostalgia for an idealized agrarian past.

## The Setting

Cereal is a uniquely American food. A walk down the cereal aisle is an experience in American vision. Unlike other sections of the store where items vary by size or shape, the cereal aisle has the same-styled box pressed one against the other. These standardized 8x11 boxes resemble hypercolor stacks of television sets, each a visual talking-head flashing sports stars, cartoons, or slim models. We find a similar, though differently hued, experience in the

Nature's Harvest supermarket section. Here, the organic cereal aisle is more like a terraced garden overgrown with images of parrots and colorful, "exotic" people. It is an interwoven expression of subaltern and popular culture. The iconic predominance of the "natural" world speaks to this association of all things green to all things good, and the multi-chromatic array of faces reinforces diversity as the path to a balanced meal. As such, the very nature of the cereal box is performative, intended to attract the attention of the consumer through culturally recognizable and emotionally resonant images.

The cereal box occupies a space, a vision, and a location all at once. After we have purchased the cereal, we are expected to sit down and read the box as part of the morning ritual. In an oddly-sustained, postmodern version of a Norman Rockwell portrait, the timeless place of the American cereal box, organic or not, is atop a breakfast table, next to an open newspaper and a half-gallon of wholesome milk. Indigenous images on organic cereal boxes are used as cultural windows that bring the meals of the "natives" into our home, and essentialize breakfasts across time and place. To more closely regard the commercial reification of the "natural," I will consider one particular brand of organic cereal found in all H.E.B. Nature's Harvest health food sections: Nature's Path's Mesa Sunrise.

## The Box

The box of Mesa Sunrise cereal is a rich desert oasis within our organic aisle garden. Orange skies and golden buttes halo a bounty of gathered grains on the front of the box, over which curls the cereal brand name in a font suggestive of petroglyphs. The carefully crafted title, Mesa Sunrise, conjures up a mythical, Southwestern landscape while subtly referencing the actual home of the Hopi Indians: Northern Arizona's Three Mesas. The brand name is quixotic, evocative, and highly poetic. In Sunrise, we are reminded how natural and timeless the morning ritual of breakfast is; the high, flat-top Mesas are the world's own breakfast table. Sunrise also recalls a pre-industrial epoch when the passing of time was not marked by the clock, but by the natural rising and falling of the sun. On the back of the box, we find a bricolage of historicized images, effluent quotes, and scientific jabber, peppered along the margins with peeling corn and flowering plants. The overall presentation of the box is intended to tell the cultural and environmental story surrounding the cereal we are about to consume. By displaying a collection of disparate images in this way, a self-reflexive framework of meaning is crafted which totals more than the sum of its parts. These images are strategic; each historic reference builds on the next to construct an overall product narrative: history is available for consumption. For example, an image of three women kneeling over their stone metates is captioned with the text, "Hopi women grinding corn."

The image is visually intimate and sepia-toned, as though we were witnessing a private moment at home. Yet, with some research, we find that the Hopi image is a photoshopped version of an early photograph taken by renowned photographer Edward Curtis in 1907, merely twenty-five years after the Hopi reservation was created. At that time, ethnographers, missionaries, and government agents were all climbing the mesas, vying for glimpses into the Hopi world. Alone, Curtis' presence as a camera-laden White man would likely render the gentle domestic scene contrived. Mesa Sunrise cereal locates itself in the landscape and constructs a stereotypical Hopi ethnicity around a "real" (though itself constructed and highly problematic) historical image of grinding maidens: no other information or details are given beside the caption. The dress, hairstyles, and posture of these women are not contemporary, and would probably only be seen in a ceremonial or performative setting today. Yet, without historic information or contextualization, we are made to believe that these three Hopi women are still grinding corn in the recesses of our mass-producing consumer present, just as Nature's Path wants us to believe that we are reading the cereal box from our own Norman Rockwell breakfast table.

Native Americans are not static cultural beings as portrayed on Mesa Sunrise; they are American consumers in their own right. Over-simplified images of "timeless natives" are used to represent a moment in time when humans had a more humble relation to nature. Disparate tribes are grouped together to further show, as the box says, "the pivotal position that corn has held in the cultural lives of indigenous peoples." Sitting just atop the industrious Hopi image is a quote regarding the Navajo, "Corn is the Navaho staff of life, and pollen is its essence." Just below, we find a brief Zuni coming-of-age anecdote: "The Zuni people of the American Southwest measured time through kernels of corn. A 'generation of corn' would be counted from when a boy received his first planting seed to the time he gave the seed to his own child to plant." These quotes are double constructions in that they offer no Native voices; only the words of the "expert" are decontextualized and used as testimony. The complexity of Zuni and Navajo cultures are reduced to single, pithy narratives constructed around cereal. While these sound bites may carry residues of historic validity, their uni-dimensionality steals from them any real chance for meaning. Native Americans represented on this box of cereal are fixed as media icons through the commodification of their tribal identity or through the market potential of their supposed traditions.

The back of the cereal box offers the central message: "Mesa Sunrise – Cereal That Whispers Secrets of the Past." The "secrets" of indigenous pasts are just that – whispers, the lifeblood of oral tradition to be counterposed to written history. As such, these whispers carry traditions that are transferred from one group to the next, as seen in the story of the Zuni boy and his father who pass time and wisdom through their heirlooms of corn. Mesa Sunrise implies that without the textual "knowledge" of "real" (i.e. written) history, fact is reduced to myth and history reduced to ethnohistory. Moreover, while these possessors of traditional knowledge may hold valuable information, their experience is neither associated with thought, nor individualism. Rather, it is assumed that oral knowledge should pass unmarred through the transmitters of human memory; critical thinking and autonomy must be subverted in the process.

For the Mesa Sunrise consumer, the "past" is neatly divided into the left- and right-hand sides of the cereal box. To oppose the North American Indians' use of corn as a spiritual and calendric sacrament (on the left-hand side), the manufacturers place (on the right) the great European "cultivation" of cereal for early scientific and medicinal purposes. Through this visually articulated division, we see two contrasting histories that serve to validate and contradict one another.

## The Message

In "Disjuncture and Difference in the Global Cultural Economy," Arjun Appadurai makes the following statement about a situation similar to the one we find on the Mesa Sunrise cereal box, "Here we have nostalgia without memory. The paradox of course has its explanations, and they are historical: unpacked, they lay bare the story of American missionizing and political rape" (3). A critical reading of the text-and-image collage on our box finds a potential naturalization and trivialization of the backbreaking labor of those involved in actual cereal production and those who ground corn on their hands and knees. Moreover, a subtle gendering occurred during the photo alteration of the original 1907 Hopi photograph. Unlike the Edward Curtis 1907 photograph, none of the Hopi women portrayed on the box of Mesa Sunrise are making eye contact with the viewer. Instead, they are all looking down, suggesting the passivity of indigenous, female labor. The presentation of passive Native women on their hands and knees asserts a contemporary "we are better off" notion that is reaffirmed through iconographic analogies between breakfast in "our world" and food production in "their world." Behind the seemingly innocuous representation lies the mechanics of power that allow one group to own another through manipulation of image and identity. Indians captured on the cereal box have been appropriated by capitalist production, a fact which must not be overlooked.

The act of naming others is an act of control through representation, as it has been observed by academics and consumers alike (see Berkhofer and Bordewich). Native Americans have long suffered the brunt of such representation. In many places, antiquated cigar-Indians still flank drug stores and cigar shop entryways. Painted or feathered Braves and Redskins still make their battle cries on the fields of sports teams. And the Land-o-Lakes butter Indian sits "Indian Style" atop her creamed throne, adorned with a single feather and two browned knees emerging from under her buckskin skirt. Aside from their lingering remnants, the classic twentieth-century images of the American Indian are now largely understood as racist caricatures. As noted by scholars and activists (see Alexie, Churchill, Dilworth, and LaDuke), these representations are far from vanquished; rather, they are being re-marketed to a contemporary audience under a different premise. There has been a significant shift from the stoic Chief and sexualized squaw, to the deeply spiritual and environmentally conscious Native American. Now, a different ideal – the natural – is being sold through a modified Native American image.

Because the vast majority of American families were once immigrants to this country, Americans have taken the liberty to "rewrite history in a self-justifying manner by redefining Native Americans as part of their own past" (Huhndorf 5). Contemporary American life is often held in oppositional tension to an imagined pre-industrial Native American world. This is not wholly a new phenomenon. As Leah Dilworth remarks in her seminal work, *Imagining Indians of the Southwest,* anthropologists were using ethnography as a tool for critically assessing popular American culture as early as the 1920's (192). Not long after his linguistic work with the Hopi, Edward Sapir published an article in the *Journal of American Sociology* that polarized the Southwest United States into "genuine" and "spurious" cultures, the former representing an ideal pre-industrial state, and the latter encompassing the fettered modern world. Much as might be seen today, "spurious" American culture was encouraged to look to indigenous culture for a cure to the spiritual, cultural, and physical woes caused by over-industrialization. Sapir writes, "Genuine culture is inherently harmonious, balanced and self-satisfactory" (314). Nature's Path uses the Hopi image of industrious small-scale corn production to invoke the fantasy that Mesa Sunrise is hand-made rather than mass-produced. It is thus more "natural"; if you eat it, you will feel harmonious and balanced.

This harmonious and balancing Indian replaces its racialized predecessor with a softer, more "authentic" and "natural" representation. Today's "Indian" is as much a creation as the cigar Indian, crafted hodgepodge from staged photographs, stolen stories, and fabricated rituals. Thus, two contradictory, but constantly intertwined, modes of imagining indigenous peoples occur. The complex and shifting valences of respect and disregard converge in the public imagery today. All such representations, whether flattering or disparaging, are fundamentally dehumanizing.

While Nature's Path cereal would not admit to representing Indians in such iconic forms, we see from the above discussion that "their" Native Americans are stereotypes nonetheless. What is unique about the marketing scheme employed on Mesa Sunrise is the very intentional tribalization of its indigenous representatives. Through early ethnography and photography, individual tribal identities can be forged into a display of cultural diversity and historical accuracy. All the while, the identities of individual indigenous actors are blurred behind generalities of tribal affiliation. The Hopi women grinding corn are neither listed by name nor differentiated in dress. Their consumer worth is not in the product of their work but in the labor of their kind: "authentic, primitive, and undifferentiated." Superficially, the cereal box attempts to dismantle this "homogenized Indian" by tribally differentiating between Native cultures in the Southwest. Likely resulting from their historic relation to the early railroad tourism industry, as well as their own successes at self-promotion, the Zuni, Hopi, and Navajo tribes have become culturally recognizable entities. I believe that the deliberate reference to these tribes serves a separate function beyond the replacement of an older generation of essentialized Indian forms.

Nature's Path does not use just any tribal identity to (re)present its cereal. The Hopi and Zuni have long been recognized as popular tourist attractions in the Southwest. They are culturally marked and seen as historical remnants of earlier times. Grand Canyon guidebooks abound with one-dimensional descriptions of their cultures and directions to the nearest pueblo gift shops selling their "traditional" crafts. The guidebook put out by the Arizona Association of Bed and Breakfast Inns and available electronically for online perusal reads: "The Hopi village of Oraibi is one of the two oldest continuously inhabited communities in the United States. While it is possible, with permission, to wander around Oraibi, you will likely learn more about Hopi culture by opting for one of the guided tours of Walpi village, which sits atop First Mesa. Throughout the Hopi mesas you will find numerous crafts shops and artists' studios where you can shop for kachinas, silver jewelry, and pottery. From the Hopi mesas, head south to I-40 and back to Flagstaff." The Bed and Breakfast Association, an exclusive echelon of the hotel industry, has marketed itself around a patron type who appreciates exotic life, "off the beaten path," with the comforts of home. Just as the language of the B&B guidebook appeals to a particular type of traveler, so too the back of the organic cereal box appeals to a selective group of consumers, perhaps the groups even overlap. These strategic marketing representations reflect the way consumers imagine their own, as well as other, cultural identities and make their choices.

The language of the cereal box relies heavily on history-rich words such as "over the millennia," "ancestors," and "generations," to develop an overall feeling of history. Yet, as mentioned above, we are presented with two distinctly different historic timelines. The history of European civilization where agricultural decrees ("800 AD Charlemagne passed laws requiring people to use flax") and medicinal knowledge ("Hippocrates used flax to relieve digestive problems") are encrypted in text ("Evidence from the writings of Hippocrates show") and are held against the traditional past of North America (presented in pictures and stories) where wizened ancestors passed on ancient farming knowledge through whispered secrets and ritual. Although it has been archaeologically established that natives cultivated both flax and amaranth in what is now the Southeastern United States well into the thirteenth century, Mesa Sunrise only shows Native Americans as raising "colorful maize." The Old World stories of flax and amaranth include dates (5000 BC, 650 BC, 800 AD) and recognizable names (Charlemagne, Hippocrates) in order to show the pedigree of an identifiable history as opposed to a New World pre-history full of undocumented ancient traditions. These disparate timelines are intended to weave through each other, imbuing Mesa Sunrise cereal with a whole world of historic and grainy diversity sanctioned by "natural" tradition and historic veracity. All the while, the methods of analysis are essentially

Hegelian; by employing the logic of dichotomy, European reason and science are deified.

The box reads, "Every spoonful of Mesa Sunrise connects you through the centuries to knowledge and traditions around the benefits of ancient grains that contemporary science is now beginning to support." We read that contemporary science is finally catching up to the wisdom gained through history. A scientific lexicon (soluble fiber, lignans, and omega-3 fatty acids found in flax) further legitimates a "traditional" past and brings this past into the present. Scientific and historical language and images are used in emotionally evocative ways. Cereal grains are bound up with symbolic meaning, and this meaning is codified in traditional food diets, historical names, dates, and places. Compared to the ancient peoples' world and their ties to nature, the present, not unlike Sapir's "spurious culture," is seen as a world of loss. Consumers now have the opportunity to reap both the benefits of contemporary scientific knowledge and colorful ancient ritual.

The organic movement is ripe with nostalgia for the "simpler" era when the process of eating was itself a ritual act. The images Nature's Path presents show the Native American past as one that is bound up with ritualistic agrarian practices. These images actively assert a valid and natural connection between food and wisdom. Moreover, the cereal box language presents the past in such a way that suggests we too can gain wisdom through eating the same ancient grains. Just as we are intended to digest the guidebook histories of the Native Americans through images and quotes, our bodies are granted effortless access to "centuries of knowledge" through breakfast cereal. The cereal goes beyond simply asserting that healthy food will make us wise. By presenting the powerful history of ritual food practices, consumers are enticed to bring ritual into their own lives through the consumption of organic foods. The pre-existing American cultural practice of eating breakfast (à la Norman Rockwell) can be imbued with meaning and enshrined in ritual when the element of moral intention is added. The knowledges and "by hand" labor of the Native are rich with tribal significance but empty of meaningful autonomous action. Today's shopper can bring individuality to the past by translating the ancient experience of eating naturally into a contemporary organic lifestyle. A ritual of healthy eating (including, of course, corn and flax found in Mesa Sunrise) will enrich the body and the mind, creating a wiser person, which in today's consumer society is equivalent to a thoughtful class of shopper. Mesa Sunrise relies on a narrative of nostalgia for the timeless yet vanquishing primitive that is validated by a scientific lexicon and a constructed Old World history.

## Conclusion

Mesa Sunrise is a cornflake cereal boasting ingredients of organically grown and processed flax, amaranth, and "Indian corn." The cereal box itself is like a miniature Levi-Straussean museum assembled from the stolen bodies and cultural sacra of the past, and reworked into a modern narrative. The images that collide and are juxtaposed on the box belong to two different visions of the past, one traditional and the other historical. Much like H.E.B.'s constructed "Nature's Harvest" environment, Mesa Sunrise cereal constructs a visual narrative around fabricated cultural identities, thereby creating a product – and a consumer – just exotic enough to be healthy.

## Works Cited

Alexie, Sherman. *Old Shirts & New Skins, Native American Series; No. 9.* Los Angeles: U of California P, 1993.

Appadurai, Arjun. "Disjuncture and Difference in the Global Cultural Economy." *Public Culture* 2.2 (1990): 1-24.

Arizona Association of Bed and Breakfast Inns. 2004. http://www.arizona-bed-breakfast.com /travelplanner-5.html

Berkhofer, Robert F. *The White Man's Indian: Images of the American Indian, from Columbus to the Present.* New York: Vintage Books, 1979.

Bordewich, Fergus M. *Killing the White Man's Indian: Reinventing of Native Americans at the End of the Twentieth Century.* New York: Doubleday, 1996.

Churchill, Ward. *From a Native Son: Selected Essays in Indigenism, 1985-1995.* Boston: South End Press, 1996.

Dilworth, Leah. *Imagining Indians in the Southwest: Persistent Visions of a Primitive Past.* Washington: Smithsonian Institution Press, 1996.

Ginsberg, Allen. *Collected Poems, 1947-1980.* New York: Harper & Row, 1984.

Huhndorf, Shari M. *Going Native: Indians in the American Cultural Imagination.* Ithaca: Cornell UP, 2001.

LaDuke, Winona. *The Winona Laduke Reader: A Collection of Essential Writings.* Stillwater, MN: Voyageur Press, 2002.

Sapir, Edward. "Culture, Genuine and Spurious." *American Journal of Sociology* 29 (1949): 308-331.

*Probably the most well known of the Harry Potter critics is Pope Benedict XVI. Then Cardinal Ratzinger thanked Gabriela Kuby in a 2003 letter for her book criticizing the Potter series. "It is good," wrote the new Pope, "that you enlighten people about Harry Potter, because those are subtle seductions, which act unnoticed and by this deeply distort Christianity in the soul, before it can grow properly." This essay examines just such conservative Christian commentary against the books.*

# "Subtle Seductions": Harry Potter and Conservative Christianity

Leslie Wilson

Here, as dusk settles on the Harry Potter series, I thought it might be useful to review the considerable criticism that has amassed from Christians writing and thinking about J.K. Rowling's books. As we travel through this bibliographic essay, we will find that, far from what we may have imagined, namely, fringe lunatics dressed like seventeenth century pilgrims wearing stockings, breeches, doublets, ruffs, and broad brimmed felt hats, tarring and feathering Professor Dumbledore, drunkenly running him through town on a pole, and tossing him into Salem Harbor, this group of Christians is quite sober and serious about saving our souls from the occult. Their opposition to the Potter books is rooted in two main concerns: first, they believe the books violate specific commandments set forth in Bible verses, and, second, they believe that Rowling, unlike C.S. Lewis and J.R.R. Tolkien, blurs conventional notions of right and wrong, good and evil, authority, and hierarchy.

One such serious Christian is Stephen Dollins who published a slim volume called

*Under the Spell of Harry Potter* through The Prophecy Club, a Topeka, Kansas, ministry dedicated to disseminating messages of biblical prophecy and warning. Dollins writes:

> So here is Satan's plan: You whet the appetites of children who are confused and not quite grounded in family morals, values, and standards (especially those young enough not fully grounded in their faith in Jesus) and introduce them to Harry Potter, a boy wizard who learns and practices the art of Witchcraft and Sorcery. You then bolster their interest in these practices and instill in them the idea that there is no good or evil, only magic, and that it's okay to practice witchcraft, because it is a moral, wholesome thing to do, as well as the fact that you will receive a reward from it. Finally when their interest in these practices is at its highest peak, offer the use of the Internet, which is exploding with information that is theirs for the taking, and teaches them how they too can be just like Harry Potter! From what the Lord has shown me thus far, I believe this is the strategy Satan is using to recruit our children into his ranks!

Indeed, Dollins may know something about "Satan's plan." For seven years, he was a High Priest at Anton Lavey's Church of Satan, and he has also published another book called *The Occult in Your Living Room* in which he documents the dangers behind the Ouija board, astrology, Tarot cards, psychics, and more. He concludes *Under the Spell of Harry Potter* by offering a list of things that "can be done about Harry." Dollins begins by suggesting prayer and quotes 2 Corinthians 10: 4-5, "For the weapons of our warfare are not carnal but mighty through God to the pulling down of strong holds. Casting down imaginations. And every high thing that exalteth itself against the knowledge of God, and bringing into captivity every thought to the obedience of Christ." He goes on to urge support for ministers and ministries that are working to expose the evil, to call for organization, and to encourage education through the dissemination of his book. He also calls for his readers to write to Christian leaders, boycott corporations promoting Harry Potter, and keep watch for other Satanic devices.

Similarly, Christian writer, producer, and occasional minister Richard Abanes worries about the impact of the series on people in general but on children in particular. In his book *Harry Potter and the Bible*, published by the Christian publisher Horizon Books, he lists the "underlying lessons communicated through Rowling's novels":

> -Lying, stealing and cheating are not only acceptable, but can also be fun.
> -Astrology, numerology, casting spells and performing "magick" can be exciting.
> -Disobedience is not very serious, unless you get caught.
> -Being "special" means you deserve to escape punishment for behaving badly.
> -Adults just get in the way most of the time.
> -Rules are made to be broken.
> -Revenge is an acceptable course of action.

Abanes counters these lessons with advice for parents, and he encourages them by offering some biblical verses: "Bear in mind that according to God's Word, the Holy Spirit dwelling in us is far more powerful than any force of darkness in the world" (1 John 4: 4). Moreover, no Christian should ever harbor fear regarding the contents of a book (1 John 4: 18), and God has not given us a spirit of fear or timidity, but one of power and love (2 Timothy 1: 7). Abanes cautions parents against banning the books, however. Instead, he suggests that "parents should give examples of where the Harry Potter series is unbiblical and explain why God is against some of the things in Rowling's books, both from a spiritual and moral perspective."

In *J.K. Rowling: A Biography*, published by Greenwood, Connie Ann Kirk documents one of the most publicized book burning events which occurred in December of 2001: "During the holiday season which just happened to coincide with the first theater release of the first film, and just days after Rowling's second wedding. Jack Brock, founder and pastor of Alamogordo, New Mexico's Christ Community Church, led his congregation in a burning of the books. Participants sang 'Amazing Grace' as they threw copies of Harry Potter books into the fire." Kirk also mentions that other congregations, notably one in Pennsylvania, have participated in book burnings. According to the website factmonster.com:

> Harry Potter fans were shocked to hear reports that the Harvest Assembly of God Church in western Pennsylvania had burned Harry Potter books. The church's minister, Reverend George Bender, called the books "supernatural." Bruce Springsteen albums, the Disney movie about Hercules, and other items deemed "ungodly" were also cast into flames. Only 30 people watched the blaze, which was held in the church parking lot in late March. But word of the event soon reached national news sources. Reverend Bender is happy for the attention, saying, "It's good to have publicity."

Another website, kidSPEAK.com documents other such protest activity: a "Jesus Party" book-cutting event, the passing of a resolution by the Arkansas Baptist State Convention protesting the sale of Potter books, a Pennsylvanian police boycott – they refused to assist the YMCA triathlon because kids attending the YMCA after-school program were read Potter books which did not serve "the will of God." In Merritt Island, Florida, Robert McGee spread "the word about the 'evils' of Harry Potter through his own anti-Harry video, which claims that J.K. Rowling's books introduce kids to human sacrifice, witchcraft and even Nazism." And in Oskaloosa, Kansas, the library dropped a Harry Potter reading program after fielding many complaints.

In the essay "Controversial Content in Children's Literature: Is Harry Potter Harmful to Children?", published by RoutledgeFalmer in the edited collection *Harry Potter's World*, scholars Deborah J. Taub and Heather L. Servaty note that many of the religious objections to the book are rooted in Deuteronomy 18: 9-12. They quote the Revised Standard Edition:

> When you come into the land which the Lord your God gives you, you shall not learn to follow the abominable practices of those nations. There shall not be found among you anyone who burns his son or his daughter as an offering, any one who practices divination, a soothsayer, or an augur, or a sorcerer, or a charmer, or a medium, or a wizard, or a necromancer. For whosever does these things is an abomination to the Lord; and because of these abominable practices the Lord your God is driving them out before you.

Taub and Servaty reference websites like crossroad.to and pawcreek.org as places to find the Christian perspective on the Internet. On crossroad.to, in an article entitled "Harry Potter & The Power of Suggestion," writer Berit Kjos argues that Rowling plants suggestions in the impressionable reader's mind. Specifically, he states that she offers the following:

1. A vision of a better world: link main characters to pagan practices.
2. Rebellion against Biblical authorities: link traditional authority figures to intolerant "muggles."
3. An idealized view of paganism: link occult images to "good" wizards.
4. A pagan alternative to Christian values: link courage and loyalty to a common quest for occult empowerment.
5. Mystical experiences that excite the emotions: link "good" spells to victory in the timeless battle between good and evil.

From this article, Kjos has links to many other pieces he has written also posted on the net. A quick click of the mouse will take you from "Twelve Reasons Not to See Harry Potter Movies" to "Bewitched by Harry Potter."

On pawcreek.org, you can find an article by Joseph Chambers, "Harry Potter and the Antichrist," in which he argues that the Potter books encourage kids to take drugs, practice astrology, glorify the devil through the character of Voldemort, believe the idea of reincarnation, and substitute Harry in for the Messiah. Chambers concludes his article by stating, "When people love imagination, superstition, paranormal intrigue, witchcraft, and sorcery better than they love truth, the Creator will allow them to be filled with their own desires. When the cup of sin is full, the King will say, 'It is enough.' My heart tells me the cup is at the brim. The King will soon have the final word and righteousness will win the day."

Taub and Sevaty also reference K.W. Gish's article, published in *The Horn Book Magazine*. In "Hunting Down Harry Potter: An Exploration of Religious Concerns about Children's Literature," librarian Gish shuns banning the books, but, as a conservative member of the Assembly of God church, she admits the texts are problematic for her. She is particularly concerned with the role of divination, possessions like that of Ginny Weasley in Book Two, and the negative, "unenlightened" portrayal of muggles. Gish writes:

> In our faith, the spiritual education of children is considered crucial. This stems largely from attention to Proverbs 22: 6: "Train up a child in the way he should go: and when he is old, he will not depart from it." Because those of my faith believe that casual exposure to the occult through media sources such as television, movies, games, and books can desensitize a Christian to the sinful nature of such beliefs and practices, any exposure is commonly prohibited. This includes reading books that portray the occult in a positive light.

In the edited collection *Reading Harry Potter* published by Praeger, we find the essay "Harry and Hierarchy: Book Banning as a Reaction to the Subversion of Authority" by Rebecca Stephens in which she pinpoints an objection somewhat different than the one Gish and others have noted. Stephens writes, "The Rowling-Lewis comparison thus raises an interesting paradox: what makes one book depicting the supernatural 'Christian' and the other somehow 'dangerous'? The answer, I believe, lies in the way that authority is represented in each set of books and the way these representations lead to different understandings of the role of values within contemporary culture."

Stephens goes on to explain what she views as the blurred moral boundaries in the Potter series, a concept perhaps most clearly articulated by John Andrew Murray in an article called "Harry Dilemma" posted on James Dobson's Focus on the Family website, family.org. Murray argues, "Rowling's work invites children to a world where witchcraft is 'neutral' and where authority is determined solely by one's might or cleverness. Lewis invites them to a world where God's authority is not only recognized, but celebrated – a world that resounds with his goodness and care." Stephens then points out what Christians like Murray fear, which is the "subversion of traditional hierarchical power structures."

In "Harry Potter and the Disenchantment of the World," published in the *Journal of Contemporary Religion*, Michael Ostling lists the Christian protests against the books:

> We learned of court challenges in Georgia; of children who had to leave the room when their teacher read Harry Potter to the class…; of Christian booksellers refusing to stock the series…; of libraries pulling the books from their shelves; even – in early 2001 – of a church-orchestrated book burning in rural Pennsylvania…. Conservative Christians rushed to press with books demonstrating the occult dangers lurking in Rowling's series, e.g. *Pokemon and Harry Potter: A Fatal Attraction…*; web sites exposed the Satanic significance of Harry's lightning-bolt scar and postulated a diabolical source for the books' amazing popularity….

Notable in this list is the book *Pokemon and Harry Potter.* The author, Phil Arms, a pastor-evangelist with radio, television, and public speaking credits argues that "a clever Satanic camouflage" conceals the "true diabolic nature" in children's games and books like Rowling's. For a writer like Arms, the Potter books are nothing more than a celebration of murder, demons, Satan, violence, witchcraft, and the occult wrapped in an entertaining, child-friendly cloak of invisibility.

Of course, the most well known of all the Potter critics is Pope Benedict XVI. Then Cardinal Ratzinger thanked Gabriela Kuby for her book *Harry Potter – gut oder böse* (*Harry Potter – good or evil?*) in which Kuby argues that the books corrupt our youth by hindering their understanding of good and evil thus damaging their relationship with Christianity in general and God in particular. "It is good," wrote the new Pope in a 2003 letter, "that you enlighten people about Harry Potter, because those are subtle seductions, which act unnoticed and by this deeply distort Christianity in the soul, before it can grow properly."

LifeSiteNews.com, who posted the Pope's letters to Kuby, has also posted a comment from the Catholic novelist and painter Michael O'Brien. He states, "This discernment on the part of Benedict XVI reveals the Holy Father's depth and wide ranging gifts of spiritual discernment." O'Brien also said that the Pope's comments were consistent with many of the statements he has been making since his election to the Chair of Peter, indeed for the past twenty years, "He is a man in whom a prodigious intellect is integrated with great spiritual gifts. He is the father of the universal church and we would do well to listen to him."

I must point out before concluding, however, that as many Christians as there are opposing Rowling's series, there are equally as many endorsing it. Critics like John Granger, described as a homeschooling Christian and father of seven, are defending the Potter series in books like his *Looking for God in Harry Potter* from Tyndale House. Likewise, in Thomas Dunne Books' *God, The Devil, and Harry Potter: A Christian Minister's Defense of the Beloved Novels*, John Killinger writes:

> There are two basic premises in this book…. The first is that the detractors are wrong and that the Potter series, far from being "wicked" or "Satanic" (one widely quoted e-mail accuses Rowling of having written "an encyclopedia of Satanism"), are in fact narratives of robust faith and morality, entirely worthy of children's reading

> again and again, and even of becoming world classics that will be reprinted as long as there is civilization. And the second premise is that much of that faith and morality is derived not only from the archetypes and legends of world literature, but from the wealth of Christian tradition that has spawned the author and her hero – a tradition that her detractors in their mean-spiritedness and narrow-mindedness (someone once spoke of an acquaintance so narrow-minded that he could peer through a keyhole with both eyes at the same time!) apparently do not know or else fail to appreciate.

For Killinger, the Potter books stir our imaginations and show us a magical world in which good ultimately conquers evil.

In Waterbrook's *What's a Christian to Do with Harry Potter?*, Christian writer, speaker, pastor, Connie Neal argues that the Potter books can provide an interesting opportunity to evangelize, proselytize, and convert. She suggests connecting events in the books to Bible passages in order to discuss "Biblical truths" and make the "Harry Potter phenomenon pay off in ministry." In her second Potter book published by Westminster John Knox Press, *The Gospel According to Harry Potter*, Neal practices what she preaches. In other words, she takes passages from the Potter books and relates them to Bible stories and lessons. In her "Afterword," she states, "I wrote this book for several reasons, but one was to extend God's welcoming invitation to you. I particularly hoped that some would hear the gospel who had never heard it before, perhaps because they were turned off by the way it has been presented." In the next paragraph, she goes on to explain, "Another reason I wrote this book was to challenge my fellow Christians to think again about the Harry Potter books. Many non-Christians share my discomfort with the fact that many critics of Harry Potter have never read even one of the...books for themselves. It is hard to be adamant if you choose to remain personally ignorant by relying only on impressions and hearsay without reading the story in question for yourself." For Neal, the books provide an opportunity to open a dialogue with non-Christians and invite them to eat in God's "banquet hall."

In our review of the literature that has amassed against the Potter series since the release of Book One, *Harry Potter and the Sorcerer's Stone* (the Philosopher's Stone in the original British version), we find that those opposed to the books are very serious about their concerns, rooting their dismay in Bible verses and the absence of a clear moral authority or God. For these detractors, Satan, magic, witchcraft, and the occult are very real, as real as the existence of J.K. Rowling herself. They believe that this fight is not only worth having but is the fight for the ultimate prize. No less, they would say, than the fight for our very souls.

# Where We Go

*In "Ridin' the Rails," John Lennon argues that hobos "can receive pleasure from the freedom that exists when poaching from the dominant culture. It is a fleeting power that exists mainly when the train is in motion: when they are in the act of stealing from the larger cultures, when they are uncounted and outside history."*

## Ridin' the Rails: The Place of the Passenger and the Space of the Hobo

John Lennon

"The body" is an idea that has been at the center of debate in cultural studies where lines are drawn and redrawn over issues including race, gender, science, and technology. As the body has been theorized, however, it has also been torn and tattooed. Pulled away from the substance of blood and tissue, it has lost some of its physical authority. Bodies, however, are not mere theoretical ideas, ethereal and unsubstantial. They are physical entities existing in time, place, space even if they choose to manipulate their own invisibility, an act frequent among marginal peoples. Remaining faithful to the physicality of the body in this study, I want to contrast the body of the rail passenger against the "invisible" body within the rail hobo subculture. By inserting their bodies within designated areas of the actual machine of the railroad car, I will argue, hobos achieve a spatiality of subcultural power.[1]

### The Place of the Passenger

The railroad line represents an invasion of place over space. Michel de Certeau, in a chapter entitled "Railway Navigation and Incarceration" from his influential book *The Practice of Everyday Life*, shows that inside the railroad car is a place of order where everything is in its right and proper place. It is "traveling incarceration" where the "unchanging traveler is pigeonholed, numbered and regulated in the grid of the railway car" (111). As passengers hand their tickets to the conductor, their movements are managed in this closed environment; they have been assigned a place to sit, to order lunch, to smoke a cigarette, and to relieve themselves: the price of a ticket allows them to perform certain bodily functions in logically organized and designated places. For the most part, though, they sit, immobile, and look out the glass pane at other immobile objects – cows staring dumbly in fields, mountain peaks covered in snow, streetlamps illuminating the night sky. As the window frames the "picture" that the passengers see, the objects, like them, become still, silent, fixed.

Like people who go to the cinema and stare at a screen, the passengers become voyeurs as they sit in their seats while the "action" outside the train is "caught" in what could be described as a frame in a film. It is not, however, the physical movement of the passengers that change the frames; rather, "vision alone continually undoes and remakes the relationships between these fixed elements" (112). These changes in their vision and the amount of scenery outside of their windows that they see and can process is therefore dependent on the machine's speed; the faster the train moves, the more their vision and the frame become blurred. Inside this module of "panoptic and classifying power," they are rational cells traveling within a rational cell (111). They are passing recognizable places (depending, of course, on the speed of the train) – places that have been scouted, mapped and, after much consideration, time and money, deemed most appropriate for the building of that particular track.

These decisions of placement are "strategies" designed by the railroad organizers only after much planning and negotiating to decide what space should come under their control.[2] Strategies, as de Certeau explains, are intimately aligned with the issue of place since they are

> the calculation (or manipulation) of power relationships that become possible as soon as a subject with will and power (a business, an army, a city, a scientific institution) can be isolated. It postulates a place that can be delimited as its own and serve those as the base from which relations with an exteriority composed of targets or threats (customers or competitors, enemies, the country surrounding the city, objectives and objects of research, etc.) can be managed. (35-36)

Strategies, therefore, are formed from bases of power and are used to manage and control objects; they are a mastery of "places through sight" (36). By dividing and bordering space, those "agents of order" strategize and therefore may be able to identify and manipulate any object within their scope of vision. And depending on the situation, the "targets" do not even know (or care) that they are being managed or controlled. This is the case with a person sitting in a seat on a train. The passengers, by paying for a ticket, have entered into a contract and agree to be managed by the railroad companies who have both the "will and power" to own the land that those tracks cover. They rely on the operators to take them on their journey and while they may not even know how they are getting there, they believe in their binding contract (the ticket) that, for example, the New York to Chicago express will somehow get them to Chicago in time for their meeting. When these lines of iron are placed into the ground, they define, categorize, and regulate the environment – something to which the passengers are mostly oblivious when they sit in the seat that has been assigned to them.

This idea of order and regulation provides a useful explication of place. As de Certeau states, "A place is thus an instantaneous configuration of positions. It implies an indication of stability" (117). There is much pleasure that can be derived from being in a stable environment even if that pleasure is based on the need to follow the "proper rules." The pleasure lies in the fact that passengers are in the place of the railroad car and that the "instantaneous configurations of positions" allow them to be cared for by the railroad companies. While their "position" is that of a dependant, the strict order leaves them, for the most part, free from worry. Sitting in their proper position, their spots are defined and stable; their role, for example, might be that of passenger number 42 on a Washington, D.C. to Pittsburg "red-eye" express and that role is strictly monitored by conductors and fellow passengers. All they need to do is to sit, relax, and allow themselves to be transported from one place to another.

## The Space of the Hobo

While the passenger occupies a place on the train, the hobo inhabits the realm of space. All actions of the passengers are regulated; if they break their contract – for example, if they light a cigarette in a no-smoking section – then they can be removed and suffer the legal penalties. As passengers, we rely on this order, so we play the passive role. When there is a break or rupture in the order of this "social contract," we realize how much we depend on others to follow their prescribed roles. Traveling through neighborhoods that we might feel afraid to walk through, we feel a sense of safety because we are confined and comfortably situated within the train. We are no longer active, worrying about our safety but passive, feeling sure that the order will prevail. Whether it is the fast speed at which we travel through the areas we fear or the feeling of invincibility riding in such a large and powerful machine, there is a cushion that comforts us within a train. As a result, when that order is disrupted, the anxiety and betrayal we feel is great.

Let me provide an example: While I was traveling on a train in Portugal from a beach town to downtown Lisbon, a group of twenty or so men in their early twenties boarded the train at a suburban stop. As the train passed by a certain spot, on cue, they began attacking the passengers, stealing jewelry and watches, and terrorizing certain ethnic groups, all in the time it took to arrive at the next stop when, all at once, they ran out of the car. When the train began moving again, no one knew what to do; we were all in a state of shock and for the most part, we sat silently in our seats and stared straight in front of us. We did nothing but remain immobile waiting for the train to rumble to our own particular destinations. Personally, I was having trouble comprehending the moments of chaos that happened within the car. Unable to rationalize the level of violence in a place of such order, I sat in my seat and waited to be carried to my station. Not once during the trip did I become other than a passive passenger. As we were leaving the car, I heard one woman ask, "Where were the conductors?" We had followed our roles as passengers, and we wondered where the agents of order on whom we all relied had gone when the rational gave way to the chaotic.

What those twenty or so youths did in the time in-between platforms was to create a space for themselves within the realm of place. Space exists when there is a rupture in the stability of the environment, when subjects enter into a "proper" place and use it for their own purposes – purposes not sanctioned by those who "own" the place. Be it political soap-boxers proclaiming their manifestos on a street corner in Manhattan, thieves grabbing chains on a train in Portugal, or hobos stealing rides on a train headed to Kansas City, all assert their own subcultural power within a regulated place and – for a time at least – transform it into their own space.

This creation of space results in instability – a tear – in the order of things. It is a "practiced place" (de Certeau 117) where subjects use opportunities that are presented to them in order to carve a space in which to assert their own power. It is, however, the power of the weak. Unable to use strategies, they are left in the margins, poaching off the larger powers and taking advantage of the opportunities that are presented to them; they must always live in the present, using tactics to play with the law that is oppressing them (37). These twenty or so youths, while powerful in the short time that it took to travel in-between stations, did not have the power of the "proper," and if they had spent too long in one place, they eventually would have been stopped and arrested for their actions. Strategies belong to the strong (I later heard that the police were "strategizing" on how better to protect passengers from these guerilla-style attacks), and the youths, therefore, had to use tactics that fragmentarily forced themselves into the other's place (xix). By using surprise, therefore, they were able to create chaos for a time and leave before order was restored. This is the power that subcultures use to create space in ordered, and therefore hostile, environments.

The hobos who have traveled and travel across the country looking for work from the late nineteenth century to the present day constitute a subculture that, much like Dick

Hebdige's punks, is "alternatively dismissed, denounced and canonized" (2). The hobo is a member of an economically mobile and socially unstable subculture that has carved a space within the culture's recognized and accepted places. The hobo – who is defined by the fact that he rides illegally on trains – is forever on the fringes of place. Never inside the train's regimented system, he is always on the outside. But he is also defined by that of which he is not a part; although never counted by the authorities, hobos are dependent on the trains for their movement and could not exist without them. There is an intimate link between the machine itself and the hobo – a bond that is essential and unique to the hobo and his lifestyle.

While de Certeau explains that both the passenger and the objects outside the window were immobile and fixed objects, he makes the important observation that it is the railroad itself that is making noise:

> There is a beating of the rails, a vibrato of the windowpanes – a sort of *rubbing together of spaces at the vanishing points of their frontier.* These junctions have no place. They indicate themselves by passing cries and momentary noises. These frontiers are illegible; they can only be heard as a single stream of sounds, so continuous is the tearing off that annihilates the points through which it passes. (113, italics mine)

It is the Iron Horse that cuts through the places – the towns, the valleys, the deserts – and at the "vanishing point of the frontier," the places disappear at the point of contact. These places are illegible, annihilated and can only be heard and no longer seen. While the railroad's speed and ubiquity has brought places in the country closer together (it has cut the time that it takes to get, for example, from Boston to Washington), spaces are still brought into being through the very act of the machine rumbling and screaming across the continent. The passenger, however, is unaware – and distant – as he sits in his seat, cushioned and protected within the place of the railroad car. The only sound that he hears is the vibrating of the window; he could put his hand on the pane and feel the rhythm or hear the click-clack, click-clack of the train on the tracks. In these places, there are only sounds. In space, however, there is noise.[3] Unlike the passive relationship between the passenger and the train, the hobo, who is physically present where the spaces rub together, is connected in a more corporal way.

Hobos, sitting in the corners of the open boxcar, are physically a part of that borderland where the frontier disappears. They are, therefore, in that space where there is no sound but only noise. Hebdidge writes that "subcultures represent 'noise' (as opposed to sound), interference in the orderly sequence," and while passengers are culturally permitted to raise their voices a bit when ordering pretzels in the bar-car, hobos, trying to keep warm in sub-zero temperatures as the train races through the countryside, may yell, stamp their feet, and run around in the boxcar in order to keep alive (90). For example, Jim Tully, in his hobo memoir, *Beggars of Life*, writes of a hazardous trip that almost cost him his life: "The cold air numbed my muscles until a stupor fought to gain control of my brain . . . I pounded the roof of the car to revive the ebbing circulation of my blood. I shook my head violently, as a pugilist does to drive the effect of a grueling smash from his brain" (230). Unable to stop the train, Tully had to endure as much as he could. Since he was not in the place of the railroad car, however, he was able to take actions not permitted (or warranted) to passengers. Since the hobos cannot be heard above the roar of the engine or seen in the darkness of the night, they can use their voices to yell and hoot; they can laugh or curse; they can stomp around to stay warm or simply because they're bored.

By stealing a ride, hobos are outside of history; there is no seat assigned, no money exchanged for a ticket, no knowledge that they are even there on the train and, therefore, they do not officially exist. And while the railroad engineers may suspect that the hobos are there, they do not count. When people exist in the spaces of society (and as a homeless wanderer participating in an illegal activity, the hobo fits this category), those who are connected to places will not recognize them.[4] When de Certeau, upon examining the incarceration of a passenger in a railway car, correctly wrote that "history exists where there is a price to be paid" (113), he was probably aware that there are those who are outside of history and who cannot afford or do not wish to pay the price to "ride the cushions," yet still take the train.

Official history exists only in areas that can be seen; spaces of darkness need to be illuminated and forced into the accepted hegemonic discourse of the time by the culture's regulators, for space is dangerous to the established order precisely because the actions taking place there are unseen and therefore cannot be regulated. As Michel Foucault showed when using the theory of the panopticon, there is much advantage in keeping people under the (illusory) constant gaze of the state rather than plunging subcultures in the dark where they can gather strength in secrecy. For in established places, people can be seen and therefore there is "a power through transparency, subjection through illumination" (Foucault 162). But what Jeremy Bentham did not realize when he revolutionized surveillance and the prison system, which Foucault is quick to point out, is that some subjects would resist this gaze and would seek to create spaces not monitored by cultural forces. Not everyone is passive, and "there would always be ways of slipping through their net" (162).[5] The hobo is not a passive figure and resists the gaze by stepping outside of history. While the passengers are always under the gaze of established authority as they sit within the place of the railroad car, the hobo exists in the space of noise and movement as the train cuts through the recognized places of the country. And while the distance between points has been diminished by the speed of the locomotive, there is still the moment of contact, the "rubbing of spaces" created by the train's movement that is unobservable and outside of history. As the hobos hold on to the train for dear life at that moment of contact in this realm of chaotic "noise," they become part of the Iron Horse. Unlike the everyday passenger who is cushioned and protected, the hobo is actually intimately intertwined with the machine. And, if de Certeau is correct and the machine is a producer of space, then so too are the hobos when, as my figures show, they becomes part of the inner workings of the train.

While the "machine is the premium mobile, the solitary god from which all action proceeds," de Certeau could also be describing the hobos themselves as they becomes part of the machine that cuts through the landscape (113). One of the most dangerous ways of stealing a ride between stops and thus the one that hobo autobiographies brag about the most was "riding the rods." Kenneth Allsop, who wrote *Hard Travelin': A Hobo and His History*, described this perilous way of traveling:

> Beneath the old boxcar – not on today's streamlined models – the iron frame was underbraced by gunnels, or iron bars, running lengthwise eighteen inches below the belly of the car, leaving a space into which a reasonably slim hobo (and they were seldom fat) could sidle and so be borne, stretched flat on his back like a kipper on a grill, cradled between the thundering wheels and a few inches above the sleepers and spraying cinders. (159)

The hobos would find a piece of wood or board and make an improvised seat a few inches above the gravel. If the hobos fell asleep, or if they slipped, or if an angry engineer with a grudge threw a bolt under the car where it then became a lethal weapon to knock the hobos off their perches, certain death would follow. This position was extremely dangerous because the distance between the hobo and the machine was non-existent – arms and legs intertwined with bolts and steel. Drawings and photos corroborate this amalgamation. For example, the popular photo by A. J. Carrel Lucas clearly shows this intermingling of steel and flesh: the hobos are laying flat on their stomachs with the wind blowing fiercely in their faces (although somehow one of the 'bos has his hat on!). They are only inches away from the wheels of the train; their bodies become engulfed by the machine itself. The hobo closest to the viewer's eye has his head stuck out into the wind, his arm forming a sideways "L" with his palm flat on the steel and his elbow almost connected to the wheel. With his look of determination and forcefulness, he seems as if he is propelling the train forward; he is not being carried by the train; rather, he is moving with the train, urging it onward. While this is certainly a romantic reading, I would argue that numerous photos of hobos riding the rods substantiate my claim. As the photo from Jack London's hobo autobiography *The Road* clearly shows, there is no protection from the elements and the hobo's arm is literally a couple of inches from the rails. Any movement – either by him or the train – that separated him from the machine would mean certain death. Thus, as the machine enters the "disappearing frontier," so too enters the hobo.

While "ridin' the rods" was the most dangerous thing hobos could do, any place on the train could be transformed into space by the hobo. It would take pages to account for all of the places that have been transformed into spaces by hobos.[6] And while they might have been arrested or suffered physical hardships if they were caught or if they slipped from their spaces, their intimate, physical connection to the train – the lack of distance between the flesh and the steel – showed that the ordered environment of the railroad car could be penetrated by those with the desire (and skill) to do so.

It is this ability to use their bodies to create space that locates the hobos' source of subcultural freedom and power within the dominant culture's regimented order. While de Certeau's major thesis in *The Practice of Everyday Life* is that average, everyday people offer resistance within the constricting environments of society, the hobo, by intermingling with the train itself, goes one step further: By creating a space outside the gaze of authority and coupling himself with the machine that is creating space at the moment of contact in-between places, the hobo exists in a realm within which the everyday passenger, in the ordered environment of the railroad car, can never be included. The hobo's power, therefore, exists when the train is in motion and breaking through the frontiers – when he is intimately connected to a force of such magnitude and strength.[7]

It is when hobos are physically and intimately connected to the train by their illegal riding that they have the most freedom and – even though death or maiming is just a slip away – control. The train is thousands of pounds strong and traveling at fast speeds; the hobo, if seen at all, is a blur. Unlike passenger number forty-two commuting from Washington, D.C. to Pittsburg on "red-eye" express, the hobos, unseen and therefore outside history, have a certain control because they are invisible and part of the "noise" of the machine. Only when the whistle sounds and the engine dies in the terminal does the power of the hobo and the train disappear: "In the mobile world of the train station, the immobile machine suddenly seems monumental and almost incongruous in its mute, idol-like inertia, a sort of god-undone" (de Certeau 114). Back in a place that is regimented, ordered, and under surveillance, the hobo has to worry about being seen and, more importantly, about the consequences of being caught without a ticket in the train yard. With the metal god no longer spitting smoke and sparks, the hobos must untangle themselves from the machines and slink along the tracks until they can find a safe haven in the hidden jungles on the outskirts of town. The space that they create, therefore, is temporary and must be replicated every time they want to catch another ride.

The body, and the ability to control its visibility, is at the heart of the hobo's subcultural power. An analysis of Charles Chesnutt's *The Marrow of Tradition (*1901), a fictionalized, historical work about the Wilmington, North Carolina, race riot of 1898, might be useful to explore this unique power of the hobo as compared to a "normal" passenger who is subservient to rules and regulations of a particular society. One of the main characters, Dr. Miller, an educated man who had received favorable press and prestige in the Northeast and in Europe for his surgical operations, is returning to Wilmington to open up a hospital when he meets his former white mentor, the renowned Dr. Burns. A few hours into the trip, however, the conductor informs both parties that they would have to separate and that Miller would have to move into the "colored" car – for in the ordered environment of the railroad system, only some members of certain races can sit in particular cars. When the two object, the conductor warns, "I could simply switch this car off the next siding, transfer the white passengers to another, and leave you and your friend in possession until you were arrested and fined or imprisoned" (55). The law of surveillance and order cannot be bucked and Miller submits to the rules and regulations of the railroad company (which are the rules and regulations of the larger State of Virginia); thus he moves to the car that is designated for him.

After being thrown out of the "Whites Only" railroad car and forced into the colored section, Miller looks out the window, and, with both shock and sadness, he spots Josh Green, a large African American man who had snuck aboard and hidden himself on the train.

> As the train came to a standstill, a huge negro, covered thickly with dust, crawled off one of the rear trucks unobserved, and ran round the rear end of the car to a watering-trough by a neighboring well . . . He threw himself down by the trough, drank long and deep, and plunging his head into the water, shook himself like a wet dog, and crept back furtively to his dangerous perch. (59)

Josh Green, however, an uneducated man of quick temper and fearless action who had been employed as a dock-worker for Miller's father, is in this instance not subject to the same laws as Dr. Miller. Stealing a ride and avoiding the gaze of the agents of the law, he is not under the power of the law in the same way as Miller, who was forced to surrender to the white conductor his own personal dignity. And while Miller – who spots Josh from his seat in the train – passes judgment on the dirty hobo and concludes, "Blessed are the meek . . . for they shall inherit the earth" (62), Josh was, however, being more active and resistant to the oppressive powers than the doctor who passively followed the rules that governed him. While Miller calls Josh meek, it was this dusty, parched hobo who (in a place – the railroad car – that was race-sensitive) was able to remain unobserved and uncounted while the train was in motion. He was able to create a space that allowed him to ride "in-between" the law and, therefore, outside of history. It was a dangerous space, one that caused Josh to exclaim, "I kind er 'lowed I was gone a dozen times, ez it wuz" (62), but it allowed him to fulfill his goals of being unobserved and getting to the place where he wanted to go. Due to his willingness to travel in-between and, therefore, place himself outside of the law, Josh was able to travel without money and with his personal dignity by creating his own particular space on the train.

This is the power of subculture. John Fiske, in *Television Culture*, states that "there is a power in resisting power, there is a power in maintaining one's social identity in opposition to that proposed by the dominant ideology, there is a power in asserting one's own subcultural values against the dominant ones" (19). It is the power of a subordinated class of people, who, because of their (lack of) social position, can be – for a time at least – outside the reach of the law. The passenger can receive pleasure from the lack of effort it takes to be a controlled subject in the railroad car because "pleasure results from the production of meanings of the world and the self that are felt to serve the interests of the reader" (Fiske 19). Hobos, on the other hand, once they define themselves as hobos, can receive pleasure from the freedom that exists when poaching from the dominant culture. It is a fleeting power that exists mainly when the train is in motion: when they are in the act of stealing from the larger cultures, when they are uncounted and outside history, when flesh and steel become one, and spaces emerge from places. Only then does the subversive power of the hobo manifest itself. It is a power that exerts itself only in moments – "for what it wins it cannot keep" (de Certeau 37) – and this power continually succumbs to the hegemonic forces of the larger culture. Regardless, though, it is a power that shows the cracks – spaces – that can be created by a subordinated subculture.

## Notes

1. Who exactly is a hobo? This is a question that has been debated (both in academic circles and also around the jungle campfires). The traditional definition is as follows: a "hobo" is a migratory worker while the "tramp" is a migratory non-worker and the "bum" is a non-migratory non-worker. Obviously, though, these definitions bleed into each other: As most hobo autobiographies attest, many who considered themselves "hobos" at one time or another were forced to beg on the road (so according to this strict definition, they should then be considered "tramps"), and many times they spent long stretches in cities (thus they could be considered "bums"). In any event, everyone would agree that in order to be a hobo, you must beat your way by train. There has also been debate about whether or not there is a current hobo population. While the scene has certainly changed since the first 'bo hopped a train after the Golden Spike was knocked into the ground at Promontory Point, Utah, in 1869, men and women continue to hop trains in the twenty-first century. For a well documented and authoritative cultural history of the hobo, particularly in terms of the racializing and gendering of the term, see Todd DePastino's *Citizen Hobo*. For a great discussion of the Hobo in terms of his economic and cultural force in the Midwest from 1880-1930, see Frank Higbie's *Indispensable Outcasts*. See also Eddy Joe Cotton's *Hobo* and Jessica Hahn's *Transient Ways* for two perspectives on the present day rail-riding community.
2. This, of course, is a highly complex set of negotiations and dealings involving class, race, and gender ideologies. While Stephen Ambrose understands the building of the line and the Big Four who were predominately involved in the building process in a mostly positive light, see John Robinson's book *The Octopus: A History of the Construction, Conspiracies, Extortions, Robberies, and Villainous Acts of Subsidized Railroads* for a scathing look at how the Big Four ruined California. See also Frank Norris's *The Octopus*, the first novel in his Epic of the Wheat trilogy, which is a fascinating and insightful portrayal of the power that the railroad had over farmers.
3. For example, in a recent luxury car commercial, a sleek, shiny car is placed in the middle of a loud, chaotic construction sight. In the first frame, the windows to the car are down, and the noise of the mechanical world is grating and disturbing. But then, with the flick of a switch, the window of the car goes up. Suddenly, the noise is gone, and there is only the sound of low classical music on the car

stereo. The noise belonged to the uncivilized and unsafe construction world (space); the sound belonged to the world of the (high-priced) civilized and ordered car environment (place).

4. This does not mean that the hobo is necessarily alone. While many hobos that I have interviewed enjoy traveling alone, most do travel in pairs or in small groups. Jessica Hahn, for example, who did travel and squat alone on occasion in the 1990s, usually did have a traveling companion when "catching out" and traveling across the United States. This was done, she explained, for both safety issues as well as camaraderie. When hobos "disappear," they rely on each other for food, information, protection, and comfort. As Todd DePastino astutely points out in *Citizen Hobo,* "If hoboing was, to a degree, an individually chosen strategy for minimizing wage dependency and insulating oneself against exploitation then the success of this strategy hinged on informal networks that made hoboing a collective enterprise as well" (69). If there were not other individuals forming these loose webs of interaction on the fringes of place, then the lone hobo would have an extremely hard time surviving and making it down the line. The key, however, is to keep these interactions out of sight from those who have the power to regulate the bodies of these illegal train riders.

5. Ted Grossardt, in his article, "Harvest(ing) Hoboes: The Production of Labor Organization through the Wheat Harvest" explains the result of what happens when illegal bodies have the ability to disappear: "When the activities of a mobile group of people are no longer observable and thus cannot be fully known, those people become potentially omnipresent to the fixed observer. The observer suddenly faces the possibility of being the observed" (285). Large groups of mostly single men traveling unseen throughout the country produces much anxiety in those who are rooted to their places. While passive bodies are easy to control, active bodies who use their invisibility for their own subcultural pleasure are quickly deemed dangerous and laws (both vigilante and state sponsored) are produced and enforced. Hobos, therefore, must continue to stay hidden from those who wish to identify and regulate them.

6. Kenneth Allsop, who was one of the first to write extensively about the hobo figure, writes of some of the spaces: "He rode on the iron plate, yet another toehold in the 'guts,' or lower berth, of a steam car. He rode the 'death woods,' the couplings themselves – the whipple trees or swingletrees – and the bumpers. He burrowed in the coal of the engineer tender. He rode among the sheep and cattle of the livestock cars. He rode in open gondolas piled with granite. He rode on the top deck, the boardwalk along the center of boxcars, and, if that was loaded in harvest time, he rode on the garb irons and the ladder on the side. He rode 'possum belly on the tool or supply box under a car. He rode the toe path, the narrow looking platform bolted on the walls of some rattlers. He rode the footrail at the rear end of the tankers. He even rode, if desperate to be on his way, under the headlight on the pilot or cowcatcher, the grilled scoop that projected afore the front wheels to clear obstructions from the line" (160).

7. Indeed, there is a distinct power to a moving train unlike anything else. When I went to the National Hobo convention in Britt, Iowa, I stayed in the jungle that was located a few hundred yards from the railroad tracks. Sometime early in the morning, I woke up to the sound of the train roaring past my tent. In my confusion, I woke up startled, and because the sound was so loud and powerful, I was convinced that the train was soon to bear down upon me. Fumbling out of my tent, I crawled out on my hands and knees and looked up at this machine roaring past me – it was, to use an overused term, awesome. Its strength, its muscle, its loudness, its beauty was magnificent. Gaining my senses, I looked around and saw a few of the older hobos staring at the machine as well. Some waved, some whooped, some just stared but all, it seemed to me, were in wonderment of the train.

## Works Cited

Allsop, Kenneth. *Hard Travellin': The Hobo and His History.* New York: The New American Library, 1967.

Ambrose, Stephen. *Nothing in the World Like It.* New York: Touchstone, 2000.

Chesnutt, Charles. *The Marrow of Tradition.* New York: Penguin Books, 1983.

Cotton, Eddy Joe. *Hobo.* New York: Harmony, 2002.

De Certeau, Michel. *The Practice of Everyday Life.* Berkeley: U of California P, 1988.
DePastino, Todd. *Citizen Hobo: How a Century of Homelessness Shaped America.* Chicago: U of Chicago P, 2003.
Fiske, John. *Television Culture.* New York: Methuen Drama, 1988.
Foucault, Michel. *Power/Knowledge: Selected Interviews and Other Writings, 1972-1977.* New York: Pantheon Books, 1980.
Grossardt, Ted. "Harvest(ing) Hoboes: The Production of Labor Organization through the Wheat Harvest." *Agricultural History* 2 (1996): 283-302.
Hahn, Jessica. *Transient Ways.* Hawaii: Passing Through Publications, 1996.
Higbie, Frank Tobias. *Indispensible Outcasts: Hobo Workers and Community in the American Midwest, 1830-1930.* Illinois: U of Illinois P, 2003.
Hebdidge, Dick. *Subculture: The Meaning of Style.* London: Routledge, 1979.
Norris, Frank. *The Octopus.* New York: Penguin Books, Reissue Edition, 1994.
Robinson, John. *The Octopus: A History of the Construction, Conspiracies, Extortions, Robberies, and* Villainous Acts of Subsidized Railroads. United Kingdom: Ayer Co. Pub., 1981.
Tully, Jim. *Beggars of Life.* New York: Albert and Charles Boni, 1924.

*In "Through the Looking Glass of Silver Springs," Wendy Adams King uses the tourist destination as a specific example to make her larger point that "the quest for and construction of the sublime, beautiful, and scientific in nature are often found throughout the history of American environmental tourist attractions…and are inseparably intertwined with American concerns about national identity, culture, and industrialization."*

# Through the Looking Glass of Silver Springs: Tourism and the Politics of Vision

Wendy Adams King

## Introduction

An Enya musical score drifts down from the white rafters of the Victorian boat dock then floats around the meticulously manicured curves and intense colors of the surrounding tropical landscaping. In the company of strangers, my family and I wait in a small line to board the Chief Yahalocee, one out of a small fleet of Silver Springs's famous glass-bottom boats. I cannot help feeling a bit skeptical. How can an old-fashioned tourist gimmick, such as the glass-bottom boat, compete with the cyberspace spectacles and multi-media extravaganzas so readily available today? My barely nine-year-old daughter is already a seasoned veteran of Space Shuttle launches, the Museum of Science, IMAX surround-sound movies, Disney and Busch Gardens virtual reality rides, all supplemented with a daily diet of DVDs and video games. What fascination can plying across the river, peering down at aquatic life through a transparent pane of glass encased in the bottom of a small boat hold for sensation saturated and technologically savvy tourists of the twenty-first century?

At the turn of the twentieth century, however, much of the appeal of Silver Springs (Florida's oldest tourist, theme park) and the glass-bottom boat tour was not unlike the interest that Space Shuttle launches and IMAX movies possess for many tourists today.

During the nascent days of Florida's budding tourism industry, in the late 1870s, Phillip Morell invented the glass-bottom.[1] (Later, Hullam Jones' 1878 version was made from a three-foot hollowed out cypress log.[2]) The relative transparency of the Silver River's waters coupled with the glass bottom of the boat promised Silver Springs tourists beauty, motion, and spectacle while also offering them a scientific education, a sense of national pride, and a sense of cultural progress. As cultural historian Susan Davis contends, "Every culture uses nature metaphorically and the natural world provides not only all means of material life but a common, human currency for representing ideas about that life as society and culture" (30).

Illustrating Davis's point, the privileging of vision (an outgrowth of the scientific revolution)[3], a privileging which informs the design and promotion of the glass-bottom boat, intertwines with American social constructions of nature over the last 125 years. Upon the Silver River's waters and within the glass-bottom boat, the social significance of America and its landscape is negotiated within tensions between romantic, scientific, and cinematic visions. An amalgam of Western myth and Renaissance, Enlightenment, and Romantic ideals is used to frame Silver Springs as an edifying landscape of personal, spiritual, and scientific national importance. Like the destinations of the American Grand Tour, rhetoric surrounding Silver Springs is indicative of the larger role tourism and spectacle play in the quest for a national cultural identity bubbling forth out of an America in the wake of modern industrialization.[4] As cultural critics such as John Sears, David E. Nye, and Mark Neumann suggest, in many ways the act of tourism and the national park itself, in the United States of the nineteenth and twentieth century, functioned as a public space that attempted to help define and unify American culture and its heterogeneous population.[5]

## A Romantic Vision: The Quest for the Sublime and Picturesque

As the craggy, yet cheerful, voice of our gray-haired captain welcomes all aboard, each of us dutifully awaits our turn to climb up and then down into the belly of the boat. Sinking into the water, now fully loaded with shorts-wearing tourists, armed with shiny cameras of all varieties as well as with the occasional juice-stained sippy cup, the boat slowly slides backward from the dock. "Bubbles!" squeals a toddler. To everyone's delight, thousands of tiny bubbles, like those in a freshly poured ginger ale, start zipping across the glass. In these shallow waters, the captain briefly lectures over a small buzzing speaker, trying to compete with the scratchy grind of tall river grasses rubbing against the boat's transparent bottom. As we reach a clearing, the captain instructs all passengers to look down at the dizzying depths of the first Silver Springs cavern on our tour. "What is under water you will be able to see clearly," repeats the captain. At this point in the tour, he proclaims that the glass-bottom makes visible the overwhelming beauty and scientific knowledge encased within the Silver River's crystalline waters. As he promotes the park, I muse to myself that it has changed very little in the 125 years since Silver Springs first captured the imaginations of nineteenth century travelers.

By the mid-nineteenth century, Romantic and Transcendentalist views of nature as a sublime and picturesque landscape had become an essential part of experiencing nature for many leisure and middle-class Americans. Patricia Jansen argues in reference to tourism in Niagara Falls, for example, "The importance of the sublime as an element in both elite and popular culture was well established by the late eighteenth century.... The craze for sublime experience entailed a new appreciation of natural phenomena" (8). John F. Kasson as well contends that aesthetics of the sublime and picturesque commonly superimposed onto the

American landscape at the turn of the century exemplify the hegemonic genteel values promoted by elite "official" culture. Leisure class values such as the quest for the sublime, according to Kasson, filtered down to the masses (who would later visit Florida and Silver Springs) via mass-produced periodicals and the agents of culture such as museum curators and educators. "Genteel reformers founded museums, art galleries, libraries, symphonies, and other institutions which set the terms of formal cultural life and established the cultural tone that dominated public discussion," writes Kasson, "as nineteenth-century cultural entrepreneurs sought to develop a vast new market, they popularized genteel values and conceptions of art" (4-5).

The genteel values and aesthetic conventions constructing a Romantic sense of the sublime and picturesque greatly contribute to American notions of national identity and leisure.[6] During the nineteenth and early twentieth century, these values and conventions were central to the history of Silver Springs as an image of America as paradise. The American leisure class traveler's quest for the sublime and beautiful in Florida is revealed in images of Silver Springs even before the glass-bottom boat was invented. In 1860, Hubbard Hart expanded his successful stagecoach line that ran between Palatka, Silver Springs, Ocala, and Tampa to include a steamboat that toured the Ocklawaha and Silver rivers. Hart's steamer passengers embarked on a two-day journey that followed the coffee-colored waters[7] of the alligator lined Ocklawaha River (Upper St. John's) up into the crystal clear water of Silver Springs.

The first written accounts of the Silver Springs steamboat tours illustrate the significance of genteel aesthetics, Romantic conventions, and American nationalism in the early reception and twentieth century development of Silver Springs as a tourist attraction and registered Natural Landmark.[8] And as Nye argues, "The American sublime transformed the individual's experience of immensity and awe into a belief in national greatness" (43). The nineteenth-century travelers, who had the time and could afford to travel to Florida in significant numbers, often used the Western literary and fine art canon to frame their experience and the Silver Springs steamboat tour as a sublime spiritual journey. Florida history and architecture historian Margot Ammidown, for example, contends that "many of the written descriptions of the early trips to the springs seemed to equate the journey with a spiritual transition to the afterlife, or to refer to the time-honored notion of the river as a metaphor for a spiritual journey to the source, which, with the advent of tourism, became a regular mini-pageant acted out on the Ocklawaha" (245). For instance, Ammidown cites the letters of nineteenth-century anthropologist Daniel Brinton (who is also quoted in the contemporary Silver Springs book) who described his journey as "one of the most dramatic transitions from darkness into light that a traveler can make anywhere on the continent" (qtd. in Ammidown 245).

Such nineteenth-century visitors as Daniel Brinton, Constance Fenimore Cooper Woolson, and George McCall described Silver Springs using Western myth, Romantic ideals, and European and American landscape oil painting conventions. Brinton, Woolson, and McCall's imagery evokes the iconography of the sublime described by American transcendentalists like Emerson, painted by Hudson River School artists, and later examined in the twentieth century by philosophers such as Heidegger. In the 1856 history *Notes on the Floridian Peninsula,* Brinton exclaimed, "Slowly drifting in a canoe over the precipice I could not restrain an involuntary start of terror, so difficult was it, from the transparency of the supporting medium for the mind to appreciate its existence" (186). Woolson commented in 1876 that "the water was so clear that one could hardly tell where it ended and the air began…the fish swimming about were as distinct as though we had them in our hands; in short…it was enchantment" (30). And George McCall, while serving in Florida during the Second Seminole War, wrote, "We were stationary…in a moment all was still as death. The line of demarcation between the waters and the atmosphere was invisible. Heavens! What an impression filled my mind at that moment! Were not the canoe and its contents obviously suspended in mid-air like Mahomet's coffin?" (150).

The intensely disorienting and enlightening collapse of space and time, described by Brinton, Woolson, and McCall, is an essential component of the Romantic and Transcendentalist vision of the sublime, vast, natural landscape. The blurred boundary as the celestial and terrestrial dissolve in the transparency of Silver Springs's waters resonates with Emerson's transcendentalist vision of the transparent eyeball. Like Emerson's communion with the natural world recounted in *Nature*, the water and surrounding landscape of Silver Springs act as a catalyst to the sublime experience believed to initiate a similar reintegration with the divine. Woolson and McCall become "a transparent eye-ball," "nothing," "all," "part or particle of God" (17). The disconcerting elements (a degree of danger and powerless to the experience itself) implied in Brinton, Woolson, and McCall's choice to compare experiences on the Silver River to "terror," "enchantment," "death," and suspension "in mid-air" illustrates what Heidegger regarded as the "sublime moment, in which anxiety is preparation of insight into the whole" (Wilson 155). The anxiety and sense of the ineffable present in Brinton, Woolson, and McCall's portrayal of Silver Springs also recalls Kant's 1870 (about the same time the glass bottom boat appears) distinctions between the aesthetics of the sublime and picturesque. The Kantian sensation of the sublime is characterized by a mix of pleasure and pain experienced in a moment when the mind is overwhelmed, pained at its inability to grasp fully ideas intuiting, not imagining, the infinite, the total (Wilson 20). The disorienting amorphous space described by Brinton, Woolson, and McCall also exemplifies the asymmetry, the formlessness versus the harmony of form of the picturesque as defined by Kant.

Today, the sublime and picturesque qualities of Silver Springs are interrupted by the activity of tourists and toddlers and the motion of the boat. Now, we float above the Spring of Fire, and our Silver Springs glass-bottom boat turns dramatically leftward as the captain explains that the spring's name comes from the tiny volcano-like forms spewing out of the cavern. Like liquid in a slow turning glass, I feel as if I am moving in the opposite direction of the boat, only to meet back with myself at circle's completion. "Whoa," whisper several fellow riders. Disoriented and a little woozy, the majority of the tourists nonetheless remain hunched-over, looking through the rectangular frames of glass in the boat's bottom at the luminescent fish and rock formations below. The boat glides to its next stop entitled the Blue Grotto. Frances Kenneley's *Discover Silver Springs: Souvenir Book* reports that the Blue Grotto's "moniker came from the cerulean hue reflected from sunlight filtering through the water" (14). I'm not entirely convinced. In addition to the spring's blue waters, the well-known, exotic Blue Grotto of Italy or even the infamous Love Grotto of Tristam and Isolde, made popular by Romantic writers, must have influenced its naming.

The captain announces the next stop as The Bridal Chamber. Written over sixty years before my *Discover Silver Springs: Souvenir Book (*first copyrighted in 1994), a 1930s Silver Springs brochure exemplifies how the promotion of Florida and Silver Springs as a rejuvenating, romantic paradise (in the genteel Romantic tradition) changed very little even as the demographic of Florida tourism drastically shifted.[9] As the nineteenth century gave way to the twentieth, so did the steamer to rail and car. By the mid-1920s, the Florida vacation was no longer restricted to the elite. The leisure class Victorian travelers, with which early Florida robber barons like Flagler sought to fill their luxury hotels, eventually were outnumbered by a new wave of middle class tourists owning automobiles. The affordable mass-produced cars and subsequent American highway systems, financed by the Coolidge Prosperity, made the state available to middle class tourists and homesteaders (Allen 227). Tin Can Tourists packed up in the new family car and left for vacation. They flocked southward to visit the state's attractions and even scrambled to purchase small pieces of Florida paradise. Record numbers of tourists even landed permanently in South Florida to live in communities, steeped in Mediterranean fantasy architecture: towns such as Coral Gables, Hollywood-by-the-Sea, and Venice-of-the-South. Evidence to Florida's popular appeal, Miami alone experienced an influx of 2.5 million people in 1925 (Gannon 77).

Although more middle-brow educational exhibits and working-class snake milking and alligator wrestling side shows were added to Silver Springs when Ross Allen opened his Reptile Institute in 1931, the genteel promotion of the park as a sublime and picturesque paradise changed very little. Writers of the 1930s brochure compared the park to the idyllic Elysian Fields, and like the much earlier descriptions of Florida by fifteenth-century French explorer Ribaut, much of the pamphlet is devoted to framing Florida and Silver Springs as a picturesque earthly paradise. Descriptions of the multitudinous plants and animals in Florida focus the reader on the fecundity of the earthly garden. The brochure boasts of rare aquatic life visible through Silver Springs's crystal clear waters. In fact, the brochure told readers they would see "more than 43 varieties of fish, turtles and fresh water shellfish." Also attesting to the Eden-like fertility imagery used to promote the park, the pamphlet notes that plants even "bloom and bear fruit under water." Not only are the plants and animals abundant in Florida's bountiful landscape, they are "bewitchingly beautiful, rare and exotic."

While the long lists of plants and animals at Silver Springs evoke the natural abundance most often associated with earthly paradise, the descriptions of the individual's experience within the park's surrounding natural beauty best illustrate the construction of the park as earthly paradise in the romantic image. Stressing feeling and the exotic, the text places the reader in an utopian fantasy landscape by making promises to "all who enter." Silver Springs, according to the depression era brochure text from Richter Library, intrigues and fascinates:

> Here is a scene that intrigues the imagination – more fascinating than anything you have seen, more beautiful than dreams can imagine, for Silver Springs is in truth the Elysian Fields of America. They who enter here leave all cares behind them. Individual worries become petite and insignificant when one is communing with Nature at her loveliest.

This text reflects the Romantic and Transcendentalist desire to escape from civilization into the rejuvenating arms of sublime nature. Simultaneously evoking the dwarfing landscapes often associated with the sublime and restorative powers of nature, the text boasts, "Worries become petite and insignificant when one is communing with Nature." Also, the description of the caves and springs suggests the overwhelming and sometimes limitless rocky landscapes, rushing waterfalls, and flowing rivers frequently seen in Romantic landscape paintings and poetry. The text further emphasizes emerging, flowing water and a large cavern: "Silver Springs is really a subterranean river springing from the earth through a vast cavern 65 feet long and 12 feet high." Including the aesthetic quality also integral to the Romantic view of nature, tourists do not only get the opportunity to commune with Nature at Silver Springs; they commune with "Nature at her loveliest."

The direct comparison to Elysian Fields also works in conjunction with the images of the sublime and beautiful nature connoted in the text. The mythical reference not only evokes the image of paradise so often associated with Florida, it also suggests the exoticism, myth, and idyllic past used so often by Romantic poets and painters. As Wordsworth wrote in "The Prospectus to the Recluse,"

> Paradise, and groves
> Elysian, Fortunate Fields – like those of old
> Sought in the Atlantic man – Why should they be
> A history only of departed things,
> Or a mere fiction of what never was? (399)

Silver Springs as Elysian Fields metaphor goes from Romantic nostalgic reference to idyllic mythological landscape to edifying sublime nature, elevating the springs to authentic space contrasted against the artificial man-made trappings of civilized society. The metaphor illustrates the efforts to exult American landscapes in order to characterize American culture as equal to, if not superior to, European culture. The beauty of North America presented as "evidence" to a unique presence of the divine in the United States also supported the popular notion of Manifest Destiny. Charles Sanford noted that American artists Thomas Cole and William Cullen Bryant, for example, "had need of the sublime to celebrate what they felt was peculiar and unique about American scenery" (qtd. in Nye 24). Neumann, Nye, and Sears contend that American romantic landscape tourism ironically functioned as a source of cultural production. Within the context of the America First tourism campaign, Silver Springs as the true Elysian Fields connotes that the American landscape even exceeds in importance and authenticity the one imagined by the culture of the Golden Age of Greece so revered by American gentility and the European elite. As Neumann argues, the effort to frame places such as Silver Springs as the true site of ancient myth and literary reference "fits well with the federal mandate to promote American scenery as superior to that of Europe; it's part of a quest for antiquities." The presence of Romanticism and the quest for American antiquities remain at Silver Springs today in the "Indian legends" and ancient fossils featured so prominently at the park.

The Chief Yahalocee moves forward. Several adults join the small children who much earlier abandoned the official position of scientists leaning over microscopes, examining the invisible world revealed by its lens, in favor of letting the wind blow on their faces as they stare at the open-air view of trees, terrestrial animals, and the surface of the water available through the open deck windows. At our captain's request, many passengers again look down through the glass bottom of the boat at the rock formation and jetting spring below. Stopping to float above the Bridal Chamber spring, the captain tells its legend. The Bridal Chamber is named after the tale of the ill-fated love affair of Indian Prince Chulcotah and Winona. She hurled herself into the deepest point of the river in a moment of agonizing grief over her forbidden love for the Prince.

It is interesting to note, however, that the Legend of the Bridal Chamber told today is different from that quoted in the Silver Springs brochures spanning from the first half of the twentieth century.[10] Still a romantic tale of "star-crossed lovers," earlier promotion cites the tale of Aunt Silla, "a 110-year-old negress," who recalls when her "honey child," Bernice Mayo, a poor, yet beautiful maiden, who wasted away after her wealthy lover's father refused to let them marry. On her deathbed, the withering Bernice, asked Aunt Silla to drop her into the big Boiling Spring (now the Bridal Chamber). Like Ophelia, Bernice's frail, porcelain white body gracefully spiraled downward as the crevice in the riverbed opened welcoming her. Her lost love, Claire, happened to be rowing by the spring with his new fiancé (a cousin-bride chosen by his father). The sparkling light from Bernice's bracelet, a token of his love, captured his attention. Knowing it was his old love reaching upward from the rock, Claire dove downward into the opening that shut and enclosed him within the riverbed with Bernice for eternity.

The changing Bridal Chamber legend is yet another example of the ways in which issues of race, class, and gender are often played out within Florida's tourist spaces. Interestingly, the "negress" tale metamorphoses into an "Indian" version of Romeo and Juliet as more progressive attitudes toward African-Americans evolve. Unfortunately, the Aunt Silla caricature, an example of the age-defying "primitive" seer stereotype (African-American film director Spike Lee recently coined "the magical Negro") is not the only example of racist imagery in Silver Springs promotion, past and present. Women and minorities are most often shown in servant roles or as park attractions on brochures. African Americans, for instance, were smiling servants (glass-bottom boat captains) or minstrel performers. On Emancipation Day 1949, Silver Springs even opened Paradise Park, a segregated Silver Springs for "colored people only." Seminole Indians were often featured as alligator wrestlers and colorful, picturesque natives living in the domestic realm of the Chickee. The tale of the ill-fated love affair of Chulcotah and Winona still told today, however, illustrates the continued presence of Native-American and gender stereotypes at Silver Springs.[11]

## Technological Vision: Science, Power, and the Sublime

Ironically, the exotic characters, danger, and excess illustrated in the ill-fated love stories so often told by Silver Springs tour guides starkly contrasts with the controlled experience and relatively homogeneous riders depicted in the park's glass-bottom boat promotion. The promotional rhetoric of Silver Springs and the glass-bottom boat embody the tension between the total abandon of sublime experience and the positions of power and containment that often appear in American conventions of sublime representation. As travel scholar Chloe Chard contends, "The sublime entails not only a disruption of the state of immobile contemplations, but also a re-imposition of that state" (137). The 1930s promotional brochure exemplifies the magisterial gaze that is part of the representation of Silver Springs as a sublime landscape. Signifying the sublime experience as often realized in Romantic and American Transcendental conventions, a god-like perspective similar to the elevated viewpoints repeatedly shown in landscape oil painting is presented to the reader in the opening paragraph of the 1930s Silver Spring brochure:

> Picture if you will a palm-fringed strip beside a lake of sapphire blue giving rise to a river of sparkling transparency and you have a birds-eye view of Silver Springs; but the water is blue only when viewed from a distance, for its crystal depths when seen from the surface are so clear that every fish and aquatic plant is an open-sesame.

As Allan Wallach asserts, in the conventions of travel literature established by James Fenimore Cooper, Washington Irving, and Nathaniel Hawthorne, "The tourist climbs to the top of a mountain, hill or tower – confronts a panoramic landscape – first overhauled by feelings of sublimity" (82). The "birds-eye view of Silver Springs" presented to the reader provides the expected panoramic vision so often associated with the sublime as experienced by tourists. Reminiscent of the Romantic landscape tradition, the omnipotent view allows the reader "to see" the spring in its entirety: "Navigable to its very source and fed by innumerable smaller springs, each a gorgeous beauty spot in itself, the stream meanders through forest primeval to join the Oklawaha nine miles away." Not only is the reader given a birds-eye view of the formulaically beautiful "palm-fringed strip" and "sapphire blue" surface of Silver Springs, but a panoramic view of the "crystal depths" below the surface is also revealed. Instead of looking down into the valley atop a mountain-ridge (like the romantic figures of Durand), Silver Springs's visitors experience the sublime through glass-bottom boats that make visible everything underwater. The tourists stare down from above, through the glass and "sparkling transparency" of the water, at the sublime landscape below the subterranean river's surface. From the omnipotent perspective of the tourist, "every fish and aquatic plant is an open-sesame." The concluding paragraph even suggests that the mysteries of nature are revealed in all their beauty at Silver Springs. Nature is no longer "nature." Instead it is a theater, a panorama, an invisible place made visible:

> Glass bottom boats ply over Florida's Subaqueous Fairyland. The underwater scenery is as gorgeous and varied as terrestrial plant and animal life is multiple; for here at Silver Springs Nature has drawn aside the curtain of mystery that shrouds other waters and revealed the living panorama of a world unknown to those who have never seen beneath its surface.

Cultural critics Mary Louise Pratt and Allan Wallach have examined the power and conventional beauty intimated in omniscient views like the one constructed for modern tourists in the quoted Silver Springs description. In the groundbreaking text *Imperial Eyes: Travel Writing and Transculturation*, Pratt contends that nineteenth-century travelers often used promontory views with pictorial conventions to present themselves as a "discoverer" who has the power/authority to evaluate, if not to possess, a scene (205). In his 1993 essay, "Making a Picture of the View from Mount Holyoke," Wallach uses the term "panoptic sublime," to describe issues of power and control he sees in the Romantic visions of Nature. Wallach argues that the omnipotent panoramic position of vision seen so often in Romantic and transcendentalist landscape painting correlates to the surveying control described by Foucault. In the nineteenth century, only the ruling class had the time and money to tour because of the expense of transportation and travel. Wallach writes, for example, "Having reached the topmost point in an optical hierarchy, the tourist experiences a sudden access of power, a dizzy sense of having suddenly come into possession of a terrain stretching as far as the eyes could see" (83). And in the panorama, the viewer is shrouded in darkness, invisible, surveying and psychologically taking possession of all that is laid before him. Like the "open-sesame" and "living panorama" of Silver Springs, nineteenth-century panorama paintings, according to Wallach, present the world in the "form of totality; nothing seems hidden to the spectator, looking down upon a vast scene from its center, appears to preside over all visibility" (82).[12] Using Pratt and Wallach's thesis, the birds-eye view of nature written into the 1930s Silver Springs brochure and created by picture frame glass-bottom boats located at the park, not only reflects the Romantic aesthetics and values of the old genteel culture; they offer the tourist the invigorating experience of possession and power over terrestrial and aquatic Nature.

The supremacy of vision and genteel notions of the sublime and beautiful expressed within the Silver Springs brochure's Romantic rhetoric are also intertwined within the scientific gaze connoted in the very design and experience of the glass-bottom boat itself. In many ways the frame and transparent glass of the boat's bottom, in which the world below the surface is even more clearly made visible, functions much like the transparent lens of a microscope. Like a variety of technologies of observation that were invented and perfected during the period between the early Renaissance and the nineteenth century, the microscope made objects that were invisible visible. These optical technologies revealed an overwhelming vision of a vast and intricately beautiful view of the cosmos (both micro and macro). The relationship between the individual and larger natural systems highly influenced transcendentalists like Emerson's concepts of the sublime as revealed by science. As Wilson contends, "Under the scientific gaze, organisms become pattern of holistic force, energy, life; an insight into the relationships between part and whole becomes sublime vision" (10). Inducing an aspect of the sublime reported by some of its visitors, the scientific gaze inherent in the glass-bottom boat, like that of the microscope and telescope, reveals more clearly the overwhelming depths and biology of the diverse aquatic "universe" below the Silver River's surface. The text of the 1930s brochure, for example, rather flamboyantly boasts that the transparency at Silver Springs "has drawn aside the curtain of mystery that shrouds other waters and revealed the living panorama of a world unknown to those who have never seen beneath its surface." Similarly, Emerson once stated when speaking of the night sky, "One might think the atmosphere was made transparent with this design, to give man, in the heavenly bodies, the perpetual presence of the sublime" (15).

The vision of the sublime constructed for Silver Springs tourists by the transparency of the water and the scientific gaze connoted within the frame of the glass-bottom boat has, in many ways, more in common with representations of the panoptic sublime as discussed by Wallach. Unlike the eye level sunsets and upward reaching mountains created by Romantic painters like Casper Friedrich, the glass-bottom boat riders are situated high above the vast caverns, jutting rocks, exotic plants, and abundant fish of the Silver River that they are watching. Like the amateur naturalist travelers examined by Pratt, they examine the natural world through the privileged "lens" of science. Although elements of the sublime (i.e. anxiety inducing vertigo, disorientation from movement, and insignificance in relation to the vastness of the depths of the water) are present, the scientific gaze and the sense of the picturesque created by the frame of the glass-bottom boat functions to contain and manage the experience of nature. Like the canvases of nineteenth-century transcendentalist American landscape oil paintings or the outer edges optical devices like the Claude Glass, the "picture window" of the glass-bottom boat functions to contain and mediate the experience of the vastness of natural landscapes. As Neumann argues in relation to the optical devices and park-sanctioned Kodak photo spots made available at the Grand Canyon by the National Park service, "The general view of the Grand Canyon is so overpowering that separating a section of it for a moment and making it a 'framed picture' – brings it better within one's comprehension" (152).

## Cinematic Vision: Nature and Technology Hollywood Style

As our Silver Springs tour nears completion, our captain slowly turns the boat around and heads back to the Victorian dock. This time, however, the boat travels northward, tracing the opposite side of the bank. During the trip home, the captain boasts about Silver Springs' cinematic history. He instructs all passengers to look at the right bank in order to catch a glimpse of a horseshoe-shaped "lucky palm" where movie stars such a Frank Sinatra, Dean Martin, Doris Day, and Don Johnson got their picture taken while at Silver Springs. The captain reminds everyone not to forget to get his or her picture taken there before leaving the park. "Make sure to make a wish," he adds. The boat momentarily stops. As the boat hovers, the captain says that he would like to introduce us to the Silver Springs' celebrities in permanent residence. After instructing everyone once again to look down through the frame of glass embedded in the boat's hull, he points to white, fiberglass statues and states that they were featured players in the television shows *I Spy* and *Sea Hunt* and in several James Bond feature films. As the boat begins to move again, the captain recommends that everyone take the Jungle Cruise glass-bottom boat in order to see the set of Johnnie Weismuller's television program *Tarzan* and the film sets of Marjoire Kinnan Rawlings's novels *The Yearling* and *Cross Creek*.

The moving images created by the frame of the glass-bottom boat and the passivity of viewers sitting and watching sections of the world below float past place the natural world within the culturally sanctioned aesthetics of science, the sublime, and the picturesque – and is not unlike watching a film. As Walker Percy asserts, "The very means by which the thing is presented for consumption, the very techniques by which the thing is made available, as an item of need-satisfaction, these very means operate to remove the thing from the sovereignty of the knower" (62). Jonathan Crary too points out that "technologies of vision not only suspended the coordinate of a lived time and space, they equally implicated the spectator in a real and fictional landscape of successive images effortlessly moving across the eyes" (158). Anthony D. King also explains, "The window . . . in modern times functions as a mechanism for consuming the landscape not only visually (as is the "picture window") but also economically and socially" (136).

## Conclusion

Influenced by the fact that his Florida essays were part of a series about the social and economic conditions in the post-Civil War South commissioned by *Scribner's Monthly*, Edward Smith King writes about a Silver Springs that is a peaceful, harmoniously beautiful, Edenesque garden. While still maintaining some elements of the sublime, King frames Silver Springs as picturesque by evoking the Romantic pastoral conventions like the wandering poet or painter, the prelapsarian landscape, stylized foliage, and a highly aesthetic setting sun. He writes:

> Yes, what of fiction could exceed in romantic interest the history of this venerable State? What poet's imagination, seven times heated, could paint foliage whose splendors should surpass that of the virgin forest of the Ocklawaha and Indian rivers? What "fountain of youth" could be imagined more redolent of enchantment than the "Silver Spring," now annually visited by 50,000 tourists? The subtle moonlight, the perfect glory of the dying sun as he sinks below a horizon fringed with fantastic trees, the perfume faintly borne from the orange grove, the murmurous music of the waves along the inlets, and the mangrove-covered banks, are beyond words. (145)

Silver Springs as an uniquely American landscape, as a sublime and picturesque earthly paradise, and the glass-bottom boat as a privileged way of seeing, all have their roots in European aesthetics and scientific traditions that attempt to elevate and contain the natural landscape. By the mid-nineteenth century, Romantic and American Transcendentalist representations of nature as a sacred space for transcendence and aesthetic pleasure, which contrasts against the artificial trappings of industrial civilized society, became an essential part of the visual paradigm of many upper and middle class Americans. Thus, the quest for and construction of the sublime, beautiful, and scientific in nature are often found throughout the history of American environmental tourist attractions such as Silver Springs and are inseparably intertwined with American concerns about national identity, culture, and industrialization. The construction of Silver Springs as a worthwhile tourist destination, as an edifying, scientific landscape, as picturesque, as sublime is illustrated in the nineteenth-century travel narratives of Daniel Brinton, of Constance Fenimore Cooper Woolson, of George McCall, in the promotional brochures and souvenir books of the twentieth century, in the narratives performed by glass-bottom boat captains today, in the essays of Edward Smith King, within twentieth-century, park-sanctioned promotional materials, and through the looking glass in the bottom of the boat itself. Even today, the rhetoric of Silver Springs promoters promises to entertain glass-bottom boat riders with beauty, motion, and spectacle, but also offers them a scientific education with a sense of national pride and cultural progress as well. This rhetoric surrounding Silver Springs is indicative of the larger role tourism and spectacle play in how Americans define themselves as individuals and as a nation.

## Notes

1. In Florida, later than many destinations on the American Grand Tour, tourism as an industry did not really see its modest beginnings as a significant tourist destination until the region became a territory of the United States in 1821 and a state in 1845. Florida historian Rembert W. Patrick asserts that it was during the territorial and early statehood periods that small numbers of visitors/tourists started to replace the earlier adventurers and journalists who came to Florida. Patrick further argues that printed journals such as Ralph Waldo Emerson's *Reminiscences,* amongst other publications by lesser-known visiting authors, "were responsible for an ever-increasing number of visitors who sought the warmth and sunshine of Florida before the Civil War" (ix). As early as 1869, according to Patrick, over 25, 000 travelers were reported to have visited Florida; less reliable sources boasted even twice that number (xiii).
2. According to both the official Silver Springs website and the *Discover Silver Springs: Souvenir Book* available today, it was Phillip Morrell who first invented that glass-bottom in the late 1870's. But it wasn't until 1890s that the glass-bottom boat was commercially developed.
3. John Berger's seminal work *Ways of Seeing* first exposed me to this contention.
4. According to John Sears, the American Grand Tour encompassed the Hudson River, the Catskills, Lake George, the Erie Canal, Niagara Falls, the White Mountains, and the Connecticut Valley.
5. Most of the culturally "sanctioned"/"certified" American tourists sights, however, were constructed with little concern or knowledge of working class or minority tastes and values until later in the twentieth century. John Kasson, for example, examines the ways in which the nineteenth-century genteel culture that dominated early American tourism is eventually subverted (but never completely) by the more working class aesthetics available at mass culture entertainment parks like Coney Island and become even more readily available in the twentieth century. This cultural shift can also be seen in the snake milking and Alligator wresting shows that appear in the early 30s when Ross Allen brings his "Reptile Institute" to Silver Springs.
6. Sears, Nye, Neumann, and Leo Marx all examine the importance of romanticism, nature, and tourism in the construction of American national identity.
7. The dark color of the Ocklawaha River is attributed to the tannins present in the water.
8. According to Kenneley's *Discover Silver Springs,* the area was designated a Registered National Landmark in 1925. The U.S. Department of the Interior stated: "This site possesses exceptional value in illustrating the natural history of the United States."

9. The brochure was obtained from the Richter Library of the University of Miami. It is undated. The dress and cars shown in one of its photographs approximate the date.
10. "Prince Chulcotah, son of Chief Yemassee, fell in love with Winona, daughter of Ikehumpkee, and enemy chief. When Winona's father learned of her desire to marry the prince, he declared war on Yemassee's tribe. Prince Chuloctah was killed, causing Winona great grief. The story says she lost her will to live, and on a clear, moonlit night, leapt into the water and was drowned," read the contemporary *Discover Silver Springs* guidebook (Kenneley 14).
11. I have yet to obtain brochures from after the 1950s; thus, I'm not yet certain when the legend changes in the official guides books. The first glass-bottom boats were also named after the park founders. My current research includes discovering when the boat names changed to those of famous Florida Indians.
12. In the paintings of Casper Friedrich, for example, the figures most often are positioned at the horizon even when standing on mountaintops. In many of the Hudson River School painting, however, the figures are looking down upon the sublime landscape spread before them.

## Works Cited


Allen, Frederick Lewis. *Only Yesterday: An Informal History of the 1920's.* New York: Harper & Row, 1931.

Ammidown, Margot. "Edens, Underworlds, and Shrines: Florida's Small Tourist Attractions." *The Journal of Decorative and Propaganda Arts* 23 (1998): 239-259.

Berger, John. *Ways of Seeing.* London: BBC, 1972.

Brinton, Daniel. *Notes on the Floridian Peninsula and Its Literary History: Indian Tribes and Antiquities.* 1859. New York: AMS Press, 1969.

Chard, Chloe. "Crossing Boundaries and Exceeding Limits: Destabilization, Tourism and the Sublime." Ed. Chloe Chard and Helen Longon. *Transports: Travel, Pleasure, and Imaginary Geography, 1600-1830.* New Haven and London: Yale UP, 1996.

Crary, Jonathan. *Techniques of the Observer: On Vision and Modernity in the Nineteenth Century.* Cambridge: MIT Press, 1990.

Davis, Susan. *Spectacular Nature: Corporate Culture and the Sea World Experience.* Berkeley: U of California P, 1997.

Emerson, Ralph Waldo. *The Collected Works of Ralph Waldo Emerson. Nature: Addresses, and Lectures 1.* Cambridge: Belknap Press of Harvard UP, 1971.

Gannon, Michael. Florida: *A Short History.* Gainesville: UP of Florida, 1993.

Jansen, Partricia. *Wild Things: Nature, Culture, and Tourism in Ontario 1790-1914.* Toronto: Toronto Press, 1995.

Kasson, John. *Amusing the Million: Coney Island at the Turn of the Century.* New York: Whill & Wang, 1978.

Kenneley, Frances. *Discover Silver Springs: Souvenir Book.* Ed. Daniel Le Blanc. Florida Leisure, Inc, 1994.

King, Anthony D. "The Politics of Vision." *Understanding Ordinary Landscapes.* Ed. Paul Groth and Todd W. Bressi. New Haven: Yale UP, 1997.

King, Edward Smith. "The Southern States of North America: Florida." *The Florida Reader: Visions of Paradise from 1530 to the Present.* Eds. Maurice O'Sullivan and Jack C. Lane. Sarasota: Pineapple Press, 1991. 144-148.

Marx, Leo. *The Machine in the Garden; Technology and the Pastoral Ideal in America.* 1964. New York: Oxford UP, 1998.

McCall, George A. *Letters from the Frontiers.* 1868. Gainesville: U of Florida P, 1974.

Neumann, Mark. *On the Rim: Looking for the Grand Canyon.* Minneapolis: U of Minnesota P, 1999.

----. Personal interview. 20 Oct. 2002.

Nye, David. American Technological Sublime. Cambridge: The MIT Press, 1996.

Patrick, W. Rembert. Introduction. *Guide to Florida.* By "Rambler." Gainesville: U of Florida P, 1964. vii-xix.

Percy, Walker. *The Message in the Bottle: How Queer Man Is, How Queer Language Is, and What One Has to Do with the Other.* New York: Farrar, Straus and Giroux, 1975.
Pratt. Mary Louise. *Imperial Eyes: Travel Writing and Transculturation.* New York and London: Routledge, 1992.
Sears, John. *Sacred Places: American Tourist Attractions in the Nineteenth Century.* Amherst: U of Massachusetts P, 1989.
*Silver Springs.* University of Miami Richter Library Special Collections, undated brochure.
Wallach, Allan. "Making a Picture of the View from Mount Holyoke." Ed. David Miller. *American Iconology: New Approaches to Nineteenth-Century Art and Literature.* New Haven: Yale UP, 1993.
Wilson, Eric. *Emerson's Sublime Science.* New York: St. Martin's Press Inc, 1999.
Woolson, Constance Fenimore. "The Oklawaha." 1875. *Old Florida 100.* Ed. Skip Whitson. Albuquerque: Sun Publishing Co., 1977.
Wordsworth, William. "The Recluse." *Wordsworth's Poems.* Vol. 3. Ed. Philip Wayne. London: J.M. Dent & Sons LTD, 1955.

*Famed for being the fastest place on earth, the Bonneville Salt Flats have long attracted racing enthusiasts. In this essay, Jessie Embry provides a brief history of the "bastion of Hot Rodding."*

# The Last Amateur Sport: Automobile Racing on the Bonneville Salt Flats

Jessie Embry

The Bonneville Salt Flats – a 200 square mile area east of Salt Lake City near the Utah-Nevada border – is world famous as the place where drivers broke the Ultimate Land Speed Record from 1935 to 1970. Yet the area remains a mystery to most. I visited car museums and archives in England during the summer of 2002. The employees accurately described the salt flats to me, but they could not locate them on a map. Many Utahns have never noticed the exit off I-80 just east of Wendover for the raceway.

My only contacts with the salt flats in the 1960s were looking at Ab Jenkins's Mormon Meteor car in the Utah State Capitol Building and reading newspaper articles about Craig Breedlove's jet car, the Spirit of America. I was unaware of the subculture of amateur, make-and-fix your own car group that has used the salt flats each year since 1949 (weather permitting) until Ron Shook, an English professor at Utah State University, and Wes Potter, an active member of the Utah Salt Flats Racing Association (USFRA), introduced it to me.

The story of driving at the salt flats starts in Southern California, the capital of the car culture and home of the hot rod movement. In February 2003, I visited the archives of the Southern California Timing Association (SCTA). That organization was the beginning of the amateur experience at the salt flats over fifty years ago. Its records are stored in Jack's Garage, literally the garage at Jack Underwood's home. Each weekday morning, men gather to share driving stories, to discuss ways to improve their cars, and to plan upcoming trips. They join other car enthusiasts almost every Saturday morning from 6:30 to 9:30 a.m. in the parking lot near a doughnut shop in Orange County. A few are there to sell, but most want to discuss their cars with the regulars and the tourists who wander by. Nearly all are men, many over sixty who became involved in the hot rod movement in the 1950s and who remember the "good old days." The few women are usually with men. While they share the same passion for cars, they are the observers.

Underwood put me in touch with Chuck Embrey who lives in the Los Angeles area, and when I suggested that we meet at the Saturday event, he knew exactly what I wanted. After most of the cars had left, Embrey and I walked around the parking lot, and he told me in detail his experience with hot rods on the streets, at drag races, and at the Bonneville Salt Flats. He had been to the salt flats only a few times, and he said with a sigh that he wished he had gone there more often. He felt a camaraderie there that he missed and tried to recapture by coming to Jack's Garage. He also longed for a legal place to drive fast.

Unlike Embrey, when I attended USFRA meets in 1993 and 1994, I met men who had focused their racing on the salt flats. When I went to World of Speed in September 1993, I was surprised to find an ant bed of activity in the desert. Everyone was madly running around working on his or her assigned task. I stopped at the souvenir stand, and Ellen Wilkinson, fondly referred to as "the t-shirt lady," talked to me briefly between customers. She reminded me that we had been in the same high school class in northern Utah. Other women sold food, operated the timing devices, and ran errands. I visited the pits, which were full of men working on cars. Nearly everyone was working. Few were spectators.

Activities stopped when an announcer broadcasted that a car was ready to make a run. All eyes focused on the track. A truck pushed a car to the starting line, and then it took off. The driver built up speed, went through the measured mile, and then slowed down. The whole process took just minutes. After a break, the car returned. Then things went on as they had before.

I walked along the racecourse past a few cars full of observers. The heat was unbearable, so I was delighted when two men offered me a ride. We exchanged greetings. They were from Connecticut and had driven across the United States to experience something that they had only read about. We shared stories. They were interested in my research; I wanted to know their impressions of the salt flats and the racing.

The next year I returned to the salt flats for the Land Speed Opener in July (an event which is no longer held because the salt is not always dry). I brought a tape recorder and walked through the pits, looking for friendly men who might be willing to talk. Several took the time to answer my questions and share their views of the racing. All the interviews were short though; they wanted to get back to work. Unfortunately, their work did not pay off. A car spun out on the wet salt, and the organizers decided it was not safe to continue. Once officials cancelled any more runs, everyone packed up and went home.

I had not been to the salt flats for almost ten years, so in August 2003 I decided to return. A lot of things had changed. For the last six years, Reilly Industries, Inc. had worked with the Bureau of Land Management and the racers to transfer salt back to the track. It was the second year that SCTA had two tracks – one nine miles long and one seven miles long. Before the meet started, SCTA expected nearly 400 cars; they got 320 entries. The heat was unbearable, but drivers and crews waited for hours in the hot sun for their chance to run the course. One driver got to the starting line and then had to pull aside because the visor on his helmet did not meet the safety code. I was boiling; I could not imagine what it would be like to wear a fire suit and helmet in that heat. Everyone was very busy. The BLM woman assured me that the men and women working on the cars would talk to me, but I decided not to interrupt their work.

Each time as I drove home, I thought about what I had seen. Here were people who were excited about what they were doing. Despite the heat and the salt, they were having fun. They were trying to break each others' records, but at the same time they were an extended family, always helping and sharing stories, equipment, and advice. They were not going after cash or even a trophy. In fact, no one received any prizes. Their reward was the sense of accomplishment – theirs and others who had the same vision.

These events happen three times a year. SCTA sponsors Speed Week in August and World Finals in October. USFRA holds World of Speed in September. The organizations spend all year planning for a weeklong activity. In September 2002 though, after USFRA had made extensive plans and had media coverage, World of Speed had to be cancelled three days before the event because a rare fall storm flooded the salt flats.

Despite these setbacks, the events attract men and women who enjoy fixing up their cars, creating new cars, driving as fast as possible, and watching other cars speed down the course. Those who participate often brag that they are the last amateur sport. They receive no pay; very few have sponsors. They work on their own cars and pay their own way. Very few people are spectators; either they run cars, or they are involved in setting up and making the event run. While most Americans focus on professional sports, the SCTA and USFRA events are a remaining sport that is a "leisure activity – a type of escape from the tensions and worries of life," typical in the late nineteenth and early twentieth centuries (Layton vii). H.F. Moorhouse studied the hot rod culture, which has some professional elements. The racing at the Bonneville Salt Flats is an amateur subset of that story.

## Racing on the Bonneville Salt Flats

The Bonneville Salt Flats did not start out as a racing venue. The Native Americans avoided the area because there was no water and nothing would grow there. Emigrant trains like the Donner-Reed Party learned how difficult it was to travel across the thin salt. Bill Rishel, later president of the Utah Automobile Association, introduced the concept of automobile racing on the salt flats. He first crossed the salt on a bicycle in 1896 as part of a nationwide contest. That crossing was slow, but Rishel recognized the potential for automobiles. In 1907, he and two Salt Lake City businessmen tested the area with a Pierce-Arrow. Encouraged, Rishel convinced a barnstorming driver, Teddy Tezlaff, to test his "Blitzen Benz" there. He drove faster than drivers at Daytona Beach, but the automobile community did not recognize his achievement. Rishel claimed that Ab Jenkins brought fame to the salt. When the salt flats portion of a cross country highway was completed in 1927, Jenkins drove a car and beat the celebrity train from Salt Lake City to Wendover, a distance of 125 miles (Jenkins and Ashton 29, 34-35).

Jenkins continued to use the salt flats for racing. In 1932, he set an unofficial record for driving twenty-four hours nonstop (112.94 mph), but even the local newspapers refused to carry the story for a week. "Bigwigs of the automobile concern" told him it was foolish to take "a wild ride on a sea of salt somewhere in the middle of the Utah desert" (Jenkins and Ashton 17, 34-36). Those opinions changed, however, when the most prominent land speed driver of the time, Britain's Sir Malcolm Campbell gave up trying to break the 300 mph barrier at Daytona Beach and accomplished his goal at the salt flats in 1935 (Embry and Shook 165-166).

From 1935 to 1970, the Bonneville Salt Flats was the place to set the Land Speed Record. During the 1930s, British drivers George Eyston and John Cobb brought their carefully designed cars to the flats and challenged each other for the fastest mile record. In 1938, they each set a new record within a month of each other. They also exchanged twelve and twenty-four hour records with Ab Jenkins. World War II stopped the racing, but in 1947 Cobb returned and drove 394.2 mph, a record that stood for fifteen years. During the 1960s, American amateur drivers such as Mickey Thompson and the Summers brothers – Bob and Bill – and British professional driver, Donald Campbell, the son of Malcolm, drove faster than Cobb in conventional cars. But it took jet cars to set extremely fast records. Americans such as Craig Breedlove, Art Arfons, and his brother Walter Arfons brought their homemade designed cars and broke each others' records, sometimes within a week of each other. In 1970, Gary Gabelich broke the record for the last time on the salt flats at a speed of 630.39 mph (Embry and Shook 166-71).

## SCTA and USFRA

The land speed records were set in cars especially designed for that purpose. But ever since the automobile was invented, men have tried to see how fast they could go. At first, they drove cars designed to be driven on roads; then they supercharged them to go even faster. In the United States, this racing included driving on open roads, hills, deserts, and oval tracks. But the drivers started looking for better places to go fast. In 1931, the Gilmore Oil Company sponsored speed trials for the first time at the El Muroc Dry Lakes in California. But those driving on the dry lakebeds there often had poor driving conditions that led to crashes and injuries, sometimes even death. As a result, car clubs had poor press. To counteract that, several formed the Southern California Timing Association (SCTA) in 1937 and started to look for better sites to race (Noeth 41).

The Bonneville Salt Flats with its Land Speed Record history seemed like a logical place to the SCTA since it was a flat, open place, which had already shown that cars could drive fast there. So ten years after their organization, members of SCTA examined the salt flats and then wrote to the American Automobile Association asking to use the flats to establish hot rod records. The AAA refused the request, arguing that it was "highly unlikely a 'hot rod' could ever achieve the speed of 203 miles an hour," the existing record for that category of cars. Car classes are determined by the style and size of engine. Many hot rods fit in the C Class (Parks).

But the amateurs did not give up. At the time, the Salt Lake City Bonneville Speedway Association, a Salt Lake City Chamber of Commerce committee, scheduled the salt flats. A group of Southern California men representing SCTA and *Hot Rod* magazine drove to Salt Lake to visit with Gus Backman, the chamber's secretary. After studying the situation, Backman agreed to let the SCTA use the salt. With that permission, SCTA formed a Board of Management. Otto Crocker, the American Power Boat Association chief timer, agreed to time events. Union Oil, Hot Rod, Grant Piston Rings, and Service Sales of Texas all agreed to be sponsors. Lee Ryan, the publicity manager, told Firestone's racing director, that the event would become "the biggest thing in this country in the way of time trials" (Noeth 42, 44-45).

SCTA scheduled the first event for 1949. By mid-August, 200 roadsters, lakesters, streamliners, coupes, sports and racing cars from eleven states had signed up. Eventually only sixty showed up. Three divisions of cars – roadsters, lakesters, and streamliners – using four sizes of engines drove on the salt flats the first year. According to Ak Miller, "The people who went, loved it. We could race flat out and the cars would disappear over the horizon, taking their exhaust note with them, on this beautiful, hard, smooth surface. We saw right away the salt was a rolling dynamometer, you just followed the black line up and over the peak power curve" (Noeth 50-53). The racers established ten new records. The *Salt Lake Tribune* reported in 1949 that "these boys" agreed "there's no place like it for real speed." SCTA lost $300 on the first meet, but they got enough positive feedback that they decided to return, and the Bonneville Speedway group agreed to let them ("Bonneville Flats Offers" 20).

The next year, ninety cars showed up and completed 1,307 runs. Mickey Thompson, a hot rodder who went on to set speed records, worked at a garage and could not miss work the first year. But he took vacation time to come in 1950. He later said, "The whole show was the dream of a lifetime come true, of pinch-penny kids turned loose on the world's greatest race course" (Noeth 50, 55-56). In 1953, the AAA came for the first time and the hot rodders created the 200 Club to recognize those who drove over 200 mph and set a record on the salt. In 1971, the National Hot Rod Association (NHRA) sanctioned the meet, providing insurance. That was the first year that the international French organization recognized the event so that Land Speed Records could be set (Bonneville Speed Week Program 1971).

Over the years, Speed Week continued to grow. The 1952 program reported, "There is no racing. Rather, competition is between the machine and time." In 1953, *Life* explained, "The glistening salt flats of Bonneville, Utah were overrun this month by some of the oddest shapes the motor age has produced" ("Speaking of Pictures" 17). The Speed Week program that year agreed, but added while not all hot rod designs had practical application in car production, they focused on design, engineering, and construction. For those involved, hot rodding was a "fascinating hobby." The program concluded, "We do not strive to outguess the engineers. We deeply hope to make their best efforts more interesting, and in the long run, more usable" (Bonneville Speed Week Program 1952). For many, there were no winners or losers; Speed Week, like the Olympics, was "an experience more than a contest" (Bonneville Speed Week Program 1953).

Each year was similar: cars broke records, drivers joined the 200 mph club, a few drivers went over 300 mph, and some had accidents. There were even a few fatalities although not very many. In response to each accident or possible problem, SCTA added safety rules. In 1957, a driver put the first parachute to a car. That year, Ray Leslie set a new American record of 266.204 mph. It was the second time he had broken the record in three day ("German Cyclists" 6). In 1966, Bob Herds and Bob McGrath had two way runs of 301 mph in their B-Class Streamliners. The wide open space helped those who had accidents survive. A Lakester rolled at 220 mph, but the driver walked away without any injuries ("Two Cars" 8). Nolan White had neck and back injuries when his modified sportster rolled at 230 mph, not bad considering the car rolled four times and was completely demolished (Colbath 86).

In August 2001, Don Vesco drove his brother Rick's car, named the Turbinator, and set a record for that class at 458 mph ("Vesco Brothers"). At the same time, Nolan White set the record for a piston/wheel driven automobile on the salt flats at 413 mph. Seventy-two-year-old White averaged 420 mph in the last measured mile and had a top speed of 434 mph. He blew his right tire at 430 mph, and his main parachute ripped off the 5,000 pound car. Thanks to White's forty-five years of experience at the salt flats, he turned into an open area with little salt. He wore out his braking system, but the car stopped when he sank into the mud. He was not as lucky two months later. A shortened racetrack meant White had only five timed miles, and he planned to decelerate after the fourth mile, allowing room to stop. His first run was perfect, reaching a 422 mph four mile average speed. However, his first parachute ripped off, and the other two also failed. White attempted to steer off the course as he had in August, but as he turned to avoid the highway, the car slid and then flipped. Sadly, he died from internal injuries ("Tribute to Nolan White").

Over the years, there were a few similar accidents, but they were the exceptions. Most of the time drivers were protected because of the wide open spaces and the way the tires held to the salt. The annual articles in *Hot Rod* magazine from 1949 to 1976 described the August event as a friendly, family event where drivers and families came each year to drive as fast as they could and renew friendships. They rarely mentioned the discomforts of the salt flats: the heat, the unpredictable weather, the concerns about less salt, spinouts, and accidents. In fact, the magazine pointed out, and racers continue to explain, that there are very few accidents, and those who do suffer everything from broken bones to death are doing what they love. Current racers mourn the loss of friends, but, interestingly enough, they would like to go the same way.

According to Louise Noeth, the "Golden Age" for the SCTA ended in 1969. She explained, "It was certainly the period of greatest change, engines, techniques, body styles, and, of course, an explosion of new faces" (109). Since then, the track has been unpredictable, but even without a "golden age," the racers continued to come. The fiftieth anniversary of Speed Week in 1998 was a celebration; forty-two of the original forty-nine racers returned. SCTA honored Bob Higbee, known as Mr. Salt, for his continuous attendance and role as safety inspector. But many who had been faithful attendees had passed on, and Speed Week was dedicated to them (Noeth 127-28). In 1987, for example, Mrs. Hospitality, Vera Aldrich, who had greeted the racers for fifteen years, died. For Aldrich, "the racers [are] my family. I just love being a part of it all" (Noeth 150).

For a quarter of a century, SCTA sponsored the only amateur event at Bonneville. In 1976, racers in Utah formed the Utah Salt Flats Racing Association. Several factors led to the creation of the new organization. By then, control of the salt flats had shifted from the Salt Lake Chamber of Commerce to the state of Utah then to the Bureau of Land Management. While the Southern California racers complained that the salt flats and their race track were disappearing, the government said it was difficult to respond to these complaints from an out-of-state organization that only used the salt flats for a week a year. Another concern came from Utah racers who wanted another time other than Speed Week to use their cars. While the SCTA members could use the dry lakes in California, the Utah racers did not have another place to go. For a while, they took their cars to the dry lakes, but that was a long way to go for testing. So Utahns started testing on the salt flats (Potter; Wilkinson).

When insurance issues made just having a timing event too expensive, USFRA started its own event on the salt flats, World of Speed in September. The organization planned its first World of Speed in 1985. The scheduling was bad; that year there was so much water that rivers flowed down the main streets of Salt Lake City, and the Utah state government put pumps in the Great Salt Lake to control the overflow. It took a couple of years for the salt flats to dry out so the Utah group did not sponsor its first event until 1987. According to the *Salt Lake Tribune*, "The salt will come alive for the second time in 45 days following the annual 'Speed Week' in August. It is sanctioned by the Federation Internationale Automobile in Paris so they can go for official Land Speed Records. The event is an attempt to focus more attention on the world-famous salt flats, which have been used only sporadically for high-speed runs since the early '70s" (Rosetta 7). For a while, USFRA members also sponsored a Land Speed Opener in July, but, like the year I went in 1994, the salt was often too wet. In addition, the volunteers did not have vacation time or resources to run both (Potter; Wilkinson). SCTA added the World Finals in October 1990 to use the salt more.

As with all new organizations, some members of the SCTA resisted the Utah group. For years, they had controlled amateur racing at the salt flats, and they did not want to share. Others saw increased exposure to racing at the salt flats as positive. The more people who understood the successes and the problems, the more the government might work to improve the salt. Members of both organizations acknowledge that personality conflicts and territory claims created tensions, but they insist that over the years the two organizations have developed a good working relationship. There are still some Californians who do not like sharing with Utah; there are Utahns who dislike Californians taking over part of their state. But their voices are muted as most see the overwhelming benefits.

Over time, the two organizations created their own place and learned to support each other. The salt flats became a negotiated space rather than a contested space. Speed Week attracts 200-300 entries each year. To make sure everyone has a chance to run, SCTA adopts very strict rules, and cars must meet the requirements. The organization refers those who do not have cars that meet their rules to the more relaxed World of Speed event. Since the event is much smaller, USFRA is not as strict. It has also added its unique events. For example, it created the 130 mph club where, with a few modifications, drivers can test how fast their street cars can go. USFRA even has an electric bar stool competition (Wilkinson).

In 2003, most see advantages for both organizations. According to Jack Underwood, the SCTA historian, the USFRA has given more political pull to the racers and their attempts to force Reilly Industries, a mining company to return salt to the racetrack. USFRA members formed "Save the Salt," a nonprofit organization that publicizes the disappearing salt and works with the federal and state government and Reilly to improve the track. Utahns and even the BLM listen to those who live in the same state as the salt flats. They are reluctant to respond to out-of-staters – especially Californians – who only come to the state twice a year. In addition, SCTA and USFRA share inspectors at their meets. USFRA maintains the trucks used to mark the track and lay the timing wires, so SCTA does not need to bring them from California each year. Both organizations recognize records set at all events. (Potter; Wilkinson). Phil Freudiger, an SCTA member, summarized the values of most about the new organization, "The USFRA is the greatest. They really work hard on saving the salt."

## Racers at the Bonneville Salt Flats

To understand why the SCTA and USFRA members go to the salt flats, it is essential to listen to their individual stories. I learned them at the Land Speed Opener in 1994 and at Jack's Garage in 2003. They show men dedicated to hard work at what most consider play.

Ben Zimmerman first came to the salt flats in 1958. After reading hot rod books, he "wanted to come down and see all these famous people do what they did best which was drive fast." Mickey Thompson and others were "kind of my heroes. They could do nothing wrong." With the possible exception of Mickey Thompson (who had many enemies and some understand why a still unknown person murdered him), racing at the salt flats was not about hero status among spectators. First, there are very few consistent fans. Those who only came to watch either stopped coming or got involved in a pit crew or assisted with the racing. Second, most drivers focus on the event and not the observers. They improve their cars and then give parts and advice to others who are competing for the same record. Zimmerman followed that pattern. He came to see drivers, and then became a driver. He continued to come to drive and see the "kids that came down the same time I did [who] are all grown up and . . . are still coming back" because coming to the flats "is kind of a fever."

Zimmerman recognized the dangers of racing, but felt safe on the salt. He had "blown [his cars] up three or four times." He added though, "I look forward to coming down and breaking something. If you don't break something, you are not trying hard." But there was more to the experience, "It is not just running a car. It is just being around here." He enjoyed the low key, lack of pressure missing in other associations, "This is just a really layback kind of place" (Zimmerman).

Charles Salmen's father was a professional racecar driver, so Charles was always interested in cars and driving fast. He got his first roadster, a 1932 model, in the 1940s when he was sixteen or seventeen and started racing in the Long Beach and Los Angeles area on Saturday nights. It was, as Salmen noted, "illegal drag racing." By 1957, he figured he had done it all, and he wanted to try the salt flats. So he built a car, a "1957 two door Chevrolet sedan with a hopped up engine." Not content to use just one car, in 1968 he brought a new Mustang fastback, "a street legal car" and spun it four times at 160 mph. He added, "That was pretty scary." In 1991, after he retired and had time to work on cars, he built a roadster like the one he started with. His new car had the same dimensions as the 1934 Ford. In three years, he had had one-way runs of 239 mph and 233 mph, but he had not put together the return (Salmen).

For E. J. and Mark Lingua, coming to the salt flats was a male-bonding, father-son affair. E. J., a physician, first came in 1965 because another doctor from Burbank had come the year before and E. J. wanted to do better. He broke the record in a 1965 Chegelle Malibu SS that he drove up, raced, and then drove home. After the first time, he continued to come because it was "an addictive enlightment." E.J.'s son Mark came for the first time when he was twelve and worked on the car along with his brother John. Mark remembered the time he set four motorcycle records on four different motorcycles in 1976. For him, driving on the salt was "kind of like driving in the rain at 50 or 65 mph where the tires are not quite sticking. It is just on the edge of hydroplaning" (Lingua).

J. D. Tone represents another male generational story. His father loved cars, and Tone grew up with a dream of driving, not setting records, on the salt flats. In 1981, he purchased the Bantam from Gary Barrious and Bob Minall, a car they built in 1969. Over the years, Tone gradually modified the car. His goal was to go as fast as he could with his equipment. In the 1990s, his son expressed an interest in racing and being a member of the 200 Club. Tone realized that his car would never go that fast, so he teamed up with another racer, Joe Fontana in 1997. They put Fontana's engine in Tone's car, and in 2002 Tone's son went 202 mph.

Tone is among the men who gather at Jack's Garage. Tone told me how he had purchased a car that did not match the standard – a 1928 Ford – and pushed the SCTA rules for size, always staying just inside of them. While Tone complained about the close inspections his car received, Underwood laughed and suggested that he was trying to join a club where his car did not exactly fit. Maybe he should form his own club! Underwood convinced Tone whenever he needed work done on his car to do it himself. So Tone learned how to work with fiberglass and paint.

The men that I talked to at the flats and in California did not mention their wives. Underwood's wife came into the garage, shared greetings, and then left for work. While Underwood has retired as a contractor and explains he has enough to live comfortably, his wife continues to work at a candy store for "something to do." Although cars did not appear to be her thing, she was very kind. She teased the men when I was working and Ron Shook, my co-researcher, joined the car discussion. I felt anyone who would allow her garage, driveway, and half her backyard to be taken over by cars, parts, and the SCTA archives supported her husband's passion.

There are women, however, who share the excitement of Bonneville. Jonathan Amo's brother, Joe, and his wife went to the salt flats for their honeymoon. It was a compromise they worked out. Joe wanted to go to the flats for the first time and get married too. The couple has gone to the flats every year since. I did not see any children when I went to the salt flats, but the Amos do bring theirs. Their first daughter Kyaera was born in January 1993 and went to the salt flats that August. Their son Aero (named for aerodynamics) went when he was only three days old. The Amo brothers race their Kawasaki ZX10 in the MPS-F (modified partial streamlined--fuel 1000 cc) class. Joe set a record on his honeymoon at 189 mph and since gone 223 mph (Amo).

Most women go as spectators or workers; they do not drive on the salt. They go to cheer on their husbands, fathers, brothers, and others. Because they enjoy the event, they find something that they can do. For several years in the late 1960s and early 1970s, Ginnie Geisler, wife of a member of the SCTA board, published an article in the annual program. She explained that her first date with her husband-to-be was at a SCTA award dinner. She went to Bonneville with him while they were dating and later after they were married. For her, "Bonneville was excitingly different – a combination of heaven and hell…. I was commanded, reprimanded, sun burnt, wind blown, and ignored" (Bonneville Program 1971). She decided to become more a part of the Bonneville experience, so she read the rule books and learned about what was happening. Her editorials explained how the SCTA officials prepared for Speed Week and described her experiences there. While she never drove a car across the salt, she kept her fingers crossed that her husband's runs would be successful.

Ellen Wilkinson and Mary West are essential parts of USFRA and Save the Salt. Mary was the first secretary for USFRA and kept track of everything. Her home was the club's office. Ellen got interested in the salt flats because she and her husband Gary wanted something that they could do together. They enjoyed skiing, but it was too hard on both of their bodies. They tried dirt bike riding, but Ellen had an accident. So they started going to the salt flats. Gary worked in the pits; Ellen enjoyed watching the cars and meeting the people. But she wanted to do more. So one day when Mary West seemed overwhelmed trying to arrange t-shirts for sale, Ellen said, "I can do the t-shirts." And she had a job.

Since then, Ellen has replaced Mary West as secretary. She collects dues, prepares the organization's quarterly newsletter and annual World of Speed program, assists in setting up and taking down the equipment, serves as a go-for at the meets, and, of course, she is still the t-shirt lady. She does not always get to watch the cars race down the track, but she listens to the announcer. And sometimes those who had successful and less than successful experiences come around and tell her what happened. She loves the people at the meet; they are a special extended family. Ellen also goes to Speed Week, but she only goes for a day since she has no responsibility. She enjoys the experience, but as she talked about being busy at World of Speed, I could tell that she wanted to be involved. As she explained, everyone has a job to do, and everyone else depends on her doing hers (Wilkinson).

Over the years, some women have actually driven on the salt flats. For professional drivers, it was usually because the men wanted to keep the competition off the salt flats or for novelty. The women went for a separate women's record rather than the land speed. For example, Paula Murphy, a professional driver, used Art Arfons's car in 1963. Two years later,

Craig Breedlove had his wife Lee drive. Breedlove broke the record, but he had scheduled the salt for another week. Rather than let Arfons use the salt and break his record so soon, Breedlove asked his wife to come and drive for the first time (Breedlove 169-71). As with many other sports, women became more acceptable as part of the women's liberation movement. They were allowed to drive at Speed Week for the first time in 1972 although the decision came too late to include their entries in the program (Bonneville Speed Week, 1972). Since then women have set records on the salt, and they no longer have to go into a separate record book.

I did not see any women driving racecars on the salt, and my impression is that men dominate the sport. When I asked why more women were not involved, the answers varied. Wes Potter told me that most men drive their own cars that they fix up and maintain. They are very picky who they allow to drive – men or women. Most women do not have the mechanical interest. There are two female members of the 200 Club, an exclusive club for people who have gone over 200 mph and broken a record. But they drove someone else's car. Ellen Wilkinson told me that she would love it if someone would offer to let her drive a car. She has driven equipment trucks and her own car on the flats, and even at the slower speeds, she enjoyed the experience. She described driving on the salt flats as hydroplaning – a feeling of being in control but also out of control. Jack Underwood, diplomatically refused to speculate: "The girls drive some very fast cars and motorcycles. I have no idea how many or why more don't."

## Sports and American Popular Culture

Sports like the amateur racing at the Bonneville Salt Flats are an important part of American popular culture and illuminate American values. As major league baseball commissioner A. Bartlett Giamatti explained, "It has long been my conviction that we can learn far more about the conditions, and values, of a society by contemplating how it chooses to play…than by examining how it goes about to work" (13). In 1917, historian Frederick Paxman even explained that sports were the new safety valve for Americans after his fellow historian and mentor Frederick Jackson Turner declared that the frontier had closed in 1890. Paxman argued that as Americans moved to cities and worked in factories they needed an escape and sports brought them together (143-68).

Paxman described amateurs, defined by Webster Collegiate Dictionary, as "one who engages in a …sport as a pastime rather than a profession." Since then athletics have become professional. Most Americans still see sports as an escape, but they are spectators rather than participants. This shift is true of some forms of automobile racing, the most watched sport in America. Yet some elements of hot rodding remain on an amateur level. For me, the activities on the Bonneville Salt Flats fit that description because no one does it for pay. A few get sponsors to help with parts, but most do all the work themselves. The drivers take their vacation time to bring their cars to the desert to set records.

Some scholars who study hot rodding would disagree. H.F. Moorhouse explains in *Driving Ambitions: An Analysis of the American Hot Rod Enthusiasm* that since there is some media coverage and some drivers have sponsors, the salt flats are no longer an amateur sport (98-99). Yet the media coverage is very small, and even Moorhouse's main source, *Hot Rod*, rarely covers the events at the salt flats anymore.

But the debate over whether the salt flat racing is an amateur sport is not the most interesting question. More important is what the SCTA and USFRA tell us about American culture. Several scholars have tried to answer that question about hot rodding in general. In

1953, Robert H. Boyle referred to hot rodding as a sport for lower middle class men looking for fulfillment in a world in which the economic system will not allow them to get ahead. Boyle also argued that the men used cars to deal with sexual insecurities (146-47). In his Ph.D. dissertation published in 1978, James Preston Viken described drag racing as a social community based on play, but one requiring a lot of work. Quoting a 1952 article on the "Psychological Components of the Hot Rodder," Moorhouse argued in 1991, "The hot rod movement involved a more vital working out of basic cultural values than the rather flabby and cluttered life of advanced capitalism now allowed" (157). He defines four elements of the American dream: a do-it-yourself attitude, a desire to succeed in a war-like activity, a substitute for women, and an outlaw breed similar to the western American gunmen breaking the law and getting away with it (173-76, 187, 190-97).

Boyle, Viken, and Moorhouse's theories on gender, race, and class apply here as well. Nearly everyone who races is European American. They have to be rich enough to be able to afford the time and money to buy and maintain their cars. Yet they do not have the luxury or the sponsorships to make racing their life's work. It is, as Moorhouse explains, their enthusiasm that keeps them going. Minorities are not excluded; early National Hot Rod Association publications clearly state that anyone is invited. Moorhouse argued that the hot rodders feel like a minority and, therefore, would never leave someone out. Women are not excluded, but they fulfill the support roles typical of traditional, middle-class homes, or they have to be as good as the boys in mechanical and driving skills (185). As these theories explain, the salt flats are one place where men feel empowered.

But beyond theory, professional and amateur drivers alike enjoy going fast. They take risks as a means of adventure. As automobile expert Ron Shook explained, men are attracted to speed and noise. Fast cars provide both. Ralph Keyes explained in his book *Why We Take Risks*, "We do our best to make life safer…Yet we find most memorable those moments when all our efforts are for naught" (13). He cited Michael Cooper-Evans, a British race driver, who believed that, as a driver, "[H]e alone has the authority to decide between life and death." Keyes continued, "By tempting death – [racers] choose life – repeatedly. And in doing, they confirm and reconfirm who's in charge of their destiny" (113-14).

George Eyston, a professional car racer who set records during the 1930s at the Bonneville Salt Flats, explained, "Conquering the unknown always has had a thrill for me." For Eyston, that unknown was going faster than anyone else because "in order to get a record, one has to outdo the best that has ever been done. In racing, the opponent may fail, allowing victory, but in setting records the race is against the clock" (1-3). Many SCTA and USFRA members would agree. Going fast is the goal whether they are in a streamliner going over 400 mph or on an electric bar stool clipping along at five mph. The challenge of breaking a record at the salt flats is their goal.

Those at the salt flats do what they enjoy not to exclude others but to meet their own goals. They are a close extended family, but they are willing to let me, a female historian from a conservative religious university, look in and participate as much as I want. The USFRA invites anyone who wants to test their cars' speed drive as long as they meet the safety requirements. The SCTA needs to be stricter because their time on the salt is limited. There is no attempt to leave people out because of class or race. While at one time sport cars may have been the elite and not as accepted by hot rodders, as Moorhouse argued, they are now accepted. While the ideal roadster may still be a Ford, those at the salt flats let others participate if they meet the guidelines. For those who go to the salt flats, the experience is hot and miserable but still fun. According to Mary West, Art Arfons's favorite saying was, "I can't wait to get here to race. When I get here, I can't wait to leave, and after I've left, I can't wait to come back" (Wilkinson).

Women can take part where they feel comfortable. Sterling Moss, one of the greatest race drivers of all time, may have been right in 1963 when he explained he had "never found a woman who . . . enjoyed speed for its own sake." That is still true for many women (the author included), but some women like Ellen Wilkinson do want to go fast. Her limitation is mechanical interest. Those who drive cars on the salt flats do all the work on their own cars; the cars are their babies and they will not let just anyone drive them. Although historian Charles Sanford argued in the 1970s, "women have virtually swarmed into the car repair business," that has not been my experience (540). In the automobile shops I go to, men fix the cars and women are the office staff just as they are at the salt flats.

## Summary

A 1980 Speed Week program summarized what the Bonneville Salt Flats mean to the SCTA and the USFRA: "Bonneville is many things to many people. To some a vacation, to others fruition of a dream, to all Bonneville is an American tradition. This is the bastion of Hot Rodding. The diversity of equipment and machines as well as personalities gives credence to that. Bonneville is a legacy to the future generation of those who will quest after speed. Let's hope they take the road not taken. That has made all the difference" (Bonneville Speed Week Program 1980).

Today in a world of professional sports, the SCTA and USFRA members stand out as people who are willing to spend their own money and vacation to take a risk and do something they love. Like others who participate in extreme sports though, they are part of American popular culture. They enjoy the challenge of a sport and take a risk to show that they control their own destiny. Racing on the salt flats is a work-play experience that provides adventure as the western frontier did for European American men in the 1800s and sports did in the early twentieth century.

## Works Cited


Amo, Jonathan. E-Mail to the author. 2002.

"Bonneville Flats Offers Unique Show with Hot Rods." *Salt Lake Tribune* 24 August 1949: 20.

Bonneville Speed Week Programs. SCTA Archives. Jack's Garage. Fountain Valley, California.

Boyle, Robert H. *Sport – Mirror of American Life*. Boston: Little, Brown, and Company, 1963.

Breedlove, Craig. *Spirit of America: Winning the World's Land Speed Record*. Chicago: Henry Regnery Co., 1971.

Colbath, Lyle, "Bonneville Records Fall." *Salt Lake Tribune* 24 August 1966: 86.

Dulles, Foster Rhea. *A History of Recreation: America Learns to Play*. New York: Appleton-Century Crofts, 1940.

Embry, Jessie and Ron Shook. "'These Bloomin' Salt Beds': Racing on the Bonneville Salt Flats." *Red Stockings & Out-of-Towners: Sports in Utah*. Ed. Stanford L. Layton. Salt Lake City: Signature Books, 2003.

Eyston, Captain G. E. T. *Fastest on Earth*. Los Angeles: Floyd Clymer, 1947.

Freudiger, Phil. Interviewed by Jessie Embry. Bonneville Salt Flats Oral History Project. Charles Redd Center for Western Studies. L. Tom Perry Special Collections and Manuscripts. Brigham Young University. Provo, Utah. 1994.

"German Cyclists Eye Salt Flats." *Salt Lake Tribune* 23 September 1957: 6D.

Giamatti, A. Bartlett. *Take Time for Paradise*. New York: Summit Books, 1989.

Jenkins, Ab and Wendell J. Ashton. *The Salt of the Earth*. Los Angeles: Cymer Motors, 1939.

Keyes, Ralph. *Chancing it: Why We Take Risks*. Boston: Little, Brown, and Co., 1985.

Layton, Stanford J. Introduction. *Red Stockings & Out-of-Towners: Sports in Utah*. Salt Lake City: Signature Books, 2003.

Lingua, E. J. and Mark. Interviewed by Jessie Embry. Bonneville Salt Flats Oral History Project. Charles Redd Center for Western Studies. L. Tom Perry Special Collections and Manuscripts. Brigham Young University. Provo, Utah. 1994.

Moorhouse, H. F. *Driving Ambitions: An Analysis of the American Hot Rod Enthusiasm*. Manchester: Manchester UP, 1991.

Noeth, Louise Ann. *Bonneville Salt Flats*. Onceola, WI: MBI Publishing Company, 1999.

Parks, Wally. "After Thirty Years It's Still the Greatest." Pamphlet 18415. Utah State Historical Society Library. Salt Lake City, Utah. 1978.

Paxman, Frederick L. "The Rise of Sport." *Mississippi Valley Historical Review* 4 (1917): 143-68.

Potter, Wester. Telephone conversation. April 2003.

Rader, Benjamin R. *American Sports: From the Age of Folk Games to the Age of Televised Sports*. 2nd ed. Englewood Cliffs, NJ: Prentice Hall, 1990.

Rosetta, Dick. "Drivers Chase Land Speed Records." *Salt Lake Tribune* 28 September 1987: C7.

Salmen, Charles. Interviewed by Jessie Embry. Bonneville Salt Flats Oral History Project. Charles Redd Center for Western Studies. L. Tom Perry Special Collections and Manuscripts. Brigham Young University. Provo, Utah. 1994.

Sanford, Charles L. "Woman's Place in American Car Culture." *Michigan Quarterly Review* (1981): 532-47.

"Speaking of Pictures." *Life* 28 September 1953: 17.

"Tribute to Nolan White." http://www.landracing.com/nolan.htm.

"Two Cars Top 300 mph at Bonneville Nationals." *Salt Lake Tribune* 24 August 1966: 8B.

"Vesco Brothers Regain World Speed Record for USA with the Thundering 458 mph Average." http://teamvesco.com/wr_press_release.htm

Viken, James Preston. "The Sport of Drag Racing and the Search for Satisfaction, Meaning, and Self: Work and the Mastery of Accrued Skill in Suitable Challenge Situations." Diss. U of Minnesota, 1978.

Wilkinson, Ellen. Interviewed by Jessie Embry. Bonneville Salt Flats Oral History Project. Charles Redd Center for Western Studies. L. Tom Perry Special Collections and Manuscripts. Brigham Young University. Provo, Utah. 2003.

Zimmerman, Ben. Interviewed by Jessie Embry. Bonneville Salt Flats Oral History Project. Charles Redd Center for Western Studies, L. Tom Perry Special Collections and Manuscripts. Brigham Young University. Provo, Utah. 1994.

*In "Quacks, Yokels, and Light-Fingered Folk," Joseph Ugoretz argues, "Oral performance art, with its performers, audiences, and performances, while it is often valorized and culturally sanctioned, as with African griots or Baptist preachers, for example, is also frequently marginalized and transgressive, as with gangsta rappers and beat poets. When people come to the fair, they are already coming to a site where this same contradiction exists."*

# "Quacks, Yokels, and Light-Fingered Folk": Oral Performance Art at the Fair

Joseph Ugoretz

> There is something magic about a fair…The smell of trampled grass, the flaring lights…
>
> -Patrick O'Brian, *The Yellow Admiral*

> There is a great quantity of eating and drinking, making love and jilting, laughing and the contrary, smoking, cheating, fighting, dancing, and fiddling: there are bullies pushing about, bucks ogling the women, knaves picking pockets, policemen on the look-out, quacks (other quacks, plague take them!) bawling in front of their booths, and yokels looking up at the tinselled dancers and poor old rouged tumblers, while the light-fingered folk are operating upon their pockets behind.
>
> -William Thackeray, *Vanity Fair*

## Introduction

The county fair carnival, in time and space, occupies an important place in the imaginations and reactions of audiences. The fair broadcasts itself, sending out forerunners. Before the time it arrives, there are advance men with posters and arrows, newspaper ads, and prepared promises. On the way to the place it occupies and creates, audiences begin to experience sights – the rides, the lights, a tethered balloon, and the streams of traffic – and sounds – music, shouting, crying children, screams of riders, and the amplified talk of the pitchmen – as well as smells – animals and their excrement, dust, roasting meat, sugar, and hot fat.

The entrance to the fair is guarded; there are gates and ticket takers, and these limits establish a zone, a space of changed rules, and different expectations. All the sensations which are broadcast into the surroundings are, inside the zone of the fair itself, intense, invasive, and uplifting. There is risk and possibility, fun and danger, the confirmation of what is mundane and allowed, as well as the challenge and violation of these same established norms and perceptions. There is also, at the fair, a performer whose natural environment this is. There is a performer who, by the nature of his art, most particularly represents and belongs to this environment.

Standing on a small raised platform, wearing a microphone on a harness around his chest, the pitchman begins his spiel. "Step right up" or "give it a try before you buy" (or even, for other types of pitchmen, "dearly beloved" or "once upon a time"). A crowd gathers, with one or two people, together, joining to start, and others, seeing them standing, joining them as well. In serried ranks, the crowd, the "tip," begins to form – some close, some on the fringes, to be, if the pitch is successful, drawn in. The pitchman engages them, together and individually, and the nervous laughs give way to more involvement as the audience gives their attention and enters the constructed physical space of the performance. The audience may buy or they may walk on, but for a moment or more they are entertained, involved, engaged in the performance.

Since 1993, I have visited more than twenty different fairs and have been part of the audience for over 200 performances. I have photographed and recorded (audio and video) performances and performers and interviewed pitchmen and their audiences. As a literary scholar, I am interested in the goals and techniques of literary artists who translate the pitchman's oral performance art into their written, literary art. As a folklorist, I am interested in the social and aesthetic dimensions of the pitchman's specific contemporary, popular, oral art form.

## The Setting

The fairs I observed, whether held in a street, a fairground, or a gymnasium, are set up to walk through. They are constructed as a pathway (or set of pathways), a passage to be traversed. There is no one place that may be identified as "the fair," because the experience of the fair requires movement through time and space.

The booths are arranged along the sides of aisles, so that stopping to look closely, to touch, or to talk requires moving to one side, out of the flow of the crowd. This arrangement of a passageway with walls of booths promotes a certain pace, which I observed in myself at the first fair I attended. This pace is an even stroll, slower than normal walking speed, yet constant. The booths on one side flow by and are observed, but to stop and engage with any one booth requires a conscious effort. There is an observation of each booth, but very little involvement or real connection.

Another element of the fair as a setting is one that is contained in the description by Thackeray I quoted above. The diversity of the fair, the great number and variety of activities, purposes, and moods – along with the conflicts this type of diversity inevitably causes – are present as clearly at the fairs I observed as at Thackeray's fictional Vanity Fair. It is the conflicts inherent in this diversity, however, which I think are most significant. Between the crowds and the people working the booths (as well as within the crowds themselves), even in the friendliest exchanges, there is an undertone of distrust, a question of whether the deal at the fair is really fair, or the merchandise worthwhile, which would only rarely be found in other commercial exchanges.

No one lives at a fair, and for the people who do live or run a business in the place where a fair occurs, the conflict and hostility (at least the inconvenience) may be even more powerful than for the crowd at the fair (Kate Walter, representing her Greenwich Village neighborhood, explored this topic in her *New York Times* piece, "Who Needs Street Fairs?"). Fairs occur in a space that is made into a different place specifically and uniquely for the fair. The space is fenced and gated, with an admission charge and a ticket required for entrance. The fair is, physically and psychically, a separate zone. Everyone in the crowd who visits this place is a newcomer (a "yokel," according to Thackeray, or a "mark" in traditional carnival language). As newcomers, no one in the crowd, even someone who lives right on the same street, is really at home.

This fact is especially apparent at the county fairgrounds. Here, space – the fairgrounds – is set aside for these fairs. This space is usually on the edge of towns, on the margins. While it is set aside for the fairs, marking them as valued visitors, it is still space set aside for visitors also space set off as separate from the "hometown" region. Most of the spaces sit empty and unused during the off-season. Even when the livestock and crafts contests are considered, we must remember that these are exhibitions of the talents and achievements of people (and animals) who are local to the counties, but not to the specific localities of the fairs themselves. The traveling, independent carnival operators (such as Reithoffer's Amusements or Amusements of America) who inhabit the space during the time of the fair are not locals. However, on the fairgrounds, even the locals are not locals, but the "carnies," in a sense, are.

Connected to this outsider status, to the fact that no one lives at the fair, is the fact that communities, in a way, and to an extent, welcome the fair. Even when this welcome is contested, there is some perceived advantage, financial, nostalgic, or otherwise, in having the fair visit. The fair and the performance that belongs to it are familiar in form, although different at each instance; fairgoers know what to expect. At the same time, they expect to be surprised. The fairs return to communities, and the communities return to the fairs. "You know where the animals are," I heard one woman tell her child, "you've been here every year I have, and a couple I haven't."

In addition, the fair is a zone of excess, and more particularly, of display of excess. From the grand flashing lights and blaring music to the sights and smells of huge amounts of tasty and aromatic food, the fair is where there is much of everything, and everything is too much for the senses. People stand and stare at this excess, watching huge roasts of beef and whole pigs turning on spits, giant Viking ships turning screaming teenagers upside down, and row after row of massive hogs, cows and cucumbers. More than watching, though, people join and become part of this display, buying and wearing large, garish hats, and carrying giant purple Chihuahuas, four-foot-long fluorescent pink inflated plastic bones, or clusters of three orange-headed wonder mops – "buy two, get a third one absolutely free!" All of this excess, its display, and the participation and inclusion of its audience, are elements of the fair as setting in which the oral performance art of the pitchman, with his display of verbal virtuosity, is inextricably intertwined.

## The Performers

Many of the features of the fair as setting connect directly to features of the pitchman as performer. The job of a pitchman as a performer is an intense and challenging one. Many performances have to be presented over the course of a fair, and there is often no clear demarcation of the ending of one performance and the beginning of another. A pitchman has to catch the attention of his audience, hold it long enough for them to hear the pitch, and then close the deal. The appreciation for this type of performance may be expressed by laughter or even applause, but for the performer, the only really valuable appreciation is when the audience hands over some money.

The pitchmen I observed were a diverse group of performers. They had varying degrees of skill and success in obtaining their audience's attention and appreciation, and varying degrees of engagement with their tasks. It became clear, as the research went on, that as in so many other artistic endeavors, there are far more pitchmen than there are talented pitchmen.

I spoke at some length with several of the pitchmen I observed. Time is money for these performers, and time spent talking to a researcher is time not spent performing. I did briefly introduce myself and ask a few questions of all the pitchmen, although more than this was often impossible. Interestingly, the ones I spoke to longest – the ones who were willing, even eager, to take the most time away from their work – were also the ones who seemed to me to be the most skilled and successful.

One woman, who was pitching chamois cloths at the Long Island Hunting and Fishing Expo, told me that she traveled and sold at fairs and expositions throughout the region and throughout the year. She was her own boss, buying the cloths wholesale, and had twelve people working for her, covering fairs that she was unable to attend. She was very aware of her own work as performance, and defined the main skills required: "You can't be afraid to talk in front of people. You have to be aggressive and be able to close. There are lots of people who can make the pitch, but you have to know just when to push for the sale. You have to be able to close." This ability to close, she said, was something that had to be sensed, a kind of intuitive, performative skill. She was unable to train people in this skill, and when I asked her how she did train her employees, she told me that she really just gave them "certain information, the facts about the product" and let them develop the pitches themselves.

As we were talking, she kept the microphone she was wearing switched on, but no one stopped walking by, no one paused to listen. After the interview was over, without noticeably changing her volume or tone of voice, she looked up and said, "Makes cleaning a breeze, you know." The difference between conversation (or interview) and performance was made completely clear: a man walking by with three children slowed and smiled. "C'mon over and take a look," she said. "Care for a demonstration?" The man came to a complete stop, glanced the other way, and walked over to stand in front of her booth. She began her pitch, ended up with a crowd of eight or nine people, and closed it by selling four packages (at ten dollars each).

I observed another example, a negative example, of the principle of sensing the moment to close in a young man with blue sunglasses pitching chamois cloth mops at the Chelsea fair. He gathered large crowds and had them laughing and responding positively to his pitch, but would perform for long periods (four to six minutes) without mentioning the price or asking for the sale. At one point, I saw a woman with money in her hand give up and walk away. The pitchman had missed the moment, failed to close, and the balance of the performance tilted away from him.

At the opposite end of the spectrum, I observed and spoke briefly with a man pitching PermaSeal Shampoo at the Lower Columbus Avenue Festival. He told me he had only been to two previous fairs and was about to quit because, he said, "There's no money here."

This pitchman was more aggressive than any of the others I observed – "Come over here, don't miss this one. You gotta see this. Best bargain at the fair. Special price today." His pitch drew larger crowds for the beginnings of his pitches. As he continued his pitch, however, and some people began to drift away (as I noticed happening with every pitch I observed, at every fair, to greater or lesser degrees), he challenged them with direct questions, "Hey, don't you want to see? All right, your loss." These questions never actually brought people back, and while he was challenging the drifters, more people, who had seemed involved, turned and left. On several occasions, he lost an entire crowd in this way. He had pushed the moment too hard and too soon, and, again, the balance of the performance tilted away from him.

Part of the nature of oral performance art, its direct approach to a present audience that must be attracted and convinced to stay, requires an aggressive, almost hostile attraction. Audiences must be forced, and the force may be aggressive, but it cannot be aggravating. The pitchman must control an audience that is not necessarily amenable to being controlled. This presents difficulties for the performer and defines the performer's character and how he or she is perceived.

All the pitchmen kept themselves, in some way, separate from their audiences. This separation was connected to the fact, which I discussed above, that no one lives at the fair, that the pitchmen are always and automatically outsiders to the community they visit, and only insiders to the zone of the outside, the fair. In *Verbal Art as Performance*, Richard Bauman notes "the persistent association between performers and marginality or deviance," and how performers are separate, "away from the center of…conventionality, on the margins of society."

The pitchmen's separation was frequently physically marked. The pitchmen I observed were marked in some way, generally by their position behind a counter or on a podium or stage. Frequently, this marker of separation was embodied in a microphone, sometimes a large one with a colorful foam head, sometimes worn around the neck and positioned upright in the middle of the chest, and sometimes worn over the head and floating directly in front of the mouth. Other times, I noticed that the pitchmen I observed had some article of clothing or other personal accessory – cowboy boots, a bolo tie, an unusual hat or a heavy silver bracelet, for example – which was unusual and flamboyant when compared to the general appearance of the audience, and of the community in which the fair was taking place. This kind of physical marking was an embodied sign of a difference in status and regard, which was noticeable and ambivalent.

Pitchmen as performers, as someone on display in a contest for control, sometimes needed to present themselves as inferiors, asking for attention from a subordinate position, even setting themselves up as a figure of fun. At other times, even during the same performance, they set themselves up as superiors, with more knowledge and ability than their audience, even condescending to them.

John, a water-race pitchman at the Dutchess County and Bloomsburg fairs, told me that he enjoyed working the water-race game particularly (he had worked several others) because of the numbers of children who played. "I especially like the little kids. I wanna pick 'em up sometimes, help them shoot. Parents don't really like it when I touch them." I had noticed this myself, in observing his and other games. Parents prevented children from coming too close to performers, showing a distinct uneasiness about even direct verbal contact. There is a sense that these performers, even those working the games most explicitly directed to small children (a game with floating plastic ducks, in which "every one's a winner," for example), are not really to be trusted with children.

These performers have a need to balance aggressiveness and pleasantness, sensing the moods of their audiences. The different phases of their task – the drawing in, the holding of attention, and the close – must receive a delicately balanced rationing of time and skill. This balancing, along with its connected interaction with the audience, lies at the core of the successful practice of their performances, and it is a talent that may be separate from the actual content of the performances.

These performers' need for control of their audience is a direct result of the live, oral nature of their art. This control is practiced with varying degrees, varying balances of aggression and flattery, by all oral performance artists. It has consequences and effects for the audiences and for the performances themselves.

## The Performances

The performance of pitchmen at fairs, like other oral performance art, is characterized by particular textual features, most noticeably including repetition, rhythmically structured catalogues, rhyme, and alliteration. Pitchmen also use a kind of exaggerated language and emphatic overstatement. These features exemplify the pitchman's characteristic display of verbal virtuosity; they convey information but also delight and maintain a hold on the audience by the use of sound. All of these techniques and features, all of this virtuosity, are used by the pitchman to enable his successful control of the audience. "You have to have an answer for everything," the man pitching the Painless Hair Remover told me. As I observed, he had exactly that. Even more significantly, his "answers for everything" were generally neatly matched in sound with the audience's questions or objections, or the next point he wanted his pitch to reach.

The use of stock answers to audience questions, challenges, and responses, of repeated formulas strung together differently and with the appropriate elements substituted into the appropriate slots, is an essential feature of all oral performance art. When an audience member interrupted a performance to ask, for example, whether the PVA mop would scrub up scuff marks from shoe heels, the pitchman's response to the challenge included three euphonious formulas, the "thirty-pound soaking-wet string-mop," "lefty-loosy, righty-tighty" and the "ketchup sandwich," which the audience had already heard several times before.

This way of using the performance to control the audience, to allow for any of their responses, continued throughout all the successful pitches. The repeated phrases: "just like that," "make it damp, then you wipe," "thumb on top, that's where your power is," "one hand on the top, other hand goes on your handle, all you do is you turn it," and so on, are a familiar form to the audiences. They become expected and anticipated (sometimes even being mouthed or muttered along with the performer). They allow the audience to feel at home and drawn into the performance, as well as giving the pitchman a way to fill in gaps and make transitions in the rhythm of the performance.

When an audience member asks a question or expresses doubt – "What if it breaks?" or "Seven dollars each?" – the pitchman can respond immediately with a phrase that the audience has already heard and is already prompted to accept – "That's not a ninety-day, not a sixty-day, that's a lifetime guarantee," or "It's not a matter of cheapness, ma'am, it's a matter of true, priceless quality."

Another feature of the pitchmen's performances, which is also a recognized quintessential feature of oral poetry, as noted by Walter J. Ong in *Orality and Literacy: The Technologizing of the Word* and Franz Boas in "Stylistic Aspects of Primitive Literature," among others, is the catalogue, a long list of items, linked together sometimes without connecting conjunctions, sometimes with repeated, not strictly necessary conjunctions. These catalogues work without logical coordinations, using a paratactic rather than a hypotactic structure. Oral catalogues derive their accumulated power and effect from their sound, the oral virtuosity they demonstrate, rather than from any logical, narrative or emotional sense. The PermaSeal salesman at the Bloomsburg Fair made extensive use of these catalogues, often drawing a smile or chuckle, and an extended stay, from an audience about to desert him.

"It cleans Dacron," he began in one such instance, "also nylon, herculon, linoleum. Wool, wood, cotton, canvas, muslin. Rattan and bamboo, and Scotchguard and concrete…." The list went on even longer, although I could not write fast enough to record it all. When I asked him about this listing (he used others – types of stains, products you might try which wouldn't work, and so on), he said, "I just try to make it as long as possible. Sometimes I don't even know what I'll say next, but I try not to repeat myself."

The elements in these oral catalogues often rhyme or alliterate, or are similarly aurally connected, presenting and emphasizing the pitchman's skill and verbal virtuosity. In addition, further emphasizing the catalogue as a virtuosic performance rather than a mere list, pitchmen frequently insert incongruous, unexpected and humorous elements, which emphasize, by interrupting, the aural flow of the catalogue. The EZ Chopper pitchman opens his bowl and puts in "cabbage, carrots, parsnip, potato, tomato, rutabaga, lemon and lime, and obviously I could put more but no one's gonna eat it anyway." These humorous elements are frequently hostile and insulting (at least mildly) or refer to the body and its functions in ways that are not generally considered appropriate or polite in public. The PVA mop, for example "picks up sand, salt, dog hair, cat hair, fish scales, toe nails…."

Often the humorous elements of the pitchman's performance represent thinly veiled attacks on children, wives, husbands, parents, and, particularly, in-laws. With the Sportsman's Dream (a knife set) "you get the utility knife – you can use for PVC and carpeting or radiator hose and still slice that nice tomato – or my wife…. She uses it for bagels." The implication, that the utility knife can slice a wife as well as a nice tomato, cannot be left standing. The moment of hesitation, though, before the bagels are mentioned, and the pitchman's smile and the audience's chuckles, emphasize both the veil (the bagels) and the attack (the slice).

These performances may skirt the boundaries, through humor and innuendo, of what is acceptable. The control the pitchman exercises is threatening to audiences, but some of this threat is simultaneously strengthened and diluted by redirecting it with humor. "Just checking if you're listening" is the way in which pitchmen often respond to audience's laughter at this type of humor, and this kind of response aptly emblematizes the way in which the pitchman's humor simultaneously diffuses and emphasizes the uneasiness provoked by this type of performance.

Pitchmen also use, sometimes separately from these catalogues and sometimes simultaneously with them, other displays of verbal virtuosity. They use polysyllabic synonyms, rattling them off with mellifluous ease. They recite, with relish, drawn out chants and convoluted constructions that roll off the tongue. Their own pleasure in their artistic invention and enjoyment of it, of the creation of impressive sound, is one of the most definitive elements of their performance.

Another technique used by pitchmen, like other oral artists, is storytelling. Many pitches I observed included long narrative segments, formulaically structured, with sequential plots, characters, actions and resolutions. Stories beginning with "I had a customer last year…" or "The other day a guy told me…" ended with "and he came back and bought a whole case this time" or "and after all that, he's still using the same drill bit." What came between these beginnings and endings, the narrative of past experiences, worked as good stories often do, to keep audiences listening and involved, to connect them to experiences and events. Often, the stories were brief, and the descriptions they included were presented in a kind of shorthand, with a small detail standing in for a lengthier passage. The descriptions and the stories, though, were extremely evocative, for reasons that are specific to oral performance art and its familiarity of form.

These stories, and much of the pitchmen's performances, contain specific references to places, events, dates, and people, all of which serve as referential pegs for the audiences. This technique is part of oral performance art's familiarity of form. When a pitchman says to the audience, "let me tell you what happened just across the river in New

Paltz" or "right there in New York City, in Mount Sinai, they're ordering fifteen cases a week," he or she makes the performance seem more real and accurate and trustworthy and gives the audience a feeling that the performance is tailored specifically to them. There is meaning immanent in these descriptions – they call to mind the entire constellation of connections the audience carries from previous stories and previous descriptions – and they can be adjusted by both the performer and the audience to each audience member. The audience knows that their life is part of the performance and the performance is part of their life – as real places they know and identify from experience are called to mind.

When a pitchman's performance is at its best, there is an engagement, a working together of the performer and the audience, and the structured orally composed formulas of the pitch only strengthen and confirm this engagement. This case was apparent in the performance of the chamois cloth pitch at the Long Island Hunting and Fishing Expo, where the woman told me, "When I'm really on, I know just what they're gonna ask, but I can't answer until they do ask it, so I'll just pause and wait for them to come in with the question." Without "them to come in with the question," the performance cannot work. The performance is co-constructed. While the pitchman is the performer, this role is, in the best pitches, actually shared with the audience, and both parties are active and essential.

## The Audiences

The key feature of the audiences for pitchmen's performances is one that I have already peripherally discussed in the contexts of the setting, the performers, and the performances. The audience for a pitch is mobile, shifting, and far from guaranteed. The strolling pace, the browsing mode of fairgoers means that they must be stopped, their pace must be interrupted, in order for them to become an audience.

I noticed on many occasions, every one that I observed, in fact, that the initial approach of a fairgoer to a pitch is tentative and punctuated by pauses. Sometimes people make the actual step (really a stop), and other times they pause only momentarily before continuing their stroll. Sometimes people stay for the whole pitch, sometimes they walk away before the close.

One important aspect of this mobility is that the pitches' audiences almost always consult in some way before making the actual step into the role of audience. Two people will glance at one another, or a single person will look away, towards other people, as they approach the pitch. Joining an audience for this type of oral performance is a negotiated communal decision, which is undertaken in common with another person, not individually.

Several of the pitchmen with whom I spoke expressed an explicit awareness of this to me. "Sometimes one is enough," one woman told me. "It depends on the flow of people, but you've got to get someone to break the ice. Once there's a few people listening, more will come."

This communality is involved not only in the beginning of the pitch, but throughout its performance. In watching audiences, even when the pitch seemed most successful and engaging, I frequently observed a glance, away from the performer and toward other audience members. A person would look away from the pitchman, and briefly check, seeming to gauge the response of the person standing nearest.

At first I noticed this in myself, and thought it was because I was there as a researcher, but as my observations continued I realized it was almost universal, occurring even when the person standing nearest appeared to be a stranger to the glancer. Being a part of an audience for a pitch, it would appear, involves being a part of a group, and being involved and concerned about measuring the behavior of the other members of that group.

This glance is, I believe, subtly related to the outsider status of fairgoers I discussed above. To be at a fair and to be in the audience of a pitch is to be engaged in an activity that, however familiar it may be, is not quite comfortable. There is a discomfort about being a "yokel," which is related to an awareness of the possibility of being cheated or taken advantage of. The pitchman's audience carries an air of caution, of guardedness, and seeks solidarity with other audience members to provide confirmation that it really is safe (and even that it is really morally acceptable) to listen and engage with the pitch.

On one occasion, when a woman had just bought a Kitchen Magic at the Lower Columbus Avenue Festival, she turned to the stranger next to her and said, "You should buy one, too. It's a good deal, isn't it?" This remark brought about another sale for the pitchman and a satisfied smile from the first buyer. She had received the confirmation she needed to be comfortable with her purchase, and the stranger she addressed had received the confirmation she needed to make a purchase. Again and again at the fair, I saw and participated in interactions of this type, sometimes supporting the performer, sometimes banding together against him.

In pitches where there is real cause for distrust (not, presumably, the ones included in this study), such as sidewalk three-card Monte games, it is common practice to hire a "shill," a confederate who poses as an audience member and provides this confirmation. I do not believe that anything of this type occurred at the pitches I observed, but it was certainly clear that the confirmation was needed, and that in successful pitches it did come.

The undertone of distrust, of caution and awareness of dangers in the pitchers' audiences was sometimes more than an undertone. As I have mentioned, questions and even direct challenges from the audience are not uncommon, and pitchmen must handle them. At times, these challenges went beyond subtle distrust into outright hostility. One well-dressed woman yelled furiously at the Kitchen Magic pitchman with his pile of sliced and diced vegetables and cheese, "You should give all that food to the homeless!" "Lady," he answered, "I haven't got the time. I'm tryin' to work for a living."

While this was perhaps not the most effective response to audience heckling, it did get a laugh from the rest of his audience, and it did not allow the heckler to stop the pitch. It also exemplified the pitchman's most common style of response to outright hostility. He used a familiar (almost proverbial) phrase, returned her hostility by belittling her, and answered her directly. He did not insult her directly, which could have led to an escalation of the exchange. He continued the contest for control, using the heckler and his contest with her to engage the rest of the audience further, and redirected the audience's attention to himself. As Amanda Dargan and Steven Zeitlin note in "Turning the Tip: The Art of the Sideshow Carnival Talker," this type of response to hecklers is common – for example, talkers might respond with comments like "I remember my first beer."

In one game in particular, "Soak the Bloke," this kind of hostility is thoroughly used to the "bloke's" advantage. In this game, the "bloke" sits behind a protective netting, above a tank of water, and taunts and insults his audience (sometimes, as the evening grows later, quite obscenely) to provoke their anger. The angrier they get, the more they want to spend money to soak him in water by throwing a baseball at a target, which, when struck, releases a trap door under his seat. While this game is atypical in the amount of anger, of insult, which is not just tolerated but desired, it does typify the ways in which this kind of response is provoked and then used to the performer's advantage.

The audiences know they are being fooled, they know they are being provoked, but because it's "all in fun," they can be hostile and aggressive in a sanctioned forum. The expressions of people throwing baseballs at this "bloke's" target included some anger, but more a kind of embarrassed humor. Some of the roughest jibes (for example, a joke at the expense of a teenaged boy's overweight mother – "Whoooeee, thar she blows!") provoked derisive laughter from the audience, as well as maniacal cackles from the "bloke," but no active hostility, beyond the sanctioned attempt to "soak" him.

The pitchmen's audiences, although they share in the performance of the pitch, both among themselves and with the performer, are nevertheless engaged in a contest for their attention and appreciation. The control of the audience ultimately does belong to each audience member, but in joining together to become an audience, they share some of this control with one another, and more importantly, it is the pitchman's task to take it over for a while. They give up this control when they stay and listen, when they give their attention, their acceptance and ultimately their money, but it is never a complete surrender. There are resistances and rebellions, discomforts and distrusts, to varying degrees and with varying results.

## Conclusion

Oral performance art, with its performers, audiences, and performances, while it is often valorized and culturally sanctioned, as with African griots or Baptist preachers, for example, is also frequently marginalized and transgressive, as with gangsta rappers and beat poets. When people come to the fair, they are already coming to a site where this same contradiction exists.

When oral performers and their audiences create their art at the fair, they are participating in a tradition, a tradition that has value to communities. This tradition includes elements of celebration and nostalgia, of community pride and esteem. In these elements, there are also negative sides. The community is defined and identified against an Other. Attitudes about the Other are reflected in the performers' attitudes about their audiences and the audiences' about the performers. The pitchmen who run children's games cannot be trusted with children, and the audiences who pay pitchmen's wages cannot be trusted with the products – "I only give them an empty container if they want to check the label. No sense taking chances," the Clenz-All pitchman, afraid of being robbed by an audience similarly afraid of being robbed by him, told me.

Leslie Prosterman's "The County Fair Carnival" recounts how people "lament" the "deterioration" of the "nice old" county fairs caused by the carnivals that ruin them. I would suggest, as her historical research concludes, that it is not the carnivals that "ruin" county fairs. The carnival is an integral part of the county fair. It is for both what is transgressive and what is valorized that people come to the fair. And it is both of these that people find in oral performance art.

Oral performance at the fair provokes smiles and frowns, distrust and acceptance, trust and fear, exploitation and enjoyment, because that is exactly the function of the fair as a whole. These performances both define and reflect their specific nature and that of the culture and context within which they occur.

In addition, oral performance art contains referential pegs, a familiarity of form and accessibility, which comes from the fact that audiences simultaneously know what to expect and do not feel entirely confident that what they will expect will occur (or will be pleasant or even acceptable). The past which is referred to in oral performance art is one about which the audience holds ambivalent feelings – nostalgic longing as well as superiority and anxiety. Oral performance art at the fair is a part of every contemporary landscape in post-capitalist, transnationalist America, and it is part of the nostalgia for and rejection of what is "old-timey" as well.

Because of the live human audience, there is also an interplay, growing out of the pitchman's contested control of the audience, which is always present in oral performance art. Richard Bauman refers to "the inherent sociability of performance." However, this sociability (like many other sociabilities) is a striving sociability, competitive and cooperative. There is a struggle for control – an unresolved, active striving for mastery – with the audience and the performer negotiating and together creating the performance. There is also, often, an outright and explicit reference to this interplay – "now I know you're gonna say…" In this way, the interplay is pointed out and pointed up, and the fact that the performer's authority is subject to question is emphasized even as those questions are partially and temporarily avoided or resolved.

The contest between the performer and the audience also includes an emotional and moral charge. There is the fear of approaching the performer, the fear of allowing children to come near. There is the off-color or slightly risqué humor and humorous, occasionally vicious, personal insult. There is a tendency, variously expressed, toward violating or at least teasing out the boundaries of morally acceptable behavior.

At the end of the day, sometimes late in the night, audiences leave the fair. They rarely leave empty-handed, although they often leave empty-pocketed. There is a certain type of exhaustion, a certain type of satisfaction, as well as relief, at the end of a day at the fair. Audiences head for their homes, having been drawn together with strangers and now separated, glad to have attended, and glad it has ended. There will be another year, another fair. There will be another experience of oral performance art, another experience of the pitchman in his context. The pitchman in print, as well, will continue to shock and amaze, delight, threaten, entertain, intrigue, and educate, as long as audiences are willing, even half willing, to

step up, step in
give it a try
give it a spin
we'll see who's the fool
or by golly you win.

*Ride along with Alan Pratt as he explores Bike Week in Daytona Beach. "The decadent and nihilistic flavor," he argues, "suggests that the burden of modern life is becoming ever more oppressive."*

# Modern America and Its Discontents: The Ride-Hard, Die-Free Fantasy of Bike Week

Alan Pratt

The biggest motorcycle event in the world, Bike Week in Daytona Beach, Florida, is a contemporary social mechanism for venting psychic energy. Examining its antecedents and character reveals a uniquely American ploy for mediating the stresses of modern civilization, one inspired by the outlaw biker counterculture, popularized by the media, and, as a direct reflection of the times, successfully commercialized for popular consumption. The decadent and nihilistic flavor of Bike Week coupled with its enormous popularity suggests that the burden of modern life is becoming ever more oppressive.

New Year's celebrations, Mardi Gras, and Bike Week are well-known examples of popular festivals that temporarily relax public order and allow participants to indulge in otherwise discouraged or forbidden activities. These rites of reversal share several features: they are performed in special places that remove participants from the banalities of daily life; they temporarily free revelers from the customary restraints and hierarchies of society; and because everyone is doing the same things, the atmosphere, while sometimes volatile, gives participants the confidence to act out aberrant behaviors (Nachbar and Lause 378).

In terms of creating an atmosphere for unrestrained revelry, Daytona Beach's Bike Week probably surpasses all other reversal rituals in the world today. From its relatively modest beginnings sixty years ago as a weekend affair for motorcycle race fans, it has become ever larger and more elaborate, and ever more difficult to control. Today, it is a massive, ten-day, outlaw fantasy of hedonistic rebellion representing a new chapter in the long history of reversal rituals.

## The Origin of Reversal Rituals

One of the first recorded instances of something approximating a reversal ritual, over 3500 years ago, were the festivals of Osiris in ancient Egypt. In the sixth century BC, Athens sponsored the raucous celebrations honoring Dionysus, festivals filled with feasts, processions, wild dancing, wine-drinking competitions, and ritual obscenity (Boardman 264). During the Roman Empire, reversal rituals like the Bacchanalia, Liberalia, and Saturnalia allowed patricians, plebeians, and slaves, alike, to abandon the constraints of civilized society so completely that the affairs reached levels of civil disorder and licentiousness that are probably still unparalleled (Durant, *Caesar* 66).

Rites of reversal continued to be popular in medieval Europe. The Festival of the Fools included a blasphemous mock Mass, and The Festival of the Ass recollected pagan fertility feasts (Durant, *Faith* 841). The medieval Catholic church found it impossible to eliminate such events and ultimately was forced to integrate them into church activity (Cohen xxiii). Mardi Gras celebrations now associated with the Christian Lent, for example, have their origins in ancient pagan rites celebrating fertility and the onset of spring ("Carnival" 931). And just like those of antiquity, medieval revels (from the Old French *reveler*, to rebel) were difficult to manage. In 1263, for instance, decrees were issued aimed at curbing what was perceived to be the relentless moral decline of the Venetian carnival (Feil). In the twenty-first century, the pattern persists as public revels continue to test moral boundaries.

The long and vexatious history of reversal rituals suggests that the psychological needs that such events satisfy are profound. Sigmund Freud understood why: it may have been easy for the barbarian to be healthy; for the civilized man, the task is a hard one (*Outline* 85). In *Civilization and Its Discontents*, he argued that civilization exacts a heavy psychic toll on humans by suppressing their narcissistic and aggressive instincts (30). With its emphasis on rationalism and secularism, modern civilization is especially repressive; and to maintain social stability, various mechanisms are required to vent or at least blunt repressed needs. Without cathartic opportunities, societies will spontaneously erupt in widespread antisocial behavior or, if draconian social controls are enacted, slowly burn down to a smoldering malaise (*Civilization* 99). Some of the mechanisms Freud describes in *Civilization and Its Discontents* for keeping aggressive instincts in check include voluntary isolation (27), aesthetic pleasure (29), and religion (32). Other strategies he observed are destructive such as nationalism, bigotry, and war (73); and some are problematic such as intoxicants (28). The reversal ritual, a relatively benign substitute satisfaction, uses fantasy as a psychic palliative (23). Anthropologists generally agree with Freud's analysis: public festivals that condone or celebrate antisocial behaviors are beneficial for maintaining social stability (Gluckman 109).

## A Modern Reversal Ritual

While Bike Week is similar to reversal rituals of old, it is different in the details. It is, for instance, strictly of this world; there are no recognized supernatural or pagan antecedents. And whereas other reversal rituals are based on themes drawn from other cultures or the distant past, Bike Week is unusual in that the dominant themes are derived from popular culture, specifically from Hollywood's fanciful vision of the outlaw biker. It is different from other revels, too, in that participants are predominantly male and, in the last decade, primarily middle-aged and middle-class.[1] And, as a reflection of the times, it is a highly consumption-oriented affair. The most obvious feature of Bike Week, however, is that it emanates from, is inspired by, and revolves around a mechanical gizmo.

Raw, loud, dangerous, and supremely phallic, the motorcycle could easily become the central motif for a modern American reversal ritual.[2] Americans have historically embraced technology, and their relationship with the motorcycle is particularly interesting. As one of the last great inventions of the industrial age, it may well have become the primary mode of transportation had it not lost out to automobiles when it became more expensive than the Model T. From that point forward, the machine became increasingly viewed as impractical, little more than technological fluff, and a dangerous form of entertainment. For these very reasons, however, the potent emotional thrills evoked by the motorcycle have transformed it over the years into a ubiquitous icon of popular culture, a fetish for some, symbolizing values associated with power, freedom, escape, high fashion – and rebellion.

## Outlaw Biker Style

Rebellion is one of the defining themes of Bike Week, manifesting itself most obviously in the outlaw biker style. The motorcycle's association with rebellion and lawlessness is a relatively recent one, dating to the July 4th weekend in 1947 when four thousand-motorcycle riders rioted in the small town of Hollister, California (Polhemus 48). In the 1960s, outlaw motorcycle gangs, generally composed of males alienated from the white working class, gained national notoriety, primarily as a result of the violent antics of the California Hells Angels. By the 1970s, motorcycle gangs were viewed as a significant threat to public order and decency.

The motorcycle was far more than transportation for these gangs. A widely circulated police report from the time confessed that it was impossible to understand the near mystical bond between a biker and his chopper ("Dangerous" 16). Easier to understand, however, was the outlaw bikers' basic philosophy summarized by "FTW." (These letters were often seen on club members' clothing and mean "F--- the World.") FTW, the report continued, is their motto and is the arrogant attitude by which this subculture attains its goals and objectives.... They don't want to be like the normal citizen or dress like them. This is why they have created their own dress code, which is filthy, repulsive, and often offensive (14).

While the filthy costume and outrageous demeanor of the outlaw biker were calculated to shock and disgust citizens, the report noted that it also gave him a powerful sexual appeal:

> Strangely enough, an unlimited number of good-looking females, it seems, are attracted to the macho image...to a life which seems as exciting as a roller coaster ride, fast motorcycles, macho men, drugs, alcohol, parties, guns, topless bars, and any-way-you-want-it sex. (23)

The menacing sexuality, penchant for violence, and in-your-face rebellion that outlaw motorcycle gangs exhibited was irresistible to the media, and outlaw bikers made for sensational reportage. In his best-selling *Hells Angels* (1966), for example, Hunter S. Thompson wrote that "they command a fascination, however reluctant, that borders on psychic masturbation" (262), and Tom Wolf's still popular *Electric Kool-Aid Acid Test* (1968) provided yet another lurid but fascinating image of the outlaw biker counterculture.

Hollywood cashed in on the phenomenon by launching a new genre, the biker film. In one of the first, Hollywood's version of events in Hollister, was László Benedek's *The Wild One* (1954). In it, Marlon Brando (Johnny) helped to create the outlaw-biker image when he played a brooding, nihilistic biker in black leather. While his gang terrorizes a small town, he attracts the attention of a respectable girl who is irresistibly drawn to the outlaw biker persona. The success of the film spawned dozens more like it such as *Wild Angels*, *Born Losers*, *Cycle Savages*, and *Easy Rider*.

Freud speculated that criminals intrigue us, at least in books and films, because they can freely pursue predatory impulses without guilt (*Narcissism* 19). That's why we are fascinated by Hollywood's gunfighters, mobsters, rogue cops, Hannibal Lectors – and outlaw bikers. The Hollywood image of the outlaw biker – the chopper-riding savage, the threatening figure in black leather and chains, oozing danger and sexual power – was a heady, intoxicating fantasy, one that captured the imagination of the public and undoubtedly influenced the character of the outlaw clubs themselves. Motorcycling would never be the same, nor would the modern American reversal ritual.

## Commercializing Outlaw Biker Fashion

In a stroke of marketing genius, Willy Davidson, of Harley-Davidson, is credited for mainstreaming the outlaw biker image when he borrowed styling cues from the stripped-down choppers preferred by motorcycle gangs (Yates 134). In the last fifteen years, the outlaw biker image has been the dominant fashion model for motorcycling, and the trappings of the outlaw biker counterculture have been bowdlerized and co-opted by otherwise respectable motorcyclists. In the last fifteen years, coincidently, interest in motorcycles has grown dramatically with double-digit sales increases for nearly every manufacturer.

Every marketing angle is now being explored to tap into the outlaw biker fantasy. The Hells Angels themselves are marketing Big Red, their own brand of custom motorcycles, and replicas of the choppers ridden in *Easy Rider* sell for more than $25,000. Motorcycle advertising frequently encourages readers to abandon social conformity and celebrate the suppressed barbarian. An advertisement for mufflers, for instance, incorporates the image of a leather-clad, tattoo-covered biker emerging from under a three-piece suit and the line, "Inside every good guy there's a real bad ass." Other advertisements encourage bikers to "Raise some hell" or pose the question "Who cares where you are going?" or remind the reader that "You've got the attitude" or inspire him to "Take the Low Road." A Harley-Davidson motorcycle advertisement tells readers, "That's not Silicone, Friend," and no one has been more aggressive than Harley-Davidson in capitalizing on outlaw biker chic. One can even order a nihilistic factory paint scheme featuring grinning skulls. The company licenses beer, dolls, cloths, bed sheets, dishes, knives, watches, and shoes; even Christmas decorations now sport the black-and-orange Harley logo.

Derived from a genuine outlaw counterculture, popularized by the media, and mainstreamed by market forces, the outlaw biker fantasy is now a billion-dollar idea. And the phenomenal appeal of this anti-establishment, rebellious fantasy to an otherwise law-abiding middle-class clearly reflects an urge to escape the onerous constraints of modern civilization. It's a fantasy that, for a price, hundreds of thousands of motorcyclists can act out every spring at Bike Week.

## Bike Week: A Ride-Hard, Die-Free Fantasy

Pilgrims from around the world come to Bike Week, the largest gathering of believers on the planet. The size of the event is unprecedented, colossal – 600,000 in 2000 – and every motel, hotel, condo, campground, and fish camp within fifty miles is booked solid. Parking lots everywhere overflow with motorcycles. This revel boasts the most people, the most arrests, the most dead (fifteen in 2000), and the most alcohol consumed. As with other rites of reversal past and present, some form of intoxicant that reduces inhibitions is crucial.[3] Imagine this: Boot Hill Saloon during any ten-day period might sell two hundred cases of beer. During Bike Week 1999, that number was 8,300 cases (Truett 2). Along with a tolerance for public drunkenness, local prohibitions regarding decency, modesty, and safety are relaxed in favor of an FTW-style fantasy.

It is no surprise that festivals that nullify public order have always been just barely tolerated by their hosts, and Bike Week is no exception. Horrified residents, law enforcement, and emergency services brace themselves for the March invasion. (The Halifax County Hospital, for example, prohibits time off during the event.) "Deadly Week," shouts the 11 March 2000 Daytona *News-Journal* with a two-inch headline, "The Bloodiest on Record."[4] Alarmed editorialists write about noise, traffic, drunkenness, nudity, and criminal behavior – all of which, they argue, seems to slip closer and closer to total anarchy with each passing year. "Boobs, bellies, and beards," one grumbles, "[we can't] sleep through the night without being awakened by a piercing blast" (Hasterok 4). And, in fact, for ten days the rumble of motorcycles goes on twenty-four hours a day as the biker crowd jams the town to the breaking point. Near the beach, traffic is often gridlocked, while along Main Street, the concentrated core of the event, crowds stand elbow to elbow to gawk at the endless, thundering parade of thousands and thousands of motorcycles of every conceivable color and every conceivable decorative motif, including flames, cartoon characters, animals, nudes, sorcerers, dragons, and death heads.

Anonymity helps to facilitate an atmosphere in which norms can be abandoned, so for reversal rituals there is usually some form of costume that cancels or blurs social distinctions. For Bike Week, the prominent costume accessory, commonly associated with the outlaw biker, is black leather. Black leather boots, pants, chaps, jackets, hats, belts, bras, and vests are ubiquitous. (The color black, incidentally, represents the absence of light and has archetypic associations with evil and wickedness.) While the few participants who are actual motorcycle gang members – the fashion aristocracy here – wear their colors, most of the Bike Week leather merely mimics the outlaw biker costume by sporting advertisements for a particular brand of motorcycle and perhaps decorated further with patches and pins available at bars and shops.[5] T-shirts, usually black, often sport skulls, snakes, saloons, vulgar messages, or manufacturers' logos. Silver jewelry, large and numerous rings, bracelets, wallet chains, and boot chains are *de rigueur* for communicating the sexy and menacing outlaw biker style.

The central icon of the event and the requisite accessory, of course, is the motorcycle. The "mystical relationship" that the biker has with his motorcycle, the one that baffled police in the 1970s report, is readily apparent during Bike Week. Most of the motorcycle owners, for example, have replaced quiet exhaust systems with louder, often earsplitting, after-market pipes. Bikers argue that being loud saves lives, but it is also conveniently exhibitionistic, the power of additional decibels enhancing the phallic power the machine embodies. Beyond the satisfaction of thundering from one partying venue to another on a motorcycle, there are biking events everywhere: club reunions, brand get-togethers, contests for best American bikes, British, or Italian, best customs, biggest, smallest, oldest, and rattiest.

As the focal point of the Bike Week hell-bent, lead-and-leather fantasy, the motorcycle is also the centerpiece of daring exploits and destructive celebrations. A common sight is bikers roaring out of parking lots or, less common, doing wheelies on their 600-pound machines. There are also the popular Wall of Death daredevils, like Rhett Rotten, who ride without hands twenty-feet high on the rim of a huge wooden barrel to grab dollar bills from the crowd. Racing at the International Speedway culminates with the Daytona 200 where motorcycles rocket around the banked track at 200 mph. There are the ceremonial "bike drops" where "Jap rice burners" are violently smashed and torched before huge cheering crowds (who imagine they're participating in a patriotic rally). In the burnout pits, particularly bold or intoxicated bikers rev their motorcycles through the gears, filling the air with acrid, black smoke as they burn off the rear tire, the cheers of the crowd lost in the earsplitting staccato from the red-hot engine.

Fueling all this drunken revelry are the most famous biker honky-tonks in the world: Boot Hill Saloon, Iron Horse Saloon, Dirty Harry's, Last Resort, and the Cabbage Patch – and there are a dozen other less well known biker hangouts throughout the county. Mostly empty during the year, they are jammed for Bike Week; and every day and late into the bonfire-illuminated nights, there are free rock-and-roll concerts featuring twenty-five-year-old music that can take "outlaw" baby boomers back to their youth.

Reversal rituals have always included a strong sexual focus. Bike Week is no exception. In fact, it is probably the most sexually charged public revel now in existence. As noted, the motorcycle itself is powerfully phallic and certainly one explanation for the machine's profound allure and the unusually raucous character of Bike Week. Recall, too, that the police report quoted above claimed that the biker image seemed mysteriously to enhance a man's sexual appeal.

It is the relatively few women of Bike Week who provide a focus for the display of ostentatious machismo; and, not surprisingly, the competitions for women are designed to objectify and celebrate female sexuality. There are Miss Budweiser, Miss Jim Beam, and Miss Bike Week contests. Nearly naked women compete in pudding, creamed corn, and cole slaw wrestling events that are witnessed by thousands. No other reversal ritual features biggest breasts, best breasts, wet t-shirt contests, best ass, hottest buns, best topless dancing contests, best popsicle or pickle licking, best banana eating, longest tongue, and nude beauty contests. In these salacious spectacles, enthusiastic women are cheered and ogled by appreciative crowds of mostly middle-aged men, who no doubt relish the opportunity for fantasies of sexual prowess and license.

Bike Week gluttony manifests itself nearly everywhere, and for this modern carnival one must pay a high price to flaunt propriety. The fact is, as a reflection of our consumer culture, Bike Week is enormously materialistic. No other rite of reversal requires so many accessories. As a result of a wildly successful marketing ploy, the motorcycle of choice is the Harley-Davidson, which new runs anywhere from $15 to $25,000. Not surprisingly, Bike Week is an orgy of spending, a whopping $320 million in 1999 (Miller 4), and hundreds of itinerant vendors sell every conceivable carnival accessory. At what other event could Camel Cigarettes merchandise lighters, cigarettes, and, of course, boot shines by buxom women?

The most popular foods of Bike Week also reflect the intemperate nature of the affair. Where else are four-pound steaks, three-pound pork chops, smoked turkey legs, and huge fried sausages smothered in onions so common? Such fare is washed down with thousands and thousands of gallons of beer, often peddled by bikini-clad women who pull cold cans from ice-filled garbage pails. (These positions, incidentally, are prized because the women typically earn more than $2000 in tips.)

## Bike Week and Burgeoning Discontentment

Having fun is serious business, and in the last fifteen years of the current boom in motorcycling, evidence of the popularity of the outlaw biker fantasy is readily apparent. Bike Week is not the only motorcycle rally that is exploding in size. Other established rallies like the seventy-six-year-old Laconia rally in New Hampshire and the Black Hills Classic in Sturgis, North Dakota, are growing ever larger while new venues for the biker-focused rite of reversal are springing up all over the country. Arizona now has its own Bike Week, and there is the new, huge Laughlin, Nevada, carnival and the Myrtle Beach revel in South Carolina. Like Daytona's Bike Week, all feature drinking and feasting, boisterous crowds, loud motorcycles, and the requisite symbols of outlawry, hedonism, and nihilism.

Demographers looking at the size and constitution of the Bike Week crowd might conclude that interest in such affairs is faddish, that it is but another symptom of a relatively affluent baby-boom generation's uncomfortable transition to mid-life. And trends analysts predict that the decade-long motorcycle fad has just about run its course ("Indicators"). There's some truth to both conclusions, and no doubt the size of the event may erode.[6] However, the source of Bike Week's popularity is more complex and resonates more deeply than a mid-life crisis, and unless the motorcycle, as some predict, is simply outlawed as too dangerous for modern society, the event and others like it will continue to thrive.

Freud said there are three sources of human suffering: the superiority of nature, the inherent weaknesses of the body, and the failure of institutions that regulate human relationships (*Civilization* 37). Of the latter, he made it clear that civilization will never work well, and its failures are largely responsible for human misery. Males, particularly, chaff at civilization's demands for social conformity, and they must find or create outlets for satisfying repressed needs.

During Bike Week, the imagery and ritual of subversion and nihilism abound creating a context for acting out a ride-hard, die-free fantasy. For ten days, participants are allowed to show the world what they think of themselves and the world around them, and for many this means assuming, to one degree or another, the exaggerated masculinity of the "peacock" male in one of its most outrageous contemporary manifestations – the outlaw biker. For all of its sound and fury, however, the flaunting of anti-establishment attitudes during Bike Week is primarily symbolic fantasy, and with each passing year a growing burden of tradition continues to formalize the affair. Just as other reversal rituals, then, Bike Week is narcissistic theater, a uniquely modern and American version of an experience that is apparently as old as civilization itself. Accordingly, when it is over, most of the 600,000 "outlaws" must again suppress antisocial inclinations and return to lives of middle-class conformity and respectability.[7]

Still, if Freud is right, then as our society becomes more crowded and complex, more competitive and controlled, the inevitable result will be even higher levels of frustration and psychic suffering. Such pressure will manifest itself as a fascination with forbidden things that will become more extreme, and acts of hedonistic rebellion will become more frequent. No doubt this is true because not just the size and number of motorcycle-focused revels are increasing. Twenty years ago, before interest in Bike Week skyrocketed, anthropologists observed that popular festivals relaxing public order and established standards of decency were flourishing throughout the world while more and more were being created (Manning x). And if the Bike Week-style revel is any indication, reversal rituals are becoming longer, more decadent, more difficult to control, and more lucrative. Such realities suggest that the oppressive burden of modern life is taking its toll and that an FTW sentiment runs deep.

## Notes

1. Of the 5.7 million motorcycle owners nationally, about 60 percent are between the ages of 37 and 64 with nearly half earning more than $50,000 a year and 25 percent above $75,000 a year (Fost).

2. In *Interpretation of Dreams*, Freud wrote that "it is highly probable all complicated machinery and apparatus occurring in dreams stand for the genitals (and, as a rule, male ones)" (391). Straddling loud, complicated machinery, then, has unmistakable phallic authority.

3. Freud rightly concluded that as a tool for curbing aggression, intoxicants have held an especially important place among civilizations: "The service rendered by intoxicating media in the struggle for happiness and in keeping misery at a distance is so highly prized as a benefit that individuals and peoples alike have given them an established place in the economics of their libido. We owe to such media not merely the immediate yield of pleasure, but also a greatly desired degree of independence from the external world" (Civilization 28).

4. Bike Week 2001, the 60th, was a first in that in June 2000 the State of Florida repealed its mandatory helmet law. In the past, Bike Week helmet requirements were usually met with non-DOT approved novelty versions, and, as such, served as little more than another fashion accessory. Replica Nazi helmets were noticeable, as were helmets sporting spikes and Viking horns; and most, if not all, sported stickers expressing FTW sentiments. For Bike Week 2001, approximately one-third of motorcycle riders wore helmets, and many of those were of the novelty sort. Six motorcyclists were fatally injured during Bike Week 2001, ten in 2002.

5. For the motorcycle club member, the leather vest or denim jacket that displays the club insignia are his "colors." (The Outlaws, for example, wear the infamous red-eyed skull above crossed pistons.) These vests also display other souvenirs of accomplishments, parallel in significance to a soldier's medals and ribbons. Real bikers lament the faddish popularity of their counterculture fashion: "And what about what used to be the standard apparel? The plain black t-shirts, the engineer boots, jeans with the little battery acid holes. Remember them? Mostly all gone now. Each item replaced by its designer counterpart to impart a carefree sense of tasteful rebellion. In essence, nothing more than a costume that only gets put on to ride the bike. The vest was a place to hang your experiences. These days that $170 vest is nothing more than free ad space for Harley-Davidson" (Arby 86).

6. Right now Bike Week is primarily a middle-aged male phenomenon. As participants grow older, they will be less inclined to tolerate the discomforts associated with riding a motorcycle. Younger motorcycle riders have shown little interest in Bike Week because the black-leather, outlaw fantasy is not part of their life experience; rather, it is a fantasy of bygone days. Instead, they prefer the streamlined, high technology of "crotch rockets." In this version of the motorcycle-related fantasy, speed and technical superiority are the measure of masculine power. The demographic is indeed shifting. While baby boomers continue to represent the largest market for motorcycles, manufactures are beginning to target riders in their late twenties and early thirties, which means moving away from products derived from the outlaw biker style (Frederick 53).

7. True outlaw bikers are not the kind of crowd that the bourgeoisie want to associate with. The fact is, that even within the context of Bike Week, fantasy outlaw bikers would be afraid or embarrassed to be seen with true desperados. Hardcore bikers are alternately amused, puzzled, or annoyed by the Bike Week phenomenon: "Harleys have become a toy for every yuppie rub [rich urban biker] jerk off out there. They get to play 'Biker' without havin' a clue what it's really all about. A half million people at Bike Week and maybe fifty thousand bikers at best. Like the t-shirt says, 'You used to hate us, now you want to be us.' I just hope there's some of us around when they're gone" (Frog 38).

## Works Cited

Arby. "See no Evo." *Full Throttle.* August 1999: 86.

Boardman, John, Ed., et al. *The Oxford History of the Classical World.* Oxford, England: Oxford UP, 1986.

"Carnival." *Encyclopedia Britannica.* Chicago: Encyclopedia Britannica, Inc., 1990 ed.

Cohen, Hennig and Tristram Potter Coffin, Eds. *The Folklore of the American Holidays*, First Ed. Detroit Michigan: Gale Research Co., 1987.

"Dangerous Motorcycle Gangs." *An Inside Look at Outlaw Motorcycle Gangs.* Boulder, CO: Paladin Press, 1992.

Durant, Will. *The Age of Faith*. New York: Simon and Schuster, 1950.

----. *Ceasar and Christ*. New York: Simon and Schuster, 1944.

Feil, D.K. "How Venetians Think about Carnival and History." *The Australian Journal of Anthropology*. January 1998. http://www.britannica.com/bcom/magazine/article/0,5744,53801,00.html

Fost, Dan. "Growing Older, But Not Up." *American Demographics* September 1998. http://www.demographics.com/

Frederick, John. "The New Wing." *Motorcycle Tour and Cruiser* April 2001: 53-60.

Freud, Sigmund. *Civilization and Its Discontents*. Trans. James Strachey. New York: W.W. Norton and Co., 1961.

----. *Interpretation of Dreams*. Trans. James Strachey. New York: Avon Books, 1965.

----. *On Narcissism*. Reprinted in Freud's "On Narcissism": An Introduction. Ed. Joseph Sandler, et. al. New Haven: Yale UP, 1991.

----. *An Outline of Psychoanalysis*. Trans. James Strachey. New York: W.W. Norton, 1949.

Frog. "The Readers Write." *Dixie Biker* April 2001: 38.

Gluckman, Max. "Rituals of Rebellion in South-East Africa." *Custom and Conflict in Africa*. Oxford: Oxford UP, 1955.

Hasterok, Pamela. "Is This All There Is, Daytona?" *The News-Journal* (Daytona Beach) 10 March 2000: 4A. "Indicators." *American Demographics* January 1999. http://www.demographics.com/

Manning, Frank, ed. *The Celebration of Society: Perspectives on Contemporary Cultural Performance*. Bowling Green, OH: Bowling Green UP, 1983.

Miller, Bonnie. "Bikers' Impact on Daytona." *The News-Journal* (Daytona Beach) 14 March 1999: 4A.

Nachbar, Jack and Kevin Lause. *Popular Culture*. Bowling Green, Ohio: Bowling Green UP, 1992.

Polhemus, Ted. "The Art of the Motorcycle: Outlaws, Animals, and Sex Machines." *The Art of the Motorcycle*. New York: Solomon R. Guggenheim Museum, 1999: 48-59.

Thompson, Hunter S. *Hell's Angels*. New York: Ballantine Books, 1966.

Truett, Richard. "Bike Week's New Faces." *Orlando Sentinel* 26 February 1998: 2B.

*The Wild One*. Dir. László Benedek. Perf. Marlon Brando and Mary Murphy. Columbia Pictures. 1954.

Yates, Brock. *Outlaw Machine*. Boston: Little, Brown, and Company, 1999.

*In this essay, Paul Lindholdt explores the world of rodeo, beloved by some and protested by many others.*

# The Contested Grounds of Rodeo

## Paul Lindholdt

> I rejoice that horses and steers have to be broken before they can be made the slaves of men, and that men themselves have some wild oats still left to sow before they become submissive members of society.
>
> –Thoreau

In the northern Rockies of Washington State, where Ice Age floods carved channeled scablands 15,000 years ago, I wait with my seven-year-old son for the Cheney Rodeo to start. The show's official sponsor has emblazoned its name on glossy programs and arena banners. It is U. S. Smokeless Tobacco, the owner of Copenhagen and Skoal. On the bleachers where Reed and I sit, paint has flaked from decades of hot sun. In our sandals and shorts, ball caps and t-shirts, we are out of place; the coarse slats promise a rash if we lean back. In his tower, the announcer, as though praying for the gathered multitude, names the U.S.A. "the greatest nation on God's green earth." Country music booms at top volume, shuddering the steel frames beneath our feet.

A radio hit by Toby Keith is playing, a militant threat of a song entitled "Courtesy of the Red, White and Blue." Its lyrics reference a roster of enemy nations. "Hey Uncle Sam put your name at the top of his list, / and the Statue of Liberty started shaking her fist." The singer alludes to a hit list, a pantheon of foreign nations soon to fall. "Man we lit up your world like the Fourth of July," the belligerent chorus roars. "It's gonna feel like the whole world is raining down on you, / courtesy of the Red, White and Blue!"

The rodeo season is upon us – the sport living and kicking in the Inland Northwest towns of Cheney, Lewiston, Omak, Moses Lake, and Worley. Ropers, riders, queens, and clowns will be thrashing limbs and stirring up dust in matches that pit humans against much-larger mammals. This pastime gratifies a throwback urge to subdue animals. It also functions to comfort audiences nostalgic for the rough-and-tumble origins of the Old West. In his peeling seat on the rodeo bleachers, my son hunkers down between my legs, his tender eyes sheltered from the sun and his ears from the booming music. It is a hot day.

In the locker room of a health club in Spokane, Washington, bull rider Steve Lebsack peered over his left shoulder, grimaced before a mirror, and dabbed salve on the healing scars from a recent shoulder surgery. It was a morning in late July, the pinnacle of the season for his favorite sport. His afternoon and evening would be spent driving west for some seven hours, across the channeled scablands toward Puget Sound. He would rent a room, rest well, and be cocked and ready Saturday morning for bull-riding contests in the coastal towns of Vancouver, Oakville, and Sedro Wooley. On Sunday morning, he would aim his Chevy pickup back across the Columbia Lindholdt River, across the scablands where Ice Age floods had rushed, to Winchester and Grangeville in the neighboring state of Idaho. Steve weighs more than two hundred pounds, big for a bull rider, narrow at the hips and waist, broad-shouldered. When he competes, he wears a pink shirt with a white cowboy hat, if the weather is hot, a denim shirt and black hat for cooler days. In a fashion flourish common among thirty-something men like him, he wears his hair buzz-cut below and dyed in wispy tips on top. Beneath his tight blue jeans he favors blunt-nosed packer boots, their fringed tongues lapping, their sloping heels slung low. In his bag with his workout gear lay the book *Idaho's Greatest Mule Deer*, confirming him as a hunter of big game. His shoulder surgery would not hold him down.

Healing in her own way that same day, Naomie Peasley was taking notes in an economics class at Lewis-Clark State College in Lewiston, Idaho. A member of the Colville Confederated Tribes, Naomie hails from a long line of horse fanciers, rodeo buffs, mountain racers, and stock contractors. A former rodeo queen, dark-eyed and articulate, she was blazing a trail away from the ranch where she grew up in Omak, Washington, toward some species of financial independence.

A coarse ordeal laid her low in 2002. Galloping downhill in the Suicide Race of the Omak Stampede Rodeo, she fell beneath the hoofs of the other riders' horses. They crushed her skull, lungs, hands, and ribs. Afterward, she damn near died. En route to a hospital in Spokane, she flat-lined twice, her anxious parents sitting vigil beside her in the helicopter. "I still have flashbacks and dreams," Naomie admits. "The start of the race is signaled with a gun, and I get anxious and nervous and scared when I hear fireworks or other big bangs." Like Steve Lebsack, she plans to down a dose of rodeo again, though, as soon as her neck and back pains abate. During the 2004 school year, she played guard for the Eastern Washington University basketball team.

Aside from the rodeo, Steven and Naomie share little else. He is a bull rider, she a horse fancier and a former rodeo queen. He is a Euro-American, a slow talker with an economics degree, who works as a sales representative for the Spokane-based Adams Tractor Company. She is a student, an Indian whose great-grandfather, Leo Moomaw, founded the Omak Stampede rodeo in 1934. Naomie's dad, Larry Peasley, is a stock contractor, furnishing animals to rodeos around the region. In gentlemanly dismissal, he names stock contracting his "expensive hobby." On his ranch, his daughter came of age under the spell of horseflesh, and she still rides every chance she gets. The Peasleys strive to keep ranching alive, adapt to the sport's growing commercialization, integrate Anglo and Native cultures, and define fit roles for women in this male-centered sport.

Inside the thousands of officially sanctioned Western rodeos every year, gender lines are evident. Rodeo queens and their courts heighten awareness of the sport in public appearances. Aiming to be eye-catching in tight blouses and high-domed hats, they are in charge of enhancing the image of rodeo, glamorizing it a bit, and getting the emphasis off the suffering of animals. They ride and preside in barrel races and grand entries. Wardrobes for national rodeo queens (never use the word *costume*) can cost $15,000. While men like Steve Lebsack do most riding and roping, and wear the biggest belt buckles and hats, the women who orbit them, dubbed "buckle bunnies" by unkind pundits, can prove useful for dressing and undressing wounds. Other women, like Naomie Peasley, never seem content simply to flutter, flatter, and adorn the scene.

The queen and her princesses kick off our Cheney Rodeo with a race around the arena known as the wild breakout. They whip the necks of their horses and dirt spurts from the hooves. All six women wear leather chaps (pronounced with an *sh-* sound, as in *sham*) adorned in glitter, fringes, and calfskin bleached and dyed red, white, and blue. Reed and I still are suffering from the heat, the itchy bleacher seats, the noise, the dust. On the heels of the breakout, the grand entry begins; then the women parade to display "the greatest flag of all, the flag we call Old Glory." The announcer in his tower invokes the flag in low tones as though in mourning. When the national anthem solemnizes us all, wearers of cowboy hats doff them and become humble as beheaded flowers.

The show is underway. Wolfy the clown starts making his rounds, goofing in sneakers and suspenders and oversized bloomers, scaling fences maniacally, returning catcalls, flirting with the girls. He wears a microphone, making sure everyone is privy to his wit. The announcer, goofing too, dubs him "a guy who wears makeup. Of course you're from California, the land of fruits and nuts." The rapid prattle from their microphones is lost on my son. Attending his first rodeo, he is frankly bored. A chute opens, a lasso yanks a calf off all four feet and slams it down, and madcap laughter bubbles from the crowd.

Beneath the laughter, the grounds of rodeo are under siege. People for the Ethical Treatment of Animals, in its latest volley in the culture war, dubs a website "Buck the Rodeo." A photo features half-clad *Baywatch* actress Bonnie-Jill Laflin, tousled and unhappy after a supposed roll in the hay, the whole spread captioned by the sentiment that "no one likes an eight-second ride." Rodeo fans, defending the eight-second ride and their right to do it, claim that rodeo enhances family values, brings together relatives and friends, and builds self-esteem that endures a lifetime. To frustrate animal advocates who might blight the fun of rodeo, an industry-supported front group, the Animal Welfare Council, aims to cut such advocates off at the pass. The AWC works to "support the use of animals in recreation, entertainment and sport."

For rural economies that have depended historically on natural resources, rodeo carries the status of custom and culture. It hearkens back to a time when all the skills on display in rodeo arenas had actual application on a ranch. Rodeo filters out the political ambiguities and challenges of urban lives. Rodeo also turns a profit, thanks to corporate sponsorships, a large following, and recent coverage by the mass media, including ESPN and *Sports Illustrated*, and regional newspapers aplenty. Chambers of Commerce also have long boosted rodeo as a homegrown entertainment to market local wares.

Rodeo is an extreme sport. The events include bull riding, bareback bronc riding, saddle bronc riding, bulldogging (aka steer wrestling), steer roping, calf roping, team roping, barrel racing, and more. Steers bred for wrestling can weigh half a ton, while bulls used for riding might run a full ton. These creatures possess intelligence and complex emotions that often prove seductive to the cowboys. If some girls find bad boys hard to resist, cowboys always lean toward volatile beasts. Other extreme sports entail the manipulation of kayaks or bikes, carabiners or skis. But muscular bulls and horses fight back against rough handling, all the more so when flank straps and electric prods make their moods more rank. Stockmen look for bulls and broncs that are resistant, tough, willing to buck. These are the rank trophy animals. The flank strap agitates the animal's groin, and the rider holds a chest rope with one hand. Just before the chute opens, the animal may receive an electric jolt to persuade it to perform. After the chute opens, a game of strength and wits ensues. Rider and mount each want to outlast the other, making roughstock events akin to hunting – a contest to the death.

Several days a week, Steve Lebsack can be found in the gym shaping up for the bulls. He lifts weights and runs, taking extra time to stretch. Already in his early thirties, his remaining days as a competitor are few. "I'm old for this game," he confesses, insisting he will give it up after one more year. A johnny-come-lately to rodeo, he admires Brant Collier, 28, and former bull riding champion Rob Sweeney, 34, now retired and owner of a Spokane-area construction business. Standing beside them, Steve says, he feels as if he's "barely fit to carry their lunch," and he was disappointed not to make the roster to ride the bulls in the Cheney Rodeo this year, a consequence of his low earnings. Bull riding never had practical application in ranch work. It is pure show, although it proves to be the show that draws the biggest crowds and cues the rowdiest songs.

If hero exaltation contributes to rodeo as pastime, there is also reverence for the animals, akin to the respect that some hunters extend toward their prey. Success for individual riders depends on which animal is chosen, in the case of racers, or drawn in the case of buckaroos. Officials, that is, select the names of particular animals to match with competitors in roughstock events. Points get awarded for the animal's difficulty, the rider's technique, and for keeping one hand in the air. A cowboy's flailing arm may get stretched out during a rough ride, or so the announcer at the Cheney Rodeo quipped. A rank bull or bronc earns a rider a higher score, but every ride has to last a full eight seconds to earn any points at all. Steven Lebsack sustained his worst injuries on Slingshot, and veneration creeps into his voice when he names that bull. Maybe Slingshot had been eating too much gunpowder, another gag in the patter that pours from announcers' boxes.

Shoulder injuries are common among bull riders, but less fortunate riders also suffer head or face injuries, making hockey helmets standard-issue now. Collier got "whipped down" once, slammed by a bull's skull, and he has metal in his head. Lebsack carries two plates and twelve screws in his left arm, four plates and ten screws in his face. One has to wonder if patched-up cowboys set off metal detectors in airports or become magnets for Frankenstein jokes. If rodeo is a young man's sport, it is also a game played mostly by single men. Many wives and steady girlfriends would object to such rigorous agendas. When the Cheney Rodeo began on July 9, 2004, Lebsack was flying to Oregon to ride in rodeos in Cottage Grove, Sweet Home, and places in between.

Frank "Bo" Campbell, a government major at Eastern Washington University, rode bulls when he was in his teens and twenties. Now fifty-two, he looks fondly on his "rodeoing" at seventeen years of age and 140 pounds in weight. He moved to Oklahoma in 1970 to study under Freckles Brown, the legendary cowboy and bull rider who is said to have broken every bone in his body but remained competitive into his fifties. Bo wised up and retired decades ago. More interested now in philosophy and politics, more concerned about U.S. foreign policy than bulls, Bo would not have favored the patriotic hoo-hah at the Cheney Rodeo.

"In 1970 I landed funny on my shoulder in Libby and dislocated it," he recalled. Physicians in that Montana town were weary of patching up busted cowboys. And so dislocations sometimes had to fix themselves. "They'd load you up with morphine and wait till it came back." His physician, rushed or impatient, wrenched some ligaments in Bo's shoulder. Bo's injury worsened. "Later my opposite side got strong and pulled my back out of whack, so my spine curved." Finally Bo had surgery, and a big scar encircles the rotator cuff on his shoulder now. Asked how rodeo animals were treated, he admits, "Some contractors took better care than others. Some kept animals in hot pens, with barely adequate water and feed, trucking them a long ways."

Dr. Jim Gjesvold, a veterinarian and former board member of the Omak Stampede, scoffs at the notion that rodeo animals are subject to abuse. Fifteen or twenty Suicide Race riders on their steeds chase down a 225-foot grade of sixty-two degrees, swim the Okanogan River, scramble up a dirt ramp, and sprint 100 yards to the finish line. Since 1983, at least eighteen horses have died in the race, just as Naomie almost died in 2002. Gjesvold claims that the Suicide Race is safer than flat-track horse racing, a claim disputed by both PETA and the Progressive Animal Welfare Society. Still, in 2004, three horses died in the three days of the race. PAWS calls it "the deadliest horse race in North America." Defensive, Gjesvold says, "No horse worth taking down that hill could be forced down the hill. Like the riders, they love to do it." Rodeo has its vocal supporters, some more invested than others. But Gjesvold's comment brings to mind an erstwhile sweetheart. Fresh from a stressful marriage and a husband who had physically abused her for years, she admitted in a moment of sad candor that she felt as if she needed to be injured just to trust that she was loved.

The first rodeos took place in Mexico. The Spanish name for cowboy, *vaquero*, comes from cow, *vaca*. Vaqueros roped horses, bulls, anything that moved, even grizzly bears, which are now extinct throughout the region. Those grizzlies must have thought that they had ascended into heaven when the "slow elk," cattle brought from Europe, began to low among them. Rather than rope their cows, vaqueros pursued and hamstrung them with sharp, curved knives. By 1888, rodeos spread to the United States and Canada by way of Indian reservations and reserves.

For the pleasure of paying customers, Buffalo Bill's Wild West shaped proto-rodeos. Its extravaganza is hard to appreciate today. It featured reenactments of bison hunts, attacks on helpless settlers' cabins, and Custer's Last Stand. Some of the scenes he brought to life, scalping for instance, were grisly. All were patriotic. (Scalping, known historically as "the unkindest cut," did not definitely originate with the Indians, and its derivation is still a subject of debate.) In 1887, Buffalo Bill Cody's pageant toured Europe to grand huzzahs. The 1976 Robert Altman film about him, *Buffalo Bill and the Indians, or Sitting Bull's History Lesson*, stars Paul Newman as the alcoholic Cody flattered by impresario Ned Salsbury, played by Joel Grey. William Cody earned his name by the way he earned his pay: an early railroad corporation awarded him $1.67 for every bison he shot. A $500 one-month salary penciled out to 300 bison slain.

Mexican horsemen were the first buckaroos, in the multiculturalism that colored early rodeos. In the Wild West show that Cody led, Indians like Sitting Bull were objects both of ridicule and wonder. In a competing show, Geronimo, from the back seat of a car, made a spectacle of blasting captive bison, whose meat his employers barbecued up for visiting dignitaries. African American cowboy Bill Pickett, "the Dusky Demon from Texas," as his employer advertised him, invented the sport of bulldogging. At only 5'7" and 145 pounds, Pickett leapt from the backs of galloping horses, tackled fleeing steers, grabbed their horns, wrenched their necks, and bit their upper lips till they gave in. Today's rules forbid rodeo contestants to bite steers. Animal welfare groups won a 1913 battle to outlaw the bite-'em technique that Pickett had learned by watching crossbred Texas bulldogs clamp on the lips of cattle and bring them to their knees. In England, Pickett upset animal-rights advocates, who felt that twisting necks was "horrible steer torture." English police arrested him in 1914 and fined him $25. His boss coughed up the fine, every week, considering it fair trade for all the lush publicity. And so the show went on. Control of nature was in Bill Pickett's blood, and while he was trying to lasso a wild coyote in 1928, his horse stepped in a hole, flipped, and broke its neck. He lay beneath the dead horse for an hour.

Early rodeos held particular values for Indians. Animals, known among some Indians as "Ones Without Fires," harbor powers not given to humans, it was believed, and certain tribes attributed their own gift powers to particular horses. Rodeo also enhanced the skills needed in raiding, which offered the means to increase horse herds. Then, too, wild horses needed to be tamed, subdued or "broken" before they could be ridden. Broken horses also needed to be taught to turn, stop, and accelerate on command. Rodeos in those days honed such practical skills.

The various events evolved partly in Native communities, and so it proved to be a biting irony when certain early rodeos barred Native entrants. High entry fees and long travel times thwarted them as well. They suspected some non-Indian judges harbored prejudices or grudges, awarding them low scores in the competitions, depriving them of rightful prizes. In the pageantry that made up rodeo until recent decades, Natives were consigned to stereotypical roles – mugging in sham encampments, wearing fake headdresses, and mock-scalping peaceful sodbusters. Such roles ultimately proved demeaning, so Indians formed their own organizations, like the All Indian Professional Rodeo Cowboys Association, and their own rodeo events, like the Suicide Race in Omak, Washington. Hundreds of all-Indian rodeos take place every year in the United States and Canada and help maintain traditional ties, much as powwows do. Annual rodeos become ritual occasions. Families and friends return from soft jobs far away, gather and swap stories, compare injuries and awards. An abiding sense of place grows stronger, ancient ties with animals too, in ways that may infuriate activists for animal rights.

Euro-Americans and Natives today are facing protesters when they enforce perceptions that they use animals for needless food or callous sport. The Makah Indian tribe's harpoon hunt for gray whales is only one of the high-profile battle in the nature wars that are being waged across the American West. In 1999, they killed a whale and now display its skeleton in a tribal museum in Washington State. Of those Makah tribal whalers, though, my blacksmith buddy Darryl Nelson said, "If they want to water-ski behind a fifty-foot whale, let 'em have at it."

Western civilization long has followed laws that safeguard animals from harm. Americans can not beat or starve or mutilate a domestic animal without threat of legal reprisal today, may not drive motor vehicles into wilderness areas since the passage of the Wilderness Act of 1964, may not "harvest" or otherwise take threatened creatures since Richard Nixon signed the Endangered Species Act in 1973. Such laws, designed to protect nature, extend it specific rights. We depend on nature, the argument goes, and when we harm it we jeopardize ourselves. Similarly, children exposed to animal cruelty may be damaged by that exposure, in the worst cases evolving into serial murderers like Ted Bundy and Jeffrey Dahmer, who began their forays into sadism with animal abuse.

Organizations like the Illinois-based SHARK (an acronym derived from SHowing Animals Respect and Kindness) are organizing effective boycotts of corporations that sponsor rodeo. SHARK's "tiger video" truck features four programmable LED signs. Its mammoth video screens, one hundred inches high, project images of rodeo abuse. When Indian riders or hunters find their traditional practices blockaded by animal activists, a most ticklish mix of ideologies may arise. So few Americans side with the animal advocates that fur-farm saboteurs and "ecoteurs" have tended to top the lists of domestic "terrorists" for decades. Such semantic sleight of hand mysteriously associates liberators of foxes and minks from factory farms with Middle East "suiciders," as George Bush named Muslim bombers in a speech defending his War on Terror.

Besides traditional military wars and culture wars, there is also the battle between the sexes. Naomie Peasely has always liked to vie against the guys. Growing up riding horses on the steep hillsides of her Omak ranch, she practiced rodeo skills. She also got hurt. "I had a couple of emergency room visits. Just look at my face." The marks I saw resembled acne pocks. "Those scars are from trying to cut off a group of horses and turn them towards home, but running into a thick tree and brush wall instead." Twigs were protruding from her cheeks that day, she claimed, and blood was running down her face. "Yeah, after that episode they called me 'The Woman from Snowy River.' I've also been called 'Crazy Bitch' because nobody seems to be able to keep up with our bucking horses in a rocky, cliff-like pasture except me." Basketball cemented and legitimized her drive to compete brutally. "I have been playing since I was about in the second grade. There was also soccer, baseball, tetherball, and other activities on the playground that I could beat all the boys at." She had always dubbed herself a tomboy, so it came as some surprise to her family when she decided to run for Okanogan County Junior Queen at the age of nine, then for Nespelem Junior Rodeo Queen at sixteen. She won both those runs. She was nineteen when she rode in the

Suicide Race. At the age of twenty-two, finishing her college degree in English Education, she was still attending rodeos, but only as a spectator and fan.

Fitting into the mold of a rodeo queen was not very difficult. "I had to fix my hair. Speak properly. Smile a lot. Sit up straight with my legs crossed; I think this was the hardest thing to remember. Back home I was the same old me. I beat up the boys and sat like one too." She had to show skills with a horse, deliver a speech, address impromptu questions, and appear in "fancy western wear, tucked in, yes. I had a crown and a sash I had to wear in public. I had to ride in parades and go to luncheons." She had to compete.

For the book *Rodeo Queens and the American Dream*, Joan Burbick interviewed women who were queens in the 1940s through the 1990s. In the early decades, the rodeo queens were more apt to be appointed than named winners. Some of them believed that boosters and promoters – out to salvage rodeo's flagging fame – had manipulated them. Others saw rodeo as an opportunity to advance economically and socially. All former queens had photo albums they cherished, as Peasley herself still does, and several of them displayed portraits of themselves in full Rodeo Queen regalia in their living rooms.

Peasley is proud of her family's traditional footing in rodeo. "My uncle Don, who has passed away, was a Tribal Council member. My aunt Patty runs a logging company and has been a secretary or judge of the Omak Stampede and Suicide Race for many years. My granddad, Ed Peasley, was a well-known horse trainer, trader, and breeder." Having grown up in a town known more for its rodeo than for any other cultural or natural feature, she sees little difference between Natives and whites as competitors, and in fact she insists that rodeo as an institution has afforded her an uncommon seat at the table: "It is not really a matter of race. Rodeo is a culture in itself. If you rodeo, you are part of a whole community." That culture entails a swagger. She characterizes it as, "Hey, I'm tougher and more talented than you."

The Suicide Race, known generically as a mountain race, had called her from an early age. Endurance racing is deeply embedded in the culture of the Colvilles, whose large reservation covers 1.4 million acres of wild, rugged lands. She had grown up with many of the former Suicide Race champions, and knew she could succeed against them. "Women had competed in the past," she said. "Either they were in the back of the pack or they ended up where I did, the hospital." Yet she set out to put her proud American boast right there beside the guys. The President of the 2002 Omak Stampede, the late "Cactus" Jack Miller, said Naomie was leading the pack of riders down the steep hill to the river, until she fell at the water's edge. The horse she rode, Black Charlie, had previously won the race, and he might have been too much for her to handle. As he was "setting up" before plunging in the Okanogan River, Black Charlie slowed so fast he ejected Peasley, who had been in the lead and was whipping hard with one hand to increase her speed. She takes complete responsibility for the crash. Miller listed her injuries as a fractured skull, a broken hand and an injured rib. The leader of the pack, she ended up being trampled by it.

In the helicopter bound for Sacred Heart Hospital in Spokane, she was having seizures and ceasing to breathe. Her scalp had a laceration at least six inches long, and she was losing blood. Her lungs had to be pumped to remove river water that she inhaled when she fell, and one lung collapsed in the process. For more than a year after, she needed a neurologist's care. Her ego was wounded, too. "I didn't know how to deal with it, turned to alcohol, and became depressed for months." Cognitive problems continue to compound the emotional distress today. "Names and numbers are still hard for me, when before I never had a problem. This may sound weird, but I had to learn how to remember all over again." The news media were conspicuously absent in the coverage of her ordeal, as if reporters or editors were too nervous to take on the story and risk darkening the already dark cloud that has been gathering over the Suicide Race since it began in 1935, three years after the Omak Stampede itself kicked off. No one seemed to want to call that cherished cultural tradition into question.

The first year after her ordeal, after wrangling with the rodeo, Naomie Peasley returned to the course as a spectator, and "all the emotions came flooding back to me." A part of her strongly wanted to be in that race again. Another part wanted "to escape, to run away, to grab every one of those guys by the throat and ask them, 'What the hell are you thinking?'" When she let loose the eloquent floodwaters of that event, it was hard to shake the feeling that she was speaking as a person who had come back from the dead. A trial-by-fire tranquility invests her; a prophet in long black braids, she alone had escaped to tell the truth. It was tempting to ask how her parents would respond to the prospect of her return to the arena as a competitor. Would they support her as they did before? Buy her clothes, help her train, take her photos, and cheer her on?

Rodeo is in the eye of a storm. It kills and injures many people and animals every year, yet it continues to enjoy canonical status in America. It appeals, just as popular Western dramas in the 1950s did, to people homesick for the stark simplicities of the Old West. By 1959, forty-eight Western shows had been produced for prime-time television. DVDs are still for sale and reruns scheduled for the viewing of *Gunsmoke*, *Maverick*, *Bonanza*, and *The Rifleman*. In the novel *Fencing the Sky*, by James Galvin, a character yearns for "the other world, the world before this world, the way of life that promised never to end and then ended." If fans believe that rodeo enhances family values, it is certainly hard to argue with parents who find roping and riding preferable to drugs, motorized recreation, and a host of other destructive teenage pastimes.

Back in the day of more wholesome family entertainment, chautauquas originated in an upstate New York town by that name. For decades, they proved to be popular outlets for roving educators and entertainers, and they have much in common with rodeos. Both institutions arose in late nineteenth-century America, and both occur in so-called dedicated spaces. Rodeo's space, known as the arena, remains idle for most of the year, yielding only to an occasional tractor pull or demolition derby. Rodeos, like chautauquas, fuse music, dramatic performances, and public lectures. The music of rodeo is invariably country. Its drama comes from clowns in makeup and baggy pants, from rodeo queens in tight jeans and sparkling tiaras and colorful chaps, and from human and animal athletes locked in contests that may end in injury or death. Rodeo's equivalent public lectures issue from homey and wise-cracking announcers who offer moral and political guidance under entertainment's guise. Also like chautauquas, most rodeos occur during the summer, in outdoor settings, as part of a particular circuit. One footloose rodeo contestant's circuit might include six rodeos in a weekend, covering three or more days, several states, and a thousand miles.

Instead of educating in the way of the liberal arts, though, instead of engaging in intellectual views, rodeos build their *esprit de corps* by making appeals to patriotism, conservative values, and the control of nature. Rodeo is a rural diversion, a stunted Chautauqua where platitudes abound and human athletes wrangle with their animals. Rodeo riders are a kind of barnyard drag queen whose spurs, spangles, boots, chaps, jeans, hats, and big-buckled belts are as stylized as stockings and high heels. Formulaic in its trappings, rodeo sells a standardized consumer product, a set of ritual gestures and moves that find their way into mainstream culture through music videos, wardrobes, and advertising. Rodeo embodies a desire for escape to a prior and simpler time when values seemed to be closer to some comfy absolute, and the shock of the modern had yet to impart scars.

Part of rodeo's appeal is that it satisfies a conflicted yearning for a bygone time. It satisfies "imperialist nostalgia." The phrase derives from anthropologist Renato Rosaldo who used it to typify Euroamericans' romanticizing of cultures their ancestors tried to destroy. Such intricate nostalgia allows immigrants to cope with the neo-colonial guilt that comes from being economic beneficiaries of centuries of conquest. Many rodeo fans share family roots in rural landscapes and in the sport of rodeo, a legacy that grew out of manifest destiny, and Rosaldo's definition of imperialism applies well to the American territorial imperative. "The peculiarity of their yearning," he wrote of the nostalgic, is that they "long for the very forms of life they intentionally altered or destroyed." The term *nostalgia* hails from the late seventeenth century, when a Swiss physician combined the Greek *nostos*, a return home, and *algos*, a painful state, to characterize "pathological conditions of homesickness among his nation's mercenaries who were fighting far from their homeland." True to form, the reenactments of wilder times in rodeo events have a certain pathological smack, nowhere more so than in the "dressing" of animals. Cattle or donkeys, goats or sheep, more rarely horses or bulls, will be made to wear hats or frilly shirts. Such an act of humanizing the animal, and in the process demeaning it, is the ultimate expression of culture over nature. It is the complicated behavior of humans who seeking to vanquish more-powerful beasts.

Rosaldo identifies "a particular kind of nostalgia, often found under imperialism, where people mourn the passing of what they themselves have transformed." In the case of rodeo, that past includes generations when cattle roamed free on the plains, when Natives were not demoted to reservations, and when wildlife encountered no barbwire, guns, or knives. An original function of the cowboy boot was to guard against snakebite, but the tables now have turned. In an ad for cowboy boots, a rattlesnake, subdued beneath the heel of the boot, is used to market the same boot that subdues it. In that ad, a hand reaches down with a big knife to behead the vanquished snake.

Rosaldo analyzes how "someone deliberately alters a form of life, and then regrets that things have not remained as they were prior to the intervention. At one more remove, people destroy their environment, and then they worship nature." At a further remove, every American has witnessed the subtle ways we help to bring about the end of nature in formerly wild places, and then name cars and shoes and office parks after those same razed places and exterminated species.

It bewilders, the process of yearning for what one has destroyed, but rodeo as a cultural category had to be invented. Rosaldo reminds us that "during the last decade of the nineteenth century, as the frontier was closing, racism was codified and people began to deify nature and its Native American inhabitants." Although the frontier has long been closed, rodeo remains a forceful demonstration that the frontier's sense of wildness and rank possibility may still be conjured up.

The quest to subdue animals, if only for the eight seconds of a ride on a bucking bronco or pinwheeling bull, confirms the rodeo contestant in his more elevated identity and bestows upon him the powers of those bareback beasts. Just as the successful hunter comes to identify with his prey, so does the rodeo rider. In Richard Slotkin's fitting phrase, it is a form of "regeneration through violence." The rodeo bull's master borrows traits from the bull, just as the rider of a racehorse takes upon herself the fleetness of her steed. Few people have the capacity, Rosaldo notes, both to "yearn for the old ways and acknowledge their warrior role in destroying them."

Today in North America, when the non-animal Cirque du Soleil has a broader following than the other circuses do, rodeo still draws audiences. Supporters claim it is the most popular spectator sport on the continent, surpassing football in the United States and hockey in Canada for the number of paying watchers it draws. As hard as this claim may be to believe, many Americans had an equally hard time believing that George W. Bush would be elected for a second term by margin of 3.5 million votes. Rodeo's leisure and liberty go hand-in-hand with Texas, the home of President Bush, and imperialist nostalgia might help explain support for both American institutions.

Attending the Cheney Rodeo with my son, we stray behind the bleachers to find him some late lunch. At every fast-food stand the smoke curls up, grilled and barbecued meat and more meat, a food we don't eat. Reed settles on fry bread, a doughy pastry sold on a paper plate by an Indian man who is overweight and sweating. Grease speckles his thick lenses. The fry bread is yummy, Reed says, crisp on the outside, soft within, drizzled with honey and loaded with carbs. It is just what he needs after our ordeal of a drive through the channeled scablands, an afternoon in the hot sun, and the blitz of stimuli from speakers high on poles around the grounds. He has seen animals ridden, roped, panting, spurred and jerked. He has watched the clouds of dust rise from their fun.

*In "From Beatniks to Britney and Beyond," Joshua Long and R. Dawn Hawley state, "In a very real way, the evolution of the American coffeehouse has emerged as reflective of American popular culture. From the counterculture emergence of the 1960s, to the materialization of new consumption cultures in the 1980s, to the postmodern consumerism of recent years, socio-cultural paradigm shifts have paralleled the creation of unique social space within the coffeehouse. Today, there is little question that the coffeehouse landscape has become an important feature of American popular culture."*

# From Beatniks to Britney and Beyond: The Socio-cultural Evolution of the American Coffeehouse

Joshua Long and R. Dawn Hawley

Each day, Americans drink over 300 million cups of coffee (SCAA). The American love affair with coffee has endured a long and intricate history, but in recent decades the mechanisms of consumption have become increasingly complex and multidimensional. In previous years, the majority of gourmet coffee consumed in the United States was still home-brewed, but 2005 marked the first year in which over 50 percent of gourmet coffee was purchased away from the home (Abelson; NCA; SCAA). As the number of coffeehouse patrons has increased, so has the diversity of consumption sites – a process that has mirrored the appearance of parallel cultures of consumption.[1] In a very real way, the evolution of the American coffeehouse has emerged as reflective of American popular culture. From the counterculture emergence of the 1960s, to the materialization of new consumption cultures in the 1980s, to the postmodern consumerism of recent years, socio-cultural paradigm shifts have paralleled the creation of unique social space within the coffeehouse. Today, there is little question that the coffeehouse landscape has become an important feature of American popular culture.

In our current age of Starbucks and Internet cafes, it is difficult to imagine a world without baristas, frothed milk, or cardboard cup sleeves. Coffee has long been a staple of the American diet, but our popularized fixation with the specialty cup has created eclectic cultures of consumption that would have shocked even the most diehard Berkeley beatnik. Propelled by the growth of corporate giants and fostered by niche independents, the coffeehouse has become a trendy, iconoclastic social hub. Tracing its roots to the counterculture cafe of the 1960s and the corporate consistency made famous by Howard Schultz, the American coffeehouse has become a widespread and *expected* cultural phenomenon. At the onset of the 1990s there were just over 500 coffeehouses in the United States. By 2005, there were an estimated 18,000 (SCAA). The exponential growth that occurred in the late 1990s is just as revealing of a cultural phenomenon as it is a corporate marketing success. As the number of coffeehouses multiplies daily, it becomes increasingly important to investigate the place – and even *placelessness* – of the American coffeehouse, and to see the changes demonstrated by niche and corporate establishments as they make their transition into icons of popular culture.

## The Recent History of the American Coffeehouse

The socio-cultural importance of the American coffeehouse is well over a century old – some would argue older.[2] But it was in more recent decades that the coffeehouse became a pronounced symbol for cultural identity. During the 1950s and 1960s, beat generation writers facilitated a cultural movement that attracted a new generation wedged between the disillusionment of World War II and the controversy that would become Vietnam. The works of Burroughs, Kerouac, and Ginsberg garnered a cultural following that required a safe social space in which to communicate "radical" ideas. As a result, in cities like San Francisco and New York, the coffeehouse began to take on a new form. The diner image of 1950s coffee shops was abandoned for dimly lit, smoke-filled cafes where "poets of the movement" read aloud and penny philosophers debated (Gitlin xiv; McNamara 317). As the beat generation gained popularity, and the conflict in Vietnam heightened, the counterculture movement eventually spawned other groups in need of the social sanctuary of the coffeehouse. The New Bohemians in Greenwich Village could now drink espresso and write songs in the safe space of places like the *Limelight* or the *Peacock* (Pendergrast 266). In Berkeley, *Peet's Coffee and Tea Company* became the popular west coast hang out for the hippies of the 1960s and 1970s, where they were more commonly referred to as "Peetniks" (Abecassis 16).

While some of the earlier establishments seemed wary of the counterculture audience they were attracting, others realized the commercial viability of these groups and quickly created an atmosphere that would cater to the emerging demographic. What had been a movement tolerated by cafe owners was fast becoming a new business trend. The new coffeehouse – the counterculture coffeehouse – was appearing in large numbers, attracting groups like the hippies, beatniks, and new bohemians. As a result, the term "coffeehouse" became synonymous with the counterculture crowd in the minds of many

Americans – a seemingly negative stigma which would prove useful in the creation of a future niche trend.

The counterculture coffeehouse continued to exist throughout the 1980s, but hippies and beatniks were soon overshadowed by a new cultural phenomenon – that of the "yuppie," the young, upwardly mobile, urban business professionals who were widely regarded as materialistic. Despite the apparent cultural contrast, the yuppies fueled the coffeehouse movement by demanding specialty coffee, subsequently increasing the marketability of the industry. While most yuppies spent little or no time in the coffeehouse, this emerging culture of conspicuous consumption increased the demand for higher quality beans. Indeed, during this time the rhetoric of gourmet coffee translated into a form of cultural capital to be exchanged as a class demarcation (Mathieu 123). The coffeehouse entrepreneurs seemed to recognize the importance of differentiating between the safe social space loved by the counterculture crowd and the landscapes of gourmet consumption relished by others. As a result, the American coffeehouse scene soon splintered, reflecting either corporate mores or counterculture ideals. While numerous owners took notice of the differing coffeehouse cultures, one envisioned a coffeehouse that would become a popular culture icon through the creation of what has been dubbed "placeless" social space (Smith 503).

When Howard Schultz began working for Starbucks in Seattle in 1982, it was a small but reputable purveyor of coffee beans. Starbucks was not truly a coffeehouse at this point, and the original owners disapproved of any expansion that would involve them in the "restaurant business" (Kotha and Schilling). It was the owners' resistance to expansion that pushed Schultz to open his own coffeehouse, *Il Giornale*, in 1985. Inspired by a 1983 trip to Italy, Schultz recognized the potential for translating the romanticized image of the Italian cafe into an American institution. Within three years of opening *Il Giornale*, Howard Schultz had purchased the original Starbucks chain, applied the name to his existing *Il Giornale* locations, and expanded to markets in Vancouver and Chicago. Within the next decade, Starbucks became a household name and had subsequently created a clear social rift between coffeehouses patronized by two dichotomous cultural groups.

Without question, Howard Shultz's brainchild served as a catalyst for what became the 1990s corporate coffeehouse movement – a cultural phenomenon that has seen not only the emergence of new coffeehouses, but also coffeehouse cultures. Curiously, the coffeehouse corporation that, in many ways, defined itself against the counterculture crowd, has spawned a growth of niche independents popular because of their *anything-but-Starbucks* attitude (see Thompson and Arsel). A popularized anti-corporate idealism has fueled the demand for alternative coffeehouses throughout the United States, and the result has been coffeehouses that have created loyal – and at times cultish – followings. Alternatively, the obvious success of Starbucks has spawned a new wave of corporate chains that seek to mimic the Starbucks expansion strategy while marketing a unique image. The following sections discuss some of the generalizations still apparent on both sides of the coffeehouse rift, but more importantly, discuss how the widespread popularity of the industry is continuing to facilitate the emergence of new coffeehouse landscapes.

## The Coffeehouse as Corporate Consistency

In contrast to counterculture coffeehouses, most corporate chains depend on uniformity, consistency, and convenience to attract their consumers. For this genre, there is no better example than the aforementioned Starbucks. From its humble beginnings in Pike Place market, Starbucks has become the idealized model for corporate expansion. With more than 9,500 retail locations worldwide and an expected 1800 new stores in fiscal 2006, Starbucks has become the world's largest coffeehouse chain.

An analysis of the Starbucks landscape is an analysis of highly effective corporate marketing and design. Fundamentally, Starbucks offers consistency, comfort, and convenience. Deeper examination, however, reveals a deliberate strategy offering escapism, luxury, and an implied sense of sophistication. These key themes, repeatedly conveyed in Starbucks around the globe, have become a benchmark of postmodern design in the coffee industry. Subsequently, they have led to a design and marketing revolution that has influenced a multitude of coffeehouses, both corporate and independent (Thompson and Arsel 631).

When Howard Schultz first envisioned the new Starbucks in the early 1980s, his main goal was to bring the prototypical European coffeehouse model to the United States, albeit with the Americanization of certain design characteristics (Smith 504-508). To have a taste of Italy in Pike Place Market, to escape from the rigors of urban living to the sophistication and leisure of the Old World – these are the ways in which Starbucks provided a place of respite. This creation of removed space – detached in sense and experience from its surrounding environment – is what makes Starbucks a unique, comfortable place to be. Ironically, the subsequent repetition of this formula is also what makes Starbucks "placeless." The Starbucks escapist experience can happen anywhere, regardless of the consumer's physical location; the corporate chain is ubiquitous.

When we step into a Starbucks, we are confronted with what is essentially an escape vaguely evocative of Europe, but with all the comforts necessitated by a "globally connected" American culture. Many of the same walls that contain internet outlets are often adorned with black and white photographs, chosen to hint at the sophisticated placidity of the Old World. The Venetian Gondolier cruising slowly down narrow water channels, the stoic face of an aging Italian proletariat drinking his morning espresso, the snapshot of young lovers in a pigeon-crowded Piazza San Marco – all of these visions promise an escape as affordable as a *venti* cup of Starbucks' smartly named Cafe Verona.

Also heightening the escapist environment is the regular practice of territorializing coffee beans. This marketing strategy conveniently adds a mental place association, most often of an exotic, far-away locale. Starbucks "designates, evaluates, and organizes coffee production according to its own taxonomy of regions" (Smith 516). By including the place name and geographical origin of each of their brews, Starbucks creates an exoticism that brings sophistication and luxury to the typical cup. Instead of drinking a common cup of joe, Starbucks patrons enjoy the luxury of imbibing Indonesian Sulawesi, Ethiopian Yergacheffe, or Arabian Mocha Sanani. To add further place meaning to the coffee names, the company adorns each brew or blend with an idyllic statement about the particular type of bean that is offered. These lyrical captions seem vaguely reminiscent of a dime store romance novel. A paragraph about Zimbabwe beans speaks of "bold African skies," "plains at sunset," and "lions, cheetahs, and elephants [gathering] beside watering holes" (Starbucks).

While innovative coffee taxonomy, deliberate design, and the territorializing of beans and blends add to the international and exotic mystique of Starbucks coffeehouses, the formulaic repetition of these ideas adds a contradictory element to the Starbucks sense of place. While each Starbucks location unquestionably represents place – or at least the fantasized image of place – there are rarely any distinguishable characteristics between Starbucks coffeehouses. For each of the almost 10,000 stores around the globe, a specific layout and decor is generally outlined by the corporation. Adherence to these design layouts and the formulaic replication associated with franchising has allowed Starbucks to become one of the most recognizable institutions in the world, a phenomenon once restricted to chain retail stores and fast food restaurants.

In this way, most loyal Starbucks patrons become members of a "corporate culture," a culture that has been created and perpetuated by corporate consistency and corporate symbolism. A Starbucks patron in Seattle can order the same beverage, by the same name, with the same logo on the cup, in the same atmosphere as the Starbucks patron in Montreal. This fact does not imply that Starbucks customers have no real sense of attachment to their favorite coffeehouse. Without question, Starbucks patrons are at times fiercely loyal to the corporation that provides them their morning jump-start and have even been known to plan trip routes with regard to Starbucks availability. Starbucks has proven that product and corporate loyalty supersede established place loyalty for those consumers who value convenience and consistency.[3] Indeed, Starbucks has itself become a pop-culture icon. Analysts agree that the Starbucks logo is now one of the most recognizable images in the world, and iconization on such a scale carries with it an overwhelming amount of cultural significance (Holmes).

## The Coffeehouse as Counterculture Hub

The corporate revolution has, however, had its detractors. In keeping with the "traditional" anti-establishment or counterculture coffeehouses of prior generations, contemporary independents have created a strong place in the American landscape and have reemerged as a major facet of American culture. The bohemian cafe of the 1960s can be found just as readily in Berkeley, California, as in San Marcos, Texas. Adorned with used furniture, chalkboard menus, and cigarette ash-dusted tables, the counterculture cafe of the present is a sanctuary for the liberal minded. New age bumper stickers decorate the walls alongside rotating art displays in this promised land flowing with soy milk and turbinado. Woe to the patron who orders anything "vente" or "doppio." "Starbuckian" is not spoken here, and if you look closely at the tip jar, "ihatestarbucks.com" has been scrawled below the larger, more colorfully written "Instant Karma."[4] The above description is obviously replete with stereotype, but the commonalities between these establishments and the socio-cultural groups that patronize them should not go unnoticed. For instance, these coffeehouses engender an anti-corporate mentality – a popularized idealism that is a common localist attribute of the counterculture crowd. Whether in a downtown Portland punk cafe, or in a musician's coffee klatch in Austin, there persists an overall distrust of the "establishment" among counterculture patrons. Often it is the distrust of a company's devotion to the bottom line that bothers many patrons, an idea that was repeatedly expounded upon during research and interviews.[5] It should be noted that many of these locales gain their image by defining themselves against larger corporations. As with anti-establishment movements, the counterculture coffeehouse relies on an "othering" of what could be perceived as mainstream American consumerism. The irony, of course, is that many patrons of these establishments are themselves fostering a form of conspicuous consumption.

A common feature of the counterculture coffeehouse is its displayed commitment to the environment and its outspoken support of ethical practices in the coffee trade. Many of these establishments regularly advertise the fact that they recycle, and most provide fair trade and organic selections. Interestingly, this attitude carries over into the overall atmosphere and space of the coffeehouse itself. To borrow from one independent coffeehouse patron in Flagstaff, Arizona, "This coffeehouse has such an organic feel." In this particular interview, the subject was attempting to describe the difference between her coffeehouse and others in the same city. Whereas some chains seemed "sterile" and "uninviting," her coffeehouse was "organic" and "natural." Dusty wooden floors and second-hand furniture provide a contrast to the comparably clinical look of the local corporate chain, and this visual perception carries multiple layers of meaning for the consumer.

Even though several corporate chains offer organic, fair trade, and shade grown selections, many counterculture consumers overlook these features because of the antiseptic, "corporatized" image. By contrast, the tolerant, open-minded, and/or "organic" image projected by the counterculture coffeehouse provides a visual litmus test for the large number of consumers who search for specific social messages in the spatial landscape. To many consumers, "organic" and "natural" are ideological messages to be communicated through the social space of the coffeehouse. When asked to describe why they were first attracted to the coffeehouse, some patrons "knew" they would like this place when they saw the band flyers on the poster board, the political bumper stickers on the wall, or the numerous vegan and vegetarian selections in the display case. In a sense, all of these features become cultural symbols within the coffeehouse, combining to create a spatial landscape that communicates specific messages to potential and returning patrons.

Probably the most significant feature of the counterculture coffeehouse is not a spatial feature, but instead a cultural characteristic. Patrons often display an intense personal attachment to their local coffeehouse. This attachment goes beyond consumer brand loyalty, creating a sense of community based around the place rather than a placelessness of the corporate coffeehouse. Research revealed that in some cases, the coffeehouse environment fostered specific cultural traits. This materialized in different ways. Often, the core patronage dressed alike, shared political attitudes, and formed a distinct kinship system.[6] Certainly, research indicated that counterculture coffeehouses depend not only on image building, but also on the social networks that focus around the place or environment of the coffeehouse and its safe social space.

## The Coffeehouse as Pop-Culture Icon

> Niles: Double cappuccino, half-caf, not-fat milk, with just enough foam to be aesthetically pleasing but not so much that it leaves a moustache.
> Waiter: Cinnamon or chocolate on that?
> Niles: Oh they make this so complicated. Um, cinnamon.
>
> - NBC's *Frasier*, "A Midwinter Night's Dream"

Somewhere during the 1990s, the coffeehouse became a pop-culture phenomenon that was fast outgrowing classifications like *corporate* and *counterculture*. While these monikers were still applicable to many establishments, hybridized and novel coffeehouse landscapes emerged that were not easily categorized. As coffeehouse consumption increased, so did the specialization of the industry in an attempt to target niche demographics. In many ways, popular media helped to drive this phenomenon, creating place and space identification, and connecting in or across social space. The coffeehouse of primetime television, for instance, not only showcased contemporary trends in the coffee industry, it has helped fuel a new generation of patrons who considered the local cafe to be the social space of choice. In some respect, the sitcoms that have featured a coffeehouse have also reflected changes in the coffeehouse landscape. When *Seinfeld* debuted in 1989, there was no mention of "lattes" or "macchiatos." Instead, the key characters visited "Monk's Cafe," a traditional New York diner without the frills evident in shows aired just a few years later (after the number of coffeehouses in the U.S. had twice doubled). *Friends*, which debuted in 1994, showcased a casual coffeehouse where the main characters lounged on couches and sipped jumbo lattes.[7] As the decade closed, the writers of *Frasier* were setting more and more scenes in "Café Nervosa," a Seattle coffeehouse where ordering the perfect cappuccino was satirized as an aristocratic art form.

The popular image of the coffeehouse has not been limited to the small screen. From *What Women Want* to *Miss Congeniality* to *You've Got Mail*, several movies have filmed both pivotal and conventional scenes in the confines of the coffeehouse. Ironically, despite the unabashed product placement displayed in most of these mainstream films, it is often overlooked because the scene on film so closely resembles an everyday coffeehouse experience for much of the population. Film critic Roger Ebert noticed this in a 1998 review of *You've Got Mail*, when he said "The characters walk into Starbucks and we never for a moment think 'product placement!' because, frankly, we can't imagine them anywhere else" (rogerebert.com).

Within ten years, the sitcom coffeehouse had made the transition from traditional diner, to trendy coffee hangout, to sophisticated bistro. Art is both imitating reality and fostering a climate for new fads or identities in coffee consumption. For instance, companies like Peet's – once an icon of the Berkeley beatnik – recently expanded with a new, worldly image focused on attracting the sophisticated consumer. With over ninety stores across the U.S., Peet's counterculture roots draw a sharp contrast to the coffee connoisseurs and urban foodies who now frequent the establishment.[8] The Coffee Bean & Tea Leaf, once a local whole bean and loose-leaf tea purveyor, has seen an incredible growth in sales after gaining the reputation as the coffeehouse of choice for entertainment stars like Ashton Kutcher, Madonna, the Olson Twins, and pop singer Britney Spears, who reportedly requested a latte flown by jet to an out-of-town concert (Boyce).

As the number of coffee outlets continue to increase, new trends have emerged in the specialty coffee industry that actively deviate from both the corporate and counterculture image in order to garner mainstream acceptance. Independent coffeehouse entrepreneurs have capitalized on popularized trends and quickly expanded, donning new themes and creating new atmospheres to cater to unique demographics. Whereas coffeehouse institutions like Peet's and Coffee Bean & Tea Leaf have redefined their image with new advertising and marketing strategies, those new to the industry have taken advantage of the latest factionalized niche created by highly specialized cultures of consumption.

Many coffeehouses now seem to focus on attracting a core following that – like the corporate and counterculture cafes – identify with each other both socially and culturally. Similar to the more commonly observed social specialization of bars and nightclubs, coffeehouses are increasingly appealing to unique demographics. The result is a sweeping pop culture phenomenon factionalized to meet the individual needs of specific cultures of consumption. Some examples include a completely wireless coffeehouse in Lawrence, Kansas, where the laptop crowd goes to get connected; a "bubble tea" and espresso bar in Columbia, Missouri, that attracts teens and college students with its innovative design and unique tea concoctions; a Spanish-only coffeehouse in Phoenix that serves Latino fare; a franchised, Christian coffeehouse in Portland, Oregon, that sponsors bands and holds weekly prayer meetings.

It is important to note that the diversification of contemporary coffeehouses has not diluted the image of the coffeehouse as a pop culture phenomenon. Instead, many still perpetuate similar traits, and in some cases, appropriate the social symbolism of the coffeehouse. Ten years ago, the words "barista," "half-caf," "macchiato," "crema," and "venti" were unknown to the majority of Americans. Now they are the essential lexicon of coffeehouse patrons across America and are a part of everyday vernacular in advertising and popular media. Indeed, even the social significance of the word "coffeehouse" is so strong it has been appropriated as a pop culture icon in cyberspace, where the term is synonymous for thousands of internet chat rooms, fan sites, and religious forums. Today, there is either a tangible or symbolic coffeehouse available to every kind of consumer, even those who don't drink coffee.

## Conclusion

The recent history of the American coffeehouse is easily traceable to its roots in counterculture idealism and corporate consistency, but these quintessential forms no longer dominate the coffeehouse landscape. What was once a social space regularly associated with one or two identifiable groups is now a popular culture icon appropriated and specialized in order to target numerous unique cultures of consumption. While corporate and counterculture still remain important archetypes, coffeehouses landscapes are not as easily catalogued as they were just two decades ago.

The diversity of coffeehouse landscapes speaks volumes about what might be the most significant feature of the present day coffeehouse: its popular image. Appropriated and romanticized by mass media, the imagery of the coffeehouse has been transformed into a pop culture icon – a social symbol recognized throughout America. As a result, the social significance of the coffeehouse will likely persist, and the image of the coffeehouse will certainly continue to evolve. Simply put, two key attributes of the American coffeehouse – its social significance and its relatable iconography – will perpetuate its popularity. The nostalgia of the coffeehouse will continue to reinforce its position as an important feature of the American landscape, and the popular imagery of the coffeehouse will both maintain traditional patronage and spawn new, specialized cultures of consumption.

## Notes

1. *Coffeehouses* are defined as those establishments whose chief sale product is coffee or coffee-related beverages and foods, and in this case those establishments that provide some form of seating or space for their patrons.
2. Daniel Webster was once noted as saying that Boston's coffeehouse, the *Green Dragon*, was the "Headquarters of the Revolution" since before the Tea Party (Ukers 613-614; Pendergrast 15).
3. Furthering this idea is the news that Starbucks plans to expand the number of drive thru locations throughout the United States and Canada (Gillespie).
4. These generalizations are remarkably accurate considering the sheer number of counterculture coffeehouses throughout the U.S. During a research trip from Flagstaff, Arizona, to Columbia, Missouri, we noted easily identifiable counterculture cafes in Albuquerque, New Mexico, Norman, Oklahoma, Oklahoma City, Oklahoma, Wichita, Kansas, Lawrence, Kansas, Kansas City, Kansas, and Columbia, Missouri. The use of "counterculture" as a taxonomy for this type of establishment creates problems in and of itself. Certainly, there is a diversity of coffeehouses that fit under this term. But while the landscape of each location is unique, certain spatial characteristics seem to permeate this

genre. Additionally, ethnographies of these establishments have revealed specific cultural characteristics unique to the patrons of each coffeehouse.

5. Perceived as "unethical," "money-hungry," and "elitist" by counterculture patrons, Starbucks did not receive positive marks during interviews. Interestingly enough, when asked to supply adjectives to describe each coffeehouse, the term "corporate" was given more than any other term. When asked whether this term had positive or negative connotations, the response was easily predictable: "Negative, definitely negative" stated one patron. Other words used by this crowd were "bourgeoisie," "manufactured," and "trendy."

6. Interviews often revealed a close personal attachment between patrons and the place of the coffeehouse, and many said that it was a second home or family for them. Interestingly, many said that they did not necessarily go for the coffee, but for the sense of community created at the coffeehouse. In an extreme case, unique religious values had emerged within the coffeehouse, and the coffeehouse had begun holding weekly religious meetings.

7. "Central Perk," the fictional coffeehouse patronized by the six "friends," has become a pop-culture icon unto itself. Not only has the fictional cafe become a merchandized image (available on sweatshirts, coffee mugs, etc.), it is the commonly adopted moniker for *Friends* Internet fan sites and has even gained status as a Wikipedia encyclopedia entry.

8. Peet's has again recently expanded and now sells its products in supermarkets and grocery stores.

## Works Cited


Abecassis, Andre. *Peet's Coffee and Tea: A history in honor of its twenty-fifth birthday.* Berkeley: Heyday Books, 2003.

Abelson, Jenn. "McDonald's Brew a Java War." *The Boston Globe* 28 October 2005: http://www.boston.com/business/articles/2005/10/28/mcdonalds_brews_a_java_war/

Boyce, Breanna. "Stop and Smell the Coffee." *The Daily Nexus* 16 September 2004: http://www.dailynexus.com/artsweek/2004/7768.html

Gillespie, Elizabeth M. "Starbucks Sees Growing Demand for Drive-Thru Coffee." *USA Today* 21 January 2006: http://www.usatoday.com/money/industries/food/2005-12-24-starbucksdrivethru

Gitlin, Todd, ed. *Campfires of the Resistance: Poetry from the Movement.* Indianapolis: Bobb-Merrill Company, 1971.

Holmes, Stanley, Drake Bennett, Kate Carlisle, and Chester Dawson. "Planet Starbucks: To keep up the growth, it must go global quickly." *Business Week* 9 September 2002: 100.

Kotha, Suresh and Melissa Schilling. *The Starbucks Corporation: Competing in a Global Market.* University of Washington, School of Business Administration, 1997. http://bschool.washington.edu/gbc/starbucksfinal.pdf

Mathieu, Paula. "Economic Citizenship and the Rhetoric of Gourmet Coffee." *Rhetoric Review* 18 (1999): 112-27.

McNamara, Brooks. "Something Glorious: Greenwich Village and the Theater." Eds. Rick Beard and Leslie Cohen Berlowitz. New Brunswick: Rutgers UP, 1993.

National Coffee Association of U.S.A (NCA). "NCA Works For You: NCDT Finds Coffee Consumption Up, Market Penetration Ties Soft Drinks." 2006. http://www.ncausa.org/custom/headlines/headlinedetails.cfm?id=412&returnto=1

Pendergrast, Mark. *Uncommon Grounds: The history of coffee and how it transformed our world.* New York: Basic Books, 1999.

Rogerebert.com. *You've Got Mail.* 2006.

SCAA Market Report. 2006. http://www.scaa.org/index.cfm

Smith, Michael D. "The Empire Filters Back: Consumption, Production, and the Politics of Starbucks Coffee." *Urban Geography* 17.6 (1996): 502-524.

Starbucks Company Website. http://www.starbucks.com

Thompson, Craig and Zeynep Arsel. "The Starbucks Brandscape and Consumers' (Anticorporate) Experiences of Globalization." *Journal of Consumer Research* 31(2004): 631-642.

Ukers, William H. *All About Coffee.* New York: The Tea & Coffee Trade Journal Company, 1935.

# The American Identity

*In "Constructing 'Godless Communism,'" Thomas Aiello argues that the "nation's virulent anticommunism during the 1950s and 1960s could have been a product of political manipulation, or American politicians could have simply responded to a national consensus left over from the First Red Scare after World War I. Either way, the virtual anti-communist consensus existed, and the commonly held American view of Communism included a lack of Christian faith. By the time the cultural climate allowed dissent on Soviet policy, atheism had established itself as the one touchstone of agreement to an otherwise divided nation. Belief in America meant a belief in the God who created it, thus defining out an atheistic minority from full citizenship."*

## Constructing "Godless Communism": Religion, Politics, and Popular Culture, 1954-1960

Thomas Aiello

James W. Fifield, minister of the First Congregational Church of Los Angeles, recalled in 1954 that a man once speaking with John Dewey commented, "Mr. Dewey, I don't see how you can believe all this collectivist thinking and all these collectivist things and still call yourself a Christian," to which Dewey responded, "I don't" (Fifield 51). Although Dewey eschewed religious supernaturalism, he embraced a pragmatic vision that allowed any new experience in hopes that it could make the world somehow better. He argued for social improvement, so long as, on the way, it not become detrimental to the concept of freedom or personal liberty. "It is this active relation between ideal and actual to which I would give the name 'God,'" wrote Dewey in his 1934 treatise *A Common Faith* (Dewey 51).

Conservative thinkers twenty years later, however, remained skeptical of Dewey's pragmatic educational models, increasingly concerned that they prepared American children for globalization. Pragmatism left little room for the idea of a preordained universe, and globalization signaled the possibility of economic and political ties to nations neither capitalist nor religious. Mid-twentieth century America clung to the Manifest Destiny of earlier generations, claiming a superiority and godliness diametrically opposed to communist claims of superiority and godlessness. American religiosity tempered and shaped American anti-communism, creating the pervasive sentiment that the United States engaged in a religious battle with a religious foe, rather than a political battle with a collectivist answer to capitalism. This American pietism shaped the American character. It defined Americanism. But a definition of Americanism that categorically included religious belief dispossessed a disbelieving minority in a nation whose First Amendment had consistently been interpreted as offering freedom of and from religion.

Throughout the nation's history, majority opinion tended to substitute for truth – such was the nature of democracy. An outspoken and proactive electorate ensured that prevailing public opinion essentially became the American Way. That public's opinions were subjective perceptions spread through the media outlets of cultural discourse. National images and patriotic feelings necessarily tainted any decision maker's self-perception, as well as his or her received image of a presumed national foe. The American perception of the Soviet Union in the 1950s found a base in atheism, totalitarianism, and communism. It fostered a public belief that no nation could positively engage with a counterpart perceived by so many as evil. Popular Christianity became the zenith of popular culture.[1]

That counterpart survived throughout the 1950s and 60s, ensuring that the domestic discourse would turn primarily on U.S.-Soviet relations. Internal security would be paramount. The House Un-American Activities Committee (HUAC) began its search for potentially subversive individuals and organizations in 1938, and by 1954, the congressional interrogators reached the zenith of their power. In the Senate, the Government Operations Committee, chaired by Wisconsin Republican Senator Joseph McCarthy, expanded its investigative scope from simple concern with government waste. The Permanent Subcommittee on Investigations hunted communist infiltration in the executive branch, stretching the limits of its authority and eventually culminating in McCarthy's 1954 Congressional censure (Ritchie xiii). That censure and the continued inquiries of the House Un-American Activities Committee only heightened a popular paranoia steadily accumulating throughout the first post-war decade. There was a clear enemy, and communists became scapegoats for American trepidation. American Christianity throughout the Cold War decade pitted itself as both the primary target of communist annihilation and the most effective weapon against the atheistic scourge.

American claims that communist philosophy was fundamentally atheistic had obvious merit. Communist thinkers from Marx to Lenin to Trotsky to Stalin advocated an abandonment of a religion they felt to be superstitious and unproductive. Thus mid-century Americans referred to "godless communism."[2] Throughout the post-war years of the Second Red Scare, "godless communism," along with similar variations, rooted itself as a functional epithet and cautionary tale to a reluctant America in a changing global environment. As the communist threat to the American way of life grew, so its godless materialism continued to threaten a Christianity increasingly tied to America's self-image. The choice between Americanism and communism was vital, without room for compromise.

President Dwight D. Eisenhower began attending church regularly in the 1950s. Former President Herbert Hoover called communism "human slavery." Walter R. Courtenay, minister of the First Presbyterian Church of Nashville, Tennessee, insisted in 1957 he "would personally rather see [his] nation die cleanly under the H-bomb than rot away under Socialism" (Fried 5). When Brooklyn clergyman William Howard Melish suggested in 1954 that Christianity and communism could coexist, he was immediately labeled a communist. For the majority of Americans, the idea that a Christian could be a communist became almost universally inconceivable. The paranoia associated with Soviet policy and global change subtly shifted to fear and hatred of atheistic philosophy – the godlessness of "godless communism." Excoriating Russia's lack of faith and emphasizing a more semantically potent "godless communism" label, United States political and religious leaders gave the populace a simple yet profound point of divergence from the confusing glob of collectivist policy they were supposed to despise. It was a metaphor of good versus evil, and a reinforcement of the notion of American divine right. That metaphor, however, became definition, thus defining American disbelievers out of their citizenship (Belfrage 224).

American church membership, approximately 49 percent of the population in 1940 irrespective of denomination, increased to 65 percent by 1970, pushed in part by the absolutist rhetoric of Cold War American politicians and evangelicals. Due to an economic climate that caused many to move and an overall growth in church construction, large numbers of Americans throughout the 1950s began changing church membership, either shifting denominations within Protestant Christianity or simply transferring membership to a new house of worship (Smith 99). The growth of American religious participation was a response to communism's unqualified rejection of God, according to commentators such as Billy Graham, igniting a virtual revival and an increasing resort to the Bible for battle with the communist foe ("Satan's Religion" 42).

Evangelists such as Graham fueled the revival spirit in America. The minister was a popular voice for fundamentalist, nationalistic conservatism, arguing that Christian salvation was the only vaccine against communism.[3] "The greatest and most effective weapon against Communism today," wrote Graham in 1954, "is to be born again Christian" (42). He encouraged a new religious turn in America, as he portrayed communism as Satanic, an anti-Christian religion competing with Christianity for American souls ("Our World in Chaos" 21). Individual atonement with God by each loyal citizen was necessary. The only way for America to combat communism was through faith, prayer, and religious revival. America without the Bible could not survive ("A Christian America" 69-72).

Billy James Hargis, another conservative fundamentalist evangelist, also saw a vital need for American Biblicism, warning from the pages of II Timothy that "the time will come when people will not tolerate sound doctrine." "For there have been some intruders," Hargis recalled from the book of Jude in 1957, "who long ago were designated for this condemnation, godless persons, who pervert the grace of our God into licentiousness and who deny our only Master and Lord, Jesus Christ" (Hargis 189). In this formulaic evangelical conception, any Biblical reference to evil was a *de facto* reference to communism.

"Ye shall know them by their fruits," offered the most common preparatory encouragement for the American religious community. "Prove all things," wrote the apostle Paul, "hold fast that which is good" (Matthew 7: 16; Thessalonians 5: 21). Verses such as these argued that Biblical knowledge was the best defense against communism. Paul's letter to the Romans taught that renewing one's heart and mind with God protected against evil (Romans 12: 2). His first letter to the Corinthians reminded Americans that understanding the duality of man offered a weapon against communist tactics (1 Corinthians 15: 45-47). While progressive ministers such as theologian Reinhold Niebuhr and Episcopal Bishop G. Bromley Oxnam quoted Acts 4: 32-37 as an example that early Christians were themselves communistic, if not simply communal, religious patriots responded with Jesus' parables of the "talents" and "pounds." Christ, they said, believed in private property. In an article published in the January 1964 edition of the *American Mercury*, conservative theologian T. Robert Ingram utilized the Bible's ninth commandment, which warns against bearing false witness, to argue for the necessity of full disclosure of Communist suspicions by the general religious public. When Paul's second letter to the Corinthians warned of false prophets, it warned of communist infiltration of liberal, socially conscious clergy (Ingram 51-55).

The most commonly referenced scriptural reference for the supposed capricious nature of liberal ministers was the story of Jesus and the moneychangers. In this tale, Jesus entered the temple of Jerusalem, and upon seeing merchants selling goods on holy ground, drove them away, chiding them for turning a religious place into "a den of thieves." Conservative ministers, calling on the story, argued that socially active clergy were using their temples for something other than prayer – turning themselves into makeshift moneychangers in the house of the Lord (Lovell 122-23). With a growing clerical correlation between social activism and Communist affiliation, more conservative houses of worship became closed sanctums rather than tools of community improvement.

Despite the differences in activist and fundamentalist dogma, U.S. religious leaders used the Bible to convince Americans that their freedom, liberty, and citizenship were inextricably tied to Christian faith. Often, ministers ignored Jesus' command to "stop judging and you will not be judged. Stop condemning and you will not be condemned," as a simple matter of political expediency (Luke 6: 37). The growing threat of a "godless communist" menace pushed many Christian teachers toward a different passage from the Sermon on the Mount as a bedrock of moral instruction, carefully reminding America that "no man can serve two masters" (Matthew 6: 24).

The American reliance on religion for ideological legitimacy blended the Christian and patriotic ideals, making Christianity a prerequisite for patriotic citizenship. Louisiana Representative George Long portrayed the battle between capitalism and communism as a battle between fear of men and faith in men, referring to Christianity as "our religion" and claiming it as the primary reason for public education and other public services (Long 13977-13979). "We are richly endowed with a spiritual treasure," said Minnesota Senator Hubert Humphrey in 1959, "that can, and does, give us overwhelming strength in any contest between totalitarianism and freedom" (Humphrey 5346). Louis Rabaut of Michigan claimed from the House floor that communism was antithetical to the American way of life on the basis of its lack of religion, citing that Christianity was the fundamental element of Americanism. Rabaut noted that America was "a Christian nation which believes in God; a nation founded upon and imbued with a fundamental faith in our Creator," while "communism, with all that it stands for, is an odious and abhorrent monster" (Rabaut 19391-2). Judging Russian action by American moral standards led to stereotyping and overemphasized a sense of U.S. superiority. "You can no more talk Communists out of Government," cried the pages of the *American Mercury*, demonstrating the stark U.S. caricature of its foreign foe, "than you could talk an onrushing lion out of molesting you" (Aldo 140).

Pundits contradictorily used freedom as the principal argument against a communist ethos, then told their audiences how to exercise that freedom. Television fueled a growing consumer culture in the 1950s and 1960s, and, when combined with "majority rule," encouraged conformity and made dissenting choices reactionary responses to the American will. The dissenting choice to disbelieve was tied to communism in the American mind, for "Communism is the deadly foe of belief in God and of all organized religion," according to former President Truman in 1953 ("Text of Truman Talk"). Freedom of religion was *de facto* freedom not to ascribe to religion, but governmental verdicts such as the Supreme Court's incremental removal of public school prayer became interpreted publicly as a tacit approval of anti-religious attitudes.

American practice and tradition made it a Christian nation, so went the prevailing belief, despite judicial First Amendment interpretations. In making the argument that the fight against communism was the fight to preserve Christian civilization, many forgot that totalitarianism disrupted the entire world – a world in which the majority of the citizens were not Christian. Commentator Max Eastman, though in the minority among conservative thinkers, argued that Christianity's focus on heavenly rewards and forgiveness made it less able to maintain the ruthlessness required to fight Soviet Communism. Eastman portrayed the battle against totalitarian Communism as a worldwide necessity, and wrote in 1964 that "to regard it as a Christian struggle seems to me parochial and self-defeating" (Eastman 58).

Of course, Communist paranoia did not exist in a vacuum, and the nuclear threat and the fear it provoked were both palpable and legitimate. That fear spawned a turn against reform, as liberality became both the model cause and symptom of postwar change in the conservative mind. It fueled racial unrest, a burgeoning women's movement that challenged traditional female roles, and a growing nuclear threat from a godless Communist menace. The national racial unease – and its particularly violent form in the American South – was similar to a subtler conservative reaction to feminism. Emerging from a violent, world-changing conflict in which women answered a national call to leave the home for the sake of the country's economic and military viability, a society wary of change countered attempts to sustain that progress with a maternal, subservient image of womanhood. "Over and over women heard in voices of tradition and of Freudian sophistication that they could desire no greater destiny than to glory in their own femininity," wrote Betty Friedan in 1963. "A thousand expert voices applauded their femininity, their adjustment, their new maturity" (11). The nation that had required so much wartime domestic change of its citizens attempted to redirect its energies on regaining an idealistic prewar society exemplified by the potency of a uniform, homogenized, white, Christian male. This backlash stifled groups representative of change – be they atheistic, black, or female – creating a situation in which legitimate fears fed irrational hostility to activism (McEnaney 448-49).

The intellectual group under some of the most intense scrutiny by anti-communist Americans were liberal theologians, principal among them Reinhold Niebuhr. Prior to, during, and after the Second World War, Niebuhr took the lead among American theologians in attempting to construct a new, progressive religious counter to Marxist conceptions of religion, history, and social change for the working poor. His theology allowed liberal social theory to coexist with more traditional forms of belief. It was anti-communist in that he argued against the presence of a utopia and the human need to achieve it. Along with his brother, H. Richard Niebuhr and fellow theologian Paul Tillich, who argued for a change in traditional Protestantism to confront the challenge of collectivization, Reinhold Niebuhr became a relative celebrity. The popular media portrayed the thinkers as divine authorities as America searched for anti-communist justification through religious leaders. Paul Tillich appeared on the cover of *Time* magazine in 1959, the accompanying article lauding the philosopher as an intellectual giant and declaring his theology as an "edifice. . .densely packed and neatly shaped against the erosion of intellectual wind and wave" ("To Be or Not to Be" 46).

But all was not praise. Conservative pundits labeled Niebuhr a communist in the pages of the *American Mercury* for his liberal theology, his "malodorous materialistic philosophy...poisoning the mainstream of dogmatic theological teachings in our country for four decades" (Benedict 18). Union Theological Seminary, Niebuhr's principal institution, endured a variety of communist-tinged epithets for its social activism. "Niebuhr," chided the *American Mercury*, "is one of a coterie of intellectual mediocrities centering at Union whose pernicious influence has spread like a pestilential stream along the conduits of denomination control" (Matthews, "Christ and Communism" 121-22). In 1958, the Seminary opposed the continuation of rigid hostility to communism, both politically and religiously, instigating a flood of fundamentalist response.

Fundamentalist discontent over Niebuhr and Union highlighted the struggle between traditionalism and progressivism in U. S. Christendom, the former represented by evangelicals emphasizing God's salvation of the righteous, the latter represented by activist ministers emphasizing God's benevolence in social causes. Conservative theologians such as Graham and Hargis stressed the moral evils of Communism. Every conflict was a battle between good and evil, between the Godly and the damned. "Either Communism must die, or Christianity must die," wrote Reverend Graham in 1954, "because it is actually a battle between Christ and anti-Christ" ("Satan's Religion" 45). Conversely, the religious progressives of the Union by no means approved of Communism, but stressed that building a socially conscious infrastructure was America's best defense against the Red Menace. Activism was the extension of religious belief. This seemed logical enough. But groups bearing names such as Christian Crusade, the Christian Anti-Communist Crusade, and the

National Association for Evangelicals used patriotism as an arguing tactic replacing logic. The groups combined political and ecumenical rhetoric to the point of creating an overgrown right-wing perversion of Christianity. The National Association for Evangelicals, which carried over ten million members in the 1950s, consistently tied its message of salvation to strong denunciations of the Red Menace, emphasizing the Christian duty to "safeguard free enterprise from perversion" (Berlet and Lyons 201). The Christian Anti-Communist Crusade, led by Fred Schwartz, did the same. By 1961, Schwartz's Crusade earned over a million dollars annually, promoting the belief that no bilateral negotiation could exist with communism. The anti-morality of the Reds, for Schwartz, suggested that "the battle against Communism is the battle for God" (Schwartz 92). Billy James Hargis' Christian Crusade reached millions each month through print and radio, and earned over a million dollars annually. Hargis consistently referred to the free enterprise system as a fundamentally Christian entity. It was Hargis's hope that "the atheistic regimes in Communist lands might fall and Christian governments might rise in their place" – "Christian" blatantly replacing more common modifiers such as "democratic," "popular," or "elected" (qtd. in Redekop 61-62).

These groups secularized the Christian battle. They did not attack communists as the mortal enemy of Christian faith, they attacked them as representations of that mortal enemy – Satan. They attacked the secular manifestation, whether wittingly or unwittingly, instead of the religious one. When Fred Schwartz declared that "Stalin is the fulfillment of Communism," or Billy Graham described communism as "Satan's religion," each created a broad caricature – a metaphor that everyone could understand. Leaders such as Schwartz, Graham, and Hargis took relative American pietism and made it absolute. They offered totalitarianism to guard against totalitarianism.

Virulent anti-atheist, anti-communist rhetoric, however, was not just a feature of the fundamentalist fringe. Frederick Brown Harris, chaplain of the Senate in 1954, referred to "atheistic world communism" as the "most monstrous mass of organized evil that history has known," claiming that the philosophy was "lower in its practice than primitive, cannibalistic tribes. Even they," wrote Harris, "will not turn on their own." The text of his message so inspired West Virginia Senator Matthew Neely, that the legislator read it into the Congressional Record (Neely 2390). Senator Richard Nixon, former member of the House Un-American Activities Committee, equated communism with pure evil, arguing in 1952 that the only way to combat "the netherworld of deceit, subversion, and espionage which is the Communist conspiracy" was Christian religious faith – "a faith based not on materialism but on a recognition of God." Nixon asserted that Western-style freedom was impossible without Biblical Christianity (570).

Archbishop Richard Cushing enunciated a common Christian belief (and a common propaganda tactic) when he wrote in 1958 that the primary goal of communism was the worldwide dismantling of all religious institutions, establishing "an enforced atheism for all men through what the Communists call 'dialectical and historical materialism.'" "What does 'dialectical materialism' mean?" asked Cushing. "It is the enunciation of atheism as Communism's world outlook – that there is no God or soul or world of the spirit" (33-34). The *American Mercury* made the argument that faith in God was the principal point of separation between humans and animals and that anyone who did not believe in God was fundamentally animalistic and untrustworthy. "We can love and trust our fellow man only because we know him to possess certain qualities transcendent to his animal nature," explained the October 1963 *American Mercury*. "Take away this divine spark and you are up against a dangerous beast" (Ingram 62).

Demonizing opponents was a recurring practice throughout the Cold War period. Regardless of logical merit, attacks on the godlessness of communism habitually referred to Satan and the Antichrist. The only tactic more frequent was the call to patriotism. Pundits assured Americans that the founding fathers, despite their political differences, all shared a similar belief in God. Billy Graham equated the Constitution's relation to the United States with the Bible's relation to Christianity – both documents acting as time-tested arbiters of time-tested entities ("Our Bible" 123).

Communism, commented Idaho Senator Henry Dworshak, only found sustenance through revolution. Capitalism found sustenance through belief in God, so destroying capitalism through revolution would subsequently destroy God. Citizens of the United States had to remain eternally vigilant against godlessness (Dworshak 14007). J. Edgar Hoover wrote that the American ideal, from its inception, based itself on a fundamental belief in God. "It is time for all of us," declared the FBI Director, "to reacquaint ourselves with our historical treasures and the moral values which inspired our forefathers to lead our country to the pinnacle of world leadership" ("The American Ideal" 100). As the arguments mounted, the full citizenship of the disbelieving minority became more and more tenuous.

"Communism, like homicide, must be met with direct action," wrote conservative commentator and former HUAC investigator J. B. Matthews ("An Anti-Communist's Guide to Action" 21). In August 1954, passage of the Communist Control Bill deprived the Communist Party of any legal rights and forced any party member to register with the government. The House Un-American Activities Committee received only one negative response to its 1954 appropriation, and the full house overwhelmingly endorsed the Communist Control Bill. Conservative politicians and commentators alike justified HUAC's appropriation as necessary for national and philosophical survival in the face of a clear and present danger. "The Soviet threat is real, a non-controversial assumption shared by the entire spectrum of non-Communist opinion in this country," wrote William F. Buckley, arguing for the Committee's validity eight years later in 1962 (17). Liberal attacks on the committee appeared periodically through the 1950s and 60s, making the general case that abusing individual rights for the sake of an intangible national ideal was itself an un-American activity. They were, of course, unsuccessful. "This annual assault has come to be expected by the Committee," taunted the pages of the *American Mercury*. "The Left Wing clique tries to cut the Committee appropriation to the bone. . .[but] the position of this courageous committee seems reasonably secure" (Stanley 89).

HUAC scrutinized propaganda exporters such as Voice of America and the National Book Committee, but it also investigated activist churches as suspected importers. Methodist Bishop G. Bromley Oxnam's prominent role in the World Council of Churches exacerbated suspicions about his loyalty. His HUAC testimony, however, reaffirmed his belief in moral absolutes. American rights were a gift from God, not the state, a result of the country's divine parentage. The state simply facilitated God's plan. "I reject Communism," Oxnam told the committee, "first, because of its atheism" (671-72). Another activist minister, Martin Luther King, Jr., admired communism's attempt to redress the underprivileged, but could not support the atheism inherent in Marxist doctrine. He insisted on the addition of the word "Christian" to the title of the Southern Leadership Conference, formerly the Southern Negro Leaders Conference, so as to deflect charges of communism (Garrow 90, 97).

Intellectuals beyond the ecumenical fraternity were also suspect. A 1956 study in the *American Sociological Review* showed an academic community troubled by a reduction in its freedom through the decade ("The Climate" 354, 357). Espousing atheism, wrote J. Edgar

Hoover, did not necessarily create a communist intellectual, but it paved the way for communism and influenced younger Americans to become communists. "Their pernicious doctrine of materialism," he wrote of the atheist community, "fed to young Americans as something new and modern, readies the minds of our youth to accept the immoral, atheistic system of thought we know as communism" ("God and Country" 13). Following Hoover's logic, noncommunist atheists and intellectuals needed to be stopped, as well. "Reactionary politicians have managed to instill suspicion of all intellectual efforts into the public," Albert Einstein declared in 1953, "by dangling before their eyes a danger from without" (668).

The culture of suspicion, however, received a blow on 17 June 1957, known to anti-communists as "Red Monday." A series of three Supreme Court decisions in Watkins v. United States, Sweezy v. New Hampshire, and Yates v. United States set new federal and state standards for just cause in investigations and inquiries. The Court's ruling in Yates established that Communist Party membership was not advocacy of governmental overthrow. "The distinction between advocacy of abstract doctrine and advocacy directed at promoting unlawful action," wrote Justice John Harlan, author of the majority opinion in Yates, "is one that has been consistently recognized in the opinions of this Court" (Yates v. U.S.).

The Court's Yates, Watkins, and Sweezy decisions, while discouraging to anti-communist America, did not receive the amount of violent criticism that Brown v. Board of Education and the Court's other education decisions received. It was the teaching system that could make good children into atheists. The United States remained suspicious of its children's education, whether in the form of Dewey's pragmatism or UNESCO's globalism. The United Nations Educational, Scientific, and Cultural Organization frightened many parents by offering a secular education program to American children. Secularism was atheism by any other name. "UNESCO," wrote a contributing editor of the *American Mercury*, "is the nearest thing to a 'managed' world culture that has emerged in this confused postwar world" (Moore 154). Veterans' organizations such as the American Legion and Veterans of Foreign Wars took a primary role in advocating religious belief as patriotic duty and denouncing UNESCO as an atheistic organization ("Legion Urges").

In 1956, New Jersey attempted unsuccessfully to remove religious references from school Christmas celebrations to comply with the state's anti-discrimination laws. The barrage of parental denunciations that followed prompted an investigation into the motives of the school superintendent who initiated the change. Fear that secular education would become atheistic indoctrination, however, was not confined to New Jersey. J. Edgar Hoover assailed its inherent atheism. Belief in God, according to Hoover, was the foundation of free inquiry, Christian faith the only avenue to American happiness and success. The foremost duty of any patriotic parent was to bring children to church. "The parents of America can strike a telling blow against the forces which contribute to our juvenile delinquency," wrote Hoover, "if our mothers and fathers will take their children to Sunday School and church regularly" ("Should I" 19). Religious practice would ensure that children would grow up properly American.

A study of college students at Dartmouth College and the University of Michigan in the early 50s and late 60s demonstrated a sharp decline in students' willingness to curtail the civil rights of suspected communists. In the study, religiosity directly related to a student's fear of communism and willingness to suspend individual freedoms. Religious orthodoxy heightened the possibility of support for social constraints and concern about communist infiltration (Hoge 182-84, 189). Similar studies acquired similar results, pitting American godliness against the blanket assumption of "godless communism." As the 1950s turned into the 1960s, the belief that collectivism and Christianity could not coexist remained.

Churches throughout the decade had varying reactions to Soviet political ideology. A 1954 Roper study showed that the Methodist church, a member of the National Council of Churches, was the least likely among Protestant groups to support Joseph McCarthy and his subcommittee (Lipset and Raab 230). The Baptist World Alliance came under anti-communist scrutiny for the appearance of globalism, while Pentecostals adhered to a more personal theology, effectively removing them from the political discourse. The Presbyterian Church publicly rejected McCarthyism as a violation of civil liberties. "The shrine of conscience and private judgment," declared the General Council of the Presbyterian Church, U.S.A. in 1953, "which God alone has a right to enter, is being violated" (Nutt 64-5). Any religious debate on the finer points of political philosophy, however, could congeal at a mutual disapproval of the menace of atheism.

The nation's virulent anticommunism during the 1950s and 1960s could have been a product of political manipulation, or American politicians could have simply responded to a national consensus left over from the First Red Scare after World War I. Either way, the virtual anti-communist consensus existed, and the commonly held American view of communism included a lack of Christian faith. By the time the cultural climate allowed dissent on Soviet policy, atheism had established itself as the one touchstone of agreement to an otherwise divided nation. Belief in America meant a belief in the God who created it, thus defining out an atheistic minority from full citizenship. Americans were loyal believers. And despite John Dewey's essential contributions to the philosophy of education, no loyal American parents would have let him near their child's classroom.

## Notes

1. This study concerns the creation of a domestic mindset – a cultural creation. Certainly, foreign policymakers had more on their minds than religion, as a policy of containment was understandably based far more on strategic maneuvering to protect U.S. interests. (The prospect of a godless world couldn't have gone unnoticed in the State Department, but such is far from the purview of this work.)
2. The U.S.S.R., however, conducted public opinion research through the Public Opinion Institute, as did Soviet Bloc countries such as Poland. One such Polish poll indicated a vast majority of religious citizens, although the government was ostensibly atheistic. This demonstrated, if nothing else, the ability of Polish citizens to speak relatively freely about their beliefs. According to the communist model, religion was simply a collection of superstitions that took time and energy from true progress. The Soviet Union was not necessarily anti-Christian, it was post-Christian, meaning that communism – created by Marx, who left the Christianity of his youth for Hegelian atheism – drew influence from a Christianity that was there first. The state did not remove God, it replaced him.
3. As of 1957, 85 percent of the American population could positively identify Billy Graham and his religious affiliation (Gallup 1490-91).

## Works Cited

Aldo, Reginald. "The American Universities and Senator McCarthy." *American Mercury* December 1954: 137-142.

Belfrage, Cedric. *The American Inquisition, 1945-1960*. Indianapolis: The Bobbs-Merrill Company, Inc., 1973.

Benedict, John. "What Religion Does Reinhold Niebuhr Peddle?" *American Mercury* October 1959: 18-27.

Berlet, Chip, and Matthew N. Lyons. *Right-Wing Populism in America: Too Close for Comfort.* New York: The Guilford Press, 2000.

"Billy Graham – Survey #583-K, Question #25a, 2 June 1957." In *The Gallup Poll: Public Opinion, 1935-1971, Vol. 2, 1949-1958.* Ed. George H. Gallup. New York: Random House, 1972. 1490-1491.

Buckley, William F., Jr. "A New Look at a Controversial Committee." *National Review* 16 January 1962: 15-21.

"The Climate of Opinion and the State of Academic Freedom." *American Sociological Review* 21 (1956): 353-357.

Cushing, Richard J. "The Godlessness of Communism." *American Mercury* March 1958: 32-34.

Dewey, John. *A Common Faith.* New Haven: Yale UP, 1934.

Eastman, Max. "Am I Conservative?" *National Review* 28 January 1964: 57-58.

Einstein, Albert. "A Letter from Albert Einstein." *Thirty Years of Treason: Excerpts from Hearings before the House Committee on Un-American Activities, 1938-1968.* Ed. Eric Bentley. New York: The Viking Press, 1971. 667-668.

Fifield, James W. "Freedom Under God." *American Mercury* June 1954: 45-51.

Fried, Richard M. *Nightmare in Red: The McCarthy Era in Perspective.* New York: Oxford UP, 1990.

Friedan, Betty. *The Feminine Mystique.* Tenth Anniversary Edition. New York: Dell Publishing Co., 1974.

Garrow, David J. *Bearing the Cross: Martin Luther King, Jr., and the Southern Christian Leadership Conference.* New York: William Morrow & Company, Inc., 1986.

Graham, Billy. "A Christian America." *American Mercury* March 1955: 68-72.

----. "Our Bible." *American Mercury* December 1955: 123-126.

----. "Our World in Chaos: The Cause and Cure." *American Mercury* July 1956: 21-27.

----. "Satan's Religion." *American Mercury* August 1954: 41-46.

Hargis, Billy James. "Communist America…Must It Be?" Mid-Eighties Update. Green Forest, AR: New Leaf Press, 1986.

Hoge, Dean R. "College Students' Value Patterns in the 1950s and 1960s." *Sociology of Education* 44 (1971): 170-197.

Hoover, J. Edgar. "The American Ideal." *American Mercury* October 1957: 99-103.

----. "God and Country or Communism?" *American Mercury* December 1957: 7-13.

----. "Should I Force My Child?" *American Mercury* February 1958: 18-19.

Ingram, T. Robert. "The World Under God's Law." *American Mercury* October 1963: 59-79.

----. "The World Under God's Law." *American Mercury* January 1964: 51-67.

"Legion Urges U.S. to Cut UNESCO Tie; Calls for Inquiry." *New York Times* 13 October 1955: 1, 18.

Lipset, Seymour Martin and Earl Raab. *The Politics of Unreason: Right Wing Extremism in America, 1790-1970.* New York: Harper & Row, 1970.

Lovell, J.A. "Jesus and the Money Changers." *American Mercury* December 1960: 121-123.

Matthews, J.B. "An Anti-Communist's Guide to Action." *American Mercury* May 1954: 21-28.

----. "Christ and Communism." *American Mercury* May 1959: 116-123.

McEnaney, Laura. "Atomic Age Motherhood: Maternalism and Militarism in the 1950s." *Women's America: Refocusing the Past.* Ed. Linda K. Kerber and Jane Sherron De Hart. New York: Oxford UP, 2000. 448-454.

Moore, Harvin, Jr. "UNESCO: 3¢ Worth of Poison." *American Mercury* August 1955: 151-154.

*The New American Bible*

Nixon, Richard. "Plea for an Anti-Communist Faith." *Thirty Years of Treason: Excerpts from Hearings before the House Committee on Un-American Activities, 1938-1968.* Ed. Eric Bentley. New York: The Viking Press, 1971. 569-571.

Nutt, Rick. "For Truth and Liberty: Presbyterians and McCarthyism." *Journal of Presbyterian History* Spring 2000: 51-66.

Oxnam, G. Bromley. "Testimony of a Bishop." *Thirty Years of Treason: Excerpts from Hearings before the House Committee on Un-American Activities, 1938-1968.* Ed. Eric Bentley. New York: The Viking Press, 1971. 669-680.

Redekop, John Harold. *The American Far Right: A Case Study of Billy James Hargis and Christian Crusade.* Grand Rapids, MI: William B. Eerdmans Publishing Company, 1968.

Ritchie, Donald A. Introduction. *Executive Sessions of the Senate Permanent Subcommittee on Investigations of the Committee on Government Operations.* Vol. 1. 83rd Cong., 1st sess., 1953. Made public January 2003. http://www.acess.gpo.gov/congress/senate/senate12cp107.html

Schwarz, Fred C. "Communism – Murder Made Moral." *American Mercury* April 1957: 92-97.

Smith, Peter. "Anglo-American Religion and Hegemonic Change in the World System, c. 1870-1980." *The British Journal of Sociology* 37 (March 1986): 86-105.

Stanley, Herbert W. "Who Wants to Abolish HUAC?" *American Mercury* June 1960: 89-92.

"Text of Truman Talk Decrying 'Hysteria' in Fighting Communists." *New York Times* 11 November 1953: 20.

"To Be or Not to Be." *Time* 16 March 1959: 46-52.

U.S. Congress. House. "America's Challenge Today." *Extension of Remarks of Hon. George S. Long of Louisiana.* 83rd Cong., 1st sess. *Congressional Record* 100, pt. 11 (10 August 1954): 13977-13979.

U.S. Congress. House. "Communism: A Threat to Freedom." *Extension of Remarks of Hon. Louis C. Rabaut.* 86th Cong., 2nd sess. *Congressional Record* 106, pt. 14 (1 September 1960): 19391-19392.

U.S. Congress. Senate. "The Christian and the Challenge of Communism." Henry Dworshak. 87th Cong, 1st sess. *Congressional Record* 107, pt. 10 (29 July 1961): 14007-14008.

U.S. Congress. Senate. "Eastertime and the American Will for Peace." Hubert Humphrey. 86th Cong., 1st sess. *Congressional Record* 105, pt. 4 (20 March 1959): 5345-5347.

U.S. Congress. Senate. "Spires of the Spirit-The Truce of the Bear." Matthew Neely. 83rd Cong., 1st sess. *Congressional Record* 100, pt. 2 (1 March 1954): 2390-2391.

Yates v. United States. 354 US 298 (1957). http://laws.findlaw.com/us/354/298.html

*For Nathaniel Naddaff-Hafrey and Zoe Trodd, protest artists "debunk the myth of American history as a series of fresh starts and of America as a perpetual New World. Excavating and reconstructing, protest artists fight attempts to stamp out the country's radical past. They refuse to discard history or to participate in the 'sloughing of the old skin, towards a new youth,' termed 'the true myth of America' by D.H. Lawrence."*

# The Turnaround Point: Vietnam Movies, Protest Literature, and the Feedback-Loop of Contemporary American Identity

Nathaniel Naddaff-Hafrey and Zoe Trodd

[M]ight as well say that Vietnam was where the Trail of Tears was headed all along, the turnaround point where it would touch and come back to form a containing perimeter.

-Michael Herr, 1977

We've all adjusted…And I fear that we are back where we started. I wish we were more troubled.

-Tim O'Brien, 1981

[P]eople were doing what they'd seen on television...This is the loop.

-Salman Rushdie, 1999

The music plays throughout the day, Hendrix, the Stones, the Who, music from a different war.

-Anthony Swofford, 2003

"If we could tell you the story, we would change mankind," said Elie Wiesel in 1977, ventriloquising Second World War veterans. "If we could tell you the tale, history would take a different course, and there would be no more wars because now we know what wars look like." And so, he continued, veterans "told the tale," only to realize "[t]hirty years later [that] their testimony appears not to have been received." Vietnam unfolded, "and I do not know what to do," Wiesel sighed (333).

Wiesel's despair notwithstanding, war veterans continue to offer their tales as a usable past: thirty years on *again,* veterans of Vietnam give "testimony" and protest America's new war. The group Vietnam Veterans Against the War (VVAW), its members committed to teaching preventative lessons, oppose George W. Bush's Iraq war. Insisting that the administration's justifications for war were as misguided as those used to send *them* to Southeast Asia, VVAW has inspired the formation of a group called Iraq Veterans Against the War, visible at the 2004 Democratic Convention. Vietnam veteran Ron Kovic, who marched with VVAW in August 1972, made a controversial appearance at the 1976 Democratic Convention, and challenged the potency of the country's warrior masculinity in his 1976 memoir *Born on the Fourth of July*, also came out against the Iraq war. In 2005, he released a revised edition of *Born on the Fourth of July,* with a new introduction. Kovic's memoir had focused on the legacy of the Vietnam war: the veteran experience and the changing relationship between protestors and the government. The new edition pointed to yet another legacy of Vietnam. "I have watched in horror the mirror image of another Vietnam unfolding," he writes, and again he has "the task of…shouting from the highest rooftops, warning the American people." Reaching for what Wiesel called history's "different course," Kovic concludes that he is still "pleading for an alternative" (10, 14): from Saigon to Baghdad, it's a mantra and a manifesto for anti-war protest literature.[1] John F. Kennedy's 1960 Democratic Party Nomination acceptance speech described a new frontier: "From the lands that stretch 3000 miles behind me, the pioneers of old gave up their safety, their comfort and sometimes their lives to build a new world here in the West," he said. "But the problems are not all solved and the battles are not all won, and we stand today on the edge of a new frontier." Seven years later, seemingly engaged in another Indian war on that "new frontier," American politicians and generals called hostile Vietnam "Indian country" and referenced "Daniel Boon Squads." In *Dispatches* (1977), Michael Herr claims that a captain invited him to play cowboys and Indians, and a scene in the documentary *Interviews With My Lai Veterans* (1971) features three veterans discussing the scalping of dead Vietnamese ("people were on an Indian trip over there," observes one). Some even wondered if the government was riding roughshod over Native Americans at home as further preparation for its war abroad: "we used to talk about 'bringing the war home,'" said Bruce Elison later. "[T]he FBI…thought that that was really a good idea, and many of the tactics that they used in Indochina and Central America and other places in this world, they decided to try out on the Pine Ridge Reservation." Herr's description of soldiers with a "wild haunted going-West look" (74), illuminates an America caught in a dangerous feedback-loop: unable to find Kovic's "alternative" and bound by thematic undercurrents that encourage the recycling of past actions and myths.[2]

If the myth of the West was informing America's ongoing struggle in Vietnam, then this was specifically a *silver screen* myth. Herr describes the film-like unreality of the war (comparing life to film a dozen times) and his prose jump-cuts and freezes frames, the filmic style elucidating the idea of Vietnam as a movie: approached by politicians like a Western, run by cowboy-Generals, and fought by soldiers with expectations of what Kovic called "the glory John Wayne war" (158). As the first-edition cover to his memoir put it, Kovic felt like "your John Wayne come home," while Herr describes the "John Wayne wetdream" enacted in Vietnam: "Somewhere all the mythic tracks intersected," writes Herr, "from the lowest John Wayne wetdream to the most aggravated soldier-poet fantasy" (20). Vietnam seemed full of kids "who got wiped out by seventeen years of war movies before coming to Vietnam to get wiped out for good," he adds (209). Richard Slotkin discusses this looping process in *Gunfighter Nation*: the "historical past was itself encoded in the terms of myth…the scenarios and game-models developed by the policy-makers were not very different from the imaginative projections that were developed by fiction writers and filmmakers…Tropes and symbols derived from Western movies had become one of the more important interpretive grids through which Americans tried to understand and control their unprecedented and dismaying experiences in Vietnam" (446, 546). The feedback loop, concerned with reification and representation, not recon and recovery, provided this "interpretive grid" and more: a surreal plane through which would-be warriors learnt about combat.[3]

But by 1968, the ongoing struggle had begun to undermine Americans' confidence in their classic cowboy and Indian narratives, and in the once-glorious John Wayne feedback-loop. Kovic's disillusionment with the war echoed across war journalism, veteran memoirs and interviews. One veteran recalled: "When I went to Vietnam, I believed in Jesus Christ and John Wayne. After Vietnam, both went down the tubes. It don't mean nothin'" (qtd. in Mahedy 33). Another recounted: "I lost my footing and slipped into a ditch, went under the water and came up and out, screaming, 'This ain't a war movie! This ain't a John Wayne movie!'…[Movies] could no longer help me to deflect reality" (qtd. in Bird 11). Doctors eventually dubbed a post-Vietnam stress disorder the "John Wayne Syndrome," and protestors turned the pervasive language of this "syndrome" back on those perpetuating the frontier myth. If history was repeating itself, then – contrary to Marx's famous dictum that it repeats first time as tragedy, second time as farce – Vietnam repeated a tragedy. As one individual remarked in a letter to *Life* magazine: "history repeats itself and this is not the first time that American soldiers have murdered women and children…how about Wounded Knee?" (White 46). American Indian Movement (AIM) members, many of whom were Vietnam veterans, identified with anti-war protestors and linked American imperialism abroad and at home. "The best analogy is South Viet Nam," said Kenneth Tilson, an attorney fighting the government's illegal invasions of reservations. "Most obviously, there is a corrupt government of natives, who are set up, armed, supplied, financed, propagandized for, and maintained in power by the U.S. Government" (*Voices* 128).

The Native American, Civil Rights, feminist, and gay rights protest movements perhaps rendered ridiculous the John Wayne myth of a white, all-male, heterosexual frontier, while the anti-war movement certainly rejected that frontier's warrior-identity. "[M]ight as well say that Vietnam was where the Trail of Tears was headed all along," writes Herr in *Dispatches*, then immediately describing the crisis of a closed frontier: "the turnaround point where it would touch and come back to form a containing perimeter" (49). By 1970, it seemed the center could not hold, as the journalist Saul Pett observed: "The unthinkable multiplies until it seems 'things fall apart – the center cannot hold'…America, we seem suddenly to have discovered, is no longer infinite in space or resources or hope. There is no next valley or virgin forest to tread" (qtd. in Roberts and Olson 586). Echoing Frederick Jackson Turner's 1893 pronouncement of the closing of the frontier, Pett's article re-declared the end of cowboy dreams. America was finding no regeneration through violence in Vietnam.[4]

Herr's "containing perimeter" also described the cyclical undercurrent, or feedback-loop, in the substructure of American society. From his first Vietnam columns in *Esquire Magazine* (1968-69) and his adaptation of these articles into *Dispatches*, to his involvement in the screenwriting process for Stanley Kubrick's *Full Metal Jacket* (1987), Herr chronicled the dimensions of this feedback-loop: its restatement of frontier values and its regeneration of American war-glory. His *Esquire* articles and *Dispatches* highlight American's love of war – the insane romance between the line soldiers and their profession: "the Grunts themselves knew…They were hip to it, and more; they savored it," writes Herr in "Khesanh" (122). Herr himself refers lovingly to the war numerous times in *Dispatches*, observing that "[f]lying over jungle was almost pure pleasure" (10) and insisting that while "most of us felt that [Vietnam] had been merely wonderful," for some "the experience had been a glorious one" (244), then quoting journalist Tim Page's exclamation: "'Take the glamour out of war! I mean, how the bloody hell can you do that?'" (248). Donald Ringnalda observes of *Dispatches* that it is "a deep-recon probe…it catches the weird, secret subtext of the war and its 'smaller darker pockets'" (83). This subtext is, in part, the secret to American war-love: a war-love both created and reinforced by the feedback loop.[5]

These blitzkrieg fantasies – the "John Wayne wet dreams" and the "secret subtext" of war-love – haunt *Full Metal Jacket* as well. Adapted jointly by Kubrick and Herr from Gustav Hasford's 1983 novel *The Short-Timers*, one of the film's pivotal points is the obsession with war. During one scene, a soldier named Eightball explains the aggressive behavior of a comrade: "Under fire, Animal Mother's one of the finest human beings in the world…all he needs is someone to throw hand grenades at him the rest of his life." Animal Mother requires war in order to be a "fine" human being, and other members of the squad share his desire for war. Crazy Earl, the squad leader, tells an interviewer and his camera-team: "Do I think America belongs in Vietnam? I don't know; I belong in Vietnam," also claiming that "these are great days we're living" and that "after we rotate back to the world, we're gonna miss not having anyone who's worth shooting at."

As in *Dispatches,* soldiers allude to movies throughout as a way to articulate their experiences. This compositional strain of cinema-DNA suggests that they are attempting to fight an idealized war – one that conforms to their film-informed notions of how war should look (for example, when Animal Mother asks Joker, "You seen much combat?" he replies: "Well I seen a little on tv"). The most telling example of this obsession with performing war is the scene in which a film crew captures the squad as they prepare to go into battle. Joker quips, "Is that you John Wayne? Is this me?" His questions expose the powerful hold that Wayne has on him and raises the issue of autonomy: is Joker or Wayne fighting this war? At one point, Cowboy shouts, "Hey! Start the cameras, this is Vietnam the Movie!" The soldiers respond in turn: "Joker can be John Wayne; I'll be a horse," "I'll be Ann Margaret," "Animal Mother can be a rabid buffalo," "I'll be General Custer," "Who'll be the Indians? Hey, we'll let the gooks play the Indians!" There is nothing new under the Vietnam sun – everything has already happened on film screens, as Herr explains at the end of *Dispatches*: "There's nothing happening there [Vietnam] that hadn't already existed here, coiled up and waiting, back in the World" (250-51).

*Full Metal Jacket,* released in 1987, functions as a warning for the post-Vietnam era. The feedback-loop, "coiled up and waiting" to structure the combat experience and organize the narrative shape of war, reappeared during the 1980s. In an interview, Herr claimed that "the Vietnam war ended in 1975. It's over. It really is over." He acknowledged that "the coverage turned the war into something that was happening in the media wonderland that we are all increasingly living in," but insisted that the "first and last chapters" of *Dispatches* were intended as "a kind of... perimeter," as though to contain the Vietnam experience (qtd. in Schroeder 37-38). Yet Vietnam seemed far from "over." Though cowboy dreams were challenged – and though the frontier seemed firmly closed – America's frontier-mentality reared its dusty head in Reagan's America. Some Vietnam films tried to rehabilitate the lost myth of warrior-masculinity: *Uncommon Valor* (1983), *Missing in Action* (1984), and *Rambo: First Blood Part II* (1985) all ask the question, phrased by Rambo in this last movie – "Do we get to win this time?" The films' plots all answer "yes." The feedback loop of movie-magic and some veteran accounts recycled metaphors and symbols, embracing the battle of the individual soldier, the thrill of a fresh kill, the love of war, and the joy of survival. If the actions of American boys, "wiped out" by retold stories, as Herr put it, were a direct product of the culture loop then their every representation after the war was recycled back into that loop.[6]

The loop also incorporated presidential self-fashioning: Reagan's self-conscious cultivation of his image as a "western" president marked another attempt to rehabilitate the cowboy myth. Reagan, who had starred in the 1953 Western *Law and Order*, and eulogized Wayne in a 1979 article called "Unforgettable John Wayne," was frequently photographed in cowboy attire riding around Sky Ranch. Two famous photographs taken in 1982 and 1984 show him raising a white cowboy hat and triumphantly waving cowboy boots. The French press may have disdainfully dubbed him "Le Cowboy," but Reagan's cowboy persona suited a nation ready to believe in traditional heroes again: perhaps Reagan would alleviate the pain of defeat in Vietnam by *winning* the Cold War. Lynda Boose discusses the deliberate attempt on the part of the Reagan administration to rewrite the national story of Vietnam: "thus reconceived, the problem [of Vietnam] was no longer the excessive deployment of militarized values, but the failure to deploy them strongly enough" (586). The story of Vietnam is rewritten so that John Wayne didn't fail us – we simply didn't let him do his job. "We lit a prairie fire a few years back," concluded Reagan in 1988. "But we can never let the fire go out or quit the fight, because the battle is never over...There's still a lot of brush to clear out at the ranch, fences that need repair and horses to ride" ("Remarks" par. 52-53).[7]

By the 1990s, the Persian Gulf war seemed another way to relight that "prairie fire" and to reinvigorate America's pugilist identity. But when the language used to justify war echoed the frontier language of the Vietnam era, the protest literature of the early 1990s in turn drew on Vietnam-era protest culture. Seeking a "turnaround point" where history might turn in a *new* direction, anti-war artists and writers re-challenged America's cowboy dreams and tried to turn the feedback-loop back upon those embracing it. Edwin Starr's "War" (1970) and Freda Payne's "Bring the Boys Home" (1971) were re-released. The AIDS activist group ACT UP produced postcards of George Bush Sr. on horseback, with lasso and cowboy hat. And, like numerous Vietnam writers, June Jordan recalled America's Indian Wars, running a thread from the Old West through the Far East to the Middle East: "This was Custer's Next-To-Last Stand / I hear Crazy Horse singing as he dies," she wrote in her poem "The Bombing of Baghdad"; "this is for Crazy Horse singing as he dies... And this is for the victims of the bombing of Baghdad / because the enemy travelled from my house / to blast your homeland / into pieces of children / and pieces of sand" (46, 48).

To some, the Iraq war now seems yet another attempt to kick "the Vietnam syndrome once and for all," as George Bush Sr. infamously claimed of the Persian Gulf war (qtd. in Dionne A21). In April 2003, historian Marilyn Young observed: "If Vietnam was Korea in slow motion, then Operation Iraqi Freedom is Vietnam on crack cocaine. In less then two weeks a thirty year old vocabulary is back: credibility gap, seek and destroy, hard to tell friend from foe, civilian interference in military affairs, the dominance of domestic politics, winning, or more often, losing hearts and minds." Back too are America's cowboy dreams. Six days after the terrorist attacks of September 11, 2001, Bush was asked at a press conference whether he wanted Osama Bin Laden dead. He responded: "I remember that they used to put out there in the old West, a wanted poster. It said: 'Wanted, Dead or Alive.' All I want and [what] America wants [is for] him [to be] brought to justice." On other occasions, he expressed a determination to "ride herd" over resistant Middle Eastern governments and branded Iraq "an outlaw regime" (qtd. in Baard 27). Reverence for Bush's frontier rhetoric was so great that in May 2005, Wyoming senator Craig Thomas introduced a resolution establishing July 23 as the "National Day of the Cowboy." Thomas wrote to Bush seeking his support, from "one cowboy to another" (qtd. in Hardy). In July, Bush signed the resolution into law and was featured on the cover of *American Cowboy Magazine*, next to the headline: "The Cowboy Gets His Day."[8]

One protest against Bush's frontier rhetoric came via Marvel Comics. In 2002, the company announced it was pulling from retirement a gun-slinging cowboy character that had lain dormant in its archives since 1979. First introduced in 1955, and one of the most popular comic-book cowboy heroes ever published, Ron Zimmerman and John Severin's Rawhide Kid was now gay. On December 21, 2002, literary critic Carla Freccero told the BBC that the series dealt "with the crisis of masculinity" and critiqued "mainstream masculinity" (qtd. in Shields). *Marvel* editor-in-chief Joe Quesada then confirmed that the series took "what has been for decades a symbol of American hetero masculinity (think John Wayne, Clint Eastwood)," and showed "a whole different point of view on the heroic ideal" ("Interview"). It was a new cowboy story and a subversive challenge to the newly-resurrected heterosexual "John Wayne" myth. It was also an explicit critique of Bush's cowboy identity. In the second issue, "Mayor Bush" explains to Matt: "We're comin' up on election time and I need a second term. People are still a little shaky cuz I only won by a few votes last time." Matt responds: "And we know yore daddy and brother bought those." Then, in the fourth issue, Bush tells the Kid: "I will bring these evil-doers to JUSTICE. Terrorism will not be tolerated and the evil ones will be punished. Cisco Pike may think he can hide, but I promise you, we will be holding him accountable. BET ON IT!" The Kid insists upon a united effort to punish the terrorists, asking Bush to "gather the townsfolk." He explains: "I'm gonna need some help taking care of these hideous outlaws…We've got to work TOGETHER."[9]

Announced in December 2002, with the first issue published in February 2003, the Kid series critiqued America's bypass of the United Nation's weapon inspection process: on August 28, 2002, the Bush Administration stated they would seek to oust Saddam Hussein regardless of whether UN inspectors were allowed back into Iraq; on September 18, the Administration formally rejected Iraq's offer to allow the UN unfettered access and called for "regime change"; on September 20, Bush presented his new doctrine of preemptive invasion. Now, as the Kid asks "Mayor Bush" to "work together" with the "townsfolk," Bush's sidekick calls this strategy a "tired cliché." Mayor Bush agrees: "'member when Will Kane pulled this kinda stunt, tryin' to rally up townsfolk to stand up against outlaws? He damn near got everybody killed… I'll be damned if I'm gonna let that fancy-pants gunfighter rope us into a thing like THAT." Echoing John Wayne's famous 1971 assertion to *Playboy* that he was no "panty-waist" (92), Mayor Bush's resistance to the "fancy-pants" request for a united effort is the *real* "tired cliché." By implication, the foreign policy of *President* Bush –

whose "W" stands for "Wayne," according to several right-wing websites – enters the realm of bygone fictions.[10]

While a cultural feedback-loop has created another self-styled cowboy-President who utilizes a "smoke 'em out" rhetoric, so too have protest writers crafted a parallel loop. The protest voices of Saigon echo across the sands of Baghdad. These voices have even threatened to invade the White House rose garden. In February 2003, Laura Bush decided to hold a symposium on "Poetry and the American Voice." She scheduled it for February 12 and invited poets to take tea in her garden. They would discuss Emily Dickinson, Langston Hughes, and Walt Whitman. Poet Sam Hamill received an invitation, and on January 26, 2003, he emailed fifty other poets, explaining that he had felt "a kind of nausea" when he read the invitation. Only the day before he had heard about Bush's proposed "shock and awe" attack, and he said in his letter that "the only legitimate response to such a morally bankrupt and unconscionable idea is to reconstitute a Poets Against the War movement like the one organized to speak out against the war in Vietnam" ("Open Letter"). He asked all poets to forward his email and make February 12 a day of Poetry Against the War. He intended to compile a protest anthology and present it to Laura Bush.

Within three days, Hamill had received 1,500 responses. He created a website for the poems, and by March 1, 2003, more than 13,000 poems were posted. He delivered 13,000 to Congress and many entered the Congressional Record. Mrs. Bush shut down the symposium and office issued a statement: "While Mrs. Bush respects the right of all Americans to express their opinions, she, too, has opinions and believes it would be inappropriate to turn a literary event into a political forum." Banished from the White House rose garden, Hamill and Poets Against the War helped organize hundreds of poetry readings, many scheduled for February 12 – the day of the cancelled symposium. On February 1, poets attended "A Counter-Intelligence Symposium" in New York, titled "Poetry is News." Echoing Hamill's Vietnam reference, the organizer, Anne Waldman, explained: "I am reminded these days of the American/Vietnam wars…This is a *war for the imagination*…We may all resound as magnificent groaning Cassandras here, prophets of doom, but we might also reclaim our world" (335-6, 357). February 2003 also saw poets sign a "Not in Our Name Statement of Conscience," which observed: "We…draw on the many examples of resistance and conscience from the past of the United States: from those who fought slavery with rebellions and the underground railroad, to those who defied the Vietnam war by refusing orders, resisting the draft, and standing in solidarity with resisters" ("Original"). In January 2005, the "New Not in Our Name Statement of Conscience" appeared in the *New York Times.* Signed by 15,000 people, it called upon the example of Vietnam protestors and declared: "The movement against the war in Vietnam never won a presidential election. But it blocked troop trains, closed induction centers, marched, spoke to people door to door – and it helped to stop a war" ("New"). Groaning Cassandras sifted the rubble of history, becoming not "prophets of doom," nor lonely keepers of the future's secrets, but empowered activists and united custodians of the *past's* inspirations.

Mrs. Bush's symposium was reminiscent of President Johnson's "White House Festival of the Arts," scheduled for June 14, 1965. Though Johnson's event went ahead, poets (including Robert Lowell) declined the invitation. The Poetry Against the War readings were also reminiscent of New York's "Angry Arts Week," January 29 to February 5, 1967. Out of "Angry Arts Week" came *A Poetry Reading for Peace in Vietnam* (1967), edited by Peter Whigham. Similarly, Poets Against the War issued an anthology (followed in 2004 by Vietnam poet Robert Bly's edited collection, *The Insanity of Empire: A Book of Poems against the Iraq War*). Poets Against the War continue to publish poems on their website and, like the

"Not in Our Name" statements of 2003 and 2005, Waldman's remarks on "Poetry is News," and Hamill's original email about Laura Bush's symposium, numerous submitted poems connect the wars in Iraq and Vietnam – forty-one explicitly, and dozens more through allusion. Echoing much Vietnam literature, several of these new anti-war poems allude to movie-Westerns. Jim Harrison's "Poem of War" reads: "The theocratic cowboy forgetting Viet Nam rides / into town on a red horse…Clint Eastwood / whispers from an alley, 'George, they / were only movies'" (98). Harrison's February 2003 challenge was to the frontier mythology re-infusing political discourse and was eerily prophetic of observations like that of Pvt. Curtis Lawrence: "It was like out of a movie," said Lawrence in December 2003 of a battle in Iraq (qtd. in Daniszewski).

Beyond Poets Against the War and Marvel Comics, numerous contemporary dissenters have connected Vietnam and Iraq as part of their protest strategy against the feedback-loop that drives Bush's self-styling. In 1968, Norman Mailer's *The Armies of the Night* had offered an answer to the question phrased in the title of his novel *Why Are We in Vietnam?* (1967): Americans were in Vietnam to cure their insanity through brutality. "He came at last to the saddest conclusion of them all for it went beyond war in Vietnam. He had come to decide that the center of America might be insane," wrote Mailer. War was "the only temporary cure possible for the condition – since the expression of brutality offers a definite if temporary relief to the schizophrenic" (188-9). Then in 2003, Mailer observed the invasion of Iraq, returned to his central question, and wrote *Why Are We At War?* The answer was still Americans' "mad-eyed mystique" (53).

Similarly connecting America's wars, the Vietnam protest poet John Balaban wrote "Collateral Damage," which ends: "I often think of Miss Tin's pillared house in Hue / and those events now thirty years ago / whenever leaders cheer the new world order, / or generals regret 'collateral damage'" (128). At first Balaban didn't think the analogies drawn between the two wars were accurate. "Vietnam was a war of national liberation," he explained in a recent interview. "Its historical profile entirely different from Iraq's, and our own interests also utterly different. There was no Saddam Hussein. No oil. No one plausibly marked the Vietnamese as threatening American interests. No Vietnamese terrorist ever blew up anything in the U.S. (Not that any Iraqi did either). Vietnam had never waged war on a neighbor, threatened an American ally." But as the war unfolded Balaban changed his mind, realizing that "as the consistent blunders of reading the Iraqis became more evident, and as the indifference towards civilian deaths became more of a given, it began to remind one of Vietnam. Just as we were ignorant of the abiding aspirations of the Vietnamese, we failed to have a clue about what the Iraqis might want, might do…Finally, as in Vietnam, in Iraq we have no exit plan."

But reading contemporary poetry that protests the Iraq war has confirmed for Balaban that the poetry of the Vietnam war has an aesthetic legacy. "Once, walking with David Ignatow and Robert Bly after a reading at the Y in New York City, I voiced skepticism about the enduring value of the protest poetry of the war," he remembered in this interview. "Bly berated me saying that I didn't understand that a 'whole, new genre was being written.' Now I think he was right." Balaban, who notes that he disagrees with Auden's statement that "poetry makes nothing happen," is yet another who refuses to adopt Wiesel's despair about the possibility for literature to change history's "course" or redesign its feedback-loop. He calls upon the memory of Vietnam – and of its "whole new genre" of protest poetry – in order to acknowledge this moment as one of "conscience and responsibility." As ever, "testimony is required of each of us," Balaban concludes, going on to quote John Winthrop's "City on the Hill" sermon: "'The eies of all people are uppon us.' Once again, as in Vietnam, we are 'made a story and a byword through the world.'"

Still another with faith in the "enduring value" of Vietnam-era testimony, as Balaban puts it, is Joe McDonald. McDonald, who sometimes claims that his band Country Joe and the Fish stopped the war in Vietnam, explained in a recent interview that one "legacy of Vietnam protest is contemporary anti-war protest." His most famous song, the "I-Feel-Like-I'm-Fixin'-To-Die-Rag" (1965), has been adapted by Clinton supporters, advocates for the Martin Luther King, Jr. holiday, and critics of the Iraq invasion – indicating that the ongoing soundtrack of Vietnam is a persistent, alternative feedback-loop. This loop exists with regard to the Iraq war, McDonald suggests, because the cartoon simplicity of the Bush Administration's "we need to take out the bad guys" approach – and the right-wing perspective which assumes opposition to the war is support for Saddam Hussein or some notion of "Islamo-fascism" – makes the "war on terror" almost impossible to protest. It's a "new challenge for those who write about war," McDonald explains. He believes that, far from exposing a lack of imagination, the reliance of contemporary anti-war protestors upon the memory of Vietnam is an attempt to fashion effective protest: only by remembering that this is just "another war like Vietnam," might writers, artists, and musicians find a way to protest it. The feedback-loop that put John Wayne into the jungles of Vietnam, and has made the "Vietnam syndrome" a spectre in Iraq, offers protest artists a way to reclaim Iraq war culture.

One of the most profound explorations of Vietnam memory as ongoing protest has come from Vietnam veteran Tim O'Brien, whose stories fuse past and present in an attempt to remind America *how* it got to where it is. "My writing protests American systems of memory, national and cultural erasure," he explained recently. "It protests the attempt to simply put the past behind us and 'heal.' We're asked to forget, but sometimes picking at a scab is helpful." Far from trapping America in a feedback-loop, writers might teach us not to repeat error by recalling it, he says: "The role of the artist is to keep a culture remembering, subvert the attempt at erasure, and uphold a sense of personal and national honesty." Long ago, he observed that evil had no place in the country's mythology, and in 1994 he protested America's "Lone Ranger" attitude in an article for *The New York Times*: America had fought aimlessly in Vietnam and "in a war without aim, you tend not to aim," wrote O'Brien. "You close your eyes, close your heart. The consequences become hit or miss in the most literal sense." The same attitude then celebrated "sleek laser-guided weaponry beating up on Saddam and his legion of devils," he added (51, 53). Now, in an interview, he points out similarities between the Iraq invasion and the Vietnam war – the same quagmire, the same doubletalk, the same suspect justifications for the war. "There hasn't been the same sense of national outrage because we have no draft," he notes.

But stories can save us, O'Brien insists, pointing in this interview to the last story of his Vietnam collection *The Things They Carried* (1990), titled "The Lives of the Dead." It ends with a connection across time and space through story: "I'm skimming across the surface of my own history, moving fast, riding the melt beneath the blades, doing loops and spins," he writes; "and when I take a high leap into the dark and come down thirty years later, I realize it is as Tim trying to save Timmy's life with a story" (273). Wiesel had mourned the lost opportunity of veterans' testimonies, ignored in 1977 – "[t]hirty years later," as he put it. Thirty years later still, echoing and reversing Wiesel, O'Brien and contemporary anti-war protestors replace mourning with militant memory. Creating "loops and spins" from Saigon to Baghdad and back, they offer their own feedback-loop of historically-charged anti-war protest. Vietnam-era and contemporary recycling of John Wayne and the Old West by politicians, along with the Bush administration's reliance upon Vietnam-era language of "seek and destroy," "hearts and minds," all reveal the existence of an American feedback-loop. As Sam Mendes' film *Jarhead* (2005) has it, the feedback-loop lends soldiers a vernacular and a series of images, so legitimizing their own experiences as consistent with previous representations of war. Adapted from Anthony Swofford's book *Jarhead* (2003), and set in the Persian Gulf war and by implication the current war in Iraq, Mendes' film depicts the continuing presence of America's Vietnam experience. The Marines prepare for war in the film's early sequences by watching *Apocalypse Now* (1978), singing along to the "Ride of the Valkyries" sequence. In his book's introduction, Swofford explains that Marines "concentrate on the Vietnam films because it's the most recent war, and the successes and failures of that war helped write our training manuals." He continues: "We rewind and review famous scenes, such as Robert Duvall and his helicopter gunships during *Apocalypse Now*… we watch Willem Dafoe get shot by a friendly and left on the battlefield in *Platoon*; and we listen closely as Matthew Modine talks trash to a streetwalker in *Full Metal Jacket*." Anti-war films are reinterpreted as pro-war, he notes:

> There is talk that many Vietnam films are antiwar, that the message is war is inhumane and look what happens when you train young American men to fight and kill…But actually, Vietnam war films are all pro-war, no matter what the supposed message, what Kubrick or Coppola or Stone intended…Corporal Johnson at Camp Pendleton and Sergeant Johnson at Travis Air Force Base and Seaman Johnson at Coronado Naval Station and Spec 4 Johnson at Fort Bragg and Lance Corporal Swofford at Twentynine Palms Marine Corps Base watch the same films and are excited by them, because the magic brutality of the films celebrates the terrible and despicable beauty of their fighting skills…The supposedly antiwar films have failed. (6-7)

Recycled imagery here fuels a stagnant feedback-loop: Swofford – and Mendes – show us the risk taken by writers, artists, and filmmakers who continue to tell the story of Vietnam. By this logic, the approach of contemporary writers and artists who use the rhetoric and referents of Vietnam does not work as anti-war protest. As the platoon in Mendes' *Jarhead* trudges through the sand, an aircraft passes overhead blasting The Doors' song "Break on Through" (1967). One Marine complains: "That's Vietnam music. Can't we get our own…music?" By connecting Vietnam and Iraq, contemporary anti-war writers and artists run the risk, ironically, of *not* breaking "on through to the other side" – of not shifting past cowboy dreams: rather than re-imagining their country, perhaps protest writers are deepening the cultural rut that has long-since trapped its wagons.[11]

Slotkin, however, believes that America is evolving, its myths changing: "By our way of remembering, retelling, and reimagining 'America,' we too engage myths with history and thus initiate the processes by which our culture is steadily revised and transformed" (660). After all, even *Jarhead* signals the loop's shift toward becoming an open curve in a new direction – "this is not Rambo time," confirms Kaczynski at one point. It is not combat but rather the *lack* of it that pushes the Marines to near-insanity: the film shows no violence whatsoever. Even the Marines' homecoming parade is an anti-climax, tempered when a Vietnam veteran climbs onto their bus. In addition, this moment echoes the opening scenes of Oliver Stone's film, *Born on the Fourth of July* (1989), when the young Ron Kovic, watching a parade, exchanges a glance with a Second World War veteran played by the real Kovic (a scene reminiscent of O'Brien's "Tim trying to save Timmy's life with a story"). Gesturing at a different kind of veteran – beyond the dysfunctional victim who brought the war home with him – *Jarhead* recalls the empowered and politicized veterans, like Kovic and O'Brien, who went on to protest the Vietnam war and now protest the war in Iraq. Summoning Vietnam means summoning not *only* a glory John Wayne war but also the 1960s moment of political protest and social upheaval. Activist history becomes the contemporary activist's muse: protest writers and artists are seeking a replacement for the feedback-loop – perhaps a new national DNA, a kind of double helix that more closely resembles our human DNA. Battle songs are stripped to their tonal origins, war flags are unravelled to their threadbare beginnings, and the possibility of a legitimate deconstruction of American war-culture emerges.

This double helix model is at the heart of the American protest literature tradition. The creation of protest literature has always been a folk process – old tunes with new words in new cirumstances. It is a form of intellectual *bricolage*; ideas, images, and language stored across time, then transformed by new contexts into a living protest legacy. Building on the past, protest artists have chosen and reshaped their ancestry: "We do not even know that the literature of America is above everything else a literature of protest and of rebellion," complained Floyd Dell in 1920; "not knowing the past, we cannot learn by its mistakes…We only slowly come to learn that what we sometimes contemptuously call 'American' is not American at all: that it is, astonishingly enough, *we* who are American: that Debs and Haywood are as American as Franklin and Lincoln" (46). Contemporary anti-war protestors, as though heeding Dell's warning, reclaim the protest moment of Vietnam and find a palpable past for their protest literature.

In so doing, they debunk the myth of American history as a series of fresh starts and of America as a perpetual New World. Excavating and reconstructing, protest artists fight attempts to stamp out the country's radical past. They refuse to discard history or to participate in the "sloughing of the old skin, towards a new youth," termed "the true myth of America" by D.H. Lawrence (60). It is the frontier myth, explained by Turner in 1893 and embraced by celluloid cowboys and cowboy-Presidents alike, from Theodore Roosevelt to John Wayne, from Ronald Reagan to George W. Bush. "American social development has been continually beginning over again on the frontier," said Turner. "This perennial rebirth, this fluidity of American life…furnish the forces dominating American character" (2-3). Resisting this myth, protest writers also disprove the particuarly pervasive idea that writing on the Left is without lineage, memory, or historical education; that it is a writing that never puts down roots. Though they seek and find new countries, then set sail for better ones, protest writers carry from the wreckage of history what O'Brien once called "odd little fragments that have no beginning and no end" (39): fragments that might fuse into a new turnaround point for the American feedback-loop.[12]

## Notes

1. The theme of emasculation continues in Sam Mendes' Gulf war film *Jarhead* (2005), where snipers are thwarted on their only mission by the arrival of air power. In frustration at reaching the war's end without firing their rifles ("I never shot my rifle," observes Swofford), they begin an orgasmic group-release of firepower into the night air. For more on the genre of "American protest literature," see Zoe Trodd, *American Protest Literature.*

2. In *The Things They Carried,* veteran and writer Tim O'Brien also explains: "It's like you're in a movie…You think of all the films you've seen…and you can't help falling back on them as models of proper comportment" (233). Discussing Wayne's portrayal of "the traditional American male" as

someone who "performs, delivers the goods, is a loner, has the equipment...and knows what he is doing," Loren Baritz explains: "It is astonishing how often American GIs in Vietnam approvingly referred to John Wayne, not as a movie star, but as a model and a standard. Everyone in Vietnam called dangerous areas Indian country" (51). See also H. Bruce Franklin, *Vietnam and Other American Fantasies*; Lloyd B. Lewis's argument that war films provide "a cinematic frame of reference for structuring experience," and "also a cluster of significant symbols for interpreting it" (23, 25); Donald Ringnalda's claim that in "America's trillion-dollar Vietnam movie, we all were actors, not audience" (83); and John Hellmann's argument that the "more developed veterans' literary accounts connect the authors' actual experiences to the American myth they had previously assimilated from popular culture" (102).

3. For more on the FBI at the "Pine Ridge Reservation," see the film *Incident at Oglala* (1992). The concept of a "feedback loop" originates with the systems dynamics model: in the 1960s, Jay Forrester applied concepts from feedback control theory to the study of industrial systems. See his 1961 book *Industrial Dynamics.* The concept of a "feedback loop" was later popularized by Peter Senge in *The Fifth Discipline.* For a pre-Vietnam Old West loop, see Bill Mauldin, *Bill Mauldin's Army*, which includes a World War II cartoon of a general putting down his jeep (marked cavalry) as if it is a horse.

4. For more on regeneration through violence, see Richard Slotkin, *Regeneration Through Violence.*

5. For more on war-love, see Chris Hedges, *War Is a Force That Gives Us Meaning*, in which Hedges, a *New York Times* war correspondent, describes his addiction to the simplicity of war and its capacity to give meaning to an otherwise sterile, monotonous life. Hedges also told PBS's "Religion and Ethics" show, on January 31, 2003: "It's very hard to make antiwar films or write antiwar books, because even if you look at a movie like *All Quiet On The Western Front,* you may recognize how horrible war is, but at the same time, you yearn for that kind of comradeship, which is not friendship. It's very different. You yearn to be tested like that. That's part of the way the myth is sold to us, that we're not finally complete human beings... until we've been through the experience of war." See also Eugene Jarecki's film *Why We Fight* (2005), and the marines' comments in Mendes' film *Jarhead*: "I was hooked," "I wanted the pink mist" and "I love this job; I thank God for every ...day he gives me in the Corps. Hoo-rah."

6. Civilians began to attend combat schools and, according to the U.S. Bureau of Alcohol, Tobacco and Firearms, two to three million military rifles were sold by 1989. For more see James William Gibson, *Warrior Dreams: Paramilitary Culture in Post-Vietnam America.*

7. See also Chris Hedges' comments to PBS's *Religion and Ethics* show, on January 31, 2003: "After the Vietnam War, we asked questions about ourselves and our nation. It made us a better people...We struggled, perhaps for the first time in a long time, to see ourselves as the outsider saw us...But gradually...love of power and that glorification, that myth of war, rose during the Reagan years, culminating in the Persian Gulf War, where war became not only respectable, but enjoyable – war as entertainment...That's what frightens me so much now."

8. See also David Ignatius' mention of a "Vietnam feedback-loop," in "Dangers of Defaming a War Hero," *The New York Times,* August 24, 2004; Paul Krugman, "The Lies About Iraq Bring Back Memories of Vietnam," *The New York Times,* April 16, 2004; Todd S. Purdum, "Flashback to the 60's: A Sinking Sensation of Parallels Between Iraq and Vietnam," *The New York Times,* January 29, 2005; Danny Schechter, "The Unreported Vietnam-Iraq Parallel," CommonDreams.org, May 1, 2005; General William Odom, "Iraq through the prism of Vietnam," *Commentary,* March 8, 2006, the Nieman Foundation for Journalism, Harvard University; and Marine General Anthony Zinni's comments to a group of Marine Corps officers on September 4, 2003, as reported in Thomas E. Ricks, "Ex-Envoy Criticizes Bush's Postwar Policy," *Washington Post,* September 5, 2003.

9. Wayne's on and off screen personas were unambiguously straight: on screen, he idealized a vision of virile straight men who waged battle by day and wooed women by night, and off-screen, his personal demeanor and values seemingly mirrored those of his cowboy characters. He espoused conservative causes, repeatedly expressed a personal distaste for homosexuality, particularly its pervasive presence in Hollywood, and proclaimed himself disgusted by Tennessee Williams' *Suddenly Last Summer* (1959).

10. For another critique of Bush's cowboy persona, see Erik Baard, "George W. Bush Ain't No Cowboy," in *The Village Voice.* Baard explained that the doctrine of pre-emptive war means the President in fact *broke* the cowboy code written by screen cowboy Gene Autry in 1939: "The Cowboy

must never shoot first, hit a smaller man, or take unfair advantage" (27). For a comic-strip protest that connects Vietnam and Iraq see G.B. Trudeau, *Got War?* and *The Long Road Home.*

11. The marines in *Jarhead* also watch *The Deer Hunter* (1978) and a party scene from *Platoon* (1986) is replayed in *Jarhead*'s Christmas Eve scene. Mendes pays Mendes pays homage to *Full Metal Jacket* (1987) with boot camp scenes, the "this is my rifle" scene, which is drawn nearly exactly from *Full Metal Jacket,* and the scene when Fowler unveils the dead Iraqi ("I gotta show you something, this is my new best buddy man"), which replays a *Full Metal Jacket* scene of the Lusthog squad pulling back the cover on the dead NVA. Swofford is a second generation American soldier: "My uncle and my father served in Vietnam, so I'm proud to serve my country here," he tells an interviewer at one point during the film." But even if still a loop, history is moving at a different pace in *Jarhead*'s war: "this war's gonna move too fast for us," says Troy. "Alright, we can shoot 1000 yards. To go that far in Vietnam that would take a week, in World War One a year, here it's gonna take about ten fucking seconds."

12. For "new countries," see Oscar Wilde, "The Soul of Man Under Socialism" (1890): "A map of the world that does not include Utopia is not worth glancing at, for it leaves out the one country at which humanity is always landing. And when humanity lands there, it looks out, and seeing a better country, sets sail. Progress is the realization of Utopias" (34). For "wreckage of history," see Walter Benjamin, *Illuminations: Essays and Reflections*: "Where we perceive a chain of events, he sees one single catastrophe which keeps piling wreckage upon wreckage and hurls it in front of his feet. The angel would like to stay, awaken the dead, and make whole what has been smashed. But…[a] storm irresistibly propels him into the future to which his back is turned, while the pile of debris before him grows skyward" (257-58).

## Works Cited


Baard, Erik. "George W. Bush Ain't No Cowboy." *Village Voice* 29 September 2004: 26-30.

Balaban, John. "Collateral Damage." *Locusts at the Edge of Summer.* Port Townsend, WA: Copper Canyon Press, 1997.

----. Interview with Zoe Trodd. 13 July 2005.

Baritz, Loren. *Backfire: A History of How American Culture Led Us Into Vietnam and Made Us Fight the Way We Did.* New York: Morrow, 1985.

Benjamin, Walter. *Illuminations: Essays and Reflections.* New York: Schocken Books, 1969.

Bird, Thomas. "Man and Boy Confront the Images of War." *The New York Times* 27 May 1990, sec. 2: 11, 16.

Boose, Lynda. "Techno-Muscularity and the 'Boy Eternal': From the Quagmire to the Gulf." *Cultures of United States Imperialism.* Ed. Amy Kaplan and Donald E. Pease. Durham: Duke UP, 1993: 581-616.

*Born on the Fourth of July.* Dir. Oliver Stone. Universal, 1989.

Bush, George W. "Guard and Reserves 'Define Spirit of America.'" Remarks by the President to Employees at the Pentagon. Pentagon 17 September 2001. http://whitehouse.gov/news/releases/2001/09

Daniszewski, John. "Troops Tell of Street Fight With Dogged Foe." *Los Angeles Times* 2 December 2003: A1.

Dell, Floyd. "Our America." *The Liberator,* III, January 1920: 44-46.

Dionne, E. J. "Kicking The 'Vietnam Syndrome': Victory Sweeps Away U.S. Doomed-To-Failure Feeling." *The Washington Post* 4 March 1991: A1+.

Elison, Bruce. Forum on "Human Rights in the United States: The Unfinished Story." 14 September 2000. National Archives and Records Administration.

Forrester, Jay. *Industrial Dynamics.* Waltham: Pegasus Communications, 1961.

Franklin, H. Bruce. *Vietnam and Other American Fantasies.* Amherst: U of Massachusetts P, 2000.

*Full Metal Jacket.* Dir. Stanley Kubrick. Warner Bros., 1987.

Gibson, James William. *Warrior Dreams: Paramilitary Culture in Post-Vietnam America.* New York: Hill and Wang, 1994.

Hardy, Cameron. "Thomas to Announce 'National Day of the Cowboy." Press release for U.S. Senator Craig Thomas. 18 March 2005. http://nationaldayofthecowboy.com/senate.aspx
Hamill, Sam. "An Open Letter." January 2003. http://www.poetsagainstthewar.org/whoweare.asp
Harrison, Jim. "Poem of War." 13 February 2003 *Poets Against The War.* Ed. Sam Hamill. New York: Thunder's Mouth, 2003.
Hedges, Chris. *Religion and Ethics.* PBS Interview. 31 January 2003.
----. *War Is A Force That Gives Us Meaning.* New York: PublicAffairs, 2002.
Hellmann, John. *American Myth and the Legacy of Vietnam.* New York: Columbia UP, 1986.
Herr, Michael. "Khesanh." *Esquire Magazine* September 1969: 118-123, 150-156.
----. *Dispatches.* New York: Knopf, 1997.
Interviews With My Lai Veterans. *Dir. Joseph Strick. Laser Film Corporation, 1971.*
*Jarhead.* Dir. Sam Mendes. Universal, 2005.
Jordan, June. "The Bombing of Baghdad." *Kissing God Goodbye.* New York: Anchor, 1997.
Kovic, Ron. *Born on the Fourth of July.* New York: Akashic Books, 2005.
*Law and Order.* Dir. Nathan Juran. Universal International, 1953.
Lawrence, D.H. *Studies in Classic American Literature.* 1923. New York: Penguin, 1977.
Lewis, Lloyd B. *The Tainted War: Culture and Identity in the Vietnam War Narratives.* Westport, CT: Greenwood Press, 1985.
Mahedy, William P. "It Don't Mean Nothin': The Vietnam War Experience." *The Vietnam Reader.* Ed. Walter Capps. New York: Routledge, 1991: 33-39.
Mailer, Norman. *The Armies of the Night.* New York: New American Library, 1968.
----. *Why Are We At War?* New York: Random House, 2003.
Mauldin, Bill. *Bill Mauldin's Army.* New York: Sloane, 1949.
McDonald, "Country" Joe. Interview with Zoe Trodd. 20 August 2005.
*Missing in Action.* Dir. Joseph Zito. MGM/UA, 1984.
"New Not In Our Name Statement of Conscience." 2005. http://www.nion.us
O'Brien, Tim. *The Things They Carried.* Boston: Houghton Mifflin, 1990.
----. "The Vietnam in Me." *New York Times Magazine* 2 October 1994: 48-57.
----. Interview with Zoe Trodd. 12 July 2005.
"Original Not In Our Name Statement of Conscience." 2002. http://www.nion.us/NSOC/original.htm
Quesada, Joe. Interview. CNN Live on Location. CNN. 12 December 2002.
*Rambo: First Blood Part II.* Dir. George P. Cosnatus. TriStar, 1985.
Reagan, Ronald. "Unforgettable John Wayne." *Reader's Digest* October 1979: 114-19.
----. "Remarks to 1988 Republican National Convention." New Orleans, LA. 15 August 1988. National Archives and Records Administration.
Ringnalda, Donald. *Fighting and Writing the Vietnam War.* Jackson: UP of Mississippi, 1994.
Roberts, Randy and James Olson. *John Wayne: American.* New York: The Free Press, 1995.
Schroeder, Eric. *"Vietnam, We've All Been There": Interviews with American Writers.* Westport: Praeger, 1992.
Senge, Peter. *The Fifth Discipline.* New York: Doubleday, 1990.
Shiels, Maggie. "Rawhide Comes Out of the Closet." BBC News. 21 Dec. 2002. http://news.bbc.co.uk/1/hi/entertainment/arts/2595301.stm.
Slotkin, Richard. *Regeneration Through Violence.* Middletown: Wesleyan UP, 1973.
----. *Gunfighter Nation.* New York: Atheneum, 1992.
Swofford, Anthony. *Jarhead: A Marine's Chronicle of the Gulf War and Other Battles.* New York: Scribner, 2003.
Trodd, Zoe, ed. *American Protest Literature.* Cambridge: Harvard UP, 2006.
Trudeau, G.B. *Got War?* Kansas City: Andrews McMeel, 2003.
----. *The Long Road Home.* Kansas City: Andrews McMeel, 2005.
Turner, Frederick Jackson. *The Significance of the Frontier in American History.* 1893. New York: Ungar, 1963.
*Uncommon Valor.* Dir. Ted Kotcheff. Paramount, 1983.
*Voices from Wounded Knee, 1973, In the Words of the Participants.* Rooseveltown: Akwesasne Notes, 1974.

Waldman, Anne and Lisa Birman, eds. *Civil Disobediences.* Minneapolis: Coffee House Press, 2004.
Wayne, John. "Candid Conversation." *Playboy* May 1971: 75-92.
White, Water. "From Harrisburg, Pennsylvania." *Life* 19 December 1969: 46.
Wiesel, Elie. *Against Silence*, volume I. Ed. Irving Abramson. New York: Holocaust Library, 1985.
Wilde, Oscar. "The Soul of Man Under Socialism." *De Profundis and Other Writings.* London: Penguin Books, 1986.
Young, Marilyn. "Historians Reflect on the War in Iraq: A Roundtable." OAH Annual Meeting 5 April 2003.
Zimmerman, Ron and John Severin. *Rawhide Kid: Slap Leather* 1: 1-5. New York: Marvel Comics, 2003. First published in magazine form as *Rawhide Kid #1-5.*

*In this essay, the author argues that the resurgence in nostalgic melodrama theater performances "evoke(s) a prelapsarian past." In other words, the "melodrama theatre is a secular ritual of collective nostalgia in which a simpler time in America is resurrected, a vision of communal identity."*

# Rituals of Nostalgia: "Old-Fashioned Melodrama" at the Millennium

James M. Cherry

As in its nineteenth century heyday, the melodrama, in all its various forms, reigns triumphant in today's cultural marketplace. The television detective series, the western, the science fiction film, the horror flick, and the action blockbuster are all its progeny. Many, if not most, of the popular films of our age contain that same heady mix of excitement, comedy, and pathos found in the famous stage adaptations of melodramas like W.H. Smith's *The Drunkard* (1844), George Aiken's *Uncle Tom's Cabin* (1852), and Augustin Daly's *Under the Gaslight* (1895). With the arrival of cinema at the turn of the century, the stage melodrama was eclipsed by a medium that could transmit thrills with ever-greater verisimilitude. Stephen Spielberg said of his own films: "In my work, everything is melodrama. I don't think I've ever not made a melodrama. *E.T.* is melodramatic, and so is *The Sugarland Express.* I mean, there's melodrama in life and I love it. It's heightened drama, taking things to histrionic extremes and squeezing out the tears a bit" ("A Dialogue" 1).

If American popular culture seems melodramatically inclined, it is perhaps due to the myth of America as nation in adolescence. The popular conception of "America" is of a young nation proud of its identity, muscular in clout and fair in temperament, and decidedly different from its older, effete European ancestors. Eric Bentley noted in *The Life of the Drama* that "theatre corresponded to that phase of a child's life when he creates magic worlds," and he continued: "Melodrama belongs to this magical phase, the phase when thoughts seem omnipotent ... in short when the larger reality has not been given diplomatic recognition" (217). The youthful American narrative is set in that earlier, "magic world" in which anything can happen, but everything always turns out right in the end.

In the first chapter of *Over the Footlights* (1923), Stephen Leacock describes the classic melodrama and its presentation on the stage of his youth:

> Everybody who has reached or passed middle age looks back with affection to that splendid old melodrama *Cast Up by the Sea*. Perhaps it wasn't called exactly that. It may have been named *Called Back from the Dead*, or *Broken Up by the Wing*, or *Buried Alive in the Snow*, or anything of that sort. In fact I believe it was played under about forty different names in fifty different forms. But it was always the same good old melodrama of the New England coast. (3)

What follows Leacock's rumination is a chapter-long exegesis of the plot of the play along with the recreation of its fictive performance and the audience's reactions to it. For Leacock, this ideal melodramatic performance of memory can be favorably compared with the film and theatrical productions of the present; it is a production so thrilling that as a spectator he was too excited to eat the popcorn and peanuts purchased in the lobby. Leacock's whimsicality is a typical response to the passage of time and the idealization of certain childhood events. The fact that melodrama of his youth came in "forty different names in fifty different forms" is immaterial as it is "always the same."

This resolute sameness, this desire for immobility afforded by nostalgia, is the hallmark of the modern "melodrama theatre." If Leacock views melodrama as a form from a bygone age and looks back with a parodic glance at its simplicity, melodrama theatres throughout America actually present these same performances of imagined memory in the form of "old-fashioned melodrama." No matter how inaccurate historically, the perception of melodrama as an arrested form of unswerving regularity and consistency has caused the genre to be emblematic of those thrilling, yet comforting, days of yesteryear.

Every summer, in locales like Cripple Creek, Colorado, Virginia City, Montana, and Victor, Idaho, melodramas are performed for audiences desirous of a taste of an old-fashioned aesthetic. The form, the "melodrama theatre," is one of the most widespread theatrical formats in America. It lives in small community theatres in Iowa, tourist traps in Colorado, and up and down the coast of California. In these performance, stock characters escape peril, reveal tell-tale scars at opportune moments, and follow the comfortable narratological arcs in which virtue always triumphs over vice. This theatre of nostalgia calls up a prelapsarian past, one that predates the complexities of modern America. And with hisses and cheers, audience members take part in a liturgy in which the past is repeated, evoked, and summoned up, sacralizing the "authentic" "America."

Far from incorporating melodramatic elements as a part of an ironic, postmodernist pastiche, melodrama theaters aim to maintain a collective cultural memory. Advertisements for such productions frequently invoke the elders of the community – "see the theatre of your grandfather!" – situating audiences in a trans-generational moral/aesthetic continuum. It is not simply the presentation of a performance, but the transmission of the experience of a performance of the past. A bridge, in a sense, to the nineteenth century. This essay examines the implications of this type of melodrama performance as a secular ritual of collective nostalgia.

Time, of course, generates the possibility for nostalgia – we cannot have nostalgia for something that occurs in the present. Like parody without the teeth of critique, nostalgia is a repetition, a return of the past to the present. It is instinctively uncritical as the past is idealized rather than analyzed. In the recent *Time Passing: Modernity and Nostalgia*, Sylviane Agacinski considers how nostalgia necessarily moves counter to the teleological conception of human progress, as "[a]ttachment to the past or returning to old forms thus appears suspect, indeed even regressive, in light of the necessary movement of history" (106). If parody, as the Russian Formalists noted, compels generic evolution through critical repetition, nostalgia forces an uncritical return.

While all artistic forms try to command the interest of the viewer, melodrama as a genre is specifically designed to keep the viewer engaged with the story through the use of various plot devices and strong appeals to the emotions. One of the most frequent mechanisms for the maintenance of audience interest is the plea for audience sentiment, often seen in a character in an unwarranted plight. The sickly, but cherubic Eva in the performances of *Uncle Tom's Cabin* and the scenes of drunkards and their spells of D.T.'s amid their impoverished families in the temperance dramas elicited primal responses from audiences.

But in the modern melodrama theatre, nostalgia for a sepia-hued era takes the place of sentiment toward a character in peril. The figure in unwarranted plight is the performance itself. A website advertisement for the Diamond Circle Melodrama of Durango, Colorado describes its productions as putting forth the genuine article: "In today's world of electronic reproductions this is real entertainment. Red velvet curtains, checkered tablecloths, brass chandeliers and authentic

Victorian costumes create an atmosphere that is truly unique, and a memory you'll treasure for years to come." Both melodrama and the nostalgia for the simpler time it has come to represent always seem to be on the verge of eclipse in the national memory. In the dedication to *Melodrama Classics: Six Plays and How to Stage Them*, Dorothy Mackin, the co-founder of The Imperial Players (now The Cripple Creek Players) melodrama theatre, protests against neglect of melodrama in the American theatrical repertory:

> It is my sincere hope that this book may be instrumental in helping to move melodrama out of the theatrical trash heap into which it has been tossed, and back into the realm of "legitimate theatre" from whence it came. (4)

This is a familiar plea made by theatre scholars like Tom Postlewait and others who view melodrama as an undervalued form.[1] But Mackin also calls for a theatrical evangelism. Her book, along with others like *Between Hisses: A Book of Songs and Olios for Melodrama* by James Burke and Paul T. Nolan, attempts to assist in the production of melodramas by community theatres and high schools with a great deal of proselytizing along the way: melodramas are packaged as easily-produced and readily acceptable to a wide variety of audiences. The acting style is portrayed by melodrama enthusiasts like Mackin as a nice departure from Stanislavsky, "introduc[ing] young actors and actresses to a wide variety of audience responses at close range" (19).

The performances of melodrama in the "melodrama theatres" constantly reaffirm a desire not only to invoke the spirit of the past, but also to situate audience members within it. Long running "melodrama theatres" like The Great American Melodrama in Pismo Beach, California, The Gaslight Theater of Tucson, Arizona, and The Golden Chain Theatre in Oakhurst, California are garbed in the trappings of the bygone era. Velvet curtains, wooden planking, and footlights are used to give the theatre an old-fashioned aura, just as modern amenities like air conditioning and imported beer undercut this aesthetic. These theatres allow audiences a seat within a pre-media age while giving them the comfort and superiority of distance. Their signature is not simply the presentation of a performance, but the transmission of the imagined experience of a former performance.

The "melodrama theatre" repertory includes either genuine melodramas (temperance melodramas and adaptations of David Belasco's *The Girl of the Golden West* and Dion Boucicault's *After Dark* are frequent favorites) or what can be termed "old-fashioned melodramas," plays in the style of nineteenth-century melodramas. I would define the "old-fashioned melodrama" as *the staged version of the idea of "melodrama" as conceptualized in the popular imagination.* It is a honed-down, always-already, parodic vision of heroes and villains; the plots of the plays are always highly formulaic; they always follow the same familiar narrative arc in which good triumphs over evil.[2] A good example of "old-fashioned melodrama" would be *The Girl of the Frozen North; or, Condemned to a Dead Man's Glacier* by Eddie Cope and Buster Cearley which includes the villainous hotel-owner Mr. Cesspool, a damsel in distress and a dynamic, but naïve, red-coated Canadian Mountie ready to save the day.

There is a wide gap between this description and its supposed pre-text, the aforementioned high-brow, "villainless melodrama" of David Belasco that evolved in the late nineteenth century (Gerould 26). Dramaturgically, the "old-fashioned melodrama" is close in shape to the 10-20-30 melodramas, but if the 10-20-30 melodramas were vehicles for spectacle, the present day "old-fashioned melodrama" is both medium and message. The clearly distinguished and exaggerated characters of the hero-heroine-villain triangle and the simplified plot attempt to summon up the "Gay Nineties" as filtered through one hundred years of media. Certainly, the Canadian Mountie figure reads like the title character from the cartoon "Dudley Do-Right," itself a parody of melodramatic extremes. Just as nostalgia can collapse time into itself, it can also collapse one form of media into another.

Geographically, most "melodrama theatres" are in the western half of the United States and this particularly geographic setting plays an important part with audiences exposed to a condensed, sanitized vision of the Old West. In other words, the audiences that frequent these theatres seek a vision of the West that is inherently melodramatic and romanticized, free from the influences of modernity. A century ago, stars like "Buffalo Bill" Cody summoned up a vision of the West for Easterners, one abounding with war dances, scalping braves, and large helpings of fancy rifle-shooting. The success of Cody and his "Combination" codified the West as a place where moral absolutes still held fast in the face of danger. As Robert G. Athearn wrote of the effect of the West on stage: "If believed ardently enough, long and strongly enough to shape the way in which we live our days, anything becomes true" (274). The popularity of melodrama theatres in western communities signifies an attempt to "shape the way in which we live our days." But as François Lyotard suggested in *The Postmodern Condition*, the postmodern moment always denies "the consensus of a taste which would make it possible to share collectively the nostalgia for the unattainable" (81). Hence, a changeable, postmodern culture takes the place of Indians as the prevalent threat to a more "natural" American culture.

It should not be surprising, therefore, that the harsher side of the American westward expansion is rarely explored in melodrama theatres. For nostalgia to operate, the displacement and genocide of Native Americans must remain outside the scope of the invocations of the American West. *Uncle Tom's Cabin*, the most significant American play from the period melodrama theatres seek to invoke, is never performed, symbolizing as it does another uncomfortable element of the American past. In this way, the melodrama theatre performances are modern equivalents of the Wild West exhibitions of the late-nineteenth and early-twentieth centuries. The extravaganzas of Buffalo Bill Cody were condensations of the mythologized West for primarily urban audiences, especially "recent immigrants who had never known the Indian or the West but relished stories and legends about frontier life and the frightfulness of Indian captivity" (Brasmer 213). Richard Slotkin has written that "If the Wild West was a 'place' rather than a 'show,' then its landscape was a mythic place, in which past and present, fiction and reality could coexist; a space in which history, translated into myth, was reenacted as ritual" (166). While Buffalo Bill and others brought the West to Brooklyn, the melodrama theatres continue to perform a similar simplified version of the West for visitors today. Paul Reddin has described the Wild West shows as "particularly important reflectors of American values because they were self-consciously American institutions devoted to defining their nation's values and history through the lens of the frontier experience" (220). Just as Wild West shows "glossed over the negative aspects of the westward movement," melodrama theatres remain engaged in the performance of a legacy sterilized of the painful events of the past (221).

The evolution of stage melodrama toward a romanticized, nostalgic version of itself reveals how a genre deemed dead after the rise of cinema took refuge in its own outdatedness. The dwelling upon obsolescence that characterizes "old-fashioned melodrama" necessarily connects it with the myth of a once-idyllic America. Melodrama theatres frequently incorporate the use of historical relics in performance as a way to have the audience engage nostalgically with the performance. For example, the Virginia City Players of Virginia City, Montana, include a vintage cremona in performances. A cremona is a self-contained instrument that attempts to replicate a full orchestra for small theatre spaces. The cremona of the Virginia City Players is described in detail on their website:

> It is sixteen feet wide and features two side chests containing flute, violin, and bass pipes, a xylophone, bass drum, crash symbol, tom tom, tympani, snare drum, sleigh bells, tambourine, castanets, wind siren, cathedral chimes, triangle and train bell. It was manufactured in Chicago by the Marquette Piano Company, whose wide variety of coin operated player pianos, orchestrians, and photoplayers sold under the Cremona trademark and were regarded as "top of the line." No expense was spared in their creation, from the piano keys of genuine ivory, to the double-veneered hardwood cases, new-scale (imparting the piano with an extraordinarily rich tone most noticeable in the mid-bass range).

The cremona acts as a trace of a long ago past that continues to exist and, most importantly, to perform in the present. The tones of the same cremona are heard upon entrance to the website dedicated to advertising the group. Its use presents a past that appears indefatigable even in the present. The gap between past and present is foreclosed in a way that recalls Jean Baudrillard's description in "The Precession of Simulacra" of the "repatriation" of the cloister of Saint-Michel de Cuxa from the Cloisters in New York to its original home in Paris. Baudrillard describes the return of the cloister to its "rightful place" not as a laudable act of restitution but as instead "supplementary subterfuge, acting as if nothing had happened and indulging in retrospective hallucination" (528). For Baudrillard, acting as if one can ever go home again is an exercise in pantomime. Similarly, the use of the cremona musically creates the illusion of the erasure of time passed; in the "melodrama theatre" "acting as if nothing had happened" is the mode to ensure its survival.

Given an aesthetic that always makes the past present, melodrama theatres can also serve as centrifuges of community. The melodramatic distillation of that which is good and that which is evil encourages the creation of community, one that Anthony Cohen in *The Symbolic Construction of Community* has explained as a conception of boundary and the manifestation of the similar and the different. Similarly, Sonja Kuftinec notes in "A Cornerstone for Rethinking Community Theatre," "In order for a community to distinguish itself, its members must differentiate themselves in some way from other communities through boundaries of land, behavior, or background" (92). The obligatory audience responses in a melodrama performance create that very vision of community through a ritualistic performance of moral binaries, "highlight[ing] social and aesthetic representations that embody, enact and mythologize community" (19).

An example of such a communal moment happens regularly every year during the melodrama performance at Mahoney State Park in Nebraska. Located in Ashbury, Nebraska, the Denman and Mary Mallory Kountze Memorial Theatre has been the site of melodrama performance since 1993 and is part of a trio of melodrama theatres in and around Lincoln. [3] In a newspaper interview with Jim Delmont of the *Omaha World-Herald*, Suzanna O'Hearn, the concessions manager of the theatre, pointed out a reoccurring trope: "In the second act of all the shows, the villain is chased into the audience by the hero – so you can hit him with the popcorn."[4] The tradition is good-humored and playful, owing in spirit as much to going to the movies as the theatre, an elision of different responses to different forms. It is a part of the response expected from an audience in many melodrama theatres and a reaction that seems to be an attempt to call up an outdated performance form. It is watching a play "in the style of" an earlier audience, underlining the essential tension of these performances as they attempt to evoke a prelapsarian past. With hisses and cheers, audience members take part in a liturgy in which the past is repeated, evoked, and summoned up, sacralizing an "authentic" form of theatre. The melodrama theatre is a secular ritual of collective nostalgia in which a simpler time in America is resurrected, a vision of communal identity.

Melodrama theatres articulate the sense of a fixed, sanitized national identity through the presentation of its plays. Just as the term "melodrama" is synonymous today with mustache-twirling villains, always-incorruptible heroes and ever-virtuous heroines, its particular distillation in the "old-fashioned melodrama" is highly useful for the propagation of ideology. If, as Northrop Frye noted in *Anatomy of Criticism*, "In the melodrama of the brutal thriller we come as close as it is normally possible for art to come to the pure self-righteousness of the lynching mob," the "old-fashioned melodrama" of popular classification serves as perfect venue for the propagation of ideology (47). Baudrillard noted that Disneyland is "a deterrence machine set up in order to rejuvenate the fiction of the real in the opposite camp" (529).[5] In the Baudrillardian sense, melodrama theatres act as localized Disneylands that perpetuate the perception of a true, youthful "America," beneath the suburban sprawl.

## Notes

1. See Thomas Postlewait's "From Melodrama to Realism: The Suspect History of American Drama" in *Melodrama: The Cultural Emergence of a Genre*, pages 39-60.
2. The quotation-marked term "old-fashioned melodrama" will be used for the remainder of this essay to denote the modern, already-parodic version of the melodramatic genre. These plays are usually published cheaply and singly. A rare compendium of "old-fashioned melodramas" is entitled *Gay Nineties Melodramas: A Collection of Old-Fashioned Melodramas of the Gay Nineties Period,* and includes twenty-three plays by Leland Price, James Floyd Stone, and notably Arthur Kaiser, the author of "The Filming of Uncle Tom's Cabin" (1922). Interestingly, half of the plays in the volume are described as either "burlesque" or "parody," yet they, either in subject matter, dramaturgy, or tone, differ little from plays described as merely "old-fashioned."
3. In addition to the Mahoney State Park melodrama, the "Freemont Dinner Train" in nearby Freemont frequently performs melodramas a part of a dinner theatre. In addition, melodramas are also performed on the Missouri River aboard the "Sprit of Brownville" riverboat. See "Melodrama!" Melodramas at Mahoney State Park. http://www.melodrama.net.

4. It should also be noticed that the expulsion of the villain from the community recalls Satan's fall from the community of Heaven, a scene represented in the English mystery plays. See John D. Cox, *The Devil and Sacred in English Drama, 1350-1642*, pages 19-38.

5. Not surprisingly, melodrama theatres are frequently a part of exhibits in theme parks. The Bird Cage melodrama theatre (which has recently closed) located inside Knott's Berry Farm in Buena Park, California began comedian Steve Martin's career.

## Works Cited


Agacinski, Sylviane. *Time Passing: Modernity and Nostalgia.* New York: Columbia UP, 2003.

Athearn, Robert G. *The Mythic West in Twentieth-Century America.* Lawrence, KS: U of Kansas P, 1986.

Baudrillard, Jean. "The Precession of Simulacra." *Simulacra and Simulation.* Trans. Sheila Faria Glaser. Ann Arbor: U of Michigan P, 1994. Rpt. in *Media and Cultural Studies: Keyworks.* Ed. Mennakshi Gigi Durham and Douglas M. Kellner. Malden, MA: Blackwell, 2001. 1-42.

Bentley, Eric. *The Life of the Drama.* New York: Atheneum, 1967.

Brasmer, William. "The Wild West Exhibition: A Fraudulent Reality." *American Popular Entertainment: Papers and Proceedings of the Conference on the History of American popular Entertainment.* Ed. Myron Matlaw. Westport, CT: Greenwood, 1979. 207-214.

Brings, Lawrence. *Gay Nineties Melodramas: A Collection of Old-Fashioned Melodramas of the Gay Nineties Period.* Minneapolis, MN: T.S. Denison, 1963.

Cohen, Anthony P. *The Symbolic Construction of Community.* New York: Youngstock, 1985.

Cox, John D. *The Devil and Sacred in English Drama, 1350-1642.* Cambridge: Cambridge UP, 2000. 19-38.

"Cremona." Virginia City Players. 2004. 13 December 2004. http://www.vcplayers.com/cremona.html

"A Dialogue on Film with Steven Spielberg." American Film Institute. 2002. 10 October 2005. http://www.fathom.com/feature/122046

Delmont, Jim. "Don't just sit there. Booing, repeating lines and throwing your popcorn at the villain aren't just tolerated at the Mahoney State Park melodramas – they're encouraged." *Omaha World-Herald.* 6 July 2003: 1AT.

Frye, Northrop. "Comic Fictional Modes." *Anatomy of Criticism: Four Essays.* Princeton: Princeton UP, 1957.

Gerould, Daniel C. "The Americanization of Melodrama." *American Melodrama.* New York: PAJ, 1983. 7-29.

Kuftinec, Sonja. "A Cornerstone for Rethinking Community Theatre." *Theatre Topics* 6.1 (1996): 91-104.

Leacock, Stephen. *Over the Footlights.* New York: Dodd and Mead, 1923.

Lyotard, François. *The Postmodern Condition: A Report on Knowledge.* Minneapolis: U of Minnesota P, 1984.

Mackin, Dorothy. *Melodrama Classics: Six Plays and How to Stage Them.* New York: Sterling, 1982.

Postlewait, Thomas. "From Melodrama to Realism: The Suspect History of American Drama." *Melodrama: The Cultural Emergence of a Genre.* Eds. Michael Hays and Anastasia Nikolopoulou. New York: St. Martin's Press, 1999. 39-60.

Reddin, Paul. *Wild West Shows.* Urbana and Chicago: U of Illinois P, 1999.

Slotkin, Richard. "Buffalo Bill's 'Wild West' and the Mythologization of the American Empire." *Cultures of United States Imperialism.* Ed. Amy Kaplan and Donald E. Pease. Durham and London: Duke UP, 1993. 164-184.

"What is Melodrama?" Diamond Circle Melodrama, 2005. 10 October 2005. http://www.diamondcirclemelodrama.com/melodrama-information.htm

*Jenny Alexander Lewis examines the issues young Latinas face concerning body image through an examination of the independent film* Real Women Have Curves.

# Body Image and the American Popular Culture Landscape: The Shifting Identity of Young Latinas in *Real Women Have Curves*

Jenny Alexander Lewis

*Real Women Have Curves*, the 2002 film based on Josefina López's two act play, politicizes the female form by strategically exposing and subverting dominant ideals about body image. López takes the overweight form, so often marginalized (like the immigrant) by society and popular culture, and redefines this form as a source of strength and integrity. Ana (America Ferrera), the main character, an intelligent, eighteen-year-old Latina, deconstructs both the American and Mexican values that are forced upon her as she becomes a woman between two cultures. In non-fictional society, young Latinas are often forced to grapple with a confusing composite of body images. As will be discussed, a curvier body often has been viewed as acceptable in Latino culture, but, as United States-based, Latina-focused media has begun to present the idea of thinness as equal to beauty, perceptions of body image have become more polarized for young Latinas. As María Figuero has noted, "Popular culture can be seen, and has been interpreted by some, as a structure of dominance that perpetuates and enhances a dominant ideology invested with the social construction of whiteness, and correspondingly, with capitalistic commodification." *Real Women Have Curves* serves as an excellent representation of timely, real-world cultural and body image issues facing young Latinas today. Ana, of her own will, shuns Mexican and American cultural norms by accepting her body "as is" – thus rejecting both Latino culture's demands she stay thin to be marriageable, as well as Anglo body image standards delegated by unattainable, popular culture-induced beauty myths.

Latina/o ideas about a woman's place as the caretaker of a family are evident in the film. For Ana's mother, Carmen (Lupe Ontiveros), the primary concern is that Ana's weight will prevent her from finding a suitable mate. The value of her education and intellect is ignored. The Latino community has at times undervalued women who were not defined in some way by their attachment to a male. According to Carla Trujillo, "For many Chicanas…identification as women, that is, as complete women, comes from the belief that [they] need to be connected to a man. Ridding [oneself] of this parasitic identification is not always easy, for we grow up…defined in a male context: daddy's girl, some guy's girlfriend, wife, or mother." These ideas extend into the point of view held by some in the Chicano community that women are not complete until they are mothers: "Many Chicanas are socialized to believe that [their] chief purpose in life is raising children." Carmen already believes that it is too late for her older daughter Estela (Ingrid Oliu); Ana's "possibilities" give her a renewed sense of hope. Ana, however, has other ideas, and is a disquieting force for the traditional Mexican wife and mother. Sandra Guzmán has written of the delicate cultural balance young Latinas must deal with when faced with the traditional expectations of their community:

> Marriage or a committed relationship takes us to territory that will bring out our mothers or abuelas in ways we didn't expect. And when we find ourselves in that territory…we struggle against her – that traditional wife who carries her home on

> her back. We fight like hell against the automatic servant and nurturer within us. Some [Latinas] call this the dreaded "Mexican-maid complex."

Ana is perhaps most unsettling because she is the antithesis of the non-threatening "good girl" ideal perpetuated by the cultures that surround her – ideals that seem to tie weight to traditional women's household roles, obedience, and marriage on the Mexican side, and magazine-inspired expectations of thin, silent beauty on the Anglo side. The film illustrates how Ana is not appreciated for her intelligence, progressive views, or independence. In response to her father's statements that Ana wants to go to college and be educated, Ana's mother replies that she can "educate" Ana – to sew, raise children, and care for a husband. When Ana tells Carmen that she is old-fashioned, proclaiming that a "woman has thoughts, ideas, a mind of her own," Carmen's response is bafflement: "Thoughts? Ideas?" The factory workers label Ana a know-it-all, she knows everything except her proper place. Ana is clearly not the traditional, meek, "good girl" Carmen wants her daughter to be.

Carmen makes derogatory comments about Ana's weight throughout the film. On Ana's first day in the factory, she looks longingly at a beautiful size seven black dress. Carmen tells her not to get her hopes up about fitting into it and that she is telling her so for her "own good." As Maria Teresa Marrero relates, for her "own good" refers to Ana's ability to "catch" a suitable husband. When Ana counters that her mother is also overweight, Carmen replies firmly, "Yes, but I'm married." This is to say that she has already caught a man, case closed, no more to be concerned about – except her daughter managing the same triumph. But Ana does not fit into this traditional mold. Instead, her identity is shifting to meld with modern, feminist ideas about women's roles in society. According to Marrero, "Ana assumes a feminist position that her body is her own, meant to please and serve her, not fulfill a biological/social function." Self-validation is more important than the validation of a man, as Ana tells her mother: "I do want to lose weight. But part of me doesn't because it says to everybody…How dare anybody tell me what I should look like or what I should be when there's so much more to me than just my weight!" Thus, Ana refuses the containment and marginalization of fat by the general public. As Jana Evans Braziel has discussed, "The excessive feminine…threatens the limits of containment and confinement," refusing society's molds and throwing the system into chaos. For Carmen, Ana's rejections of the conventional values and expectations the older generation holds so dear toss everything she knows and accepts into disarray. Carmen does not know what to do with Ana. Where is the obedient, self-sacrificing daughter she expected? The film thus puts forth a shift in Latina identity with body image as its starting point; Chicana women become both "perpetrators" and "innovators" of cultural values," Marrero argues, and push the personal into the political arena. *Real Women Have Curves* also rejects body image ideals forced on Latinas (and, indeed, all women) by media. Latino/a culture, in the past, has often been viewed as accepting of a curvier, larger body size, as discussed by María Figueroa and Linda Delgado. Delgado claims that weight in the Latino community shows that one is eating well enough to deal with family and home burdens. Skinniness can be equated with unattractiveness and an unhealthy lifestyle, with not taking care of oneself. What picture does this present of the Latina body? When tied to the home and domestic duties, it gives an image of the female body primarily as a place of comfort, a home and refuge. The food women prepare in their kitchens is meant to be taken in, to nurture. However, a woman must not be too fat; that could ruin her chances for marriage. The idea that a certain amount of weight is necessary for family strength, combined with the idea that crossing the line with too much weight makes one incapable of catching or keeping a husband, creates a dichotomy of body image. Weight is inextricably tied up with the home and the family, with traditional women's roles. Sandra Guzmán, a former editor of *Latina* magazine, recounts how during her girlhood, gordita was an endearing term, and to be flaca or skinny was to be fea or ugly. Guzmán laments that this has shifted as a result of acculturation to the United States.

Hence, when Latino/a culture crosses wires with mainstream U.S. popular culture, the female body takes on a particular image of a particular beauty in the public's imagination. Figueroa criticizes *Latina* magazine as a case-in-point for "advancing an assimilationist paradigm that perpetuates the dominant ideals of white beauty for Latina access into the mainstream." This includes *Latina's* beauty tips for straightening hair and lunchtime body workouts. Cover models are usually already highly visible in mainstream American culture; they include Jennifer Lopez, Mariah Carey, and Salma Hayek. Figueroa points to the thinness of these models and their Americanized beauty; their clothes and styling do not "disclose any ethnic or racial markers" that would brand them as ethnic women. Figueroa does not indicate what she might mean by this statement, but she does express disappointment that *Latina* is not working to accomplish its vision of representation of Latinas of diverse sizes, shapes, and colors – in short, the magazine's covers ignore the heterogeneity of Latina identity.

Cherrié L. Moraga has concurred with the putting on a pedestal of "whiteness" in the Chicano community. In her essay "La Guera," Moraga writes, "I was educated; but more than this, I was 'la guera' – fair-skinned. Born with the features of my Chicana mother, but the skin of my Anglo father, I had it made. No one ever quite told me this (that light was right), but I knew that being light was something valued in my family, who were all Chicano, with the exception of my father. In fact, everything about my upbringing…attempted to bleach me of what color I did have." Moraga feels that the fact she is well-educated has had less value to her family than her appearance. In *Real Women Have Curves*, Ana must also deal with her mother's concern with her physical appearance overwhelming any indication of pride over her daughter's achievements in education.

Desire to assimilate into United States' society, to achieve the "American Dream," seems to perpetuate this esteem of one race's features over another's. In *Chicano Professionals: Class, Culture, and Identity,* Tamis Hoover Rentería has detailed how the blonde, thin, Anglo woman has symbolized the "American dream of success, of moving up the ladder from blue-collar immigrant to white collar American…To possess a Blonde, or to be oneself the possessed Blonde, conjured up images of the 'Good Life,' White Anglo Saxon Protestant middle-class style." This desire for a better life, for the America portrayed in film, television, magazines, and advertisements, at times even spills over into Mexico's consciousness. Rentería writes:

> In Mexico, attractiveness is often associated with European rather than Indian physiognomy. Advertising billboards in Mexico regularly depict upper-class looking, blue-eyed blondes curled around various products (liquor, perfume, dishwashers) thus symbolically linking the consuming of certain goods with social mobility, status, and European and/or "Anglo" looking women…in many Chicano…families, children [have been] classified as attractive or not according to how light-skinned or light-haired they were, and whether or not they had green or blue eyes instead of brown.

In taking a look at a recent issue of *Latina* magazine, produced in the United States, I noted that this value of white, "economically viable beauty" certainly exalts thinness as well.

*Latina*'s December 2004 cover blurbs tout promises such as "5 ways to eat what you want and not gain weight! (frijoles and flan included)." The article itself, written by Karen Grimaldos, begins with a refrain we have seen many times in "mainstream" magazines, but with a Latina twist:

> It seems that every January, many of us chicas glumly perform the same holiday ritual: We reach into the dark depths of our closets, pull out our gordita pants, and walk around feeling more plump than Papá Noel – a consequence of having spent weeks piling our plates with typical (and fattening) fiesta foods such as lechon, tamales, and turión…The good news is that you can indulge in just about anything you like (even Abuela's dulce de leche) without plumping up, as long as you follow some basic guidelines.

Like Carmen's nickname for Ana – "Butterball" – the article clearly demeans the fat body, making it ridiculous through the connotations of its language. Snickering mentions of "gordita pants," "more plump than Papa Noel," and "plumping up" imply that the fat body is silly and to be shunned. The female body must be contained in its proper place before its girth grows too wide. The "good news" according to the piece, and the message imparted to Latinas young and old in the grand tradition of American media, is that such a horrifying form can be – and indeed must be – avoided at all costs.

This idea is reiterated in a fashion spread, mentioned on the cover as "The Sexiest Party Dresses for Your Curves." This blurb is not necessarily derogatory, but in the actual fashion spread, body shapes are polarized once again in the spectrum of beauty versus undesirability. A "long, lean frame" is described as flattering, but the larger form is apologized for, by the women pictured and the magazine itself. A twenty-five-year-old woman photographed for the spread states of her body, "Even though I have bigger hips, I have a small waistline." Not to worry, the article suggests that a cinched waistline will draw "attention away from the hips." If *Latina's* simple guidelines are followed to the letter, you too can look like Hayek.

In the set directions for the play version of López's *Real Women Have Curves*, the factory staging is meant to contain collages of "magazine runway 'fashion' clippings." Once again, we are back to society's containment of women into small packages fit for consumption, back to Ana's mother's obsession that her daughter be thin and beautiful to be sellable to society and a husband. As Figueroa reminds us, "*Latina* leans toward assimilation through bodily transformation." Sandra Guzmán, for her part, has admitted perpetuating what she calls the established "mentality (and trend) within the ranks of the magazine industry that considers a light-skinned, light-haired, tall, skinny woman the ideal of female beauty."

In *Real Women Have Curves*, Ana rejects this phenomenon. Instead of assimilating into American popular culture exemplars, Ana remains on the border, refusing to accept the ideals perpetuated in magazines and the telenovelas her mother adores. As Josefina López has stated in a 2003 interview with Monica Brown: during the process of growing into a woman, the "message was clear that you had to be skinny…it's very clear…especially when you watch the telenovelas or…Mexican or Spanish-speaking TV, it's always the guera, the skinny gueras that are on TV. Even though it's Mexican TV." Tamis Hoover Rentería agrees with this point: "The 'novelas' or soap operas produced in Latin American countries (and viewed daily in many Chicano households in the United States) feature light skinned, European looking, often blond heroes and heroines, occasionally depicting maids and country bumpkins with more 'mestizo' or 'Indian' features." As in other media, the telenovelas champion the "white" ideal of beauty as a result of commodification of this beauty by dominant culture. In *Real Women Have Curves*, Ana's mother is enthralled with such soap operas, and subconsciously wants her daughter in some way to resemble the women portrayed in them. Instead, while Carmen recounts the latest episode breathlessly, Ana sits outside of the television room, having a private chuckle at the program's ludicrous plot. She does not fall for consumerist views of "beauty" and lives of excitement and drama.

This, along with Ana's refusal to lose weight, irritates Carmen. Ana's body protects her from cultural paradigms and permits her to control her own destiny. The "right" clothes, designed for the "right" bodies as dictated by the telenovelas and magazines, are irrelevant to Ana. Estela, Ana's sister, agrees with this point. In one scene, she brings Ana a beautiful red dress, stating: "Pretty dresses aren't just for skinny girls…I cut this especially for your body." Estela discloses that she is designing her own line; this will no doubt include fashions for larger sizes which is a triumph over Ana's lament early in the film when she holds one of the factory's dresses commenting on how much work goes into each design: "I never realized how much work…was put in into it…but it's not for me." Ana hangs the dress back up with a sigh. Estela, in designing beautiful dresses for curvier forms, has scored a coup. "Such a move constitutes both a recognition and acceptance of [the factory women] as women of fashion, elegance, and beauty," argues Margo Milleret, even if they are not in the cast of a soap opera or on the cover of *Latina*. It also reclaims the task of making the tiny dresses for skinny women that before would serve to remind the factory workers of their supposed "inferiority" in terms of body size.

Unfortunately, for a growing number of young Latinas, society's voice is too indoctrinated to resist. As Guzmán also notes, a 1997 study on the influence of fashion publications on young women's satisfaction with their bodies found that women who were heavily exposed to fashion media "preferred to weigh less, were less satisfied with their bodies, were more frustrated about their weight, were more preoccupied with the desire to be thin, and were more afraid of getting fat" than peers who were not exposed to such media (see Turner, Hamilton, Jacobs, Angood, and Dwyer). Anorexia and bulimia, once believed to be a strictly "white" problem, have risen in Latinas with the process of American acculturation. As young Latina girls conform to the dominant culture, they put more and more emphasis on thinness. A 1995 medical study found that Latinas who were born in the U.S. tended to esteem a thinner figure, while those who immigrated after seventeen years of age had less desire for a thin body. The study attributes this to the fact that those arriving in the U.S. later in life were not socialized early on to the prevailing fashion of thinness perpetuated in U.S. culture and media.

As Susan Bordo relates in her fascinating book *Unbearable Weight: Feminism, Western Culture, and the Body*, "Culture not only has taught women to be insecure about their bodies, constantly monitoring themselves for signs of imperfection, constantly engaged in physical 'improvement'; it also is constantly teaching women (and, let us not forget, men as well) how to see bodies. As slenderness has consistently been visually glamorized, and as the ideal has grown thinner and thinner, bodies that a decade ago were considered slender have now come to seem fleshy." Bordo also notes that the "equation of slenderness and success in this culture continually undermines the preservation of alternative ideals of beauty." In contrast, Ana is not concerned with taking up space. Ana's lack of concern is shown in a rather humorous scene with Carmen. When seated in a café with her mother, Carmen tells Ana she could be beautiful if only she lost weight. "Don't eat the flan!" Carmen commands. Ana pops the flan into her mouth with relish, a look of defiance on her face. She does not hide her eating like a dirty secret, throwing the accepted system of the shame an overweight person should have about eating dessert in public into disarray. Ana's greatest revolt against the norm occurs near the end of the film when she encourages all of the women in the factory to disrobe because of the stifling heat, regardless of their weight. Then, the women try to take the prize for who is the fattest, comparing stretch marks proudly. Ana thus gets the women to liberate themselves from the garments that encase and restrict their flesh, to show who they really are. They accept one another as is. Only Carmen will not join. Ana lifts her mother's shirt and Carmen protests, but not before Ana sees a large scar on her mother's abdomen. When Ana asks about it, Carmen replies, "This one is you." The caesarean scar revealed through Carmen's own display of flesh shows much about the sacrifices she has made in life. Her flesh and blood sacrifice has not been to the beauty myth. Her sacrifice has been for her family, and she views Ana's independence and desire to leave to go to college as a rejection of that sacrifice to the family unit. As Carla Trujillo states: "Personified by the Virgen de Guadalupe, the concept of motherhood and martyrdom go hand in hand." Carmen walks out of the factory, leaving the other women behind to complete the dress order. Ana stands firm, telling her mother goodbye.

Ana, in using her body as a vital element in expressing her views, liberates herself by the internal self rather than the external, programmed by culture's uncompromising rules and restrictions. By staying in tune with personal convictions, Ana rejects the oppression that surrounds her. Margo Milleret is accurate in her assertion that the overweight characters in *Real Women Have Curves* are "real" in that they do not conform to fantastical market standards of what a woman should look like. Instead, they maintain true individuality through their supposedly unacceptable, marginal forms, and through this extra weight, learn to honor each other as women. Magazines, telenovelas, and cultural expectations can be ignored. The factory becomes a sort of "test kitchen" where they can be visible in their real bodies. The idea of the factory as a private, feminine space is interesting in that it is outside the home, outside of that space traditionally associated with femininity and, not coincidentally, with food – the kitchen. The women depend only upon one another for influence, marveling, "Look at how beautiful we are!" This is a safe, empowering space. It "offers an opportunity to redesign how young women grow up and how they are welcomed into the larger society. Most of all, this model can influence/infiltrate the worlds around it transforming them into better places to grow up," Milleret states. Acceptance of the body resists all of culture's dictates, allowing young women to be proud of what they look like.

This scene is unique in the context of the majority of performance. Film and theater are usually the domain of the temptress – the blonde vixen and beauty in high heels illuminated in the stage lights. The fat body as a source of integrity and power is rarely, if ever seen in these mediums. The dilemma of the overweight performer, playwright, or screenwriter is to present the fat female body without ridiculing it or making it a laughable spectacle in the face of society's indoctrinated associations of fat with gluttony and an overall lack of self-control. But can society's influence be entirely ignored? After taking off her clothes in the factory, Ana encourages the women to get back to work without dressing. "Who cares what we look like when no one's watching us?" she says. But someone is watching them: the audience. The presence of these bodies on stage and screen forces audience members to face their own oppressive ideologies about the female body, to question what is "real" about these bodies and what is false about their own expectations for them. As Petra Kruppers notes, much feminist thought has put forth that the "possibilities that lie in [an overweight actress's] fatness can be revalued, wrested back from patriarchal discourse, and made into a trope for female empowerment." Ana has served to influence society through the presentation of her body on stage, rather than the other way around.

For young Latinas in the real world, progress is being made. In addition to this film, there are current American-produced handbooks for young Latinas growing up in a world influenced by multiple cultures, including Sandra Guzmán's *The Latina's Bible* and *Border-Line Personalities: A New Generation of Latinas Dish on Sex, Sass, and Cultural Shifting* by Michelle Herrera Mulligan, et al. Such books work to guide Latinas through conflicting traditional family ways and modern women's opportunities. Even *Latina* magazine in December 2004 featured an interview with Josefina López (though the weight issues presented in *Real Women Have Curves* are not touched). Perhaps such changes in identity associations with weight demonstrate that attention to the issues can indeed have an effect on the world at large.

In her work *The Last Generation*, Cherrié Moraga writes of a desire to create a picture of the Latina woman "before the 'Fall,' before shame, before betrayal, before Eve, Malinche, and Guadalupe; before the occupation of Aztlán, la llegada de los españoles, the Aztecs' War of Flowers. I don't know what this woman looks like exactly, but I know she is more than the bent back in the field, more than the assembly-line fingers and the rigid body beneath him in bed, more than the veiled face above the rosary beads. She is more than the sum of all these fragmented parts…How did we become so broken?" In short, Moraga longs for a time of Chicana women before all of the oppression and corruption of time and social conditioning, when a woman could be herself, fully, without outside influence to cloud her thinking.

In Ana, we get a glimpse of a woman well on her way to this unbroken, complete beauty, born of self-validation and the refusal to be corrupted by the chatter outside her. The conclusion of the film shows Ana, newly arrived in New York to attend Columbia University. She struts down the city street with confidence, "walking like a lady" as her mother told her to do. But, as we see in the way Ana boldly holds her head high and bravely faces the path ahead of her, it is Ana's own personal interpretation of what "walking like a lady" signifies. In following her own inner voice, Ana has shifted her identity from the expected to the desired, on her own terms, with her own interpretation of "real" beauty.

*Debbie Hallett mounts a defense of* Hustle and Flow *in her article "Consuming the Black Body": "At first glance, this film seems to reinforce negative constructions of American blackness…. Yet, a closer analysis of character dialogue and narrative technique reveals the film's subtle critique of socially prescribed racial identities."*

# Consuming the Black Body: Identity Politics and Optic Blackness in *Hustle and Flow*

Debbie Hallett

Craig Brewer's critically acclaimed film *Hustle and Flow* tells the story of a Memphis pimp who attempts to become a rapper. Through collaboration with two friends and one of his prostitutes, DJay, played by Terrence Howard, creates a music track that he then attempts to promote. In his efforts to promote his music, DJay becomes involved in a conflict with a famous rapper, Skinny Black, and shoots Black's bodyguard. Ultimately, however, due to the persistence of DJay's prostitute, Nola, the track gets played on the radio, and, although he is in jail, DJay achieves his dream of becoming a famous rapper.

At first glance, this film seems to reinforce negative constructions of American blackness. The narrative only features two masculine identities, the gangsta rapper and the pimp. Much like the sambo and coon performances in minstrel shows, these essentialist identity categories have become naturalized in contemporary culture. The film's plot structure and character development are heavily invested in the gangsta and pimp tropes. Yet, a closer analysis of character dialogue and narrative technique reveals the film's subtle critique of socially prescribed racial identities. The film does not condemn the gangsta and pimp tropes, nor does it question their authenticity; rather, the film exposes the limited options for identity formation available within black youth culture. As a character, DJay complicates American audiences' desire to consume certain types of black bodies, he performs the pimp persona while simultaneously articulating his identity, and black identity as a whole, as constituted by sociopolitical forces. The film does rely on and invoke the commodification and stereotyping of black bodies to ensure financial success, and therefore cannot be interpreted as wholly productive in terms of African-American body politics. However, a subversive and powerful critique is embedded within the narrative, and, in this way, the film exposes the constraining nature of socially prescribed black identities.

The first scene of the film takes place in a parked car where DJay and Nola converse as DJay attempts to pimp Nola to other men as they drive past. DJay begins the film with a monologue, delivered in vernacular speech as he deeply inhales cigarette smoke:

> See, man ain't like a dog, and when I say man I'm talking about man as in mankind, not man as in men. Man – we a lot like a dog…But man, he know about death. Got him a sense of history, got religion. A dog don't know shit about no birthdays…they goin' through life care free…But, people like you and me, we always just wondering "what if" you know what I mean? So when you say to me "hey, I don't think we should be doing this" – I gotta say, baby, I don't think we need to be doin' this neither. But we ain't gon' get no move on in this world lying around in the sun licking our ass all day. I mean, we man. I mean, you a woman and all but, we man.

In this monologue, DJay highlights themes that become the subtext for the remainder of the film. He addresses two pertinent issues: man as an individual versus humanity as a whole and the commodification of the body as simultaneously debilitating and mobilizing.

DJay begins by making a distinction between man and mankind. Man, as an individual, is like a dog lying in the sun and is oblivious to larger issues that extend beyond the scope of pleasure and self-preservation. Here DJay explicitly links his conception of individual men to wealth and privilege, as this identity is detached from labor and struggle and is defined by comfort and freedom. Mankind, on the other hand, is defined by a connection to death, history, and religion. Humanity is unified by its sense of the past as a struggle fraught with tragedy. For DJay, mankind is a community of marginalized people whose identities are constituted by sociopolitical forces.

As a member of mankind, DJay is aware of the implications of his actions, and he understands his identity as part of a larger cultural fabric. He constructs his identity as a pimp, and Nola's identity as a prostitute, as concurrently deliberate and forced. As a man, he must engage in his profession as a means of survival but as a part of mankind, he is aware of the economic and historical forces that have dictated his life. He emphasizes the plight of oppressed peoples who always straddle the line between fighting for personal gain and fighting for the betterment of humanity. DJay wonders "what if" he could escape his profession, and he regards being a pimp as an activity, rather than a definitive persona; it is something that he does, not who he is. Although he struggles with his identity as a pimp, DJay reconstitutes his actions as evidence of another identity. Because he is not oblivious to the complexities founding his black pimp identity, he interprets himself as a part of mankind, a community of oppressed peoples who work and struggle.

DJay continues in his monologue to address the commodification of the body. In his attempts to articulate his subjectivity as a pimp, DJay calls attention to the ways in which "scripting, as a paradigm, is not just about stereotypes and negative images; it is about how the treatment of Black *bodies* as commodities has persisted for hundreds of years and continues today" (Jackson 12). In the scene within the film, DJay is not selling his body; in fact, he is selling the body of his white prostitute, Nola. Yet his word choice clearly shows that DJay is also selling something additional. It is important to note that DJay's speech functions simultaneously as a monologue addressed to the viewer, as well as a response within a conversation with Nola, which is *en media res* as the film begins. DJay's speech bridges the "real" world of the audience with the on screen reality of the film. His entire speech is a response to an extradiagetic query posed by Nola, to which the viewer is not privy. DJay responds by saying "So when you say to me, "hey, I don't think we should be doing this" – I gotta say, baby, I don't think we need to be doin' this neither." It can be assumed that Nola has questioned the necessity of prostituting herself, but Djay's reply broadens the scope of inquiry. He aligns himself with Nola, as a commodity that is being sold, through his deliberate use of the subjective pronoun "we." Additionally, DJay is speaking directly to the camera, and the viewer is not even aware of Nola's presence until after the monologue is complete. In this light, DJay can be read as the prostitute that is selling his body for popular consumption in the "real" world of the viewer, in much the same way that Nola sells her body within the filmic narrative. He completes his speech by admitting that he is complicit in his own commodification and insists, "we ain't gon' get no move on in this world" without prostituting ourselves. Thus the film begins with a self-reflexive commentary on the commodification of the black body within American visual culture.

The black identities that are available for consumption in this film are the pimp and the gangsta rapper. These identities are preferenced within the film and, indeed, are presented as the only acceptable masculine roles. DJay articulates the role of the black pimp in American culture when he responds to his friend Key's comment, "I see you still doing the same." DJay replies by comparing his profession to "the post office" which is present and reliable "through rain, sleet, or snow." Here DJay explicitly verbalizes that the black pimp identity (and the conjoined expectation to hustle and sell drugs) is a foundational element of American culture; it has been institutionalized, like the post office. This statement is particularly poignant in light of Key's initial comment that DJay "is still doing the same" because DJay is literally enacting the same role that has been assigned to black men throughout American history. A role that is not only defined by the literal profession of pimping but also by the overt sexual, criminal, and exploitative connotations associated with that occupation. Because hegemonic power structures connect blackness with these negative traits, Djay's profession seems fitting and natural – the logical life path for a young black man. DJay's pimp identity and his black body are linked in the American psyche and thus he, as an individual, is performing and maintaining the traditional masculine identity assigned to his race.

However, DJay is not content with his life as a pimp and aspires to occupy the only other masculine identity available within the film, the gangsta rapper. These identities create a false dichotomy within the film; the pimp represents the demeaned black man while the gangsta rapper represents the successful black man. Although other black male identities are featured within the film, each character idealizes the gangta rapper as the paramount, authentic black identity. Characters such as Key and the prison guards idolize the rapper persona and express dissatisfaction with their current professions and lifestyles, which are presented as disingenuous. At separate times within the film, both Key and the prison guards communicate feelings of disconnect with their current lifestyles, as if their jobs are not representative of their authentic identities. These characters display the negative psychological ramifications of essentialist identity prescriptions and show that, although essentialism is an abstract concept, it has a material presence which can be seen in its affects on the body and the psyche.

Both of the black masculine identities within the film are deeply embedded in street mythology and the ghetto lifestyle. These identities are presented as authentic and real; all other identities are simply masquerade. Yet the consequences of essentialist logic are manifested through the characters' struggle with identity formation. For example, although Key appears to be financially successful and happily married, he feels inadequate because he is not fulfilling the street identity that is inextricably linked to blackness. He is psychologically emasculated by his inability to successfully perform his race within normative codes.

DJay further enunciates the failure of essentialist logic toward the end of the film when Key shows him a picture of the prostitute Shug's baby daughter. DJay postulates that the baby is going to "dream big and ask me, 'when she grow up, can she be president?' And I'm gon' look her in the eye and lie because sometimes that's what you gotta do." DJay understands the ways in which the baby's identity will be inscribed onto her body, and he knows that the identity of president is not available to her. More specifically, even allowing her to dream of being president is a lie; goals and aspirations become essentialized and are a component of prescribed identities. Only certain types of dreams are available to black bodies. DJay never explicitly attacks white sociopolitic forces; instead he struggles against an abstracted power structure. Yet, as bell hooks points out, critiquing essentialism "challenges colonial imperialist paradigms of black identity which represent blackness one-dimensionally in ways that reinforce and sustain white supremacy" (28). In street vernacular, DJay addresses the same issues with which bell hooks wrestles in her theoretical writings.

According to essentialist logic, blackness is disconnected from ideology and can be understood, instead, in terms of biology. Stuart Hall asserts, "The essentializing moment is weak because it naturalized and dehistoricizes difference, mistaking what is historical and cultural for what is natural, biological, and genetic" (29). Blackness is not a biological essence but instead is constructed through the interplay of economic, political and social forces. The commentary and actions of the black characters in *Hustle and Flow* clearly express the confining and repressive nature of essentialist identity prescriptions. Yet, it is through the interracial relationships within the narrative that other elements of blackness are explored.

Throughout the narrative, it is clear that one of the films primary objectives is the deconstruction of oppositional binaries, such as male/female and black/white. In his opening speech, DJay includes Nola in his unifying definition of mankind by telling her "we man, I mean, you a woman and all but, we man." Later DJay admires Nola's strength of character and describes her as having "big gorilla balls." Although Nola and DJay exist on opposite sides of traditional binary frameworks, they identify with one another. Through the lens of binary hierarchies, DJay wields power over Nola because he is a man and her pimp. Conversely, Nola holds power over DJay because she is white and he is black. Yet, while they are divided by these factors, they are united through their simultaneous struggle as oppressed subjects. Nola often functions as a conduit through which their shared experience is expressed. For example, at a critical point in the film, she cries, "Everybody's got something important going on in their lives. I want something. I WANT SOMETHING." Although Nola cannot express what it is she wants she knows it is "not this." Here Nola gives language to the emotions plaguing almost every character in the film: they want to be relevant. Society has determined that the individual identities that they occupy are excess, useless, and disposable, therefore robbing them of meaning, purpose, and relevancy.

In many ways, Nola invokes W.T. Lhamon's notion of optic blackness. She is not black, but through her relationship with DJay, she is able to articulate her own struggles with identity and oppression. Nola also performs blackness, or at least the socially prescribed concept of blackness, through her language, lifestyle, and physical appearance (specifically her hair). She embodies optic blackness, that is "a particular blackness that disaffected peoples of every ethnicity in the United States evoke to signal their dissatisfied relation to American and Atlantic history" (Lhamon 111). Nola sheds light on the lack within understandings of blackness that link it to phenotype at the exclusion of the psychological and symbolic.

Although Llhamon specifically states that all ethnicities can leverage blackness, he qualifies optic blackness as inherently oppositional to whiteness (Lhamon 111). The contention then that Nola, a white character, can perform optic blackness inevitably calls into question the nature of whiteness. The film clearly expresses that whiteness and blackness are concepts that are entangled with phenotype but not limited to it. This maneuver is accomplished through the talented white sound mixer, Shelby. Upon Shelby's entrance into the narrative, DJay is initially disgruntled and asks Key, "Who…is this? He's white." Key responds by telling DJay "No, he's just light skinned." Later Shelby proves he is not white by enacting behaviors socially linked to blackness. He is musically talented, impoverished, and a drug user. Moreover, he is nonjudgmental of DJay's lifestyle. Shelby is, in fact, white according to his skin color, but he does not perform whiteness nor does he represent white power structures.

Nola and Shelby disembody blackness from phenotype and instead connect it to bodies that are for sale. They are labeled and oppressed by a system that has deemed them irrelevant. The metanarrative that unites the male and female African Americans to the male and female Caucasians is one of consumption and commodity. Each character within the narrative possesses a body that is available for purchase as laborer, sexual plaything, or visual spectacle. It is not surprising that a menial laborer and a prostitute would invoke optic blackness; these characters are commodities, and commodification has long been linked with blackness.

Shelby and Nola's invocations of optic blackness begin to desuture blackness from phenotype and essentializing biological identity formation. This project is furthered through the introduction of music, more specifically, the tracks "It's Hard Out Here for a Pimp" and "Whoop that Trick" on which the narrative is centered. Although they are two distinct songs, they overlap and enmesh throughout the narrative and can be discussed collectively as they simultaneously serve as the musical self-representation created by DJay and his friends.

As the characters attempt to record the tracks, several key events occur which reveal the complex relationship between blackness and music.

The way in which the film deliberately addresses gender representations in rap music is particularly interesting. When DJay begins to rap the lyrics to his first track, which eventually evolves into "Whoop that Trick," Key asks DJay to stop and think about his lyrics. Key suggests that the lyrics "beat that bitch" and "stomp that ho" might be perceived as misogynistic by mainstream audiences. It is at this point that Key, DJay, and Shelby enter into a discussion about language and its relation to knowledge, gender, and culture. DJay insists that he "ain't trying to call no hoes no bitch" while Shelby asserts, "most of the bitches I know are guys." Again, although the characters employ street vernacular, they are clearly grappling concepts that are crucial to the work of theorists such as Jacques Derrida and Richard Wright. Here DJay is grieved and angered that the message he desires to convey will not be transmitted or received intact. Through conversing with Shelby and Key, DJay is able to show that language is unnatural and has no inherent or essential meaning, "Language is constructed socially; and its group-defining forms and functions emerge out of the contexts, contingencies, and communities that constitute it and which, in turn, are constituted by it" (Wright 86). The language that DJay employs is that which his community created. Yet, as he attempts to deploy the language of his community, the language is misunderstood and mistranslated by hegemonic audiences. That language, and the new meanings which have been ascribed to it, then becomes a lens through which hegemonic audiences interpret and, in effect, recreate the initial discourse community. This process is narrated by DJay and his friends as it occurs because, it is important to note that, even though Key prevents certain lyrics from being included in the track (and getting radio play), those lyrics have already been transmitted to audiences via the film.

DJay, Key, and Shelby point out the disconnect between the intended meanings and the received meanings in rap music lyrics. Although Key points out that the chorus of "Whoop that Trick" appears sexist, DJay's message becomes clearer through the context of the song's verses. In fact, because many of the pejorative terms, such as bitch, trick, and ho function interchangeably, it is almost impossible to link each noun to a subject without context, despite traditional word associations. DJay's song begins with a threat, "If you violate off the top trick you gotta go / I done held in a lot of shit and I'm 'bout to flip / Now I think it's time to show you bitches." Clearly, in this sense, DJay is using the word "trick" to refer to prostitutes, and "bitches" can be understood as the men who pay them for sex. DJay claims that he will protect his prostitutes and will not allow them to be abused or victimized. Later DJay asserts, "Security be the main ones acting like some hoes" and "We some straight hood niggaz from the ghetto and the projects / F--- the police cause we know we the suspects." Here DJay overtly identifies juridical power as an oppressive and antagonistic force. Throughout the song, DJay verbally attacks men who interfere with his lifestyle, and he uses pejorative labels to leverage his assault. At no time does DJay usethese phrases to insult women. In fact, the content of the song is devoted almost exclusively to depicting various types of masculine subjects. Although exaggerated gender stereotypes are deployed in ways that reinforce traditional, nonproductive readings of masculinity and femininity, a close reading of the song shows that women are not the intended subject of degradation or assault. Indeed, it is the police, security, and other masculine identities that are "bitched" in this song.

The Academy Award winning song "It's Hard Out Here for a Pimp" further complicates gendered qualifiers within hegemonic language systems. For example, DJay continues to use the words bitch and ho as synonymous with a variety of objects and subjects, invoking literal meanings and symbolic meanings. Yet, DJay explicitly refers to his prostitutes, Nola and Shug, as "a snow bunny" and "a black girl." He goes on to describe his exploitation of their labor as "making change off these women." Here Djay uses the subjective identifiers "bunny," "girl," and "woman," which are not traditionally disrespectful and cannot be interpreted as misogynistic (with the possible exception of "bunny" which has been associated with *Playboy*). Yet, within the context of the song, the message is perceptibly sexist as he is describing the ways in which the bodies of these women are exploited and commodified for his profit. DJay's lyrics show that he is aware of his complicity in objectifying and oppressing women. However, the word "bitch" is not linked to female bodies in the song and is never used to describe a woman. The song's structuring and word choice shows that, even though these women are being commodified, their individual subjectivities are not being verbally degraded or "bitched."

Indeed, the women to whom DJay refers in the song are presented as victims of the same power system by which he is victimized; "Done seen people killed, done seen people deal / Done seen people live in poverty with no meals / It's f----- up where I live, but that's just how it is / It might be new to you, but it's been like this for years." DJay is simply describing his experience living in the ghetto and forcing audiences to realize that hegemonic power structures brought the ghetto into existence and sustain the presence of ghetto lifestyle by refusing to make necessary legal and social changes. There are minimal economic options available to individuals raised in impoverished communities. DJay is not pimping Shug and Nola because he thinks prostitution is the natural and rightful role of women, he is pimping them because he believes he has no other way to make a living. DJay demonstrates that, while these individual women are commodified for his profit, ultimately they are all victims of American culture at large, which judges their lifestyle while simultaneously recreating and enforcing the power structure that makes that lifestyle necessary.

Moreover, the women in the film are hailed by the music in a manner that is unambiguously positive and powerful. Shug is an integral part of the creation of the song "It's Hard Out Here for a Pimp," as she sings the refrain or "hook." Shug explicitly demonstrates her feelings of empowerment via the song when she thanks DJay for letting her sing on the track. The song becomes a vehicle for communication between these two characters, who have a love relationship fraught with complexities and built on the pimp/prostitute hustle. Shug is able to nurture DJay in a way that has been previously unviable in the film; he empowers her by including her in his musical project, and she, in turn, helps him to fulfill his desired identity as a rapper. Shug exhibits joy and exhilaration when she hears "Whoop that Trick" on the radio, showing that she perceives the success of the song as a personal triumph.

Nola, also, is empowered by the music, as it resolves her aforementioned desire for "something important" to do with her life. When DJay is arrested, he elects Nola to be "in charge" and tells her, "In two weeks I want to hear my shit in the [prison] yard." Nola makes it her life's purpose to get "Whoop that Trick" played on the radio and to circulate DJay's story. Nola's character undergoes a psychological transformation due to her connection with the music. She begins to experience life as an individual whose presence and actions have impact and meaning.

For each of the characters, the music becomes a liberating, empowering force. Although the lyrics overtly address DJay's personal experiences and worldview, the struggles of Nola, Shug, Key, and Shelby are represented in the music. Ultimately the musical score within the film emerges as a palimpsest on which the stories of the oppressed can be written;

the songs are a unifying musical rhetoric that expresses the collective psychological outcry of optic blackness.

The music created on screen functions in the same capacity as the film itself; a cursory inspection displays pejorative stereotypes and misogynistic themes yet a more detailed analysis reveals the interplay of progressive theoretical issues. Through strategic deployment of language and an invocation of optic blackness, *Hustle and Flow* leverages a powerful critique against essentialist identity formation and the sociopolitical forces that sustain ghetto living. DJay's monologue overtly addresses American audiences' desire to consume black bodies that perform the street while Nola articulates the visceral and emotional pain experienced by optic black bodies. Further, the music created within the film is an empowering force that infuses each character with agency and confidence. The struggles of the black, white, female, and male characters in the film intertwine and unify to create a narrative that reveals their collective oppression and commodification. The film displays the consequences of essentialism, as each of the characters is stunted and confined by the limitations of their assigned identities. Ultimately, *Hustle and Flow* does not simply tell the story of a pimp but, moreover, presents a critique of sociopolitically prescribed identities, which are exposed as psychologically and physically destructive.

## Works Cited

Hall, Stuart. "What is This 'Black' in Black Popular Culture?" *Black Popular Culture*. Ed. Gina Dent. New York: Bay Press, 1983.

hooks, bell. *Yearning: Race, Gender, and Cultural Politics*. Massachusetts: South End Press, 1990.

*Hustle and Flow*. Dir. Craig Brewer. Perf. Terence Howard. Crunk, New Deal, Homegrown, and MTV Films, 2005.

Jackson, Ronald. *Scripting the Black Masculine Body: Identity Discourse, and Racial Politics in Popular Media*. New York: State U of New York Albany P, 2006.

Lhamon, W.T. "Optic Black: Naturalizing the Refusal to Fit." *Black Cultural Traffic*. Eds. Harry Elam, Jr., and Kennell Jackson. Michigan: U of Michigan P, 2005.

Wright, Richard. "The Word at Work: Ideological and Epistemological Dynamics in African American Rhetoric." *Understanding African-American Rhetoric: Classical Origins to Contemporary Innovations*. Eds. Ronald Jackson and Elaine Richardson. New York: Routledge, 2003.

# Casebook on Health Issues

*In "Plague of the Century: Thoughts on Crowd, Conformity, and Contagion," David Raney explores the language of disease and its meaning in our culture.*

## Plague of the Century: Thoughts on Crowd, Conformity, and Contagion

David Raney

> As men grow more alike, each man feels himself weaker in regard to all the rest.
>
> -Alexis de Tocqueville

In April 1924, Franz Kafka wrote to a friend from the sanatorium where he would die two months later, complaining that no one would speak to him frankly about his illness: "Verbally I don't learn anything definite, since in discussing tuberculosis…everybody drops into a shy, evasive, glassy-eyed manner of speech" (Sontag 7). Thirty years later, a decade after publishing *The Plague*, Albert Camus observed in a 1957 symposium that euphemism still ruled the discussion of grave diseases:

> In our well-policed society we recognize that an illness is serious from the fact that we don't dare speak of it directly. For a long time, in middle-class families people said no more than that the elder daughter had a "suspicious cough" or that the father had a "growth" because tuberculosis and cancer were looked upon as somewhat shameful maladies. (176)

This remains true to some extent today: cancer is frequently "the C-word" in conversation and AIDS a "lingering illness" in obituaries. But in an age in which diseases, particularly of the contagious type, seem to be on every magazine cover, paperback rack, and movie marquee, it can no longer be said that as a culture we are generally "shy" or "evasive" about our maladies. In fact, it might be fair to twist Camus's axiom into a contemporary corollary: in our society, we realize that a phenomenon is serious from the fact that we speak of it as an illness.

Naturally an era's predominant concerns will be reflected in this sort of metaphorical figuration, so it is unsurprising that in our day computer phenomena and nuclear proliferation are referred to as "infectious." And perhaps it is inevitable that such analogies should sometimes collapse, the metaphor veering toward the real. When the computer lexicon borrowed the word "virus," for instance, to name a species of rapidly multiplying computer failure, it spawned a subgenre of science fiction thrillers – a recent example is Graham Watkins's *Virus* (1995) – in which superviruses transfer themselves from machine to user and threaten millions. This sort of narrative seems a clear demonstration of anxiety over the ambiguous boundaries, in this case between man and machine, that are put into question almost daily by developments in artificial intelligence, robotics, and other advanced technologies. Non-fiction books on high-tech subjects can take nearly as grim and sensational a tone as their fictional counterparts: *Silicon Shock: the Menace of the Computer Invasion* (1985), for example, or *Computer Viruses, Worms...Killer Programs, and Other Threats to Your System* (1989). The language and images of technology, medicine, and fearful fantasy are interdependent.

Language itself, in fact, has often been conceived of by our century as contagious. Poet Louise Glück echoes William Burroughs's famous claim that "language is a virus" when she invokes "the contagious vernacular" (*First* 123). Memoirist Anwar Accawi tells of his parents referring to cancer as "that disease" not out of a concern for euphemistic delicacy but "because they were afraid that saying the word itself would bring the sickness upon them" (19). The Russian theorist Mikhail Bakhtin suggests something similar in positing that language "lies on the borderline between oneself and the other…exists in other people's mouths…is populated with the intentions of others" (293-4). And Stephen Pinker, a cognitive neuroscientist, draws the analogy still more clearly. Language innovation, he theorizes, "must spread and catch on like a contagious disease until it becomes epidemic"; in this way, learning is "contagiously spread from person to person [as] minds become coordinated" (243, 411).

These are fairly recent developments, though. Certain fears, or more precisely fears of certain Others – differing by race especially, but also by class and gender – have been particularly persistent in our century and have been cast in terms of contagion ever since the scientific breakthroughs of the 1870s and 1880s. Of course these fears, like the general figurative use of disease, long predate the modern period. But germ theory offered a new and versatile way to conceive of boundary loss and shifting identity, and while this phenomenon is hardly exclusive to America, the peculiarities of our culture and history have rendered such metaphor-making a compelling, pervasive project for us.

One way to understand the American reaction to theories of contagion is to view it through the lens of our conflicted ideas about individuals and crowds. Deep in our national mythos is the glorified figure of the loner: the farmer, backwoodsman, cowboy, gold miner, or other adventurer who lives by wit and grit a step from the frontier, needing no organized religion or government to show him the way. At the same time, though, America has struggled since its beginnings to define itself geographically, culturally, and politically and in so doing to assert some communal identity. Our democratic institutions have similarly striven to reconcile the warring demands of individual and group, avoiding both anarchy and the "tyranny of the majority" which, de Tocqueville warned, "represses not only all contest, but all controversy" (273).

We resist conformity on principle, it seems, but indulge it in practice. Despite expressions of horror about "mass man" during the Red Scare 1950s, for instance, Americans were already growing increasingly homogenous in behavior and taste. Max Lerner in his 1957 book *America as a Civilization* caricatured Americans as robots "performing routinized operations at regular intervals":

> They take time out for standardized "coffee breaks" and later a quick standardized lunch, come home at night to eat processed or canned food, and read syndicated columns and comic strips. Dressed in standardized clothes they attend standardized club meetings…. They are drafted into standardized armies, and if they escape the death of mechanized warfare they die of highly uniform diseases [and] are buried in standardized graves. (261)

It is important to note that there is nothing uniquely American in the fear of conformity, either. Scotsman John Robison in an influential 1797 tract railed against the French Revolution as a conspiracy to "reduce mankind to the state of one undistinguishable mass" (Davis 39). But sociologist David Potter, in his 1963 Commonwealth lectures on "Freedom and Vulnerability," suggests a reason that America's vaunted individualism should so often express itself as conformity. "No other nation," Potter argued, "has had the same combination of compelling experiences with pioneering, mass immigration, and urbanization – *all* of which tended to intensify the fear of isolation and the feeling of dependence on the group" (23). America has nevertheless tended, except in wartime, to emphasize its *pluribus* rather than its *unum*. I would argue that this psychosocial ambivalence plays a large part in both our fear of contagion and our insistence on using it to express other, unrelated fears. Contagion, after all, threatens natural borders (self and other) and artificial ones (class, race, nation), both individual and communal. And, in doing so, it imposes a paradoxical combination of difference and unity: it alters individuals but dissolves the distinctions between them, resulting in both the pariah's isolation and a forced community of shared symptoms.

If American culture has been divided against itself on the relative value of individuals and groups, however, precision requires that a distinction be made in the latter term between "the people" and "the masses." Just as the Greek philosopher Proclus distinguished "the people" – a group "united to itself" and worthy of democracy – from "the populace" – an incoherent rabble – so in our own national rhetoric "the people" are lauded from the first words of the Constitution while the "crowd," "mob," or "masses" merely threaten social disruption (Stafford 290). The difference goes beyond semantics, for the second set of terms generally carries a class stigma. Matthew Arnold labelled culture "an *internal* condition" and felt, as Lawrence Levine observes, that anything producing "a group atmosphere, a mass ethos, was culturally suspect." An 1894 article in *Century* magazine defined "the masses" as those delighting in "eating, drinking, smoking…dancing, music of a noisy and lively character," etc. By contrast, anyone demonstrating "a permanent taste for higher pleasures," went the argument, "ceases, ipso facto, to belong to the masses" (Levine 164, 225). And it is these "crowds" and "masses" (not the noble "people") who are most often constructed as contagious. Military historian John Keegan, for example, writes in *The Face of Battle* (1978) that "a crowd is the antithesis of an army" and is characterized by "inconstant and potentially infectious emotion which, if it spreads, is fatal" to discipline (175). John Adams, writing two centuries earlier, opined that America with all its open land might avoid the unruliness of crowds: "Where large numbers live in small places," he reasoned, inevitably there are "contagions of madness and folly" (587).

Our imaginative literature has made similar connections between crowds and contagion. Nathaniel Hawthorne in "My Kinsman, Major Molineux" (1832), writing before germ theory had taken hold, nevertheless describes a gathering mob as a disease symptom: "[It was] as if a dream had broken forth from some feverish brain, and were sweeping visibly through the midnight streets" (561). Mark Twain, writing after that seismic paradigm shift, links mobs specifically to contagion in claiming that "men in a crowd…don't think for themselves, but become impregnated by contagious sentiments uppermost in the minds of all who happen to be *en masse*" (Mills 69).

What is at stake here is not so much behavior as identity: madness, fever, and uncontrolled emotions take us out of ourselves, whether violence follows or not. Expressing that identity purge as a contagious phenomenon acknowledges that contagious disease, like the engulfing crowd, dissolves the fragile membranes by which we distinguish ourselves from others.

Wallace Stegner's novel *On a Darkling Plain* (1940) also clearly links identity, crowds, and contagion. Set during the 1918-19 influenza epidemic, the novel presents a protagonist who "could stand...individuals" but not mankind "in pack." Only "in isolation," Vickers contends, could people "stay human [and] keep their dignity. When more than three of them got together it was a pack, and the pack was immoral, treacherous, lying...full of reasonless hatred for the foreign and different" (67-8). Yet in those "packs," too, lies the danger of a specific, infectious *agent* of the foreign and different. The flu then ravaging cities was "one good argument for living alone," he reasons: "The plague [was] a symbol of the manifold sickness, physical and spiritual, that affected mankind in the mass" (157). Holed up in a remote camp on the Canadian plains, Vickers considers his hut walls "a bulwark...an affirmation of tentative identity" (122) during the long storm-blast of the flu. Another character, venturing into town and "almost certain contagion," is likewise described as "trying to hide his identity, as if he could escape the disease" (161). When Vickers finally comes down with flu, the narrator again implicates contagion in a loss of identity. He becomes just "another patient...part of the town's collective sickness" and feels "poised over his own body, separate from it...as if he walked with another person" (225, 207).

These last few examples end fifty years ago, but contagion as a figurative device has hardly vanished from our lives since then. Contagion metaphors are everywhere: we are confronted daily in the news media with the "virus" of sexism, road rage, doubt, war, and witchcraft; with "epidemics" of hate, handguns, disrespect, eating disorders and even, in a bizarre recent instance, historical novels (Dee 77). Virtually no facet of American life is immune to such treatment (as the phrase "immune to" itself suggests), and the phenomenon goes beyond popular journalism. Essayist William Zinsser remarks that our Alamo martyrs are "immune to the virus of revisionism" (77). Roger Shattuck in *Forbidden Knowledge: From Prometheus to Pornography* (1996) shares imagery with early 20th-century book censors – though he presents a more sophisticated argument than the banners and burners – when he explicitly compares stories appealing to our violent or prurient interests to "bacterial and viral disease" assaulting "our moral immune systems" (296-7). And Jean Baudrillard claims in *The Transparency of Evil* (1993) that thought itself is "a sort of network of antibodies and natural immune defences" against a broad spectrum of phenomena which render us vulnerable to "the evil genie of otherness." These can be as trivial as fashion fads, which "fade away like epidemics once they have ravaged the imagination, once the virus has run its course," or as potentially catastrophic as "AIDS, terrorism, crack cocaine or computer viruses." All of these, Baudrillard maintains, "hew to the same agenda of virulence and radiation, an agenda whose very power over the imagination is of a viral character" (61-70).

Nor has actual contagion, of course, been relegated solely to theory and imagination. This fact is clear enough from the recent media attention given to resurgent ancient diseases like tuberculosis and cholera, plus such new horrors as hantavirus, Ebola, flesh-eating bacteria, the so-called "X" virus from Sudan and, of course, AIDS. Bacterial and viral diseases still kill about fifteen million people annually worldwide (Lemonick 62-9). Ironically, in fact, we may be to some extent victims of our own success in the battle against germs. In barely a century, science has learned to slow, halt, kill or cure most of the scourges of our recent ancestors, but as Darwinian natural selection would predict, these conquests have cleared the field for some new entries and occasionally for stronger versions of old ones. The drug-resistant strains of streptococcus and staphylococcus in hospitals provide examples. Another is the set of emergent tropical diseases – AIDS is thought to be among them – which have beset us as a result of our destruction of the rainforest, a process which itself only became possible once we devised vaccines and treatments for known tropical killers. Historian William McNeill numbers polio, too, among the century's "new diseases of cleanliness," in that "minor infection in infancy produced immunity…whereas persons whose sanitary regimen kept them from contact with the virus until later in life often suffered severe paralysis or even death" (254).

This is not to argue, it need hardly be said, for a cessation of efforts to control or eradicate disease. But it does point to the likelihood that contagion will always be with us, tapping deep fears and questioning our notions of individual agency and identity. In this way, microbial contagion, and the metaphors which deform or translate it into other realms of understanding, will continue to shape our conception to the point where, in Louise Glück's phrase, self ends and "the blur of the world begins" ("Dreamer" 80).

## Works Cited


Accawi, Anwar F. "The Cave." *The Sun* February 1999: 18-21.

Adams, John. *Works IV*. Ed. C.F. Adams. New York: Little, Brown, 1856.

Bakhtin, Mikhail. "Discourse in the Novel." *The Dialogic Imagination*. Ed. Michael Holquist. Austin: U of TX Press, 1981. 259-422.

Boudrillard, Jean. *The Transparency of Evil: Essays on Extreme Phenomena*. New York: Verso, 1993.

Camus, Albert. "Reflections on the Guillotine." *Resistance, Rebellion and Death*. Trans. Justin O'Brien. New York: Vintage, 1974.173-234.

Davis, David Brion. *The Fear of Conspiracy: Images of Un-American Subversion from the Revolution to the Present*. Ithaca: Cornell UP, 1971.

Dee, Jonathan. "The Reanimators: On the Art of Literary Graverobbing." *Harper's* June 1999: 76-84.

De Tocqueville, Alexis. *Democracy in America*. 2 vols. New York: Vintage, 1945.

Glück, Louise. *The First Four Books of Poems*. NY: Ecco, 1995. 123-4.

----. "The Dreamer and the Watcher." *Singular Voices: American Poetry Today*. Ed. Stephen Berg. New York: Avon, 1985. 75-82.

Hawthorne, Nathaniel. "My Kinsman, Major Molineux." *The Norton Anthology of American Literature*. Shorter Fourth Edition. Ed. Nina Baym et al. New York: Norton, 1995: 551-563.

Keegan, John. *The Face of Battle*. New York: Penguin, 1978.

Lemonick, Michael D. "The Killers All Around." *Time* 12 September 1994: 62-69.

Lerner, Max. *America as a Civilization*. New York: Simon & Schuster, 1957.

Levine, Lawrence. *Highbrow/Lowbrow: The Emergence of Cultural Hierarchy in America*. Cambridge: Harvard UP, 1988.

McNeill, William. *Plagues and Peoples*. New York: Anchor, 1989.

Mills, Nicolaus. *The Crowd in American Literature*. Baton Rouge: Louisiana State UP, 1986.

Pinker, Steven. *The Language Instinct*. New York: Harper, 1995.

Potter, David. *Freedom and Its Limitations in American Life*. Stanford: Stanford UP, 1976

Shattuck, Roger. *Forbidden Knowledge: From Prometheus to Pornography*. New York: St. Martin's, 1996.

Sontag, Susan. *Illness As Metaphor*. New York: Vintage, 1979.

Stafford, Barbara M. *Body Criticism: Imagining the Unseen in Enlightenment Art and Medicine*. Cambridge: MIT Press, 1991.

Stegner, Wallace. *On a Darkling Plain*. New York: Harcourt Brace, 1940.

Zinsser, William. *American Places*. New York: Harper, 1993.

*In "Paraih among Pariahs: Images of the IV Drug User in the Context of AIDS," Dennis Lensing argues that "voices must be raised to challenge the one-dimensional representations of IVDUs... Until such voices gain sufficient power and number to provide audible counterpoint to the dominant simple-mindedness, IVDUs with AIDS will continue to bear the brunt of societal victim-blame."*

# Pariah among Pariahs: Images of the IV Drug User in the Context of AIDS

Dennis Lensing

The instant the camera cuts to a close-up of a spoon, we know what is coming. A dash of powder, white (usually) or brown, a spray of water, a match-head bursting into flame. Powder dissolves in boiling water. Water is soaked up in a tiny wad of cotton. Cotton is sucked dry by a needle. We wince as the needle finds the vein and blood blossoms into the barrel of the syringe. Down goes the plunger, and the camera relents, pulling back to show our antihero's eyes roll back into his (rarely her) head, blissfully, as if to confirm Brian Johnson's assertion that "[s]imulating substance abuse has become a kind of pornography." As a recurring and familiar landmark on the protagonist's journey into addiction, the eroticized image of use stands in stark counterpoint to the dehumanized image of user.

"The Ritual," as many films refer to it, is presented so compulsively and uniformly in filmic depictions of addiction's woes that images of the IV drug user's paraphernalia and the process of fixing have become staples of the drug-movie genre; the art of "works" has entered the age of mechanical reproduction. The Ritual sequence appears, for example, in *Sid & Nancy* (1986), *Drugstore Cowboy* (1989), *Rush* (1991), *The Basketball Diaries* (1995), *Trainspotting* (1996), and *Requiem for a Dream* (2000), just a few of the numerous addiction films of the past three decades. All participate to a greater or lesser degree in what Jonathan White has called "the Addiction Narrative," in which the protagonist "falls" into poverty and desperation as a result of addiction. The story is told over and over; indeed, so common and popular is this particular narrative that we might be tempted now to agree with a commentator in a 1916 edition of *Variety* when *The Devil's Needle* was released: "The drug story has been so often sheeted [screened] that there's nothing left to it" (qtd. in von Busack). Of course, nearly a century has passed since that weary proclamation, and drug use, like everything else, has changed much over the decades. Since the 1960s, the variety of pharmaceuticals available for injection has exploded, as has the range of pleasurable sensations and ill effects they can cause. Perhaps most notably, today's IV drug user (IVDU) has, on top of addiction, withdrawal sickness, impurities, overdose, and the threat of HIV transmission to worry about. In light of this, one of the most remarkable aspects of recent movies featuring IV drug use is the almost complete absence of mention of HIV and AIDS, as though to focus on the addict means necessarily to forget about the person with AIDS.

Of course, many of these films are set in the decades just prior to the AIDS epidemic. However, even those which could address the dangers of HIV avoid mention of the virus. In *Requiem for a Dream*, for example, almost everything imaginable happens to the four characters as a result of drug use except AIDS: Harry's (Jared Leto) arm is infected and amputated, his mother (Ellen Burstyn) becomes psychotic and undergoes electroshock therapy, Tyrone (Marlon) Wayans) is imprisoned, and Marion (Jennifer Connelly) becomes a sex worker to support her coke habit. In a movie obsessed with addiction, abjection, and loss, the absence of HIV is remarkable. In fact, of all recent mainstream drug films, only

*Trainspotting* mentions AIDS at all, and then only in a simplistic manner, in reference to a rather minor character. While Renton (Ewan McGregor), Sick Boy (Jonny Lee Miller), Spud (Ewen Bremner), and Allison (Susan Vidler) all shoot up heroin on a regular basis, and without much visible attention to precautions, they all manage to avoid HIV. Their straight-laced friend Tommy (Kevin McKidd), however, contracts HIV almost immediately upon trying heroin when his engagement falls apart; he proceeds to full-blown AIDS and death with remarkable speed, almost entirely offscreen. In effect, his story serves as a cautionary tale that "good boys" should not dabble; "real users," like the main characters, need not worry – not, at least, about AIDS.

However, it would be a mistake to think that the drug film genre is exceptional in its limited and simplistic portrayal of AIDS. Rather, these movies participate in a system of representation whose remarkable uniformity transcends genre, operating in news reports, scientific studies, activist writings, and novels pertaining to IV drug use and AIDS. Whereas movies dealing with IV drug use consistently elide the realities of HIV, discourse focused on HIV consistently elides or demonizes the IV drug user; these discursive moves are two facets of a single system of marginalization. The AIDS epidemic has been with us now for decades and continues to take a disproportionate toll on gay men, ethnic minorities, and IVDUs: meanwhile, media representations have moved far from the first panicky articles and newsclips attempting to get a handle on the "new Black Plague" in the 1980s. The fevered search for a cure and heated exchanges on how best to deal with this new disease have been largely replaced by calm reports of newer, more promising regimens for controlling the syndrome once HIV has been contracted. But from this steady murmur of reassuring news occasionally bursts forth something deemed newsworthy enough to merit more than a few column inches of technical jargon. Unfortunately, these hot stories are reminiscent of earlier times in more than tone; they remind us that, however far we may have come in the treatment of AIDS, we have barely progressed at all in our representations of the disease, or in our popular understanding of how to live in a world with AIDS. The astonishing announcement by Jesse Helms in March 2002 is a case in point. What could be more newsworthy than archconservative Jesse Helms, never afraid to go on record that gay men or IV drug users with AIDS deserved what they got, suddenly proclaiming his shame at not having done more to combat AIDS over the last twenty years? Reading the specifics of this newfound shame, however, one finds that this newsflash is really just the same old story.

Helms's call for government assistance to help stop the spread of AIDS is really quite specific. As has been spelled out in his editorial "We Cannot Turn Away," Helms's shame derives specifically from not helping to combat the transmission of HIV from mothers to infants in Africa. For all his rhetoric of shame and regret, and despite his closing statement that "we cannot turn away when we see our fellow man in need," Helms continues to turn his back on the realities of AIDS and to refuse to see the epidemic in terms of health rather than of morality (Helms). His new stance on AIDS shows that the same old "us/them" categories are in use, and that some "risk groups" are more deserving than others. In this particular case, African women and babies are posited as the ultimate "innocent victims," while African men, gay men in general, and IV drug users are all consigned to oblivion, presumably because they are in some way to blame for their HIV+ status. In short, Helms's epiphany has much to tell us about how far we have not come in developing our understanding of AIDS. Helms's "conversion" serves as a call for us to reflect upon present realities of AIDS, and upon the roots of the pernicious representations which have helped foster the spread of AIDS.

When attempting to get "the facts about AIDS," we cannot help but encounter the phrase "risk groups," an ubiquitous though misleading phrase, which is at once essential to the understanding of the way AIDS works in the United States and harmful to the understanding of the way HIV works in the human body. Time and again, in article after article, the litany of such "risk groups" has played itself out, naming all those "others" who are deemed likely to be infected: "gay men, Haitians, drug abusers, hemophiliacs, addicts' female sexual partners and their babies" (Shilts 429). That the category "gay man" is invoked first is hardly accidental, since AIDS has from the start been associated with the so-called "gay community," the social group hardest hit by AIDS and most able to respond. As Cindy Patton points out, "It was largely the groups based in gay community traditions which formed the basis of what was to become an AIDS service industry" (12). Other groups, such as sex workers' rights organizations and the National Hemophilia Foundation, later mobilized to represent their communities in various conflicts and crises regarding AIDS, which are often as much about representation as about "reality," as much about images as about resources.

Only one of these "risk groups" has not to any great degree entered the fray: IVDUs. As a result, discourse regarding AIDS issues relevant to IVDUs has largely been controlled by members of other groups and has been denied thorough and serious consideration. Although as of March 2002, 57% of all AIDS cases among women and 31% of cases among men have been attributed to injection drug use or sex with partners who inject drugs, it is virtually impossible to locate information specifically about or directed specifically towards IVDUs (CDC). Rather, a few pages in any given work will mention IVDUs in passing, usually in a series or phrases such as "women, IVDUs, and others with lower incomes" (Christensen 11), "other risk groups such as intravenous drug users or Haitians" (Shilts 232), and so on. In both "fictional" and "nonfictional" discourses of AIDS, IVDUs have been defined and characterized by and for others, with little attention paid to the actual situations and needs of IVDUs themselves.

Before addressing the unpleasant social realities and inaccurate representations of life as an HIV+ IVDU, we must recognize that identity as an IVDU is no more clearcut than identity based on social constructs such as race or sexual orientation. The idea that shooting up once makes one a "junky" is no less absurd than the notion that any man who has had a sexual experience with another man suddenly "is" (or "reveals himself to be") gay. The myth of either/or categorization regarding drug use has been fostered by decades of the "War on Drugs" and its propaganda, often assisted by popular culture representations of addiction, and it grossly distorts the realities of drug use and addiction, erasing all distinctions between the various drugs and between habitual and non-habitual use. Although studies of "risk groups" and how they function to control discourse about AIDS are essential, it is necessary at the same time to keep in mind the fictional, oversimplifying nature of all such "identities" and "communities" based on race, gender, sexual orientation, IV drug use, and so on.

## Realities

The realities of life as an HIV+ IVDU reveal just how deleterious identification as a "community" from the outside – that is, "diagnosis" in Patton's sense (127) – can be. As Edith Campbell of the Methadone Maintenance Program states:

> VDUs are a population that until now has not even been acknowledged as existing in terms of being entitled to any attention from the rest of society. Suddenly,

> because there's a threat coming through AIDS, everyone wants to know what's going on. (qtd. in Carlomusto and Juhasz)

IVDUs are thus "scapegoated as vectors of transmission," "receiving attention only insofar as non-IV drug using populations are threatened" (Saalfield 124). IVDUs are among the "guilty victims" who transmit the virus to their "innocent" lovers and children. Randy Shilts, whose 1988 book *And the Band Played On* set the terms of most subsequent AIDS discourse, puts it thus: "Intravenous drug users would be wiped out in astounding numbers, taking with them their sexual partners and infant children" (460). Although Shilts predicts the effects of the epidemic on gay men, hemophiliacs, and equatorial Africans in the same paragraph, only IVDUs are portrayed as vindictive murderers of innocents. The Centers for Disease Control and Prevention to this day also adhere to this policy of worrying more about the effect of the IVDU on others than about the effect of HIV on the IVDU him- or herself. The CDC website delineates nine "Populations at Risk." The descriptions of these populations begin similarly for the most part, stating the impact that HIV has had on the group in question. The one exception comes in the first sentence of the description of HIV among IVDUs, which reads as follows: "Sharing syringes and other equipment for drug injection is a well known route of HIV transmission, yet injection drug use contributes to the epidemic's spread far beyond the circle of those who inject" (CDC). Concern moves away from the IVDU halfway through the very first sentence of the informational site devoted to the spreading of HIV via intravenous drug use.

Feeding the fires of public outrage against the criminally irresponsible junkies are the fears engendered by the associations linking IVDUs with sex workers, both construed as, and only as, "link[s] between high- and low-risk groups," vectors first and victims second if at all (Harcourt and Philpot 155). Although this association, as will be shown, does have some basis in reality, its prevalence in AIDS discourse is also driven by a logic that is purely representational. Knowledge about AIDS in the United States has from the very beginning been predicated on the dichotomy self/other. This has been articulated in a multitude of ways: "homosexual and heterosexual," "normal and abnormal," "guilty and innocent," and "United States and Africa" (Treichler 63-4). The heterosexual "general public" of the United States has consistently projected the possibility of "non-gay AIDS" onto Africa, imaginatively containing the danger within the borders of the Dark Continent. Once the statistics came to prove all too well that heterosexual transmission does, in fact, occur in the United States too, another means of denial was required, and a new fiction was generated: "Heterosexual AIDS in the U.S. is related to drug use, while 'African AIDS' will be related to (African) heterosexual practices" (Patton 66). And, since prostitutes have played such an important role in understanding the spread of AIDS in Africa, many of the fantasies about IVDUs in the United States are played out on the bodies of sex workers. Thus, the peculiar logic of displacement and projection generated the portrait of one of the more vile demons of the epidemic: the junky whore. Shilts again proves reliable in uncritically articulating popular myth, referring to New York City's "drug-shooting hookers" as "legion," an openly demonizing characterization (513).

The interweaving of discourse about IVDUs and about prostitutes reflects the complexity of the overlapping of categories in real life, despite the efforts of sex workers' rights groups to distance themselves from the issue of IV drug use. For example, in 1988, Carol Leigh, a member of COYOTE (Call Off Your Old Tired Ethics), claimed that "seropositivity in prostitutes *is confined* to IV drug users, who comprise only ten percent of prostitutes" (180, emphasis added). This absurdly extreme generalization is telling; the stigma of IV drug use is the last thing the already beleaguered community of sex workers can afford to shoulder. Once again, IVDUs are treated as "other," even by those stigmatized by the general population, and are condescended to as "victims" whose primary need is "drug treatment programs…designed to meet the needs of IV drug using prostitutes" (Leigh 180). This ubiquitous and misguided attention to "treatment programs" as a necessary good for drug users, as well as the characterization of such institutions as representative of the "IVDU community" will be examined and problematized later in this paper.

Perhaps another cause of such vehement assertions that IVDUs and prostitutes are mutually distinct categories having little to do with one another is the constituency of such groups as COYOTE and US Pros; the very existence and effectiveness of these organizations attests to a higher degree of awareness and power than sex workers not affiliated with such advocacy groups can be expected to have. Many studies undertaken regarding sex workers and IVDUs have, in fact, discovered a hierarchy, with "the highest levels of intravenous drug use…found among street prostitutes" (Harcourt and Philpot 149). Higher-class prostitutes and "call men" were discovered to have lower rates of IV drug use, resulting in skewed data, since "most studies have been conducted among street prostitutes" (Venema and Visser 52). Recognizing such studies as skewed, and wishing to avoid the additional stigmatization of association with IV drug use, spokeswomen for sex workers' organizations distance themselves from the issue of drug use, contributing to the silences and misrepresentations surrounding the issue.

## Fiction

The myths which masquerade as knowledge about IVDUs in such "factual" discourses as the theoretical and scientific works cited thus far are by no means confined to those modes of representation. In the fiction of AIDS (I include Shilts's purportedly factual work in this category as well, due to its narrative structure and rhetorical style), the "twin threats of oblivion and diagnosis" are played out again and again (Patton 127). In those works which do not entirely elide the IVDU, a certain characterization arises: the IVDU is threatening, irresponsible, even animalistic, and invariably doomed to continued addiction until death comes, which never takes very long.

Although mentioned repeatedly in Shilts's *And the Band Played On*, IVDUs are almost never considered in and of themselves, but only as one group in a litany of "risk groups" as shown above, or as an important "similar mystery" in the days of Gay-Related Immune Deficiency (GRID) (56). Only once in the course of 621 pages is there an actual representation of an IVDU, who is, predictably, a prostitute. The portrait of Silvana Strangis that emerges in the three pages he devotes to her is less the portrait of an individual than the construction of a stereotype. Silvana is not "that different from the other prostitutes who worked the Tenderloin" (508). She is strung out, irresponsible, and ignorant enough to go along with the suggestion of the police that she get tested; it takes "a reporter to tell…about her profession…and her urgent need for AIDS screening" and the head nurse to worry "about issues like confidentiality and civil rights" (509). Shilts's statement that "years of heroin addiction had undone whatever Silvana Strangis had learned of discretion" so that she readily talks about her boyfriend's HIV status to the police who have just arrested her is about as implausible as fiction can be. The notion that heroin addiction leads one to be more confiding in police officers about anything, much less about something so sensitive, is an absurd extension of the mythic stupidity of the junky. Although Silvana tries to go straight by getting into a methadone program, seeming "repentant and eager for a new life," she, of course, fulfills the demands of the stereotype, in which addiction automatically equals doom (512). Her boyfriend Tony, "with a terminal diagnosis" and "little incentive to quit drugs," drags Silvana down with him (515). The myth articulated by Silvana is completed: "It's like what they say on TV. You get in but you can't get out" (510). And as if the function of Silvana's grim tale within Shilts's larger narrative were not already painfully clear, he spells out the moral of the story: It is "emblematic of the complicated problems that intravenous drug users presented in the AIDS epidemic. *These people* weren't optimistic gay men who would spend their last days doing white-light meditation with their Shanti Project volunteer; they were addicts" (515, emphasis added). Rather than *having* a problem in the AIDS epidemic, IVDUs *present* a problem in Shilts's representation; it sounds almost as though he expects an apology.

In *People in Trouble*, Sarah Schulman's popular 1990 novel, IVDUs receive similarly stereotypical treatment. Often, they are utterly dehumanized, used as scenery, as are homeless people throughout the work. During the scene which takes place in the "hellhole" of the Bellvue emergency room, the litany of horrors Molly and Fabian witness includes, but only in passing, "many, many drug overdoses" among the myriad street people, prisoners, and criminals (211-2). This infernal scene is reminiscent of one earlier in the book, in which Peter passes "a line of street people not being too rowdy…waiting to get into a soup kitchen" (134). Again, in the midst of the list of outcasts arises the death's head of addiction: "that junky/crackhead zombie look with sunken or distracted eyes and missing teeth" (135).

Only three times in this novel do IVDUs gain any semblance of humanity, in the persons of the unnamed man with the bandaged hand, Charlie, and Sam. In the first two instances, the IVDU is the stereotypical junky: the deceitful, exploitative black man. In the case of the injured man, even the "green tinge" of his hand and his "wrinkled prescription" are not enough to stop Peter and Molly from treating him like a subhuman parasite (139). Peter wonders "if the guy was just laying it on thick, trying to get some money out of him," while Molly asks him, in an accusatory tone, "Do you need a painkiller?" (139-40). Even the suspicion of drug abuse is grounds for condescension and accusation. In the case of Charlie, who is without any doubt an addict, always "looking hungry and wanting to get high," the rhetoric of blame is even clearer (172). In fact, Molly even provides a working definition of the drug addict, in case the reader is not sure what stance should be taken:

> …while drug addicts are real people in that they get hungry and cold and sick and die, there is a big hunk missing from them somehow. And for that reason they couldn't be treated as fully human because they would just rip you off and exploit you every chance they got. (172-3)

Charlie, in fact, cannot even be trusted "to not pocket the waitress' tip" (173). The dehumanization of IVDUs (who are human only in getting sick and dying), as well as the racist coding of the "junky," are here completely overt.

Sam, the cowgirl who becomes Molly's lover, comes closest to escaping the junky stereotype, perhaps because, in this novel, there is no such thing as a bad lesbian. Rather than being a "junky," Sam is a person who is "a good liar and a smooth operator and a real drinker with a few secrets," one of which is IV drug use (179). Both Sam and Daisy, the latter of whom is briefly mentioned as having done drugs in the past, to explain her seropositivity while maintaining her lesbianism intact, are differentiated from the stereotypical junky by their ability to stop. "Real junkies" being less than human and doomed to die addicted, it is essential that Schulman tell the reader that Sam "got off drugs" (226).

Here, the distinction between the IVDU and the junky is created; even when the IVDU is treated as human, the junky must be retained as the subhuman "other." Even so, the IVDU is represented as self-absorbed, with little if any social consciousness. Sam wants to "get stoned" on the day Justice plans its credit card strike (195). Molly has to convince her to go, insisting, "It's real" (195). Shilts"s optimistic gay man vs. depraved addict dichotomy is inscribed here; IV drug use is incompatible with social responsibility. Even in its most sympathetic IVDU character, *People in Trouble* perpetuates the myth that IVDUs are hard pressed to care about anything but themselves and their next fix, and that they, therefore, must be led by more socially conscious groups.

We might expect that mainstream ideas would be reproduced in mainstream publications like *And the Band Played On* and *People in Trouble*, turning to "fringe" or "underground" writing to challenge these characterizations of drug use and drug users. However, many of the pieces anthologized in *High Risk*, presented on its opening page as "uncompromisingly truthful," also reproduce these common stereotypes of the addict. IVDUs are reduced to scenery again in Cooper's "Wrong": "Times Square was spooky; too many junkies out, pissed eyes way back in their heads" (117). Kathy Acker, in "A Young Girl," denies IVDUs even the quality of life: "On the New York City streets, children play with used needles. Therefore, it's the dead who determine how the living act" (145). Pat Califia's "Heroin" is rather better, in that it does represent the actual act of shooting up, which is as absent from most AIDS writings as is the act of sex in governmental "safe sex" pamphlets. However, she does lean towards the idea that shooting up just once can result in a loss of free will: "of course I am not addicted but I am going to make sure I can get my hands on some more of this" (64). This slippery-slope mentality and the image of "the ancient reptile in me," which inscribes animalism in IV drug use, play into the old stereotypes, despite the straightforward descriptions of the experience that came before. That such dogmatic and stereotypical representations of the IVDU are present in the same collection as William S. Burroughs's "Just Say No to Drug Hysteria" is ironic, to say the least.

In light of the oppressive mass of stigmatizing, marginalizing, oversimplifying representations of IVDUs, of which the works discussed thus far form only a small sample, any work which runs counter in any way to the dominant images is surprising and noteworthy. In the realm of fiction, David Wojnarowicz proves an exception to the condescending, accusatory tone which is the rule. His collection of lyrical and polemical essays, *Close to the Knives*, problematizes the presumptions of dominant discourses regarding the IVDU.

Wojnarowicz is exceptional from the start among AIDS writers in that he writes as (among other things) a drug user himself. In *Close to the Knives*, he describes his experiences with a number of drugs: alcohol, marijuana, speed, mushrooms, peyote, ecstasy, and heroin. He seems to be virtually alone in his willingness to admit that "there is nothing worse to [him] than witnessing a friend's addiction to dope accelerate" without regarding addicts as voiceless subhumans (208). He can even go so far as to state, referring to Dakota, an IVDU, that "I learned so much from him spiritually – he pulled me up from the bottom of the ladder," a far cry from the dead eyes, zombie looks, and larcenous souls found elsewhere (208). Without shying away from the destructive, dehumanizing effects of chemical dependency in the United States, Wojnarowicz manages to portray IVDUs as complex human beings, not victims who must be condescended to in order to save them from themselves. In his own life, too, he explodes the mythical binary opposition addict/non-user. His description of "flirting with heroin" escapes such binary logic, falling somewhere between the idea of the junky and the idea of the "normal" person. Such complexity in IV drug use representation is exceptional, very nearly unique. And very sorely needed, to contradict the simplistic characterizations and condemnations of the IVDU that have been dominant now for well over a decade.

## Consequences

Among theoretical and scientific discourses of IVDUs and AIDS, the stereotype of the self-destructive, irresponsible, subhuman junky has perpetuated an oversimplified, uncritical focus on "rehabilitation programs" as the means by which the spread of AIDS can be checked. Even those bold enough to depart from "Just Say No" rhetoric to espouse the expansion of treatment programs tend to invoke these programs as a simple, straightforward panacea. Only a very few works go beyond the invocation of the phrase, and actually examine the nature of these programs as they are usually proposed and implemented.

While Catherine Saalfield is correct in asserting that "an IVDU who is HIV+ must have access to treatment for her or his HIV infection as well as her or his addiction," this statement fails to consider that the types of treatment available at present, even if the usual waiting period of many weeks were eliminated, are hardly ideal (125). Essentially, three types of cure exist for chemical dependency: individualized abstinence programs like Narcotics Anonymous, drug substitution programs like methadone maintenance, and "alternative" cures such as apomorphine and acupuncture. At present, only the first two are widely available, although their rates of success are far from admirable. Programs like Narcotics Anonymous, which require that one submit to a "power greater than oneself" and view "addiction as the primary disease in an HIV-infected 'addict'" are hardly adequate (Patton 11). As Patton points out, this method causes the IVDU to rewrite "her/his social identity (as 'irresponsible addict') as a medical identity or as sufferer from the disease of addiction" (12). Such programs, aside from being offensive in their insistence that the addict accept some form of religious belief, are certainly less effective than therapies that take into account the user's actual social contexts. That Patton lists Narcotics Anonymous among her AIDS Service Organizations, raising it to the level of the Gay Men's Health Crisis, for example, is problematic. By analogy, we could expect from the inclusion of these two groups on the same list that an efficient means of stopping the spread of AIDS would be to institute a twelve-step program in which gay men submit themselves to a higher power, admitting themselves to be "irresponsible homosexuals" and seeking the strength to become straight. Such groups do exist, in the Catholic Church, for example, but they are hardly considered admirable or even tolerable by most gays and lesbians. The essential problem with the twelve-step approach is that it misses the point: HIV is spread by *unsafe* sex and by *dirty* needles, not by gay sex or IV drug use *per se*.

More widespread than these self-help programs are methadone maintenance programs. While referred to as "rehabilitation," methadone maintenance is in actuality merely the substitution of one addiction for another, the only difference being that methadone is not pleasurable, only serving to forestall withdrawal pains, and that it is subsidized and provided by the government, thus preventing the accidental overdose, dangerous impurities, and financial hardships associated with heroin use. IVDUs get a prescription each week, which may or may not gradually be reduced. In the United States, it generally is reduced over time; in this case, as in the case of Narcotics Anonymous, "the treatment is old-fashioned withdrawal, with a very high incidence of relapse" (Burroughs 79). That methadone is just as addictive as heroin is made clear by "recovered addict" Jan

Wessels: "I've been taking it for half a year now, it's far out. They can take anything from me…my beer, my wife…so long as they keep their hands off my injectable methadone" (Kools 5).

Apomorphine and acupuncture therapies, on the other hand, operate by supplementing the body's own supply of endorphins or by stimulating the body's manufacture of its own endorphins, in order to lessen the pains of withdrawal. Such treatments, although mentioned in passing by Catherine Saalfield in her essay "Intravenous Drug Use, Women, and HIV" (126) and vehemently championed by Burroughs in numerous essays, are hardly ever mentioned as means of rehabilitation, though they could hardly be less promising than "old-fashioned withdrawal." The cursory and superficial attention given to the real issues of IV drug use and AIDS by writers whose only knowledge of IVDUs comes from popular stereotypes prevents the realization that "treatment" can mean many different things, not all of them terribly worthwhile. Thus, calls for "treatment programs," when not specific and substantive, often amount to little more than a plaintive cry to "do something about these people."

Some few voices have managed to break through the propaganda surrounding IVDUs and see more clearly that IVDUs are, indeed, human, that IV drug use does not automatically mean depravity or irresponsibility or an inability to think beyond the next fix. Some have realized that injectable drugs do not cause AIDS any more than does sex. It is the sharing of needles or of bodily fluids that transmits HIV from one body to another. Studies have shown that the primary reason for sharing needles is that "many states have paraphernalia laws that have been used by police against addicts and other IVDUs for years" (Waldorf and Murphy 118). Such laws discourage users from carrying their own works and actually serve to foster such institutions as the shooting gallery, which provide drugs, (previously used) works, and a place to inject. In response to such unsafe practices, needle exchange programs have been established. Government-sponsored programs are rare, but illegal street-based programs have been organized effectively in many United States cities, San Francisco's Prevention Point Needle Exchange being one highly successful example, in operation since November 1988. Such programs are sorely needed, not only to make clean works available, but also to challenge the public perception of the IVDU as irresponsible and the assumption that drug use is essentially connected to AIDS. Speaking from her experience with PPNE, Patricia Case challenges the myth of the irresponsible junky, saying, "substance abusers are receptive to exchange programs: They are interested in preventing HIV" (Saalfield 127).

## Conclusion

The stigmatizing stereotypes of the "junky," which largely determine public attitudes and actions regarding IVDUs, have, unlike myths about "fags" and "whores," remained for the most part unchallenged in the vast majority of AIDS discourse. In many cases, in fact, these negative images have been fostered by other stigmatized groups, as in the voices of Randy Shilts and Carol Leigh, in an attempt to destigmatize themselves in the context of AIDS. In both fiction and nonfiction, IVDUs have been diagnosed time and time again as parasitic, self-involved, subhuman, half-dead beings, or have been condemned to oblivion, as in the Denver Principles (the Founding Statement of People with AIDS/ARC), which nowhere refer to IV drug use or chemical dependency. IVDUs have been the "other" for just about every "risk group" trying to distance itself from the social stigma attached to AIDS. Rare are the voices that talk back, telling of IVDUs who are actually human, who are not, in the end, "only junkies."

While it is true that, in the United States today, dependence on substances like heroin will almost certainly do violence to a person's livelihood and dignity, voices must be raised to challenge the one-dimensional representations of IVDUs which form the bulk of discourse concerning the issue. Until such voices gain sufficient power and number to provide audible counterpoint to the dominant simple-mindedness, IVDUs with AIDS will continue to bear the brunt of societal victim-blame, and all the progressive asides generously included by AIDS writers regarding the "treatment" and "education" of IVDUs will continue, and will do about as much good as the "Just Say No" philosophy which has been with us over two decades now. And Jesse Helms will continue to receive astonished praise for his sudden "conversion" into a caring human being, as he urges the appropriation of funds to stop the spread of AIDS in Africa – certainly laudable – while scorning and ignoring hundreds of thousands of "guilty" people with AIDS in the United States – undeniably inexcusable. Human beings will continue to die, victims of an epidemic of ignorance and blame which continues to run rampant.

## Works Cited


*The Basketball Diaries.* Dir. Scott Kalvert. Perf. Leonardo DiCaprio and Lorraine Bracco. New Line, 1995.

Carlomusto, Jean and Alexandra Juhasz. *Living with AIDS: Women and AIDS.* New York: Gay Men's Health Crisis, 1988.

Centers for Disease Control and Prevention. "Drug-Associated HIV Transmission Continues in United States." *Divisions of HIV/AIDS Prevention.* 4 April 2002. http://www.cdc.gov/hiv/pubs/facts/idu.htm

Christensen, Kim. "How Do Women Live?" *Women, AIDS, and Activism.* Boston: South End Press, 1992. 10-22.

*Drugstore Cowboy.* Dir. Gus Van Sant. Perf. Matt Dillon and Kelly Lynch. Image, 1989.

Harcourt, Christina and Ross Philpot. "Female Prostitutes, AIDS, Drugs, and Alcohol in New South Wales." *AIDS, Drugs, and Prostitution.* Ed. Martin Plant. New York: Routledge, 1990. 145-163.

Helms, Jesse. "We Cannot Turn Away." 24 March 2002. *The Republican Website of the Senate Committee on Foreign Relations.* http://www.senate.gov/~foreign/minority/press_template.cfm?id=182203

Johnson, Brian. "The Stoned Screen." *Maclean's* 16 Apr. 2001: http://www.mapinc.org/drugnews/v01/n629/a06.html?177

Kools, John-Peter. "Policy for Supplying Methadone." *Mainline* July 1992: 5-7.

Leigh, Carol. "Further Violations of Our Rights." *Cultural Analysis/Cultural Activism.* Ed. Douglas Crimp. Cambridge: MIT Press, 1988. 173-182.

Patton, Cindy. *Inventing AIDS.* New York: Routledge, 1990.

*Requiem for a Dream.* Dir. Darren Aronofsky. Perf. Ellen Burstyn and Jared Leto. Artisan, 2000.

*Rush.* Dir. Lili Fini Zanuck. Perf. Jason Patric and Jennifer Jason Leigh. MGM, 1991.

Saalfield, Catherine. "Intravenous Drug Use, Women, and HIV." *Women, AIDS, and Activism.* Boston: South End Press, 1992. 124-129.

Scholder, Amy and Ira Silverberg, eds. *High Risk.* New York: Penguin, 1991.

Schulman, Sarah. *People in Trouble.* New York: Penguin, 1990.

Shilts, Randy. *And the Band Played On.* New York: Penguin, 1988.

*Sid & Nancy.* Dir. Alex Woods. Perf. Gary Oldman and Chloe Webb. Zenith, 1986.

*Trainspotting.* Dir. Danny Boyle. Perf. Ewan McGregor and Ewen Bremner. Miramax, 1996.

Treichler, Paula. "AIDS, Homophobia, and Biomedical Discourse: An Epidemic of Signification."

*Cultural Analysis/Cultural Activism.* Ed. Douglas Crimp.Cambridge: MIT Press, 1988. 60-72.

Venema, Petrien and Jan Visser. "Safer Prostitution: A New Approach in Holland." *AIDS, Drugs, and Prostitution.* Ed. Martin Plant. New York: Routledge, 1990. 50-64.

von Busack, Richard. "Shoot-'Em-Ups: The Perennial Appeal of Movie Addicts." *MetroActive* 1 Sept. 2002: http://www.metroactive.com/papers/metro/08.01.96/trainspot2-9631.html

Waldorf, Dan and Sheigla Murphy. "Intravenous Drug Use and Syringe-Sharing Practices of Call Men and Hustlers." *AIDS, Drugs, and Prostitution.* Ed. Martin Plant. New York: Routledge, 1990. 110-129.

White, Jonathan David. "Extreme Prejudice, Excessive Force, Zero Tolerance: Cultural Political Economy of the U. S. Drug Wars, 1980-1996." Diss. George Washington U, 1997.

*In "Encountering the Other, SARS, Public Health and Race Relations," Da Zheng turns his attention to "the surge of racial and ethnic discrimination...in response to the SARS scare."*

# Encountering the Other: SARS, Public Health, and Race Relations

## Da Zheng

In spring 2003, when scientists were scrambling to search for the causative pathogen and mode of transmission of SARS, the public was tormented with anxiety and fear, which in some cases fermented xenophobia and created racial and ethnic tension.

On an MIT website, an insidious April fool's hoax surfaced, warning of infected employees at a restaurant in Boston's Chinatown. The rumor spread quickly by mouth and email that there was widespread contagion in the area. Meanwhile, in New York City, a healthy Vietnamese owner of a Chinese restaurant was bombarded with consolatory phone calls, online postings, and the local newsprint about his own death caused by SARS. Needless to say, these hoaxes and rumors swirled and swept like hurricanes; as a result, businesses in both communities suffered a tremendous blow from the "unfounded blather" (Schram). Across the nation, anxiety and fear, generated by the news about the invisible and indeterminate contagion of the epidemic, were visible on the streets and corners of Chinatown communities in San Francisco, Los Angeles, Chicago, Philadelphia as well as in Boston and New York. Restaurants lost their clientele, and tourists stayed shy of the districts. Wedding banquets were cancelled, and the crowded Chinatown streets suddenly appeared deserted (Hopkins). As David Baltimore, a Nobel laureate, commented in *The Wall Street Journal* on April 28, "Just as the media recently gave us a...particularly intimate experience of war, we're now getting a new and particularly fearsome experience of a public-health crisis with SARS – in which a media-transmitted epidemic of concern for personal safety outpaces the risk to public health of the actual virus" (qtd. in Pierce 20).

Needless to say, the public soon discovered that the "epidemic" in those areas had been a hoax, and the businesses slowly resumed their former momentum. However, the surge of racial and ethnic discrimination in the community in response to the SARS scare is worth our close attention.

What Judy Collins of Massachusetts had experienced during the SARS scare was just this kind of discrimination. Judy and her husband, Dick, went to Guangzhou, China, in

March when the news about the mysterious disease had just broken out. Having previously adopted two girls from China – eight-year-old Brittany and five-year-old Madison – the Collins went there again to bring back a third child, this time a two-year-old boy, Sean. When Judy and Dick were there, the American consulate had dismissed all nonessential personnel in response to SARS, but it remained open for adoptions. Judy stayed alert. Even though she knew that the place where Sean came from had no SARS cases, she kept herself informed by calling epidemiologists, checking the Center for Disease Control's website, and monitoring everyone for any SARS symptoms. When they returned to Massachusetts, however, the local community panicked. The school requested their children be kept home for ten days though they had no symptoms at all. Similarly, Dick developed a rash after sitting in their hot tub; despite the fact that a rash is not one of the primary symptoms of SARS, his physician refused to treat him and sent him instead to the emergency room where he had to enter through a private door. The neighbors came to visit the new child, but they stopped at the end of the driveway, inquiring if everyone in the family was all right. No one in Judy's family got SARS; nevertheless, people feared they carried the disease because of their recent trip to China and their adopted children (Pierce 21-22).

The level of anxiety was nearly tangible. In Great Britain, SARS was referred to as "the next AIDS" in newspapers, though the claim was later proven to be unfounded. In fact, the 7,000 probable cases worldwide by early May paled in comparison to the two million victims of tuberculosis each year. SARS traveled fast, but fear traveled even faster. The widely-circulated stories made it seem as if people in the North American Asian communities were carriers of the disease even though SARS is not a disease of ethnicity. Fueled by fear, these stories were prejudicial and discriminatory.

Such widespread fear of an epidemic and its consequences is not unprecedented in American history. The San Francisco bubonic plague in 1900 was another such case. On March 6, 1900, the assistant city physician, Dr. Frank P. Wilson, was called to the basement of the Globe Hotel in San Francisco to examine the dead body of Wing Chung Ging, a forty-one-year-old Chinese resident (Shah 120).[1] The doctor noticed swollen lymph nodes in the groin of the body. After the smears of the glands was tested, Dr. Wilfred Kellogg, a city bacteriologist, read the preliminary microscopic study and suspected that Ging had died of bubonic plague. While the smears were rushed to the bacteriological laboratory for further examination, the city ordered an immediate quarantine of Chinatown. Early the next morning, thirty-two police officers were dispatched to the Chinese quarter, removing all whites from the affected area and allowing no one to enter it. The area was sealed off from the rest of the city by noon on March 7 (Shah 120).

Bubonic plague had a notorious history. In the 1890s, the epidemic hit major cities in China and India, causing devastating consequences. The recorded death toll in India alone exceeded twelve million from 1896 to 1930 (Shah 125). Because of the plague, trade ports in Hong Kong, Honolulu, Bombay, and Sydney took a beating. Even though bubonic plague had never attacked North America before 1900, public health authorities, white businessmen, and the Chinese residents in America all followed the news.

When the story about the Ging case broke out, the San Francisco municipal and federal health officials believed that they could contain the epidemic through quarantine, which was an extraordinary measure. It was based on the "logic of public health measures" that "routinely conflated deadly disease" with "Chinese race and residence." Hence, dividing the contaminated from the uncontaminated "along racial lines" would be the most effective way to contain the horrible bubonic plague (Shah 121). In other words, public health management and inadequate medical knowledge inflamed prevailing prejudices and fears about the menace of Chinese immigrants and Chinatown. Chinatwon was an easy and natural target since it had long been perceived as deficient in sanitary measures and thus a hot bed of diseases. One of the features of the epidemic disease is its transgression of boundaries, as Nayan Shah and Susan Craddock have observed, hence the need to draw lines, to quarantine.

In fact, Wing Chung Ging probably did not die of bubonic plaque. He had been ill for six months before his death. On February 7, he called for a doctor, complaining of pains in the chest, back, and bladder. A week later, his fever and pains had subsided, but he suffered from urethral discharges, swelling in his right groin, and a lame right leg. The doctor suspected that he had been afflicted with gonorrhea. His conditions worsened in the subsequent two weeks, and he collapsed suddenly and died on March 6. Even though some of his symptoms – the fever, severe headache, extreme fatigue, painful swelling of lymph glands in the groin – signaled bubonic plague, some believed that he could have died of typhoid or venereal disease since bubonic plague patients usually died more rapidly. Regardless, many expressed their astonishment at the city's decision to quarantine the entire Chinatown community (Shah 132). With all whites being removed from the district while no one was allowed to enter, Chinatown was blockaded like "a besieged city" from the rest of San Francisco overnight (Craddock 128, 133). Some Chinatown business owners protested because such large-scaled quarantine seriously disrupted Chinese business. Chinatown, "the conflation of race and place," "provided the illusion of impermeable boundaries" of racial geography which seemed to promise containment. But, as we can see now, the "blockade of Chinatown" was an "explicit act of racial discrimination against Chinese residents" (Shah 129, 132).

In late April, when four suspicious deaths were reported in the Chinese quarter over three days, the Public Health Service intervened to recommend a mass inoculation of San Francisco's Chinese population. The secretary of the treasury then ordered a restriction on public travel for "Asiatics or other races particularly liable to the disease." With this ordinance, the government confirmed the putative racial susceptibility to bubonic plague (Shah 133).

Racial tension was high. Many Chinese gathered protesting against the mass vaccination campaign. Some noted that, since the vaccination was different from the smallpox immunization, the inoculation would be life threatening to a frail person. Others proposed to shut down Chinatown businesses in protest, a suggestion that won overwhelming support from the crowd. Many businesses did indeed shut down when physicians and health workers went to give inoculations in Chinatown. Circulars accused the Board of Health of attempting to "poison the Chinese by injecting drugs under the skin" (Shah 134-35).

These actions then led to rumors about the source of bubonic plague and suspicion about the motivation of the public health officials. When the health officials tried to eliminate rats by nailing dead fish on wooden boards and placing them in the sewers, they filled the fishes' abdominal cavity with arsenic paste. But the rumor began to circulate that the officials filled the fish with bacilli of bubonic plague and fed them to the rats so that "these animals would contract the disease and carry it among the Chinese." The fear, mistrust, and suspicion of the Chinese toward the public health officials came, in turn, from racial tension resulting from the racially discriminatory policy of the city government (Shah 135).

On June 15, 1900, Judge William Morrow ordered quarantine to be lifted. The quarantine of the Chinese, he argued, was "an act based more on discrimination than on maintaining the public's health." While recognizing that the purpose of quarantine was to isolate those infected from those who were not, Morrows believed it wrong to enact the "cordoning of an entire district composed overwhelmingly of uninfected individuals" (Craddock 136). He "admonished the health authorities for making Chinese residents more vulnerable by not strenuously isolating the houses of plague victims within the quarantined district." The Board of Health was ordered to stop the general quarantine of Chinatown and to quarantine only individual buildings where plague victims or their contacts had resided (Shah 144).

Many recent studies have called our attention to how "race, place, and culture" could have been fused together into an essential triangle to explain epidemics (see Anderson, Craddock, Deverell, Shah, and Stern). For example, Kay Anderson and Susan Craddock have shown respectively that Chinatown, being in Vancouver, San Francisco, or elsewhere, was preserved as the headquarters of disease. In a government report prepared by the City of San Francisco in 1880, Chinatown was called "a nuisance" and a "cancer spot" that "endangers" the otherwise "healthy conditions" of the city (Craddock 69, 80). Such constructions of Chinatown often created an image of pathologized space and promoted "racialized spatialization and racial tension. Even scientific research could be tainted to serve that rhetoric. Physicians in America, attempting to pinpoint patterns of susceptibility to germ access, ascribed the plague to Asians. Surgeon General Walter Wyman even called the plague a 'rice-eaters' disease'" (Craddock 130).

Indeed, fear of epidemic is related to the fear of the unknown, often expressed during our contact with different ethnic groups. Debbie Liu, a thirteen-year-old Chinese-Canadian girl, sent a letter to *Langley Advance* in May 2003, complaining that she and her sister encountered unexpected racial slurs in May while taking a walk on a street. Two unknown teenagers in a passing car called them "SARS," which made the two girls feel "insulted and angered." Liu wrote:

> We can't blame Asian people that they started SARS. It's totally unfair and rude. SARS doesn't have eyes or anything; it can't see which people it's going to.
>
> My sister and I have never left Canada since we arrived here seven years ago. I'm only 13 years old and I'm being called, "SARS." Do you want to be called, "SARS," huh? How would you feel if a stupid person came up to your face and called you "SARS"?
>
> When I first came to Canada, I thought people in Canada were nice, friendly, and polite people. Then I've been called this.
>
> My thoughts were destroyed, and I've begun to think that they're rude, unfriendly, and immature. But I don't want to think like that. They're acting like Germans in World War II, calling Jews "Dirty Jews." (Liu)

It is important to note the change in the girls resulting from this incident, the reverse racism they felt toward others. In addition, the comparison of this racial encounter with fascism and anti-Semitism during WWII is frighteningly and strikingly accurate. In their study of the U.S policy concerning the U.S.-Mexico border in the first two decades of the twentieth century, Alexandra Stern and Howard Markel trace the development from several cases of fever in El Paso in 1916 to the U.S. Public Health Service's unilateral decision to implement quarantine on "all persons coming to El Paso from Mexico" in 1917 (Stern 104). Stern argues in another essay that "the discourses and practices of medicine and social control that were critical to inventing multiple boundaries in the 1910s were folded into eugenic theories of difference and moved into the national imaginary in the 1920s." The exhortations of eugenicists "pathologied the extremities of the body politic and helped to shape restrictive legislation as well as justify the establishment of the Border Control in 1924" (81). Because of the dominant view that tended to stereotype Mexicans as "a class of equally degraded, poverty-stricken laborers living in rat-infested congregations," the outbreak of the plague epidemic in Los Angeles in 1924 became, in William Deverell's term, "peculiarly Mexicanized." To many whites, the plague "had rendered Mexicans unusually dangerous" (188, 191). The disease, in other words, had been associated with ethnicity. Such racial and ethnic discrimination had happened to Jews, Germans, Haitians, Irish, and other ethnic groups as well in relatively recent cultural history. In the mid-nineteenth century, for example, with the arrival of millions of immigrants from Europe, "vague fears of strangers" coalesced into specific stigmatization of the Irish. Many Irish immigrants were in New York, and a large number of sick or disabled newcomers strained existing medical facilities. Coupled with the preexisting anti-Catholic sentiments and the large scale of immigration, this development sent shock waves of apprehension through native-born Americans. When confronted with the threat of cholera and Irish Catholics, the officials of the public health chose to go beyond quarantine to the "exclusion of those foreign-born who menaced the community's health and well-being" (Kraut).

In addition to the recent SARS scare, there have been a number of other cases in nature, which have triggered horror and brought on racialized rhetoric. For example, Chinese mitten crabs have been said to be "stealing" anglers' bait and constituting "a threat to levees" in the Sacramento region. Mitten crabs are Chinese natives, and they are inclined to burrow holes in levees and stream banks. They damage rice crops and carry a lung fluke that has caused symptoms similar to tuberculosis in millions of Asians. In 1992, the first Chinese mitten crab was captured by a South Bay shrimp fisherman; in 1996, it was said that only forty-five crabs had been found in the Delta; and then, by 1997, 20,000 were caught. So far, no crab damage has been observed, and the government is not dealing with this issue. But the prospect of the spread of crab larvae in currents out of San Francisco Bay has already triggered alarm and worry in some who ask, "If these things are multiplying to the levels they're estimating, what's going to happen in two or three years?" (Vogel).

In November 2002, the Great Lakes Fishery Commission took emergency action to defend against, as P. J. Perea termed it, the "Asian Carp Invasion." According to the news release, three U.S. federal agencies, the International Joint Commission, and the Great Lakes Fishery Commission worked jointly to "defend against an invasive species threat" to the Great Lakes region. "These fish are extremely prolific, rapidly advancing their way up the Mississippi River toward the Great Lakes via the canal and threatening the biological integrity of the Great Lakes" (Great Lakes). It is said that Asian carp grow fast – up to 100 pounds and four feet long. Well-adapted to the climate of the region, they would "compete for food" with other "valuable" fish and could potentially develop to become a "dominant species" in the Great Lakes. Government agencies provided backup power hardware for an electrical barrier in Chicago to protect against the vicious invaders. The system uses electricity to repel fish. Officials hope to block the migration of species between the Mississippi Rivers and the Great Lakes.

The racialized rhetoric in these reports is alarming. Words such as "migration," "threats," "invade," "steal," and "compete" recur throughout, and such rhetoric is not entirely unfamiliar; it echoes the language directed against immigrant aliens. A Canadian politician, for example, was forced to apologize for her own racist remarks at the University of Winnipeg in November 2000. In her speech, she told the audience that she was concerned about the immigration system of the country. She mentioned problems such as immigrants in Toronto who supported Tamil terrorists and an influx of Asians on the West Coast. She then said, "I call it the Asian invasion…the Asian students that have come over to Canada have pressured the university system" so much so that Canadian students "could not even get into some of our university programs in Vancouver and Victoria" (Ditchburn).

It has been two years since the epidemic strain of SARS was last reported in June of 2003. In Beijing and Guangzhou, "public hysteria about the disease" is said to have subsided, giving way to "public nonchalance." Dr. Kathryn V. Holmes, a prominent microbiologist, has recently been quoted as declaring that "SARS no longer existed in the wild and that the virus no longer presented a serious health threat to the world." Very few people, in China and North America alike, talk about it, and the epidemic seems to have become part of history (Yardley).

Nevertheless, the cultural and racial impact brought on by the SARS epidemic, and of course the other cases I have cited in this paper should never be forgotten. No one knows for sure at this point if SARS will ever strike again. But it is certain that we will confront various forms of epidemic and serious disease sometime in the future. Fear, suspicions, and tension could corrode already tenuous racial and ethnic relationships. It is crucial for us to remember the past and understand that encountering the Other has become an inevitable necessity in our global, cultural environment today. While this fact has created unprecedented opportunities, it has also posed formidable new challenges. Being open-minded and willing to respect and even embrace the Other is the key to mutual understanding and a racially harmonious relationship, not to mention our success in fighting epidemics and other unknown diseases.

## Note

1. The name of the patient has also been identified as "Chick Gin." See Craddock, 126-27.

## Works Cited

Anderson, Kay. *Vancouver's Chinatown.* Montreal: Mc-Gill-Queen's UP, 1991.

Craddock, Susan. *City of Plagues.* Minneapolis: U of Minnesota P, 2000.

Deverell, William. "Plague in Los Angeles, 1924: Ethnicity and Typicality." *Over the Edge: Remapping the American West.* Eds. Valerie J. Matsumoto and Blake Allmendinger. Berkeley: U of California P, 1999. 172-200.

Ditchburn, Jennifer. "Alliance Candidate Laments 'Asian invasion' on West Coast." *The Canadian Press* 18 November 2000: http://www.canoe.ca/CNEWSElection2000News/1118_ca-sp.html

Great Lakes Fishery Commission. "Agencies Take Emergency Action to Defend against Asian Carp Invasion." 18 November 2002. http://www.state.gov/g/oes/rls/prsrl/press/15389.htm

Hopkins, Jim. "Fear of SARS hurts business in Chinatown Customer traffic said to be down by 60% or more." *USA Today* 25 April 2003: http://www.usatoday.com/usatonline/20030425/5104035s.htm

Kraut, Alan M. *Silent Travelers.* New York: Basic Books, 1994.

Liu, Debbie. "Intolerance: SARS spreads racism." *Langley Advance* 6 May 2003: http://www.langleyadvance.com/051103/opinion/051103lc2.html

Markel, Howard, and Alexandra Minna Stern. "Which Face? Whose Nation? Immigration, Public Health, and the Constitution of Disease at America's Ports and Borders, 1891 to 1928." *Immigration Research for a New Century*. Eds. Nancy Foner, Ruben G. Rumbaut, and Steven J. Gold. New York: Russell Sage Foundation, 2000. 93-112.

Perea, P. J. "Asian Carp Invasion." *IPO*. N.d. http://www.lib.niu.edu/ipo/oi020508.html

Pierce, Charles P. "Epidemic of Fear." *Boston Globe Magazine* June 2003: http://groups.yahoo.com/gropu/asianamericanartistry/message/1875

Schram, Justin. "How popular perceptions of risk from SARS Are Fermenting Discrimination." *BMJ* 23 April 2003: http://bmj.bmjjournals.com/cgi/content/full/326/7395/939

Shah, Nayan. *Contagious Divides*. Berkeley: U of California P, 2001.

Stern, Alexandra Minna. "Buildings, Boundaries, and Blood: Medicalization and Nation-Building on the U.S.-Mexico Border, 1910-1930." *The Hispanic American Historical Review* 79.1 (1999): 41-81.

Vogel, Nancy. "Mitten crabs fan out in area: Species could be a threat to levees." *New Jersey Fishing* 27 August 1998: http://www.fishingnj.org/artmttencrb.htm

CPSIA information can be obtained at www.ICGtesting.com
224165LV00003B/1/P

9 780978 904180